LETTERS TO SARTRE

Letters to Sartre

SIMONE DE BEAUVOIR

Translated and Edited by
Quintin Hoare

Preface by
Sylvie Le Bon de Beauvoir

Arcade Publishing • New York

First Arcade Paperback Edition 1993

Originally published in France under the title *Lettres à Sartre*

Library of Congress Cataloging-in-Publication Data

Beauvoir, Simone de, 1908–
    [Lettres à Sartre. English]
    Letters to Sartre / Simone de Beauvoir; translated and edited by Quintin Hoare;
preface by Sylvie Le Bon de Beauvoir. — 1st U.S. ed.
    p. cm
    Translation of: Lettres à Sartre.
    Includes index.
    ISBN 1-55970-153-6 (hc)
    ISBN 1-55970-212-5 (pb)
    1. Beauvoir, Simone de, 1908– — Correspondence. 2. Sartre, Jean Paul, 1905–
— Correspondence. 3. Authors, French — 20th century — Correspondence.
4. Feminists — France — Correspondence. I. Le Bon de Beauvoir, Sylvie.
II. Hoare, Quintin. III. Title.
PQ2603.E362Z49513   1992   91-73949

Published in the United States by Arcade Publishing, Inc., New York,
by arrangement with Little, Brown and Company, Inc.

Distributed by Little, Brown and Company

10 9 8 7 6 5 4 3 2 1

MV-NY

Printed in the United States of America

CONTENTS

Introduction

Simone de Beauvoir (born 1908, died 1986) was for the last four decades of her life – indeed is still, after her death – not just one of the most famous women of the age, but also one of the most public. Six autobiographical works were published in her lifetime (four volumes of memoirs, and her accounts of her mother's and Sartre's deaths). Innumerable interviews covered all her various personae: existentialist philosopher; prize-winning novelist; courageous political campaigner; pioneer theorist and role-model for the women's movement internationally; Sartre's lifelong companion – in that notorious 'morganatic union' allowing contingent loves. A vast secondary literature, in many languages, has been devoted to her life and works. All this taken together might lead one to believe that everything had already been told and retold, so De Beauvoir could now go gentle into the good night of easy oblivion that so often swallows up public figures for a while after their physical demise. It has turned out, however, that nothing could be farther from the truth.

Within two years of her death, De Beauvoir was once again at the vortex of a controversial maelstrom, investing the central core of her entire public being – her very integrity, as a valid inspiration to successive generations of women pursuing the elusive grail of equality and freedom (and, of course, to men identifying with those goals). What unleashed the maelstrom? It was the publication of her correspondence with Sartre, translated in the present volume. This revealed what a very partial segment of the human truth had, in reality, ever been disclosed, in all that welter of biographical and autobiographical coverage. It also demonstrated the radical incompatibility of her and Sartre's whole conception of free human relations – *as they actually lived it* – with the somewhat rose-tinted, soft-edged public image she had herself at times helped to create.

Of course, it had long been manifest that De Beauvoir's own account of her life had been ruthlessly censored, pruned and sanitized to present the public facade she deemed fitting. People important in her life or Sartre's had been concealed behind one, two, three, even four successive pseudonyms. Friends' susceptibilities and Sartre's good name had alike been jealously protected. What was much more of a surprise was how successful she had been in taming any too impertinently intrusive lines of enquiry on the part of her biographers. Taking them into her apparent confidence – admitting them to the privilege of her friendship, adroitly burdening them with gratitude – she blithely misled them as she pleased, making even the best of them into unwitting hagiographers. Outsmarted, they underestimated her toughness and savvy – and turned the old iconoclast into a benign totem. How she must have chuckled into her whisky, on evenings after their earnest visits!

What provoked the outraged reaction of so many to the posthumous publication of these letters? At least three strands converged here. First, traditional sexism: eager for revenge on the woman who, more than anyone else, had come to symbolize the whole 20th-century assault on male privilege and masculinist values; newly emboldened, in the late-eighties climate of modish, cynical 'post-everything'. Secondly (overlapping with the first), ideological Reaction: the posturing apostles of intellectual yuppiedom who – back in the seventies, under the banner of the marvellously misnamed 'new philosophy' – had emerged to challenge the long dominance in Paris of the Left intelligentsia of which De Beauvoir had been such a central figure. But these two categories of detractor were predictable. More significant was a third strand made up of former or still-would-be sympathizers, who now felt De Beauvoir had revealed herself in her letters to be dismayingly *other* than the idealized image of her they had so long been nurturing.

What kind of letters are these, then? Described banally, they trace the gaps in the joint existence of De Beauvoir and Sartre – so rarely separated for any length of time. By far the longest such separation was imposed by the Second World War, with Sartre's mobilization and subsequent imprisonment; it is thus from this period that the largest number of surviving letters – a *daily* correspondence – date. A second large batch were written during the lengthy stays De Beauvoir made in the United States between 1947 and 1951, especially after her passionate affair began with Nelson Algren. Apart from these (and the year Sartre spent in Berlin in 1933-4, from which regrettably no letters survive), De Beauvoir and Sartre were parted – hence, corresponded – mainly during separate holidays. At all such times, the letters of each provided the other with the 'everyday dust of life' of which Sylvie Le Bon de Beauvoir speaks below – the news, the gossip, the progress-reports on work, the passing reflections, the daily moods, fears, hopes – thus maintaining the continuity of a shared life that extended over almost half a century.

But beyond this banal description, De Beauvoir's letters to Sartre have two other, more dramatic, dimensions: they are love letters (from first to last), and they are concurrently the unsparing account of those other – 'contingent' – loves allowed for in her pact with Sartre. In the war years at the centre of this volume, De Beauvoir is settling down into a long friendship with her former lover Olga Kosakiewitch, detaching herself from her most recent lover Bianca Bienenfeld, edging towards a new loving relationship with Natalie Sorokine, pursuing an intermittent affair with Olga's partner and future husband Jacques-Laurent Bost. Meanwhile Sartre – by letter – is sustaining a passionate affair with Olga's sister Wanda, likewise detaching himself from Bianca with whom he had had a whirlwind prewar fling, and negotiating tortuously with other recent ephemeral lovers. All this complex web of interlocking liaisons is recorded, analysed, agonized over, smiled at, on a daily basis by the central couple – whose exchanges are thus love letters of a radically unconforming kind. It is this, above all – the hint of voyeurism, the whiff at times of Valmont and Mme de Merteuil – which some readers have found disconcerting.

But how misguided. For it is precisely this blazing, disconcerting truthfulness that forms the bedrock of De Beauvoir's lifelong passionate relationship with Sartre, giving it its radical edge. In this sense, sexual freedom for them had as much – indeed ultimately far more – to do with freeing a marriage (albeit a morganatic one!) from sex as with freeing sex from the ties of marriage. Love and ethics themselves were being redefined, not just mores. The modernist creation that is pehaps how best to view their union – embedded in its time, yet possessing a durable charge; seminal, yet never to be repeated – was, like *Ulysses* or 'The Bride Stripped Bare', always going to remain a hard bite to swallow, digest or, of course, spit out. De Beauvoir herself is a validly heroic figure, not as some kind of bloodless *image d'Epinal*, but for the specific way she resolved (while assuming) her human contradictions – in her life as well as in her work. For she always remained the dutiful daughter as she rebelled, the matriarch of the Family as she theorized the supersession of the traditional family, the puritan as she broke taboos, the loyal friend as she 'deceived', the apolitical woman refusing to read newspapers as – into her old age – she took to the streets and challenged the law, the observer of formalities as she gave rein to her emotions: strong as she was weak, and weak as she was strong. Above all, of course, she stepped back from the ordinary human realities of her own existence – love and passion (straight or gay), frustration, disappointment, frigidity, jealousy, fear, anger, hope, wish, dream – and produced a work which stands and will stand as the baseline of all aspirations for equality between the sexes in the modern world.

★ ★ ★

The selection of De Beauvoir's letters translated here represents some two thirds of the French edition published in 1990. It was easy to omit a number of letters included there, which were addressed not to Sartre but to 'Toulouse' (see note 63 below) and recuperated after her tragic death. It also seemed preferable to leave out material overlapping with De Beauvoir's autobiographical volumes or, in particular, her book on the United States. Other cuts were harder to make, but the overriding aim was to produce a shortened version as close as possible to the original in terms of both tone and content. To leave the overall balance as little changed as possible, while preserving the essential *exchange* with Sartre – as well as all discussion of De Beauvoir's own or Sartre's work; everything touching on their mutual relations, her relationship with Algren, or their respective more contingent or ephemeral liaisons with others; her reflections on the War or politics; and everything likely to be of specific interest to feminists. I have further sought to do all this without altering the quotidian (often literally) and sometimes mundane character of letters crammed with details of books read, films seen, cafés frequented, friends encountered, parties attended, or natural beauties admired.

The translation itself requires little comment, except perhaps for the endearments and salutations exchanged by De Beauvoir and Sartre. Nothing in English can convey, of course, the idiosyncratic flavour of a mode of address between them that always maintained the formal *vous* (in speech and writing alike). Nor, for example, the sheer perversity of the ungrammatical *vous autre* – inadequately rendered here as 'yourself'. I have attempted to compensate for the loss of these untranslatable features of De Beauvoir's style by elsewhere preserving – more than I should otherwise have done – forms of address striking an unfamiliar note in English. I have also kept the obsessively repeated use of the adjective 'little' – so characteristic that it has been the subject of scholarly exegesis! Finally, in explanation of my preference for the translated form of De Beauvoir's nickname *le Castor*, I shall just quote the passage from her *Memoirs of a Dutiful Daughter* where she explains its origin: 'One day he [René Maheu] wrote on my exercise-book, in large capital letters: BEAUVOIR = BEAVER. "You are a beaver," he said. "Beavers like company and they have a constructive bent".'

Quintin Hoare
October 1991

PREFACE TO THE FRENCH EDITION

When Simone de Beauvoir published the letters Sartre had written her (*Lettres au Castor*, Paris 1983), her friends were puzzled: 'How about your own, Beaver?', they asked. That was my reaction too. I still retain a sharp memory of how my pleasure in reading them was tinged with frustration: 'How about your own, Beaver?' We were, of course, suffering primarily from disappointed curiosity: so many allusions, jokes and details remained enigmatic or hung fire. Simone de Beauvoir herself could not always fill in the gaps, or revive that 'everyday dust of life' that was the contingent and irreplaceable matter of the letters she wrote to Sartre. But the loss and forgetfulness further affected, at a deeper level, the truth itself of their relationship, interrupting and muddling the correspondence that relayed their 'sustained conversation': in other words, their very life. For speaking – speaking to one another – was for them like breathing. At all events, she would always meet enquiries with the same response: 'My own letters? They're lost.' And this is what she believed to the end. In March 1984, a Canadian feminist magazine interviewed her at length:

'– After the appearance of *Lettres au Castor*, many people wondered why you hadn't published your replies. We feel the lack of them. Do you intend to do that?

'– No. In the first place, my letters have mostly been lost, because they weren't in my possession but in Sartre's. And since there was a bomb attack at his place, lots of his papers were lost. Secondly, I don't feel that I ought to publish letters of my own during my lifetime. When I'm dead they might perhaps be published, if they can be found.'

I did find them. One gloomy day in November 1986, while rummaging aimlessly in the depths of a cupboard at her place, I unearthed a massive packet: letters upon letters in her hand, most of them still folded in their envelopes. Addressed to 'Monsieur Sartre'. It was as unexpected and moving as suddenly discovering a secret chamber in a pyramid explored countless times. She had been mistaken, her letters did exist. A strange mistake for her to have made, but no stranger than the one she had made earlier in connection with Sartre's letters, likewise supposedly lost. For in *The Prime of Life* she had written in error, with respect to Sartre's wartime service at Brumath in 1939: 'He used to write to me almost every day, but I lost this correspondence during the exodus.' And a few pages later, about leaving Paris in June 1940: 'I packed my bags, taking only essentials. I took all Sartre's letters – I don't know where or when they were lost.' Well, the letters in question were the very ones she herself was to publish in 1983. The confusion must assuredly be due to some mix-up with the fate of the earliest letters she had received from Sartre, in 1929 and 1930 while he was doing his military service, which really have vanished, alas!

Once the manuscripts had been discovered, a major obstacle still frequently impeded my labours: the Beaver's handwriting. Remarkable for the perverse resistance it puts up against its first duty – that of being legible – it subjects its supplicants to torments and contortions more reminiscent of the decoding of Linear B than of the delights of epistolary communication. Sartre used to complain bitterly about it: 'Really, my dearest, how badly you do write! It's almost unreadable . . . Here, for example, is how you write impression: imp ⟿ . Make sense of that! I think I must read you with the eyes of love, because I never go astray. But to put me even further to the test, you displace letters within the words. This is how you write 'fear [*crains*]': ⟿ . No matter, I read it all.' [3 December 1939] Very few words, in fact, have showed a determination superior to my own. I note them as they occur. This correspondence is unexpurgated. Since any reasons that may have justified cuts in 1983 no longer exist, I have made almost none. Is it not, by now, preferable to tell all in order to tell the truth? Through the indisputable power of direct testimony, to set aside clichés, myths, images – all those lies – so that the real person, as she really was, may appear? Simone de Beauvoir used to say that one of her most enduring fantasies involved the conviction that her singular existence, with all its frivolous incidents and the incomparable taste of mortal instants – her entire existence – was recorded somewhere on a giant tape-recorder. These letters, in their own way, form part of that dream of a complete recording. At all events, you can certainly hear her voice in them, its most fleeting along with its most constant tones: her true, living voice.

Sylvie Le Bon de Beauvoir

LETTERS

JANUARY 1930 – JULY 1939
Before the War

🦎 1930

[91 Place Denfert-Rochereau
Paris 14]

Tuesday [6 January 1930]

My love,

I'm writing this in bed. Yesterday, I couldn't have managed it but just slept, with gargling as my sole distraction. I had a very sore throat and even some temperature. My grandmother nursed me with the most tiresome devotion.[1] She'd come into my room every couple of minutes, to add a dash of lemon or brandy to tea I'd no desire to drink, since I was sleeping. My mother came by, and was very sweet. My sister came by as well, but too late to mail you the letter, which she must have taken to the post this morning. She took Nizan the article too.[2] She told me all the gossip, and I was very pleased with her.

If one has to be ill, it's nice to do so just after you've left, my dearest love. I'd be sliding from sleep into wakefulness and back, without ever quitting the memories of that miraculous week we spent together. There you were at my side, dearest little man, all tenderness and solicitude – like at That Lady's last Sunday[3] – and as for me, I was brimming over with love for you and happiness. Today I'm fine and my benign feelings persist. I'm still in bed, just to be on the safe side, but I've eaten two nice little boiled eggs and some bananas and I feel like reading Rabelais,

---

[1]De Beauvoir rented a room in her grandmother's flat at 91 Place Denfert-Rochereau from the autumn of 1929, shortly after she completed her studies at the Sorbonne, to the summer of 1931, when she left Paris for a year's teaching in a lycée at Marseilles.
[2]Paul Nizan (1905-40), close friend of Sartre at the Lycée Henri IV and later at the École Normale Supérieure, became a successful novelist; he was also a prominent Communist journalist until he broke with the Party after the Ribbentrop-Molotov Pact. Serving as a liaison officer with the British force, Nizan was killed during the retreat to Dunkirk.
[3]That Lady: nickname for Mme Morel, a rich Argentinian woman with a flat in Boulevard Raspail, a country house near Angers and a villa at Juan-les-Pins, who in 1926 became a close friend of Sartre and his *normalien* comrades René Maheu and – in particular – Pierre Guille, and of whom De Beauvoir and Sartre were to see a great deal until the 1950s. She figures in De Beauvoir's autobiography as 'Mme Lemaire'.

seeing my sister who's due to drop in, and playing the convalescent.

My love, I never felt our love more strongly than that evening at Les Vikings, where you gazed at me so tenderly I felt like weeping. And what a delightful train took us to Saint-Germain, my love![4] If I weren't so uncomfortably positioned for writing, I'd spend pages telling you how happy I am and how much I love you. But I take comfort from the fact that you felt it clearly yourself, didn't you, little man? Here are a hundred kisses, each carrying the same message.

I was very annoyed yesterday by a *pneu* I got from the Llama,[5] trying to be wounding in a really infantile way. I shall be very sweet to him on Wednesday, but I find such injustice towards both you and me highly unpleasant. I'm copying out his note word for word, including the significant crossings-out:

'10 o'clock. Forgive me for disturbing you amid all the tender and colourful memories that are doubtless prolonging for you your own dear love's passage. Nevertheless:

Can you be at home *on Wednesday afternoon?* I shall probably arrive at about 3-3.15, since I have a lecture at the Ecole at 1.30.[6] Otherwise (and Sartre must have shown you how unnecessary it was to put yourself out on my account) come and have lunch at Adolphe's *on Thursday at 12.15* (my apologies for not being able, alas!, to take you to Pierre's). I take the liberty of insisting – insofar as I still have any right to do so – that I see you on either Wednesday or Thursday. I have some quite important things to tell you, since it is possible I shall never see you again. For you must understand that I have had my fill of the pretty situation that now exists, as a result of that September of yours and the two months of lying which followed it, and that I deserve something better than the crumbs – the relations continued out of charity 'because I am unhappy' – that you both offer me with such elegance.

Do not be alarmed, at any rate. And, above all, do not write to me. That would be the best way not to see me again at all. As things are, I shall tell you quite frankly I am too unhappy to have been able as yet to take any final decision. I shall postpone this, *I promise you* (and my promises I keep), until Wednesday.'

---

[4]Probably Saint-Germain-en-Laye, where Nizan and his wife Rirette had a house.
[5]The Llama: nickname of René Maheu, who was very close to De Beauvoir (figuring in her autobiography as 'Herbaud') in the year of her *agrégation* (1929), first giving her the nickname 'Beaver'. He was also a friend of Sartre at the École Normale. Later director-general of UNESCO.
[6]École: the École Normale Supérieure in Rue d'Ulm, where Sartre (1924-9), Nizan, Maheu and Guille were students while De Beauvoir was at the Sorbonne.

I shall assure him, of course, that neither you nor I is prolonging our relations with him out of pity. I want, above all, to try and make him feel my affection for him – and yours too. But I shall tell him, all the same, how astonishing I find this note of his. For absolutely nothing had happened between us from the Saturday when I left him and he was so pleased with me until this Monday – he always said that he accepted this situation, and that what he feared was seeing it change. He, who finds it so easy to reconcile his affections for his wife, for me and for the Humous Lady,[7] is really the last person who can reproach me for loving somebody besides him. I feel, too, that I've put myself out for him more than once, and that these parentheses are pointlessly unpleasant. I was very upset that day at the Napoli and the Café des Sports, when I saw the Llama being so nice after the letter was discovered. I was still a bit upset at the Closerie des Lilas the other day. But this note hasn't upset me at all, because I see it as mere jealousy of a thoroughly disagreeable kind.

How are you, little man? I'm really longing for a letter from you tomorrow. We'll be seeing each other soon, won't we, my love? You promised, so I'm taking good care of myself. I love you, I love you. I am, most tenderly, your own Beaver.

S. de Beauvoir

Monsieur Sartre
Villa Polownia
St Symphorien
(Indre et Loire)[8]

---

[7]Reference to the 'Eugenic cosmology' (extracted from Cocteau's *Le Potomak*) which Maheu and his friends affected during their university years (see S. de Beauvoir, *Memoirs of a Dutiful Daughter*, London 1963, pp.321-4), and which distinguished various castes: the Eugenes, the Marrhanes, the Mortimer, etc. 'Humous' or earthy women are those who 'have a future' (De Beauvoir was one).

[8]Meteorological station at Saint-Symphorien near Tours, where Sartre was doing his military service starting in this month of January 1930, after a training period at Saint-Cyr (November-December 1929).

❦ 1935

Hôtel du Midi
Place des Marronniers
Valgorge (Ardèche)

Valgorge, 28 July [1935]

My dear love,

Here is the first of the two letters you'll find in Paris, a few days from now. I still have no news of you, of course, since I haven't yet been to Villefort; I do so hope you're not being too bored.[9] Know always how tenderly I love you, my beautiful little marvel. The days are beginning to orient themselves most delightfully towards you, and this morning I'm enjoying telling myself how, in a week's time, at this very hour, I shall be in the presence of yourself. For I shall certainly go and pick you up at 1 in the morning on Saturday at Ste Cécile d'Andorge: I can't wait to see you again, as though you'd been away from me for ages.

My poor dear love, I shall be giving you a detailed account of my trip, map in hand. It's becoming more and more agreeable. Since the day I wrote to you, the scenery has become really beautiful. Some parts are rather similar to the Hautes-Alpes, with great, bleak, undulating grasslands like the ones we saw near the Col du Lautaret. Then, just a day later, you're transported from these to spots looking exactly like Corsica. On the other hand, there are plenty of landscapes resembling nothing but themselves, very beautiful and strange. I slept 1,700 metres up in a windswept mountain hut, where I was really cold;[10] I awoke between two seas of cloud scudding above and below me at such unimaginable speeds that I'd have been carried away by the wind if I'd attempted to move. I had to wait quite a while before I could make my way down to the valley, where that very same day my feet caught the sun so badly that I was totally paralysed and reduced to an evening of immobility. I promptly bought some woollen socks and large espadrilles, so I've now managed to reduce to a minimum all the minor torments of blisters and scratches to which my feet formerly subjected me. So I spent Monday afternoon rubbing myself with ointments and reading Colette's *Sido*, which is pretty awful. Next day I could walk like a marvel, and I slept beneath the stars without feeling the least chill even at dawn. Since then I've slept twice more in barns, including last night when I was wonderfully snug, and the rest of the time in small hotels.

---

[9]Sartre was on a Norwegian cruise with his mother and stepfather.
[10]For this night spent on Mont Mézenc, see *The Prime of Life*, London 1965, p.217.

I lost my way a couple of times in woods and thickets, getting dreadfully scratched and managing to lose Collinet's guide;[11] but that doesn't matter, since I'm resolved not to buy him another. By and large I find my bearings like a dream, making 30 or 35 km. a day on excellent trails. In the afternoon I usually take a bus. They never do more than 10 km. an hour in these parts, so that covering 20 km. takes up two hours, while lunching and reading *Le Petit Marseillais* (the only paper you can buy hereabouts, since the area is a kind of suburb of Marseilles, inhabited solely by tourists and holiday-makers from the Midi) takes up another two. The hot hours of the day are usually spent in this way; I walk only in the mornings, and in the evenings after four. I also make use of private cars a lot, either when I'm tired or as part of a concerted plan; by now I stop them as easily as buses.

With everything ordered in this way, I don't have a moment to be bored, or even to wonder how to fill my time. This morning, exceptionally, having arrived at ten at a godforsaken place from which a bus I'm planning to take leaves only at three, I have lots of time to spare. I ordered a coffee, read *Le Petit Marseillais* and am now writing to you. The weather is delightful, as usual. Since I've so far been almost continuously in the mountains, there's a breeze even at noon and at the same time the sky is completely clear. I hope we shall be equally lucky.

My dear love, I'm going to take such good care of you, I'm going to be very sweet to you, I so much want you to have a nice little holiday. I'll write another note in two or three days, to give you the very latest news. Until Saturday evening, my love. If I'm not at Ste Cécile, come to Florac by noon on Sunday as arranged. If I'm not there either, go to the Hôtel Central and ask whether there's any mail for you; and if I'm not there by four in the afternoon, alert the local police. I'm really looking forward to this little trip with you. I love you passionately, my beloved.

S. de Beauvoir

I visited Vals, which is quite pleasant as spas go – perhaps partly due to the fact that it was only eight in the morning and the streets were empty.

I swill lemonade which is exquisite in these parts, being made precisely from Vals water. I eat one enormous meal daily, which is sometimes very good but always accompanied by dreadful wine, and one small, cold meal. I have plenty of money and live very well.

---

[11]Michel Collinet was a friend of De Beauvoir's lifelong friend Colette Audry, who had been a colleague at the Lycée Jeanne d'Arc at Rouen in 1932. For a portrait of him, see *The Prime of Life,* p. 120.

Do you know the story of Ortega and the bull? Or the one about a strangely invigorating hair dye? Remind me to tell you them, and also to tell you about a certain boy scout.

There are pinball machines everywhere I go, and once or twice I've almost been tempted to play.

❧ 1936

Dear little being,

Everything's as fine as can be for you, but I'm too fagged to explain it all in detail. She was overcome with regret that you could have misinterpreted things, and is thinking of writing to you.[12] She said with a meaningful smile that she hadn't changed her feelings since Saturday, 'on the contrary'. – Till tomorrow at about nine. I'm going to bed. I kiss you, o best of little men.

Beaver

❧ 1937

[probably early 1937]

My love,

I've had a night punctuated by the most passionate little *Erlebnisse* for you[13] – which has meant that I've slept very badly. I had a delightful dream about Maurice Chevalier, who was simultaneously Colette and very surprised by this: 'Isn't she a woman?', he was saying. Though hardly daisy fresh, I'm no longer feeling tragic. I just wish I could be there beside you, so handsome in your little blue pyjamas, and kiss you with all my strength. I love you. Not being able to see you during the day brings tears to my eyes (my tiredness still brings me close to tears, but the tender kind, not the sad any more). I'm afraid I won't be daisy

---

[12]'She' is Olga Kosakiewitch (subsequently Olga Bost; stage name 'Olga Dominique'; figures in De Beauvoir's autobiography simply as Olga D., and in her editions of Sartre's war diaries and correspondence as 'Zazoulich'), a pupil of De Beauvoir at Rouen in 1933 who subsequently formed an intense, triangular relationship with De Beauvoir and Sartre in 1935-6. Subsequently married to Sartre's pupil and lifelong friend Jacques-Laurent Bost. In these letters, usually K. or Kos.

[13]*Erlebnis* (plural *Erlebnisse*): term borrowed from phenomenology and meaning 'lived experience', though De Beauvoir and Sartre commonly used it in the sense of 'emotion' or 'rapture'.

fresh this evening, but you can be sure of one thing. I shall be terribly happy to see you. I love you so passionately. I'm sorry, I haven't been as sweet as I should. But I kiss your sweet self, and your darling, lovely little face.

Your charming Beaver

You did cancel the wire?
Work well, I love you.

Taverne Charley
20 Boulevard Garibaldi

Marseilles [10 September 1937][14]

My love,

I was pretty much distraught when your little face disappeared from sight, and for a moment I stood helplessly in the station, quite out of my wits. And then, all of a sudden, that evening I had to spend alone in Marseilles struck me as imbued with a kind of gloomy poetry. There was a high wind outside, no question of going for a walk round the port in my poor summer clothes. I had no real desire to do so, in any case. So I took my bag to the left luggage office, then decided to go and see the Mathurin picture at the Cinéac.[15] In the bag, I found *Eyeless in Gaza* and the little textbook, which means our losses have really been very minimal. I stowed away the bits and pieces you so kindly handed me from the train door, and set off towards the Canebière. For 3 francs, I saw a programme lasting an hour and a half; this included a kind of feature on pickpockets, demonstrating fifty ingenious methods of stealing suitcases, bags and wallets. There were also some amazing acrobatic stunts – a guy diving off Brooklyn Bridge, another crossing some American street on a tightrope 300 metres up, etc. – and a documentary film in colour on Guatemala, which at least saved me from a nasty disappointment, since the Mathurin is pretty worthless. But comfortably ensconced in my armchair, I quite recovered my spirits during that hour. My neighbour tried to play footsy with me, though

---

[14]On their return from a trip to Greece in the summer of 1937, Sartre and De Beauvoir had spent two days together in Marseilles, after which he had returned to Paris while she went off for a little trip round Alsace with Olga.

[15]In 1931-2, when she was teaching in Marseilles.

actually it was as bright as day in the auditorium, a strange, sad light which didn't impair the projected image at all.

Then I came here and ate a fillet steak with fried bread, potatoes and artichoke hearts that consoled me for all my troubles: a miracle, I hadn't thought such a thing still existed. The place is delightful, it makes me feel odd and most extremely poetical to be spending an evening in this little inn, all by myself, just like in the old days when you didn't yet love me quite so much – there are still as many photos on the walls, and the same little cushions on the wooden benches. We'll go together next year.

It's 10.30 now. I've done the crossword in *Marianne*, which is ridiculously easy, and realize that instead of *The Safety-Match Mystery* you bought me *The Adventures of Ellery Queen* – but it's just as good. I'm going to write to my mother and read a bit, then in a little while I'll go off to the station and try to find a corner, after which I'll sleep like a log. I'm so sleepy I feel as though I were drunk. I'm quite choked with tenderness for you, my love, it makes me a bit pathetic to love you so much. Did you manage to get some sleep, my little man? You had nothing for your supper, you poor little person. Write to me very soon, tell me whether your little lip is better and if the lycée's miles away[16] – write to Urmatt, Bas-Rhin, where I shall be on the *16th*. Try to have the letter there by the morning of the 16th. As for the money, don't forget that it should be sent to *Barr*, Bas-Rhin.

Goodbye, my love. I'm lacerated everywhere by being far away from you after all these days – what a delightful little face you had this morning, curled up beside me in your little cocoon. I kiss you passionately.

Your charming Beaver

Envelope:
Monsieur Sartre,
Hôtel Royal Bretagne,
11 bis, rue de la Gaîté
Paris

---

[16]Sartre had just been appointed to the Lycée Pasteur, at Neuilly (on the western outskirts of Paris), after completing a year of teaching at Laon.

[Urmatt, Alsace][17]

Friday, 17 [September 1937]

Most dear little being,

I found your letter yesterday evening at Saales, and was very happy because it was so long and loving. When I wake up each morning it makes me sad to think I'm going to spend another long day without you. I'm hoping to find another letter from you shortly at the Urmatt post office, but I'm very much afraid you won't have had the wit to send it there. I'm pissed off because I don't know what address to give you, the weather's filthy and it's impossible to make any plan. Still, I'll try and wire the name of some village in the course of the day. At any rate, I'll be seeing you soon, I think you can count on me for the *22nd in the morning*, as we probably won't have enough left for a bed in Strasburg that last night. At latest I'll be in Paris on the evening of the 22nd, I'll meet you at the Dôme an hour or so after the train gets in – I'll wire you the exact time on the 21st. I can't wait to see you again, my love.

I've been having an agreeable time up to now, but today the rain really is too heavy, we're stuck in a little café in Urmatt for the entire day, I'm afraid. And I wonder whether the following days will be any better, which is rather a melancholy thought. It's a pity, since otherwise this trip would be very pleasant. K.[18] is charming, perfectly idyllic with me, entranced by everything, and best of all much lustier than might have been thought, quite Gallic even. The rain and wind don't frighten her, she easily walks 5 or 6 hours a day; yesterday we actually walked for 7 hours, with only an hour's halt, and if she was a bit the worse for wear by the end that was only because we hadn't eaten all day and her feet were sopping wet – in any case, she made a very speedy recovery. The first day in Strasburg was very agreeable. She arrived, delighted by her journey, and I took her off for a stroll; it was cold but not raining, and we saw all the agreeable parts of Strasburg round the Pont aux Corbeaux. Behind the cathedral there's an extremely pleasing little square, with lots of old inns and shady tea houses. We went inside one of them, it was crammed with Alsatians swilling beer and I drank a little white wine. Then we went up and wandered around the first floor of the building, through deserted 'wine rooms' and tea rooms, and came across an odd kind of hall with a dance-floor in the middle and closed boxes all round, from which vague whisperings could be heard; an

[17]Trip through Alsace described in *The Prime of Life*, p.313.
[18]Olga Kosakiewicz, see n. 12 above.

Alsatian lady in a white apron, sitting on a chair, was guarding the entrance. As this bears the name 'Dance Hall', when we get back to Strasburg we'll go in the evening and spend a little time there. After that we saw the cathedral and Place Gutenberg, and at 7 o'clock we had dinner at the Kammerzell, in the downstairs room, which is charming and where the prices are extraordinarily modest. At about 9 we found ourselves in a little square, enclosed on every side and reached by way of an arched passage. We climbed the stairs to a dance hall on the first floor of one house – it was jam-packed with people and we had difficulty finding two seats, in between two Alsatian families. Though it was all shabby respectability, Alsatians dancing the tango are a sight worth seeing – we danced a bit ourselves, with everyone looking askance at us because of our bare legs. We went home fairly early, at around midnight, both dropping with exhaustion. Next morning we drank hot coffee in the little hotel café and ate delicious brioches on the way, then made our pilgrimage: K.'s lycée, which is a beautiful old house on the canal bank where we went in and traipsed through the corridors and classrooms, and where we stole a fine white handkerchief embroidered in blue; the Orangery, which is a very agreeable small park; and the neighbourhood where the K.s used to live, a wealthy neighbourhood by the canal which I well remember passing through with you.

[. . .]

This morning we arrived by bus at Urmatt, 30 km from Saales; it's raining, so we came into this inn where we may have to stay all day. If the weather lifts, we'll go up the Donon. Then K. wants to see some ruined castles again, probably we'll go down towards Selestat and Ribeauville, and I'll finally show her Riquewihr, Kaysersberg and Colmar. She's in raptures over the trip, both because she's making it with me and because it's so healthy – all that fresh air and physical exercise. But she's interested neither in the towns, nor in the villages, nor in the scenery, but exclusively in ruined castles or in her childhood memories. She has told me that the only place in France where she'd like to go – apart from Alsace – is Brittany, because she has read poetical stories about it. As for me, I'd be quite enjoying it if the weather were fine, even though Alsace is really a bit too orderly for my taste and anyway I've already seen the most pleasing things with you. I'm not bored, but it's dreary and the time passes pretty slowly. I'm dying to be in Paris with you and to see you again. Goodbye for now, my little sweet husband. Try and pinch me a really long day or evening from your parents on the 22nd. I love you,

Your charming Beaver

🌸 1938

Hôtel du Cheval Blanc
Spontour (Corrèze)[19]

Spontour, Monday evening
[Whit Monday 1938]

My love,

It's amazing to land up in this village, when you've spent all day following a tiny path along the Dordogne and expected at most to find a hamlet. First, you cross a magnificent stone bridge and on your right see a huge 'International Café-Restaurant', to your left a huge 'Modern Dance Hall', both built of wood and painted green. Next, all the buildings are cafés. Finally, there's a wedding-procession of fifty souls winding through the streets at a spanking pace. From a distance I'd seen only peaceful little houses at the water's edge, each with a little plume of smoke rising vertically above its roof. I was quite amazed.

The Cheval Blanc hotel is like that one in Uzerche where we had a meal and you wanted to throw toffees into the water for me. The big hotel café's deserted and the owners eat next door, but they've lit up for me.

This is how I ended up here. You should first know that I slept very badly on the train. A family settled in as far as Vierzon, but that wasn't a problem. And there was another fellow, but he got out on the way too, so I was left on my own. But I was tossed around like mad, which destroyed any chance of sleep. Once I even found myself on the floor, and woke myself up with a shout of 'Hey, there!'. However, I did get some sleep after Montluçon. And then I was roused by the faintest of lights, looked out of the window and saw we were in a little village, an hour away from Mauriac. There were still stars in the sky, but it was fantastically warm. I stuck my head outside for a look. It was a delightful moment, I saw the dawn and then sunrise over the prettiest landscape. The train had grown very small and was climbing slowly up the track. At 5.30 I was in Mauriac – sky overcast – I took a stroll through the town, looked at a pretty, pitch-black Romanesque church, scaled a hillock from which I gazed out across a vast, rather unappealing countryside, like a more contorted version of Périgord. At 7 I boarded a bus – a bus that stopped literally every ten metres, and took 2 hours to cover 20 km. All the people were griping like mad, but to no avail. We arrived at a village and I had a big breakfast with eggs, milk and

---

[19]Walking holiday described in *The Prime of Life*, p.326.

sausage, enough not to be hungry for the rest of the day. Then I made my way up by a road and through woods towards some big mountains – but alas! the higher I went, the thicker the fog became. By the time I reached the topmost peak of the Cantal, pretty well exhausted, I was surrounded by a sea of fog; a family of motorists huddled shivering in a tiny shelter; one of the roads was blocked by firns. It was devilishly wild and bare – in fine weather it must be rather attractive, but as things were it was fairly chilling. I had to abandon the idea of a long, carefully planned ramble through the mountains and just set off down a road, since it was too cold to sit down. I walked downhill until the fog was left overhead, soon caught sight of a pretty valley and swooped down into a village, where I rested. I wouldn't have minded eating something, but after spotting maggots in the pastries I just dried my clothes and person (the fog having changed to rain along the way). Thanks to my stout shoes and raincoat, I wasn't soaked. When the weather brightened up a bit at about 5, I set off again like a stubborn woman; I wanted to get over a pass and then down into the valley of the Lioran, it should have taken two hours or so, but I couldn't find the pass, the fog returned, and I decided to go back down. On the way down I thought I'd gone mad, for I'd left the village turning right, on the way up I'd been keeping to the right all the time, only to find as I walked on downhill that the village was on *my* left – in other words, still further to the right. I was irritated and almost worried, but then when I reached the bottom I saw that it was another village, and there was a much more comfortable hotel than in the first one, so I had an immense dinner. By 8.30 I was sleeping the sleep of the righteous.

Today the weather was perfect. I took a bus which traced the full length of a pretty valley before taking me to Aurillac, whence another bus conveyed me to Argentat. I was so pleased to be back in the Limousin, it really is a pretty part of the country. Argentat is like Uzerche, the Dordogne gorges like those along the Vézère – to my taste, it's thoroughly charming. I ate a real lunch at Argentat at 10 in the morning, with rabbit, chicken, etc. There was a fair in town, which was very entertaining. Furthermore, I'm very proud of myself because, in spite of certain female frailties, I did 35 km between 11 in the morning and 8 in the evening without feeling tired. I had some milk and eggs after 10 km. I arrived here half an hour ago and am now writing to you before going off to bed. I'm having a very enjoyable time – I love you – I think lots of nice things about you during the day, but I'm too tired to tell you them. Till Saturday, my love.

Your charming Beaver

P.S. I forgot to tell you that the novel by Mr Daly King is vaguely entertaining, but scientific.[20] The novel by M. Boileau is appalling, unreadable, but contains a neat problem with an elegant solution. I've already lost the little guidebook – and also my soap and toothbrush. I'll buy some more soap, but as for the guidebook I knew it by heart.

* * *

Tuesday

Hi, my love! I've just sent off the wire and am hoping for a letter at the Lioran. I did 30 km along the Dordogne gorges – pretty, but monotonous – then a kindly lorry conveyed me to Bort-les-Orgues. I saw the 'organ-pipes' from a distance, but didn't bother to climb up, since I'm well acquainted with sights of that kind. Instead I went to the cafe, to drink fresh lemon and write to Bianca Bienenfeld.[21] This evening I'll write to K. and tomorrow you'll have another little letter. I'm setting off by train for the mountains, because the weather's fine and I'm stubborn, I'll climb up by another route to the top of that mountain which struck me numb. I'm enjoying myself – I love you.

Beaver

La Flégère
Les Praz de Chamonix
[Haute-Savoie]

Friday [15 July 1938]

Dear little being,

It's rather meritorious on my part to be writing to you, since we're in a real hurry to go off walking again – but, after all, I love you and

---

[20]Charles Daly King, author of *The Psychology of Consciousness* (1932), published several novels in the thirties, including *Arrogant Alibi, Bermuda Burial, Careless Corpse* and *The Curious Mr Tarrant*.

[21]Bianca Bienenfeld. Former pupil of De Beauvoir's at the Lycée Molière (in the 16th Arrondissement) in 1838, of Polish-Jewish origin, who became her lover, had a brief affair with Sartre in July/August 1939 prior to his mobilization, and figures as 'Louise Védrine' or 'V.' in De Beauvoir's editions of Sartre's correspondence and war diaries. Subsequently (1941) married Bernard Lamblin, Sartre's former pupil from the Lycée Pasteur in 1939.

want you to know what's becoming of me.[22] First, in the little corner where you settled me I spent quite a good journey, but got hardly any sleep. There was an Italian beside me who had an amazing resemblance to Mussolini, and who squashed me with his fat behind. At 4.30 in the morning, I changed trains. The weather was marvellous, a clear sky still containing a bright moon and stars though it was already dawn, and white mists to be seen everywhere over the countryside, with black mountains rising above them – it was quite lovely. The train conveyed me through the most beautiful scenery as far as Annemasse, not far from Geneva, where I transferred into a little electric tram running along a road. We were entering a region of high mountains and could see snow and high peaks – I was in ecstasies. I met a woman there whom I'd known at the Cours Désir,[23] and we kept up a pitiful conversation for the entire journey. At 9 the tram halted at the foot of a mountain amphitheatre, and I found Bost already tanned and looking very nice in his yellow pullover. He recounted his journey: on the first day a lorry had conveyed him in state all the way to Dole, then he'd gone to Lausanne – in the hope of finding a sister whom he didn't in fact find – crossed Lake Geneva, and made his way back by bus after bankrupting himself among the Swiss.

[. . .]

I told Bost the story about Boutang, he was captivated and shocked.[24]

Goodbye, my love, I'm hoping for a letter from you soon, at Chamonix, I'll write tomorrow.*

A big hug and kiss – I've lots of little *Erlebnisse* for you and I'm not forgetting that you have some for me too, all teeming fresh – I love you.

Beaver

*So write to Bourg-Saint-Maurice (Savoie).

---

[22]'We' = herself and Jacques-Laurent Bost. Bost had been a pupil of Sartre's at the Lycée François I in Le Havre (1934-5), and was known as Little Bost to distinguish him from his elder brother Pierre, writer and chief editor of *Marianne*. Married Olga Kosakiewitch, and remained a lifelong friend and colleague of De Beauvoir and Sartre. For his portrait, see *The Prime of Life*, p.245-7.

[23]The Cours Adeline Désir was an exclusive Catholic private school in the 6th Arrondissement of Paris, attended by De Beauvoir from 1913 until 1924 (when she was 16).

[24]Anecdote recounted by Sartre in his letter of 14 July: see *Lettres au Castor*, vol. 1, p.185.

Col de Balme [Haute-Savoie]
Simond Frères,
Propriétaires

17 July 1938

Most dear little being,

Here I am, at that same Col de Balme above Charamillon which we never visited together when we were at Argentières: it's a pity, because there's a fantastic view over Switzerland and the Chamonix valley. We've just had lunch here – only an omelette and sautéd potatoes, since we're extremely careful with our money. I'm already quite tanned, and look like a woman of the wilds. I've my left hand all bandaged up, since I acquired a magnificent wound yesterday – I'll tell you the whole story.

First of all, the day before yesterday I finished off a letter in the hotel at Buet, where the rain finally obliged us to spend the night: a room with twin beds, all very proper, and as much hot water as you wanted – so we washed for a week. The rain came down all night. We'd asked to be woken at 6, but it was still raining and we went back to sleep until 9.30; then, opening our eyes, we saw that it was quite fine and we were in danger of wasting a day, so we set off determinedly for the mountain we planned to reach – the Buet – rising 1,800 metres above us. At first we went up a decent path winding through gorges, but then we had to scramble across scree and firns. The place was really wild and magnificent, and it was great fun crossing huge stretches of snow. We had some very fine views up to about 2,800 metres, but above that there was a thick fog – and an icy wind that chilled us to the bone. All the same we went stubbornly up and up, it was terribly steep, my heart was going like a hammer; but 50 metres from the top, as the fog wasn't lifting and there was still a big firn to cross, we decided to go back down. We opened a tin of sardines for a bite to eat but hail began to fall, so we raced down across some slate and in ten minutes found ourselves below the fog. We hurtled across the firns too, letting ourselves slide – either upright or sitting – but that's when, having picked up a bit too much speed, I tried to brake by catching hold of a rock which split my left hand between the fourth and fifth fingers, I didn't feel a thing, I noticed only a few seconds later that my blood was spurting everywhere – it was deep and quite nauseating. We made a bandage out of a handkerchief, which didn't prevent my blood from spurting everywhere, but in the first chalet-hotel we raced down to Bost washed my hand in spirits and put on a new little dressing. But he insisted I should go and see a doctor, so we went back to the hotel, packed our bags and took the little train you and I often used to take to Montroc – but this time on the other side of the tunnel, towards

Switzerland. The run was delightful, the little train sped high above splendid wild gorges, and after half an hour we arrived at Finhaut, the first hamlet on the line which possessed a doctor. We asked the stationmaster for his address, and he pointed to one of the actual passengers getting off the train. This was the doctor, who led us genially to a very Swiss kind of chalet-pharmacy, all in wood, with little bottles and mechanical armchairs everywhere: this was his house. He put on a long white smock, carefully disinfected my hand and suggested putting in a stitch, so that the scar would look better; but I rejected this with horror, so he just gave me a good, solid bandage that I can take off in two or three days. I feel absolutely nothing, and in fact am quite proud when people ask me if I'm badly wounded. Then we bought bread, chocolate and cheese and went for a melancholy stroll beside waterlogged meadows. Then I had the idea of sleeping in a barn. I asked some people to direct me to one, and they directed me to the village hall – which serves as the mayor's office, I think, at the same time as being a hotel and cafe. There, a very kind lady led us to a charming barn, with a little wooden balcony; we ate our meal sitting on the balcony, drank water from a fountain, then wandered round the village a bit while Bost smoked his pipe. The view was wonderful, mountains, clouds, little red lights in the night and I couldn't have felt more at ease. We slept well, except that the single sleeping-bag links me tightly to Bost, who kicks all night and filled my face with hay. At 7 this morning the weather was marvellous. We washed a bit at the fountain, breakfasted in the garden of the village hall, off milk and what the good lady called 'artificial' honey, then had to plunge to the very bottom of deep gorges in order to get up on the other side. Bost tried to make friends with a nanny-goat, which butted him hard in the midriff – but she didn't have horns. Then, at about 3, we reached the Col de Balme where we had lunch. I started to write to you, then we climbed to a peak from which there was an infinitely more stupendous view over the snow-covered peaks of huge mountains. Picture us constantly in landscapes resembling the Zugspitz, with that strange mixture of icy wind and blazing sun. We hared downhill to Montroc – our ski slope looks quite flat at this time of year – and just caught the little electric train running to Chamonix. There I bribed a railway clerk (it was Sunday) to hand over Bost's second sleeping-bag, and Bost bribed the postal clerk to hand over our mail: a letter from Bienenfeld and your wire, but no letter from you. I'm having everything forwarded to Bourg St Maurice, so that's where you should write until further orders. We jumped aboard a coach which in two hours travelled all the way down the Chamonix valley and up again past Sallanches to Cluses. There, dazed by sun, hunger and exhaustion, we wandered from shop to shop buying stacks of food, then looked for a spot to camp and found only an ugly patch of grass surrounded by houses. When we'd eaten and pitched our tent, we felt like kings; changing into slippers, we went back into Cluses and had a drink and a chat sitting outside a cafe, just like some sedate couple on holiday. I'm finishing off this letter while Bost writes up our travel log. He's so proud of it, and indeed it isn't half bad: 7½ hours walking and 1,200 metres climbed even today, which was a kind of rest day. Now we're off to sleep in the tent ready and waiting for us. We'll take a coach at 9.30 for the Chartreuse du Reposoir – which inspired Henri Bordeaux[25] – and we'll climb a mountain that's 'easy but vertiginous': we're afraid we may chicken out of going up, since we're rather cowardly about vertigo, but we'll have a fine outing in any case.

Bost is revelling in the story of M. Plume[26] – he likes to read me extracts out loud while I'm writing to you or sleeping.

Goodnight, my love, I'm going to sleep. I love you very much

Your Beaver

[Nancroix, Savoie]

Friday 22 [July 1938]

My sweet little husband,

I've been waking up these past few days with a keen longing to see you. And I'm beginning to count the days that separate us – still over a week to go. Yesterday, as it was theoretically a rest day – which we really needed – I took the opportunity of dragging Bost by bus to Bourg St Maurice, where I found your long letters. I read them at my ease in a little shady café, and today I've just read them again. They entertained me greatly and I'm waiting impatiently for the sequel. I find Gibert very likeable and the story elegant, but I'm shocked to see old Merleauponte abandoning his role as an impartial, tranquil monk.[27] You're very sweet

---

[25]Henry Bordeaux (1870-1963), novelist of provincial life, especially devoted to his native Savoy.
[26]By the poet Henri Michaux (1899-   ).
[27]Gibert: Colette Gibert, a drama student at the Théâtre de l'Atelier (called 'Cecilia Bertin' in The Prime of Life – p.349 – and 'Martine Bourdin' in De Beauvoir's edition of the Lettres au Castor, July 1938 passim), with whom Sartre had a brief fling during the summer of 1938. She brought Sartre back into contact with the philosopher Maurice Merleau-Ponty, who was in love with her. A contemporary of De Beauvoir's at the Sorbonne in 1929, he was to be a close friend and colleague in the immediate postwar period.

to have told me the whole story in such detail, my love.

[...]

This morning we left at 9, climbed to a peak from which there was a splendidly sinister view, then made our way down to a village called Nancroix where we've just had lunch. Bost was half-dead: he ate half his meal, but immediately went and threw it up again in the garden. I had to endure the chambermaid's commiserations. In the garden I found Bost relieved and gay, but was overcome in turn by a violent nosebleed – I don't think we'll be walking much this evening. We're now drinking coffee and writing letters like real holidaymakers. Apart from the nosebleed, I'm in marvellous shape actually, I'm full of beans today.

I've had some letters from Bienenfeld, full of passion. I'll be at Annecy on the 27th in the morning, write me a last little letter there.

I'm not doing much thinking. I'm blissful, I long to see you, I'm beginning to feel the greatest impatience to see you, my beloved, I love you quite passionately.

Goodbye, my love – thank you for your agreeable long letters – have a good time and come and join me with a thousand little *Erlebnisse* to do the courtesies to my own.

I kiss you most tenderly

Your Beaver

Envelope
Monsieur Sartre,
Hôtel Mistral,
Rue Cels, Paris 14
postmarked
'Bourg St Maurice at St Pierre d'Albigny'*

Hôtel de la gare
Albertville (Savoie)

Albertville, Wednesday [27 July 1938]

Dear little being,

I'm not going to write you a long letter, though I've hundreds of things to tell you, because I prefer to tell you them in person on Saturday. You should know, however:

---

*Letters 22 July to 20 September 1938 addressed as above

1. First, that I love you dearly – I'm quite overcome at the thought that I'll see you disembarking from the train on Saturday, carrying your suitcase and my red hatbox – I can already picture us ensconced on our deckchairs overlooking a lovely blue sea and talking nineteen to the dozen – and I feel a great sense of well-being.[28]

2. You've been very sweet to write me such long letters. I'm hoping for another this evening at Annecy. You tell me countless pleasing little items of news, but the most pleasing of all is that you've found your subject. The big page looks extremely fine with that title, just the perverse kind you like: *Lucifer* – I can find no fault with it.[29]

3. Something extremely agreeable has happened to me, which I didn't at all expect when I left – I slept with Little Bost three days ago. It was I who propositioned him, of course. Both of us had been wanting it: we'd have serious conversations during the day, and the evenings would be unbearably oppressive. One rainy evening at Tignes, in a barn, lying face down a few inches away from one another, we gazed at each other for an hour finding various pretexts to put off the moment of going to sleep, he babbling frantically, I racking my brains vainly for the casual, appropriate words I couldn't manage to articulate – I'll tell you it all properly later. In the end I laughed foolishly and looked at him, so he said: 'Why are you laughing?' and I said: 'I'm trying to picture your face if I propositioned you to sleep with me' and he said: 'I was thinking that you were thinking that I wanted to kiss you but didn't dare.' After that we floundered on for another quarter of an hour before he made up his mind to kiss me. He was tremendously astonished when I told him I'd always had a soft spot for him – and he ended up telling me yesterday evening that he'd loved me for ages. I'm very fond of him. We spend idyllic days, and nights of passion. But have no fear of finding me sullen or disoriented or ill at ease on Saturday; it's something precious to me, something intense, but also light and easy and properly in its place in my life, simply a happy blossoming of relations that I'd always found very agreeable. It strikes me as funny, on the other hand, to think that I'm now going to spend two days with Bienenfeld.

Goodbye, dear little being – I'll be on the platform on Saturday, or at the buffet if you don't see me on the platform. I'd like to spend long weeks alone with you. A big kiss.

Your Beaver

---

[28]They were about to embark for Morocco.
[29]The work in question was to become *Les Chemins de la Liberté* (*The Roads to Freedom*).

[Marseilles]

Saturday [September 1938]

Your own self, my love,

I've just called at the post office, but found no wire – I'll call back again. The afternoon papers aren't out yet, and I'm impatient and pretty gloomy.[30] When you're there, I can't be really worried. But all day yesterday, and now, I can feel the full weight of it; and it seems odd to be here, far away from Paris and you, not knowing if I'm going to stay or leave, not knowing what you think, not knowing anything. I live in expectation – and in a fog – and feel as though I'd left you centuries ago.

The weather's fine here, we could lead a delightful life. Kosakiewitch has a really pleasing room, a sixth-floor with balcony over the Old Port. From the bed you can see all the little boats, the water and the lights, and you feel as though you're sleeping right in the street. There's a little sink and a stove for doing the cooking, and when you eat there with the window open you can believe yourself on the terrace of some palace. On Thursday evening we didn't have dinner there but at the Cascade – indoors, because it was a bit cold. I had the most delicious fish soup, followed by grilled bass. Afterwards we went to the Cintra and to Charley's, and we didn't get home till about 2. I was in a good mood and happy. We talked for a long time that evening, and again in the morning after waking up very early, but I've so much sleep in reserve that I wasn't tired. When we came down at noon to have lunch at Charley's, we saw the papers, which were gloomy. We went for a long walk round Marseilles, by way of the Prado and the Corniche, then came back to drink in little cafés, have dinner in K.'s room, and spend the evening on the balcony – where I interested K. tremendously talking to her about the Arabs. I slept well, then this morning we were up and about by 9 and went for a stroll in the streets round the Old Port and near the Porte d'Aix. We had lunch – K. made me a scrumptious omelette – and we're now taking coffee in a bistro that's allegedly full of criminal types – it certainly looks that way.

All this strikes me as dreadfully contingent, and I can feel time passing never-endingly.

* * *

My beloved, I have your wire – so we're leaving. I'm amazed, since I understood things were going very badly. Summon me back at once if things do become worrying, I beg of you. It doesn't seem at all the same

---

[30]War seemed imminent – the Munich Agreement delaying it was not reached until the very end of the month.

as when I was with you. When I'm with you, nothing seems terrible to me, not even leaving you. But away from you, the slightest fear is unbearable. I love you passionately – I'm empty and miserable without you. K. has been very sweet, and the first evening I was touched by seeing her again – but already she bores and rather irritates me, and her presence at this moment strikes me as absurd. Write to me immediately at the addresses provided. I love you, with a touch of tragedy and quite madly.

Your Beaver

※ 1939

[Paris]

Monday morning [3 July 1939]

Most dear little being,

I just caught sight of a great, green shape snatching you up, so I stepped back hastily. I think I caught sight of The Step-father too.[31] It was heart-rending to see them with my own eyes taking delivery of you, my pet, and I wandered about the platform for a moment, disconcerted and desolate. Then I left and went down towards Gien, which is a real take-in. As you must have discerned there was a village fête in progress, which was like an insult. I climbed to the castle, walked to the end of the Quai – in a quarter of an hour I'd done it all and was finding the hole unbearable. I went back to the station buffet and began reading the N.R.F.,[32] which I finished on the train. I'll send it you in a little while. Clara Malraux's article is amazing. It's distressing enough that a person should think such things, but to write them down and have them published is really beyond my comprehension – she comes out as the most complete nitwit, by her own admission. The little seduction story is side-splitting. All in all, I had almost enough to keep me amused as far as Paris. I raced to the hotel and found a message from Kos., suggesting a meeting at the Café de Flore. I hope they didn't say on the telephone that I'd left with you; at all events, she didn't breathe a word to me about it during the evening. At first she was cool, but I think that's because I'd been away for the whole week – and nothing to do with the circumstances of my return – since in the end she became

---

[31]After a few days spent together Sartre and De Beauvoir had to separate at Gien, since he was obliged to spend some time with his mother and stepfather.
[32]*Nouvelle Revue Française.*

charming. We stayed on for a while at the Flore. Her audition went well, but Dullin[33] – who had a train to catch – didn't make any detailed comments. When each audition ended, he simply said: 'bad scene', or 'good scene', or 'very good scene' – and for Kos. he said 'very good scene'. The wretched Delarue was stopped in the middle of his.[34] In the evening, they all went on a junket together – at a girl friend of Madeleine Robinson's place.[35] It was a drunken orgy, at which everybody was smooching with everybody else and Delarue kissed Kos. – but he was so tipsy he couldn't remember next day, he just had a vague, dreadful impression of having behaved badly. She was tight too, but in control of herself, and she really flabbergasted me by saying haughtily: 'I can't understand how it is that when people are drunk, they smooch with just anybody; you can always behave properly if you want to' – this in naive disgust at the notion of any kind of abandon while under the influence. We went and had dinner in a little restaurant in Rue St Benoît, where everybody from the Café de Flore meets and you can eat very well without spending much – and which is not disagreeable. Then we spent a long time at an outside table at the Deux Magots. It was a lovely little evening, one on which I'd have been so happy with you, beloved little being. I got home at one and rose at seven, which means I am in fact feeling tired today. At the moment I'm supervising a fourth-year exam, and after that I've hundreds of things to do: ring Davy,[36] see Bienenfeld, have lunch with Poupette,[37] see That Lady if possible, come back to school at 5 for a staff meeting, and meet up with Kos. for a long evening. I feel a bit overwhelmed. The weather's extremely beautiful, and seeing that I can't be [with] you I'd like to be entirely alone and have nothing to do. But above all I wish you were here. I fell asleep and awoke in anguish at your leaving. I loved you so much in that little train yesterday. You're so nice, you know, dearest little being – you're far more than quite nice, you're the nicest of little men, and I'm so happy with you. But I can't wait to have you to myself for days on end, as will soon be the case.

---

[33]Charles Dullin (1885-1949), actor and producer, founder in 1921 of the Théâtre de l'Atelier. One of the foremost producers of avant-garde theatre in the years leading up to and immediately following the war, Dullin was both a friend of De Beauvoir and Sartre (living as he did with 'Toulouse' – see note 63 below) and the original producer of Sartre's first play staged in Paris, *The Flies*.

[34]Delarue: fellow drama student with Olga at the Théâtre de l'Atelier.

[35]For a portrait of the actress Madeleine Robinson, see *The Prime of Life*, p.348.

[36]The Inspector General at the ministry of education.

[37]Nickname of De Beauvoir's younger sister Hélène, married to Sartre's former pupil from Le Havre, Lionel de Roulet.

Do write to me – go on writing to Paris, as I'll be back here anyway on Friday. Look, is it impossible for me to tell Kos., if the case arises, that I'm going to spend Saturday–Sunday with you? Just Saturday–Sunday, Wanda[38] couldn't surely be angry about that, and it would give me an excellent alibi: Wednesday–Thursday La Pouèze,[39] then back to Paris, then two days seeing you. It's also quite possible that I'll have no need to, and in any case I can manage things differently if it bothers you too much. But let me know immediately about this, please – I'd like your reply by Wednesday morning. I'm afraid Kos. has not the least desire to leave before 14 July – but I won't give her much money.

Goodbye, my love, I'll write to you tomorrow. I love you quite passionately – and with a touch of tragedy – poor little prisoner, all out of reach. Till Tuesday, my love. We'll spend a huge evening, perhaps we won't go to bed all night, if the weather's still as fine. I kiss your dear little face all over. I love you, my beloved.

Your charming Beaver

I'm no longer disfigured at all.

Envelope:
Monsieur Sartre
Poste Restante
St Sauveur en Puisaye,
Yonne.*

---

*Letters 3 to 8 July 1938 addressed as above
[38]Wanda Kosakiewitch, Olga's younger sister and likewise an actress (stage name Marie Olivier), appears in Sartre's war diaries and correspondence edited by De Beauvoir as 'Tania Zazoulich'. Her pursuit and seduction by, and relationship with, Sartre loom large in the *Lettres au Castor*, and she was to remain a lifelong friend (see *Adieux. A Farewell to Sartre*, London 1984, passim).
[39]Mme Morel's house near Angers.

Brasserie Lumina
76 Rue de Rennes
Paris

Wednesday [5 July 1939]

The first page of this letter must
be torn up at once, because otherwise you'll forget.

I'm telling Kos. that I'll be
staying at La Pouèze till Monday.
No point in saying I'm at St
Fargeau, etc. I won't come back on
the Friday, as I'm only leaving
tomorrow. I'm telling Bienenfeld
too that I'm at La Pouèze.[40]

Most dear little being,

I miss you. I've received all your little letters safely, and you're very
sweet to have been such a good correspondent. But it really grieves me
to feel you so glum, there far away, and to be glum myself here. I've
just received a blow: I went to see the tax people, and they're demanding
2,400 francs from me. I'll check whether it's really true, and appeal if
need be. How much have you paid, for instance? I think I'd be allowed
to pay just half now, and the rest when school reopens – but it's still
rotten. Moreover, Gégé's[41] asking for her dough – 1,200 francs –
though that's something you ought to take care of. For my part I've had
to give some dough to Kos., who's finally leaving on Saturday, and pay
some bills – to the dentist, and for books – but I'll just survive till
Wednesday. There you are! It's none too brilliant, and I'm sorry to start
off with all this – but it's casting a gloom over my own mood. I'm so
longing to go off on an agreeable journey with you – just you – and see
things. There's no question of Norway – it's more expensive than
Holland, and they tell me no French person will set foot there this year.
I thought we might spend a week in the Pyrenees, getting about by

---

[40]De Beauvoir was getting ready to visit Bost, who was doing his military service at
Amiens. It was advisable for this visit to be concealed from both Olga (who was already
in a relationship with Bost) and Bianca Bienenfeld. Moreover, De Beauvoir could not
claim to be with Sartre at Saint-Fargeau near Saint-Sauveur, since Wanda – in love with
Sartre – was proving extremely jealous.
[41]Gégé = Géraldine Pardo, lifelong friend of De Beauvoir from 1929, when she first met
her through her sister. An artist and designer, she often used to lend money to De
Beauvoir and Sartre in the prewar period.

P.L.M. buses,[42] then take ship at Bordeaux for a few weeks in Portugal? Let me know quickly what you think – my nerves are really jangling. I'm leaving tomorrow for Amiens, where I think I'll stay till Monday morning, so write me there poste restante. Little Bost is off to the Ardennes on the 13th, and doesn't get a long leave – it's rotten.

I'll tell you how I've been living. On Monday, I spent a pretty god-awful day. I saw some tedious pupils in the morning, after writing to you while supervising an essay. Then I went to That Lady's,[43] to pay my respects for an hour or so and ask her to give me an alibi. She was charming, but glum because Mops[44] wants to go with her to Cavallo and is giving her no respite. 'You've got some idea in your head, going off alone with Geneviève', says Mops, 'you've certainly got some idea in your head.' She's sulking, because That Lady's going off to La Pouèze and leaving her on her own with her husband. That Lady and Zuorro[45] had been at the Escadrille, and found it moderately charming. But they hadn't found anything to eat there – it had been completely empty and they'd got the impression they weren't wanted. Zuorro had been quite nice, though still a bit out of sorts.

After that I went and saw Poupette, and had lunch with her at the Italian place. We ate outside – it was moderately agreeable. Then we went for a walk through Paris, along the river towards Palais Royal. She's really het up about Lionel,[46] whose glands turn out to be tubercular and who's totally downcast. We must go there next week. Perhaps I'll be a martyr and go there on Monday, before your return. She spoke laughingly to me about the mysterious way Wanda's dropping hints about 'a holiday in the Midi', and also about how Wanda tried to hide from her the fact that you'd come with her and Mouloudji[47] – which explains Poupette's comment: 'I thought I recognized Sartre's handiwork'. She talked to me about Gégé, who's beginning to drive Pardo up the wall. She was rather sweet and nice.

---

[42]P.L.M. = Paris – Lyon – Mediterranée.

[43]In Boulevard Raspail.

[44]Nickname of Mme Morel's daughter Jacqueline.

[45]Marc Zuore ('Marco' in De Beauvoir's autobiography), friend whom Sartre had got to know at the Cité Universitaire in 1929. A teacher of French language, he had been a colleague of De Beauvoir at Rouen in 1932, but had now received a Paris post. For a time he hoped to become an opera singer, but never realized this ambition. His unrequited passion for Bost altered his relations with Sartre and De Beauvoir: see *The Prime of Life*, pp.118 and 283-4.

[46]Lionel de Roulet, husband of De Beauvoir's sister Poupette and former pupil of Sartre in 1932 (see *The Prime of Life*, pp124-5).

[47]Mouloudji: Algerian friend of Olga, a child film star and fellow student at the Atelier drama classes (see *The Prime of Life*, p.349).

The Boubous[48] are spending their holidays at Cagnes, 10 km. from Juan-les-Pins,[49] and are counting on seeing us. They're pestering us. I dropped in to Nordisk Travel with her — you know already what they told me. Then I went off by Métro to see Bienenfeld, but scarcely did see her, since she was almost as exhausted as the evening before (she's fine now). I left her and went on to school, where there was a meeting. I also rang Davy, whom I'll see next week. And in the midst of all this I forgot to send you the *N.R.F.*, poor little fellow, I'm really ashamed. I'll send it off straight away, with a Claudel that has just arrived. At 7 I met Kos. in Montmartre. We spent an extremely agreeable evening, with a whole series of charming episodes. I think I'll actually tell you all about it in person on Tuesday, since it would take me three hours. Basically, we traipsed around until about 11.30, having drinks at Place du Tertre and Chez Graff. We passed by the Escadrille several times, but at 9 they wouldn't even let us in the door, while at 11 it was so deserted it was intimidating. So we went to the Ange Rouge (that dancehall full of pimps and Corsicans, where people fire off revolvers), and it was marvellous there. Some fellows quite seriously propositioned us for a grand orgy. They even brought along a beautiful woman to entice us, and above all — due to a misunderstanding — got the idea that K. took drugs, so they brought along a frightful-looking fellow who offered her heroin and coke, and haggled with her for ages, and even showed her little packets: we were ever so flattered. After we left there, there was a tiny but very funny episode with a Negro, and also some gorgeous fellows in a motor tried to pick us up. To top it all off, we were at the swing club until 4.30 in the morning; they have wonderful jazz records, and it's the most agreeable place. Rue Pigalle was charming before dawn. We walked for a while, and I took a taxi to get home to bed. Kos. was extremely nice, she's on the best of terms with me.

I slept till 1, and at 2 went to meet Sorokine at the Dôme.[50] I had a

---

[48]The 'Boubous' = the Gerassis. De Beauvoir got to know Estepha Awdykowicz (later Gerassi, nicknamed 'the Baba') in 1928, while visiting her friend ZaZa Le Coin, where Stépha — a Ukrainian from Poland — was working as governess to ZaZa's younger sisters (see *Memoirs of a Dutiful Daughter*, p.278 ff.). Stépha married Fernando Gerassi ('the Boubou'), a Spanish painter, and the two (with later their son John, or 'Tito', born 1935), were among the closest friends of De Beauvoir and Sartre throughout the thirties. They emigrated to the United States in 1940.

[49]They were staying with Mme Morel at her villa.

[50]Nathalie Sorokine ('Lisa Oblanoff' in *The Prime of Life*, see p.347 etc.), of White Russian origin, was De Beauvoir's pupil at the Lycée Molière in 1938 and subsequently became a close friend. In 1945 she married Ivan Moffatt, an American GI, and returned with him to Los Angeles where he worked in Hollywood as an assistant to the director George Stevens.

coffee and a talk with her – she's really nice, but really pitiful. I think I'll send her to the Limousin for her vacation, to La Grillère.[51] I promised to devote my whole evening to her on Monday. She went with me to the clinic, where I stayed for an hour and a half. Bienenfeld was well and very sweet, but her mother stuck like a burr – she did it deliberately, out of spite. When her father and sister showed up, I got the hell out – and arrived at the Flore a bit late. But I made a few jokes about Bienenfeld, which went down very well. Kos. was tired, and sad because of Bost and going away – but very amiable. She took the fact that I was going to La Pouèze very well. We dined in Rue St-Benoît, where you can eat sumptuously for practically nothing, and it's agreeable too – I'll take you there this week. Then we came back to sit outside at the Flore, and finally walked across Paris to the Madeleine. It was a really lovely evening, with a fat orange moon in the sky, a bit of a breeze, and the odd cloud: crossing the Seine and Louvre was so agreeable that it was affecting. Kos. and I had a serious chat – about herself, about her life, and about life in general. She told me once again that she found mine dreadfully austere. We'd never been so intimate, and at the time I almost believed her. I went home (prudently, by Métro: Monday evening apart I'm being very frugal) and so to bed. This morning I received your second letter, and a note from that woman wanting her suitcase. I went to Neuilly to see Bienenfeld, who firmly showed her mother the door so I did see her for a while on her own. I gave her your letter. I'm going back to see her now, and I'll try to go again tomorrow for a moment before leaving.

I've just had lunch at my mother's, then been to see the tax people. This evening I'm seeing Kos. again, to say goodbye.

I feel odd. There's a tremendous atmosphere of year's end. It's not entirely disagreeable. But I miss you to the point of anguish. I'd like to see you and have you to myself – just to myself – for a long, long while. Do come back quickly, sweet little being. Let me know when you're getting back on Tuesday. I'm just going to ring Pasteur,[52] and I'll put the information in a postscript. I love you, dear little being, I love you quite passionately and kiss and hug you

Your charming Beaver

The prize-giving is on the 12th, at 3 o'clock.

---

[51] For the De Beauvoir family homes near Uzerche (Corrèze) in the old province of Limousin – La Grillère, an estate some 20 kilometres away, and Meyrignac, a large house on the outskirts – see *Memoirs of a Dutiful Daughter*, pp.23-4.
[52] The Lycée Pasteur at Neuilly, see note 16 above.

[Amiens]

Thursday [6 July 1939]

Most dear little being,

I'm writing to you from the Amiens train and don't have any ink in my fountain-pen, but this pencil seems quite decent. I've just received your little letter, and I'm very touched by it. You're the best little man in the world, and I too will write to you every day. I'm in the dumps. I haven't had enough sleep these last few days and I'm worn out. Also, I've received a first tax demand – without allowances – and the amount really is 2,400 F. And yesterday Kos. asked me unexpectedly for 300 F. – for debts and rent. It's really getting me down. Bienenfeld was sad I was leaving, and I feel a bit remorseful. Kos. talked to me at length about Bost, and though I don't feel any remorse so far as she's concerned, I do have a sense of superficiality and guile, that will melt away when I see Bost but that deprives me of all pleasure in leaving. At this moment I'd like to see you and only you. Everything's so full, so necessary, and so happy, with you – your self – my true life. Come back soon. Just look at me! I'm quite overcome when I think about seeing your little face again on Tuesday.

Yesterday after writing to you I went and saw Bienenfeld. She was charming. She gave me this little letter for you, which I enclose. She told me, in all innocence, that she was amazed I should be leaving for La Pouèze at this moment. But I explained as best I could how I was alone in Paris, how it made me wretched, and how I couldn't see her properly or even very often. At this point her mother came back, and as she talked Bienenfeld – under her mother's very nose – scribbled on a paper and showed me the words: 'I'm so pleased I could talk to you. I'm all right, don't worry.' It made me ever so remorseful, to see her being so nice. Her mother wouldn't budge again, then an aunt turned up, and in the end they started bustling around me to get me to leave, which I did. At the Flore I met a very nervy Kos., who'd just seen off Wanda. We went for a stroll and ended up in Montparnasse, but as I was scared stiff of running into somebody like Zuorro or Mops, [53] I refused to stay there and dragged Kos. off to the Latin Quarter. We sat down outside the Balzar – which was agreeable – and talked about our relationship, with which she declared she was absolutely delighted. Then we went to the Capoulade, and she talked about Bost. She explained to me that again this year she'd often tormented him without knowing why, to revenge

---

[53]Since this would inevitably have destroyed the fiction of the trip to La Pouèze, see note 40 above.

herself for the past; but that this was finished now, and what she finds marvellous is to be confronted with someone absolutely alone, who has no recourse outside her. It wasn't very nice, but I found it more amusing than disconcerting. All in all, when she's at her best as she is now – serene and trusting and well-disposed – she's very interesting and even engaging, but not nice. We parted tenderly on the steps of the Saint-Michel Métro, and doubtless we'll have the most idyllic relationship next year.

Now the train's moving and it's hard to write. I slept, I got your letter, and I took the 10 o'clock train – which now has third-class carriages. I've just read *Match* and done half the crossword. The weather's pretty fine, and I'm less downcast than when I set out. I'm thinking about how I'm going to see you again soon, and how in any case I'll be spending my holidays with you. I love you, dear little being – it makes me so sad that you should be there with nothing to interest you. Do keep writing to me, I'll do the same. You've received a thesis from the Lunar Man[54] with a gracious dedication, but no other mail. There's really nothing more to tell you.

Goodbye – your self, my love, my life. I love you and long to see you. How I need you! How wretched I'd be if you didn't exist! And how nice you are to me, sweet little being! I kiss you so passionately. I love you.

Your charming Beaver

[Amiens]

Friday [7 July 1939]

Tear up these letters –
yesterday's as well

Most dear little being,

I was quite right not to rejoice yesterday – it was a premonition. I spent the whole day in a dreary café waiting for Little Bost, who never showed up. It couldn't have been more annoying. This morning, in

---

[54]The Lunar Man was Jean-André Ville, philologist husband of Marie ('Marie Girard' in *The Prime of Life*, pp.183-4), nicknamed the Lunar Woman, a dreamy French woman with whom Sartre had an affair during his stay in Berlin in 1934 and whom he and De Beauvoir continued to see after her return to Paris.

desperation, I went to ask for him at the barracks. I saw him – quite obliterated by a helmet – and he'd had to stand guard all day yesterday. He claims he'd written to warn me not to come before today, but I never received that letter. It's idiotic, especially because of Bienenfeld, whom I could have seen for another two days. But it turned out that that wait of several hours yesterday constituted excellent circumstances for reading Heidegger, whom I've almost finished and managed to understand – at least superficially. In other words, I know what he means but can't check out the difficulties, though I'm aware of heaps of them. What's more, I'm so ruthless at present that I don't regret a day like yesterday, extremely disagreeable as it was in every respect, for it provides me with a standard day highly suitable for use in a novel – and in a whole number of ways too, depending on whether it's tilted in the direction of the passions or left as it was in the contingent. I slept well, despite everything. After seeing Bost – whom I'll see properly only in a while, at 6 – I worked extremely well first in a café and then in my room. Now I'm going to do another hour's work or so at the Chanteclerc. There was no letter from you at the Poste Restante, but it will probably be there tomorrow. By Monday morning I'll be back in Paris. On Tuesday I'll see you – I'm so longing for that. I've written you a very short letter, but I'm far more eventless if possible even than you. I'll write again tomorrow, and on Sunday. Goodbye, your self, my life – I love you. The weather's filthy – my whole room's shaken by the wind, you'd think it was going to turn upside down. My tenderest kisses, beloved little being – I dreamt about you.

Your charming Beaver

Hôtel de France
Saint-Étienne-de-Tinée
[Alpes-Maritimes]

27 July [1939]

Dear little being,

I'm dreadfully sorry to have sent the money so late, but I called at the post office only after getting back from my trip. Actually, it's lucky I dropped by so quickly – I might easily not have gone there till this morning. They swore to me it would arrive yesterday evening – I hope you received it in time all the same. I've just found your little letter and it really fortified my soul. Yes, we'll stay [with That Lady] till the 20th and still have 35 little days left just for us. I love you, my sweet little one, and I'm so impatient for it to be 2 August – I'll be waiting for you at the buffet when the Annecy train gets in.

I met up with the Boubou – but I've already told you about that, and about our first day's excursion together.[55] The second was quite different. It was a Tuesday and we'd decided to climb to 2,800 metres: 4 hours' climb, and then some 4 hours down again to Saint-Étienne-de-Tinée. In the morning we took a bus at 6 to get up to a village at 1,500 m. There we had breakfast and bought provisions – it was charming. And then we began to climb. Alas, the Boubou can't climb! It took 5½ hours to haul him to the top, and even then he didn't go right to the summit, which I climbed on my own. We slept while the sun was high, tricked by a 'deceptive' wind into thinking that we ran no risk of sunburn – with the result that we got our faces, legs and arms frightfully burnt. Then we began our descent. Our route was suitable for the 'experienced tourist', but as it happened we went astray before finding it and lost our bearings for quite a while. Then we had to make the descent and, as it was stony and the Boubou only had espadrilles, it was extremely arduous. We took ages and didn't arrive at Saint-Étienne till after dark, and even then only by hitching a ride for the last few kilometres. He's utterly chicken-hearted, it's hilarious! He's afraid of stones, the sun, Italian frontier-guards, everything – there's nothing to be done with him. Yesterday, in fact, he developed such a temperature that he stayed at the hotel all day, while I made a marvellous trip – I told Bienenfeld all about it and she must have told you: 3,051 m.[56] I climbed to where there was just snow and rock, and saw one of the loveliest landscapes of my whole life, frozen blue lakes set in jagged mountains of volcanic hue – it was splendid! I came back not tired in the least, slept well, and am now fresh as a daisy. I'm writing to you from the garden of the hotel, where a few holiday-makers are taking breakfast in their dressing-gowns – it's agreeable, sunny with a little breeze, like some leisurely country morning. We're not leaving till 11, for money reasons, since the Boubou had to wire for some cash which we're now awaiting. We're planning an easy stage as far as Barcelonnette. Then I hope I'll manage to get rid of him. He made a few passes at me the first two nights (we had first a room with twin beds, then two communicating rooms) – but very discreet ones. I hope to be alone again tomorrow. I'll probably go back up towards Guillestre, but I can't give you an address – I'll wire you one more. I'll send the money as soon as

---

[55]The letter in question has been lost, but for the encounter with Gerassi, see *The Prime of Life*, p.371.
[56]Bianca Bienenfeld was at the time with Sartre in Savoy.

possible, i.e. as soon as I get it. I'll send 3,000 F., as I prefer not to carry money on me when I'm hiking.

I certainly have written to Kos., and can't understand . . . Speaking of which, I'm writing to tell her I made a little two-day trip before joining you on the 27th at Annecy.[57]

Goodbye, my love, I love you. I want only to see you – come back to me soon. We'll be happy together at Marseilles. Passionate kisses.

Your charming Beaver

Envelope:
Monsieur Sartre
Poste Restante
La Clusaz, Haute-Savoie

[Queyras,
Hautes Alpes]

[30 July 1939]

I don't have time to write you a proper letter, but you've got my news through Bienenfeld. I feel quite cut off from you, not knowing what you're doing (cut off in terms of knowledge rather than the heart). But it's impossible to give any addresses, as I don't know from morning to evening what I'll be doing. At any rate, I'm arriving in Marseilles on the 1st in the evening, and on the morning of the 2nd I'll be at the Annecy train. Rendez-vous at the buffet – wire if there's any mishap, but try to avoid one. I'm in a fever of impatience to see you. Goodbye, see you soon. Longing so much to see you.

S. de Beauvoir

Postcard
Monsieur Sartre
Poste Restante
La Clusaz, Haute-Savoie
(Forwarded to Marseilles)

---

[57]Untrue – but a fiction necessary to deceive Wanda, who was not supposed to know about Sartre's affair with Bianca.

LETTERS
SEPTEMBER 1939 – MARCH 1940
The Phoney War

[Paris]

Thursday 7 September [1939]

My love

What a joy to have your address at last and be able to feel myself in contact with you: to know where you are and that for the moment it's somewhere pretty safe.[58] I'm in a happier state than I've experienced since your departure – yes, truly, it's happiness, and the best kind, this strength of love that I feel between us, this close bond uniting us amid all this gloom. I love you so. I'm not thinking about the day when I'll see you again,[59] any more than I ever evoke our past – I too am blocked against all memory. But I don't need to see you – I'm not separated from you, I'm still in the same world as you. I'm going to write you a huge letter. I'm at the Dôme, it's 8 in the evening and I've three hours ahead of me. You should know first that I'm calm, involved, not at all unhappy – I have no regret, no desire, no hope for anything. I'm easy in my mind about you, and this ease of mind comes from the absolute certainty I now have that, if the worst were to happen to you, I should no longer live either. The only painful thing is my intermittent bouts of panic concerning Bost: such violent pangs of dread for him that I feel I'm almost losing my reason.[60] Especially in the evenings. But it seems to me that even this is diminishing somewhat.

Well, I left the station.[61] I was scared of collapsing as soon as I got outside, but no, I walked straight ahead without crying, without thinking, simply with an exhausting sense that I couldn't ever stop again, since the least pause would be excruciating – I basically lived for more or less two days in a state of feverish tension, which was so exhausting it made my whole head ache. The weather was marvellous that morning. I crossed Les Halles – amid vast heaps of cabbages and carrots – and the Luxembourg, then continued to the hotel. There I

---

[58]Sartre, called up, had left for Nancy on 2 September (see *The Prime of Life*, p.379).
[59]They were to remain separated from 2 September 1939 until the end of March 1941, though they did see each other when De Beauvoir visited Brumath in Alsace, where Sartre was stationed, in early November 1939, and again in Paris during Sartre's two periods of leave in February and April 1940.
[60]Bost, a private in a regular regiment, risked being sent to the front.
[61]The Gare de l'Est.

found a lucky distraction, in the shape of a letter from Kos. replying to my sharp letter. It was a missive of crazy bad faith, in which she waxed indignant about my having accused her in my inner thoughts of having told a lie, and offered this in explanation of her silence. This irritated me, and since I suppose it was the only living, present object upon which any action was possible, I applied myself doggedly to this business for almost the entire day. Going off at once to the Dôme, I answered her in a letter that settled matters once and for all but was still full of good will and affection. She has since sent me a very nice note in reply to my nice letter, followed by a distraught (though still very nice) one in reply to my last letter (the one settling matters). And for my part I've sent her two very tender letters and some money for her to come here. So we've made up, and we'll finish our explanations face to face. What's more, I intend to be angelic, because she's really pitiful. I was busy writing this reply when I caught sight of the Boubou's round head – he'd landed that very morning and the first person he saw was me. You can just imagine how pleased I was to see him! A human being to talk to struck me as something really precious (I'd vainly looked in on Zuorro, who has been called up, and on That Lady, who's not back yet, and I'd also rung C. Audry and the Lunar Woman,[62] who aren't in Paris; Sorokine too had left Paris – she'd sent me a *pneu* to let me know). I had lunch at the Coupole with the Boubou, wrote a few letters, then went by Métro to Boulevard Rochechouart where I saw *Trafic d'armes*. It was dubbed and not much good; too short, too, since it was only 5 when I found myself back on the Boulevard de Clichy, under a stormy sky. I called on Toulouse,[63] but she's at Férolles. I wrote, but she hasn't answered yet; neither has De Roulet, nor my family (I don't have any news of Bienenfeld either, or – more understandably – of Bost). I began to walk in the direction of Montparnasse, but stopped in a café on the boulevards where I began filling my notebook. I find it easy to keep this journal up: it's already very thick, and I'll make you read it from beginning to end.[64] I don't recopy it, but I'm using it at this moment in writing to you, so that I don't forget anything. The weather was muggy, I was sleepy and dazed. On Boulevard Montparnasse, the Tschuntz

[62]See note 54 above
[63]Toulouse: nickname of Simone Jollivet ('Camille' in De Beauvoir's autobiography, stage name 'Simone Sans'), actress and playwright. An early love of Sartre's (they met in 1925), she later lived and worked with Charles Dullin (see note 33 above). She remained a friend of Sartre and De Beauvoir, despite political differences during the Occupation, until her tragic decline into despair and alcoholism (d. 1967).
[64]De Beauvoir's war journal survives. Drawn on for *The Prime of Life*, it was finally published in 1990 as *Journal de Guerre*.

bookshop – that one where we sometimes stop and look at surrealist pictures – has put up a splendid sign: 'French family – 1 son killed 1914 – 1 son wounded – liable for call-up on day 9.' The Monoprix stores have also put up printed signs: 'French management – French staff – French capital.' I went up to the Boubou's place and dozed for a while on the couch, obsessively going over in my mind the quarrel I'd had with Kosakiewitch (this amused me, as an example of psychic defence). Then he showed up, very serious: 'Let's see if you have a heart', he said. And then he solemnly informed me that Ehrenburg had been so shattered by recent events he could neither eat nor drink.[65] I found this staggering. He knew you'd left that morning, he knew I was on tenterhooks about Bost, yet he tested my peace of mind by telling me about the mental torments of Ehrenburg. He's a funny guy, too. He hasn't been called up, and he won't be. He's a great peace-lover, and speaks with a heroic air of shutting himself up in an ivory tower and creating a pleasant life for himself, drinking, eating and having fun. He implicates me in this heroism, moreover, as if I were losing no more than he in this war. He's so totally selfish that when something affects him, he finds it quite shattering – but seeks solace, self-importantly, in the very fact of being shattered. He wouldn't enlist unless he were sure of being a major. I laughed in his face and said he'd be accepted only as a private, which made him very annoyed. Now he believes it too, and is speaking of returning to Nice where Stépha has remained.

We went and had dinner at the Crêperie Bretonne in Rue Montparnasse. I recall that moment very well. We'd taken a little table outside, and we couldn't see a thing as the street was completely dark. There were whores pacing the pavement opposite, it was late, and there was no food to be had. We went for a little walk round. The cafés close at 11 now, you know, and the cinemas and theatres at 8.30 – the evenings are unutterably bleak. Gerassi suggested I sleep at his place and I accepted, as I couldn't stand being back in my room. I looked in at home and found a letter from Little Bost, written on Thursday; he was still hopeful, yet it was a heartrending little letter. That letter, and my room which I'd not been back to since 3 in the morning – with your pipe and your little blue shirt – cast me into a storm of sobbing that lasted for quite some time. Then I met up with the Boubou again on Avenue du Maine. He chucked a sheet over the couch in his studio and took himself off to bed upstairs, while I slept well without so much as a nightmare.

Next day was Sunday. I woke up at 8.30 and went to collect my mail,

[65]The Soviet writer Ilya Ehrenburg, like Fernando Gerassi, had fought in the Spanish Civil War. The events referred to here are obviously the Nazi-Soviet Pact of August 1939.

but there wasn't any. I had a coffee at Rey's,[66] and began reading Gide's *Journal* which I'd bought the evening before – and which I'll send you as early as I can tomorrow morning. I felt wholly blocked, with a fountain of tears ready to be shed; but weeping seemed pointless, because just as many tears would still be left afterwards. *Paris-Midi* was bannering: 'Final Plea to Berlin', but it was utterly hopeless. At noon I called in again at the hotel and learnt that Gégé had rung me. Quite overjoyed, I rang her back at once. I needed people round me, anybody, in order truly to feel immersed in a world event rather than some individual adventure – which would then have turned into a dreadful calamity. I went to her place on foot. The policemen had splendid, gleaming new helmets and, slung over their shoulders, little putty-coloured satchels holding their gasmasks. A few civilians were already making their appearance with these satchels – now almost all sport either the putty-coloured satchel or the long grey cylinder, and in the evenings even the tarts patrolling the streets carry masks. The shop windows are all embellished with strips of yellow or blue paper, you'd think they were all broken and out of service. Hardly anybody on the streets and a strange, dreary atmosphere everywhere. Lots of Métro stations are barricaded off by chains and huge notices indicating the nearest station available. The Métro's very much reduced, there are hardly any buses any more, and on that particular day there were no taxis either – or virtually none – though there are some around again now. The cars are a splendid sight, by the way, with their fronts daubed in blue paint and their blue headlights resembling huge gemstones. I arrived at Gégé's place – she looked charming, with her hair all over the place and in a little pleated skirt and white blouse. She told me all about her holidays – she was hanging out with a group of those wealthy homosexuals we often see at the Zanzibar, and showed me photos of them. She gave me news of my sister, whom she went to see at La Grillère; apparently she's thriving, though sick to death of tubercular glands. Then Pardo showed up and we went to the Dôme, where we met the Boubou again;[67] we all ate chicken and rice, and there was a moment of relaxation. Pardo maintained there'd be no declaration of war and my neighbour, a well-informed Englishman, asserted the same thing – we even laid bets. Without restoring my hope, those few instants at least plunged me back into a vague state of uncertainty, so that when half an hour later I saw *Paris-Soir*'s banner headline 'War', it gave me

---

[66] A brasserie in Avenue du Maine, called Les Trois Mousquetaires, described in *The Prime of Life*, p.315.
[67] Pardo: a friend and future second husband of Gégé.

an appalling shock.[68] I broke into tears on the spot, and went home to calm down by crying my heart out. Once I was calm again, I went off to the Flore and wrote to Bost. At 6 Gégé showed up again, very wrought up and with tears in her eyes. She's worried about her family, who are in the Calvados, and is wondering how she'll support them till the war's over. She was supposed to go off again two days later with Pardo to Corrèze, to the Jouvenels' place, but she wasn't keen on the idea. Pardo (who has been declared unfit because of his heart) will be overseeing the estate, as the single man among a dozen women whom Gégé can't stand. Pardo's sister turned up – the one we saw at Juan-les-Pins – rather nice, and shattered because her boy friend has been called up. There were still people at the Flore who were saying they didn't believe in the war – they were the tough ones – but there were a lot of dismal faces. Ella Pardo told us how the pictures in the Louvre had all been packed up, and about the trouble they'd had with the Victory of Samothrace – it was quite entertaining. I got Gégé to point out lots of people for me. That long-haired fellow who's often with Sonia,[69] and whom we were so intrigued by, is an Italian sculptor called Giacometti.[70] The place was packed and everybody was shaking hands with everybody else; I felt just the tiniest scrap of collectivity – it was very salutary. We dined in a dark room belonging to a little restaurant in Boulevard Saint-Germain: Pardo, his sister, Gégé, myself and a big shot from Hachette. At first it was unbearably gloomy, but then people started blathering away about politics, and about the USSR in particular, which helped to pass the time. After that I made my own way back with Gégé towards the Dôme, and there was little Mané-Katz all dressed up as a private and very dashing. We passed Kisling in uniform too, and at Saint-Germain Breton – dressed as an officer, of course.[71] There was an extraordinary sky over Paris that evening – 'a promise of victory', the papers called it – and with all those violet and blue headlamps in the darkness it was splendid. The Dôme was packed too, and we shook countless hands. For me, it was like the first days of an illness, when you've got a temperature and every least thing is

---

[68]War was declared on 3 September 1939 at 17 hours.

[69]Sonia Mossé: see *The Prime of Life*, pp.350-52.

[70]De Beauvoir and Sartre were eventually to meet Alberto Giacometti through Nathalie Sorokine in the spring of 1941 (see *The Prime of Life*, pp.486-9), and they were thereafter to become good friends.

[71]Mané-Katz and Moise Kisling were painters (see *The Prime of Life*, p.280). André Breton, the surrealist writer, had been an early influence on Sartre, and De Beauvoir was subsequently to analyse his poetic notion of woman – as everything except herself – in *The Second Sex*.

amplified till it fills and seduces your consciousness entirely. From time to time visions of horror would nevertheless shoot through my mind – I was in a strange state. We spotted P. Bost,[72] and Gégé asked him for news of his brother – but he knew almost nothing. In front of the Dôme, a policeman was arguing with the manager: 'Still too much light.' Now all the street-lamps are swathed in thick blue wrappings, so that you can barely see the Rotonde from the Dôme or vice-versa. At 11 they cleared the café. Gégé took me off to spend the night at her place. Pardo gave me a little dose of tranquillizer, and I fell into the most beatific slumber. Next morning we all three took tea and jam together, then I went to buy *A Raw Youth*,[73] which I wanted to send to Bost; I took the opportunity to finish it, while drinking a coffee at the Capoulade. I was beginning to relax and find solace in little pleasures – like reading Gide or *A Raw Youth*. I looked in as I was passing the Guilles' place;[74] but even though there was a woman on the balcony tending flowers, it was all locked up. I read and had lunch at the Dôme. Terse communiques: 'Military operations have begun on land and sea'. At the hotel, they'd told me there'd been a telephone call from your mother, so I rang back. I first got your step-father (who was extremely polite) and then your mother, who invited me to go and see her – which I did. She was very amiable, but a real pain in the neck. I actually took this as a sign my spirits were lifting, because I was starting to find some things boring again – the day before, everything had been a godsend. She talked to me about you, I said all the proper things, and she couldn't resist a gallant: 'It'll do him good, it'll teach him about life'. There were some very strange tramps prowling about Passy. I took the opportunity of dropping in at the school to collect my gas-mask.[75] The head mistress took my measurements in person, and explained to me how the monstrous object was used. Apparently, there are unlikely to be any high schools kept in Paris, but it's not yet known for certain. For the first time I felt a moment's emotion concerning *my* life, when I saw the school courtyard all peaceful and in bloom – but that soon passed. I left with my cylinder slung round my shoulder and showed up at Gégé's,

---

[72] For Pierre Bost, see note 22 above.

[73] By Fyodor Dostoievsky.

[74] The Guilles: Pierre Guille (in De Beauvoir's autobiography 'Pagniez') had been one of Sartre's closest friends at the École Normale Supérieure, and from 1926 also the friend – and probably lover – of Mme Morel (see note 3 above). A teacher at this time, he was married and lived on Boulevard St Michel.

[75] The school was the Lycée Molière in Passy, in the rich 16th Arrondissement of Paris, to which De Beauvoir was appointed in 1936 following her stint teaching in Rouen, and where she taught until the defeat of France in June 1940 – although, from the outbreak of war on, it had been amalgamated with the Lycée Camille Sée.

where I burst in on a family quarrel. They hardly exchanged two words in my presence before Gégé rushed off to fling herself sobbing on a bed. I flung myself down beside her and have become such a *piège*,[76] and so used to these situations, that I petted her with tender little whispers of 'There now, dear' and 'There now, kid', and came within an ace of saying 'My darling' – it was hilarious. She was saying 'I'm scared, I'm scared', and trembling all over. She was afraid for Bost, whom she still loves terribly, and for Denonain[77] – who, because of some misunderstanding that was really upsetting her, had left that morning without her having managed to see him. And then there was a big fuss because she was just off to see Nogues again,[78] and Pardo couldn't contain his fury about it. Old Ma Kientz[79] is probably going to transfer the whole firm to Montfort-L'Amaury, and she'll be sending for Gégé – who thus won't lose her job. I calmed her down and accompanied her on foot to the Gare Saint-Lazare, while she talked to me about Nogues. She doesn't love Pardo at all. She told me: 'I keep telling myself all the time that he's intelligent, but then every so often I say to myself: What the hell do I care about his being intelligent, if I don't love him?' He loves her madly. When I returned to the Flore I found him virtually in tears, and he confided in me how much Gégé seeing Nogues hurt him. He was absolutely pole-axed. Then his friend from the evening before – the fellow from Hachette – turned up, and explained to us all about the Volunteers of Death. It's Péricart – that 'Dead Men Arise!' fellow – who had the idea. One letter he has received reads as follows: 'Sir, I am 32 years old, missing an arm and an eye, and had believed my life devoid of meaning; but, by restoring that word "Service" to me in its full splendour, you have given me a new existence.' The fellow ends by asking whether not just the maimed, but the half-witted too mightn't be put to some use. Thereupon Comtesse Montinori showed up (that erotic girl – the woman painter from the Gruber set – whom Poupette was for ever talking about) and announced that she was enlisting in the Garibaldi volunteers. And at that point the Hungarian popped up,[80] sat down opposite me, and informed me: 'I'm enlisting.' An airman sitting beside me said: 'Sir, allow me to buy you a drink.' The Hungarian refused in embarrassment – 'I'm not asking for any reward!' – and they

---

[76]Short for *piège à loups* ('mantrap'), a term which Mme Morel popularized in her circle of intimates for homosexuals of either sex.
[77] Gégé's first husband.
[78]Her patron and friend.
[79]Gégé's employer.
[80]Former lover of Stépha's, met at the Bibliothèque Nationale in 1929. See *Memoirs of a Dutiful Daughter*, pp.298-300.

ended up clinking glasses of brandy-and-soda. But alas! the manager announced he was closing the café next day, which he duly did, so that everybody in Paris now believes in the war – and I'm denied that little *querencia*.[81]

Gégé returned and I set off for the Dôme, flanked by two beings convulsed with tension and sadness. Exerting myself I told endless stories, after which – as everyone was talking about air raids – I went back to sleep at their place again.

My love, the Dôme's emptying and I can't manage any more. You'll have the sequel tomorrow morning – there are hundreds of things left to tell you. I'm sending you Gide's *Journal*; tell me quickly what else you want. Until tomorrow – I love you. You haven't left me.

Your charming Beaver

Gégé has given me a photo of you, which I like a lot.

Envelope:
Private Sartre
c/o M. le curé de Ceintrey
Meurthe-et-Moselle

(Forwarded to Observation Post,
Artillery Headquarters, Postal Zone 108)

[Paris]

Friday, 8 September [1939]

My love,

Here's the continuation of the letter I had to break off yesterday, because of sleepiness and the blackout. I slept well, there wasn't any air-raid warning last night, the weather's terrific and I feel fresh. So I'll go on with giving you a full account of everything.

I'd reached Monday night. Well, I'd gone off for the second time to sleep in Gégé's lovely little blue bedroom, and was sound asleep when she turned up looking somewhat haggard: 'The sirens!'. There was a wailing in the darkness that was both sinister and beautiful. I slipped on a dressing-gown, and from the window we watched people hurrying to the shelters beneath a magnificent sky. Gégé and Pardo were nervous:

---

[81]Bullfighting term, adopted from Hemingway both by François Mauriac and by Sartre, meaning a 'haven' or favourite spot.

'It's because I can't find my dressing-gown', Gégé was saying, 'I can't stand not being able to find my things'; and Pardo, all of a tremble, kept repeating: 'Let's get a move on!' We went downstairs. The concierge had already donned her gas mask, but we needed only a second's reflection before going back up to bed, convinced that it was a false alarm. I went back to sleep beautifully till the All Clear, at 7 in the morning. But then my room was invaded by Gégé, and who was doing the packing, Pardo, and some little female from the Flore – a very plain script-girl whom they were taking with them to the country, who was quite convulsed with fear. It was very entertaining, at 7 in the morning, to see people emerging from the shelters. There were two women in flowered dressing-gowns, tall and thin, who looked quite terrifying, with cloths wrapped round their faces which I think were improvised gas masks. I was still there when they left: they crammed a pile of bundles into their little car, and at about 10 they set off, leaving the flat at my disposal. Now I can put up Kos. there, which will save me some expense. There are books, records, a bath – it's agreeable. I wasn't bothered by the poverty of the resources that had been left me. On the contrary, I've always enjoyed picturing very deprived lives in which it's necessary to make the most of the tiniest little things, so I'm well set up; and though I'll probably get tired of it, for the time being the very fact of filling my days still provides me with entertainment. It's a kind of challenge that I'm meeting very well, in fact – I haven't even had time to go to the cinema since *Trafic d'armes*. After their departure, I got dressed and then called in at the hotel, where I got your first letter. It moistened my heart somewhat: when I think of your little flesh-and-bone being in its fatigues and forage-cap, I grow moist; and when I think of your boredom, your solitude and your arrested life, I feel anguished. But I'm not like Poupette, who used to meditate in the style of Loyola. I think about it as little as possible. It's only rarely and despite myself that it comes upon me, and I feel as though I were plummeting into a void – then it passes. I love you, my life's own self. I went to the Dôme to write up my diary. Fujita was there[82] – a bit calmer than usual, if anything – and I caught sight of T [...] too,[83] and lots of familiar faces. I had lunch with the Boubou, and ate that sausage and lentil dish you're so fond of, my love. But I'm beginning to be so desiccated that objects of that kind no longer appear to me like memory traps, to be

---

[82]Tsuguharu Fujita (1886-1968): Japanese painter resident in Paris from 1913, painted especially female nudes and cats. Late in life converted to Catholicism and changed his forename to Léonard in honour of Da Vinci.
[83]Illegible name.

escaped from as quickly as possible. Now, when memories arrive, they're equally dried out, embalmed, and utterly blunted. In the afternoon, therefore, seated at a table outside the Deux Magots, I was able to spend hours on that square – which reminded me of so many things to do with you and Bost – and recall it all without any echo within myself. All the Flore crowd had migrated to that spot, and I sat down just behind Sonia and Agnès Capri.[84] They cut far less of a dash than before, and were now thinking only about skedaddling to Nice: 'I can't spend another night like that', Sonia was saying as they made feverish financial calculations. The square was dead, beneath a blazing sun. There were fellows in blue dungarees shifting sandbags in front of the church. Once a man played a sad little tune on a flute, endlessly protracted. I stayed there reading Gide, especially his notes on August 1914. There were lots of similarities – and lots of differences too. It was interesting. At moments it threw me into a state of panic.

I called in at the *N.R.F.*, which is moving. I think you should write to them directly for the money, to 5 Rue Sébastien Bottin – they'll forward the letter. Write and tell them to send me the money, I'd like to have it for the Kos. sisters. I'm fairly wealthy this month. I've paid back the Boubou, settled the hotel bill, and bought Gide's *Journal*; but I'm living comfortably on 50 F. a day (I've found a restaurant in Rue Vavin where you can eat magnificently for 10 F.) and I'll have enough to keep Kos. for a week and travel to Quimper, so things are fine. There was an ambiguous piece in the paper implying that you might possibly be paid your salary, but it's not certain.

I went home to pick up my mail; there was only a nice note from Kos., which I answered as nicely as possible. Nothing from Bost, to whom I wrote a little letter – and, as I wrote, was overcome by a truly unbearable anguish. Actually, it has been like that all these days: calm mornings, then lingering afternoons sliding gradually towards a kind of horror. I had an appointment with the Hungarian at 7 in the Dôme, so I went to meet him and he took me to an outside table at a little restaurant on Bd Montparnasse (the one where Zuorro wanted to take us, I think). He began to discuss general ideas, but I couldn't say a word – I was all tensed up and in despair. To my great shame, as he was telling me how he'd last set eyes on me in June with a charming young man, I burst into tears. After that I wasn't so tense. I drank a lot of wine – and afterwards, at Les Vikings, Akvavit – and was completely blotto (well, not completely, but enough to talk a lot and get the Hungarian

---

[84]For Sonia Mossé and Agnès Capri, joint owners of a cabaret in which the latter also sang, see *The Prime of Life*, pp.350-52.

talking and not be bored). He told me he was sexually 'perverted', a masochist who can love only women stronger than himself, in whose arms he can lose himself like a little child. Once you've seen the fellow, it's hair-raising to picture his ideal type of woman. He found one capable of lifting him at arm's length, so he took her out of the brothel where she was and teamed up with her. The most entertaining thing of all is the following. He fell sentimentally in love with a slender young girl, and convinced himself that this meant she'd dominate him intellectually; he managed to sleep with her only by repeating certain words to himself, such as 'the boundless sea', or 'adrift on the ocean'. The word 'infinity', in particular, never failed to deliver for him. That's what he meant about Cherubino – do you remember? – it fits his case splendidly.[85] He also told me he was a serious alcoholic, and used to have hallucinations – but I couldn't get any details out of him. One night he did quite genuinely break a tooth, rushing at an old beggar-woman he'd seen coming in through the window. And when he wakes up in the morning, he's often being punched or slapped. All this quite entertained me, and helped on by drunkenness I managed to be so amiable that on several occasions he pounced on my hands and kissed them, apologizing for being a 'pervert'. I was in such a state that I think I'd have slept with the fellow that evening if he'd wanted, though God knows he repels me. But I'd have been very sorry next morning. For in the mornings despite everything I feel very solidly anchored in my life, whereas in the evenings I'd do anything in order really to blot out the moment. He took me to his place on Bd St Michel to read me bits of his novel about Stépha; but he mumbled them, and it became most damnably boring – so I left him and walked back to my place through pitch darkness. I went to bed, but suddenly after two hours' sleep was woken by the sound of gunfire. I leapt out of bed, astonished that no air-raid warning had been given. Still half asleep and unable to find my things in the darkness, I felt a momentary nervousness. Going down, however, at the foot of the stairs I found people who were quite calm and who told me the sirens had sounded an hour earlier. I stayed there for twenty minutes, but then as the gunfire had stopped I went back up to bed – I think the others did the same – and just kept my clothes on till the All Clear. I then slept until 10 in the morning. It's extremely pleasant having a shelter right there in the building, as you can wait to go down till the shindig actually starts. Next morning, I was at Rey's

---

[85]Probably a reference to Dullin's production of *The Marriage of Figaro*, where the casting of a 12-year-old boy in the part of Cherubino aroused controversy (see *The Prime of Life*, p.353).

drinking my coffee when they suddenly lowered the metal shutters and everyone started running – the sirens again. I went home, to find the landlady still tranquilly doing the dishes and everyone standing about in groups outside the shelters, calmly chatting. As for me, I read in my room and before long we heard the All Clear. I had lunch at the Dôme, read *Le Canard Enchaîné* – quite funny – I'm keeping it, because of its excellent collection of foolish sayings. I saw the Boubou for a moment, sent Kos. 50 F. to get here with (the trains are running normally), then spent the afternoon at the Dupont, reading, writing letters and filling in my diary. Sorokine has written me a note – she's looking after kids in the Pyrenees. I read at the Dôme again till 9. Sylvia Beach has closed down, and Monnier too,[86] and all the public libraries, but this journal of Gide's has at least filled my days. He's a man of manners – a wretched kind of life – and by the end he becomes doddery and an unspeakable bore. The rest I'd like to discuss with you, but still have too many things to tell you.

At 9 I met the Boubou, who carried me off to his place. There were biscuits and brandy, which we consumed while listening to the wireless: we had quite a fine Mozart symphony, some harpsichord music by Bach, some Russian songs, and three minutes of Chinese music (unfortunately cut short). It gave me enormous pleasure to hear a bit of music again. I'm going to go and listen to Gégé's records, and the Boubou's too. I stayed on there to sleep, thinking there'd be another raid. I slept well, and in the morning the Boubou came prowling round me – I think he's entertaining fresh hopes – but to no avail. So now it was yesterday. I went to take my morning coffee sitting outside at the Dôme, and as I was reading Gide's *Journal* a chap leaned across to me: 'What a comfort to see someone reading Gide at a moment like this!' It was a certain Adamov, a frightful wreck whom we often used to see at the Dôme – slightly hunch-backed, toothless, face all pock-marked – and who knows Wanda a bit and was supposed to read her fortune. He told me he'd long wanted to know me, and to know you too – though he didn't entirely hold with your views – and expressed astonishment that we used to be seen around formerly in the company of Kos. senior and are now seen around with her younger sister. He's vaguely surrealist, and a pan-psychist, and a total imbecile. I killed an hour talking to him. In the afternoon I saw him again at the Dôme, and he lent me his manuscript 'Endless Humiliation', which he's typing out carefully in three carbon copies. He's another masochist, but their lyricism renders

---

[86]Sylvia Beach ran a Left Bank bookshop called Shakespeare and Co., Adrienne Monnier another in Rue de l'Odéon called Maison des Amis des Livres.

totally uninteresting his accounts of women's high heels and muddy sandals trampling his chest and face. Like lots of the foreigners here, he's not too sure what's going to happen to him – they're all in a state of some perturbation. I abandoned him and popped back home, where I found your last letter. I love your letters so much, my beloved, you're so alive in them and I find so much of you there. I went to eat in my little restaurant, then drank coffee with the Boubou and read *Marie-Claire*. It was an all-purpose issue, designed to serve equally well for war or peace, with advice both about hay-boxes and about passive defence. In the washrooms at the Dôme (perhaps I told you this yesterday) I saw a tart doing her eyes: 'I'm not putting on any mascara', she said, 'because of the gas.' Then I went to the hairdresser's. I was really glad to find my hairdresser his usual self – it shows there are some limits! He gave me a lovely hair-do, which nobody will admire: it was with a pang of anguish that I found myself really beautiful. After that I read Gide, and then had your letter. I went and had some pancakes at the Crêperie Bretonne, then on to the Dôme to write to you – after which I went home and slept.

This morning I was woken by a telephone call from the Hungarian – he's leaving tomorrow. I took breakfast with him at the Dôme, and he admitted to me that he wasn't Hungarian at all but a Slovak and a Jew (that fierce anti-Semite!). He told me stories about his life, devoid of interest. I went to Bienenfeld's to collect my papers: my heart was wrung by that empty flat, and her room, and all her notes put away so neatly in her desk. I write to her almost every day, but have no news of her.

I went home and tidied up my papers, books and clothes. I'm quite settled in now, so perhaps I'll get back to writing. I met the Boubou for lunch and coffee, which we took at the Dôme. They make you pay for your order now as soon as they bring it, because people leave in such a rush when there's a raid. The Boubou had seen Ehrenburg yesterday, and Malraux – who's been declared unfit for service and about whom he told me nothing interesting. I'm finding him more and more exasperating. He talks about doing some painting, full of self-wonder: 'You know, Ehrenburg thinks what I'm doing at present shows extraordinary energy!' But he doesn't do a thing except trail around after all and sundry – it's all so spineless that it's sickening.

Nothing from Bost at midday – I'm once again filled with unbearable dread. But how lucky I still am, my love! If you were in the front line, what would my days be like? Even as it is I have moments of real torture. If something bad does happen to him, perhaps I'll be so accustomed to the idea I shan't be devastated – but getting used to it still involves a few jolts. Apart from that, I'm not at all unhappy. The objects:

'happiness' and 'unhappiness' quite simply no longer exist. I no longer have a 'life' – not for a second so far have I had the reflexive attitude that might allow regret or hope. I'm conscious either of a specific object – a page of Gide, or a face – or else of the situation in general, which excludes tenderness and suffering alike. Even my fears have no face, no regrets, no sweetness – I'll talk to you again about all this.

At the same time as this letter, but under separate cover, I'm sending you a note from the *N.R.F.* and a letter from Wanda. I've read the letter, and I'm afraid it may make you a bit sorry to have left her so hurriedly. On the other hand, my love, having you with me uninterruptedly for those last few hours was so very precious to me, that I hope it will take away some of your remorse. I think I've told you everything properly – I'll write to you every day. Write to me too, every letter gives me so much peace of mind, confidence, and even happiness. I don't feel alone for an instant, I'm with you, I feel your presence in every one of my thoughts – we really are one person, my beloved. I kiss all of your dear little face.

Your charming Beaver

What books do you want? Only good ones, or rubbish too if any comes my way?

Envelope:
F.M.[87]
Private Sartre
c/o M. le curé de Ceintrey
Meurthe et Moselle
(*Forwarded to:*
Observation Post, Artillery Headquarters
Postal Zone 108)*

116 rue d'Assas, VIme[88]
[Paris]

Saturday [9 September 1939]

Most dear little being
I've received another little letter from you – it must be Tuesday's – in which you tell me about your bucolic existence picking plums. You're

---

*Letters 8 to 11 September 1939 addressed as above

[87]*Franchise Militaire*: military exemption (from postal charges).
[88]Gégé's address.

the best little one in the world to write to me every day like this. I received a letter from Bost at the same time, and felt as though my soul were being released from a vice – for after writing to you yesterday I did indeed go through hours of the most terrible distress. For the time being he's in absolute safety, standing by. He doesn't seem excessively dejected, merely bored. His address is 51st Infantry Reg., 5th Company, Postal Zone 170. You ought to write to him – I'm going to send him some books. This is my first really relaxed and even happy day for a week. Kos. arrived yesterday evening: she's as nice as can be and really thoroughly likeable. But I'll tell you everything in order.

First, after writing to you yesterday and sending you Gide's *Journal*, I met the Hungarian at 5 at my place; he brought me some books and a huge, spherical glass timepiece weighing a kilo, which I've since given Kosakiewitch as a present. He'd drunk too many Pernods in celebration of his departure, while I was in great distress – it had suddenly gripped me, I had a lump in my throat and conversation was impossible. I got rid of him almost at once, then took the Métro to Montmartre and began walking round the boulevards like a madwoman. I wanted to try and face things and think them through, but it was impossible: from the first images, my stomach would contract and all I could do was try not to think at all and walk straight ahead, utterly empty. No letter that evening. I dined off two pancakes, while reading *Grand Cap* by Thyde Monnier – which is dreadful. But I was forced to skip the descriptions of trenches, for if I'd let my thoughts dwell on them I'd have burst into tears in front of everyone, or screamed. I went inside at the Dôme – it was just like a catafalque, more gloomy than ever – to continue my reading and write up my diary. And I thought how everything was just beginning, and how it hadn't done me much good to have husbanded and reinforced myself so carefully to get through the past eight days, since I had Heaven knows how many times that number still to get through.

[...]

I think some lycées are going to be kept on in Paris, so I really hope they'll leave me here.

I'm still living from one day to the next, but if I could only retain this peace of mind I'd be able to work and get by all right on my own. How about you? You're not too bored, are you, beloved little being? Do tell me everything about yourself. You're still just as present to me, my love, and I kiss you with all my might.

Your charming Beaver

[Paris]

Sunday [10 September 1939]

Most dear little being

Thank you for writing so well to me. I have your letter bearing the number 1, i.e. Wednesday's, so I don't think any have been lost. You must have seen from my two long letters (if you've indeed received them) that I too am not at all existential, but like you — albeit with more resources — simply get through life from one day to the next. In the first days this primarily represented a kind of flight. But since achieving a temporary peace of mind yesterday, I'm abandoning myself to the day in hand without fleeing — but without seeking anything either. It must be said that Kos. is a magnificent resource. Perhaps for the first time in my life, conversation no longer seems like a kind of difficult, ritual game, but I'm in the know. And she seems very open, and absolutely ready to understand. Moreover, she's as decent and estimable as possible in incredibly rotten circumstances. Did I tell you she's talking of finding a job, of writing? Yes, I think I did.

Yesterday after writing to you we went and posted our letters, then ensconced ourselves at the Deux Magots. The weather was sultry. There were lots of people we knew, as there are again today: Agnès Capri in a ravishing print dress, and Sonia — who hasn't yet skedaddled — and lots of others. We chatted for a long time, then dined at a little snack-bar in Rue Vavin, where we spotted Gerassi. We had a drink at the Dôme before going home, and when we got in we tried to put some music on, but I don't know which is worst out of the records, the needles or the gramophone — so Beethoven's 7th Symphony came out all mangled. As we were sleepy, we soon gave up and went to bed.

Now that there are no more false alarms, you can sleep wonderfully in Paris because it's so quiet. This morning I got up at about 9, and Kos. brought me tea in some charming and mysterious cups belonging to Pardo (for we've ransacked the whole place). Then I wrote to my family — my mother now composes 'lofty' letters about war — and called in on my mother's instructions to get some news of my aged grandmother. How it did move me, finding myself back in that apartment from the days of your military service.[89] Heaps of old, old memories came back to me — I already loved you very intensely. My aged grandmother's senile. She had a fat woman with her, who's a friend of my Aunt Lili and involved in civil defence. She was urging my grandmother to leave: 'Children and old people have to be evacuated at once', she was saying. But my grandmother placed her hands on her round belly and said with

---

[89]See note 1 above.

a mutinous, obstinate air: 'I'm not a child, though.' She's spry rather than dull-witted in her senility. I quickly left her and went to the hotel. Disaster! – I hadn't slept there, and the Boxer[90] and Lili had been there yesterday evening and left a note under my door saying: 'We're at number 8, come and see us tomorrow at 9.30'. It was now midday and they'd left, and I'm afraid they may take it as a sign of ill will – and quite apart from that I'd have liked to see them. There were two huge letters from Sorokine, who's tending and wiping hundreds of children somewhere in the Pyrenees. She's gloomy, but still just as agreeable. Also a mysterious telegram notification. But the notification has to be stamped before you can go to the post office, and in order to get it stamped at the police station you need a residence certificate, and as it was Sunday I wasn't able to do anything at all – I'll go tomorrow morning. I think it must be Bienenfeld, in a panic because she hasn't had any news of me, or because she knows I haven't had any news of her. There was your letter too. I met Kos. at 1, and we had lunch at the little restaurant in Rue Vavin, then drank coffee at the Deux Magots. After that, we went for a walk in Montmartre. You know, now I really understand that story which I used to find so literary, about the fellow who sees his wife and child die without shedding a tear, but then weeps over a slave. There are tiny memories which tear at my heart – in Montmartre, for example – whereas I'm left quite unmoved by the big, serious things.

We went to Place du Tertre – which was very crowded – then to Wepler's for a drink, and now here we are back at the Dôme. We're going to have dinner, go home, probably chat for a while, then sleep.

I'm quite peaceful as you can see, dear little being. It seems to me too as though we were talking, when I write to you or especially when I receive a letter – it makes me feel close, so close. From time to time I look at your photos, and then I'm tempted to feel sad. But I feel so joined to you that I haven't yet realized I won't see you for a long while. I love you, my beloved, I cover your eyes, your cheeks, your whole dear face with kisses.

Your charming Beaver

---

[90]Alphonse Bonnafé had been a teaching colleague of Sartre at Le Havre 1931-3 and 1934-6, who had initiated boxing classes for some of the pupils in which Sartre had participated enthusiastically. He and his wife Lili remained friends of Sartre and De Beauvoir after Sartre moved to Laon and subsequently Paris.

116 Rue d'Assas
[Paris]

Monday 11 September [1939]

Dear little being

No letter from you today. On the other hand, I've had another two from Bost – who's very affecting. He explains how he really likes digging trenches, how he isn't at all gloomy, and how he's just wondering if he'll be scared to death when he gets shot at. He asks for tobacco and books, which I'll send him. When you've finished Gide's *Journal*, perhaps you could send him that too? After writing to you yesterday we went and had dinner at the little restaurant, and as it was almost full we had to sit at the same table as Gerassi. He dropped one clanger after another, till I was in a cold sweat. 'I can't really recall any longer how I first slept with you,' he said to me. Kos. told me afterwards that I'd changed countenance, and she'd felt utterly dismayed for an instant; but he'd only meant that old night at my grandmother's. I was on the rack, and fled in disorder. We went for a long walk along Bd St Michel, and sat down at the Capoulade. After that we went home, and on the way home embarked on a big explanation that lasted till midnight. Kos. is full of resentment against Wanda, though Wanda – displeased by our tiff – has allowed her to tell me the truth, i.e. that everything was now settled between you and her. The latest news seems to indicate that Kos. wasn't lying, and that Wanda did in fact leave for Laigle while pretending to be in Paris (from where Kos. was forwarding any letters). This is also what K. told Bost – but I can't quite understand, since at the same time she told Bost she'd lied to me. Perhaps that was in the letter she wrote me at La Pouèze, and which I never received. At any rate, all this is fuzzy and unimportant. I told Kos. that I believed her and we made up effusively. We went to bed at around midnight. As I was rereading your last letter in bed, I heard frenzied voices: 'We don't need your kind of spies round here!', 'Just put a slug through their shutters! – Light! Light!'. I tried to negotiate through the window – there was a blue veil over my light – but the policemen were in no joking mood, so I eventually put it out. Then I was just having a splendid dream – along the lines of *Trafic d'armes*, with myself filling the role of heroic detective – when Kos. opened my door in some agitation and I heard the loud wail of the sirens. When I half-heartedly suggested to Kos. that we go downstairs, she accepted with alacrity; so we went down to the cellar, where we found a number of chairs in a tidy row and sat down gloomily. A few tenants then turned up with little campstools, and the concierge told us sharply that the chairs belonged to some gentlemen from across the road, who'd soon be along to occupy them. So we went back upstairs, on the pretext of fetching something to sit on, and I gently persuaded Kos. to wait a bit before going down again. We lay down side by side on my bed, fully dressed and unable to sleep because of the whistle blasts and loud voices of the policemen outside in the street. There was once the very distant sound of gunfire, but we fell asleep as soon as we heard the All Clear. It had lasted barely ¾ of an hour, and so long as you can sleep on in the morning it's really no hardship.

I rose at about 9.30 and we drank tea and talked till midday, then I went to the hotel to pick up my mail and a residence certificate I needed in order to get a telegram notification stamped. After that I went to pick up the cable from the post office – it's so complicated! The cable was from Bienenfeld, saying that she'd received my news and I should come quickly. I wrote to her to explain that I couldn't leave Kos. immediately – which is true – but that I'd come in a week or ten days. I wouldn't like her to be upset, though, so I'm a bit worried. I hid out at the Closerie des Lilas to write a quick letter to Bost. He's still asking for news of you – do write to him, he breaks my heart. I rejoined Kos. and we ate at the snack bar, which is very agreeable, then had coffee at the Dôme. It's marvellous how fellows keep staring at us and even discreetly propositioning us – they must take us for women of easy virtue, or women hard up for men. It's true that on the streets of Paris you don't see many women wearing make-up, nicely turned out, and looking carefree – other than at the Deux Magots. We were actually being real 'women on the home front' today – packing up a parcel of books for Bost, writing to the forces, and fixing up our home. We bought pots of powdered paint and Kos. mixed it with water, oil, and even Ambre Solaire, then daubed all the windowpanes artistically, while I played *Petrushka* on the gramophone and wrote letters – with an interval for tea, which involved little cakes and conversation. I don't know what Gégé will say when she comes back to her flat, but it's really successful as a mausoleum – not the least ray of light now penetrates it from outside. It's just finished now and we're about to go out. The weather has been drizzly all day. Perhaps we'll go and listen to records at the Boubou's place. It's a strange life of leisure that I'm leading, empty and devoid of much meaning, but – shocking to say – full of charm. I haven't yet realized it's for a long time – I don't think about the future. My love, is it true I'm not going to see you for a long time? Are you *sure* there's no way of taking a trip to Nancy? Do write to me, dear little being – I love you. If I could only see you again, just for a few hours even ... Have you got my letters? Tell me how you felt when you received them, do talk to me – I'll keep my peace of mind only if I can feel you really close. *What books do you want?* I kiss you with all my might, yourself, my happiness and my life.

Your charming Beaver

Remember! I haven't told you *anything about Kos. or about Wanda.*

116 Rue d'Assas
[Paris]

Tuesday 12 [September 1939]

My love,

I got your two letters this morning, Thursday's and Friday's, and they wrung my heart. You had no news of me, of course, as I got your address only on Friday. Communicating's a lengthy business – it's so far – for the first time I couldn't stifle a huge, desperate longing to see you. I'm uneasy at the idea that you're going with the artillery. You're not going to be in safety at all. The idea that you could be running risks is unbearable to me. Do write and tell me, precisely and honestly, how exposed you're going to be – I'm tormented by anxiety. I also had a letter from Bost, who has played a dirty trick on me. He was leaving on Saturday with a day's provisions and didn't know where. He was leaving – and it obviously wasn't towards the rear, so he's being sent to the front. I must get used to thinking about him as though he were dead, but my whole being rebels. I relapsed into a feeling of horror all morning – always that blank horror, devoid even of any concrete regrets.

Yesterday the day had been agreeable, as I told you, and it had ended agreeably too. I went to eat a bite with Kos. at about 9, then we called in at the Dôme, where we found the Boubou at the centre of a tableful of noisy, picturesque Spaniards. It reminded me of my first year after my *agrégation* – those big conglomerations that would split up into sub-groups and jabber away in a variety of languages. Kos. was highly entertained, and also charming. We got rid of all the people, then went and listened to music at Gerassi's – but he doesn't play us his records with very good grace. On the wireless we heard a fine 'Elegy' by Fauré, and also *Firebird*; and on the gramophone some very lovely variations by Beethoven on a theme by Mozart – then we went home to sleep. This morning everything was grey, and Kos. had toothache and was plaintive. All the same, there was an agreeable moment over breakfast. I'd been to buy eggs and milk (I enjoy this domestic life) and we talked

– even about coats and hairstyles – while readjusting to our existence. After that, I called in at my place and found that disastrous mail. There were also some little letters from Bienenfeld, who really would like me to come. But her mother's furious at the idea. Bienenfeld's asking whether I could give that money back to her father. If I get your salary and the *N.R.F.* money, I'll do so. But I really would have liked to fetch up the Kos. sisters and have a bit of money in hand – so *do please write to the N.R.F.* One thing, at least, has happened to please me: a note from my headmistress, letting me know that they're keeping me in Paris and I'll be the only candidate for my post. I went for a walk through the streets, utterly gloomy after those letters and reimmersed entirely in the war. Then I went to the Dôme and Kos. did me some good, even though she's very downcast too. I didn't tell her about Bos, it was pointless. We ate and then went to the Champs-Élysées, which was pretty deserted and absolutely dismal. After strolling up and down it for a while, we went into a cinema – only 1¼ hours, the whole programme. There was a bad thriller, a very good old Mickey Mouse, and a newsreel on the declaration of war. After that we went to my place (to 71 Rue de Rennes, I mean) and spent a long time rummaging among old things and books, which was quite fun – but I no longer have any past there.

Do you want Henry James's *Portrait of a Lady?* It's not at all bad – I found it there.

After that we went and ate in Rue Vavin, before going home. We're both tired to death – I'm not sure why – and I'm saddened to death. I'm waiting – I'm not sure what for – I think I'll be waiting till the war ends. I'm still blocked, but from time [to time] I remember something from that trip to Morocco, or Megève, and it wrings my heart. But that wouldn't be a problem – it's fear that's the worst thing – which this evening has merged into despondency and a headache. My beloved, I feel your love so clearly in your letters, I feel you joined to me, I love you so. I kiss you, beloved little being, with all my might.

Your charming Beaver

Envelope:
F.M.
Private Sartre
Observation Post
Artillery Headquarters
Postal Zone 108*

---

*Letters 12 September 1939 to 11 January 1940 addressed as above

116 rue d'Assas
[Paris]

Thursday 14 September [1939]

Most dear little being

I was very depressed on Tuesday evening when I wrote to you. I went to bed, and for the first time since you left I reread your letters and spent a long time looking at your little photos. How I love your face! I recalled lots of images of you and felt passionately how much I loved you. I shed a few tears, and that brought a kind of relaxation. Yesterday morning I had another letter from you. So far there's not a single one missing. You seemed to be working well and not being bored, which comforted me. And then Gerassi – whom I met at the Dôme – assured me that, given the address you'd sent me, you certainly weren't in any danger. I was glad to hear this. But I'd like to know precisely how matters do stand, so tell me straight. Nothing from you this morning, but it sometimes skips one delivery. I'm just anxious to know whether you got my letters and the book – I do hope so. Nothing from Bost, but that's only to be expected: since he was being transferred, he won't have written. I'm a little less anxious about him now. I think that what's going on is the 'concentration of forces' always being talked about in the papers, and that he'll be in no danger before the first serious attacks, which means days and perhaps even weeks of respite. Moreover, even if he does die nothing tangible will occur: I'll continue not to be able to see him, and doubtless my memories will continue indefinitely to remain blocked. It will be an annihilation. Alongside the *fullness* of a presence, that *nothing* constituted by an absence is astonishing – why can't it be a contrary fullness? It's as though some trick were involved. At present, I feel a kind of gloomy resignation regarding Bost. I asked Kos. what effect it would have on her if he died. She told me that she'd wondered at once about that, and that it would be a great sorrow but not a disaster, because although their relations were most agreeable there was nothing essential about them for her. I was glad to hear that. Moreover, I've no remorse where she's concerned and am more and more determined, if Bost does return, not to sacrifice him to her. What most surprises me is the fact that she hasn't even bothered to have his letters forwarded from Laigle to Paris, and that she doesn't feel a more specific anxiety. There's a deep frivolity in her, within even the sincerest and most touchingly tragic feelings. She's rotten to Wanda too – she hasn't written her a word. I don't think they're getting on very well.

I had a little letter from Toulouse yesterday, on black-bordered paper because her father died at the end of the holidays. She's at Férolles with Dullin, waiting to see how events unfold, and is getting ready to write her novel. She's kindly inviting me down for a couple of days, so I'll arrive there on Saturday and leave again on Monday. I'll probably leave Kos. in Paris for these two days, with 20 F. Then I'll spend another 24 hours with her, and on Tuesday evening I'll leave for Quimper, where I'll stay ten days or so. Apparently Mme Bienenfeld is furious about my coming. On my way back I'll spend a day at That Lady's – if it's convenient for her – since I'll almost be passing through Angers. All of this is going to cost a bit and I'll just last out on my month's pay, even though I'm living here on only 50 F. a day for two. But anyway I shall last out.

Did you get the letter in which I told you to write to the *N.R.F.* at Rue Sébastien Bottin, asking them to send me the money? I'd like to know as soon as possible how much I'll have available for the Kos. sisters. Bienenfeld's asking if I could pay her father back – I'm not quite sure how I'll manage.

[. . .]

I'm pleased at the idea of changing my life – of going to Férolles and Quimper. Go on writing to Paris, I'll have everything forwarded. Goodbye, dear little being. I'd like to know that you've got my letters. I love you, my dearest love. I'd give anything to kiss your little face. Do write to me, your letters are all my happiness.

Your charming Beaver

Établissement Dupont

Paris, Friday 15 September [1939]

Dear little being

I had a little letter from you this morning: Sunday's. They arrive late, but very regularly. I'm glad to know that you've had my first big letter – I feel properly connected with you now. I hope that you've had the second one too, and the Gide, and all the subsequent letters. There were also two little letters from B., who has reached some place or other after two days in a coach. It's dated Tuesday. He doesn't give any details. I'm most uneasy about his fate, though he is asking for books – which presumes a somewhat longer respite. Have you written to him? Still to the same address – I've given him yours. There was a letter from C.

Audry, with whom I'll spend a moment or two next Tuesday. And a demanding letter from Bienenfeld. She's angry because I didn't come straight to Quimper. I wrote explaining to her that I couldn't just run off from Paris without knowing anything about you, my family, money matters, or what job I'd be going back to, and that I absolutely had to take care of Kos. I have an absolutely clear conscience, since I really couldn't have organized myself differently. If she mentions it to you in her letters, do defend me. This situation's annoying: if I behave correctly with one of them, the other at once starts moaning. I told Kos. candidly that I was first going to stay for two days with Toulouse and then going to see Bienenfeld at Quimper, and she took it very well, without ceasing to be charming. Actually, I could have arrived two days earlier at Bienenfeld's, by giving up the idea of seeing Toulouse. But I'll enjoy seeing Toulouse, and it interests me on Kos.'s behalf. I won't tell Bienenfeld I've been there, though, as she'd think it lightminded – I'll just give Kos. as an excuse. Tell me what you think. I won't get angry this time, my love. So I'm setting off tomorrow for Férolles, where I intend to spend Saturday evening, Sunday and Monday. I don't know whether Kos. will wait for me in Paris or not. At any rate, I'll leave again on Tuesday for Quimper, where I'll arrive on Wednesday morning, and I'll there till the end of the month – I'll take books and some work with me. I'm glad to be changing my life, as things are dragging a bit here. The weather's bad, we can't even go for a stroll, and whatever efforts we may make at conversation the inactivity's still getting both of us down.

[. . .]

This morning, after a rather hasty breakfast, I went to pick up my mail. I wrote a note to Bienenfeld from the Rallye (since Rey's is closed), and another to Bost. Kos. and I had lunch at the Milk Bar, sent off some parcels and then came here, where we're writing side by side before going to the cinema to see *Snow White*. On a streetcorner we met Levillain – your pupil from Le Havre – resplendent in the uniform of a cavalry officer. He gave up medicine and went through Saumur[91] – now he's a grown man. He announced to us, with heroic and winning gaiety, that he was leaving for the front in a few days – he was so marvellously true to himself that we were really impressed.

That's all. The red benches are crowded with people and there are budgerigars in the aviary: that hasn't changed here. I'm not bored, I'm not unhappy, I'll never be unhappy as long as I have you – even far

---

[91]Cavalry school.

away from me. All in all, the war hasn't yet changed my soul. My novel still interests me, and all of my past remains rigorously valid – even the passions and jealousies relating to B. I questioned myself about this yesterday, and find that – even in the face of tragic prospects – relations with an other's consciousness (and all that's involved in them) still survive.

I can't wait for your next letter, in which you will 'answer' me. I'm in a hurry for us to be able really to talk to one another by letter. It's already good to have news of you, but when we can think things together again it will be even better.

Goodbye, dear little being – I love you – I kiss you with all my might.

Your charming Beaver

I'm really upset about Bienenfeld

116 Rue d'Assas
[Paris]

Saturday 16 [September 1939]

Dear little being

I've just had your long Tuesday letter. The fact that it was so long and affectionate gave me real pleasure, my love. We're as one – I feel that at every instant. I love you. I've received all your letters all right, and hope you haven't missed out any either. The Gide was sent c/o M. le Curé, and registered. If it didn't arrive, let me know and I'll make a complaint. Lots of letters too were addressed c/o M. le Curé. No other mail this morning, except a letter from my mother in which she describes some woman as 'a charming colonial's wife who has read everything'! She's going to come back to Paris, and though I couldn't give a damn about that, Poupette's threatening to do so too – which I'd find the hell of a nuisance.

Yesterday after writing to you we went and saw *Snow White*. The dubbing, the music, the script and many of the images are of an appalling vulgarity. There are just a few fairly agreeable touches. With it they were showing a passage from a concert by Paderewski, who plays like a god. It was a good show for wartime – but not absorbing enough all the same, since in the middle I was overcome by gloomy thoughts: still about Bost, who's the real black spot. I feel a kind of impotent, yet intense remorse when I think of the fate of all those fellows. We came home slowly, cooked some rice and pasta, and chatted in a macabre, playful vein about the expediency of killing people in given circumstances and what the results would be. We went to bed at about 10.30, but I couldn't sleep for a long time. I finished *Portrait of a Lady* – which I found hard going, because the observations at the end are all dreadfully muddled – and began rereading *Jane Eyre*, which I'm not finding too boring. I woke early, so am feeling a bit shattered today. I thought of putting Kos. in my hotel room (she doesn't want to stay at Gégé's on her own) while I go and visit Toulouse. But even if one locks away the most compromising things, one can't be quite sure what she might unearth at the bottom of one's trunks. I told her the landlady wouldn't accept that arrangement, so she's returning to Laigle this evening. I'd really like her to be able to come back in October, so I'm going to look for a job for her.

I'm going to send you Dabit's *Journal* right away,[92] and some exercise-books. Send it on afterwards to Bost (51st Inf., 5 Company, Zone 170) if you can, like all the books you've read which you don't need any longer. Tell me whether you've written to the *N.R.F.* about the money.

Tomorrow and Monday I'll write long letters about Toulouse, but they'll probably be slow in arriving, being sent from Crécy-en-Brie. From Wednesday on, I'll be in Quimper. Perhaps you could write poste restante to Quimper, but not for long, because on the 29th at the latest I'll be back and your letters arrive so slowly – one has to reckon on 4 or 5 days. I'm glad you've settled in well, you're not unhappy and you're working well. I'm not at all unhappy either, not glum in the least – in fact, I feel full of beans. Goodbye, sweet little beloved being, I kiss you most passionately.

Your charming Beaver

Mme Nizan has certainly left.

[Crécy-en-Brie]

Sunday 17 September [1939]

My love,

I'm sitting in Toulouse's garden bathed in sunlight. It's midday. They've gone off shopping, and there's just the sound of water simmering

---

[92]Eugène Dabit (1898-1936), author of so-called 'populist' novels, whose journal was published posthumously in 1939.

in a saucepan coming from the kitchen. It's so agreeable – this fine weather, these flowers, this charming little house – that I feel quite softened. You should be there too, my love, in the next room with your pipe, and every now and then you'd smile to me through the window.

After writing to you yesterday, I stayed for another hour chatting to Kos. We tidied up the flat, I went to buy you some books and paper and send them off to you, then we had a drink at the Versailles. I told Kos. to tell Wanda you were hoping for some money from your books, so there were good chances she'd be able to come to Paris, at least for a while. After that Kos. saw me to the Métro. I was rather pleased at the idea of changing my life and being without her again. And yet, as soon as she'd left me I felt somehow disoriented. It was my whole individual life I was leaving, along with her; and I was once again merely a rootless being – without either a home or expectations – absorbed in a tragic collective history. And it was as though you and Bost were yet a little further away from me. When I arrived at the Gare de l'Est, that morning I left you there still seemed terribly recent. I reread my black notebook, with all the details on your departure, and recalled exactly all the tragedy of those hours. Like you, I caught the train on Platform 1 – a stopping train to Nancy and Strasburg – and I followed the same route as you as far as Esbly. There was a violent stench of war in the station, on that wheezing train, and at every one of those innumerable stopping-places. In a sense, I took pleasure in being entirely recaptured by the world. Through the window I looked at the Marne Canal: it was gentle and melancholy in the gathering twilight, with silent bicycles on the towpath and barges and children. It was reminiscent of excursions from Rouen, or other train journeys when I'd be going to Amiens, and for a moment I really could recall what being happy was like. Yet I didn't feel it was painful to be a consciousness withdrawn from happiness and unhappiness, and I understood how one can be detached painlessly too even from the will to live – i.e. accept the idea of dying. I think it's the first time this has happened to me. I also thought about Bost. I'm almost convinced that I shan't ever see him again. This paralyses me when I write to him, and even where thinking about him is concerned. What can you make of a person you'll never see again? In this way I reached Esbly – it was past 7 and beginning to get dark. I was told there wasn't a train till 8.30, and vaguely thought how extremely crass it had been of me to announce my arrival for 7, on the strength of a railway clerk's word – but I really didn't care. I didn't think about arriving. I installed myself outside a café near the station, and it wasn't in the least like a halt in the middle of a definite journey. On the contrary, it seemed like a true moment in which I was anywhere and aimless. All the rest – my life with Kos., my visit to Crécy – appeared like some trick or rosy dream offering respite from that truth. I stayed there for an hour in the fading light writing up my journal, which was very behindhand. Beside the open window a tableful of people were drinking Pernod and talking of war and death. They were talking about some woman who'd received a cable: 'Husband dead on field of honour', and voicing their indignation. 'Normally', one fellow was saying, 'it's the mayor who comes along and tells her: "Your husband's seriously wounded, my poor madam" – that's not so cold.' Trains went through, and yet more trains, many of them filled with mute soldiers. The darkness was dense, with two or three blue lamps illuminating the tiny groups of tables outside tiny bistros. At 8.15 I took the little train to Crécy – pitch dark, with just blue night-lights. We passed through a few little stations – equally dark, with stationmasters shouting out their names in the night – and eventually I arrived. I expected to have to make my own way, but Dullin was there, wrapped in old shawls and mufflers, and he took me in his arms. Apologizing profusely, I climbed into his old cart.

After that tragic and poetical journey, another story began – with a comic dominant theme, as you may imagine. We climbed slowly towards Férolles. The carriage had one lamp missing, and the horse was often frightened. There are troops everywhere here, and we were halted once on the way. Dullin kept repeating: 'It's terrible, terrible', in that familiar voice. He's especially sickened by the people in the rear, especially Jouvet,[93] who with several films already begun has declared: 'There's nothing more to be done for the theatre. We must devote ourselves to the cinema – finish off the films already begun and then devote ourselves to supporting French production.' Giraudoux[94] has put him in charge of film production, so he's very happy. As for Dullin, he has conferred at length with Baty and the idea of going to America or some neutral country revolts him. He'd like to try tours in France – which certainly won't be subsidized, but they're going to try on their own initiative. He again expressed his respect for Kos., saying: 'Well, so her career has once again been interrupted.' I'll talk to them about her more specifically today.

Eventually we arrived at the edge of the village, where Toulouse

[93]Louis Jouvet (1887-1951), actor-manager from 1934 till his death of the Théâtre de l'Athénée, was influential in introducing Jean Giraudoux to the French public.
[94]Jean Giraudoux (1882-1944), novelist and playwright, was one of the most eminent French men of letters in the nineteen-thirties. In August 1939 he became Minister of Information in the Daladier cabinet and in early 1940 was put in charge of all government propaganda, but he resigned when Reynaud replaced Daladier in March.

appeared on the scene holding a blue torch in her hand. As she escorted us some soldiers joined the escort, making fun of the strange old boneshaker. They've bought another house next to their own and that's where we put the horse, unharnessing it by the blue light of the torch – they take as many precautions here about lights as in Paris. Then we went into the house, where Toulouse's mother was waiting with a stern look. She flung herself upon me and kissed me on both cheeks. She has aged enormously since we last saw her: she's 74 and looks it. She's still red-headed, but with white roots – and a puffy face, bulging eyes, a drooping mouth, and speech so abrupt and jerky that I thought she was mad. Not mad, however, but – just imagine! – once she was installed at Crécy in the next-door house, they realized she was a total ether addict. She'd first taken ether for her chronic asthma, but she soon became so used to it that she needed a litre a day. She had it brought up to her by all the people in the village, sniffing it openly in front of all and sundry. There was a reek of ether all round the house, and she'd often fall flat on the ground and almost crack her skull. It became particularly tragic when Toulouse's father began to develop encephalitis lethargica, which required a lot of nursing. His wife went on drugging herself, and there were lots of scenes which the village witnessed in outrage. Toulouse eventually sent her father off to a nursing home at Lagny, where she took care of him with Zina's help while keeping her other eye on her mother. Her father's final illness was lengthy and painful – apparently it was extremely traumatic. Toulouse claims that her mother kicked the habit after his death – that's a month ago – but she looks strange. She seems to hate Dullin. It was quite funny at table, because there was tomato salad and sausage, to which we helped ourselves, and Dullin asked whiningly for more sausage – saying that he didn't eat tomatoes, so could he have a little more sausage – and then his mother-in-law attacked him savagely, saying: 'I took only one slice, so as to leave more for you', and Dullin apologized, and it just went on like that. Yet she calls him Lolo and kisses him before going off to bed. Toulouse sent her off as soon as dinner was over, and Dullin told me about his war years. He actually enlisted and did 3 years in the trenches, without getting the least pleasure*. Through his stories, it all seemed to retain a human character, with ethics and freedom still operative. He interested me. I told them stories of my own, then remained alone with Toulouse till past midnight – that's when she filled me in on the family dramas. She handed me the prologue and first act of her play,[95] which I started to read yesterday evening in bed and have

---

[95]About the Princesse des Ursins.

just finished. It's neither ridiculous, nor clumsy, nor even very boring; but despite a certain liveliness of the dialogue I find it dreadfully flat. I didn't expect that at all. It's sober and lacklustre – impossible to know without the remaining acts how it would turn out on the stage. It's definitely better than *Plutus*, but one can't conceive why it was ever written.

I slept in that room Toulouse occupied one night when you had a temperature and we slept in the Corsair's Room.[96] The Corsair's Room has become even more splendid, there's an old trunk and sumptuous draperies – it's so pleasant here that it's quite affecting. I slept like a log till 11. I woke up feeling sad, but that's [. . .] too. In normal times, what exacerbates my sadness is the fact that it shocks, scares and revolts me, and reflection turns it into a drama. Whereas here – at present, I mean – I at once accept it with good grace, and anything extra that comes along is welcome.

I was just finishing writing when Toulouse and Dullin showed up in the car. I greeted them, we unpacked the provisions, and we sat down to eat a sumptuous lunch under the cloister. Do you recall how agreeable this spot is, dear little being? There was good wine and *vieux marc* and the lunch was pleasant. Dullin's relations with his mother-in-law are enchanting: 'You know', she says sternly, 'that magic dye doesn't work at all.' 'Well', says Dullin, gimlet-eyed but in a dulcet, casual tone of voice, 'is it in keeping with the principles of dyeing to hang up the object you've just dyed for two days in the rain?' The woman retorts with dignity: 'I left it in the rain on purpose.' 'Oh! Well then,' says Dullin, 'if you did it on purpose!' It's like that from morning to evening, and quite hilarious.

So we were in a fairly gay mood when Dullin's niece – who lives nearby – arrived, kissed her uncle on the forehead, smiled to the company, and said: 'Have you seen what the Russians have done, then?' We had no idea. She informed us that they'd gone into Poland, which was a dirty trick.[97] Thereupon, Dullin obligingly launched into a detailed description of the fate of light infantry in wartime. He put all his artistry into this, and it was so unbearable that I couldn't restrain myself and tears came to my eyes. However, I calmed down and managed to listen to quite a number of heroic stories and varied

---

[96]Dullin and Toulouse used to decorate their houses with old theatrical props; presumably they had a room at Férolles containing props from some past production of Marcel Achard's play *Le Corsaire*.
[97]Following the Nazi-Soviet pact, Poland was invaded by German troops on 1 September 1939; its swift collapse provoked a Soviet invasion from the east on 17 September.

accounts of war – but inside I was trembling with all my might.

When we left the table, Toulouse took me for a long walk. We crossed some fields and came out at the side of a road near a little station, where we had a drink in a bistro by the roadside. There were two soldiers guarding the track, and lots of cars full of soldiers went by – there was a strong smell of war. It wasn't like Paris, it was the very picture of the French countryside in wartime. Yet the villages were peaceful, and so beautiful at the close of the day. I felt very strongly the truth of what you once said to me – at Avignon, I think – about how precious an instant can be in the midst of tragedy. I wasn't forgetting anything, yet nothing could destroy the loveliness of the landscape. It was really powerful, that walk with the horizon blocked and dark, and then that sky and that countryside which were not part of any sad history – which were not part of any history at all – but which existed with their own meaning, with which I was imbued as though despite myself. These are the truest and best moments, better than instants of pure distraction or moments of horror either. We talked about Toulouse's play, which I duly praised; about Kos., for whom they are full of benevolence but without being able to do anything for her at the present time; and about their plans. They say that going to America would amount to doing a shameful bunk, and that something must be attempted in France – but it strikes them as difficult. Apparently Jouvet, with his monocle, used to assume the airs of a great leader. He said: 'What's needed on the radio is to raise morale. We need to put on easy, entertaining things. Claudel's *The Satin Slipper* or Péguy's *Joan of Arc*[98] – that's the kind of thing we need.' We arrived home at about 7 and found Dullin rather downcast, because his calculations and projects aren't working out well. We listened to the news and had dinner. The old woman was wearing her glasses; she was calmer than yesterday and less terrifying. At dinner we discussed Catholicism, and Dullin told me stories about priests with loose morals. He also told a charming story about the little cabaret-singer from the Vieux Colombier, who turned up in distress one day in Dullin's and Jouvet's dressing-room, because he said Gide and Ghéon kept cornering him with evil intentions.[99] And also how, one night at the Père Tranquille in Les Halles, Gide and Ghéon had picked up two little street-arabs – and then five more had turned up, stripped them

[98]Paul Claudel (1868-1955), poet and playwright, wrote his long drama set in Spain, *The Satin Slipper*, in 1925-8, but it was produced in an acting version only in 1943. Charles Péguy (1873-1914), Catholic essayist and poet, wrote three dramatic poems on Joan of Arc between 1909 and 1912.

[99]André Gide and Henri 'Ghéon' (Vanglon), author of religious dramas, were both homosexual.

naked, and demanded a big cheque to give them their clothes back. We chatted agreeably in this way till 10 at night, and then everyone got sleepy so we went up to our rooms. That's where I am now, finishing off my letter. I'll add a continuation tomorrow before mailing it in Paris. My love, shall we have to go on for a very long time not living together? Even after three years, though, we'd be just the same. Only for all that time I wouldn't really have had a life. It would be just a period of waiting – waiting for you. My love, how I long to squeeze your little arm in mine. I'm remembering – that platform in Marseilles at 5 in the morning, when I saw you appear and you smiled at me. Your love is ever-present to me, my beloved, and with it I feel strong.

Monday

This morning at 9 I was brought a cup of coffee. I got up and wrote a long letter to Kosakiewitch. Then I went downstairs and sat by the stove to read the first part of Shakespeare's *Henry IV*, where Falstaff appears. It's an excellent play and I enjoyed it. Dullin, with the diligence of a schoolboy, was drawing up endless projects, while Toulouse was wandering round the house in her dressing-gown. She's wearing mourning – a pretty stylish kind of mourning, but mourning nonetheless. It was all very agreeable, but through the open window you could hear officers' voices and whistle blasts. And I found it odd being on the side of the 'resident' on whom troops are billeted, whereas I picture you as a soldier in some resident's home. We had lunch, I talked to Toulouse for quite a while, then she drove me to the station. I caught a train and it took me 2½ hours to get back to Paris. But I was reading *The Hound of the Baskervilles*, which was entertaining, and anyway I'm never in a hurry any more. Yet I felt rather as though I were expected in Paris, because of the letters: I found an enormous packet of them. Two were from you, dated the 13th and 14th – it's more or less regular, you have to reckon 4 days. But I'm terribly upset that you haven't got my letters – they're like a real journal. Bost has received them all. There were 3 little notes from him, including one written on Saturday that has restored me to life. He isn't yet in any danger, and he's so humble and touching – quite astonished and embarrassed that anyone should be worried about him, and no longer even afraid of being afraid – that he brings tears to my eyes. He says he too is living from one day to the next: that he organizes a little life for himself, which works for two days out of three – or even a bit more. There was a letter from Sorokine, who's still wiping kids, and three charming letters from Bienenfeld, who says she understands and is expecting me whenever I like. This gave me an enormous desire to see her – I'm leaving tomorrow evening.

I came back here to write a long letter to Bost and finish off this letter for you. C. Chonez[100] came up to me and asked me at length for news of you, saying that she would gladly give the lives of ten nobodies to save yours – I don't know what the nobodies would have to say about it.

My hand's dropping off and I'm going to bed, my love. Till tomorrow. I'm so much with you – I want you to have my letters and feel how you're all intermingled with me. I kiss you, my sweet little one, so tenderly and passionately.

Your charming Beaver

Toulouse asked for your address, so that she could write to you. And her mother gave me hundreds of messages for 'Jean-Paul'. Toulouse was charming and nice. We'll see something of each other this year.

*I meant to say 'wound' not 'pleasure', but I don't think he got any pleasure either.

[Paris]

Tuesday 19 September [1939]

Most dear little being

Just a quick note before leaving for Quimper. I've had a very busy day. Yesterday I was just finishing off writing to you when they ejected me brutally from the Dôme. It's odd to see how people cling on, even though the inside of the Dôme is so gloomy, and how scared they are at the idea of finding themselves outside. I was a bit like that too; I didn't like having to go home to my room, which is so inhospitable with its blue light. Yet I was gay as I walked through the streets, because of the letters I'd received. It's beautiful – the Rue de la Gaîté, pitch dark, with just a dim little blue bar here and there. I went to bed, reread my letters, and began Gogol's *Taras Bulba* – which looks quite entertaining. The book fell from my hands, but I still took a long time to fall asleep. I woke at 8 feeling full of beans. I packed my bags and tidied my room – which I may not rent again, if I can find some empty flat. Then I went off to the Dôme, where I read while waiting for C. Audry. The weather was wonderful and I felt in an excellent mood. C. Audry showed up

---

[100]Claudine Chonez was a journalist and writer, who wrote an article on the mobilization of Sartre, the new literary success, based on a recent interview with him.

suddenly with a magnificent nickel-plated bicycle, that she'd bought on 1 September with her last few pennies. It suits her so well. She looked very sporty, with her hair in a net. She's married to Minder – as we guessed.[101] I asked her if she loved him and she said yes, but in a mild sort of way. He has been declared unfit for service and annoys her because, instead of being happy with his lot, he does nothing but moan about his luck. She couldn't tell me anything interesting about him. Apparently your poor German teacher Katia Landau is now in a dreadful situation: she has lost her husband, who has been taken away and never set eyes on again. It also seems that our friend N. is very demoralized at present. C. Audry's sister,[102] on the other hand, is in fine fettle, and her husband the general knows all the right people. They're going to stay in Paris, and perhaps J. Audry will find Kos. a job as a script-girl. I spotted Rabo, the brother of my pupil Rabinovici and admirer of Audry. It seems the preparatory classes for girls taking the École exam are being transferred to Bordeaux and Tournon, so I'll just be having a normal Bac class. It also seems that the headmistress at C. Sée is complaining that she has heard nothing from me, so I'll write to her from Quimper. C. Audry seems uneasy about what attitude to take, and is afraid of boredom and discomfort. She didn't say anything else of interest. She told me – and Dullin had told me the same thing – that at the Hôtel Continental (where Giraudoux lives) it's hilarious to see Jean-Pierre Aumont[103] hanging about in magnificent riding-breeches. Also, some wives are apparently contriving to get right to the frontier to see their husbands. Do find out about this – after all, you're only in the rear.

She left me at about midday and I went to see Stépha, who's in a state of prostration because Fernand has been having some problems – I don't think it's too serious. They've asked C. Audry and a lot of other people for help. But Stépha's nervous – and about her mother too, who was at Lvov and of whom she has had no news. At Stépha's I read a letter from Poupette, which painted an intriguing but gloomy picture of Saint-Germain-les-Belles and the atmosphere of baseless rumour prevailing there. I took Stépha to the Crêperie Bretonne and she told me hundreds of stories that I'll have to repeat to you face to face. I'm noting them down so that I don't forget anything. We had lunch, and I stayed with her for a while before calling back at the hotel, where I found a wire from Bienenfeld – who's expecting me tomorrow morning – and a strange red letter which I'm enclosing with my own letter and which

---

[101] A bilingual German specialist.
[102] The film-maker Jacqueline Audry.
[103] Jean-Pierre Aumont (1911-): pseudonym of J.-P. Salomons, actor and playwright.

seems to be from some lunatic. There was also a note from Raoul Lévy[104] asking to see me, so I phoned and made an appointment with him at the Dôme, to which I'm just off.

I do so hope you've had my letters. Everything I live through is lived through in order to tell you about it, so that it makes a little enrichment of your own life. There was nothing from you today. I do so want you to write to me – I've received your letters.

The deputy manageress of this hotel is hateful. I no longer like the Hôtel Mistral, and am rather thinking of moving when I get back.

Goodbye, my love, I'll add a note when I've seen Lévy, in case he tells me some entertaining stories. I'm a bit apprehensive about the journey this evening, because Stépha took 30 hours to get here from Marseilles. When shall I be in Quimper? My letters will take a long time arriving from there. But if only you had all the others!

I've just seen Lévy, very sweet, but he told me nothing entertaining. He says that Kanapa is well, and that they're both contemplating their future lot philosophically. Lamblin, it seems, is less satisfied. I must hurry to the station. I kiss you passionately, my love.

Your charming Beaver

I've had your little letter of the 15th. Thank you.

[Quimper]

Wednesday 20 September [1939]

My love,

I found your little letter yesterday, when I called back at the hotel to pick up my luggage. How I do hope the mail orderly has brought you my twelve letters awaiting delivery, and that you can feel me living with you. This letter will take a long time to arrive, and from now on I shan't have any of yours for a long while. Yet I'm glad to be here. I'm writing to you from a café on those quays where we used to walk together on rainy days.[105] I can remember it well. I haven't yet rediscovered that big dining-room painted by the blind painter, but I'm going to look for it.

---

[104]Former pupil of Sartre, and fellow-student of Jean Kanapa and Lamblin, in 1939 at Lycée Pasteur in Neuilly.
[105]Easter 1932 – see *The Prime of Life*, p.108.

It was a real wartime journey last night, even though the train wasn't late. I went to catch my train on that kind of big open-air terrace you climb up to through a gate on the Avenue du Maine. There were 50 carriages, all crammed with passengers and above all with suitcases, filling the racks to bursting point. I found myself a seat in a compartment containing eight women and one man. The night-light was so dim that I barely managed to read *Taras Bulba* for half an hour, virtually ruining my eyes in the process. Sleeping too was more or less impossible, because of the talking, the heat, and the shortage of room. Feeling quite numb, I dozed – undisturbed but a bit sickened by those women, who really were coming it strong. The two who were with the man were carrying huge bundles of silverware, and they never stopped telling fantastic stories about spies. They probably suspected the presence of hordes of spies on the roofs and axles of the train, since they were ever on the lookout for sounds and smells. 'I saw a flash', one would say with a shudder. 'What's that smell? There's a funny smell', would say another. And the whole compartment would hold its breath. We were next to the WC, and every time the toilet-lid was raised with a bang the people all trembled, convinced there was going to be an explosion. I don't know whether the brakes were in a bad state or the driver incompetent, but the stops were violent and abrupt. At the first of them, a woman was almost taken ill – thinking there'd been a derailment – and had to be comforted with cold tea. A fellow in a nearby compartment actually did get a suitcase on his head and had to be taken off on a stretcher. Once an hour, a madman looking just like a schoolteacher would come and gibber away about how his mission was to comfort the world, and about how Hitler's head would soon be cut into six pieces. I dozed, and was full of poetry despite everything. I've never been so accessible and poetic as since the war began – because I'm less in my life and more in things, I think. But I also thought about my life, with enormous satisfaction: it's pleasant to have behind you. I worry much less about happiness than before. Or, at least, it strikes me that happiness was for me a privileged way of grasping the world, like a symphony performed by the best orchestra; and if the face of the world itself has changed, the importance of happiness disappears. I'm explaining rather badly, because my head's still woozy after that sleepless night, but you can see what I mean. In the darkness I passed through Angers, where I'm hoping to stop on the way back (I've written to That Lady about it), and Nantes, where on a shop front I saw the words 'House of the True Beaver'[106] – I'll unmask the imposter! Then

---

[106] *Au Vrai Castor*: shop-sign for fur goods.

gradually daylight came, disclosing an ugly countryside and those squat, grey Breton churchtowers we don't much like. I was glad to see the countryside again, and to have to adapt myself to a new way of living. Glad to see B. too – albeit in a mild way. I found her on the platform, all pretty and tragic. Her mother made a dreadful scene this morning because of my arrival. She claims she has found some letter, which she's getting ready to send to the ministry to cause trouble for me. But countless signs indicate that she hasn't found anything. Moreover, my letters were passionate but not compromising, so I'm unworried. But B. was very much on edge. She told me how things are for her here – you already know from her letters, it's really hateful. She has found me a charming room in an old hotel of the Petit Mouton type. I spruced myself up again somewhat, then we took a stroll through the town, which is very agreeable. It's full of coaches and I'm counting on making lots of excursions – and first of all to the Pointe du Raz – but her mother's going to be a damned nuisance.

I lunched in an agreeable Breton crêperie, and am now writing to you while waiting for B. to come back from her own lunch. I really like her, the weather's fine, Bost wrote me a charming, touching letter yesterday, and I'm happy. I don't speak about you, because you're not variable matter, you're the base, which dulls the worst sorrows and makes joy so easily possible. Goodbye, my dear love, you're my strength, my assurance, and the source of all good things – and you're the most charming of little ones – and I love you in accordance with your merits, which are measureless.

Your charming Beaver

Grand Café de Bretagne
Quimper

Quimper, Thursday 21 [September 1939]

My love,

I'm having a good time at Quimper, it's almost like a country holiday. But in the evenings, once Bienenfeld has left me, things become quite gloomy again. It's only 7.30, and since yesterday I've known what an evening in Quimper means – so it's not without a certain trepidation that I note how I'm not in the least sleepy.

As for Bienenfeld, my feelings are rather tender. She's affecting and charming, and she was really pretty today in her print dress – the dress from her Annecy photograph. But I don't know why, I'm cold. Perhaps it's the fact of having got on so well with Kos. – that always harms Bienenfeld. Perhaps, too, I was expecting something more solid, but find just a little girl, rather lost, too pathetic, and disordered in her thoughts. What's more, I'm not in much of a sentimental mood. She has no suspicion of this – she's in seventh heaven – and, besides, I have no difficulty in being melting with her, I'm full of tenderness for her. But, my love, what barren nourishment – all these people who aren't you! How I'd like something solid, something true!

I had a dream about Bienenfeld last night. I first dreamed that at the post office they gave me a letter from you, from London, in which you were complaining of being bored for no good reason. And I was suddenly furious at the thought that I'd been hanging about in Paris, far away from you, for no good reason either. So I cabled you: 'Come back!' and told Bienenfeld I was returning to Paris to see you. She declared that she wanted those ten days in September for herself – just her and you – since she'd been so long without seeing you. So I became furiously angry and said such harsh things to her that she flung herself down on a bed screaming and sobbing, and we hated one another.

And then, today, she really did calculate: 'In six months, Sartre will get 6 days leave. You will let me spend three days with him, won't you? There'll be three left for you.' And I felt myself trembling inside with anger. Six days, in six months, how little that will be! How I shall want you to myself! We'll have to hide out like criminals. This ruthlessness of mine is very premature, of course, but I'm beginning to wait for those six days, I'm beginning to realize I won't see you before that – I'm beginning to miss you horribly. It's not yet sorrow or anything tragic, it's more like some food I'm lacking: I've enough just to vegetate, but always with an empty feeling in my stomach and a certain languor – whereas with you I used to be vigorous.

At 2 yesterday I'd just finished writing to you when Bienenfeld came to pick me up. We went for a beautiful walk which she'll doubtless tell you all about – it was wild and very lovely. There really are Breton farms and houses of great beauty: austere but pure. But the people, with their headdresses and bonnets and blue eyes, are not a whit preferable to the yokels of Rodez – in fact, they're even worse. The weather was fine and I loved being back in the country. For the first time since you left I had real desires, alive and stubborn: to go to the Pointe du Raz; to go for a bathe in the sea; to see Audierne and St Guénolé. But in the evening, when I found myself on my own again, I realized anew that it was wartime and the bistros and streets were full of soldiers. I looked for a restaurant – wanting something really cheap, because I'm a pauper and need a bit of cash for buses – and ended up in a grimy back shop, full of unwashed tramps and with food to match. They gave me a bread soup that had weevils in it, and then some other garbage. I swallowed down everything, forcing myself to do so, and after quarter of an hour I fled. I went to one of the big cafés on the quays and wrote to Sorokine, then made up my journal. No sooner was it 8 p.m. than they drew heavy blue curtains, shooed me back to the vicinity of the till, and switched off everything except three little lamps. There was just me and a customer fooling around with two whores. Luckily at 9 in the evening sleep overcame me, so I climbed up to my room and fell into a deep slumber. My hotel is an annexe of a big hotel connected to that Hôtel de l'Épée where you and I had lunch: through the windows I saw those paintings by the painter Lemordant again. I'm the only guest. There's an entrance on the cathedral square: you go through a rustic dining-room where nobody eats any longer – it looks all neglected and absurd, with its poster for the Club des Sans-Club on the wall[107] – then you go up a spiral staircase and find my little room, with its bed set back in an alcove. But at night this entrance is closed and you have to go through the garage of the Hotel de l'Épée, then through a courtyard full of thistles and stinking drains. I find this hotel charming. From my little window, I can see old turreted houses and a grassy courtyard. All of Quimper is really agreeable, and round every corner you come across the most charming windows, roofs and gables.

At 8.30 I was eating delicious croissants as I waited for Bienenfeld. I was hoping to go to the Pointe du Raz, but her mother had made such dreadful scenes again that there was no question of that. She didn't arrive until 9, and we talked. We went to the top of a little hill, where we sat in the sun and had a charming view of the town. Then she went home. I found lots of pretty little restaurants reminding me of that one at Caen, where we sometimes used to go during the exam period. In one of them I ate copiously and drank a bottle of cider: it was good, but with cold veal for the first course and roast veal to follow – too much veal! I went to the café to wait for B. I'm reading *Tête d'Or*, which I first read quiveringly ten years ago and which has stirred me again this time – the agony and death of Cébès is splendid.[108] On the other hand, it's a fascist – almost a Nazi – play. This afternoon we went for another fine walk, quite a long one since we didn't get back till 7, after which we ate a few crêpes and I came here to write to you. This is the other café, and though it has closed its metal shutters now, there are three tables occupied (two of them by officers) and it's lit up. Furthermore,

---

[107]Something similar to the Oddfellows.
[108]Play by Claudel, see note 98 above.

it's leather rather than red plush and smells less of death. I'm going to read till I'm thrown out, then go back to my room. Goodbye, my love, I miss your letters. O you – my life, my health, and the salt of the earth – how colourless the world is without you! How grey everything is! Your tenderness is still with me from afar, but I'm not able – like the reader imagined by Maheu – to reinvent your thoughts and your words. You were such an 'interesting' and charming yourself, and I'm so bored of not hearing your voice any more – I do miss you, my love. If I should forget to kill myself out of passion at your death, I'd end up withering away gently from boredom and they'd bury me just the same. Come back to me.

Your charming Beaver

Grand Café de Bretagne
Quimper

Quimper, Friday 22 September [1939]

My love,

I'm in the same café as yesterday, at the same hour. It's still light outside, but they're already closing the metal shutters. I don't have a great deal to tell you. I returned to my agreeable little room yesterday at about 10, after rereading Conrad's *End of the Tether*, which is pretty good. I went to bed and read Jouhandeau's *La Jeunesse de Théophile*, which I'm enjoying. Then I slept. I woke up in bright sunlight, came down at 8.30 and in the café found Bienenfeld with a poor little face ravaged by tears and lack of sleep, because of a hysterical scene with her mother. She more or less chucked B. out and forbade her ever to see me again. On Monday she's taking her to Paris to see her father, and B. can't refuse, which means that I'm rather kicking myself for having come all the way down here. I think I'll have three days touring around, without a rucksack – which would be provocative – but with just my big handbag, which will take all I need. I'll go and see Morgat, and the Pointe du Raz, and on the way I'll revisit Douarnenez and Locronan, where we were so happy, my love – it was a honeymoon, do you remember, my sweet little one? Then I'll go to Angers and see That Lady. I consoled B. as best I could, we went and sat in a very agreeable park surrounding the cathedral, and gradually she calmed down. At about 11 we took a coach and went to see the sea at Concarneau, which is a charming port with an old enclosed town entirely surrounded by ramparts, which jut into the sea like a tiny St Malo. We lunched off bread and rillettes on the ramparts, then set off on foot along a coast road and, in glorious weather, followed the sea, passing through some charming scenery. At 4 we took another coach back to Quimper. We went up to my room and petted one another a bit – as much as possible, actually – but I was as cold as a log. Indeed, I think I'm totally frigid, which is also one way of being blocked. At 6 we went for one more little walk round Quimper, and I stuffed myself with cold crêpes – which are not very good, but very cheap. As we were strolling along a street, some girls from the Red Cross school came up and told B. her sister had called in at the school to leave a message that she should go home immediately. She sped off at a run and I came back here. A quarter of an hour later she turned up again and told me her family had left at 2 with the car, and that there was nobody either at home or at the Perraults' place. Then she went off again and I'm left bewildered. I'm going to write to Kos. and read and go home to sleep. I felt more affection for B. than yesterday – she was so concerned and touching – but she seems alien to my life, completely alien. I'm pressing her as hard as I can to try to come and live in Paris – her existence is really wretched.

Goodbye, beloved little being. I have lots of little memories of you. I can't believe that I'm not going to find you there in Paris. I love you. I've been happy with you – what a wealth of happiness behind me, my love! I kiss you so passionately, littlest of all charms, little all-charm, little charm-all.

Your charming Beaver

10 at night – B.'s affairs seem to be sorting themselves out somewhat.

[Quimper]

Saturday 23 September [1939]

My love,

I've had two letters from you – those of the 16th and 17th. They haven't taken too long, seeing that I'm at Quimper. I'm so glad you've received the Gide and begun to receive my letters – I think you must have a lot of them by now. How good it will be when we can communicate together again – I so need to feel your thought close at hand.

I've had nothing from Bost, but last Sunday all was going well with him and nothing much seems to have happened since then. Nothing from Kos. – I wonder why. I hope Wanda hasn't been causing trouble (about Bienenfeld, for example), but I don't think so. It's probably the mails. I'm also annoyed because my parents will be in Paris on Tuesday, and I told Poupette – in order to avoid going to the Limousin – that I was staying in Paris. I'll have to think up some explanation. On the other hand, I've received a friendly card from That Lady inviting me to La Pouèze, where I'll be spending Thursday and Friday.

I've had quite a good day today. This morning in the café from 8 to 10 I read the second version of *Tête d'Or* and the second part of Shakespeare's *Henry IV* – both a bit austere. Then Bienenfeld came along, her mind wholly taken up by problems of a lost key and identity-card, going into every attendant detail. She has a frantic core that she expends on muddle-headed practical obsessions, or on puerile tragic fits. At times she moves me and at others she irritates me. This morning she irritated me – thinking all askew, attributing to some German leader or other a speech by Giraudoux, and panicking about a 10-F. lock. She left me to have lunch alone, and I ate very well, in a different bistro from the day before yesterday's but of the same type and drinking a litre of cider. I was reading *Mars ou la guerre jugée* by Alain, which I find excellent but very horrific beneath its air of dry detachment – it really shook me. At a certain moment they gave the news from Warsaw on the radio, and it was astonishing to see the Breton women in their headdresses turn utterly expressionless faces to the set, quite impervious to the Polish disasters. After lunch I met up with Bienenfeld and her sister again, and we went by coach to the seaside. We found splendid white, rocky beaches, with a sea that was full of life and colour and wide horizons. We walked about for a while, then took to the water. It was searingly cold but soon grew voluptuous, and I realized with delight that my body was floating and moving over the water with an ease it had never known – but which seemed quite natural to me. I experienced a moment of deep joy. We rubbed ourselves down quickly, dressed again, went for a little walk, then returned home. I went for a walk on my own with Bienenfeld, in a little outlying part of the town where there's a very beautiful church and old houses. There she became gloomy and pathetic. We went up to my room, where she cried from exhaustion. This life her mother subjects her to is unbearable – I really felt how painful and distressing it must be. I consoled her as best I could, but she plunged me into the dismals myself. I have the most wonderful luck to have money and not depend on anybody. It doesn't prevent tragedy and horror; but that gloom of Bienenfeld or the Kos. sisters never overcomes me, because I feel free, disposing of my own life – and if need be of my death – and not being responsible to anyone but myself.

I have only myself to blame if I let the situation get on top of me; and I have the maximum number of chances and possibilities, when it's a question of finding a way in the dark. That's why everything retains a savour of 'experience' and 'interest'.

I've come here to eat some pancakes in a very stylish little *crêperie*: the blue curtains don't disfigure it, and it's better being here than in the café.

I really understand everything you write about war being indiscernible, and about hollow dumb-bells.[109] For my part, I discern things everywhere that are a lousy, damned nuisance – but not war. That's what disappoints Bienenfeld too – but I'd never really expected anything else. Just three or four times – at Esbly (that stop on the way to Crécy), or at the Dôme, or in trains – I've really felt a black presence all round me, and this was a plenitude that was almost voluptuous. During the first week I experienced above all a kind of indefinite and somewhat debilitating flight – but then that was over and it's now a matter of living in the moment. I can't really imagine my return to Paris in a week's time and the real resumption of my life.

Bienenfeld claims that you'll certainly receive your salary. On the other hand, her mother's clamouring for that money – so I'm going to pay it back a thousand francs at a time. Gégé is offering me her flat at the same price I'm paying at the hotel, so I'm going to take it – but just for myself, since she wants to keep a room. That suits me very well. I'll try and find a place for the Kos. sisters at Zuorro's, or De Roulet's, or my grandmother's, or even my mother's. If I have only my own salary, they can come for a week each month until Kos. finds a job. Then Wanda could spend a fortnight each month in Paris. If I have your salary too, I'll give them 2,000 F. a month and pay debts with the rest; and I'll put some money aside for when we don't have your salary any longer, which may happen. I promise you I'll do whatever's best. I'm afraid I'll also have to bring Bienenfeld to Paris from time to time. Poor little girl, I'm full of pity for her, but terribly detached from her – I care much more about Kos. at the moment.

My love, *do answer* what I say in my letters, I want to talk to you. I do so long for something solid and hard to hold on to – do speak to me.

About the N.R.F., there's nothing to be said. I went there, and they told me it had moved but one should go on writing to Rue Sébastien

---

[109]In his letter of 16 September, Sartre had written: 'This war . . . flees thought; I try bravely to catch it but . . . war is always somewhere behind, impossible to grasp . . . I'm somewhat disoriented ethically . . . like the fellow who has readied himself to lift a big dumb-bell and finds that it's hollow . . . naturally, he finds himself on his butt.'

Bottin – they'll forward everything.

Write quickly telling them to send me the money. I forwarded you the letter in which they say they're still counting on your collaboration – write them an answer about that.

Goodbye, my love. I feel really tired this evening. If I were told I was going to see you I think I'd faint from joy. But that doesn't even amount to a wish, since I know only too well that I shan't see you for a long while. I love you.

Your charming Beaver

Zuorro, That Lady tells me, is in Constantine, and Guille in Dijon. So they're not badly off.

Hotel de l'Épée
Quimper

Sunday 24 September [1939]

Most dear little being

Just a short note before I go to sleep, it's already 10.30. I've just left Bienenfeld, and the separation was pathetic – at least on her side, poor creature. As for me I was touched, but coolly. It was, if anything, painful for me to rediscover in her countenance feelings that I'd had for others – and that, for weeks already, I no longer have. I'm growing hard, my love, it would take your own little person to make me melt. You say you don't approve of your tranquillity; but I don't much approve either of this kind of animal well-being to which I've been restricted for some time. This morning, while filling myself with meat and cider at lunchtime, I felt it was rather monstrous to be so violently alive; to enjoy my life and be satisfied with it, without thinking – and almost feeling – anything any more. I don't know if it's frivolity, or myopia, or selfishness. I don't know how one ought to be. But those few moments of terror that I felt about Bost – and to some extent about you – strike me as a meagre price, set beside the privilege of being sure of preserving my life. This time is so strange. I wish for your return, and wishing for that means wishing for the end of the war: in other words, wishing for the war really to begin. You don't know where to place a desire – everything's impossible.

We spent another good day. In the morning, after two hours of reading during which I finished *Mars ou la guerre jugée*, I went for a walk in the outskirts of Quimper, where I saw a charming little church. This afternoon we went for a walk in some moorlike terrain along the Odet: it was a melancholy landscape of broom, pine and grey water, a really beautiful landscape that one could love with all one's heart. I ate pancakes at the *crêperie* while reading *Rimbaud en Abyssinie*, from which I didn't learn much.[110] Then Bienenfeld came back, in spite of a scene with her mother, and we spent a dismal hour in my room. I don't know what her father will decide, but she can't go on living with her mother, who's driving her mad. She's really pitiful. Perhaps she'll live on her own at Rennes – that would be best.

You'll probably have no letter for a day or two, since I'm leaving tomorrow morning for Morgat, from where I'll be able to see the Pointe du Raz, and then Penmarch. On Wednesday evening I'll leave for Angers, and on Thursday I'll be at La Pouèze. I'll stay there till Monday 2nd, since the schools don't reopen until the 9th. From Monday on I'll be living at Gégé's – i.e. 116 Rue d'Assas, c/o Mme Pardo – so write there. I'm so glad you've had my letters. I'd like to see your little notebook.[111] Do tell me what you write in it, and in what terms you're treating yourself as you deserve. Speak to me about yourself – don't leave me.

I love you, my sweet little one, I'd so like to talk to you. I'm happy whenever I go and see someone new – but at once disappointed, since the pleasure I'm hoping for from them is that which you alone can give me. I'm mutilated without you, my love. It's not exactly painful, but it's sad. In the whole world, there's only you who count for me.

Your charming Beaver

Hôtel de Bretagne
Douarnenez

Monday 25 September [1939]

My love, my dear love

My heart's just a mush this evening, I'm consumed by passion for you and it couldn't be more painful. This has been brewing all day and it came down on me like a tornado in the streets of Douarnenez, where I

---

[110]French translation (1938) of Enid Starkie's *Arthur Rimbaud in Abyssinia* (1937).
[111]A reference to the little notebook in which Sartre had begun (on 14 September) to keep a journal of his daily existence, and also to re-examine his past – the first of the fourteen which were to become his *War Diaries*, and of which five survived.

broke into sobs. Luckily it was moonlight! My love, we were together on this little bridge where there were lots of fishermen in red trousers sitting in a row on the parapet. And just now I missed your little arm in mine and your face beside me so strongly that I didn't know what was to become of me. I've revisited Locronan – I remember it all so well. How, on the beach of St Anne de la Palud, you told me about Isoré and his loves. How, on the bay at Douarnenez, near a pine wood that I've seen again, you told me that you loved to see the sea through the pine trees, and we talked about evolutionism and mechanicism and about animals. Every morning we'd wake up in our twin beds and I'd ask you: 'How are you, my little Poulpiquet?'.[112] O my love, I do so long for your tenderness this evening! I feel I've never told you enough how I loved you, that I've never been nice enough to you. My sweet little one, how I'd like to hold you and cover you with kisses – how happy I've been with you! From all sides today the most heart-rending memories came crowding back to me.

I left this morning at 9 on a big red coach. We drove without stopping to Morgat, which I reached at 11. The route was very pretty – I really like all those Breton churches and villages – and Morgat's on a wonderful stretch of coast. I went off for a long walk all round the peninsula, which is densely covered with heather and broom. There are big sheer cliffs over a blue-and-green sea – marvellous. The sun was dazzling and I felt really intensely that particular nature of Brittany: a white background of sky, stone and water, and the presence of the sea everywhere among the moors, giving them their meaning. The people at the end of the peninsula are at least as wild as the old women of Emborio.[113] Everywhere I was regarded as a spy, and people muttered in Breton as I passed. I walked, I was gripped by what I saw, and this mingled with the regret I was feeling for you – it was poetic and intense. From the tip of the peninsula, you were right opposite Camaret and could see the Tas-de-Pois where we went when it rained so hard. And what with the wind, and the sun on the sea, and the height of the cliffs, it was really exhilarating. And surrounded by all that I felt my heart softening. I took the coach again at 5. You had to change at Locronan, so I went for a meal of eggs and milk at our hotel. But it's no longer on the same premises, it's across the way, in a Renaissance house with a dining-room done up with greater pomp – and, it must be said, very successfully. But the old premises are still there, and I revisited the old

---

[112]More usually Poulpican, a demon in Breton legend.
[113]Village on the island of Santorini in the Cyclades, visited with Bost and Sartre in 1937 (see *The Prime of Life*, p.308) and used by Sartre as the model for Argos in *The Flies*.

dining-room where on one wet day we were all alone. Then I caught another coach, which brought me here. I took a room, then went down to the harbour. It was sunset, and at the same time there was moonlight: you'd have said a nocturnal landscape lit by some extraordinary artifice – I've never seen light like that. And how charming the little boats were, with their blue nets outspread! There were girls too on the jetty, laughing aloud, and nice young people strolling in groups who were laughing too. I hadn't heard anyone laugh in public, or sing, since the war started. It was one of the tenderest evenings of peace and happiness you could dream of. I strolled beside the sea till darkness fell completely, and cried like a baby. I love you, my beloved.

I came back here to write and am in the hotel café, where there's a collection of strange individuals. There's a bearded fellow with a contorted face who produces inarticulate sounds, and another bearded fellow in a pink shirt – they're playing piquet. It's only 8.30, but I'm going upstairs to read in bed. Tomorrow I'll go to the Pointe du Raz.

I received a charming letter from Kos. – but nothing from you either yesterday or today. I'd so like to find a way of seeing you. My beloved, I love you and I'd be so nice if you were there. You're my life, my happiness and my self. You're everything for me – and this evening, above all, a tender face that I can't think of without tears (in spite of the bearded fellows). I love you passionately.

Your charming Beaver

Write to me at 116 Rue d'Assas, c/o Mme Pardo.

[La Pouèze, Angers]

Thursday 28 September [1939]

My love, my dear love

I'm happy. I have three letters from you – you're talking to me – you're so close, it's as if you were clasping me in your little arms. And I'm so much at ease here, in this beautiful dining-room at La Pouèze that I've been given as a bedroom, with a big wood fire, the silence, and the garden still light outside the window. I'm so much at ease with That Lady, with whom for the first time I can talk about you – you, just as you are (she's the first person with whom I can do so, I mean). Mops has given me lots of photos, but I'm going to keep the ones of you until they've had copies made, then I'll send you them too – you'll find them amusing. I love the one of me where I'm seated. I've got one where you're standing and looking extremely agreeable; and another where you weren't posing and look wonderful, gazing at Zuorro with a quizzical look that I know so well – and that no photo has ever caught before.

My journey here was quite a little adventure. I took the train yesterday at 6, after writing to you. There was nothing else at the post office. (I have the letters of the 18th, 20th, 21st and 22nd. The one of the 19th must have been sent to Quimper, from where it'll be forwarded on to me here, so I'll certainly get that one too. If I understand right you have all of mine, so that's fine.) I had a corner seat and till nightfall went on reading Gramont's *Memoirs*,[114] which are rather entertaining. The compartment was full, but of people who weren't too disagreeable. There was moonlight over the countryside, and I listened to the people and looked at the flat landscape with a kind of infinite patience that war has given me, and that's truly a sort of state of grace. I was at ease. I was a bit ashamed – thinking about Bost and you – to think how I'd the best of it, by such a long chalk. I know I can't do anything about that. But if one had to choose – without the others knowing – one can't be sure how one would choose (if they knew, that would invalidate it because pleasure at their gratitude would out-trump everything else). Well, however that may be, I watched the towns flit by, and the broad Loire, and the meadows – from time to time I'd doze for quarter of an hour – and I felt as though I could have stayed like that for days. But eventually we arrived at Angers. I had only 20 F. in my pocket for a hotel and a public conveyance if That Lady didn't come, so I was a trifle worried. It was 2 in the morning and my suitcase was heavy. I walked towards the exit and there a soldier stopped me: 'Mademoiselle de Beauvoir?' 'That's me.' I was a trifle surprised, but not too much. He explained to me that Mlle de Staecklin[115] – Marie-Noelle – had phoned during the day, that she'd come and pick me up next day, and that he'd booked a hotel room for me and got some things for supper. He took my case. He had a bottle of beer in his pocket and was laden with sandwiches and bananas – it was marvellous. He took my arm, saying: 'I'm forty, old enough to be your father', then led me to a very fine hotel near the station. We placed the provisions on the table, and he asked: 'Can I stay?' with a funny expression – and he was looking at me in a

---

[114]The memoirs of Philibert, Comte de Gramont (1621-1707) were largely written by his brother-in-law Anthony Hamilton and published in 1717, and offer a portrait of life in the courts first of Louis XIV and later of Charles II of England.
[115]A friend of the Morels.

pretty funny way. I never quite understood what was in his mind. It struck me as comical, unreal and copied from a novel – that arrival, and that soldier in my room at 2 in the morning, and that collation. I remained standing in some embarrassment, so he said: 'Sit down – sit down on the bed,' but I took a chair and chatted in a worldly manner. He's a painter – a 1917 Rome Scholar[116] – who lived in that same handsome building in Rue Vavin where the Nizans live. I ate the fruit and told him to drink the beer. 'I'll have to drink out of the same glass as you, if you don't mind,' he told me with the same peculiar expression. I said I didn't – and carried on desperately about Brittany, my travels, etc. Finally at 3 he withdrew, saying he'd come back at 7.30 and have me brought up some breakfast. This morning, when That Lady went to thank him, he insisted on treating me to the breakfast and the collation, while That Lady to my great discomfiture was paying for the room.

As for me I went to bed, highly amused and full of impatience to see That Lady. I woke up pretty early and was all ready by the time I was brought my breakfast at 8. I went downstairs to write in the café below, and after that in a café on the main square where I'd arranged on the phone to meet That Lady. I wrote to Bienenfeld, to Kos., to Sorokine, and a short note to the Boxers: as you know, they tried to see me in Paris but I missed them, and they've now written from Provins saying they can't live without knowing where you are. I at once sent them your address and said I'd like to go and see them in Provins one Thursday or Sunday in October – I'd enjoy that. I enjoy seeing people, especially so that I can tell you about it. I really feel in such cases as though I were living instead of you, by proxy. I'd like you to feel that too, and for it to seem like *your* life that's continuing through me rather than just an account of my life addressed to a poor hermit.

Eventually, when it was almost noon and I'd just finished Gramont's *Memoirs*, I saw That Lady's car arrive. She was as spruce as could be and accompanied by Mops, resplendent in a white jacket, and Boudi.[117] They arranged to meet me an hour later at the station, since they were going to visit Aunt Suzanne. So I went for a walk round Angers, which I found very agreeable with the cathedral, the château, the little streets and the quays. Then they met up with me again and brought me here, in the company of M.-N. de Staecklin – who looks like her mother but with a goitre. The weather was fine, I was happy. For the moment, I like entering upon a new form of life and abandoning myself to it. I was

---

[116]Scholarships awarded by the state in France to young musicians, sculptors, painters, architects and engravers, allowing them to complete their training in Rome.
[117]Daughter of Jacqueline Morel (Mops), aged six.

now placing myself in That Lady's hands, and there was a novel experience to be lived – which was my life at La Pouèze – and this interested and charmed me. The countryside's ugly and the village too, but the house is a marvel. We had lunch at once, and the meal was a sensual delight after so many hours of fasting: delectable roast veal, duck, fried potatoes, salad, preserves, apples and pears and cider. Then they showed me round all the rooms, including the study of That Gentleman,[118] who'd laid some pseudo-philosophical books out ready for me on a velvet armchair. I even went to the attic and found three cupboards full of books, so that I now dream of spending two months here just reading and eating and sleeping – it was a real delight. I've already collected a dozen of the most alluring, but if I go on writing so much I'll never get through them. I went to the post office, where there were three letters from you, and three from Bost dated the 21st, 22nd and 23rd – which is not long ago. His letters are all thick and very cheerful and incredibly appealing. What sickens him is going on manoeuvres. My God, if only (as you claim) they spare human resources – and he weren't to be killed! Do write to him – I think you'll find his letters amusing.

As for your letters, my love, how sweet you are to make them so long, and to *answer* me and *speak* to me. How close to you I feel! I read the anecdotic parts to That Lady and Mops, who laughed till they cried.

I don't at all think that Bienenfeld will let you go. On the contrary, she told me how during the first days she used to sob at the post office while reading your letters, and how she'd hoped this war would put an end to your affair with Wanda. I just think that she's so easily influenced, her thinking gets ruined as soon as she's with idiots; and that she has to be kept on something of a short leash in order to be agreeable. That's what I felt last year at Annecy too. Like you, I'm cool towards her at present; but I know that will pass, since she's very estimable despite everything and often quite winning. As for the Kos. sisters, I think both of them have shown themselves at their best under these circumstances, and that perhaps they'll be definitively marked by them for the better. I'll be curious to see them installed in Paris. I didn't understand anything either about that tangled tale of the lie.

I too feel somehow affected by the fact that Pitoëff has died.[119] I

---

[118]M. Morel, a research physician much older than his wife, who had returned from the First World War an acute hypochondriac who kept to his room and saw almost nobody. De Beauvoir herself never set eyes on him.

[119]Georges Pitoeff (1886-1939), actor and theatrical producer, born in Tiflis but with his own company in Paris from 1919 on, specializing in modern classics in translation, e.g. Ibsen, Pirandello, Shaw, Chekhov.

forgot to tell you yesterday, in connection with Brittany, how odd it was encountering literally only children, old people, or those afflicted with goitre – it really is wholly denuded of men – and then an endless stream of aeroplanes in the sky and warships in slow procession over the sea.

At the Pointe du Raz, confronted by the starry sky, I wondered why it was that human consciousness constructed a world with durations and distances and masses that are not commensurate with man. Brunschwicg would speak of progress of consciousness,[120] and of how the Greeks used to think of the world as finite, etc. But what I mean is that it's odd the *hyle*[121] should itself lead to non-human constructions. Of course, you can't ask why the *hyle* is like that, but it's strange – or isn't it?

That Lady told me she might perhaps be able to do something for Sorokine, which would really set my mind at rest. We had tea and talked until 6, and since then I've brought my diary up to date and written to you. My diary's already full up, and it's really amusing to reread. Goodbye, my sweet little one, my love, my life – I love you, and you're with me. Thank you, my love, for writing to me like that, for not leaving me. I'm overwhelmed by *gratitude* for you, and by admiration – or if you prefer *astonishment*, in the strong sense of the word – and by tenderness. I've never loved you more strongly. When I do see you again, I feel as though it will quite take my breath away.

Your charming Beaver

Do you want *Taras Bulba*? And Gramont's *Memoirs*? I have them. Let me know about this – and how about James's *Portrait of a Lady*? Or Jouhandeau's *La Jeunesse de Théophile* and Queneau's *Les Enfants de Limon*? I've got all these from the Hungarian.

That Lady's going to write to you. Guille is a telephone operator at some Army Headquarters, very cushy. Isorni[122] is in a dreadful situation – with machine-guns. Zuorro in Constantine. Nothing's known about the Pupil.[123] Maheu's letter was a big success – they're going to type it out and distribute it.

---

[120]Léon Brunschwicg (1869-1944): dominant figure in French philosophy between the wars. The themes in question figure, for example, in his *Les Étapes de la Pensée Mathématique*.

[121]Phenomenological term used by Husserl for the given material constituting a consciousness, but here meaning consciousness itself.

[122]Mme Morel's son-in-law, husband to Mops.

[123]Albert, Mme Morel's son, whom Sartre had tutored in philosophy in 1930, and to whom *L'Imaginaire* is dedicated.

[La Pouèze, Angers]

Saturday 30 September [1939]

My love

Being here is blissful. I'm enjoying most heavenly life of reading and peace. They're keeping me till the schools reopen, and I hope that's going to be late – I'm going to call Paris in a moment.

On Thursday evening after I'd written to you we had dinner, and I said I wanted to go to bed early, seeing that my previous night had been so short. That Lady and Mops started fussing round me laughing like madwomen – bringing me dozens of dressing-gowns, preparing a night-time snack with cider, preserves and chocolate, and trying out twenty forms of lighting and twenty arrangements of the cushions. It was like the queen's going-to-bed ceremony, and I thought I'd never get between the sheets. But when I eventually did, I found myself in royal comfort indeed. There was a big wood fire, and I settled down to read Bessie Cutter, which I finished. After that I read a good Simenon, *La Marie du Port*, and then a good Pierre Véry as well, *Mademoiselle Bécut*,[124] so that I didn't eventually turn the light out till past 1 in the morning. Then I still didn't sleep, but thought about you and imagined you opening the door and coming to my bedside in your lovely little white garment – my love, it was incredible! When I really see your face again, I think I'll faint with joy. I love you, dear little being, I can't believe that we'll remain separated for long. In the end I did fall asleep, but was up again by 8. I wrote to Little Bost, whom I hadn't written to the day before. I ate a delicious breakfast, with apricot preserve. Then I read *Generals Die In Bed*,[125] which left me full of black thoughts – it's an excellent book, but I can't really *believe* that it's going to be like that again. Once it all really gets started and one has to believe it, how shall we be able to stand the idea? It's going to be appalling.

I spent the morning without seeing anybody at all, which was very agreeable. I went for a little walk, with a fine, cold sky overhead, but this countryside's off-putting. I climbed up to the attic, where I stripped an entire cupboard. It's unbelievable the things they've got – old books, new ones, history, travel, detective stories, novels. I brought down a huge armful and must confide to you that I'm going to steal a few of them on the sly. Do you want Defoe's *Colonel Jack*? Gide says that it's excellent. And how about *Last Chance Saloon* by Jack London, which I've also managed to tuck away in my suitcase? I started reading

---

[124]Pierre Véry (1900-60), author of numerous detective stories of which the best known was *Les Disparus de Saint-Agil* (1935).
[125]Work published in 1930 by the American author Charles Harrison.

Campagne by Raymonde Vincent,[126] which is not too bad, and eventually saw That Lady and Mops, and That Lady took me off to the cellar to make my own choice of wine. I chose a Chambolle Musigny which was a delight. Nothing much seems to have happened at Juan-les-Pins after we left. There were some long, confused explanations that satisfied Zuorro, and war brought universal brotherhood. Zuorro took ship for Constantine, very pleased to be sent there. That Lady and Mops hastened to Limoges, where they'd fixed to meet Isorni if mobilization occurred. Isorni and Zuorro were apparently half-dead with fear during those last days, which disgusted Mops. She writes to her husband – who's still at Fontainebleau – and she even goes to see him, but she still doesn't give the least damn about him. Apparently Guille was extremely nice, and the Bel Eute perfectly decent.[127] Guille was initially in a bad situation at Supplies, but then he became a switchboard operator at Headquarters, which was a real piece of luck.

We had lunch and That Gentleman sent a written note down to That Lady: it was the communique announcing the German-Russian Treaty. What now? It's now that the war's going to begin. I'm filled with dread this morning. I did some reading in the garden, in the sun. That dog who used to be so pitiful has now become a lusty bitch of monstrous size, who fawns on That Lady with bearlike graces. Boudi's very mousy – it's impossible to hear her, and she's devoid of charm. Mops is unbearable with her. At 4 we left for Angers, where That Lady was taking a Russian princess who's a refugee here and whom That Lady maintains: she's totally deaf, and you have to write everything down on paper for her. We went to pick up Aunt Suzanne at St Martin. I shook the whole lot of them off, so that I could go for a little walk and write to Bienenfeld in a café – where they came to collect me. We took Aunt Suzanne home, then came back here. I finished *Campagne*, had dinner and went to bed. In bed I read some more – *La Tradition de Minuit*, which is a good book.[128]

I've just been brought my breakfast, with a whole set of *Crapouillot*[129] on the horrors of war – a delicate mark of attention on the part of That Gentleman, who's overwhelming me with little favours of the kind. I'll read that, and also *War* by Ludwig Renn. When I achieve faith, I'll have

---

[126]Translated into English as *Born of Woman* (1939).
[127]Nickname for Guille's wife.
[128]By Pierre Mac Orlan (pseudonym of Pierre Dumarchais) (1883-1970), author of humorous tales and novels of exotic adventure.
[129]*Crapouillot* ('trench-mortar'): satirical illustrated review founded as a soldiers' broadsheet in 1915, but continued as an avant-garde literary journal after the War – regularly until 1930, occasionally thereafter.

a fine assortment of concrete representations to animate, so I think I'll be up to scratch.

Goodbye, my love. The apricot preserve awaits me. On Monday you'll have some photos of yourself and a little one of me too. I love you. I'm hoping for a letter this morning. I kiss you most passionately.

Your charming Beaver

My love, I have your letters of the 19th and 23rd – how I do love you! What you say about Bost doesn't reassure me at all. The other day I was making some far more accurate calculations with Raoul Lévy, who specializes in probabilities. In the *infantry*, 1 out of every 4 gets killed (on average) and as many again are seriously wounded. But the truth is, one has absolutely no idea how this war is going to be waged.

I've just phoned my headmistress in Paris. School reopens on the 9th. In principle, a certificate of appointment has to be signed on the 2nd – but she told me, in veiled terms, that it could be signed later. I'll stay here till next Friday; I'm enjoying myself so much.

I began reading the 'History of the War' from *Crapouillot*, and taking notes. The brainwashing is amazingly reminiscent of today's press, it's quite sinister.

Fragment

[La Pouèze, Angers]

[30 September or 1 October 1939]

I've had a long letter from Bost, who's still leading the same little life. Luckily he has Amsellem[130], they're inseparable. Two little letters from Bienenfeld, whose affairs seem to be being straightened out. I didn't leave any letters lying around, and I kept my lips sealed when I was with Kos. She merely knows that I often wrote and often received letters – but that was only normal. Besides, being what she is, she certainly hasn't stirred up any trouble with Wanda. She wrote to me just after she'd returned to Laigle: 'Wanda's less agitated, and is probably going to write a novel.' But you've doubtless had some letters in the meantime. At all events, Kos.'s stay in Paris can't have anything to do with Wanda's silence.

---

[130] A fellow soldier with whom Bost had struck up a close friendship.

My love, not see you until Christmas or March! It has struck me that you could easily convince Wanda that your leave lasts only for whatever time you intend to give her. As for Bienenfeld, perhaps it would be possible not to tell her you have any? I'd so like to have a long time of our life together, and see *with you* the people you choose to see. But I'll do exactly as you wish, of course. My sweet little one, it shatters me to think specifically 'I'll see you at Christmas', since then I *know* I shan't see you before that.

I love you – and kiss you passionately

Your charming Beaver

[La Pouèze, Angers]

Sunday [1 October 1939]

Most dear little being

There wasn't a letter from you today – which casts rather a shadow over me. I've very few things to tell you. I'm living in clover here, in a kind of bemused state that's sometimes blissful and sometimes melancholy. I read all day. Yesterday I read or leafed through a whole set of *Crapouillot* on the war, and also books by Rathenau, Kautsky and Pierrefeu[131] unearthed from the back of bookshelves – I find it all extremely interesting. I installed myself on the sofa in one corner of the dining-room, with a lamp lit; it was raining outside, but inside there was a big fire. I was comfortable, but so dizzy with reading that it eventually gave me a headache – it's a long time since that happened to me. In bed at night I go for a change of mood and read detective stories – though this hasn't prevented me from having dreams about poison gas. And also a dream about Dullin, with whom I was having the most tender relations under the stern, critical gaze of Toulouse. This morning I stayed reading in bed for quite a long time: some Pierre Véry, who isn't such a bad writer (of detective stories), and L. Renn's *War* – which is worthless. Then I wrote a few letters and we had lunch. Before each lunch, That Lady takes me to the cellar and I embarrassedly choose the most delicious wines: a Chambolle-Musigny the day before yesterday, and yesterday a fantastic Meursault – but this morning a Pouilly that

---

[131]Walther Rathenau (1867-1922), German statesman whose many works are mainly concerned with the outcome of the First World War and ideas for a new postwar social and economic order; Karl Kautsky (1854-1938), German social-democratic leader, also wrote prolifically on the war and its consequences; Jean de Pierrefeu, *Plutarch Lied*.

was too old and tasted vinegary. Yesterday I went for a little drive in the rain with That Lady, taking her letters to the post. I don't see a lot of her, but she's charming. When I feel like it, we talk about you. We'd like – I'd like – so desperately for you to be there, drinking that good wine and talking and smiling at me. I love you. I don't know why I've chosen a moment when I'm feeling down to write to you. I don't understand anything in the papers – I can't imagine what's going to happen.

I wrote to my sister to come to Paris at my expense on about 8 October, so I'll see her for a few days. Everybody tells me that I'll have your salary – I'll send for the Kosakiewitch sisters immediately.

Goodbye, my love. I'm going back to my books on war and peace and so on. I find it hard to bear the idea of living any longer without you. I miss you so much, I'll just waste away and die.

Your charming Beaver

[Angers]

Wednesday 4 October [1939]

My love

Two letters from you – how happy I am! I don't understand why I'm denied mail every other day here: I had nothing yesterday, and today I've had two letters from you and two from Bost. I don't know either why yours take such a long time: Bost's are dated the 28th and 29th, yours only the 25th and 26th. I was really gloomy when I got up: it's fantastic the extent to which these letters have become something alive and present for me, and how abandoned I felt without mail. Now I've recovered my zest for life. I'm pleased to have your salary – I think I'll send for the Kos. sisters right away on 15 October. You don't have any taxes to pay. That's to say, taxes are still payable in principle by those who've been called up, but no measures will be taken against them if they don't pay: that's tantamount to saying they don't have to pay. On the other hand, I have 3,000 F. to pay on my own account. But with all that money I'll easily be able to pay off my debts, pay the taxes, and keep alive.

I had a letter from my mother, who's beside herself with fury because she noticed I'd gone up to her flat with Kos. and now she's accusing me of having *burgled* it! She's grumbling because I haven't been to see them in Paris. They're settling down at La Grillère, and my father will try to find a bit of work in Limoges. I invited Poupette to come to Paris for a few days – it's the least I could do. This morning for the first time I really felt like being back in Paris and moving round a bit. I'll be there tomorrow during the afternoon, and I'll go at once to collect some dough and see my headmistress. I'm settling in at Gégé's, 116 Rue d'Assas. I don't know where to put the Kos. sisters. If they need two rooms – which I think they'll insist on – I'll certainly have to give them more than 2,000 F. per month. I'll let you know about all that. Yesterday they came and picked me up from that café in Angers from which I wrote to you. Aunt Suzanne was there, still just as venomous and angry that I should be staying such a long time at La Pouèze. We took her back to her old people's home, then returned home ourselves since it was raining dismally. I was in bed by 9, where I read some Jack London, a good adventure novel by Curwood called *The River's End*, and some bad stories by Stevenson.[132] This morning I started on the history of the peace. Nothing could be more depressing to read about – it's enough to break the heart even of your average swine.

Don't shave off your beard, I like to think of you having a fine frill of whiskers.[133]

I realize that I really am going to begin a year of life in Paris, that I'm going to live as usual – and that you won't be there. It wrings my heart. I miss you desperately. You haven't told me whether it's crazy to try and obtain a pass to go and see you? If it's possible, I'll come for 1 November. I'd so like to see you, if only for an hour – just to look at you and kiss you. I love you.

Your charming Beaver

I'm rereading your letters. One of your subtleties had escaped me, though I've now noted it down carefully.[134] You're a good little one, a little far-sighted one, and I love you.

---

[132]James O. Curwood, *The River's End* (1919); and Robert Louis Stevenson, a collection of stories including 'The Misadventures of John Nicholson'.

[133]Sartre had informed her in his letter of 25 September that he had grown a round beard like Stendhal's, with a shaven upper lip.

[134]Sartre had included a coded message in his letter, to inform her of his new quarters.

Le Dôme

Paris, Thursday [5 October 1939]

My love

I'm terribly happy, because I'm almost certain I'll be able to leave on Monday or Tuesday to visit my sister Emma.[135] I was afraid they wouldn't let me have a safe-conduct, but they were charming at the police-station and quite understood that with her bone disease the poor creature couldn't make the journey alone, so I'd have to go and fetch her. They duly recorded my request and told me the papers would be ready perhaps by Monday evening, and in any case on Tuesday. I don't think there's any possibility now of their going back on it. So I'll get there either on Tuesday morning or evening or on Wednesday morning, and hope to stay till Sunday night — seeing that the schools don't reopen till the 16th. You can imagine my delight. On the other hand, they're quite dreadful to the poor wives who want to go and visit their husbands at the front. They systematically refuse passes — even for Seine-et-Marne — and the soldier's liable for punishment (if his wife does manage to join him anyway).

I made my decision yesterday morning right away, on receipt of her last letter. Yesterday morning the calm of La Pouèze suddenly became burdensome to me, and after writing my mail I felt such a desire to leave that I opened my heart to That Lady — giving her the reasons — and she was in even more of a hurry than I was to see me on my way. We spent a feverish day, and at 7 that evening they dropped me at Angers. It was dismal weather and I felt the sorrow of being separated from you so painfully that it took my breath away. I went by bus to the outskirts of town, where The Buccaneer[136] was supposed to be showing, and arrived in a neighbourhood full of barracks, with tarts accosting soldiers in the darkness and tiny blue-windowed bistros crammed with troops. It was so intimidating that I wandered for a long while along the dark avenues without daring to go in anywhere, though eventually I did sit down — surrounded by soldiers — while waiting for the cinema to open. It didn't open. There were only daytime performances. I returned through the streets on foot, wrote a letter to Bienenfeld from the café of my hotel, then went to bed and slept very badly, tossing and turning. Apart from dark fear for others, I know nothing more disagreeable than a certain kind of hope. That's my present condition, and I don't know how I'll be able to stand it for several days. I caught a train at 7 in the morning

---

[135]Coded expression, designed to deceive the censors, employed by Sartre and De Beauvoir when organizing clandestine visits to the front.
[136]Directed by Cecil B. De Mille (1938).

and arrived at noon. It was a fine day, we passed through green countryside, and on the way I saw St Cyr again, my love, and that little station where I so often left you – how I did love you in that train![137] Little Bost writes me charming letters, but I can't really manage any longer to harbour tender feelings for him. My love for you has laid everything waste – a real tornado. I'm hard and unfeeling, with just a great blaze of passion for you. I called in at Rue Cels and Rue d'Assas, where I found shoals of letters. I'd been so farsighted regarding the instructions I left for my mail, that I didn't miss a thing and had everything as quickly as possible: letters from Sorokine, so wretched that I'm going to let That Lady take her in – she can't go on like that; a very nice little letter from Kosakiewitch; a letter from Bienenfeld, disappointed not to have seen me again in Paris, but very passionate and sweet; a letter from my sister, disappointed that I didn't go to the Limousin, and who hid my trip to Brittany from Lionel because he'd have been too hurt by it; some little letters of no interest from former pupils; two letters from Bost, one written when he was plastered; and three letters from you. My love, they're so tender, so close – like a true presence. They overwhelmed me with passion for you. We had so much happiness, passion never had any opportunity to be volcanic – but I always knew it could produce earthquakes in me.

At Rue d'Assas I found Gégé who has played a trick on me, since she's still living there with Pardo. Even like this I prefer it to the hotel, since I'll have a pretty, heated room. But I wonder if it won't get on my nerves. It does save me from living with Kos., and I prefer that – I'll put them in the hotel, in two rooms. Poupette's closing her studio, so I don't know how Wanda will manage.[138] If you have the opportunity, tell Wanda I was boiling with anger in my letters about this Gégé business, since I think Kos. is going to be affected by it.

I barely greeted Gégé, but rushed off to have my photo taken at the Bon Marché (I'm not sending you the photo – I'm too ugly in it), where I ate, as there's a kind of bar-cum-restaurant where you can gulp down a 'beef with lentils' while the photos are being developed. I had some trouble getting a residence certificate, since I'm a sub-tenant. The concierge struggled with her conscience for quarter of an hour, while a taxi waited for me. Her defeat and future services cost me 50 F. – she was quite overcome, as she'd reckoned on only half that.

---

[137]Sartre began his military service in 1929 with a training period at St Cyr.
[138]Wanda, too, had been painting in Poupette's studio.

After that I went to Camille Sée:[139] a vast, splendid barrack of a building. The headmistress received me (there'd been an exchange of letters and telephone calls, in which I'd played a pitiful role – especially as my father had got involved). She's an elegant woman, to the point where I took her for some chic secretary. She's *thin*, the first thin headmistress I've ever seen, well dressed, alert, with an intelligent gleam in her eye and a thoroughly jaunty, modern little look about her: 'I'm pretty jaunty', she said herself with a smile, explaining how she isn't afraid of bombs. We couldn't have been more polite, but we shan't get on for long. At any rate, she was afraid she couldn't give me more than 8½ hours work – whereas they could make me do 14 – and I'd have at most only 20 pupils. I don't think I'll have any reduction of salary – it's my maximum hours that have been raised by 2.

So everything's going very well. From this point of view, I'll have a marvellous year. I'll get down to my novel again,[140] and have dough, leisure and a good place to live. You should write to That Lady – she was quite incredibly kind. I was rather moved when I said goodbye to her, and she was too – and quite feverishly keen for my plans to succeed.

Goodbye, my love. I'm writing with the feeling of being a bit tipsy. I'm so excited my whole body's atremble – do rejoice on my behalf – provided it's not all in vain. I kiss you passionately

Your charming Beaver

I'll go tomorrow to collect our salaries. That Lady wants us to pay her back a thousand francs, so I'll do that. She *very much* likes your 'factum',[141] and is savouring it before locking it away in the safe. My love, how sweet you are to share my life with me like this, and to take a keen interest in it. You're everything in the world for me.

---

[139]Lycée Camille Sée, with which De Beauvoir's own Lycée Molière had been amalgamated for the duration of the war; she remained there as a teacher until her dismissal in 1943.

[140]*She Came to Stay*, begun in 1938, on which De Beauvoir was to work until the summer of 1941. See *The Prime of Life*, p.387 and thereafter.

[141]The first outline for *The Age of Reason*.

[Paris]

Friday 6 October [1939]

My love

After the letter I wrote yesterday, you can well imagine what a blow your little note of 3 October, which got here this morning, was for me.[142] I was filled with such gloom that I felt I'd never be able to start living again. But then it all blew over almost at once – you get so immune eventually. I had perhaps half an hour of real inner revolt, after your letter and one from Bost, who seems to be being moved gradually closer and closer to the front line and is now being instructed on how to behave under fire. At Quimper and La Pouèze, I'd rediscovered a foolish unconcern and reaccustomed myself to the idea of happiness. But this morning I was forced to a fresh realization that things were just the same as a month ago; that they'd be like that for a long while, without respite; and that my fears would only grow. Now the balance has been restored – in pain, dread and emptiness – and it's with astonishment that I contemplate the weeks of truce behind me. They're like a slumber, a happy slumber, but one from which I've emerged.

What's to be done? Do try as soon as possible to do everything you can for me, like the other time. Find a way. I'm not sure I won't try something notwithstanding – all I risk is losing a bit of money and a few days, and for what my time is worth . . . I'll be seeing the Audry sisters tomorrow, and I'll ask their advice – but if your help arrives in time I think I'll find a way. Otherwise I'll wait till 1 November. At least it's been clearly established that it can be done.

I'm settling in. I like my room at Gégé's – I've now fetched all my things and found a place for them. I got 3,550 F. for you and the same amount for myself – it's a fortune. Here's my budget: I'll send for the Kos. sisters on the 15th, and allocate them 1,500 F. for this month; 500 F. for you; 1,000 F. for That Lady. That leaves 4,000 F. I'll take 2,000 for my rent and living expenses at 50 F. per day (since the 1st – as there's a little arrangement with That Lady who advanced me some dough). I'll put aside 1,000 for M. Bienenfeld. Then I'll have 1,000 left over for myself – for books, clothing expenses, Poupette's journey to Paris and her stay here, the Kos. sisters' journey to Paris, etc. I'm hoping to scrape together another 500 F. out of this, which will be put aside too for M. Bienenfeld. With the money from the *N.R.F.*, if they send it, I could pay off everything by 1 November. After that, I'll save up for my 3,000 F. of taxes. If everything's settled by January, I'll try and

---

[142]Sartre informed her of his imminent transfer to an unknown destination.

round off the year by paying That Lady back, since she seems to wish it. How much do we owe her? I'll give her a bit in any case, even if we do have to tap her again in the event of some disaster – it's just as good as having money tucked away. That Lady was suggesting you make another approach to Maheu, moreoever – I think she'd quite like to have her money back.[143] The real problem's going to be housing the Kos. sisters. De Roulet's flat has been sold, and the furniture's being stored at Rue Sauteuil,[144] so Wanda won't be able to go there. She'll have to work at the academy. The Boubou will look after her a bit, he tells me.[145] I'm going to find them two little rooms in a hotel. I'll keep them from 15 October to 15 December, send them off for a fortnight, then fetch them back on 1 January – how does that strike you?

Yesterday after writing to you I went to visit the Gerassis. They were charming, and bursting with amusing and tragic stories about their circle. They're extraordinarily precious in wartime, because they're full of backstage gossip and you feel connected via them to the whole world. It seems Nizan did indeed hand in his resignation just two days before the roof fell in,[146] but in total good faith apparently, seeing as he'd been in a state of complete turmoil from the outset. Malraux's trying to enlist in a tank regiment, but all his struggles are unavailing – they won't take him because of his nervous twitches. G. managed to worm loose after four days, thanks to some powerful interventions.[147] He was incredibly interesting to listen to – I'm recording everything in my notebook. I've bought a new one, since the first is jam-packed. I bought them a drink, then went to the Dôme and wrote to Bost. It was splendid being in Paris – I'd forgotten what it was like, and when I found myself outside in the dark and saw the Great Bear shining over the Vavin intersection it gave me quite a jolt. It's darker than ever on the boulevard – it's tragic and moving. Oh! I was forgetting: before going to write at the Dôme, I had dinner at the Coupole. I asked unthinkingly for a half-litre of Munich beer, and the waiter couldn't stop laughing: 'Wait till we get across the Siegfried Line', he told me. I wrote to Bost. He showers me with little letters. I reread them all from beginning to end just now and felt like weeping from pity: every one of them is good-tempered and almost carefree, but the days succeed one another against a background of deepest gloom and at times he actually feels it like that. All my

---

[143]Presumably Maheu either owed money to Sartre, or could be tapped for a loan.
[144]Where Poupette had her studio.
[145]He was also a partner, of course.
[146]In other words, before the French government began its harsh crackdown on the Communist Party, using the pretext of the Nazi-Soviet Pact.
[147]Gerassi had spent several days under arrest (see *The Prime of Life*, p.395).

tenderness for him returned at once – but I'm much unhappier than before, because I'm dreadfully scared.

I went to bed, dropping with fatigue. I fell asleep at about 10, but heard Gégé coming in at midnight and called out to her and we chatted for a bit. She has got some work at Kientz's for 2,000 F. a month, and is just the same as ever. It didn't last long, but I couldn't get back to sleep for two hours. On such occasions I tackle practical, long-term problems. How shall we hide the fact you've got leave, or how long it's for, from the Kos. sisters? How shall I see Bost, if he has some leave? A solution appears both urgent and impossible, so I end up in a cold sweat. This morning at about 6.30 there was a siren that began wailing all on its own. It didn't have the right rhythm for an air-raid warning, but people were still all woken up and shouting at each other in the street. A bad night, all in all, and this afternoon I'm still feeling shattered.

I got up in a good mood – this was before your letter – and dressed up to the nines. I put on your smart little white jacket, which suits me splendidly with a green scarf, a green turban and a black belt. I found it quite moving to be dolled up like that. I rushed off by bus to your lycée, then – in view of the size of the sums I was collecting – paid myself a taxi to my own lycée, Camille Sée, where they still needed some signatures from me. I finished settling in, then spent an hour reading *Dead Souls*, which I've bought for Bost. I'll tell him to send it on to you once he has read it – it's enjoyable. For you, I bought *The Idiot*. The *N.R.F.* isn't out yet. I'll pick up Green's *Journal*.[148] I'll send *The Idiot* straight away and Green tomorrow, so that I can glance through it – there are also some envelopes in the parcel.

I had lunch in the little restaurant in Rue Vavin, then had coffee at the Dôme while reading *Dead Souls* and writing lots of little letters: my sister, Kos., Bienenfeld. Now I'm off to the post office to dispatch parcels and money – a 500 F. postal order for you. I'll read, write to Bost and make up my journal, then at about 8 I'm seeing the Gerassis.

I phoned your mother, but there was no answer. I'll have another go, and try to see her tomorrow. I don't have a minute to be bored. On Monday, if all our fine plans have gone up in smoke, I'm getting down to my novel again. I've had your Sunday letter and the little note of the 3rd: one spoiled the pleasure of the other for me. The little note had been opened by the censors – that's the first time. The mail gets here

---

[148]Julien Green (1900-), *Journal*, vol. 1, published in 1938.

quickly now, in three days. Do write to me – and do your best for me. I love you with passion and a great deal of anguish.

Your charming Beaver

Le Dôme
[Paris]

Saturday 7 October [1939]

My love

This morning I had a letter from you – so tender, my love! All you say about me not being a 'thing in your life' gives me such strength.[149] I really do feel it. We truly are just one person, you and I, and that's a fantastic power. And when I feel it as I do now, I can envisage absolutely anything. That was Monday's letter. This evening I had Wednesday's. You should know that the *N.R.F.* no longer sells single issues – you have to subscribe. I sent you a first parcel this morning, containing *The Idiot* and some envelopes. In spite of your wanderings, I'll probably send off the second too, with Green's *Journal*, some Waterman ink capsules, the latest 'Masque' and 'Empreinte',[150] and the 'Castor'. Perhaps it'll get through to you, and not much money will be wasted anyway – I hope you'll have it by Wednesday or Thursday. I'm in a great state of emotional depression (not intellectual, just emotional), caused I think by the ups and downs of hope and despair of these past few days. Unless the difficulties grow more definite and intractable, I'm going to try something. But I'll wait for your next letters and your advice before reaching a final decision.

Yesterday after writing to you I called back to the hotel, where I saw Gégé. She told me that with Pardo returning for good, they couldn't rent me the flat. She returned me the money I'd already given her, and I at once began hunting for a hotel. I've found two very nice ones – next door to one another – in Rue Vavin next to Les Vikings. One at 250 F. incl., with well-furnished, comfortable rooms but on the small side. The other at 300 incl., the rooms a bit shabbier, but large and to my taste

---

[149]On 2 October, Sartre had written: 'If there'd been any need to feel how united we are, this phoney war would at least have had the advantage of making that felt. But it wasn't necessary. All the same, it does provide an answer to that question which used to torment us so: my love, you're not "a thing in my life" – even the most important – since my life no longer belongs to me, I don't even have any regrets for it, while you are still *me*. You're far more: it's you who allow me to envisage any future and any life.'
[150]Series of popular detective stories.

more attractive. That's the one I'm choosing for myself. The Kos. sisters
will see, but in the large rooms Wanda could paint – others have
apparently done so. I spent a long time on this hunt, then went on to
write some letters at the Dôme and read Green's *Journal:* it's wretched.
Nothing of what he records is worthy of interest, and he can't tell a
story – you feel you're confronted by an *appearance*, just like with G.
Lumière.[151] After that I went up to the Gerassis' place, where I had *poule
au pot* and played dominoes with some enthusiasm. But there's a
running battle going on. The day before yesterday, it seems Stépha made
the mistake of staying with me for an hour, whereas she'd said she was
coming back in five minutes. In itself that's not so serious, but what is
serious is the fact that by doing so she *destroyed his good mood* – that
good mood which it takes vitality and heroism to achieve. The Boubou
explained all this solemnly. Don't you think that's a really splendid new
right – the right to a good mood?

I'm being turned out. I'll send this off at once and go on writing to
you at home – but the manager's not joking. They're putting the lights
out – farewell – I love you.

S. de B.

Le Dôme
[Paris]

Saturday 7 October [1939]

My love

I'm continuing the letter I had to break off. I stayed right to the last,
at the very back of the Dôme in the chess players' corner, and when I
left it made a strange impression on me to see the café behind its blue
windows, already quite empty, with three waiters doing their accounts
at the till. Outside there were crowds of people in little groups,
hesitating to disperse – it was agreeable. I came home through streets
as dark as the darkest tunnel and am writing to you from this little flat
which won't have been mine for long. You know, it gave me a real jolt
yesterday when I decided to live in Rue Vavin. It's much better, of

---

[151]Ginette Lumière was a colleague of De Beauvoir at Rouen, whom she saw as putting
up an *apparence* or facade that had little to do with her real self. (See *The Prime of Life*,
p.128.) This notion of 'appearance' was fundamental for De Beauvoir, who applied it to
'all those who mime convictions and feelings for which they do not have the inner
resources'.

course, since I have to catch my Metro at Montparnasse, and then Kos. hates the Hôtel Mistral and I want to stay near her. But I felt as though I were separating from you, and definitively abandoning our life. So your letter this morning made me doubly happy, by assuring me that nothing would ever separate us. We'll both go back to the Hôtel Mistral, my love, won't we? We'll live together again? Promiscuously? Little being, dear little creature, I love you so much – I can't stop crying today.

[. . .]

I called in at the Hôtel Mistral to clear my room. The new landlady's a shrew – I'm glad to have got the hell out. After that I went to the hairdresser's, and was inspired by that to buy a few beauty products, then went home and gave myself splendid 'heather' coloured nails and a nicely painted face. With your little white coat, I was extremely beautiful – and the Audry sisters paid me lavish compliments. I'd arranged to meet them at 3, you see, at the Marignan. I ate lunch and read the Agatha Christie I'm sending you, which is entertaining. Then I met up with them outside the door of the Marignan, which has been temporarily closed down by military decree for staying open after 11 – so we went to the Pam Pam. Audry's sister has grown still younger – she looked ravishing – and things are going well for her too: at the moment her husband's pulling in 20,000 F. as easy as pie. So she says with a grave expression: 'A person mustn't think of their individual misfortunes, when there's such an immense general misfortune' – but she makes no bones about smiling and discussing good restaurants. She's charming, though, always full of obscene stories which she tells most gracefully. Those Champs-Élysées – it's fantastic how much they resemble a 'home front', in the most conventional sense: a 1916 home front as brought back to life by *Crapouillot*, crammed with beautiful tarts, elegant officers and obvious shirkers – and with particular stress on the word 'shirker', though I'd never encountered anything of that kind. It was pretty sickening. I got rid of them at about 5. I was dying to see a film, so I went to the Ursulines. I felt quite moved at the sight of that cinema hall – it's something which goes back to the Llama, one of the spots in Paris that represent a continuity in my life of the kind provided for others by a country cottage. There were lots of people, quite smart and also quite noisy: noisy because they were aware of the war, and because it destroys barriers and discretion. They were showing *St Louis Blues*,[152] which is often boring but has some fine passages. When I saw a night club with a band in it, I began weeping buckets. I

---

[152]Directed by Raoul Walsh (1939).

was weeping for Little Bost, utterly convinced that I should never repeat those evenings I had with him at the Nox or the Cabane Cubaine. Even if he doesn't peg it, what will he be like after a war? How will things be between us? It's not at all the same thing as the Llama, and my affair with him. It's just something that was very agreeable and precious, but that can't be revived. Above all, I think with horror but virtual certainty that he won't be coming back – and find the thought detestable. I continued to sob through *Cavalcade*,[153] which lends itself very well to that. It's terribly unappealing, but a careful piece of work and not boring. It was full of war stories, but I wasn't captured by it for a moment – I wasn't crying over the story or its heroes, but over myself. When I emerged from it, however, I was captured by the darkness. Paris is fantastically beautiful during all this period – not gloomy, but deeply and purely tragic – and especially this evening, when there was a first winter fog. I once more became the impersonal consciousness of a great cataclysm – and that stopped my tears. I went home to see if there was a letter from you, and there was one, Wednesday's, which first made me leap for joy then cast me down again – alas! my love – I'm anxiously awaiting the ones to follow. I had another good cry, then made my face up again as best I could and went to eat pancakes and chips at the Crêperie Bretonne, while finishing off the Agatha Christie. That made me late. They were vaguely expecting me at the Boubou's place for a game of poker, but I didn't go. Instead I went and wrote a letter to Bost, and was thinking I still had plenty of time to write a long one to you when they turned me out.

I'm not bored, as you see. On the contrary, I barely have time to read all I'd like to. And I'll get down to my novel again before long. I'm not gloomy either. When I see all those deadbeats, and all those weak, amiable little individuals like Bienenfeld, Kos. etc., I find it agreeable to think how sturdy we are, you and I. I feel that, so far, it's been a success for our principles and way of living. My love, it's not just our relations that you've accomplished – it truly is your *life*, your principles, and my own life too as an indirect consequence. My love, it wrings my heart when you say you're no longer affected by your little books. They're so alive for me, and so mingled with your little person. You're a lovely little accomplishment of Heaven – I love you.

How I'd like to see you, if only for a moment!

Your charming Beaver

---

[153]Directed by Frank Lloyd (1933).

[Paris]

Sunday 8 October [1939]

Most dear little being

No letter from you today. Give or take a day, that doesn't surprise me. But how is it you don't get all of mine? That does surprise – and annoy – me. It must be that little post office near La Pouèze which was the problem. I don't have a great deal to tell you. I'm awaiting your next letters – and the advice you'll give me – with fantastic impatience. I need them in order to make up my mind, and the uncertainty annoys me.[154] I'll be calmer when I've actually abandoned the whole idea. I've once again had the following thought (or rather made the following observation): that belief and desire are really one and the same thing. When I had a hope – in the train bringing me from La Pouèze to Paris, for example – I was consumed with impatience and tender images, and my desire was so violent I lived only for that. And this morning I caught myself thinking, or almost thinking: 'I don't really care, after all' – and feeling slack, and in no great hurry to make a move, and uninterested even in the possibility of success – and that indifference was precisely the certainty of failure which engulfs me. Truly, my heart no longer beats when I tell myself: 'It's possible' – and this calm is precisely a deep conviction that it's impossible.

Yesterday after writing to you I hurried off to bed, dropping with sleep. However, I did begin Le Singe d'Argile,[155] and can't have got to sleep before 1 in the morning. For a change the light woke me fully by 8, but I stayed voluptuously in bed, finished Le Singe d'Argile – which is feeble, with a stale old trick – and read more of Green's Journal. In the end it's quite entertaining the extent to which the fellow's just an appearance. That doesn't exclude sincerity, but there's sincerity even in appearance (I'm thinking of that sense of the fantastic – the beyond – which you have to believe in, since he never stops talking about it), and quite apart from that he's so diligent he reminds one of Ginette Lumière.[156] He's the kind of person you'd like to tell – when he's talking about painting or landscape, or recording little human facts – 'Oh, how diligent you are!' I read, then got up. The concierge brought me a little letter from Bost, who tells me he jumped for joy when he received your letter and broke his pipe while reading it. He's going off soon – but where? Write to him again. I think of him as a rather carefree condemned man, and feel he should be given as many pleasures as

[154]The issue was, of course, the projected clandestine visit to Sartre at the front.
[155]Le Singe d'Argile (The Clay Monkey), a detective story.
[156]See note 151 above.

possible before he pegs it. Perhaps it annoys you that I often ask you to write to him. But it's like a kind of remorse I feel towards him, when I think how you and I will meet again and so be happy, while he'll die in some hole. I know perfectly well there was nothing we could do about it. But all the same, we belong to the generation that let it all happen. Our stance does seem entirely correct to me – I mean, refusing to move in politics, but on condition we also accept everything without complaint as a cataclysm in which we have taken no part – it's correct and satisfactory when one's thinking of oneself, but for young people who haven't had time to lift a finger it's terribly unjust. We couldn't have done anything – I don't feel any remorse for not having done anything – but I do feel remorse when I think it's someone else who'll pay for our impotence. There's a regular pattern now: in the morning the day begins calmly, then by the evening I'm sunk in melancholy or pathos – but always on the edge of tears or beyond. I ought to write in the morning, but it's in the evening that I feel most like writing.

I had a coffee at the Closerie des Lilas, while finishing Green's *Journal*. Then I went and sent you a parcel, and after that ate a steak at the Milk Bar and had coffee at the Dôme while writing to Bienenfeld, Sorokine and That Lady. I also wrote at length in my diary. During all this I saw the Boubou and the Baba (separately), and Stépha grumbled about how the Boubou thinks of himself at present like a precious vase, fragile and cracked.

At about 3 I wanted to go to the cinema, in Rue Boulard just near Denfert Rochereau, where they were showing *Angels with Dirty Faces*.[157] But that performance was full up, so I went off to wait for two hours – reading Defoe's *Colonel Jack* and the end of *Dead Souls* – in that Café Oriental where you once helped to sort things out for Bost and me. Then, at about 5, I went back to the cinema: there was a huge queue – or rather three queues side by side – just very young kids, mostly. We waited for ten minutes, then the first house came out and there was a fantastic rush, people all had tickets booked in advance, and they jostled the usherettes, half demolished the doors, and half killed the boss – who was trying to stem the tide. It was a vast, densely packed cinema that was soon full up. The film was very agreeable, despite the subject, because James Cagney is so marvellously attractive. I've decided to see him everywhere, on every occasion, whatever the subject may be. Actually, the subject wasn't so stupid until the end, and then rather in the same way that Defoe's books are moral – they're all charming villainy, and then some ballast is thrown in right at the end

---

[157]Directed by Michael Curtiz (1938).

without it convincing anyone. The fights were good too.

Since coming out, I've just been for dinner and then sat down at the Dôme to write to you. Perhaps I'll go and play dominoes with the Gerassis, but what I really want is to go and sleep.

I had the following thought this morning – and reflected how it was just what needed to be got across in my novel. It's the fact that when you love someone trustingly – as I love you, or Bienenfeld loves you, or Poupette loves De Roulet (always supposing she's sincere) – you take each tender act, each word, not as *true* but rather as a signifying object: a given bit of reality with respect to which the question of truth isn't posed. By contrast, however, the tender acts or words of the said beloved person with a third party (let's say with Wanda) appear like constructed objects – they're 'bracketed off'. The difference is not that you think in one case: 'He's telling me the truth' and in the other: 'He's lying to her'. You may very well concede that he isn't lying to the other person, but truth itself is disarmed here, appearing almost a matter of luck – since it could be false. Whereas in your own case you don't even have that reflective idea of *truth* – the bracketing doesn't occur. This explains how far illusion can go: like Poupette for that woman from Oran, or Bienenfeld for Wanda. Ceasing to be as one, moreover, means effecting that bracketing off for yourself too. Even if you always conclude that it's true, this reflective faith is not the same thing as an obvious fact. I've often explained to you how, from a horror of resembling Poupette or Bienenfeld, I've sometimes done that bracketing – which is basically what corresponds to the situation of 'being a thing in your life'. I've always thought that you truly loved me, of course, but at such moments there was *your* love and *me* to whom it was addressed. When I say we're as one, however, it means we're beneath reflection: our love is realized through our every action and every word. But, you know, I think that after these last weeks and the letters you've written me, no good sense could any longer induce me to effect the conversion that extrapolating involves. My love, we're as one. I feel that I'm you, moreover, as much as you're myself. I love you, my sweet little one, and never have I felt your love more intensely.

I don't know what I'd give to tell you how I love you, and above all how happy I am that you should love me so well. O dear little clipped face, how I long to see you again!

Your charming Beaver

Le Dôme

Paris, Monday 9 October [1939]

Dear little being

I'm too tense to write you a long letter. I was so hoping to receive a letter from you with some advice – but nothing yesterday and nothing today. Nothing from Bost either today – is the post back to not working again? Yet we have all the documents ready, or pretty much so, only we can't do without your instructions – but a swift decision has to be taken. I went to bed very early yesterday after writing to you, and in bed I read a bit of Queneau's *Les Enfants du Limon*, which I'm enjoying.[158] I find that fellow has talent, and a certain grace in the way he plays with words – I'll send you the book. [. . .] I had coffee at the Dôme – alone this time – while reading *Édouard VII* by Maurois, which interests me slightly because it fills in my knowledge of those prewar years. Then I jumped on a bus to Rue Amélie, but the magazine *Europe* has stopped coming out.[159] Then I went back to Rue d'Assas, where Gégé was drawing away. I chatted with her for a while, then rang your mother – very friendly – and we arranged to meet tomorrow. There was a note from Sorokine, who's now back in Paris, warning me of a possible visit. So I waited for her – but was waiting above all for the post, which brought me only a letter from Bienenfeld. Sorokine came shortly after that, we talked, then I took her out and we had a drink in a little café at the Odéon, from which we walked to the Duroc Métro station. On the way she took my arm in a pleasing gesture, and then gave me a look and wriggled in embarrassment – I wasn't quite sure what to say to her. I feel a bit like some clumsy seducer confronted with a young virgin, as mysterious as all virgins are. Only the seducer at least has a clear mission, which is to seduce and, as it were, pierce the mystery. Whereas, in my own case, I'm simultaneously the prey. It's a dreadfully awkward situation, and one exclusively confined to *pièges*.

I left her, had a bite to eat and am now off to try and see the Gerassis or somebody. I can't stay in one place, I'm just waiting for tomorrow morning's mail.

Goodbye, my love. Perhaps tomorrow evening I'll be leaving Paris, but it's far from certain. In any case, write to me from now on at the Hôtel du Danemark, Rue Vavin. I'll write more properly tomorrow – I love you

Your charming Beaver

---

[158]Raymond Queneau was to become a friend in 1943 (see *The Prime of Life*, p.560).
[159]*Europe* was a left-wing journal in which Sartre published some short items of literary comment in 1938.

Le Dôme
[Paris]

Tuesday evening [10 October 1939]

My love

I've had three letters from you today: a little note from the 5th, informing me of a first transfer; a charming letter of the 6th, in which you describe how you're all alone in a village emptied of soldiers – I could really feel how it must have looked; and lastly the letter of the 7th, in which you inform me of a further transfer to an evacuated village. So it's over, there's no more hope. I've felt terribly agitated all day long – as I have, in fact, all these last days – but now all of a sudden I'm regaining a kind of peace, my will's uncoupled and my resignation total. My love, my love, how hard it is to be far away from you! I love you so passionately, I'm in floods of tears – but tears of love more than sorrow. You wrote to me so tenderly, my sweet little one, my dear little one, my love! It's the first time this evening that I fully realize I'm going to be living without you. That it's going to be a long, long time before I see you – I'd thought that impossible. Without you – I can't bear the idea. Yourself, my other self, o dear little being, I love you quite desperately.

I thought I was calm when I began this letter, but now I see I'm not. I'll try all the same to tell you about my life. Yesterday I went and played dominoes with the Gerassis, and we played for two hours – it was enjoyable. I went back to sleep for the last time in Gégé's blue bedroom, since Pardo had come back to Paris that very evening. This morning I began shifting my stuff to the Hôtel du Danemark, 21 Rue Vavin. Then I had a bite to eat at the Milk Bar, and after that went to see Sorokine. I found her at home – her parents no longer hate me, God knows why. She was charming, but is utterly desperate because she can't register at the Sorbonne if she doesn't have an identity card, or obtain an identity card for less than 500 F. if she's not registered at the Sorbonne. I'm going to try and get Colette Audry to do something again. I stayed with her from 12.30 till 3.30, then went to meet your mother in a cake-shop near the Gare Saint-Lazare. She was charming – really a nice woman – and told me a few little confidences about her life. Just imagine, I was so on edge today that when I was leaving her and she wished me good luck in going to see you, I shed a few tears – I'm quite overcome by it. I told her you'd be getting your salary – I think that was right? She became very anxious about what clothes you'd wear to go on leave – alas, poor woman! Just come, you'll always be handsome enough. I called in at Rue d'Assas again, to pick up my mail and a few more bundles, which I've just taken up to my room. That's when I had your letter killing all my hopes. I've put away all my things and fixed up my room – I like it enormously, far more than the one at Hôtel Mistral. It's the same kind of room, but more spacious and agreeable. There's an immense bed in an alcove, a vast table with shelves for books over it, a handsome and very roomy mirror-wardrobe, heavy curtains in worn red velvet, a sordid screen to hide the basin, and on the floor an appalling, grimy rug. My chair's padded and upholstered in grimy red, and there's another plush-covered one. What's pleasant is the fact that as the curtains are thick, my light-bulb can be left bare – so I'm revelling in decent light. And there's a bulb over my bed. I've really never been so well fixed up. It costs 310 F. a month incl. and is fantastically well-situated. If Wanda needs it to paint, I'll give it up to her – seeing as it's the larger – but I'll be pleased if she makes do with the next-door room, which isn't bad either. Tomorrow right away I'm going to get down to my novel. Now that I'm fixed up, I'm even making a few vague plans regarding clothes: I'm going to devote 30 F. to a coat in November. I still have piles of books on my shelves. And I like the idea of starting to write again. It's all this that momentarily filled my mind and gave me a sense of calm. But then, once I started writing to you, I felt desperate. Now I'm growing calm again.

Sorokine has given me a tiny photograph album in which I've put all your photos. I've just looked at them. How I love your face, how moving and strong it is! How I did love your smile! Goodbye. Now I'm waiting only for your letters. My love, you write so well to me, it's just like a sustained conversation – that's such a help. On the days when there are no letters, I'm a soul in torment.

I received a charming note from the Boxers, whom I'll go and see this very Thursday or Friday perhaps.

My sweet little one, I kiss you passionately. I wish you could clasp me in your two little arms. Saturday's precisely our anniversary: 14 October.[160] You've made such a beautiful life for me, my love, I owe you everything I have, everything I am.

Oh! this evening I can't bear not having you any more.

Your charming Beaver

Another little note from the Dôme. I had such a funny feeling just now. As I wrote to you, and again afterwards, I wept buckets. Then I washed my face, in order to go and have dinner and spend some time at the Dôme. But as I was repairing my makeup I saw a powerful picture of

---

[160]The tenth anniversary of their 'morganatic marriage' (see *The Prime of Life*, pp.19-28).

myself, which struck me as necessary. I could see the minutes I was about to live swollen by those tears I'd just shed – and it gave the most extraordinary sense of a woman in wartime. And then, with a kind of bewilderment, I thought: 'It's me, that woman! Me it's happening to.' I looked at that from the depths of Space and Time, and for a moment something in me really escaped historicity. I did actually go and have dinner in Rue Vavin, then come to the Dôme to write a little letter to Bost – but my heart wasn't in it. No letter from him for the past two days – I feel quite strange. I feel as though I were some other person, in a kingdom of shadows, and can't believe I'll ever return to being a creature of flesh and blood. It's funny, when I think about Bost I think also that if I meet up with him again, it'll be a shadow – a meeting of shadows. But if I think about seeing *you* again, then life fills me anew – there'll be earth and light again, and you'll never be a shadow. O you little absolute, my strength, my only life! I'll never pay too dearly – be it even by your death, which my own would closely follow – for this marvellous luck of being in the same world as you. My dear love.

Hôtel du Danemark
21 Rue Vavin
[Paris]

Wednesday 11 October [1939]

My love

This superb writing paper belongs to a nice young man who has squeezed in beside me at the Milk Bar – where I'm having dinner – and who's casting sidelong glances at me. He's with a pal who's about to leave, and in another five minutes he's undoubtedly going to strike up a conversation with me. Actually, I'll probably ask him for a second sheet. I'm in an excellent mood, unlike yesterday evening – it's finally resignation that has carried the day. Yet I haven't had a letter from you today. I just got out of bed on the right side.

[. . .]

I got up this morning full of enthusiasm. I went for a coffee at the counter in the Dôme, which I'll do every morning – I find it delightful. Then I called in to pick up my mail at Gégé's. There was just a letter from Bost, who's still exulting about having had one from you. Let me remind you to be sure and send him the detective stories after you've read them, and any books that might interest him. I wrote to Bienenfeld, made up my journal, wrote to Bost, then as it was midday had lunch – my restaurant's at my door, it's incredibly convenient. At 12.30 I was back in my room with some cigarettes, settling down to reread my novel. I was full of apprehension, scared I'd no longer find it interesting or it would make me wretched. In fact, I read 100 pages of it – that's half – and was really encouraged. I find it entertaining and interesting. I could spot the defects all right, but they're all easy to put right and I'm really pleased with it, that's why I'm in such a good mood this evening. After that Sorokine turned up and, as in the month of July, pulled me first onto the bed, then – amid sobs – into her arms and towards her mouth; finally, after about an hour, she even drew my hand to specific parts of her body. After this she was nervous and mistrustful, rummaging in my bag and wanting to take my diary. She's the very image of 'unripe fruit' – with moments of agreeable, floating tenderness, but at other times the convulsive movements of an adolescent girl at the awkward age. She told me lots of sweet nothings in Russian, and once in French: 'I love you so! – I love you so much, so much!' There's nothing to be done: here I am, caught up in an affair – and as she has a dreadfully demanding and authoritarian look about her, that's quite a nuisance. She loves me at least as intensely as Bienenfeld has ever loved me. As for me, of course, I was like a log – I'll be an asexual being by the war's end.

I called in at Gégé's – where there were only letters of no interest from my mother and my sister – then came here to eat. Now I'm off to say hello to the Gerassis for a quarter of an hour, after which I'll go home and work. I have an immense desire to work.

I called on the Gerassis. Alfred[161] was there with his wife, a melting blonde. I stayed for only a moment, then came home to finish reading my novel. I find it good from the point of view of atmosphere, dialogue, and episodes taken singly – and the last chapter, the big scene during the hundredth performance, I find entirely satisfying. But the subject is still evaded. Pierre's a failure, even Xavière doesn't really come off, their relations (Pierre-Xavière) are not filled in properly, and the central subject – Françoise's problem with consciousness, life, etc. – isn't posed clearly, or at any rate dramatically. There's lots to redo. But I'm pleased all the same, because it presents a really teeming world, I don't find the style bad, and there's a satisfying tone to it. Also it seems quite well

---

[161]Fernando's brother.

constructed, with lots of cross-references. When you come back on leave, it's too bad but we'll have to devote a few hours to reading it, since I'll need your advice so much. For the moment, I'll be continuing with enthusiasm. The subject strikes me as a topical one, since it basically involves the question of individual happiness coming up against catastrophe – of whatever kind. Tomorrow I'll tackle the chapter about the illness, which is already well begun.

Goodbye, my love. Now that I'll be working, my life will regain a meaning. I'll go down and post this letter, though it's raining so hard, then I'll go to bed and sleep. I love you, my sweet little one. We're as one person – I love you passionately

Your charming Beaver

I left with a smile to the nice young man, whose pal refused to leave so he couldn't engage me in conversation.

[Paris]

Friday 13 October [1939]

My love

You had a very dry little letter yesterday. That's because at half past midnight I still hadn't been able to finish it off, and I was in the street before going back home and preferred to send off what I'd done rather than nothing. The late hour was due to the appearance in my life of the Lunar Woman, whom I didn't leave from 6 till midnight and found very entertaining. But I'll tell you everything in order.

After writing to you I had lunch, then worked for a bit. Then at 2.30 Sorokine turned up, looking sulky and even wrathful. This was because, the day before, she'd pinched my little black notebook from my bag without my noticing – but then at the bottom of the stairs chickened out and given it back to me – so to scare her I'd put on a fearsome look and said: 'You did the right thing, otherwise I'd never have seen you again.' She'd brooded over this furiously all evening, and yesterday she sat down on the bed and burst out into reproaches, followed by tears – whence coaxings, kisses, passionate embraces. She has lovely tragic and despairing expressions that wring my heart. I tried to explain how I really cared for her, but she told me in despair: 'It's so unequal, though – I have the fifth place in your life!' And with sure instinct she told me she could overlook you, Bost (about whom I've told her almost nothing), and Kosakiewitch, but she hated my red-haired girl friend.[162] I was as tender as I could be – though without making any promises – and eventually she recovered her composure and began to look almost happy. Above all, she seemed relaxed and trusting, without the somewhat jarring hostility of those other times. She's charming when she's like that – her face all transfigured, and childish, and pathetic, and so on and so forth. If Bienenfeld didn't exist, I'd assuredly give her that place. Well, I'll be seeing something of her this year and we'll see, but I am slightly worried.

I left her – I'm to go to her place tomorrow evening – and called in at Gégé's, where I found a huge letter from Bienenfeld (very nice but a bit boring) and the Lunar Woman, fresh and agreeable and all dolled up, who'd come to see me. I took her for a drink at the Dôme, and then – since I found her amusing – to the Crêperie Bretonne where we stuffed ourselves with pancakes and flan, and after that – since I still found her amusing – to the downstairs bar at the Schubert. This is a little Viennese restaurant on Bd Montparnasse, which has opened a basement club with piano, lights in the corners, American Bar, and drinks that are ridiculously expensive for a place of the kind – it's 18 F. a cocktail, just like in a big place with a dance floor. Nobody dances there, though, and it's empty and sad – but it's not unpleasing and makes a change of scene. We chatted some more, but then at 11 we were turned out and I kept the Lunar Woman company to Bd St Michel, where she's living now. Then, as it was a really mild, starry night, we strolled on to Châtelet and along the banks of the Seine, after which I accompanied her back and went home myself. The streets are beautiful and sinister after 11 – almost deserted, save for constant police patrols, on foot or bicycle, with big capes and gleaming helmets. They carry electric torches, which they aim at the passers-by, and stop all the men and ask them for their papers. They even inspect the urinals to see nobody has taken cover there. But they don't ask women anything.

The Lunar Woman was full of stories – and I of patience, since it takes ages to extract the substance of these stories from the jumble of details under which she buries them. She talked almost without drawing breath. She's quite overcome by a grand passion for some Spaniard she met this month in the Pyrenees, when she was there at her mother-in-law's after her husband's departure. The fellow's a young labourer of 20, divinely handsome, who lives in the mountains half-naked and on the run. He does odd jobs, thanks to [. . .],[163] but is hated by the people

---

[162]Bianca Bienenfeld.
[163]Illegible word.

of the village (who've knocked off quite a number of Spanish refugees unwilling to enlist, with their bare hands or with pitchforks). The Lunar Woman, of course, has taken up the defence of all the refugees in the area. She's thrown herself into activity, made speeches, argued, protested, and acquired a bad reputation everywhere. Since her current dream is to 'return to the land' and live as a peasant, she has lost her head over this handsome Spaniard all the more rapidly and, indeed, had a highly romantic affair with him. He barely knows French, so I can just imagine the conversations between that Lunar Woman and that man of the wilds. She used to meet him only in secret, with the aid of countless ruses, miles from anywhere. Once she lost her way in the darkness and did 5 km barefoot through thorns, since her sandals had fallen off. She fell, she tumbled into ravines, and she came back cut to shreds. Her one dream now is to obtain papers for him and go off to live there in some village, watching a wood fire blaze all day long and sleeping with him at night.

All this was mixed up, of course, with the most utterly insipid stories about Quakers, pear trees, and peasant feuds. She also told me about her stay with the Lunar Man at the Pointe du Raz. They stayed with some fishermen, with whom they used to get drunk every evening, and whom they'd undertaken to improve. They wanted to teach them to look after their boats better, to navigate more cautiously, to drink less, and not send their children to Church schools – can't you just picture them? Actually, she gave me a good description of the lives of all those people. After that they sailed off from Nantes to Bastia, arriving with just 50 F. in their pockets, and were received by Blondie's parents – with whom things didn't go at all well.[164] She complains about your not ridding her of Blondie: if you'd only seen her twice weekly to urge her to leave him, she'd doubtless have left him by now. She talked to me about him too. Above all, she delighted me with her general attitude – on public squares, or in trains – since the declaration of war. She gets herself told off in no uncertain terms, and will end up in gaol. There were also, of course, bawdy stories about sexual goings-on, and a lovely story that happened to Leduc – that fellow from the Age Nouveau, who got the bird that day when Kos. was acting in 7 at a Time – a story about his being arrested as the result of a mix-up, which really delighted me because of the fellow's ugly mug. It all seemed the most incredibly typical wartime evening out, but romantic and agreeable. She's very reassuring actually, because she says: 'We'll be going back to the Pointe du Raz for our next holiday too.' She explains how rotten it would be

---

[164]'Blondinet' was another nickname for the Lunar Man (see note 54 above).

if her husband died: 'At our age, it isn't easy to make a new situation for yourself. You've put so much effort into securing your daily bread, and then you have to start hustling again.' I'm going to the cinema with her this evening. After that she'll be sucked dry, I think, but for a time I've found her amusing. She's nice and she's funny.

So I went to bed at around 1, slept till 9.30, then had breakfast at the Dôme where I met Stépha. We talked for a bit, looked at the papers, did some shopping, then I went back to the Dôme where I ate a *brandade de morue* and wrote to you. I'm going to work from 2 till 7, then see the Lunar Woman. My days are full up now, as you can see, and I'm having trouble finding room for my letters, my diary, and a bit of reading.

You were asking me some questions about That Lady, but what is there to tell you? The idea of war prevents her from sleeping, and she doesn't find it much fun being at La Pouèze yet seems quite resigned to it. It was I who talked, mostly. I told stories – especially about you. I avoided political conversations with That Lady, because it's painful hearing someone as well-intentioned as she is say that in 1918 we really should have pushed on to Berlin; or that the General Staff in 1914 can't really have been as bad as all that; or other things of the same ilk. She's dreadfully incoherent, and her own feelings are perpetually in contradiction with the convictions she has learnt. Nothing's known about the Pupil, who perhaps went back to Argentina.

The Dôme is still lively and entertaining – with something dark and heavy about it, which derives from the relations between the French and the foreigners. This morning there were heaps of familiar faces. I'm fantastically pleased to be in Paris. If it were a matter only of a short-term separation between you and me, I'd be having the most satisfactory of lives.

Goodbye, my sweet little one. There wasn't a letter this morning at Rue d'Assas, but perhaps one will arrive this evening. I love you, my beloved. I have all your photos in a pretty little portable album which Sorokine gave me. I kiss you most passionately, yourself, my little flower.

Your charming Beaver

[Paris]

Saturday 14 October [1939]

My love, most dear little being

How sad I am that you should have remained all this time without a letter! Do you have them now? Those were precisely the letters in which I told you of my movements and projects, my hopes, disappointments and expectations. Told you, too, about getting settled in Paris. If there are any missing, let me have the dates and with the help of my little diary I'll tell you everything entertaining or interesting over again. How much you do love me, my beloved, I'm quite overwhelmed by it. Oh! I love you so much that it's hard, really hard, to be far away from you. Your letter made me cry, and I'm still crying. You're so sweet to answer me at length; but it's unbearable to think that for months this is the only way you'll be able to answer me, in writing. You're so present to me, and I feel myself so present to you, but your face is in darkness and you no longer have a body. I've nothing to touch but the characters on the paper, and your little drawing of a lighter at the end of your letter. I find your reply to my question on infinity wonderfully interesting and satisfying. I'll read it once more in a critical spirit, but I can't see anything there to pick up on, and it strikes me as true.

Yesterday, after writing to you, I went home to work and I worked till 6. I'm no longer really used to being confronted by a blank sheet of paper, but even so it didn't go too badly. Then I made myself beautiful, dropped in at Gégé's – where I found a long and charming letter from Little Bost – then went to the Capoulade to meet the Lunar Woman. We went to the Panthéon cinema next door, where we saw a charming English cartoon: ever so poetic, with vaguely surrealist effects and a quite original style – I'd really like to see others in the same series. They were showing *Test Pilot*, which is quite entertaining, though by the end you're fed up with Myrna Loy's restrained sufferings and Spencer Tracy's doom-laden expressions – but Clark Gable is delightful from start to finish. Then we went back to the bar at the Capoulade, at 10 in the evening, and the Lunar Woman ordered steaks and Beaujolais. The Beaujolais made us a bit tipsy, and we began to exchange declarations of friendship. She told me how her father had raped her (something she claims never to have told anyone else right out), and other stuff about her life. Then, as they were turfing us out, we decided to buy some alcohol to drink at my place. But first she wanted to drop in on Youki – Fujita's ex-wife, now married to Desnos – who's sleeping with Michel, and whom Kos. used to see at the sports ground.[165] We bought a small bottle for ourselves and a bigger one for Youki, and showed up in a smoke-filled room full of people and glasses of red wine

---

[165]Nickname for Fernande Barrey (see *The Prime of Life*, p.383 and 406), formerly married to Fujita (see note 82 above), now married to Robert Desnos (1900-45), the Belgian surrealist poet.

and Fujita's paintings. That appalling exhibitionist about whom Wanda must have told you was there, reading cards in another room. In the sitting-room there were crowds of people: Youki, in a Japanese kimono; a rather lovely blonde in the alluring style, very delectable; Michel; Blanche Picard, with the visage of an intellectual and martyr; a little piège with cropped hair who's often to be seen with Michel at the Dôme, and who was smoking a pipe; Thérèse, the wife of the exhibitionist, who's the instructress at that celebrated sports club and a close friend of Kiki from Montparnasse, with a penchant for mysticism; two insignificant other women; a rather handsome blond fellow; some tongue-tied youngsters; and a drunken, blear-eyed soldier whom I've often seen at the Flore. They were all in a great pother about some letter from Desnos, who has been called up and was writing in a fairly straightforward, calm fashion describing the daily round of his life. Youki was boiling with indignation, others were finding excuses, others were admiring – it was all quite hilarious. It was simply a question of what pose to strike, and as they're in some disarray they adopt a cynical, couldn't-give-a-damn attitude. The soldier was zealously playing his role as a combatant disgusted by the 'civilian mentality': he was half weeping, or laughing hysterically, and saying: 'You give me a pain in the arse' at every opportunity. The words 'shit' and 'arse' peppered the conversation, of course, and they were all bullshitting away in a pretty contemptible and sickening fashion. It was true they all gave the most shameful impression of people who don't have a clue about war – but the soldier was a damnable bore too, with his claims as a future combatant. The atmosphere was very heady, charged with a crude and unbridled sexuality. The Lunar Woman spent half an hour smooching with the blond fellow, and all anyone talked about was screwing or jerking off. I really did understand what sort of impression all those women, all that kind of people, must have made on the Kos. sisters. For they do in fact place themselves on a feminine, sexual terrain – the Lunar Woman and Youki, for example. Yet that kind of femininity and sexuality nauseates the Kos. sisters. For my own part, I'm totally out of it in scenes of that kind. But they're in a sense on the inside, despite dominating them intellectually and morally. And their scorn is aggressive, because in a sense they're in danger (in danger not of being affected, but of being compromised in their own eyes). It's an impression I'd like to expand on in detail with you, but we'd have to be face to face. I'm incidentally going to try and get Kos. to talk about this.

Anyway, the Lunar Woman was bestowing more and more tokens of friendship upon me. She told me she'd loved me since Berlin: 'in a sense, against somebody', she added – that 'somebody' meaning you. She has still got a big grudge against you. She told me she'd had a dreadful lot of bother because of you. She also says she never had a 'passion' for you. She constantly compares you with her husband, and makes you out to be more or less equal. But she considers that you produce too slowly, and also that you overestimate people, which leads them – Wanda, for instance – to overestimate themselves. You overestimate *yourself*, and Wanda, and the Lunar Woman. I'm the only one you don't overestimate. On the contrary, you're too cool about acclaiming my perfection and she's going to have a word with you about it. As for Wanda, she sees her as a nice, naive girl who believes everything you tell her. I took care, of course, not to say a word that could be passed back to Wanda. Apparently that famous night in the waiting-room, Wanda got a thrashing, or perhaps a spanking, because she slapped some fellow. And they administered her a massive purgative under the pretext of giving her a tonic, just out of revenge – I gave the Lunar Woman a piece of my mind about that. The Lunar Woman was quite agreeable all this time. She sang, everybody sang: songs by Prevert, and also old patriotic songs from 1914 – some of which are really extreme – and obscene songs, and others too. It was very entertaining, they've an amazing repertoire. We left at around 4, and I took the Lunar Woman back to my place with the small bottle of alcohol. The blond fellow followed and they installed themselves on my bed.

[. . .]

Kos. is coming tomorrow, and I'm curiously happy. I'm a little tired because of being up almost all night, and won't be doing much work today. What with getting the Kos. sisters settled in and my sister's arrival, I'll have to reckon on a week before I can work properly. Wanda's arriving on Monday – they've arranged things that way themselves. I mean to take her out and be very nice to her, and if that goes well all three of us will go out from time to time. I was full of sympathy for her yesterday evening, because I really understood how an ambience of that kind can both attract and disgust her, and how she must be quite out of her depth.

Goodbye, my love. I so hope you'll get my letters. Do keep writing to me. I love you, sweetest little one, without much joy today. I can't believe I'm going to be a long while without seeing you, I who live only through you. I clasp your little head in my hands, my love, and passionately kiss your face.

Your charming Beaver

Le Dôme

Paris, Sunday 15 October [1939]

My love,

This morning I got your little letter of the 10th; I'd already had your big one of the 11th yesterday. I'm impatient to know whether you've finally received mine. Bost too had to wait for a very long time for my letters of the 5th and 6th, but he did get them eventually. It pains me to feel you're separated from me. I'm not gloomy today, but I'm not really happy. There's a memory that has kept coming back to me these past two days – it's your own little self in That Lady's garden, cheering me on as I swam so diligently.[166] My love, what a distance liés between those moments and the ones we're living through now. Everyone seems to think the war will be a long one. I can't manage to think concretely what two years without you will represent, but I do have some vague apprehension of what I shall be in six months.

Bost is 35 km. away from Bar-le-Duc, and will probably spend the winter there. He seemed gloomy in his last letters and he too has that heroic impatience you speak of and finds that the waiting is worst of all.

Yesterday after writing to you I went first to the hairdresser's, then to buy two little turbans, and then to Lycée C. Sée. I have only 8½ hours, very neatly distributed – but I'm also assigned to Fénelon. I dropped in there to see the headmistress, but didn't find her in – no matter, I'll telephone tomorrow. I don't think they'll give me another final-year class, since I'm only supposed to do 14 h. – I'll probably just have odds and ends. Fénelon has been moved to Henri IV, and the idea of being a teacher just there makes me feel all poetic.[167] From Henri IV I went to the Capoulade and ate ham and eggs while writing to Bost; then I went by Metro to Porte de St-Cloud to see Sorokine. She had a girl friend there, who was very ugly and not very interesting: it was that notorious friend of hers about whom she no longer much cares, but whom she wanted to show me. We chatted for a bit before accompanying the friend back home, then went for a walk along the river at Passy. The embankment was lovely in the darkness, with its trees festooned with dead leaves and yellow lights. I was very tender with Sorokine, taking her arm myself and telling her sweet nothings. And for the first time she was absolutely melting and happy and abandoned with me. Instead of the vague hostility of other days, there was a charming childlike complicity. We went up to her place, chatted a bit, and I'm still moved when I recall how she behaved like some little tamed animal.

---

[166] At Juan-les-Pins, during August of this same year.
[167] It was at Lycée Henri IV that Sartre had been a pupil in 1915-17 and again in 1920-22.

There's more and more of the 'constant nymph' about her. The presence of her parents in the next room imposed considerable restraint, but she had a way of furtively touching my hand, offering her cheek, and making me little moues of affection that were at once discreet, animal, and moving. She was really precious to me yesterday evening, with her tartan hair-ribbon, her teddy-bear in her arms, and her serious face. It'll be all right this year, because I have the time; but it's a damn nuisance for the future, because I won't ever be able to ditch her now. I went home at about 11 and found a little letter from Bienenfeld, to whom I replied at length, as I'd had a long one from her the day before yesterday. Alas! I don't miss her much at all, poor thing; I'm much gladder to be expecting Kos. at present than if I were expecting her. I'm extraordinarily glad that Kos. is turning up again: it's a piece of my real life – my life with Bost and you – that I'll regain by regaining her. And I'm really fond of her now. This morning I rose at 9, spent a long while getting dressed and doing my nails, then went and picked up your little letter from Gégé's and sent you off a parcel containing paper, newspapers and books. At the Poste Restante where he now writes to me, I found two big letters from Bost – and also a clever little supplementary note he'd sent me. You too should send me an unexpected little note over and above your letters some time. I went to the station to see whether Kos. was on the midday train, but she wasn't. So I came to have lunch here, and will be returning to the station at 5.

In the meantime, I'll go and do some work. Goodbye, my little sweet one. As soon as I have a definitive time-table, I'll give it to you. It's so precious to be able to write to one another like this, and makes me feel we two still have a single life. I do so hope you'll get my letters all right. With the most passionate kisses, my love –

Your charming Beaver

Do send Bost all the books you can – he's really clamouring for them.

[Paris]

Monday 16 October [1939]

Dear little being

I have your little letter of the 13th, but not that of the 12th. If I understand right, you did receive letters from me on the 12th – but how annoying all these delays are, and how paralysed and isolated one does feel. I'm pretty glum today, because normal life is beginning again – beginning again without you – and it's dreadfully austere. Yesterday after writing to you I worked for a bit, then went to the 5 o'clock train to look for Kos., but she wasn't on it. So I went off by Métro to the Gaîté Rochechouart, to see *Peter Ibbetson*[168] – it's atrociously bad and ridiculous. I got back to the Gare Montparnasse just in time to pluck Kos. like a flower. She was very nice, but I was rather disappointed. I'm not sure what help I was expecting from her, but she's herself one more person to be helped. I find her a bit of a burden, and imbued with a gloom that it falls to me to dispel. But that doesn't stop me from being glad of her company. She wants to take a philosophy degree, and I'm giving her strong encouragement. She's going to register tomorrow – it'll keep her busy and might be useful to her. It was 9 when we vainly sought refuge in the Dôme – which was full so we went to the Rotonde, where I ate an andouillette while telling Kos. heaps of stories, especially about the Lunar Woman. Then we went up to chat at my place till one in the morning. Wanda has a slight sore throat and will not be here for a few days. I slept from 1 to 7.30, and it was pretty painful when the alarm-clock got me out of bed. I was rather gloomy, starting my regular existence alone without the expectation of rejoining you when evening comes – I, who used to classify my days last year according to my evening assignation, and who used to be so happy on the days when it was with you. Nothing but days without you now. I walked to the Gare Montparnasse and had coffee at the counter in the Dupont – after which it's 10 min. by Métro to Convention, followed by 10 min. on foot to the Lycée. I found 9 pupils, as good as gold in their blue pinafores, and talked to them about consciousness. The Lycée's magnificent, there's a staff room, with huge club armchairs and modern tables, as big as a railway-station concourse – and everything else to match. The deputies and headmistress are friendly, in general you feel free, and it's lively and agreeable to work there. But alas! the headmistress informed me that I'd also have a final-year class at Fénelon and, furthermore, that there was some vague idea at the ministry of sending me to Bordeaux. This froze me to the marrow. I decided to go off quickly and see M. Monod, the school inspector, to have it out with him. Sorokine was waiting for me at the gate, so we jumped into a taxi and I raced off to Lycée Henri IV. How agreeable it is on the inside! But it's all under repair, so life's concentrated in one modern wing that's all tiled and very ugly. I encountered a collection of real shrews there, all dressed in black and

---

[168]Novel (1891) by Georges Du Maurier, adapted for the stage.

each with a gas-mask in its putty-coloured satchel slung over one shoulder, and the most shrewish of all was the headmistress: semi-hunchbacked, wearing a black hat, and she too with a mask and a sinister air. She handed me an impossible time-table, and when I pulled a long face she expressed great disappointment at my accepting to work at her school without greater enthusiasm. I have 17 hours! It's frightful, and I don't see how I'll manage to work at my novel, especially with all the travelling to and fro – I'm really disgusted.

[. . .]

I think I'll be obliged to give up my room to Wanda, because of her painting, which causes me some heartache – but in fact there's one next door that's not too awful. What else? I had a letter from Bienenfeld, who tells me that Kanapa wants to see me. I'll see him, it should be quite enjoyable. Bienenfeld seems really happy – she wrote me a charming little letter.

Write to me at the Hôtel du Danemark, 21 rue Vavin. Do keep writing to me, I have such need of your letters – and such need of you.

This letter is wretched, but Kos. is with me and that puts me off. I reread your philosophical letter. You're a splendid little philosopher, my little poppet. You must begin to construct a system, since you have the time.

Goodbye, my love. Tomorrow I'll find a more peaceful moment to write to you and send you a big organizational plan of my life, which I'll make this evening. I love you, my beloved – life without you bores me most desperately. I kiss you tenderly, my love.

Your charming Beaver

Café-Restaurant de Versailles
3 Place de Rennes
Paris VI

Paris, Tuesday 17 October [1939]

Dearest little being

I'm not in too bad a mood today, because although it's my hardest day of the week I realize that I won't be too tired to do some work in the evening – from 4 or 5 until 8, which is fine. Here's what I've done. First, yesterday after writing to you I went with Kos. for a bite at the snack bar, after which we went to the Dôme. We did have a chat, but we were both dead beat so we went home at 9. We were told that a lady had called, and had said she'd call back again soon as she'd nothing else to do – it was the Lunar Woman, of course. I found a little letter from Bienenfeld, who says that Kanapa wants to see me. I'll see him – it'll be quite enjoyable. I wrote to Bost, then went to sleep. I rose at 7.30 – it was to Henri IV that I was going this morning, which is not at all disagreeable: it takes me 10 minutes to get there crossing the Luxembourg, which is magnificent at present and particularly delightful in the morning mist, then I have coffee at the Capoulade before going on to the Lycée. I did 2½ hours of lessons, interrupted by a charming distraction – an air-raid drill. First, the headmistress traipsed round the corridors with a tin hat on her head and gas-mask slung over one shoulder, blowing shrill blasts on a whistle. Then we all went down in Indian file to a magnificently appointed shelter. There we sat down and, with the whistle still stuck in her mouth but now bare-headed, the headmistress put us through a gas-mask practice. 'Teachers too!', she shouted, but I hadn't got mine. She explained that we weren't to speak or move if there actually was a raid, because that uses up oxygen. You should have seen her play the general – she's a proper shrew! We ended our lessons, then I went to write to Bienenfeld and eat a bite at the Source – I'm entranced at finding myself in the Latin Quarter when I come out of school. After that I took a Métro and was at C. Sée by 1 o'clock. Two hours of lessons. The headmistress is a paragon compared with the usual run of headmistresses, she really couldn't be more affable – but it's a pity she has a blue chin. I shall be charming with her too, since after all my future lies in this Lycée. But I'd really take pleasure in teaching that other one a thing or two. I took another Métro to Montparnasse and went to the post office to pick up Bost's letters, since as I think I told you he's now writing to me Poste Restante.[169] There was a very nice letter from him. He more or less gets all my letters, but no parcels. I'm annoyed, because I'd sent him some books and a little pipe. I came here to this gloomy Café Versailles, to write to him and start writing to you. But I won't post my letter, I'll wait for yours – because I prefer calling in at Gégé's after 5 and getting both the morning and evening deliveries. Upon reflection, I'll post it all the same, in order to gain a day. I'll start to write to you again anyway this evening, because this is just a little scrap.

I'm off now to meet Kos. at the Deux Magots and finish off the evening with her. Yesterday we worked out a detailed time-table, from which it emerges that I'll be able to work perfectly well this year. That

---

[169]To avoid his letters to De Beauvoir being seen by Olga, now living in the same hotel.

calmed me down, and I'll make a serious start after Poupette's arrival. My life's full, but how insipid, o salt of my life! Till this evening. I love you, my little sweet thing.

Your charming Beaver

Le Dôme
[Paris]

18 October [1939], Wednesday

My love

I found a letter from you yesterday at Gégé's (these are not tears, but water[170]) dated the 14th, and this morning how happy I was to receive the letter of the 15th with the two photos. There's still your letter of the 12th that's missing, which annoys me because precisely from the others I can tell it was the reply to those four letters you took such a long time to receive – but perhaps it'll turn up in its own good time. The ones of mine that you haven't got – the ones dated the 6th, 7th and 8th – weren't of any great interest. I was writing in a state of over-wrought impatience, and nothing was happening to me. Thank you for all your good advice, which I have fully understood and will follow, always provided that the situation remains the same. Well, if it changes we'll see – you can give me fresh advice as appropriate.[171] You know, in the photo you have just the same face as ten years ago. I remember yourself so well, with your little forage-cap – you haven't aged a whisker.

Yesterday after writing to you I rejoined Kos. at the Deux Magots. She was in the dumps, because she'd done almost nothing all day except trail around and was exhausted. We bought some material for me, for a magnificent new red turban. Then I called in at Gégé's, and she showed me some lovely new fabric patterns. Pardo can't find a job and is probably going to enlist – in the auxiliaries, of course. Everyone's enlisting, it's quite moving – all Kos.'s foreign friends are enlisting. She showed me a comical letter from Delarue, who's in utter despair: Alain's ethics seem to be of no use at all to him.[172] Kos. and I had dinner at the

---

[170]The paper was stained.

[171]De Beauvoir could not make arrangements for a visit to the front until it was clear whether Sartre's unit was going to move, and if so where.

[172]Alain: pen-name of Émile-Auguste Chartier (1868-1951), influential essayist and, with Brunschwicg, the dominant figure in French philosophy between the wars. He was prosecuted with others in 1939 for having signed a tract by the pacifist Louis Lecoin, entitled *Paix Immédiate!*.

snack bar, then – o joy! – we went to the Café de Flore. It's reopened, you see, I'm not sure exactly since when. Lots of places are reopening: the Jockey from 5 to 11 in the evening, and Agnès Capri during the same hours – we'll go and see what's going on, I'm curious to know what people you can find there and how they're behaving. As for the Flore, it was jam-packed. Sonia was there looking splendid, and Fernandez, and Fargue, and lots of other acquaintances. Inside, it was all draped in blue, and as they now have new, bright red benches, the effect's magnificent. The cafés are far more agreeable than at the beginning of September, because at that time they were only roughly camouflaged and had to keep their lights shielded, whereas now they're all tightly enclosed behind thick curtains and fully lit – seeming almost like chapels when you come into them from the darkness. It was jam-packed, then, and one astonishing thing was that it was practically all men. There was an aroma of coarse male tobacco and political conversation, and the whole atmosphere was pretty different from what it used to be. All the waiters have changed, only the manager has remained the same. We chatted, but I had to make a big effort because Kos. was rather low. Then we walked home, fairly early, and I went to bed and read *Troilus and Cressida* for a bit, which I find delightful.

Today's my 'Thursday' – my free day.* I rose at 8, had coffee at the Dôme, read the newspaper and *Le Canard Enchaîné* – which made me laugh quite a bit – then did some work. I'm still working half-heartedly. I had lunch and at 12.30 Sorokine arrived, charming and passionate. I found it very awkward, because Kos. is in the next room and you can hear absolutely everything, but I couldn't stop her – after half an hour of falsely animated conversation – from falling headlong into my arms. We exchanged kisses and she was happy, but then she asked me greedily how many times a week I reckoned on seeing her, and I said two, which made her so unhappy that she burst into tears. Eventually I promised her 1½ hours of Kant one morning; an evening; and part of Wednesday. Actually, I do have time – it's more that it's a bit of a damn nuisance. But after this she was happy, and went off all tender and gay. I find her as agreeable as could be, especially when she's being affectionate – yet you can't conceive how bored I am by these outpourings of affection on the part of Bienenfeld and Sorokine. Still, I did receive a very warm, agreeable letter from Bienenfeld, which quite moved me. But it amuses me that with respect to Sorokine, about whom I was talking to her, she should say: 'Don't tell yourself she's nice or else you'll be caught, like with the Kos. sisters' – she recommends me to adopt an implacable hardness. It's comical, she doesn't realize it's with *her* I was caught like that. In a letter that's got lost,[173] I wrote you a whole dissertation on this privileged character one always accords to *oneself* – I'll write it again for you, if the letter's really lost. It's one of the things that most annoy me, because one can never be certain one won't fall into the trap.

I telephoned Lévy, to fix an appointment with him and Kanapa for tomorrow.

My sister's arriving this evening. That makes a dreadful day. First Sorokine, now Kos. from 4 to 8, then Poupette. But it won't be like this any more next week – I'll hardly see Kos. except in the evenings. So long as I can't see you, what I like best by far is being alone. I'm sick of putting myself out for people who don't bring me anything. My glumness in this regard comes partly from the fact that Kos. couldn't have been more sullen this morning. All right, she had a headache, but it reduced her to a snivelling despair that was hard to endure. Already I think of her only as a burden to drag around – but luckily she has her ups and downs, and will assuredly grow pleasanter. Wanda's still not here.

My sweet little one, you say you're *sustained* by my letters, whereas I find them really wretched all these days. But I'd like it to be true. It's wonderful to have somebody who sustains you, I realize that now more strongly than ever – it's so rare, so precious. My love, how grey a life without your presence is!

Goodbye, my dear love. How I long to see you! I love you, my sweet little one, and kiss you most passionately.

Your charming Beaver

*A wartime 'Thursday', falling in fact on Wednesday.

[Paris]

Thursday 19 October [1939]

Most dear little being

This morning I left too early to get the mail, but I'm hoping to have a letter this evening. The one of the 12th wasn't yet at Gégé's yesterday, but I'll doggedly keep going to look for it. I so need your letters, my love.

[. . .]

---

[173]Presumably a reference to the letter of 8 October, which Sartre complained of not having received in his letter of the 15th, but which he did in fact receive a day later.

I went to bed at about midnight and rose at 8 – I had school at 10.30. I went to the post office in Rue Littré, where I found a really nice long letter from Bost; then I went to answer him from the Versailles, which is just opposite, while eating my breakfast. I found it incredibly poetic, that gloomy café where the waiters were still washing the tables – it was like those provincial cafés where you end up when you get off a train in the early morning. It reminded me of Bordeaux, and of arriving at Carcassonne too, and it brought tears to my eyes. O my sweet little one, my love, we were still happy that morning. I remember with such emotion the ramparts, and the little open-air café, and how intensely we felt our love in the narrow streets – do you remember? I left for school. I have a lovely little locker in the magnificent staff room, in which I've put an attaché case with all my private papers – I prefer not to leave your letters or anything else lying about at home. I gave my lesson, then wandered round Place de la Convention in search of a bar-restaurant. It was 12.30 and I had to be at Henri IV by 2, which was a bit tight. I ended up in a very comfortable restaurant with tablecloths and cruets, but where I ate very well while reading *Troilus and Cressida*: pâté, sirloin and roast potatoes, strawberry dessert, all for 10 F. – perhaps I'll go back. I took a Métro which dropped me at Jussieu; it was incredibly agreeable alighting there, and I still had time for a coffee while starting to write to you. At school I found only six pupils – my class has melted away: they've exchanged one group for another, but this other as yet exists only on paper. A class of six pupils is sad, because you can't imagine to yourself that – hidden away in the back rows – there may be one or two faces lit up with comprehension. It couldn't have been more of a damned bore. At 4 I met Lévy and Kanapa at the Balzar. Kanapa was no longer crazy at all, but very nice and simple, with no twitches or glances at his watch, no affectations. But it would have been more enjoyable to see him on his own. As it was, we made only general conversation and I talked almost all the time. I'll ask them out from time to time. I enjoy seeing the odd male – however dainty a shoot he may be – since I literally talk only to women these days. After that I saw Kos. for two hours, then Poupette at the Dôme. We had dinner at the Milk Bar, from which I'm writing while she writes to Lionel. I'll write again when I get back home in an hour – but I'm going to mail this note right away. Nothing from you. My love, I'm so sad, so sad to be deprived of you.

Your charming Beaver

Le Dôme
[Paris]

Friday 20 October [1939]

Most dear little being

I wrote you a very skimpy little letter yesterday, but what with Kos., Poupette and school, I don't have a minute to spare. I'm no longer even keeping up my journal – though luckily I do have a bit of time this morning, so I'll try to bring it up to date. So we had dinner and spent the evening yesterday at the Milk Bar, then Poupette came up to my room. She was full of confidences and attempted sincerity, and fairly nice – but what an odd person! She gave me a long account of her relations with Lionel, who spent the month of September at St-Germain-les-Belles, as you know. She looked after him devotedly all that month, and Lionel began to expound a theory to her, according to which there are two women contained in her: a tender, devoted woman made for marriage and motherhood, and a very artificially constructed woman – the woman painter – whom he doesn't like. He loved her more than ever during that month of September, he used to say, because she used to wait on him and he adores being waited on. I think he'd set himself the goal of transforming Poupette into a slave-woman for his private amusement – but he must have been disappointed. After all, the very first word with which she greeted him when he arrived in the Limousin was: 'You mustn't prevent me from working.' On a subsequent occasion he proposed to her that they place their relationship on another footing, saying that he'd like a truly loving relationship with her – a male-female relationship that would spare him the need for amorous adventures. She protested, saying: 'I prefer you to have adventures, it takes the load off me.' Eventually, when his family wanted to whisk him off to Portugal, he proposed to stay at St-Germain-les-Belles on condition that Poupette devote herself entirely to him. She refused outright, because that would have prevented her from working. Apparently he really held that against her. She explained to me that he's perfect as a friend, but she's none too happy with his feelings as a lover, because he's so lacking in tenderness and so domineering. I eventually threw her out, because I was dropping asleep. I was just dozing off when I was woken by shouts of 'Madeleine, Madeleine . . .'[174]. It was Kos., who then began groaning horribly. I got up and woke her by knocking on her door. She was having a nightmare – a big dog was lying on her body. I went back to sleep after that, but then I had nightmares too, in which De Roulet and Bost were all mixed up – most unfortunately for me. I woke up an hour ago, laid low by a

---

[174]Name of Olga's nanny.

dreadful cold, and feel quite exhausted. Kos. gave me a nice little breakfast, with an egg and some milk, and I've just begun this letter to you. I'd so like to get one today! What did that one of the 12th say, that I certainly shan't get now?

The little Oranaise is lying low in Oran, and well and truly stuck so far as the diploma Lionel was going to do with her is concerned. Did you appreciate the little anecdote about the rhinoceros in the Green? I found it charming.

Lévy told me he'd met one of your colleagues, a Communist teacher of German, who made a full-scale attack on you: you deprive your pupils of all critical spirit, you divert them from the real problems – such as the problem of eating – and you give them an aesthetic attitude that makes them very disagreeable.

My love, it's half past one now. I've made up my journal, written to Bienenfeld and Bost, and read a bit of *Anthony and Cleopatra* – for Kosakiewitch has lent me her big *Shakespeare* in the Pléiade edition, and I'm going to reread the lot. Poupette came back again and we had lunch in Rue Vavin – she's sweet, and quite bearable really. We came via the Luxembourg to have coffee at the Capoulade, then she left me and I'm off to school – my cold's a little bit better. But I feel quite abandoned: still no letter from you. Nor do I know if you're receiving mine. It was so agreeable when we could really speak to each other by letter – now we're writing to each other at random. I'm going to begin my preparations for 1 November, but I'm still going to need certain kinds of advice.[175]

I looked again at your photos, which have already caused mirth in more than one quarter. It quite moved me, seeing my ski-shoes on your feet again.

I'm going to take my sister to the cinema, and then take her out with Kos., with Gégé, with the Lunar Woman, and with the Gerassis – just to liven things up a bit. The Lunar Woman saw Kos. yesterday for 1½ hours, and asked her why she didn't splash out a bit. For her own part, she was negotiating to buy a waterproof cape from a mounted policeman. Pardo told me that at Youki's they called her 'the Caca Kid', but I'm not really sure why.

Goodbye, distant little being. I'm off to see my six pupils again, and not looking forward to it – I don't enjoy myself enough.

I want to see you, and want your letters. Most dear little being, do

---

[175] 1 November (All Saints Day) is a national holiday in France.

your cheeks still smell of cake? I cover them with little French kisses. I
love you, o yourself.

Your charming Beaver

Le Dôme
Poste Restante Office 43
Rue Littré
(N.B. 43 is the number of the office,
 not the street number)

Paris, Saturday 21 October [1939]

My love

A letter from you at last – I didn't have anything yesterday or the day
before. So the letter of the 12th is definitively lost, and the ones of the
15th and 16th haven't arrived either – it's the one of the 17th that I've
had. Well, whenever you tell or ask me anything important, you must
repeat it not just once but twice. As for an address, you'd better write
as well to Poste Restante, Office 43, Rue Littré – that's the most
convenient, since I already go there to pick up Bost's letters[176] – and I'll
keep your letters in those lockers at the school. My love, how
abandoned and miserable I feel when your letters don't arrive properly!
Today or on Monday I'll begin taking steps to go and see Emma on
1 November. People say they give permission for that without too much
difficulty – I'll keep you posted.

I'm glad you approve of my plan. My idea was to stop my novel at
the *start* of the war, just as the fellows are all going off. And even if the
war's over before my novel is, I think I'll stop there. It's of little
importance what becomes of Pierre and Gerbert; and as for Françoise,
what matters is for her to be alone in front of her past and the whole
uncertain future. It makes me rather bitter to speak of this, since I no
longer have any time to work since Poupette has been here – and I'd so
like to get started again. I'm not tragic these days, I don't weep, but I
feel alone, bewildered, far from you, far from everything – nothing has
any meaning. Do write to me, my love, and make certain to put on the
right address – these lost letters and gaps are infuriating.

Well, I wrote to you yesterday before going off to school. I gave my

---

[176]De Beauvoir already had Bost's letters sent poste restante to avoid them being seen by
Olga. Now she wanted Sartre to do likewise, to avoid his letters being seen by Wanda
who was about to move into her hotel.

lesson, and there were only five pupils. But then I had a little boost to my self-esteem. While I was at the post office in Rue Cujas sending a money order to Bienenfeld (and behind me there chanced to be a teacher from Molière who'd hated Bienenfeld, and who saw me send the money – how shady I must appear!), a little girl came up to me with a letter in her hand. With a foreign accent and a pleasing manner, she told me she was glad to find me – since she wasn't too sure where to send her letter. Though I probably didn't know her, she already knew me very well. I transcribe the letter here – it really flattered me. 'I am one of those victims whom fate has plucked from your lessons and plunged into another where they cannot fail to find themselves somewhat disoriented. I regret the loss all the more keenly in that I had begun to *understand*, and your way of teaching had in any case fascinated me. I want only to tell you that already, after the few hours we have spent together, you have been able to make pupils unhappy to leave you – and all the more unhappy because the separation was so unexpected and sudden, and because we have to switch abruptly from "Consciousness" to the history of philosophy and then on to Logic . . .'

Isn't that just too romantic? I think when I'm sixty they'll be killing themselves for love in the middle of the class – for it's growing worse year by year. What's more the other teacher is Mme Meyerson, whom I've seen, and whose face explains a great deal.

I went to the Capoulade to meet Kos., who's sweetness itself with me. We chatted for two hours, then I went to the Mahieu to meet Poupette, whom I took to the little Alsatian restaurant on Boulevard St Michel for a quiche and some good white wine. Then we went to the Cinéma du Panthéon to see the end of *Silver Moth*, which is absurd even though Katharine Hepburn's so beautiful, and *Jean de la Lune*, which I found rather enjoyable.[177] We came home in the most marvellous moonlight – I never tire of those country sky effects over Paris. I never tire of Paris, actually, it's the one thing that warms my heart somewhat. In my pigeonhole I found *Spanish Testament*,[178] left there no doubt by the Boubou; I took it to bed and couldn't put it down. It's an excellent book, without artistic pretensions, but simple and agreeable in tone and incredibly moving. If I can get it on permanent loan, I'll send it you; otherwise, if you want it just say so and I'll buy it for you.

Have you sent any books to Bost? He has bags of time to read and would really like some.

I went to sleep, got up at 7.30, drank a coffee at the Dupont, then

---

[177]*Jean de la Lune:*1931 film directed by Jean Choux.
[178]By Arthur Koestler (1937, French translation 1939).

went to Camille Sée. Two hours' teaching, then I called in on the bursar, who turns out to be my old bursar from Rouen. I didn't recognize her – but it wasn't too obvious – and we had a long talk about Delort, Jahan and C. Audry:[179] 'Such a lovely specimen', she said admiringly. After that I met up with Sorokine who was there waiting for me, still all melting and delightful. She has managed to register at the Sorbonne, I've promised to see her, and she's almost happy. We went by Métro to Montparnasse, sat ourselves down at the Versailles – which couldn't have been gloomier (she likes only deserted cafés) – and held hands tenderly as we talked. I went to pick up Bost's letters – there was a little one and a big one. He's moving – only 4 km. – and reckons to stay there till March – well, there's that at least.

[. . .]

I went and did some shopping with Poupette. I'd like to get my mother to make me a warm coat. Everybody says I've never looked so good as in these lovely turbans, which I wear over my ears like a real Indian – but that's not much use to me. This evening we're going to the Jockey – Poupette, Kos. and I – it should be fun to see.

I've kept forgetting to tell you the following: at La Pouèze, That Lady showed me the announcement of M. Jollivet's death. It was formulated like this:

Mme Jollivet
Simone Jollivet
Mlle X (in religion Sister Y.)
Monsieur Charles Dullin
have the unhappy duty to inform you . . . etc.

Isn't that delightful?

Tell me *which letters you haven't received*, and tell me if there was anything important in your missing letters (perhaps I do have the one of the 15th, after all – I even think so – but not those of the 16th or 12th).

Wanda has announced her arrival for tomorrow.

Goodbye, my love – how far away you are! I have a desperate need to see you and talk to you. I can't believe all this is going to last. I love you, o yourself, and am nothing without you.

Your charming Beaver

---

[179]Colleagues of De Beauvoir at the Lycée Jeanne d'Arc in Rouen.

Tell me, when you have time, what you've written about your historicity.

[Paris]

Sunday 22 [October 1939]

My love

I've just found a letter from you at Gégé's. It's dated the 19th, so has got here fast. But in fact only half of it has come, and the one dated the 18th is missing, and the one of the 16th before that, and the one of the 12th before that again – so it couldn't be more infuriating.

I collected your friends together, and found them interesting.[180] I'm taking steps to go and see Emma. I certainly shan't manage to be there before 1 November, but there's some chance I could go there then – it's complicated, but might work out.

I'm sad, sad, sad. But not tragic. Not gloomy. I'm not bored, and even have some very good times, but the need to see you is killing me.

Don't tell Bienenfeld any longer that you're continuing with your journal – and you'd better say you've lost the first notebook. I too find her letters very boring.

I find it rather annoying that you should no longer be writing to my place. It's also annoying to think that when you get some leave, I shan't be able to show you my room or go with you to our favourite places in Montparnasse or St Germain-des-Prés, we'll have to skulk in some corner. If only it could happen at a time when Wanda was at Laigle. She hasn't arrived yet.

[. . .]

I'm going to write a note to Bienenfeld, who thinks I'm neglecting her a bit, then I'm off with Poupette to meet the Lunar Woman at the Dôme.

My love, it's true what you say: you're an absence rather than a presence for me, and that's painful. I'm living in a provisional state, everything around me and in me is provisional. I wait – quite patiently – but do nothing except wait. I wait for you, and will perhaps wait for years like this. You're everything for me, my love

Your charming Beaver

---

[180]To avoid the censors, Sartre's letter of 15 October had contained seven fictional names whose initials gave her the location of his new quarters: BRUMATH.

[Paris]

Monday 23 October [1939]

My love

I've received your letter of the 16th and am so glad it wasn't lost. It was really long and vivid, so I feel truly close to you once more – in uninterrupted conversation with you. Perhaps this evening Gégé will bring me the ones of the 18th and 20th. There's only the letter of the 12th which seems definitively lost. I love you, little being, passionately – but with a trace of distress. I so wish you'd be given back to me.

This morning I began my preparations to go and see Emma. They're well under way and all I have to do is wait, but it will take at least 8 days. I don't actually have any leave for 1 November, but that doesn't matter, I'll take the following Friday, Saturday and Sunday off. That's convenient, because on the Friday I have lessons only at H. IV, and on the Saturday only at C. Sée, so it makes only one day's absence at each school and there's no need even for a doctor's certificate.

Yesterday after writing to you I met Poupette and we walked over towards Montparnasse. There was a marvellous sunset over the Carrousel and the Seine, you can't imagine how beautiful Paris is just now. How lovely it would be to take a walk with your little arm in mine! We went to Gégé's, but stayed only an hour. I called in on Kos., then went to the Dôme to meet Poupette again and the Lunar Woman. Wanda was there too, having just arrived. She was all of a fluster and quite ugly: very fat, with a blotchy complexion and looking like a peasant. When I saw her today Kos. had cut her hair and she was a little bit better – but not much. We exchanged innumerable compliments. I think she'll take the room under her sister's, since she really likes the hotel, having met an old friend from Dreux there. This hotel's crammed full of women – it's almost like a girls' boarding school. That buxom brunette from the Dôme is here – the one who's a model, and whom Stépha thinks has a lovely body – and yesterday she knocked at Kos.'s door and asked: 'Got a cigarette, Madame?' 'Hello!' Kos. said to her, with a friendly, even intimate look. The woman stared at her round-eyed.

We left the Dôme and went off for pancakes and cider at the Crêperie. Then we went to the O.K., which is a hot, lively nightclub, quite agreeable, where I'll take you on your first leave if there aren't any restrictions on your movements. I was dropping with exhaustion, and the Lunar Woman was talking non-stop. She'd seen Thérèse – the mystical instructress – again, who told her that Yuki and the soldier were quite embarrassed next day to have quarrelled like that the night before. 'But', said Thérèse, 'it was just the kind of evening he needed.

When he gets back to the front, it'll provide him with a fantastic memory and he won't be able to think about anything else.' Thérèse was meanwhile complaining, in the presence of her exhibitionist husband, about how he was now going after children. At the same time she was singing great paeans of praise to chastity, supported by quotations from the Bible. Apparently the exhibitionist really loves it when people talk about his vice in front of him. I'm glad to have seen one of them in private, because whenever you see one in the exercise of his functions you always wonder what he can be like in conventional life. Apart from that, the Lunar Woman didn't sleep with the blond fellow. She found out he was married and her rule is not to touch a fellow when there's another woman, as it brings bad luck. She said this, moreover, without any animus – she actually likes me, and has bought me a Gilles et Julien record,[181] which is the acme of kindness since I don't even have a gramophone. Then, while walking me home, she told me: 'I lied to Wanda last year. I told her I'd had seven lovers, but I'd like you to know that isn't true. I was lying to her because she kept wheedling stories out of me. You never do that – I simply tell you them.' She told me at length the story of her Vienna lover, and also how she had 300 F. stolen from her on Sunday by the wife of the mounted policeman from whom she was trying to buy a trench-coat: they were taken from her bag while she was visiting the house. But to tell the truth I didn't find all this in the least entertaining. I felt like going to bed, and was wondering in bewilderment what the hell I was doing with those two women. I'm heartily sick of such wartime relationships – and of Poupette, in particular.

I went home to bed and collapsed in a heap, despite Kos.'s cries from the neighbouring room – which soon stopped in any case. I woke up, as always, with an almost pathological dread. I never like the alarm-clock's ring in the dark of a morning. But these days returning consciousness also brings back my wartime life and your absence – and I have a dreadful moment to get through. However, the weather was fine. I went to C. Sée and taught for two hours, interrupted by an air-raid drill that passed off as benignly as everything else, then went to the 15th Arr. police station. I had my photo taken – here's one of the snaps, in which I'm none too beautiful but in which you can see how nice my turban looks – then came back to Montparnasse and found two letters from Bost, to whom I wrote a short note from the Versailles.

You don't tell me whether you've written to him again, nor whether

---

[181]Gilles et Julien were anarchist, anti-militarist singers whom De Beauvoir had long admired (see *The Prime of Life*, p.141-2).

you've sent him the books, which would save me one parcel.

It's not *Barnaby Rudge* I liked, but *Great Expectations* – I'll send you both of them.

I met Kos., had lunch with her at the Milk Bar, then we did some shopping. I found your letter on my return to the hotel and it transformed my whole being. If only they start arriving properly again – I need them so much! As far as the shopping went, we ordered a lovely coat pattern for me and bought some splendid material: it will look like that beige coat of Bienenfeld's that was so beautiful. Then we went to the Marignan, where I'd arranged to meet Poupette at 4. It's already past 5, but she's at the doctor's. He already gave her insides a dreadful working over the other day, and is going to have another bash today.

I'll add a note this evening, once I have the letters I'm hoping for from you.

Dear little being, my love, here's your letter of the 18th – it's so tender, how it warms my heart! I'll reread it this evening when I go to bed, since I have Poupette and Gégé here with me. So you've now had all my letters, I think, and for my part I'm missing only yours of the 12th. From tomorrow on, things should proceed normally. So you did send the books to Bost – that was well done. As for the questions you ask about how much help Kos. has been, etc. you now have the answers: it's only your letters that are of any help to me. It's *fantastic* how having them changes my whole being, so that I become almost happy again. I love you, passionately.

[. . .]

Your charming Beaver

Chez Dupont
[Paris]

Tuesday 24 October [1939]

Dear little being

I didn't have school this morning – Henri IV's on vacation for the Bac exams – but in an hour (it's midday) I'll be at C. Sée. I'm at the Dupont, where I'll have lunch while writing something to you. I've reread the two letters I received from you yesterday and am full of love for you. I'm in a bad mood this morning, because of my life these days with Poupette and because of a letter from Bienenfeld that annoyed me. She reproaches me with seeing too much of Kos. and Sorokine; tells me

I shouldn't allow myself to be taken over like that; and at the same time informs me that, after the war, she'll be seeing much more of us (you and me) than before. At the same time Kos. is complaining of not seeing enough of me, and intends to make up for it once Poupette has left – though this doesn't annoy me so much, since it involves only myself. But I shudder somewhat when I think about your return, and how Wanda and Bienenfeld will have rights over you – and I become like Bienenfeld myself and would like to be the only one to monopolize you. We won't let our life together be eaten into, will we, my love? I hate it when Bienenfeld is full of blind, authoritarian advice. I didn't hide the fact from her that I was glad to see Kos. again. It's a bit spiteful to speak of her as though she were some boring company I put up with out of pity – B.'s simply jealous of her. She's talking about going to see you – should I advise her to do so, or dissuade her from it? She expatiates upon my 'ruined life' (because I see Kos. every day) in a way that greatly puts me out. What's more, I'm supposed to send for her once Poupette has left – there's one whom I shan't be in any hurry to bring back!

[. . .]

This morning I arose from 9 hours of good sleep, dressed, then went off for a couple of eggs with Kos. Wanda turned up wrapped in a thick robe – still ugly, but agreeable. We talked at length and I was terribly nice, offering her my room – which, alas!, she accepted – making plans for joint outings, and telling stories. Kos. is reading *Spanish Testament*, but when she finds certain episodes too dreadful, she simply refuses to believe them. I had a go at persuading her that it was all real, but it's her way of denying anything that might trouble her. I say this without hostility, since I like the Kos. sisters and spent an agreeable time with them this morning. After that, I went to the Dupont to eat a big helping of calves' sweetbreads and write to you. I'm now off to teach, but I'll add a note this evening once I've been to pick up your letter – I do hope there'll be one. I love you, my beloved. Tell me, will you really still go on being in no danger, even when your division goes into action?

I'm glad you've eventually had all my letters. I'll send you the books you ask for – do send Bost some, and write to him.

Le Sélect
99 Bd Montparnasse
Paris VI

Evening

My love, I've had your little letter of the 20th. How glad I am they're arriving properly again: it's just like picking up a conversation, you're with me again, and my sadness has melted away – almost – though it did in fact flare up this evening when P. informed me she'd be staying on till Sunday, but that's all over now. I told her I'd see her only in the evenings, and tomorrow I'm going to start working again. I taught for 3 hours on psychoanalysis, which my pupils enjoyed enormously. Then I spent a tender little hour at the Sélect with Sorokine, who's still incredibly charming. I took her to the Dôme, where we met Poupette and a Russian girl friend of Sorokine's fresh out of school. For the past month she'd been exploited by some dentist – just like Sorokine at her day nursery. And my star pupil from last year spends her days washing the floors of an American hospital. The fate of those girls is a hard one. I took Poupette to the Champs Elysées to see *As You Desire Me* with Stroheim and Greta Garbo – it wasn't bad. Do you recall, my love, that poetic evening at the Théâtre Montparnasse when we saw the play?

We came back to have onion soup at the Sélect and write for a while – now we're off to bed.

The *N.R.F.* isn't sending any money – perhaps one should write again. Poupette cost me 1,000 F., so although I'll get through the month I shan't have anything for M. Bienenfeld. Davy hasn't been called up, but he has been evacuated – to Bordeaux, I think. Monod's now inspector-general, and has his office at the Academy (what they call the 'Academy' at the Sorbonne). I'm furious that Mauriac should have taken our word *querencia*.

Kos. was gloomy, because she had a headache. Stopping work and Bost's absence have naturally cast her down, but not exaggeratedly – she's being terribly nice to me at the moment. I'll tell you more about that another time, now I'm going to stop. My love, how it moves me that you should be so interested in everything that happens to me, down to the route I take to school. You're within me, as the social is said to be within the individual – in every thought, every word, every act. My sweet little one, I love you so passionately, and with such tenderness! How thirsty I am to see you – I feel as though I'll faint away from happiness! I kiss you, my love. I'm calm, in the certain knowledge that nothing and nobody will sap our life, and nothing – no cataclysm, no absence – will wear down our love. I so wish that in a moment I could fall asleep beside you and see your eyes all rosy with slumber, your face all tender and blurred. I love you so intensely, my beloved.

Your charming Beaver

If Wanda makes any comments to you about me, do tell me them. I want to know if my charm offensive will succeed.

[Paris]

Wednesday 25 October [1939]

Sweet little being

I'm feeling blissful this morning, because I've got back to my work. I rose at 8.30, dressed at high speed and hurried down to instal myself at the back of the Dôme. I drank coffee while reading *Marie-Claire* and *Le Canard* – and the papers, of course – to get myself in the mood. Then from 9.30 till 12.30 I worked like a saint. I've got the whole novel so clearly in my head now that stopping at each chapter irritates me. I can't decide whether or not to work on larger chunks, and proceed as quickly as possible right to the end, then go back over everything in detail. The weather's fine. I was completely undisturbed, but at the same time could see shapes in the street, which I found delightful. I called in at Gégé's, but Poupette had carried off your letter – she's too stupid! She's not seeing me till this evening, so I'll have to wait all day for it. Then I went back to the hotel, where I've just seen Kos. She's getting dressed, we'll go for lunch and a walk round together, then I'll come back to work. She's terribly happy because the Atelier's going to start up its classes again – that will really change her life. Wanda's apparently complaining about the Lunar Woman, because when W. told her about how I was going to give up my room to her, the Lunar Woman said: 'Oh! so you're driving that poor Beaver out of her room now, are you?' – with an air of wishing to protect me from oppression. She'll end up making me take a dislike to myself! Kos. is still just as angelic – I really enjoy her company and am glad she's in Paris. Once Poupette has left, my life will become quite decent again.

[. . .]

They're saying there'll be leave for everybody over the coming four months – ten days of it. So I'll see you really properly, my love, in Paris. I'm just afraid that since it's being trumpeted in the papers, it may be terribly hard to hide the fact that you've got ten days from your family, Wanda, and Bienenfeld. I find that terribly unnerving. This ability to be unnerved by something in the future is a characteristic I have in common with Bienenfeld, which is why it so annoys me in her. I think there'll be almost no way for me to see Bost. I'd be able to invent alibis for my own part, but he'd be too scared. And you – how will it be possible to see you almost all the time, with just a little time for W. as you said? Yet I do want you to myself with all my might, my love. Well, I'm sure you'll manage things.

I went and had lunch with Kos. at the Milk Bar, then we did a few little bits of shopping on foot. We went to buy her a coat, which her mother was prepared to shell out for and which she'd seen in a shop-window on Bd St Germain and found ravishing. But the saleswoman laughed in our faces – it was a soldier's cape. I did think too that the cut was a bit austere. We went home and, just as I was starting to write to you, Wanda came into my room bringing all her things – so with her help I moved out my own. I'm now underneath Kos.'s room. It's infinitely less nice, but adequate for me to be able to work there with pleasure, and I'll have more independence.

I worked for another two hours. Now I'm off to the cinema with Poupette and the Gerassis. I'm going to get your letter – that's what I'm waiting for anxiously. I'm sad, as I often am in the evening. I'm transfixed by the obvious fact: 'I'm going to remain like this without him for a long while' – and feel like having a good cry. I go through much of my life with a kind of belief in miracles, and have never yet seriously thought that you wouldn't be here at Easter – or, if so, only at moments of crisis. My love, I miss you quite desperately.

I haven't told you that the Lunar Woman interprets the war as follows: it's a plot by state leaders to assert their power domestically. Daladier says to Hitler: 'All right, you begin'. 'O.K.', says Hitler – or something like that. And that's how matters proceed.

Here's my sister, who has just come up to my room with your letter of the 21st. Thank you, my love, for writing so well, and for being so close. Of course, I've long ago collected your friends together. I'm so happy about what you tell me regarding Emma, but for my own part I can't do anything except wait. On Saturday or Monday I'll know. I'll cable you in the event of success, and tell you the day of any definite acceptance.

I love you. I'm not in a bad mood, because my work's going well. But I'm sad and feverish. I'd so like to see you!

I kiss you with all my might, my dear little one

Your charming Beaver

[Paris]

Thursday 26 October [1939]

Most dear little being

I have your long letter of the 22nd. Dear little support, salt and joy of my life, I'm ashamed to have moaned so much in my letters. Don't worry, my love, it's only a superficial bad mood. Basically you write about things more than they exist, and that's always because, at the moment of writing, you're trying to describe an object – the gloomy world, or the wretchedness of life, etc. But if you try instead to make an hourly summary, there turns out to be not so much difference between the days and you're neither as sad nor as unfortunate as all that. At any rate, now that I've gone back to my work, I'm happy. Since this afternoon, I've also had something to hope for. Forms were handed round at school, encouraging teachers to have themselves seconded to correspondence tuition. I asked to keep C. Sée, but in place of Fénelon for my hours of duty to be made up by correspondence lessons. As I correct papers so fast, and work very fast in general, I'm sure I'd save a tremendous amount of time. At all events, it would be work at home and so much more relaxing. I think I'll go and see Monod again tomorrow, in order to back up my application.

As for Emma, I'm neither hoping nor despairing – just waiting. I've told you – haven't I? – that I'll wire you as soon as I know if it's success or failure. And I'll let you know the day of definite acceptance. But I certainly shan't know anything before Monday.

I find what you say about your novel very interesting. It's rather the same with me. Like you I don't yet have the impression of finitude, but I do already have the impression of limited matter – and it's not a very agreeable moment: one has neither the pleasure of infinite wealth, as at the outset, nor that of a well-articulated mechanism. All the same, I'm really enjoying writing.

[. . .]

Goodbye, my love. I feel your love so strongly. My life is still happiness, an immense happiness, because you exist and I love you. You haven't taken the least step away from me, you're with me, and your letters bring you so strongly back to life each day, my dear, dear love! How lovely it would be to see you, what strength I'd have for ages after that! But I shan't be disappointed, because I'm not counting on anything.

I kiss you, my sweet little one, my life

Your charming Beaver

Café-Restaurant de Versailles
3 Place de Rennes
Paris VI

Thursday midnight [26 October 1939]

My love

We're just back from the Jockey and I'm going to write you a little letter till I fall asleep – I so need to feel myself in your company, my sweet little one. When I'd finished writing to you earlier on, Poupette and I went to a pleasant little pancake house (another one) in Rue Pauline. We ate some delicious dumplings and some pancakes with jam, and drank cider. The weather was warm, and on the walls there were ugly blue nets intended to remind you of Douarnenez (which they did in fact do), while at the tables there were some rather amusing people. Then we went up to see the Kos. sisters. Real Kos. was wrapped in her beautiful orange-hemmed robe, with a splendid orange 'K' on the pocket. She seemed tired and downcast, and said she didn't want to come because of a headache. She made a strong impression on me – of disgust, pity, hostility, tenderness (in me), of poetry and squalor – you can see the kind of thing. She's so mundane to me – and yet transfigured by so many things (your former love, that of Bost) – that it makes a strange mixture. Wanda showed up too, spruce as could be and all ready for an outing. She was charming this evening, with her hair straight and pale like two years ago, a black pullover setting off her neck, a light complexion, and a young, ungainly look – rather pathetic. I found her engaging, though in her eager display of frantic amiability all she could keep saying was 'It's funny' – to Poupette and me indiscriminately – with an air of false sprightliness. Strange evening! I was somewhat concerned about Real Kos., intrigued by Young Kos. – intrigued above all to discover what it was about her that could attract you – and annoyed by a letter from Bienenfeld, who wants to go and see you. As I've already told you, I'm not jealous of your feelings for people. But I am jealous of people's feelings for you (it's not just a theme for a novel!). Wanda doesn't bother me, because in her little consciousness you're such an odd being, so different from the one I love. But Bienenfeld irritates me because it's a more serious version of you, and because she's so restless, and because she theorizes her love for you with such self-importance – it has its own solid violence, moreover. When you're there, I know quite well our love is the truest; but from afar I find it a burden to see you trailing round in other hearts. At present – as is sometimes the case – I'd so like to be alone with you, without Kosakiewitch, without Bienenfeld, just you and me. I know it's foolish – since if you were there there'd be nothing but you and me, despite all the others –

but you're far away.

O yourself, I love you so, love you in the real sense of the word. I have a passionate need for you. O little shadow, do become flesh and blood – I so need your little arms around me!

The Jockey was crowded this evening and agreeable. People were having dinner and drinking. There were lots of tarts, a sprinkling of soldiers, the beautiful panther-woman from the Dôme with her frizzy hair, and one of the Negresses – and some young couples. There were the two singers from the other day and a new one too. We took a table on the stage, right by the bar. Poupette and Wanda drank whisky and I drank Calvados. We didn't talk much, especially as Poupette always interrupted me into the bargain. But I felt there was a current of good will between Wanda and me. We watched all the people, and it couldn't have been more friendly. At 11 we were thrown out, so we went home. I went up to see Kos., who was in bed; she'd already been asleep and I wished her goodnight tenderly – I'm not quite sure if it was weariness or repentance that made her sweet and compliant. I went back down to my own room, and began this letter before going to sleep. I'll finish it off tomorrow.

My love, I do so love your letters and feel you so much with me. But I still need so much to see your face again, and to see a host of the tenderest little *Erlebnisse* passing over it. I love you passionately this evening – and even with a strange assortment of passions, o little unreal one! That's because of the darkness, the Calvados and my fatigue. I find it pleasing, actually, so absurdly to rediscover that kind of anguish for you – o yourself, my absolute, my life – for you, my other self. Till tomorrow, my love.

I've had a note from the Boxers, with a little drawing by Lili representing the Boxer. It ends as follows: 'In the firm hope of seeing you again soon' – but he suggests times we might meet on 2 November exactly during my teaching hours (for I don't think we'll have any holiday).

Friday 27

My sweet little one. I went to bed yesterday night after writing to you and slept very badly – I was in an agitated state.

[. . .]

I'm going to call in at Gégé's, to see if there was a letter from you in the 5 o'clock mail – they're my daily bread and I can't do without them. I love you today without any welter of passions – sensibly, calmly and joyfully. But I'm beginning to chafe about Emma, since the moment when I'll know is drawing close – and I'm becoming aware that if the answer's no, I'll break down.

I need you, my love

Your charming Beaver

[Paris]

Saturday 28 October [1939]

My love

Here are three letters arriving together from you – dated the 23rd, 24th and 25th – I found them at the post office just now. How happy I am! The 25th is so recent – it's really pleasing to be having Wednesday's news already. One of the letters had been opened by the censors, but they were all lovely and intact, and so tender, my love – I'm very upset to think I saddened you by my own sadness. As I've said, that's over now; I've got back to work and I'm calm. Regarding Emma, I still don't know anything, which makes me very frustrated. And regarding your leave, I still feel no concrete joy; I don't really believe in it, and lose myself in the details of how to manage things practically. Won't it seem terribly shady if I vanish just before your leave? The best thing would be to say I'm going off to see you and will come back with you, because you've got only 5 days. I'm also wondering if I wouldn't prefer to see you for 6 days, then leave you to Wanda for 3 days and see you again for 2 days. I'd like to spend the last moments with you, and I'd find it painful to know you were still in Paris but that for me it was over.

I just wrote all this, and then suddenly it came to me – I understood: more or less, with difficulty or not, I shall see you, I shall see you, I'll fall asleep beside you, I'll wake up beside you, I'll walk through Paris holding your little arm and we'll talk for hours, and hours, and even what with school and your parents there'll be a long, long time for us. My dear love, I so want that, so need it! In a month I'll see you – at worst. I love you so, my sweet little one.

[...]

I love you. I'm on edge because of Emma, but I'm wild with happiness when I think that I'll see you for almost 8 full days. It's *almost* all the same to me that you'll be visiting your family, if it's really only from 12.30 till 3, since that will partly overlap with my teaching periods –

but all the same, if that could only be avoided! I'll go and fetch your civilian clothes.

Goodbye, my love, my life. I kiss you passionately, and love you boundlessly.

Your charming Beaver

Please send the books to Bost, even if you don't write to him.

[Paris]

Sunday 29th October [1939]

My love,

It's late and I ought to go to bed, but instead I'm going to write you a long letter. I have a frantic desire to speak to you, and such a strong and – alas! – vain desire to hear you answer me! I love you, o yourself! All day I've been beset by countless memories which wring my heart. I've seen again in my mind's eye a street in Pompeii, where we walked in bright sunlight; and a terrace in Tetouan, where you squeezed lemonade for me; and a dinner at the Louis XIV, where we talked about war; and a stopping-place in the Pyrenees, on the way up to Quillan, on a wet road. My sweet little one, each time I felt such an impulse towards you that my heart was bursting; but then it was checked there, unable to reach you, and the pain was terrible. I'm also beginning to imagine a room: I'm there, it's 11 in the morning – or 9 at night – and my heart's thumping; suddenly there's a knock at the door and you come in. I feel my breath cut short when I imagine that really happening – and perhaps it's going to be true. My love, I'm so overwhelmed by waiting. I want so very, very much to see you.

Yesterday evening after I'd written to you my sister came – it was about 6.30. We went and had dinner at the pancake house on Rue Pauline: as before, dumplings – which are delicious – and pancakes. Then we went to the Dôme. I'd brought your letters along in a bundle and began reading her long extracts. It was very enjoyable. It made almost two months of your life that I now rediscovered all in one go. I could remember almost everything, but all the same there were some details that stood out more clearly. I decided to buy a folder – but of a sophisticated type, with a kind of zip – and put all your letters into it, laid out nice and flat (since they all have the same format, except for one). That'll make a real little book. How I loved you, my beloved, rereading all that!* I cast a little glance over the intimate passages en route. My little support, my dear life – you haven't left me for an instant. How you've managed to stay with me! How precious and necessary that is to me!

We came home at about 10. I washed your little white garment, which I wear with love and on which everyone congratulates me. I wear violet-red accessories with it – scarf and turban – and it's very elegant. We washed, mended, did our nails, etc. and at 11.30 I went to bed – but some old hens in the next-door room talked for hours. I did sleep all the same, but badly.

At 8.30 I got up, went to pick my sister up from my grandmother's and put her jubilantly on the train. Wanda had loaded her with chocolate and cigarettes and she was in seventh heaven. When I left her, it was as though nails were being plucked from my hands and feet. I went to the post office, but there wasn't any letter from you – which was only to be expected, since Wednesday's had already arrived yesterday. I had a note from Bost – a letter, even, and a very nice one. However, calling in after that on Kos., I was foolish enough to glance at a letter from Bost that was lying around: it gave me a jolt to see how tender it was. I accept the idea abstractly – indeed he told me expressly he was involved to the hilt – but when I really feel that he loves her, I can no longer believe he loves me too. Once again – albeit in a paler version, and against a strange background of unreality and absurdity – I had the same impression I told you about last year: something you have to swallow down quickly, without really identifying the taste on the way; something you'll keep and brood over, but that you don't have time to turn over right away to extract all the venom, so that you keep it as it is, with all its menace. For I had to go on talking to Kos., without being able to think. I left her pretty hastily and went off to the Coupole where, thanks also to the rain and a headache, I had a sticky moment – a moment of sheer absurdity, disgust and indifference. I ate, then updated my journal. I remembered the pine-wood at Juan-les-Pins, and how you'd reasoned with me so sensibly one day when I had the [same] blues, and then I felt a great, clear, violent pain – so passionate that it bordered on happiness. It's still there, and since the hour's so late it makes me weep. My sweet little one, I'll never tell you enough what you are for me. You're my strength, my ethics, and all I have that's good. I see your face again so clearly at present, so affectionate and tender – my love – I see it.

[. . .]

This time I'm going to sleep. I think I'll sleep well, because I'm fagged out. I worked for only one hour this morning, but that's all right, it's moving. And now it'll proceed regularly. My beloved, I love you even more passionately than I thought. I didn't think I'd find your absence so harrowing, but I do. Not because I need anyone – I don't feel lonely or abandoned – but because I want *you*. O yourself, little being of flesh and blood with your little round-necked pullovers, your smiles, your two tender little arms – and your beautiful face, so rich, so pleasing, so loving, my love.

Your charming Beaver

* This time they really are little tears.

[Paris]

31 October 1939

SUCCESS EMMA HOPED FOR – DEFINITE ACCEPTANCE WEDNESDAY MORNING – BEAUVOIR

Telegram
Sartre Observation Post
Artillery Headquarters Zone 108

[A break in the correspondence occurs at this point, coinciding with the visit Simone de Beauvoir succeeded in making to Sartre, stationed at Brumath in Alsace. See the account of this visit in The Prime of Life, *pp. 412-21.]*

[Brumath, Alsace]

[1 November 1939]

Your pipe has been found safely at the Taverne du Cerf – it's waiting for you there.[182]

Envelope
Private Sartre

---

[182]Note sent by De Beauvoir to inform Sartre of her clandestine arrival in Brumath.

[Paris]

Monday 6 November [1939]

My love

I'm happy, my love. I think I'm going to be happy for a long while now. I love you, my sweet little one, and am all enfolded in your affection. There were five letters from you at the post office this morning and I read them with a passion of tenderness and joy. Sweet little face, dear little being, never have I cared so strongly or so joyfully for you.

I'll tell you everything. I left Emma[183] at 8 yesterday, but I stupidly forgot to leave her any money. I ran after her almost immediately, but she'd already vanished into the darkness – so I'll send it to her tomorrow morning. I entered a little station crowded with people – soldiers, and a few civilians laden with parcels. Like the village itself, it was a country station in wartime – but the war had utterly obliterated the countryside, in spite of the fine starry sky. There was an hour in a stopping train, then I got out at a big station to wait for the express. It was 9 o'clock and everything was dark. The train was leaving at midnight, so there were 3 hours to wait – and no refreshment bar, nothing but a gloomy waiting-room full of wooden tables and chairs hidden beneath packages and people: sad people, sad evacuees' packages – mattresses, chicken-coops, etc. An airforce officer took charge of me and led me out of the station. Through a glazed door, he got round a hotel waitress: since the hotels are no longer open after 9, it was a miracle we were allowed in. I drank a lemonade and began to write up my journal, sitting there opposite that ill-favoured, disagreeable fellow. But at 9.30 they threw us out. It was pitch dark outside, and we felt really hunted – nowhere to go except that horrible waiting-room. I read there, standing up, for almost an hour, after which I managed to get a chair. A noisome stove made the room dreadfully hot, while the stench of cheap cigars made it reek still more foully. But it made an intense impression on me, since all those people no longer seemed like some secondary aspect of war – a mere consequence of war – but were really war itself in person, presenting itself in a certain guise as true as any other. Precisely because it [is] imperceptible, I truly grasped how you can perceive it everywhere – like Gide's God. From my conversations with Emma I still retained that intense intellectual exultation I've described to you – I was happy. I stepped onto the platform swarming with soldiers and stood there like a stylite, upright and unfeeling, unaware of the passage of time so full was my inner life. A train pulled in and all the soldiers made a rush for it, so that not a seat was left. But they were just announcing another

---

[183]'Emma' here obviously means Sartre himself.

one behind it, so I waited for that. This time, just as I was entering a very comfortable compartment containing only four people – three soldiers and a burly civilian – one of the soldiers asked me: 'Are you on your own? You can come in here with us.' And he vacated a corner seat for me, and urged one of his pals to lean against the door and keep it shut – which he did. One, a burly Alsatian [. . .] told me to lie down and wrapped me in his cape, while the civilian took a plump pillow from his luggage which I placed beneath my head – I felt like a queen. They began to chat and pass round Alsatian *vieux marc*, so I opened one eye and they offered me almost half a tumbler – it was delicious, and contributed to plunging me into a state of deep bliss. The Alsatian was kind enough to say: 'Put your feet on my knees', and politely to add: 'May I take your shoes off?' 'Oh!', I told him, 'you can do what you like with my feet.' But a little later, as I slept, I felt him take me at my word and start squeezing my ankles with considerable tenderness – so I pulled my feet away and he didn't press the point. He'd told me with great gallantry at the outset, when I kept digging my heels into him: 'Don't worry, it's the first contact I've had with a woman for 12 weeks.' Through my sleep I heard their stories, always the same old thing: how Germans and Frenchmen go angling on opposite sides of the Rhine; how once, when a German machine-gun had fired a few shots, a sign had promptly been hoisted: 'French soldiers! That was just some clumsy fellow firing by mistake – we aren't firing at you.' They also spoke warmly about their officers – such as a certain captain who'd gone into a bar himself and bought a litre of wine for his men. And also of the terrible plight of those whose houses had been evacuated, in order to billet soldiers there. Even Alsatians don't respect these houses. One soldier, wanting to skin a rabbit, had apparently nailed it to the doors of a mirror wardrobe. That made a real impression on those peasants – the idea that you could hack a mirror wardrobe to bits. They declared softly that they didn't understand much about this war.

The train was late. I saw a fine, mild, golden day rise over the Marne – I think it must be an Indian summer. I dressed as best I could in the train lavatory, and as soon as we arrived jumped into a taxi which took me to C. Sée. The headmistress hadn't received my apology note, but she didn't reproach me. The other one got hers, so I can't understand what mistake I can have made in the address. Two hours of teaching, then a meeting in the staff room to discuss with the headmistress how to distribute woollen garments to the evacuees – I was livid. I went by taxi to Montparnasse, where I called in at the poste restante: 5 letters from you, 6 from Bost – the clerk gave me an understanding smile. I bore my huge packet off to the Versailles, and for the first time read

Bost's letters first. They set my mind at rest – he's truly charming, he loves me a great deal and tells me so very agreeably. My heart was filled with real affection for him, though no trace of passion remained, even regarding his leave. Anyway, I'll be the first one to see him and I'll go to pick him up at the station. I'll have to reckon with him in my plans, just as you so wisely told me. After that I read your letters and, my love, they made a far more agreeable impression on me than I was expecting. I rediscovered in them an echo of all your words of yesterday – rediscovered the living yourself – and am going to reread them when I go to bed. My sweet little one, my dear love! Then I went to have my hair washed – in a quarter of an hour – which it really did need. Then I went to meet Kos. at the hotel.

My love, it's 11 and I'm so tired – I want to sleep. I'll go on with this account tomorrow morning. I saw your mother all right, and Wanda – I'll tell you all about it. W. had her photo taken today, from which I deduce that she's going to start making applications. It caused me a touch of foolish displeasure, but only the faintest and that's over now. I love you, my sweet little one. I can see you again so clearly – I feel so close to you, so enfolded, so happy. You're my joy, and my strength, and my life, and my sweet little beloved husband – and the dearest of little beings – my love.

Your charming Beaver

[Paris]

Tuesday 7 November [1939]

My dear love

I'm a bit disappointed because I was hoping to work this evening and wait till tonight to write to you. But all those hours of teaching tired me out, I've a headache and am already sleepy – I can't work. I hope that this will change in the days to come. At all events, tomorrow I've a full day's work ahead of me, with a plan already drawn up – and I'm reckoning on it going well.

[...]

This morning I rose at 7 and went to the Mahieu. I wrote a little note to Bost before school, I hadn't even replied yesterday to all his nice letters. Then 1½ hours of teaching. On the way out Sorokine was waiting for me. She was sitting on a kind of little stairway near the church, bare-legged, with heavy shoes on her feet, a red ribbon in her lovely blonde hair, and the look of a tiny little girl who'd grown too fast. She was touching and pleasing, but her eyes were full of tears and for quite a while I couldn't get a word out of her. She'd had some dreadful scenes with her mother – who'd almost broken a brush over her head – and with her father, who'd terrorized her with his shouting. She didn't want to stay with her family any longer, she was sick of being called a parasite. They're really foul. She had just one measly 10 F. coin – earned from those lessons she gives – and her father appropriated it, calling her a frightful miser. Yet she does all her journeys in Paris on foot, so she can save up for her chemistry studies. I promised to pay for those studies next year – 200 F. a term – if she's still penniless. We went to the Source, where we talked and ate pork chops. I bought some books for you: I'll keep the Cassou[184] and the Ellery Queen for two or three days to read. You should know that *Carnets de Moleskine*[185] has been banned. The others haven't yet been published, not one of them – not even the Troyat – so you'll have to send me a new list. I sent off the Jules Romains volumes, and the money to my sister and to you. At the post office I met Jolibois,[186] who'd just been to see M.P. exactly as I'd just been to see Emma – we might easily have met yesterday morning at the station. He's bored, but well. I went to school: *3 hours* of teaching. On my way out I met two pupils from last year: Goetschel – from whom you read a disagreeable letter – and one of her friends. That gave me a little jolt, because it brought last year so vividly to life. I really liked that class, and my work at that time. Now my classes are a dreadful burden to me. The girls were quite devoid of interest, actually, so I took them for a tea at Les Vikings then quickly got rid of them. I came up here and worked for 1½ hours, but then Jolibois showed up – on the pretext of asking for your address. I was so cold that she didn't dare stay. Her relationship with M.P. seems to be becoming quite serious. I was upset, because you could hear desperate sobbing somewhere in the building and it seemed to come from Kos.'s room. A woman was crying out: 'It's not true! No, it's not true!' – and although I'd seen Kos.'s key downstairs, I imagined it was her and that she'd discovered all.[187] Imagined it without really believing it. Actually, it came from down below and was the hysterical woman – but I still felt quite upset by it. Now I'm writing to you, and between now and 8 I'm

---

[184]Jean Cassou, *Quarante-huit*, Paris 1939.
[185]First World War journal by Lucien Jacques, with a preface by Jean Giono.
[186]Simone Jolibois was a friend – and later the wife – of Maurice Merleau-Ponty.
[187]All about De Beauvoir's relationship with Bost, in other words.

going to write to my mother and the Boxer. Then I'll go out for a while with Kos. and tomorrow I'm hoping for a long, studious day.

Kos. has paid 400 F. to register. If I have to reimburse her, I'll just get through the month. If not, and if I live off 50 F. a day, allowing 300 F. for Bienenfeld's trip there'll be 400 F. left over. But 50 F. a day is tight, because when I take the Kos. sisters out it's me who pays. At the end of term I'll get my extra hours, which is just as well since I'll use that to pay my taxes. There you are, my love. Yesterday I was happy, I had wings, everything seemed wonderfully satisfying. This evening I'm a bit empty and dazed. But I know I'll regain that happiness once I feel better. My love, my dear little husband – how well I recall that Boeuf Noir inn[188] where we sat side by side talking, and all the tender things you said to me. That's with me always – it never leaves me. And you're constantly with me, and you speak to me, my sweet little one.

I love you passionately

The Beaver

[Paris]

Wednesday 8 November [1939]

My love

I'm really tired again this evening – but for good reasons. I had a studious day, as you'll see. If every day was like that, things would be perfect – that's because it was my day off.

[. . .]

I am on excellent terms with Kos. – she's studying Bergson diligently for several hours a day. She was flattered by my telling her your opinion about her theme for a story – but she's not working on it. Wanda seems to be seriously dreaming of going to see you. She has some idea of procuring false papers from some fellow of Arlette Ménard's – a crooked policeman – but I told Kos. to be sure and dissuade her from that. Perhaps he'll use his influence, though, to help her get real papers.

I learnt yesterday from Jolibois that Gibert's a teacher in Argentan, which can't be much fun. I asked Jolibois about it just so I could tell you, but then I forgot. I thought it was a bit indelicate of me to ask her

---

[188] At Brumath.

that, but she didn't seem too shocked.[189]

I've had a letter from a pupil whom I met for an hour last year, when Bienenfeld was ill – I don't know if you remember, but we found the letter she wrote at that time amusing. This time she wrote saying that she'd like some advice on her work, 'but I must confess, in all sincerity, that it is only in order to see you and hear you that I shall be coming. The only reason why I am trying my luck in this way is the great admiration I have for you.' I'll see her for half an hour, but really there aren't enough minutes in the day.

I'm expecting Bienenfeld tomorrow, although I haven't heard from her. I've sent her 200 F. I don't find the prospect enjoyable in the least, but I imagine I'll be glad once I see her.

Yesterday in bed I started the Ellery Queen, which seems less good than usual. You'll have it soon.

Now I'm off to bed and to sleep. I love you so much, my sweet little one. I think I'll have a letter from you tomorrow. As from today, I'm going back to waiting to see you again – since I can already feel your absence now. My dear love, you're so much richer than any memory. I can't replace you, even with the most violent passion – it's the flesh-and-blood you I need. But I'm not unhappy – I love you so much. As I fall asleep I'm going to reread all your latest little letters. Goodbye for now, my dear, dear love

Your charming Beaver

Le Dôme
[Paris]   Thursday 9 November [1939]
Dear little being

You'll get only a little note this evening, since I'm writing to you at Bienenfeld's side before leaving for Agnès Capri's place. I went dutifully to bed last night and rose at 8, so that I could work on my novel from 8.30 to 10. I went to school, and at 12.30 on my way out I spotted Bienenfeld in the hall, while Sorokine was waiting for me somewhere else. B. told me she'd return at 4 and I shouldn't stand Sorokine up, so I took S. by Métro to the Latin Quarter. [. . .] I walked down to the Mahieu, where I saw Lévy, Kanapa, Lamblin and Bienenfeld – whose cheeks began to tremble with emotion. I took her home with me – she

---

[189]Indelicate because of Merleau-Ponty's former passion for Colette Gibert (see note 27 above).

was in an indescribable (and frightful) state, nerves on edge and pathetic. She has given up any idea of going to see you, and indeed I dissuaded her from doing so. She's reckoning to come and settle in Paris, or at least hoping to do so, at the end of the month. That's going to complicate my life dreadfully, and when your leave comes it'll mean hiding twice over. I went to warn Kos. that I wasn't going out with her – she took it very well, and couldn't be sweeter. Apparently Delarue began by joining the officer-cadet squad – hoping to gain time – but now has found another arrangement which gains him still more, though leaving him as an ordinary soldier. He has written another letter, slightly less downcast – and at all events is going to write to you. Kanapa has passed his three exams, and Lévy his one. They're going to write to you too – they're furious that Geoffroy[190] has already done so.

We spent two hours in my room, then dressed to go out. My feelings for B. haven't altered since I talked to you about them, and those first hours did nothing to change them. But I think I'm going to enjoy myself a bit.

I hate writing to you like this. Tomorrow I'll save a little hour for myself, but I'm afraid it may be difficult. I'll divert her attention by getting her to read your novel.

Goodbye, my sweet little one. I'm hoping for a letter from you tomorrow, which I'll go off to pick up secretly. I love you – love you passionately.

Your charming Beaver

Chez les Vikings
29 and 31 Rue Vavin
[Paris]   Friday 10 November [1939]
Most dear little being

I received your letter this morning. I shan't file this one in the big yellow folder at school, I'll keep it in a secret pocket in my bag and I think I'll read it every day. I love you. I love you, and feel your love as strongly as I feel my own – we're as one. You can't imagine how calm and strong that makes me. I'm happy. Never, never, have I felt so fully merged with you and alone with you in the world.

Yesterday, after writing to you, we went to Agnès Capri's place. I've

---

[190]Another former pupil of Sartre at the Lycée Pasteur in Neuilly.

charged Bienenfeld with telling you all about that – it was very entertaining. Then we went back to the hotel and she slept in my room (without letting on to the Kos. sisters). We had a passionate night – the strength of that girl's passion is incredible. Sensually I was more involved than usual, with the vague, lousy idea (I think) that I should at least 'take advantage' of her body. There was a hint of depravity, that I can't quite put my finger on, but which I think was simply the absence of affection. It was the awareness of having a sensual pleasure without affection – something that has basically never happened to me. We slept well actually, and this morning went for breakfast to the Versailles, after which I went to pick up your letter. Then I went to meet Kos. at 11.30 at the Capoulade. She was in a corner, all of a pickle because she hadn't been able to find her lectures at the Sorbonne. Now that Bienenfeld has taken charge of me and is oppressing me, Kos. is taking on something of the attraction of forbidden fruit – and I found her seductive and charming. We had lunch at the bar in the Capoulade, and she told me little stories about Delarue, Tyssen, and Lexia – since she'd spent yesterday evening with Lexia, who'd told her lots of stuff. Apparently Delarue is impotent, or a virgin, according to a mysterious statement of Lexia's which basically corroborates what Gibert told us about him. It also seems that Dullin – according to what Tyssen told Lexia – had such 'scatological' (a term of Lexia's which I fear is merely the equivalent of 'obscene') relations with Tyssen that Lexia wasn't willing to repeat them. It also seems that Tyssen thought she was pregnant and put on a big show, begging L. to help her and saying: 'Help me, because I'm so little, I've no experience. Look at my poor little hands and my little feet, and my throat's so little I can't even swallow a pill, and I'm so pure in spite of everything, I'm just a little child!' – it was all so excessive that she seemed really crazy. Kos. recounted all this to me. I told her I wouldn't be able to see her because of Bienenfeld and she was absolutely sweet about it, in a way that didn't seem put on. She went along with me to school and we saw Sorokine, who was lying in wait for me but made off when she saw Kos. Kos. laughed, but I was annoyed – I'm really too much the quarry. 3 hours' teaching, then when I left I hid away in a little café to write a little note to Bost, to whom I didn't write yesterday. After that I came and met Bienenfeld at the Mahieu – and found her *suffocating*. When I told her that I'd see Kos. tomorrow for *1 hour*, she almost threw a fit. I couldn't have felt a stronger reaction against her, and for a few moments was rather harsh. She told me she'd been angry with me for spending money on Poupette, instead of bringing her several times to Paris; and also that she wanted to get me to drop school during her stay. She's filled with a frustrated craving that I perfectly understand – we've often talked about it – but that I find hateful when I'm the victim of it. She's no longer planning to go and see you. As for your leave, she's vague about it and I think you'll easily be able to postpone it from month to month until the next one. I think your first meeting with her will be an indefinite, frantic copulation. I was overwhelmed by her till about 6 in the evening; but then we went back to my room and talked reasonably, and I analysed her psychology to such good effect that she was overcome with admiration. It was well done – one of those synthetic views which you've told me I'm good at, and in which I explained the links in her case between self-importance, pathos and seriousness – and between being demanding and self-accusatory – based upon a kind of Platonic idea of the human condition with absolute happiness and a sense of her rights with respect to that ideal. Well, I can't repeat for you that whole character sketch, which I think correct and which she confirmed to me by lots of little confessions. She practises mental and manual masturbation all day long, and I explained to her that the latter may be all very well, but the former's disastrous. I worked away assiduously to persuade her as far as possible to accept a life without us, instead of rejecting it; to make her solitude into a strength and seek an emotional independence. She seemed convinced, but it won't be much use. If she comes back to Paris, it will be a real little cataclysm – a disaster for me. But talking about all that gave me a renewed interest in her, and she listened so docilely that she was really touching. All the same, when I dropped in on Kos. for a moment, to take her some notes,[191] and saw her there with Wanda – who was eating prunes and cheese – it was Bienenfeld who seemed like the former mistress and Kos. who held a new romance.

We went and had dinner at the Crêperie, and now we're writing at Les Vikings. My love, what you say about how, together, we could be anywhere at all – that's so true for me! Anywhere at all – there's only you in the whole world who count for me. This has to be taken in the fullest sense: neither people, nor places – nothing matters in the least to me. I'd restart a life with you by making a clean sweep of everything – Paris, money, everything – with joy. I need nothing but you and a bit of freedom. I love you. I'll see you again, you who are everything to me and who are also yourself, o littlest of all charms, little all-charm, little charm-all. I've retained your smiles and your dear expressions. And I'm so happy, because I've nothing to tell you about my love that you don't know as well as I do, my dear love.

Your charming Beaver

---

[191]Philosophy notes.

No more jealousy regarding Bienenfeld – that's quite dead. It's dead along with my *esteem* – it was that esteem which used to affect me (I still esteem her, of course, but not as an equal).

I enclose a letter from M.P.[192] which amused me – send it back so that I can answer him.

[Paris]

Saturday 11 November [1939]

Dear little being

I've had your two letters dated Tuesday and Wednesday – my love, they're so tender, you're such a support, I'm so serene when I think about you. I need that support and that serenity at present. First of all, I'm finding Bienenfeld indescribably burdensome, to the point where a shiver of annoyance sometimes escapes me, or there's a nuance in my voice, which then require explanations and correctives. For example, when she told me she wanted to come for ten days for your leave, and have you for 6 days to herself – or at least 5 – and on top of that make up threesomes, and then take you over on my own days while I'm at school, I argued in the abstract – since that's not going to happen – but I found that image of you being shunted to and fro between her and me unbearable. I said: 'Perhaps he should be left to catch his breath for an hour every now and then,' and she said: 'To do what?' She admitted to me that she couldn't understand how a person could ever wish for an hour of solitude. When I said that threesomes wouldn't be all that agreeable, during so short a time – and when I also said that it would, after all, be a sacrifice for me (willingly agreed to, I added, but a sacrifice nonetheless) to leave you to her for 5 days – she was extremely surprised. 'You've no sense for threesomes, any more!', she told me. So I spent the night with her – pretty much a rerun of the previous night, but less involving. This morning: school. On the way out Sorokine was waiting for me, charming as can be, having fled the paternal roof because she'd called her father a 'filthy bastard' – in response to insults that included calling her a 'filthy slut'. She came to ask me for advice and support, but I was scarcely able to give her either, since Bienenfeld was waiting for me in a little café, in order to go with me to the Latin Quarter – where I waited for Kos. at the Dupont. Half an hour's wait,

[192]Merleau-Ponty.

during which I was able to read a detective story – what a marvellous relief! Kos. arrived, as nice as ever. She told me lots of amusing stories about Arlette Ménard (Wanda must have told you them), and the end of the story of Tyssen's pregnancy. One day T. left her room and turned up in Lexia's, all little joyful airs and brandishing a sanitary towel spotted with blood. Lexia thought Tyssen was trying to insult her and was stirred to the depths of her little rosebud soul – she almost slapped her. Then she saw that Tyssen had placed the cloth in her lap and was showering it with morbid endearments, so she grew rather frightened – at the same time as being disgusted. Kos. went yesterday to her first lectures at the Sorbonne, and they made her a bit gloomy.* She missed them this morning, because of the air-raid warning which had prevented her from sleeping. On Tuesday she's starting her classes with Dullin at the Atelier again, which I think will change her life. I left her, had lunch with Bienenfeld, then went to pick up your letters. I did tell her I'd got some, but I post-dated them in the account I gave her – which in any case was very cursory. She didn't ask to see them anyway – I'd have refused. There were also two letters from Bost. He has written me a letter full of ardent affection and understanding, accusing himself of having fulminated against me for two days – I think it was because I'd announced I might visit him, which had annoyed him immensely. He didn't want me to come – yet I think he rather holds it against me that, once I'd said I would, I didn't in fact do so. It gave me pleasure in a way, since those were living, warm feelings; but it also annoyed me to think what a touchy little soul he was – and I'm still annoyed. Especially since I slept badly last night, and ahead of me I've 24 hours non-stop of seeing Bienenfeld. She's leaving at 6 tomorrow morning, and I'm waiting for that liberation with every fibre. I think there's something definitively broken, and I'm a bit frightened about what may ensue. But almost everything she says makes me bristle up. When I let slip yesterday evening that you'd read my diary, she fell into despair because I didn't have the same intimacy with her I had with you. Yet I'd never said things were on an equal footing, and obviously she should have understood the cases aren't the same. It took hours of reasoning to get her to accept that, and she remained somewhat bruised.

Wanda must have started writing to you again, I suppose. As I told you, she wanted to get false papers so she could go and see you. Also, she has asked me for your novel to read, and I've graciously given her it.

Kos. has seen Sorokine and seems to have taken to her greatly. I think it's sincere, actually – she sees her as a little girl presenting no danger. She's none too keen on Bienenfeld, but Wanda – who met her – said Bienenfeld appeared an 'elegant young lady'. Bienenfeld found Wanda ugly. It was only a brief encounter on the stairs – they didn't even say hello – and I was rather embarrassed.

My sweet little one, can you give me the exact address of Mme Pierre?[193] The name of the village where she is? Do you think she might put me up for one night – from Saturday to Sunday – if need be, or find me a room? Could she write me a letter of invitation, which I could produce? That would be perfect. Do this as soon as possible, please, in case Bost makes up his mind. He seems really to want to see me – ever since I went out there, so that he feels I'm closer than before to his present life. Thank you. Don't forget, please.

In a minute I'll go and shut myself in the lavatory to reread your letters in peace. Bienenfeld keeps telling me: 'Hurry up!' – she's tiresome. She loves you passionately, yet it's a struggle to make her write to you every day. 'Let's write short letters,' she says, while I plead: 'We mustn't neglect him, let's write long letters.' Goodbye, my dear love. Tomorrow evening it'll be over. Then, after that, I'll have a time full of work and peace – I can feel it and it makes me happy. I'll be all at one with you, all dutiful and happy. My beloved, you love me so dearly, and I love you so dearly. I kiss you all over your face, my dear life

Your charming Beaver

* Meyerson had given her an essay to write on resentment – which had delighted her.

Le Sélect
[Paris]

Sunday 12 November [1939]

My love

At last I can write to you at my leisure, which gives me fantastic pleasure. It's 6 o'clock and I've just put Bienenfeld on the train. I really liked her today, since she couldn't have been more rational and charming – and also because I was going to leave her, so it all seemed less burdensome. But yesterday there was a big scene. As I told you, I was very much on edge when I was writing to you – and she was too. We left the Dôme, and she began to reproach me for not wanting to leave you to her for 6 days during your leave. Flushing with anger, I

---

[193]Wife of Jean Pierre, one of Sartre's fellow soldiers, portrayed in the *War Diaries* as 'Paul'.

told her I couldn't understand how she envisaged our relations; that she seemed to see the threesome as an exact tripartite division, which astonished me. She told me she did indeed reckon in future to cut our lives into thirds – and, for example, during the holidays spend one month with me, one with you, and leave one month for us. I said she was mistaken – that things wouldn't be like that – and for a moment there was a real, sharp quarrel. I said if we were to proceed in that way, then the result of her arrival in my life would be that, instead of the three months I used to have with you, I'd be given one month of you, one of her, and one empty month – which really would be too injurious. She defended herself fiercely. We went up to my room, and she said she could see I loved her less than you. I said that I loved her just as much, but hád more need of you – and, when pressed, that if I had to go exclusively with one or other, I'd go with you. She sobbed, but then calmed down, and we continued the discussion in a gentler vein. I explained my life with you to her, and that those ten years hadn't been idyllic; that there'd been separations, difficulties of every kind, etc. (exaggerating enormously); and that though this didn't constitute a stock of happiness on which to rest, it had nevertheless 'situated' me differently from her with respect to you. That our relations (yours and mine) didn't have the youth and ardour of those we enjoyed with her; but that it was necessary precisely to make up for that by their duration. That I had many fewer years than she ahead of me in which to be happy – that I'd be old while she was still young. Lastly, that our situations of life and with respect to you were so different, that dividing our lives into three equal parts would be a false kind of justice. She was quite struck by these arguments. She also remembered that until August she'd seen the threesome as a base made up of you and me, with a projecting point that was her, rather than as something perfectly symmetrical. She acknowledged that she'd formerly had a respect for our relations which she has now lost. It cheered her up to think she'd actually been of my opinion.

All this was doubtless pretty harsh to tell her, and in cold blood I'd not have done so; but I'm glad I did, because she was in the process of taking us down too dangerous a path. She really could have reproached us, moreover, with not having made things clear. I spoke in my own name only, insisting what's more on the fact that *you* loved us both equally, and it was I alone who made a distinction – one not of feeling, actually, but of need, metaphysics and ethics. It was agreed that we wouldn't bother you with these disputes, and she won't mention them to you – so don't allude to them. But I did say I believed you also thought those ten years of life in common had given me rights over you of a kind no one else could have – that you thought you *owed* yourself to me first. Speak along the same lines when the opportunity arises, stressing that idea of 'being situated' which convinced her. She's amusing, actually, since she says things like the following: 'But I feel anguished precisely because you're older than I am – I must take advantage of you before you're too old!' And she wonders what'll become of her 'afterwards', when we're too old. She told me she loved us exactly the same, and wouldn't be able to choose between leaving one of us or the other. That you were gayer, more sensual, coarser, and with an indescribable character deriving from the fact that you're a male. In my case, it's more serious, purer, more religious. I explained to her at great length that she must theorize *her life* rather than us; that you and I theorized our lives, and if she adopted that viewpoint her life with us – allowing for all the restrictions I'd imposed – would perhaps strike her as less simply idyllic than she was hoping, but rich and beautiful for all that. She was convinced, and told me today that she found this new viewpoint rather hard, but seductive – because more complex. You can't imagine how relieved I am to have warned her like this. For she must be taken seriously, you know. She'll insist on every promise made to her being kept. But she no longer strikes me as dangerous in the way she was before. What's more, my relations with her seemed infinitely more genuine today, and have become quite precious to me again. I thought perhaps you'd rebuke me – and, to tell the truth, it was for no good reason but out of annoyance and agitation that I began that outburst. But, after this day spent with her, I'm satisfied. It has wrenched her abruptly out of her disordered fits and brought her back to reflection, good will and above all a sense of reality – and she was infinitely more engaging.

Yesterday from 7 to 10 we talked in my room, then ate at the Sélect and went to bed: a pathetic, passionate night. I felt quite sickened by passion – like foie gras, and poor quality into the bargain – and was afraid of today's day. Quite to the contrary, however, she was very pleasing. We rose late, had lunch at the Milk Bar, then went for a long walk to Montmartre. The weather was mild and melancholy. Lots of nightclubs are still partly open – from 7 p.m. to 11 p.m. – while lots of others are dead. We had a drink at Montmartre's red café, then strolled here, there and everywhere. The Maison Rouge lives on, but was empty – the Escadrille too. We talked about her work, her life, her future, and our relations – and I rediscovered a bit of that truth there used to be in our relations with her, and at the same time rediscovered a great deal of affection for her. Above all, there was something very touching about the way she thought she was going to undergo an intellectual reformation, down there in Rennes, and reflect upon the situation – also about all that diligence of hers. She was interested, and although she found what I told her pretty painful, she was glad to have a field of mental activity to which she could apply herself. I told her to be sure and write to me how it all worked out in her mind. We returned to Montparnasse, I put her on the train and now I'm writing to you. [. . .]

I've reread your two letters of yesterday at leisure, my beloved. I love you – and how strongly I feel your love! I'll get another tomorrow, perhaps two. Do let me know what you think about everything I tell you. Goodbye, my little beloved husband, most dear little being. I kiss you most passionately

Your charming Beaver

I've had a charming letter from That Lady, to whom I'll write tomorrow.

La Coupole
102 Bd du Montparnasse
[Paris]

Monday 13 November [1939]

My love

Here are two long letters from you – dated Thursday and Friday. I'm quite moved that you should speak to me so tenderly, and be so full of precautions and delicacy regarding Bienenfeld and Wanda. It's so charming of you, my love, to have included with your official letter a long note for my eyes only, and to have sought to forestall and disarm anything that might be disagreeable to me. I love you – we're as one. I'm so overwhelmed by your love that I feel an agonizing happiness within – you know, one of those moments of happiness that would make up for a whole year of gloom and tears. I have no words to tell you how much I love your little photo with the anemometer. I've never had such a good one. I looked at it after reading your first letter and was quite overcome by suddenly seeing that dear, lovely mug of yours after reading your tender words. I'm happy, my sweet little one.

As it happens, the letter arrived after Bienenfeld's departure, so I'll forward the little note for her along with her photo. As I've told you, she didn't ask to see your letters, and I post-dated them – verbally – which made perfect sense.

Yesterday, after writing to you from the Sélect, I went to the hotel to meet up with Kos. I felt vague, tired, sticky from those days of passion and at the same time touched by that last afternoon and the last images of Bienenfeld, which were charming. I wondered too how Kos. was going to greet me. She was extremely edgy for her part, with a strange expression: a determination not to be hostile, but with something resentful beneath her amiability – it was painful to see. We went to the Sélect and had a bite to eat while she told me animatedly about her life, and stories about Wanda that W. must have told you. And then her animation dwindled and I could feel her tensing up again. She learnt from the landlady of the hotel, who's an absolute blabbermouth, that Bienenfeld had slept at the hotel. She told me this in passing, but with annoyance in her voice. Apparently, the morning after that night of the air-raid warning – when Lexia too had slept at the hotel – the good lady gave Wanda a real earful, asking: 'What on earth are the four of you up to? There were visitors in every room!' (the 4 being Kos., Wanda, Arlette Ménard and I). Kos. added, in a voice tense with anger: 'It really is a bit much, Wanda getting an earful because of Lexia and Bienenfeld.' I let her finish her stories, then talked about Bienenfeld (transposing certain facts, since you weren't part of the picture) – but Kos. listened without the least sympathy and with a pretty frosty expression. We remained at the Sélect for a while in a glum state, then went out and she relaxed a bit. She told me she was in the dumps because, for several days, she hadn't written to Bost and she was afraid she wouldn't be able to start up again. 'He finds my letters cold,' she said, 'but I'm not thinking things about Bost all the time and I can't make them up.' And she asked me, with renewed trust: 'Can you imagine being able to maintain relations over 4 years with someone you see for 10 days a year? What becomes of it? There's nothing of it left.' – this with hostility not so much towards the war as towards Bost. But it's because he reproaches her that she's paralysed and resentful like that. All the same, here once again I felt a spurt of idiotic pleasure – and the pleasure's still persisting today. I like to think that Bost is safer in my hands than in Kos.'s, and that in his decent little life I really do have a role she'll never be capable of filling. What's more I found it all amusing, because I couldn't help wondering if it weren't by contrast with my letters – which are always long and full of observations regarding the war, Bost's life, etc. – that Bost found Kos.'s empty and cold.

[. . .]

This is the first day since the war began that – without external assistance – I've been immersed in the humdrum and the contingent, as happy as in the days of last year. That's thanks to you again, my love, to your love and your dear letters – thank you, my sweet little one. How I love your little photo! Do good work of your own at the Écrevisse.[194] I kiss you most passionately, my love.

Your charming Beaver

I must reproach you a bit for having quarrelled with the Cerf.

Wanda is thinking of going to see Emma, but she hasn't yet even got an identity card.

[Paris]

Tuesday 14 November [1939]

Most dear little being

I'm still really happy today. My love, it's incredible how much good you've done me. When I wake up – today, yesterday – I at once think with satisfaction how there's a whole day of life and work ahead of me, and I feel really joyful. That's thanks to you, my dear little one – because you're truly with me, and it's my life with you I'm still leading. I'm writing to you from the Mahieu. It's 11, and I've just given my lesson at H. IV, then written up my little diary. Those lessons are a bit of a bore: as I've told you, they took away twenty of my pupils and then, a week ago, gave me twenty others in exchange – there are only three left from the first batch – so everything has to be started over again. I get the old ones to explain things, and devise hundreds of new methods, but it's boring just the same.

I wrote to you from the Coupole, before and after eating a gorgeous pork chop with apple. From 11 till a quarter to 2, I did nothing except write to you and write up my journal, which I've brought almost up to date. Now I'll keep it dutifully, for at least half an hour every day, which will be much more enjoyable. After that I set off for school. The weather was misty, and everything was not so much gloomy as austere. You have the impression the world has grown poorer, so there's now just one thing for each place and one place for each thing, as in certain Populist streets in Berlin[195] – do you remember? – and yet it remains Paris with all its poetry. It's something like a poetical abstract, all immersed in grey and in autumn. I think that – like Roquentin[196] facing

---

[194]Brumath inn where Sartre used to go and write.
[195]See *The Prime of Life*, p.180, for De Beauvoir's visit to Berlin.
[196]In Sartre's *Nausea*.

the public park – you'd have to live through an entire 'wartime-afternoon-in-Paris-in-autumn', then you'd perhaps feel that very particular nature which I felt yesterday. In front of a leather-goods shop in Rue Vavin there stood a fellow in rags, gaunt, bearded, slightly deranged, who was returning from some kind of 'other world': he was neither outraged nor admiring – just pure, boundless astonishment. He talked to himself, glued his nose to the window and talked to the objects within, recoiled, came back. Once he tried to go off, only to come back, caught fast in the snare – and I too was in the snare as I watched him. And it was nothing less than astonishing to see that couple – the shop and the man – and for them to be able to exist together. Metaphysically astonishing, like the coexistence of non-communicating worlds. That gazing consciousness was one absolute, while the shop referred to an *other* absolute. And it was something so blatant as to be almost shocking – that plurality of absolutes. I crossed the Luxembourg. There are no leaves left on the trees, but the ground's still covered by a thick russet carpet. In a few days the soil will be bare too, and then it'll really be winter. After that, in Rue Soufflot, I had the strong impression of Paris in wartime that I've described to you. It was a day like those described by Rilke, but in the seriousness of war – simultaneously a halo of misty mystery and a hard glaze. It's much the same today, but less intense.

[. . .]

Goodbye, my love – I can't prevent myself from sacrificing my journal to these letters. I love you so much. I so love talking to you. I'll see you in 40 days at the latest – I'm happy. How I love that good old mug of yours in the little photo.

Your charming Beaver

[Paris]

Wednesday 15 November [1939]

My love

Something very pleasant has just happened to me: I've had a cheque for 5,000 F. from Gallimard, and he says the statement of your account has not yet been drawn up and I'll be sent any balance there may be. I'll send off 4,500 once I've got the cheque cashed – by old man Gerassi, probably – since it's crossed.[197] The remainder will help me get through

---

[197]Neither Sartre nor De Beauvoir had bank accounts of their own at this time.

this month, which is a bit tight, because of Bienenfeld, my trip, the Kos. registration fees and 200 F. worth of books I'll be sending you. I was quite upset to see how impatiently you were longing for books. Listen, I'm sending you Kos.'s *Shakespeare* without telling her. Read it without damaging it, then send it back to me in a month's time – or even earlier, if you read it fast – that will save me 200 F., which is not to be sneezed at. I'm also enclosing Cassou's *48*, and in a few days' time I'll send you a big parcel. I'll finish paying off the Bienenfelds out of my December salary, and use my extra hours to pay my taxes. Out of the December money, since I'm sending the Kos. sisters off on the 15th I'll only have to give them 1,000 F., so that even with Poupette's rent (350 F.), and the Atelier (250 F.), I'll have masses of money left over for trips, your leave, etc. Then in January I'll start the year without a single debt, which makes me really glad. I'll even be able to bring the Kos. sisters back to Paris as from the first of January.

My sweet little one, your Saturday letter – which I received yesterday – was quite melancholy, and it wrung my heart. My love, your existence is very austere – you're a true little stoic to keep that nice smiling mug in the photo. You know, as soon as I feel myself touched by melancholy, I take it out of my bag and gaze at it, and my happiness is restored. How gay and charming you are! – I love you forthwith.

Yesterday, just as I was finishing writing to you, I spotted Gibert – but she had nothing more to tell me. Then at midday Sorokine showed up, looking quite wild. I took her to the little Mirov restaurant where I'd been with Bienenfeld, and where for 11 F. you can eat quite good Russian food. She wouldn't eat a thing, and wouldn't speak either. I painfully dragged out of her that she'd gone back to live with her family, but wasn't speaking to her father. She's doing chemistry and finding it a bit too much for her. I think she was beside herself with jealousy because of 'my red-haired girl friend'. She walked with me across the Luxembourg as far as the Montparnasse Métro station – with me talking and her sulking. After she'd left me and I was going down the passage of the Métro, I heard her galloping at my heels and she planted herself in front of me, looking upset. I was late and said brusquely: 'What's the matter? I'm in a hurry.' Then she galloped off in the other direction, without answering. That's how she is, all little sudden spurts – of pride, or of affection. It's sometimes irritating at the time, but all in all it's pleasing. She's going to come along in a minute, so I'll tell you the sequel this evening.

[. . .]

Kos. rejoined me for lunch, since this evening she's going out on her own. She was resentful at the world, but charming with me – confiding in me regarding her resentment. She talked to me about Bost, to whom she hasn't written for a week. She complains that their correspondence is made up of monologues: Bost's letters irritate her, while he complains discreetly of her being too cold. This was her starting-point for a condemnation of relations via correspondence, and of absence, and even of all her relations with Bost since last year – saying that they existed in two different worlds and it was better to break everything off. I pleaded Bost's cause with total honesty, and entreated Kos. to search her heart and write. But, of course, I was also pleased – because their relations, and that mysterious correspondence, are at once depoeticized in my eyes.

I came back here to work for another 2 hours, then went to the post office to send you *Shakespeare* and pick up your letter. How tender it is, my love! How I love you! I'm waiting impatiently for the letter in which you'll pass judgement on my conduct with Bienenfeld. I'm ashamed to say I never ask myself: 'Have I done well?', merely: 'Will he think badly of me?' I've had a very downcast letter from Bienenfeld; however, by a strange defensive reflex, she's less worried about the definite things I said to her than by a vaguely intuited lack of confidence regarding the black notebook. I regret and don't regret. I think she'll accept it, and that it would have been wrong to let her continue down the path she'd embarked on.

I've sent tobacco, halva, ink-capsules – they must already have arrived. A. Ménard's stories are legion, my love, and not very amusing.[198] Perhaps it has to do with some night she spent in the jug after being in a clandestine club – but I can't throw much light on it. As for W.'s preparations, they barely exist other than in her little head, seeing that on Saturday she still didn't have her identity-card and I don't think she has got it since then. I'm going to take W. out with her sister one of these evenings, especially now that I'm allotting myself 300 F. extra.

That's all, my dear little one. It's 5.30 and Sorokine's about to arrive. Then I'll write heaps of letters: Bienenfeld, Bost, That Lady, mother, sister, etc. and at about 9 I'll go to the Gerassis'. I'll tell you all about that tomorrow. I thought I didn't have anything to tell you, but actually there has been quite a lot. My love, I think you must be pleased with me, since I'm happy and dutiful. I've never felt so violently that you loved me. I no longer read your letters without tears of happiness. How

---

[198]Wanda's friend Arlette Ménard appears in the *Lettres au Castor* as Arlette Jacquart.

I love you! – as you know, sweet little being. It's so strong, so warm, so happy! My love

Your charming Beaver

[Paris]

Thursday 16 November [1939]

Most dear little being

It's 7 and I'm at the Mahieu. I'm acquiring a certain affection for this place, which is comfortable and quite a laugh. Just now there was a very Latin Quarter group of old men, with white hair and heavy make-up, arguing over *Les Morticoles*[199] and the music of Massenet, and humming tunes in support of their views – it was all a bit much. My head's throbbing a bit, for I've been working almost non-stop – school, journal, novel – since 8.30 this morning. There's a good programme on at the Ursulines and I'm dying to go to the cinema, but I don't know if Kos. will want to.

My love, I got your Monday letter. There's a tiny hint of sadness about your letters now, which wrings my heart. I think it's your poor little tired eyes that pain me so, and a touch of resigned dejection in all that you recount. My beloved, I love you so. This morning, while dressing, I could see you again at the Boeuf Noir, talking to me about my jealousies with respect to Bost, and suddenly my eyes filled with tears – tears of love, with no sadness. It seems such a young, fresh love, my sweet little one, like our spring idylls: do you remember how, in springtime, we often take brand new honeymoons? It's like that, but far stronger and more serious. It's a fine success, my love, and you'll just have to resign yourself – you can't hope for any advance over that. It's perfect and there's nothing to be done about it.

Well, Sorokine showed up yesterday just as I was finishing my letter to you. She was all smiles and quite charming. She told me: 'Turn your back, don't look!' and when I turned round she'd pinned two funny little drawings on the wall, rather like those ones Kos. used to make. There's a skeleton in a transparent blue dress, with a monstrous Tartar's head and a bloody knife in its hand, which I find quite delightful. I asked her to explain her capricious behaviour of the previous evening, but she wouldn't and I didn't press her. We talked, we embraced, and I was full

---

[199]Satirical novel (1894) by Léon Daudet.

of tenderness – I really love those wild, tender ways of hers. What Bienenfeld doesn't understand, as I think I've already written to you, is that you have to take the other person into account even during an effusion of passion. You mustn't hand out passion to them like a slap. It must remain a gift made in order to be received, an expression of feeling, a gift granted to and intended for someone – rather than being a mere organic outburst. The Kos. sisters, on the other hand, reject the gift – which is also a none too agreeable form of egoism. Sorokine's just exactly as she should be, and that's one of the things about her that attract me.

[. . .]

I was at the Dôme by 8.30 and spent an hour writing up my diary, to which you've got me quite attached by taking an interest in it. I also wrote to my mother and my sister. Then I called in at the post office, and in the Métro read your letter and Bost's. In Bost's letter there was an absolutely charming photo of him, and this sudden appearance gave me the strangest jolt. He looks as if he has put on a bit of weight, he's smiling, and he's not really much to look at – but so alive, compared with the withered images that were all I had left! I don't know if I've told you, but I've noticed that when I get emotional about you, my emotion's all tension, fever and active agitation, whereas with Bost it turns at once to a sick feeling. Often passionate sentiments are superimposed on this and create a tension; but the first impulse is a kind of nauseous dread – which is what I felt this morning looking at his photo. I think it's because 'you and I are one', so if I'm afraid, or irritated, or nostalgic about you, it's like feeling that about part of myself. It's something that makes me dependent upon myself, and there's always the possibility of effective action, with a promise of success. Whereas Bost is a little independent island out there, and there's nothing to be done about him – so my emotion regarding him is impotent.

[. . .]

I've had a little note from Bienenfeld, deliriously affectionate because when I sent her your letter I added a very affectionate note of my own. She says everything's all right because I love her – I'm awfully pleased. If she could only not be too unhappy about what I said to her, while nevertheless holding it in her mind, that would be a success. I wrote her a long letter yesterday, sensible and passionate – I've high hopes.

I wasn't thinking precisely of Aristotle's eudaemonism in connection with her, for that consists in seeking man's happiness in the human condition, without any idea of rights. Whereas she seems to imagine an intelligible world in which absolute, ideal, total happiness is realized – and to consider she has rights to this. I don't understand her very well, since I've always wished for happiness but without thinking I had any right to it: thought of it as something constructed by me, rather than as manna fallen from on high. It would never have occurred to me to *complain* about my parents, for example. You had to win your happiness, as I saw it, amid conditions some of which were burdensome, others favourable. Whereas she waxes indignant at the least obstacle, as though it were an outrage. I told you how hard I found her with her mother and sister, for example. It's a kind of presumption, like her intellectual presumption. There's a right she claims to the truth – a naive belief in *her* thought – which goes together with her right to happiness and her sentimental illusions. It's just the opposite of the kind of humility I find in Bost, which so touches me when he refuses to wax indignant over his fate, and refuses to let one pity him. But that presumption of Bienenfeld's is actually just a shell, which is the most disagreeable thing. She's like the madman who thinks he's Charlemagne, but if you point out to him: 'You're a barber', he agrees tamely: 'I'm a barber.' In that sense, she's utterly lacking in pride or any kind of self-esteem. And that acceptance of humiliation – after an initial puffed-up presumptuousness – strikes me as terribly Jewish. I thought all this a few days ago – and I still think it – but I have touching images of her at present, and great affection for her.

This time – goodbye, my love – I'll post my letter tomorrow at 8, I can't face going down. I love you, my dear little one – you're right here with me. You've once again given me happiness and I am happy – altogether with you.

Here are lots of nice little French kisses all over your little face.

Your charming Beaver

[. . .]

[Paris]

Friday 17 November [1939]

Most dear little being

How it vexes me that your eyes should be so tired – do rest them. Does it tire you to read as well? Tomorrow I'll send you the two books, and Bost tells me he's sending *Moll Flanders* and *Dead Souls* – so you'll have enough to keep you busy. My sweet little one, you don't say if this leave business is making you sad. You're going to be shut away for ages in that little out-of-the-way place of yours! For my own part, it doesn't cast me too much into despair since in any case I'll be seeing Emma at Christmas. I'll almost be able to take better advantage of you like that – but it's not the same for you. Bost will probably come in December. In any case, I prefer your leaves not to coincide – it would actually risk being embarrassing, since no one would be really free in their movements, especially him. And in sentimental terms it would be so much benefit lost, since the pleasure of seeing him would be submerged in that of seeing you. But how nice of you to suggest it, little being! You're so sweet, my love. You know that, so far as I'm concerned, when I talk about 'spending 6 or 8 days' with you, I don't mean to place you under lock and key. I'd even once thought that we'd see lots of people, together – I'd like to see both Toulouse and That Lady, and whomsoever else you'd enjoy seeing. Thank you for Mme Pierre's address, but that sensitive fellow[200] doesn't want to see me there, so I won't be going – unless he changes his mind, which would amaze me.

I've had some letters from Bienenfeld which are truly affecting, because of the effort she's making not to make any more 'demands'. She writes to tell me that it's enough for her that we love her, and that she doesn't want to make any more comparisons or demands. I'm going to write her a tender letter. But when the issue arises again, I'll maintain my point of view. I think it has in fact now been hammered into her head, which considerably reduces the threat she represents for us. I too can see ahead, and imagine her demands two or three years from now. It's just as well for them to be limited in advance, and all you need to do – like me – is affirm your feelings passionately, but restrict your practical promises. You can actually put it all on my shoulders, if you like. There's no reason to be too concerned, actually. She won't have all that much opportunity to come to Paris to see you, in seven months' time, because of her family – and that blessed family will save you for a long while to come.

I'm dead tired this evening – though it's only 6.30. But I've got a tart and a Negro in the next-door room who were talking and laughing all night long, so I didn't get to sleep till 2. Then I got up at 7.30 to take Kos. to the Sorbonne, but Kos. stayed in bed – it's true that she was feeling sick. I went and worked for 3 hours at the Dôme, then went on to the Biarritz where I met Kanapa and Lévy – very friendly. I told them about my trip to Brumath, while eating an omelette and some pâté. Then

---

[200]Bost.

3 hours of teaching. Then I worked for almost 2 hours at the Mahieu. Kos. joined me there, on her way back from a lecture by Bayet. She's working beside me on *Creative Evolution*.[201] We're going to the cinema in a little while, and I'll have an early night.

Can you do me *a little historical account* – a concise one – *of the year that has just gone by, from the angle of the threats of war*, from September to September. Something very short, but quite precise – it's for my novel. I need dates, to within a month. Thank you very much – and do it for me at once, please, I'm terribly embarrassed by my ignorance.

I was so tired I had to stop even this letter. We took the Métro from St Michel to Barbès, then came down here to have dinner in the basement of the Dupont-Barbès, which isn't too disagreeable at all – it's almost empty, with benches in acid-yellow, and I dined extremely well. I'm just taking off a moment to finish my letter, before going to the cinema next door to see *The Return of the Cisco Kid:*[202] the posters are splendid and I'm counting on really enjoying myself.

I'm ashamed to have written such a poor letter, when I love you so much – but it'll be better tomorrow. Goodbye, my sweet little one, I kiss you most tenderly

Your charming Beaver

[Paris]

Saturday 18 November [1939]

My dear, dear love

How sweet your letters are! – they give me happiness for the whole day. You can't know what deep joy they bring me, to the point where I find myself as peaceful and contented as I've ever been. For my own part, I wrote poorly yesterday and this evening it's almost midnight and my head's throbbing. Tomorrow I'll write a really long letter, since I've got my whole Sunday to myself. For now, I want just to tell you about my life, since I absolutely must write to Bienenfeld before going to sleep.

So yesterday we went to the cinema. We saw – on purpose – the end of the Shirley Temple film called *Stowaway* – that brat is even more

---

[201]By Henri Bergson (1907).
[202](1939) Second in a series of Westerns starring Warner Baxter; it was directed by Herbert Leeds.

repellent than I'd imagined. Then a gloomy newsreel – in particular, Maurice Chevalier singing to an audience of soldiers – and then a good cowboy film, *The Return of the Cisco Kid* with Warner Baxter, which was marvellous. We made our way home. My neighbours were making as though to start talking again, but I gave them a good earful – after which they were silent as the grave. I slept well, but for barely 7½ hours, and woke up tired. Two hours of teaching. At the post office I got your letter and one from Bost, who's very good and sends a little note every day – he seems glum at present. He's sending you *Moll Flanders* and *Dead Souls*. Please send him *Barnaby Rudge*. I worked for an hour and a half at the Versailles, and finally shifted off Chap. 9 – the big chapter on the illness, with acceptance of the threesome – and began Chap. 10 on Elizabeth, which I'm enjoying. I want to show her during a fit of sincerity, in a black mood of the Renée Ballon type.[203]

[. . .]

Has Wanda written to you yet? Her silence coincided with her big evening out at the Hoggar, with the Lunar Woman and Ménard. They picked up three men who took them to Mme Feldmann's hotel in Rue Cujas, I think. They were Poles, and divinely handsome. Ménard took a room with one of them, and the Lunar Woman hesitated: 'Do you want me to stay with you?', she asked Wanda, 'I'm not so keen on the whole business, you know.' 'I don't want to make you suffer', Wanda said. So the Lunar Woman turned to the 3rd Pole and said: 'You mustn't lay a finger on that one, she's a real case' – so he spent the whole night caressing Wanda's hair. Wanda was anyway feeling dreadfully sick. In the morning, Wanda went to wake up first the Lunar Woman, then Ménard – who'd shamelessly slept with their fellows – in their beds. Wanda must have told you the story, but if not, mum's the word! – I don't want to play the telltale. I haven't seen her for ages. She has done an ugly portrait of Ménard, and started one of Lexia which seems very pleasing – but she works for only one hour every three days. We'll go out together one of these evenings.

I'm the proud owner of some splendid coral-and-gold earrings that Poupette has given me – they've been made into clips for me and look really lovely with the turban.

Wouldn't you rather send me the films to develop, instead of developing them yourself?

Tomorrow I'll send off the two books.

---

[203]Renée Ballon was a friend from De Beauvoir's Rouen days, portrayed in *The Prime of Life* (pp.167-79) as 'Louise Perron'.

Goodbye, my love, I'm dropping with fatigue. I love you, my dear little one, my life, my happiness, my little absolute. I kiss you more tenderly than ever.

Your charming Beaver

I'll do my best to see Nizan when he comes on leave — write and tell him to see me.

[Paris]

Sunday 19 November [1939]

Most dear little being

Here's your Thursday letter — the post's functioning regularly and fast now, which is agreeable. I don't regard Gibert as really mad (she never called by on Friday, so I haven't seen her again), but there's still more there than just playacting — there's some pathological 'crux'. As for Wanda, as I've told you she didn't write because she doubtless felt too shy to tell you the story of that night at the Hoggar. Has she written since then? You must have the *Shakespeare* by now, and I hope you're pleased with it. Send me the negatives of your photos, then, so that I can have them developed here — that'll be far better. Don't fail to send me a little outline history of the war (if I may make so bold) between September '38 and September '39. Thanks a lot.

Bienenfeld is writing me lots of touching little letters, to tell me that everything's all right since I love her, and that the problems she has to confront are serious but not alarming — so that's perfect.

Yesterday evening after writing to you I scribbled a note to Bost, but for Bienenfeld my strength failed me — I flopped into bed and took advantage of the clocks changing to sleep for 8½ hours. I'm driving myself pretty hard, as you can see — never lying in late, or going for an idle stroll — but that's how it has to be if I'm to combine novel, letters and diary simultaneously. The truth is that at this pace the novel has taken giant steps forward in the space of six days, and I'll grant myself a bit of respite later on. For the moment, it's all right like this and I'm even enjoying it.

[. . .]

Kos. and I had dinner after that at the Milk Bar, then went up to her room where we looked at a marvellous thing together — some 'Letters to Dead Soldiers' in a 1932 issue of *Europe*. These are letters that the post-office administration kept because the addressees were dead, and the selection's amazingly well done. There's a homosexual fixing an appointment with his little pal, whom he's paying lavishly: 'Above all, don't wash before coming', he tells him, 'I want to have you just as you are out there.' There's the story of a peasant who screws chickens (the winged variety[204]): 'I haven't been there to see what he does to them, but it utterly wrecks their rear ends.' And the story of a soldier's wife (it's his parents who are writing to him) who's totally under the influence of her maid: 'they walk about naked in the garden, kissing' – and they're slowly poisoning his daughter, who's dying. And heroic letters as well, and desperate ones – they're absolutely hilarious.

Now I'm going to sleep. Till tomorrow, my sweet little one. I'm still happy and as satisfied with myself as can be, because I'm working so well. I'd just like to read a bit more. I love you, my darling, and feel myself well loved. I kiss you with all my Beaver's might

Your charming Beaver

I've had the most touching, disarming letter from Bienenfeld, who tells me she's well on the way to becoming 'all right', and who does indeed seem to be quite perfect all these days. She's perhaps going to come back to Paris, and I'll be miraculously gentle with her.

[Paris]

Monday 20 November [1939]

Most dear little being

I'm at the Coupole, where I've just had lunch. I got your letter at 11. Every time I'm sure you won't be able to write me such a sweet letter as the day before, and every time it's still sweeter. My beloved, how I love you! You explain very well what it means to have someone as an absolute. Yes, it's exactly like that for me. A world in which you are – and in so far as you're in it and aware of it – cannot be condemned. I don't know why, precisely, but at this particular moment I'm pretty overwrought. Is it a modest glass of red wine? Or the story I've just read by St Exupéry?[205] Or both? Well, something has given way and I'm filled with what he calls 'tender sufferings'. I'm sending you the book, because although the fellow talks drivel when he's thinking abstractly and in

---

[204]Not quite translatable pun: in French *poule* can mean 'hen', 'fowl' or 'chick' – in the slang sense – or 'whore'.
[205]*Terre des Hommes* (Paris 1939), partly translated as *Wind, Sand and Stars* (London 1975).

general – for example, in the last chapter: 'The Men' – he did on two occasions grip me in the stories he tells. Perhaps it's because I read so little. But I really like 'In the Middle of the Desert'. That's where he explains something that I've felt – and still feel – very strongly: that 'tender sufferings are still riches'. He says of thirst: 'I no longer form saliva, but neither do I form the sweet images over which I might have groaned. The sun has dried up the well of tears.' Meditating upon this, images at once formed within me; and though they remained dry and lifeless, it was enough for me to recall that they'd been alive – and to measure the distance between the two.

After that, I abandoned my novel and I'm now writing to you, my little support, which calms me – for our love is resistant even to drought and far beyond all those sweet, vanishing images.

[. . .]

I can see perfectly well what I'm suffering from at present. Images have come back to me, but not sufficiently swollen with life to give me a real plentitude of heartbreak – merely enough for me to be amazed not to be heartbroken by them. It's not my disturbed peace I regret, but the violence of the suffering I do not feel.

(Some fellows next to me are eating coffee parfaits. On finishing their delicious meal, they say: 'I think it's immoral to dance' – for there's talk of reopening the dance-halls on Sundays – 'the soldiers out there aren't dancing, are they?' It reminds me of my grandmother refusing butter with her boiled egg, because the Good Lord would have added some if He'd wanted to, while at the same time sprinkling it with salt.)

It's now 6 p.m. I walked across the Luxembourg to school today, and couldn't have felt more sensitive. It was a fine grey-blue day, the sky blue but not clear, with masses of clouds and every so often a clear gap. Not a leaf left on the trees, or on the ground either. The weather almost muggy, albeit cold. I went along to the school and gave my lesson: that class at Henri IV looks a bit more promising than the other one. On my way out – while crossing that first dark, yellowing courtyard, which is so old and pleasing – I thought of yourself when you were a pupil there, and my heart was filled simultaneously with love-admiration and with love-affection for yourself. And then I sent you the books and came to the Mahieu, where I wrote for 2 hours. That makes another 3 hours of work today, even though it's one of the busiest days at school – which is pretty good. Sorokine was working dutifully in one corner at the Mahieu, but I merely greeted her – it's not her day. I'm going to do a little bit more work, then at 7 Kos. is coming and we'll go to the

Ursulines to see *The Petrified Forest* with Bette Davis. I'll tell you what the film's like tomorrow.

Goodbye, my dear little one. This letter's short on anecdotes, but my life's so peaceful! My heart bleeds for you somewhat, when I see how austere such days of clear conscience and work seem in the long run. And yet I've ten times as much distraction and variety as yourself. Goodbye, dear little beloved one. In two months' time you'll be in Paris and we'll career all over the place together. But I find it a bit painful to imagine for you – that brief break. My love, my dear little one, as soon as I've cashed the cheque I'll send a huge parcel of books, since that's all I can do for you. You seem all poetic and fragile to me this evening. All perfumed. And it's just as though I can feel you imprisoned inside yourself, which fills me with anguish. A little absolute has nothing to fear – but a perfumed little being suffers from eye-ache, boredom, regrets and the sullens, when the fancy takes him. I love you so, little being. I kiss your poor eyes, and the whole of your dear face, most passionately

Your charming Beaver

[Paris]

Tuesday 21 November [1939]

Most dear little being

Your Saturday letter brought tears of laughter to my eyes. It's a real little anthology item, that account of the medical inspection, along with your preamble. I'm glad you were pleased with the *Shakespeare* – but it's a secret, don't mention it, take good care of it and send it back as soon as possible. Send me the Romains volumes – and *48* once you've read it. Send me back *Spanish Testament* and St Exupéry too, otherwise I'd have to buy new copies.

[. . .]

At 4.30 I was at the post office, where I found your letter and three from Bost – one of them posted only on Sunday. He's outraged by Kos.'s behaviour: she has written to him at length, telling him how during that week of silence she'd hated him like in their first year, how she'd remembered all their most disagreeable moments, and how she'd wanted to break off their relations. He found that lousy, and asked for my advice – which I didn't refrain from giving him. At once he wrote me a letter that was almost passionate – tender and charming, at any rate. He'll not be coming after all until 1 February. I'd like that not to coincide with you but to come straight afterwards – since I too, my love, shall be pretty Goethean after seeing you for all that time.[206]

I think you've done the right thing with Bienenfeld, you know. The future isn't so black. If we affirm that we love her, she can accept everything. It's enough to signal clearly our intention to keep our own relations intact and not allow ourselves to be invaded, and she'll behave sensibly. All that's needed is a passionate tone in the moments we do give her. Moreover, she has her parents and will always have something or other on her hands, since she's an active soul.

[. . .]

There! I've been out with Kos., who was all sweetness and light. We merely went and had dinner at the Dôme, where I had sauerkraut in memory of you. I'd eaten a kind of Polish sauerkraut this morning too – which makes a lot for one day. Kos. told me that Dullin had been extraordinarily nice to her, and she was in seventh heaven. She talked to me again about Bost, with whom she has resumed relations by correspondence. She says this business has been a very good thing, because it has shaken up their routine and it was this routine that was hateful. I find that conception of things profoundly stupid, preoccupied as it is with surface appearances. Moreover, it'll all inevitably become routine again – then she'll need some fresh tempest. 'That makes three months I haven't set eyes on the fellow,' she told me resentfully.

Alas! my love, what a tedious letter – and I've nothing else to tell you. I'm working too hard, there are no adventures left in my day and scarcely any thoughts in my head. I'm going to write Bienenfeld a little note, read *The Idiot*, and go to sleep.

Till tomorrow, my dear little one. This letter has the sole merit of reflecting my life, which is like that, dry and featureless. I love you, o yourself, who know so well how to express your love for me, and whose day-to-day relations with me – for ten years now – have been ever sparkling fresh. O yourself, my daily bread, and my little sun, and my life, and my joy! I love you, my dear little one. I feel your affection strongly, oh! so strongly, as though you were folding me in your little arms – my dear love

Your charming Beaver

---

[206]In his letter of 17 November, Sartre had written that De Beauvoir's letters gave him: 'a kind of Goethean wisdom, which allows me to *attend* the various events in my life without taking part in them. With your letters, I'm Olympian at small cost, because I rediscover a world common to you and me which (whether there's war or peace) is *good*, like a turbulent novel that ends well.'

[Paris]

Wednesday 22 November [1939]

My love

I have the impression I've been sending you really short and lousy letters all these last days. But the fact is that absolutely nothing's happening to me, either outside or inside. Today I'm free as the wind, and am going to write for as long as I've anything to say. But there's still just the same void – my novel's consuming my time and my thoughts alike. How obliging you are, my dear little one! I've received the huge outline, and despite your admonitions I'll stick to that for the time being.[207] First, it conjures up for me a host of rich, precise memories. That year didn't glance off me entirely, after all – it's simply that what I needed above all were dates and specific facts. Anyway, I don't want to lose my momentum. When I get really sick of labouring away like an inventive ant, I'll take a week off and go into the matter more deeply – but later on. For the work I'm doing at present, your answers are quite sufficient. Thank you, my love, it's a whole little exam paper you've sent me.

[. . .]

Goodbye, my dear love. I'm living with a tranquil austerity that's not burdensome, because my eyes are fixed on the Christmas holidays. If that doesn't work out, it'll be a dreadful blow. But the chances are that it will work out.

I'm waiting impatiently for your next letter. Are you finding little *querencias*? Will you be as well fixed up as you were? Do tell me in as much detail as the censorship will allow.

Thank you again, dear little being. You've really put some work into it. I love you, my beloved. This morning before getting up I imagined for quite a while that you were beside me, and that when I opened my eyes I'd see your little morning face – without glasses, with your hair all tousled and your eyes all rosy, and with such a tender look. How I long really to see it! I kiss it most passionately, my love

Your charming Beaver

---

[207]Sartre had enclosed with his letter of 19 November an outline history of the past year (which has unfortunately not survived), but had also urged De Beauvoir to go and read the newspapers of the period at the Bibliothèque Nationale: 'I *exhort* you to inform yourself a bit; you can't just be satisfied with this [i.e. his outline].'

[Paris]

Thursday 23 November [1939]

My dear love

I've got your little Monday letter. It's a little one, but I'm glad because it tells me that you're happy – then I'm happy too. I've begun a new chapter, which I'm pleased with. It's a bit exhausting to work as I'm working now, because you have to invent all the time. But it's enjoyable too, and I think composing all in one go like this ought to provide a certain unity. And polishing it all up afterwards should be an absolute delight.

Yesterday, I did some more work after writing to you. As it was going well, I lingered at the Dôme until 10 to 5; then, just as I was passing through the door, I saw a little fury advancing towards me with a ferocious air – it was Sorokine, with whom I'd had an appointment in my room at a quarter to. She told me that I'd forgotten the appointment and was disgusting. That annoyed me, so as we reached my room I told her, if she was going to whine like that, she'd better leave. 'Good, I'm leaving', she said dully and went out of the door – but without closing it. I let her stew for a while to see what she'd do, but then I felt ashamed; so I opened the door and saw she'd just – ever so slowly – moved down a few steps. So I called her roughly back and she clambered up again, dragging her heels. I told her curtly to sit down opposite me for her lesson. I understood then – in miniature – those huge, reprehensible, but irresistible fits of rage which sometimes grip you in the face of weak, defenceless little individuals, and which come from the very annoyance one feels at not being able, or willing, to control oneself better. I experience that with Sorokine, and it's really shameful. She's not at all annoying, she's actually charming with her mysteries and her caprices – it's with myself that I'm annoyed. I gave her the lesson – an hour on the notion of substance, so she'll be able to understand Bréhier's lectures on the *Monadology*[208] – and after an hour she looked at the clock and said mysteriously that we 'wouldn't have time'. By an adroit and casual manoeuvre we went and sat on the bed, and I told her what I'd been doing – while her feet and legs shook with a nervous tremor, heightened by a kind of play-acting that was itself nervous. This too annoyed me, so I said – with a crudeness that I myself can't get over – 'Just hang on a moment!' I blushed for it – a Kos. would have left for ever. But she didn't bat an eyelid, merely calmed down, and after 5 min. I began kissing her. But we didn't have much time, so after 5 min. I let her go – whereupon she rolled herself into a ball on the bed, half in tears. I

---

[208] By Leibniz.

tried to console her, but as I didn't want to be late at the Opéra I eventually left her and got ready to go out. I took her with me – looking grim as death – and in the taxi tried to cajole her a bit, but to no avail. She left me in front of the Opéra and vanished into the night, her spirits as sombre as the night itself. To finish with her – I met up with her again this morning at 12.30, as on every Thursday, serene and charming, bringing me philosophical problems to solve and toffees. I had lunch with her in the quiet little blue brasserie in Rue Lecourbe where I'll take you some day. Then I took her by Métro to Sèvres, and from there on foot across the Luxembourg to the Latin Quarter. She confided her troubles to me sweetly – the chemistry, her parents, myself – but added that in my case it was still far better than nothing. I was tender as could be with her, and told her lots of little stories. From now on, we're going to separate the philosophy lesson from the kissing sessions – those kissing sessions in any case set her nerves dreadfully on edge, but she insists on them – and I don't want to go any further. It's a little problem. Have I told you that a pupil from some lycée or other is paying her for private lessons at 20 F. an hour, in order to have at least a pale reflection of my lectures? And also that the pupils at Molière used to call me 'the Beauvoir babe', which is disrespectful to say the least.

[. . .]

We got home and Kos. – who was dead tired – said goodnight at once. I couldn't be more delighted since I feel fresh in the evenings, even though I'm sleeping barely 8 hours and doing hard mental work. I finished off *The Idiot* and the last hundred pages are fantastic – so much so, that I think I'll send it off to you after all. Bost tells me he has sent you some books, so you're rich now.

As I was falling asleep, I heard a vague screeching through my earplugs and great bursts of laughter over my head. These inform me more surely than the sirens, since an air-raid warning's a festive occasion in this little world – an opportunity to get together in your nightshirts and jabber away noisily. I rammed my plugs in deeper and slept till morning. It seems you could hear the guns so clearly that lots of people went down to the shelters – but with my earplugs I no longer fear anything.

This morning I went to work at the Dôme. I really like Thursday mornings at present, from 8.30 to 10: they have the charm of a brief, threatened pleasure – seeing that I have school afterwards. I went to pick up my letters: a little one from you, which I read at the post office, and a long one from Bost which I read on the Métro. He seems to love me particularly just at the moment, and has a most agreeable way of saying so. He wonders what effect seeing me again will have on him – and so do I: it makes me feel quite queasy in advance. What's more, it's funny, but when you write: 'end of the war at Christmas', that makes me more scared than joyful. I don't believe it enough for joy to carry all before it, and there remains a vague fear of expecting too much from that return of life: a fear of myself faced by the happy event; a fear of craving, disappointment, tension – I don't know. In a sense, it's so comfortable being glum and hopeless.

Two hours of school. They've reopened the Vaugirard station, so I'm only 3 min. away from the Métro (to school). Then Sorokine – and then two hours at H. IV, where I had the class in stitches about magic. Then I bought myself some books, of which I was in sore need, with the library money – I'm still waiting for my 5,000 F. Then I worked at the Mahieu. And I'm still there – Kos. is going to meet me here.

I'm glad, because this time I've written you a long letter.

My love, I live in the certainty that I'm going to see you in a month's time. Perhaps I'll be disappointed, but for the moment that makes everything easy for me. My love, never, never, have I felt your love so intensely

Your charming Beaver

[Paris]

Friday 24 November [1939]

Most dear little being

Well, so I wrote you a long letter yesterday evening. It was just 7.30 when I'd finished – I was at the Mahieu and expecting Kos. precisely at that time. No Kos.! I wrote to Poupette, then wrote up my little journal at length – which I enjoyed doing. By the end I was getting twinges in my elbow, from having written for 2½ hours without drawing breath. For with the novel you have to wait for the phrases to come, but with the correspondence or the journal your hand's always lagging behind your thoughts. All that time on my own was like a real godsend, since with Kos. and Sorokine I always have a festive feeling when they deprive me of their presence for a while. I so like being alone, and above all I've such a plethora of pastimes I enjoy – like my journal, or reading. All the same, at 9 I was beginning to worry – and on such occasions the idea that 'she has found out something' comes to haunt me, and I have a dreadful feeling of impending disaster. Meanwhile, a fellow came along and offered me some little sets of folding images, which could be combined in such a way that Hitler's head could be attached to the bodies of a gorilla, a pig, or a hippopotamus, depending on the purchaser's taste. It's the first time I've seen that kind of patriotic vulgarity – and it doesn't seem to be having much success, actually. Meanwhile, in the washrooms at the Mahieu, an old woman peddling toiletries, filthy and toothless, prowled round me saying: 'It's pretty that little turban. Did you make it yourself? How many metres did it take? But you have to be young to wear that.' Meanwhile, Kos. still wasn't arriving.

Finally, at past 9, she showed up with a distraught air. She'd been trying to get some suitcases moved (the suitcases left behind last year at that hotel in Montmartre) and had been held up. And quite apart from that, ever since she has begun working at the Atelier again she has been like last year, in a perpetual frenzy. She'd worked all day learning to speak verse and, though she'd achieved some results, was nevertheless looking very drawn. At a singing class with Abondance, however, she'd had a success: she'd found she had such a big voice that she'd drowned out all the rest and Abondance had congratulated her warmly. I took her to have dinner at Mirov's, where you can eat well, undisturbed, and with excellent music. She explained to me that at the Atelier she was constantly 'on display' to other people, and I recalled the Kos. of last year – that constructed, arrogant, stupidly vain personage whom I detest. With me she's really touching, for even when she's all nerves, she strives to remain confiding, amiable, friendly. But then our moralism always supervenes – esteem has crumbled – and I view her like a spectacle. I think: 'she says that . . .', 'she thinks she feels that . . .', 'she claims to think that . . .' – and I no longer 'feel with' her, it's finished.

I've also had the following thought about my relations with her: that the strength of a relation with somebody comes from the fact that you indicate yourselves together in the future (to use Heidegger's vocabulary). But Kos. doesn't indicate herself in the future – or in so far as she does do so, she indicates herself alone. That's why, at best, you can say: 'at this moment I'm fine with her' – it remains something immanent. It's always Proust's passive idealism, in the sentimental domain. The connecting link: transcendence, future, activity of consciousness, reveals itself as profoundly true in the sentimental domain.

[. . .]

Goodbye, my dear little one – it's thanks to you that I'm happy. And if my happiness makes you blissful, that forms a judicious circle. I love you and am altogether with you. I kiss you with all my Beaver's might

Your charming Beaver

[. . .]

[Paris]

Saturday 25 November [1939]

Most dear little being

I've been happy today, happy because of your letters. First, this morning I received your Wednesday letter, which moved me very greatly. Dear little being, of course you should write whatever comes into your head, without any feeling of responsibility towards my expectations. The miraculous thing about your letters is that precisely I don't expect anything. I tell myself every time that the next letter you send me will be a bit more humdrum (as happens with me, I think), and if that were to occur I shouldn't be at all troubled – it would strike me as merely normal. But then, every time, the short and somewhat perfunctory letter I was quite reasonably expecting turns out to be for the next day: every time it's a long letter that arrives, rich and tender, to surprise me. But don't feel obliged to give me that surprise – please understand that. Follow your heart, but also your exhaustion and your mood. That's what I do myself.

So there was this very moving letter written at the Ecrevisse, and then Bienenfeld had the charming kindness (she's recovering those pleasing inspirations of old) to send me the letter you'd written her about our relations. And that touched me, my dear little one, even though you weren't being sincere with her. It touched me that you should speak of me like that. And it at once clothed your relations with herself – and herself – with a kind of authenticity in my eyes that had long been lost. Moreover, she enclosed it with a very sensible, ordinary letter that I'm sending you with my own. All in all, lies and truth correct one another admirably, and you and I have done good work. We just need to take a bit of trouble, and that little person will succeed in being happy without bothering us too much – don't you think?

I've also had a truly charming letter from Bost. He's quite inventive now in his tenderness, and graceful when he's being inventive, and my relations with him are worth more than those silly passionate jealousies. After I'd read your letter and his this morning, I felt fulfilled as no woman in the world can ever have been. But what overwhelms me most of all, my sweet little one, is to feel in your cold (as you claim) little self so many fresh, teeming little *Erlebnisse*. A plague on whited sepulchres, my love! – I won't speak of it again for a long while.

So I worked yesterday till 7 at that Cujas, where I happened to be: novel, journal, letters to Bienenfeld and Bost. That made more than 4 hours of novel in my day. Alas! my love, I shan't be able to show you anything when you come on leave – the draft's too muddled. Unless, that is, your approach makes me change my style of work, so that I finish a few chapters in January – but I don't think so. What I shall ask you to do is reread the whole beginning carefully in one go – it'll take you 3 or 4 hours – and give me general advice, then compare this with my own critical comments and discuss the whole thing at proper length. Simply writing this fills me to the brim with impatience and longing.

At 7 I went to the Mahieu. It was raining cats and dogs. At the Mahieu were Gégé and Gerassi, but not Stépha, who was confined to her bed because they'd spent too long and impassioned a night of poker. Gégé was in transports because Pardo's on holiday somewhere or other, and she's sleeping with Nogues every night – after which she'll pass back into Denonain's hands, after which she'll return to Pardo, with whom she's not getting on at all well. Gerassi was depressed about money matters; they're penniless and wondering what to do. They're thinking of leaving for America as housekeeper-and-butler: apparently it brings in 4,000 F. each per month, with board and lodging, at dollar rates – but it's not much fun. We chatted for a while in a tiny bar opposite the St Jacques church and I ate some pâté and some chocolate – since they didn't want to have dinner. Then we went to the Ursulines. We arrived in the middle of a film of which we saw the beginning later, and which is fantastic: *The Edge of the World*. It all takes place on a faraway island in the Orkneys, with cliffs and storms, and perilous climbs, and magnificent camera-shots. And then there was a film with Mae West, *Every Day's a Holiday*, which was incredibly funny – it's impossible not to take to that woman. We left the cinema and Gégé took a taxi to rush off and join Nogues, while I came back on foot with the Boubou.

[...]

I rose at 7.30, went to C. Sée, called in at the post office, and read my letters at the Versailles – with the joy I've told you of – then worked. I've begun the chapter from Gerbert's viewpoint, which I'm really enjoying. I made up Bost's parcel, ate at the Dôme while rereading your letters, then worked some more. At 5 Sorokine came to my room. She was terribly affectionate – all yielding and confiding. She asked me in a whisper if I kissed my Russian girl friend in the same way I kissed her.

I told her I didn't any longer. She told me she'd like to discuss all that with me. And then we did some philosophy – Descartes' *Meditations*. She's not at all stupid, she could be really good at philosophy – it's a pity.

[...]

I love you, little being. I'm moved by your love, it's a brand new happiness for me, it'll amaze me till the day I die that you should love me like this. My heart's content if, through my love, you can feel how you're all perfumed yourself. I kiss you, my dear little one, as if you were at my side, with your eyes all rosy with sleep, and we were falling asleep together.

Your charming Beaver

[Paris]

Tuesday 28 November [1939]

Most dear little being

This time, even in the evening mail there was no letter from you. No letter from Bost either – I'm feeling a bit abandoned. But not over much, since I know I'll get some tomorrow. I've just found out something rather annoying: my family's returning to Paris tomorrow evening. If it's only my parents that's all right, it'll even save me from having to go down to the Limousin. But I'm scared stiff that Poupette may be coming too and I'll be obliged to see her. I'll have to give her at least one evening a week, and even though it'll be an evening of movies or at the Opera I'm appalled at the prospect, since she won't be satisfied with that. Bienenfeld too is making threatening noises about coming back to Paris, and then – what a regiment of women on my poor hands! But I hope that since Poupette no longer has a studio in Paris – thanks to the clever furniture-storage arrangement – she'll hang on down there at least for a while. I've just had a card from my mother, saying my father has found a job (which is one comfort) and they're returning post haste.

Yesterday evening, we didn't go to the Poisson d'Or after all. There'd been some mix-up, and Wanda had an appointment with the Lunar Woman – and who knows what else? – so just Kos. and I went and had dinner at that little Restaurant Pagès. Then we went to sit in the front section of the Dôme, which was quite surprising and delightful. There are no brasiers but just the tables and chairs, which are widely spaced and where nobody was sitting anyway. The floor's covered by thick yellow matting the colour of horse manure – and the windows, of course, are shrouded in blue material. I don't know if you can picture what it looks like – something comfortable and temporary, like an encampment or the interior of a log-cabin – with its own quite particular charm. It was very well heated too. Kos, had a *Baudelaire* with her, which I leafed through in her company and was delighted by – partly thanks to the war, because like my memories the masterpieces of the human spirit now have a retrospective character, which makes them all perfumed and precious. They appear situated in a finite history and no longer immersed in an indefinite time. Moreover, there's no poet in the world quite like him and, if that's poetry, I like poetry. Often quite rhetorical – and with platitudinous lapses even in the best poems – but it's marvellous. Kos. was practising reciting a poem about a 'soft enchantress',[209] which is beautiful but has an almost obscene couplet in the middle which she finds too embarrassing; so she'd chosen one of the poems entitled 'Spleen' – the one beginning: 'I have memories and to spare for a thousand years of life' – and was reciting it as though it were a semi-madman speaking, part ironical but pretty nutty. It made a fine effect. I wonder what Dullin will think of it – I'll know in a little while and tell you all about it. It's interesting to see beautiful lines being worked on like that. It's the only way of exploring all the nuances and giving them their full weight – i.e. the usual old story of objects being enriched only through the variation of techniques, and through the wealth of uses to which they're put. In that sense, the performer's art is incredibly valuable.

[. . .]

Goodbye, my love. I feel odd without a letter, and stupidly anxious. But it must be just the mails. Tomorrow morning I'll rush to the post office. I love you, my dear little one, my darling, as strongly as ever. In less than a month, I'll be seeing you.

Your charming Beaver

I'm going to have 10 pupils for private lessons – 2 hrs a week, as a group. How much shall I ask for? 20 F. per head, per hour? That would make a splendid sum, but I don't quite dare. It's only till Christmas, but it'll make 8 hours at least. I'll pay all our debts.

---

[209]*Le Beau Navire*: only an extremely prudish sensibility could find anything obscene in this poem.

[Paris]

30 November [1939] – Thursday

My love

I've just bought you a huge bundle of books. I'll send half off tomorrow morning (there was such a queue at the post office that it discouraged me), and keep the other half for a week to read, then they'll go off too. I've had your letter of the 27th, and really enjoyed the story of the quarrel with Pierre. As for what you tell me about your mother, the funniest thing is that according to what she told me yesterday, Tante Marie probably won't send a thing and it's your mother who'll have to take care of the parcels.[210]

As for me, I called in at the post office after seeing her and doing a bit more work. I found a charming letter from Bost there, and have had two more today that have really cheered me up, especially since he explains how with Kos. he has always missed a certain spiritual kinship, complicity and deep commitment – and he agrees with lots of things I was saying to him about her. With me directly, moreover, he's really pleasing and affectionate – which delighted me. He has received my illegal parcel safely.

[. . .]

At half past midday Sorokine was waiting for me, all idyllic. We ate in the little brasserie near my school, then went by Métro and on foot to H. IV. She expounded to me all the reasons why she liked me so much, and handed me a long letter in which she asks me to talk to her about everything, tell her all about my life, force her to work – and hundreds of other things too. She makes demands all the time but does it with considerable grace, and I'm becoming more and more attached to her. School. Then I bought your books, and then called in at the post office: your letter and two from Bost, which I read at the Versailles. I came back here, then went to see the dressmaker again – I'm going to be beautiful. Wanda had just been seeing Mouloudji; she's going to put him in her room and move in with the Lunar Woman (they're going to live in some shared studios – something I fear may turn into an escapade). She and the Lunar Woman told me some 'marvellous stories' about a real tough guy, a lover of Youki's and friend of Mouloudji's, whom they'd just seen at the Dôme. The Lunar Woman was trying on

---

[210]In his letter of 27 November, Sartre had reported that his mother had asked him – on behalf of his aunt Marie Hirsch – for the names of 20 indigent soldiers to whom parcels could be sent. Sartre had managed to comply (despite the middle-class character of the HQ personnel), and had been very amused by his mother's subsequent request that he should write to *thank* his aunt.

an extremely lovely dress, but I saw her bosom – it's worse than anything I'd been led to expect.

There you are. I came back down here to write, it's 7.30 and I'm going to do some correspondence until Kos. arrives at about 9. All three of us are going out, and I'll enjoy seeing Wanda. I haven't done any work, but I was too tired in any case. I'll get down to it again tomorrow – since after a good night I'll be feeling fresh for sure.

Goodbye, my love. I'm annoyed not to know if you're leaving or not. I love you, my beloved. Every evening I think of the next day's letter and that justifies the coming day. I live only through you and for you, my sweet little one. I have a burning desire to see your little face again, to kiss it, and to squeeze you in my arms.

Your charming Beaver

[Paris]

Friday 1 December [1939]

Most dear little being

Another very sweet letter from you today. But how annoyed that Emma business makes me. In order to do things properly, I'll need to begin applying on the 10th and to have the papers by then. If the worst comes to the worst I'll do without them, but at least I need some specific information. That casts a shadow over my day. If it weren't for that I'd be blissful today – it's wonderfully agreeable to find oneself restored to good health and with a clear head. I still have my horrid spot, but I've resigned myself to that.

It upsets me that you should be getting agitated about Wanda.[211] What am I to tell you? No one has mentioned Blin to me again, but the fact is no one really tells me anything about her life these days. She certainly does often go to the Rhumerie Martiniquaise. She's absolutely not painting at all, and not drawing much either. She sees a bit of the Lunar Woman, a bit of Ménard too, and yesterday she met up with Mouloudji.* The soldier in Kos.'s room was a certain Jean-Paul, who lives in the building opposite. Wanda did once go dancing at his place with Ménard, but she despises him (he's a revolting fellow, a rich brat with a taste for orgies) and rags him scornfully. That's all I know. I went

---

[211]Sartre had been expressing growing alarm about Wanda's relations with Atelier actor Roger Blin.

out with her just yesterday evening, actually. Kos. didn't arrive till 9.30, so the three of us simply went to grab a bite at the Rotonde. Wanda was combed and powdered in the most charming way, and I really like her face; but her body's a bit terrifying – she had a white blouse on which made her look almost matronly. The dressmaker has made her a lovely black velvet coat, which suits her very well – but it didn't brighten her up. Kos., on the other hand, was bubbling over with stories about little fellows from the Atelier who flirt with her and malicious jokes of Vallon's at her and Lexia's expense, and with tedious stories about characters to be played. She really floored Dullin when she recited him those lines by Baudelaire. As for Dullin, apparently the other day he kissed Olga Keshelevich on the forehead – you know, that dark-haired girl we've often seen at the Dôme, and whom you've certainly heard about – and she exclaimed in ecstasy: 'Oh! how happy I am, Monsieur Dullin, you wicked thing, you!' The Atelier's going to reopen in January with *Richard III*, which gladdens my heart. Wanda talked a bit too – about Ménard's sexual encounters, and about Yuki's lover (the new one, who smashed in the face of Michel the tough guy), who's fantastic because he has ever so many affairs with women but only one real love in his life – and that's for his wife. Both Kos. sisters exclaimed over how splendid this was: a sentiment extending throughout a life and surviving despite any number of amorous adventures. I didn't know where to look, upon my word! But they oscillate in their view of things. At any rate, we conversed in friendly fashion and then went home to bed, Kos. swearing that next morning she'd be at the Sorbonne by 9. I fell asleep while reading a bit of Paul Morand – who's hardly readable any more, you know.[212] And this morning, as usual, at 8.30 Kos. was in her dressing-gown on the landing in a complete daze. I went to the Dôme and worked for two and a quarter hours. Then I called in at the post office to send you the books and pick up your letter. I felt just the same as you about Saint-Exupéry. It's not all that good, but it represents a radical change of scene, so that you feel strongly – so very, very strongly – the general possibility of another life for the human reality in general which each of us is. It's one of the rare books in a long while that has made me dream, and I felt touched that it should have had the same effect on you. After that I went by Métro to the Latin Quarter, to buy some books for my pupils and then have lunch at the Biarritz with Kanapa and Lévy. I have a sort of affection for them, because they

[212]Paul Morand (1888-1976), diplomat, poet and author of sardonic stories and novels depicting cosmopolitan life in interwar Europe, especially in its intellectual and worldly aspects.

represent 'last year' for me. Kanapa vaguely spoke of going winter-sporting with me. If I do go winter-sporting, I'd really enjoy it if he came too – but it was all very much up in the air. They told me that the little cinema had reopened, on Sunday afternoons. That delighted me, but it's stupid that it should be on the same day as the concert.

[. . .]

Goodbye, my love. I kiss and hug you. Little poetic one, little all-perfumed one, all-so-little perfumed one, little all-perfuming one! I love you, and so long to hold your little arm – I love you so much

Your charming Beaver

* The Lunar Woman, Wanda and Mouloudji are going to live together, with the three of them sharing two studios. Mouloudji was wanting to enlist, but the women have adopted him.

[Paris]

Saturday 2 December [1939]

Most dear little one

I think you'll be reassured regarding Wanda if I tell you that she's going back to spend the coming month at Laigle. I don't know how she has managed it, but the 600 F. I transmitted to her yesterday via her sister – intended to last until 15 December – weren't enough even to pay her debts, so she asked me for another 200 F., which I handed her this morning. Yet her rent should have been paid out of the November money. This annoyed me. If I can, I'll give them a bit more next term. But the fact is that Kos. gets by with it, even while paying the Atelier – and last month 200 F. in registration fees at the Sorbonne as well. It's true that I take her out, whereas nobody takes Wanda out – but she often pays her share on our outings, and with her Atelier expenses that must more or less balance out. At all events, that ought to allow Kos. to live just the tiniest bit more easily, which doesn't strike me as too unfair seeing that last year her existence was infinitely tighter than her sister's.

[. . .]

I arrived at the Dôme. I made a detailed plan, chapter by chapter, of the whole final part. There's action enough and to spare, but it's indispensable that there should be a real brutal murder at the end.

Without that, it's all in the realm of 'ideas' – an idea of murder, based on an idea of relations of consciousness. A real act is needed, so that everything can be realized. And that's causing me trouble technically – but I'll talk to you about that. Otherwise it all works out so well – the sleeping around with Gerbert and everything – that it might seem almost too necessary. I worked for over an hour, then ate and wrote this note. I'm just off to buy your photographic materials. Tomorrow, I'll have so many things to tell you that I shudder to think of it: evening with Wahl,[213] day at Toulouse's. I'll begin this very evening when I get back from Audry's place.

I'd like to begin making the arrangements regarding Emma's situation immediately after the 10th – on the 12th or 13th at the latest. But I need to have papers. Insist on her sending me them *as soon as possible*. I know it's a bit tight, but she should be able to manage it. If she gets down to it right away, I'll probably have them in time. I'd so like it to work out.

It's Lévy who had the idea all on his own to send you *Pylon* – at least I think so.[214] If I'd spoken to him about it, that would be very corny.

I've just come home and reread with pleasure all that I've done this term – it's turning out well. But what a labour to redraft all that! And there are still three huge chapters to do before getting to the third part, i.e. the declaration of war and the end. I'll tell you the plan in detail when I see you.

Goodbye, my love. Sorokine's arriving in half an hour, and I'll see her then go to Audry's. Tomorrow, when I get back from Toulouse's, I'll write you a long letter. I love you so much, my dear little one – I'm beginning to have a feverish longing to see you again. You stand at the end of these weeks like a warm little light towards which I'm running as hard as I can. But what a disappointment, if it's further away than I was hoping. My dear love, if it were only possible for me to kiss you in three weeks' time! I love you so passionately, I need you so much, my dear little one.

Your charming Beaver

I'm glad you like *Spanish Testament* – I too like the beginning in Malaga. Please send it to Bost, along with Saint-Exupéry and *Barnaby Rudge*. I haven't yet got your Romains volumes. My boil's beginning to

---

[213]Jean Wahl, French philosopher, influenced by Kierkegaard.
[214]By William Faulkner.

subside gently and is no longer painful. In three or four days the skin will be quite smooth again.

[Paris]

Sunday 3 December [1939]

My love

It's been like a little day without you today, since I wasn't able to collect your letter this morning – we left too early for Toulouse's. But I'll get two tomorrow, which gives me the impression of a real little appointment with you: 11 o'clock at the post office. It's only 9.30 p.m., yet I'm already dropping with sleep; but there are hundreds of things to tell you, so I'm going to write you a long letter all the same. My love, you should first know that I'm full of memories of you all these days – of you, and our life – and it seems so tender, it moves me to tears, and I'm quite overwhelmed to have known such happiness. For, in a sense, one can actually live very well without it. It's such a luxury that you'd never dream of even wishing for it, if you hadn't had it – and in fact you couldn't even invent it. As things are, though, it comes back to me in sudden spurts and I'm filled with longing to recover it. All the same, it's not too painful, because it's against a background of tranquil certainty: I'll recover you and everything else along with you.

Yesterday Sorokine came to see me: conversation interrupted by ardent kisses and philosophy. We went together, on foot and by Métro, as far as C. Audry's place. She's still relaxed and happy with me. She told me how she'd wanted to make my acquaintance from the start, and tenderly recalled a host of memories. I left her at quarter to 8 on Boulevard Exelmans, and went up to C. Audry's apartment. She was dressed all in black, with a little white bonnet and her hair in a net – looking rather good, but very much the officer's wife. She led me into the huge dining-cum-drawing room, which looks like a furniture repository and where Minder and Wahl were waiting. I hadn't remembered Wahl as quite that ugly, with his long, filthy hair. They were talking about a certain Landsberg, whom I don't know – a fellow from the *Esprit* group – who on Tuesday is giving a lecture on 'The Nation State'. The conversation was pretty desultory at first, but as soon as we'd sat down to table it livened up a bit. There was a delicious meal prepared by C. Audry, who's becoming more and more of a domesticated woman. Minder at once [adopted] a cordial, and almost intimate, tone with me, which rather surprised me after the other day. He'd loosened up, and was joking about being a linguistic hermaphrodite and talking quite a lot. I find he has a certain intellectual charm beneath his cool exterior, and every word he utters seems warranted – you feel there's something solid and clearcut behind it. Infinitely more than with Wahl, who's the floundering type. He (Wahl) had been at a meeting of the *N.R.F.* the previous day,* and had seen heaps of people there – including Aragon, in lieutenant's uniform, who'd been sequestered in one room because Thierry Maulnier was there and a meeting would inevitably have been ticklish.[215] Maulnier was in civvies for his part, and they did actually end up being brought face to face without any disaster. Aragon seems to be sticking to his position, claiming that there's indeed a civil war under way but not an external war. Malraux was there and wants to enlist with the Czechs; before judging Stalin, he's waiting for him to decide whether he's 'sovietizing' or 'protecting' Finland – the distinction's a pretty fine one. Apparently he said lots of things but Wahl didn't remember or understand any of them. That Wahl doesn't seem to take very easily to people. Benda was there, and Petitjean – about whom he'd nothing to say – and Chamson, who's clamouring for a real fight and claims the troops are all fretting at the bit. Wahl got them to give him proofs of *L'Imaginaire* – though it's not being published for another five months – and he has read the end, which he finds lyrical and superb. Apparently Gide's in the Midi, actively involved with refugees – it seems fated. Minder talked a bit about propaganda and showed us some leaflets, but it wasn't very interesting. He claims to have information that things are going pretty badly in Germany – but neither he, nor Wahl, nor the other people we were speaking of, could think of anything definite. Wahl was funny, taking the most hypocritical precautions before peddling little stories like one about searchlights or the one about Aragon's opinion on the war. C. Audry didn't say a word, despite the banality of the conversation. What amused me – since it's an experience I've almost never had – was the following. In the beginning, when I see people talk they strike me as 'serious', and situated on a level where my own thought isn't valid – or isn't good coin, at any rate. But then I realize that the tiniest idea of yours – or mine, or ours – which I advance creates an effect of bottomless profundity, taking pride of place in the conversation. There was an example yesterday, when they were asking if the present state should be called peace or war

---

[215]'Thierry Maulnier', pen name of Jacques Talagrand (1905-88), in the thirties a disciple of Charles Maurras and Action Française, later to become a member of the Académie Française and columnist for *Le Figaro* (in which he violently attacked Sartre during the Algerian War). Louis Aragon, the surrealist poet, was of course a line-toeing Communist.

and – basing myself on you – I spoke about developing a more flexible concept of war.

[. . .]

Goodbye, sweet little being. Till tomorrow, when I'll get some letters. I hope this one will have entertained you somewhat. I feel happy, my love, and so strong – because you exist. I'm going to see you: that's the background of all my thoughts, and the meaning of all these days. I love you, little dear being, so passionately and tenderly, tenderly

Your charming Beaver

*Paulhan comes to P. once a month for the Review.

[Paris]

Monday 4 December [1939]

My dear love

For quite a while now, I've been gazing round-eyed at your last two letters. Since I might just as well, I'll write to you about them. First, about Emma: I'm resigned in advance, but I'll try an approach to her parents anyway. That can't impair whatever I may be able to do later – and if I fail, too bad. I'll wait till 13 December to have all the cards in my hand,[216] as that should give time for them to reach me. If I do get them, I'll have a good chance of success despite everything. It's pretty thin, of course – but I'll try anyway. Next, the news of your possible return.[217] That would be absolutely wonderful! Even if you're at Béziers, that'll mean the Easter holidays and summer vacation are assured, plus two or three days we can spend together here and there. I'm saying nothing to the Kos. sisters, of course, and you mustn't say anything either to begin with. We have to arrange things between ourselves, so that everything's settled in our best interests. If my Christmas holidays are free, I'll go winter-sporting: either to Norden with C. Audry and Peltier, or to Megève with Kanapa – which I'd enjoy more. I'm writing to the Idéal-Sport[218] to find out whether it's open. But I don't want to go alone – with skiing, that's not possible. I'd prefer it even to visiting

---

[216]In other words, to know Sartre's exact address.
[217]Sartre for a time thought he was going to be transferred to the rear.
[218]The Chalet Idéal-Sport at Megève (Haute-Savoie).

That Lady, since I'll always be able to find time to go and say hello to her, after all.

[. . .]

I wrote to Bost, had a dismal dinner at my parents', then went to the Rotonde with Kos. I can't emphasize too strongly how nice that girl is with me. She was dreadfully nervous about Bost, but she now treats me as a partner in her nervousness, so she's all confiding and friendly. She told me lots of little stories about Lexia and the Atelier. She'd just seen Delarue, who'd graciously brought along the *Carnets de Moleskine* for you – I'll send them off later, as I'd like to have a look at them. We came home, it's now 11, and I'm off to bed to spend a quarter of an hour reading. I'm anxious about Bost too. He's certainly moved up to the front – no further doubt's possible. It's an anxiety buried deep within me – rather like an aching tooth, that's temporarily numb – as though I felt too lazy to think about him or revive my feelings and suffer. But it's not agreeable – and I sense that the first half-living little image of him will be painful. Simply while writing this, I've recalled his last letters – which were so tender – and it has brought tears to my eyes. I know perfectly well that, even out there, there's not much fighting – but it's none too reassuring all the same. My God, how I'd hate anything to happen to him! I don't think I'd get over that too quickly.

Goodbye, my love. I suddenly feel agitated, and would so like to have you with me – just at this moment – my dear little one, my love! Must I wait two months to see you? I kiss you, beloved little being, all over your little face.

Your charming Beaver

[Paris]

Tuesday 5 December [1939]

Most dear little being

I've at last had a short, sleepy note from yourself (whatever you may maintain about it). And I've accepted it without disappointment, just as I thought. But I didn't understand the mysterious reference to springs for rheumatic patients.[219] I wracked my brains in vain for quite a time.

---

[219]The village of Morsbronn where Sartre was about to be relocated had thermal springs, to which he had alluded in order to inform De Beauvoir about his new quarters without arousing the censors' suspicions.

I've had a note from Bost, saying that he's constantly being moved from one place to another, as he'll tell me in detail later. But he seemed extremely calm, which reassured me on the whole. To tell the truth, I have a craven need for tranquillity. I want to work, in the belief that you'll soon be sent to Orléans or Tours – I find tragedy a bore. All the same, I'd like a more explicit letter.

A wire from Bienenfeld, informing me that she's arriving on Thursday. That annoys me – I feel she might consult people in advance, instead of simply dropping on them like manna from heaven. I'd precisely written to her yesterday to wait until the 15th, since Kos. would then have left and it would have been better. As her father is coming on leave on the 15th, obviously she has to show up before that – but I'd still have liked to be warned earlier. I have certain appointments – for example, on Saturday with the Lunar Woman, whom I haven't seen for such ages – which it's rude to cancel. What's more, I think she'll be angry with my letter of yesterday. I'll send her a wire to say I'm expecting her on Thursday, but since in her letter she's already grumbling that I don't write to her enough, I foresee that there'll be a bit of friction even so. I'll do my best to be an angel, but once again I'm awaiting her with no pleasure, whereas I'd expected to feel some.

I've had a note from Merleau-Ponty, who'll be on leave on the 18th. I'll have a long evening out with him, which will be fun. On the 17th I'm going to see the Boxers. It seems Bienenfeld won't come to live in Paris this year in any case, so there's that comfort at least. Perhaps next term I might manage to have a bit of time to read, which I'd really enjoy.

[...]

Listen, little one, do put pressure on Emma to do everything she can, and then I'll do the same – I'd so like to see her! It doesn't matter there being no trains – that didn't stop Simone Jolibois in similar circumstances. If she'll just invite me to come down, in a letter I can show to my mother, they'll let me leave. Otherwise I'll go winter-sporting – I've already written to Megève.

Till tomorrow, my love. I'll write more properly. But it's really a dull day – not dismal, I'm never dismal, but dull. Why didn't you tell me to send some money sooner? I'll send some off without asking your opinion – I'm angry you should be eating nothing but sausage. Goodbye, little beloved. Send me some nice photos. I kiss you most tenderly, my love

Your charming Beaver

[Paris]

Wednesday 6 December [1939]

My love

I've just received your long letter of Sunday. I think I understand perfectly what ethic you mean — but I'd like to talk to you about it.

[. . .]

So, after leaving you yesterday evening, I went to meet Kos. downstairs at the Dupont. There was another wire from Bienenfeld, which depressed me. She's coming on Thursday for 4 days, and her mother's allowing her to attend lectures at the Sorbonne — which means she'll be coming every week. Seeing her one evening a week wouldn't bother me, but she's bound to be terribly demanding. I'm going to talk to Kos. about it in a minute, and that's bothering me.

[. . .]

My handwriting's so bad because I'm writing too much. Also, I never have enough time for everything I want to tell you — so I write flat out. Bost complains bitterly about not being able to decipher a thing. I'll make a bit of an effort.

You know, my love, I think it's a bit difficult for me to tell your mother you won't be sleeping at her place — it's better you do that.

I've finally got the joke about the rheumatic patients — but it was really hard.

I worked at the Dôme, then Kos. asked if she could bring Mouloudji along to lunch with us — at her expense. I accepted and we went to the Rotonde, where we had salt pork with red beans — delicious! It was lucky Bost had admitted he'd been to Marseilles,[220] since Mouloudji came right out with the fact that he'd seen him, in a way that left no possible doubt. He's really agreeable — even more so than last year — and I found him delightful.

I arrived home to find an extremely affectionate note from Merleau-Ponty, who says he'll be most happy during his leave to see me for a long day 'in the same way that people see each other on a boat or a walking-trip'. I've also had a letter from Bienenfeld, very sweet, saying that she won't be demanding and will let me keep all my appointments. At once, I'm glad to be seeing her. I spoke about her to Kos., who took

---

[220]In July 1939, having a period of leave during his military service, Bost had visited Marseilles and met up with De Beauvoir and Sartre (see *The Prime of Life*, p.372), but had hesitated before telling Olga.

it with nobility of soul: that girl has become a veritable angel.

I'm finishing off quickly since at 6 I'm expecting Sorokine, with whom I'm going to *The Damnation of Faust*.[221] I'll tell you about that tomorrow.

Goodbye, my dear little one. How sweet your letters are, and what savour they impart to my life! In my own, it always seems to me that I'm unable to tell you sufficiently how I love you, and all that you are for me. O my love, how I long to see you! I'm beginning to be in agonies. I love you, my sweet little one

Your charming Beaver

Are we going to tell Bienenfeld I'm returning to see Emma again? Concealing, of course, how I persuaded her.

[Paris]

Thursday 7 December [1939]

My love

This morning I had your Monday letter, which once again filled me to overflowing with love for you. I'm glad you've finally received the books and that you're pleased with them. I'm longing to know how you're going to be billeted, and what resources you'll have there. Also, whether you'll find some friendly laundress[222] – that's so important.

Well, Sorokine arrived at 6 yesterday and, by sundry signs of nervousness, made clear to me that we should get down to kissing right away – which was done. After that, we went and caught the A.F. at Montparnasse – having first bought some cakes, bananas and dates. We ensconced ourselves in a little café next to the Opéra, and I told her lots of stories – she was in seventh heaven. Then we took two seats at the back of a ground-floor box and listened to *The Damnation of Faust*. You know its merits – there are some very agreeable bits. The singing was lifeless and the production absurd, but I still enjoyed hearing it from beginning to end. Sorokine was clasping my hands and kissing me in the dark. She was really happy, and her happiness and affection made her quite beautiful. She's unlucky to have come into my life so late – I could have cared a great deal for her. We stayed till the last interval,

---

[221]By Hector Berlioz.
[222]Who would agree to rent a room if De Beauvoir was able to make a visit, or for Sartre to work in.

when – on perceiving to our astonishment that while the orchestra was playing *Invitation to the Waltz*, the curtain was rising upon a Louis XV salon – we fled into the night. We had a lot of trouble finding a café willing to serve us, because it was almost 11. After that, we circled for a further 10 minutes round our Métro stations. She said she loved me ever so much more than her girl-friend, and recounted to me all her happy and unhappy memories concerning her relations with me. She's pleased at the thought that we've made so much progress in 3 months. I said: 'Yes, things couldn't be better than they are now.' But she protested vigorously, considering on the contrary that lots of improvements could still be made. Here, I think she'll be disappointed. She howled like a banshee, of course, when I finally went down to my Métro, so that we almost parted in anger. However, at 12.30 this morning she was all smiles – bringing me a chocolate treat, and paying me hundreds of other little attentions. Whatever shall I do with her? I really don't know. I've warned her that all this is exceptional, and after the war I'll have much less to give her; but I've also told her I'll never drop her. All the same, I'm not worried. I *know* I'm going to work and to see you – the rest will always fall into place. Arriving home, I fell asleep at once and carried on till past 8 this morning. I went to the post office, then to the Versailles to read your letter. I did an hour's work. Since yesterday, I've been revising the novel from the beginning. I've had enough of inventing drafts; everything's in place now and I want to write some definitive stuff. I'm enjoying it enormously, and it seems terribly – quite seductively – easy. I went to school, had lunch with Sorokine, then Henri IV, then I came home and am writing to you while waiting – neither joyfully nor sullenly – for Bienenfeld, who's arriving at about 5.30. So I'm reading those gloomy *Carnets de Moleskine* – which are quite good, really.

Goodbye, my dear little one – tomorrow I'll tell you in detail all about Bienenfeld. She'll be less oppressive than last time. I still have no news of Bost.

Till tomorrow, my love. I do so, so long to see you without delay. I'm living in impatience and uncertainty these days, and wholly focused upon this uncertain Christmas. I love you, my little one – with a tender, tender love, young and fresh and even a little moist. I kiss you, most passionately.

Your charming Beaver

[Paris]

Friday 8 December 1939]

Most dear little being

So you're a switchboard operator now? I laughed at the thought of you in front of your infernal machine, like the fat woman outside the washrooms at the Dôme. But I do hope it won't take up too much of your time, my luckless pet. I'm waiting impatiently for tomorrow's letter, which will tell me the whole story – and also perhaps tell me where things have got to with the Emma business.

Yesterday, as I waited for Bienenfeld and the dressmaker, it was the Lunar Woman who turned up – she'd come to see the dressmaker. She told me her husband had written to me, which astonished me, but I haven't actually received the letter. She also told me she was delighted to be going out with me on Saturday and would put on her beautiful dress. And she added with a smile: 'Just for the sake of it – I still feel all dolled up in my Sunday best when I wear it.' You probably know about Wanda helping her compose a letter to her lover, the Pole. The lover was so moved by it that he came back to her, telling her she was wonderful. We chatted like this for a while. No dressmaker. But Bienenfeld did turn up, disconcerted in the first flush of her passion by the Lunar Woman's presence. The three of us conducted a proper, worldly conversation. The Lunar Woman said she was anti-semitic in general, but not in particular – which really made Bienenfeld laugh. In the end, I left the Lunar Woman in my room to wait for the dressmaker (who never turned up actually), while I went off with Bienenfeld. We went to the Coupole, where I stuffed myself like a pig. But there was a modestly-dressed fellow next to us who was stuffing himself far more shamefully. He ordered good wine, red caviar, and a truffle cooked in the embers – which is a really splendid dish. They bring you a big buttered-paper package, covered with embers; you pierce the paper, and take out a splendid little puff pastry; you open the pastry, and inside you find an enormous truffle. He ate it with an air of calm restraint. After that we went to Les Vikings for a glass of akvavit – it was altogether deserted. My feelings for Bienenfeld were quite tender, but as so often it was all gentle to the point almost of boredom, against a background of benevolence and esteem. She's probably going to come back to Paris, but that doesn't dismay me. I'll give her two evenings a week, taken from Kos. who'll still have 5 – she doesn't ask for more, plus an hour gleaned here and there. It makes no difference. We chatted – about her work and her life – and she was charming. I could feel the charm in the object, but without warmth in myself. Yet, you see, it's quite different from the other time, since there's affection and friendship this time, and moral approval. I at once recovered the normal tone of our physical relations: easy and limpid like rock water. We anyway skimped the embraces rather, leaving more time for sleep.

[. . .]

After that I went to school, and I'll tell you the rest tomorrow. I'm with Bienenfeld and don't have time now. Till tomorrow, when I'll have further entertaining things to write to you about. I love you, my sweet little one.

Your charming Beaver

Le Dôme

Paris, Sunday 10 December [1939]

Most dear little being

I've hundreds of little stories to tell you, but I don't know if I'll have time, since I'm expecting Kos. at any moment. I'll start anyway, and tomorrow I'll be able to write a long letter at my leisure.

[. . .]

After leaving [the Opéra-Comique] we kept to the boulevards, and Bienenfeld confessed to being upset, because she'd read a little note I'd written to Kos. – but never sent – and found it tender. It had struck her, above all, as something concrete. I explained carefully how things like that are always concrete, saying she was too straightforward and needed to see things in their complexity – and we talked rationally and agreeably about love, jealousy, freedom, etc.

[. . .]

My love, I can really feel how your life is, at the Hôtel Bellevue.[223] You describe it so well, and I can feel how it's like a strange kind of nature. I'm sad today, which is the first time for ages. It's not a matter of being gloomy or anything, but precisely sadness – because of the Christmas holidays, because I'm losing hope. I'm scared of going really crazy once that's definitely lost.

Following my conversations with Bienenfeld, I've started an investigation regarding men's opinion of me physically. For normally it's only women who find me pretty. Kanapa thinks I'm good-looking, but not

---

[223] At Morsbronn.

the pretty kind. Lévy, on the other hand, thinks I'm pretty and even quite beautiful. The Lunar Man thinks I'm very good-looking. I've seen a hilarious letter from him, in which he tells his wife he's going to write to Poupette and to me, seeing that upon reflection he has concluded he basically doesn't know us well at all. I've recovered my warm feelings for Bienenfeld, in a calm way – but they've always been like that.

Goodbye, my sweet little one. Tomorrow I'll write you a nice letter. I miss you, my love, and have such a need to see you. Solitude may well be of benefit to me, but how hard your absence is for me! I long for your little face, your voice, your gestures, and your tenderness. I'm quite melting with tenderness for you today – and it's painful. My love, I don't know what I'd give to see you. I kiss you passionately, little beloved.

Your charming Beaver

Since Kos. isn't arriving, I'll begin my story. You can reread the beginning along with tomorrow's letter to make a whole, since it was entertaining.

The Lunar Woman turned up at the Dôme, truly splendid – with a fur-lined coat, the most beautiful brown moleskin hat that suits her to perfection, a shoulder-bag, and an extremely modish umbrella. Wondering where to go, we chose La Villa – you know, on the corner of Rue Vavin, one of the few nightclubs we've never been into. It's comical, a bit like a provincial dancehall – and, in particular, like the Royal at Rouen: same shoddy decor, poor band, hostesses in worn satin. The Lunar Woman ate a cold platter, and we drank a bottle of Chablis between us. We chatted, while the hostesses dressed themselves up as chorus-girls and came out to do little turns on the dance-floor. People were dancing, moreover, which greatly surprised us – but it was only yesterday the dancehalls reopened. The chorus-girls were atrocious. They turned up first in Eton collars, with short, pleated skirts, tartan bows in their hair and tartan collars, leaving just their breasts bare as in certain Chinese sculptures – isolated in this way they had the look of unwholesome excrescences. The Lunar Woman studied them with interest, since she's interested in women just now, and particularly appreciated those that were really large and heavy. After that, they came on disguised as Polish, English, etc. soldiers, to the strains of the Madelon,[224] and it was just like a bad parody of some music-hall in

---

[224]Madelon (Quand): popular French soldiers' song from World War I.

1917. After that they made further costume changes – but it was always just as wretched. The one pleasing thing was that at about 1.30 the cops turned up – with their fine gleaming helmets and torches strapped to their chests – and mingled with all those satins, and that music, and those glittering officers (for there were some), and asked people for their papers. That made it like a real wartime evening – it was powerful stuff.

At first the conversation was rather glum, since the Lunar Woman subsequently confessed she'd come along with no desire to tell me any of her stories – having the idea that relations between us had soured – but little by little I got her talking and she told me some marvellous ones. Just imagine, the other evening at Youki's there was another session of the same kind as that one I attended. Everybody left gradually, leaving Blanche Picard (that former actress from the Atelier with the dark, passionate soul who hates Kos. and Toulouse, and whom people used to call hysterical because she no longer screwed around), whom they sent to bed; Youki; her latest pimp Pierre, whom the Lunar Woman and Wanda admire, and who whenever he sleeps with a woman binds her hands behind her back; and the Lunar Woman herself. She wanted to leave, but Youki made her stay on. Youki took off half her clothes and started dancing and doing gymnastics; then, at a certain moment, she went off to throw up the alcohol she'd drunk during the evening and came back saying: 'I've taken off my panties, that'll be easier,' and sat down on Pierre's lap, having first taken care to dress him in a Japanese kimono. The Lunar Woman began playing and listening to a gramophone record, which she put on four or five times without daring to turn her head while the others were screwing – though she later blamed herself for her timidity. Once that was over, Youki rushed off and fetched a tiny basin and, in front of the two others, sat on it and began washing herself. 'It was funny', the Lunar Woman said, 'because all three of us were so big and the basin was so very small.' After that, Youki invited the Lunar Woman to stay the night – so she obediently went and stretched out beside Blanche Picard, who was whimpering with rage. B. Picard has slept with Youki, and is jealous of her privileges. Youki and Pierre screwed again in the dining-room, then – when the Lunar Woman was already asleep – Youki arrived, turned on the light, and made such a noise she woke everyone up, before stretching out next to the Lunar Woman who was thus sandwiched between Blanche and her. Youki began toying with her breasts, saying: 'I can't sleep', but the Lunar Woman disengaged herself. In the end, however, albeit refusing any reciprocal favours, she had to resign herself to 'putting Youki to sleep', while next to her Blanche was fuming with rage. Don't you find that a lovely story?

[...]

After that they threw us out. The Lunar Woman was still thirsty for alcohol and *Stimmung*,[225] but as I could offer her neither one nor the other I let her vanish into the streets alone while I went home.

Now I've told you the lot, it's 3 o'clock and Kos. isn't here yet. So much the better. You can see how conversation, alcohol and the setting interlocked to provide a really entertaining evening.

[Paris]

Monday 11 December [1939]

My love

I've just received your letter and one from Bost, and a great, gloomy coldness has spread across the world. Partly because of Emma – if she can't do anything, what shall I be able to do with only three or four days left? I'll make an application on Thursday, but almost without hope – but above all because of Bost. He has written me a letter from the other world, and I'm paralysed by the thought of writing to him – I feel as though I'd be writing to a spectre. Even his handwriting has changed. I'm sending you it – a copy should be made of it *in toto*. It's not gloomy, it's worse – he's somewhere else and lost. It's almost as strange, coming from Bost, as though he'd gone mad.

Well, I wrote to you yesterday until Kos. arrived. She was sweet and charming, and in the loveliest weather we walked as far as the boulevards. We sat down for a while in a café, then went to the concert at the Conservatoire. We found the same conductor – Charles Munch – whom we'd seen once before with Zuorro, and whom we liked a lot. He has a strange, drug-addict's face and conducts like a god – and he didn't let us down. They first had a tedious Requiem, by a living composer – a first performance and deadly boring. But after that there was an absolutely marvellous Franck symphony, I don't think I've ever heard anything so beautiful – I was in seventh heaven. We left there, Kos. and I, still on the most idyllic terms, but when I told her I was going to meet Bienenfeld at St Germain-des-Prés, suddenly her mien changed dramatically and she said I'd given her no warning. It's possible that I'd been a bit vague. Actually, I'd offered her my whole afternoon in exchange for the evening, and I'd told her basically that I didn't have a free evening till Monday. She made the most frightful face and said

[225] Mood.

coldly that this wasn't the first time, that it had already happened on the occasion of Bienenfeld's last visit – which is absolutely untrue. Actually, she's merely fuming about Bienenfeld, and any formal incorrectness on my part simply served as a pretext. I made lengthy apologies, pleading my good faith, but she flounced off like an offended queen. At the Flore I met up with Bienenfeld, who was scared stiff of being tipsy – since she had got tipsy, as she must have told you. Actually she wasn't tipsy at all, but quite charming. Sonia was there, with a big satin bow in her hair, and lots of other people. We'd made an appointment initially Chez Lipp, but Lipp was crammed with people eating sauerkraut, so we just had a snack of chocolate and preserves and went on to the College Inn. The lady pianist's still there, but the male pianist has left and there's a new barman, and waiters in a kind of blue uniform with gold braid – it was quite pleasing. Bienenfeld and I talked at length, about seriousness in life and the way she looks at existence as an investment. She was absolutely charming, and I rediscovered my maximum feelings for her – she was gay and grave as in her best days, movingly interspersing smiles and deep looks. She's funny, because what depresses her is to think that in 10 years we'll be too old for her to love us in the same way. That depresses her, and yet as she has admitted she *wants* it, since the detachment she foresees will be free, and it's freely that she foresees it and accepts it today. She also wonders if it wouldn't be more 'advantageous' to her if she didn't know us. She also says you're dead for her: that, despite the letters, it all seems wholly frozen, distant and abstract, and the idea of having to reconstruct everything terrifies her. She's a strange person, who isn't equal to her own passions; but she's far more interesting for her positivism and deep concern for herself than for the exaggerated outbursts she goes in for. We arrived home and some passionate embraces ensued – the truth is, I've developed a certain taste for such relations. And then we slept. I left her this morning to go to school. I got my letters, then came to the Dôme to write to you. I'm all the same going to write to Bost, then I'll write up my journal at length and have lunch. I'm not calm enough for the novel.

Haven't you had the parcels of books and photographic materials yet?

Goodbye, my dear little one. Implore Emma to make an effort – there's still just time. And even late it might still help me. I'm afraid I've been very wrought up this past fortnight. My love, in six weeks at the latest – and perhaps in four, or perhaps in two – I'll be seeing you. I have such a need to see you. I kiss you passionately.

Your charming Beaver

What if you were to tell Bienenfeld they're going to send you away from the front, and explain the absence of leave in that way? It would make it less hard for her. You wouldn't have to say anything till February. I think it would be better to tell her you're not getting any leave *after* it has taken place, so as not to start her thinking.

[Paris]

Tuesday 12 December [1939]

My love

I was really moved yesterday to find at the hotel a little package addressed in your hand. It made me sad, because it was Seltzer it seems who'd dropped it there, so he has exchanged his leave with someone else and it won't be with you. Moreover, the little note you enclosed with the diaries must date from Sunday, and it leaves almost no hope. I'll make an application on Thursday, for form's sake, but I'm not counting on anything. As for your notebooks, I'm glad to have them. I just dipped into them for ¾ hour yesterday in bed, looking for nice anecdotes, and then this morning while eating breakfast returned to your autobiography – and found it incrdibly enjoyable. I'll go on with it this afternoon. I didn't know that story about the political meeting your stepfather took you to, and I enjoyed the part about your relations with Nizan. One entertaining thing: I read a passage about yourself, dated Friday 10 November, which surprised me by a certain slightly pompous tone of repressed pathos and strained simplicity: 'I must learn to tear up my past images like old, cancelled photos . . .', etc. There's a page of this, whose content I perfectly understand but the sound of which did surprise me. And then, three pages further on, I read: 'I must record what lies behind the 3 preceding pages, where I detect a few traces of grandiloquence' – and you explain your state of mind very amusingly. I was relieved and contented – but it's extraordinary the extent to which – through that text and your subsequent explanations – I could empathize with you writing those three pages. My love, as I read that far away from you, it seems much more detached than at Brumath – almost like the work of a stranger – and I'm charmed to read it in that way. How nice you are, my sweet little one, and how intelligent! I've just received a letter from you, in which you copy out your ethics for me. It's dated Saturday and I've put it aside, since I prefer first to read the two notebooks – which I'll do as soon as I've finished this letter – then read the rest of it later. My love, I read in the Métro

– or while waiting to give my lessons – and it delights me to have my life all intermingled with yours like this. I've had two letters from Bost, which seem a bit less spectral. He's still too amazed to be bored.

[. . .]

This morning, lesson at H. IV. I wrote up my own diary – which was really behindhand – then had lunch at the Capoulade with Sorokine, went to C. Sée, called in at the post office, and I'm now at the Versailles. I'm going home in a minute, to read your notebooks and do a good stretch of work.

Goodbye, my love. I'm sad – I'd like to see you. I've been wholly with you since yesterday evening, which delights me. I love these little notebooks, and your good little, right-thinking, fine-sounding self. I kiss you, my love – and I'd so like to see you!

Your charming Beaver

[Paris]

Wednesday 13 December [1939]

Most dear little being

I'm rather downcast this afternoon. I've just been to the police station, and there's nothing to be done about Emma; supporting documents are needed that she no longer has time to send me, and in any case it takes a month. So I've written to the Idéal-Sport to book a room – but my heart isn't in it. Bienenfeld certainly won't be coming, Kanapa isn't certain – it'll be pretty austere. But I'll take books and work with me, and mingle skiing with meditation. Send me *The Castle* and Cassou's *48*, please, and above all the *Shakespeare*, since I don't want to have to buy a new copy. I really want to do some reading, or it'll be too gloomy. In addition, I've had a rotten day: two hours of extra lessons; a skimpy hour's work; and then the Lady Boxer arrived – she'd announced her visit yesterday – and had lunch with me, then stuck to me like a burr. She was terribly sweet, but very tiresome. I promised to go down to Provins on Sunday, which only half delights me. I took her with me to the police station, then went to see your mother for an hour at the Lutétia – and that wasn't much fun either. Now I have to spend two hours with my Russians,[226] and the evening with Kos. It's really insipid,

---

[226]Sorokine and her girl friend.

this series of people who don't interest me – what I'd like is solitude and work.

Yesterday I worked well: two and a half hours without lifting my head – it was a real pleasure. In January I'd like to show you at least 100–150 pages in final draft. Then I read your notebooks (I lent one of them to the Lady Boxer, but with countless admonitions – and I'll recover it on Sunday), and I had more than an hour for this, since Kos. didn't arrive till 8.15. My love, tomorrow I'll write you the long letter you request – about the ideas – but I'm only just starting on the ethics. Up to now, there have been autobiography and anecdotes – and a passage on will that I read too fast, so I'll go back to it. I've reached over halfway through the second notebook. I find it *absolutely marvellous*. You found a method and style for that study of yourself which just couldn't be improved on – highly effective as literature, at the same time as throwing the object into relief with maximum accuracy. I was so moved yesterday while reading one passage, which brought back to me the whole atmosphere of the Guille-That Lady period – it seemed very poetic. It was still a youthful period, because we were still making ourselves in an unsettled world. And the world settled for darkness, while you settled things for yourself. You're made now – better than could ever have been hoped for – to the point where you can now take stock of yourself. And Guille's made too, and so am I, and all that tender uncertainty has been lost for ever. I didn't formulate it like that yesterday, but I had a strong affective memory – of an intellectual and moral climate in which we then lived. And also a certain nostalgia – although in a sense we're better now, you and I – for, notwithstanding, at this very moment I feel a kind of faintly desolate harshness in us, with these hard bones we've developed. On the other hand, you really made me laugh with that big quarrel between you and Pieter, in which you were so monstrously in the wrong and demonstrated such skilful bad faith. And there were other bits too that really made me laugh – those notebooks are so alive and rich, they'll be one of your best books, you know. And what strikes me is the novel character of the genre and technique you've invented in them – it couldn't be more individual and successful.

[. . .]

Nothing from Bost – nor yesterday either. He's too depressed to write, and that makes me dreadfully sad. I've bought him a huge parcel of sausage and smoked bacon.

Goodbye, my dear little one. What restores me to a degree of happiness is the piece of news you allude to. I'm not expecting anything much from your leave – your mother, the need to hide, and all the rest, is going to make me very nervy, I'm afraid. What's more it'll be short and hurried. But to spend a long holiday with you at my leisure is something I'm beginning to hope for quite passionately. At any rate, it'll be a month or more before I see you, my little one – my little one. I miss you so. I kiss you, my love, with all my Beaver's heart

Your charming Beaver

[...]

[Paris]

[14 December 1939]

My love

How charming and tender your letter was. It's so nice of you to take care of my summer holiday. I realize that your suggestion pleases me. I'll walk in the mountains, I'll work on my novel, and I'll have interesting company – isn't that magical? It has cast a golden glow over my whole future. The idea of your leave too gladdened my heart today, because I believed in it with all my heart: I saw you arriving with your trim frill of beard, and I saw us in Paris, deep in conversation, deeply happy. All this brings succour to my soul, which really needs it, resembling as it does this snowy weather that has engulfed Paris. It's not that the cold is unbearable, but there's ice everywhere, it's neither wet nor dry, it's foggy and pretty dismal; and there's the fact that 'Emma' has to be abandoned; and there's the fact that Bost is off to the front in a week, which does frighten me actually, in spite of what he says and what you say too – there must be risks involved, at least. I'm wondering whether I should go to Megève. I'm frightened of being so far away, though I do need some *querencia* and am finding Paris terribly oppressive. And then I don't think I sleep enough, I'm always tired out by 7 in the evening. Once again, don't imagine I'm gloomy – it's more that all my thoughts and my whole way of feeling are flagging. You know, you tell me I've changed with respect to happiness, but that's not true. At most I've qualified the idea of happiness, but basically I'm still happy. Life, love, work – they're still fine, hard objects around me, very real, and if they present themselves more austerely, through less pleasant moments, that doesn't change what's essential. If those objects were to disappear, that would be quite different; I can't at all imagine how that would be.

I've finished your notebooks. I'd have liked to write you the big letter you ask for – about your ideas – but it all makes the same impression on me as Bergson (forgive me) when I was young: so absolutely true and definitive that I can find nothing to say. It's extraordinarily interesting, and so true that one thinks: 'Well, yes, of course!', though it's devilishly ingenious. All that part about human will and ethics is convincing – I can't find any fault with it. So I'm quite dazzled by the proof of what a good head you have, my sweet little one. Only I'm greedy for the continuation – I can't at all see how the transition to practical ethics occurs. So far it remains formal – just like Kant's good will, which is defined by the will to be a good will. I've just read it through again, but really I can't comment without having read the continuation. I find everything right line by line, I only wonder how you'll resolve it; what I must assume; and, when I assume my freedom, what I do with that assumed freedom. Send me the continuation as soon as you can – it's really, really interesting.

I'll tell you about my life. Well, after I wrote to you yesterday, I went home to find a light on in my room. It was Sorokine, fixing bright yellow-and-red blotters on my work table with drawing-pins. They were charming and I duly showed my gratitude. We were supposed to work, but we began by tender embraces and when the hour to work came she still held me in her arms. Then, after five minutes, she said nervously: 'I'd like us to either work or talk.' I tried to stand up, but she clung to me and kissed me. It was more passionate than ever: she removed a pin from my blouse and a shoe from my foot, in a symbolic disrobing, and attempted clumsy caresses through my clothes. Then – more and more on edge – she seized her notebook on Kant and said: 'Let's work, but let's stay here.' Then, five minutes later, she burst into tears: 'We're not working – I'll never make any progress.' I told her I wasn't fooled. That it was these physical relations which made her edgy, and that in fact the whole thing was a mess and perhaps we'd better put an end to them. She sobbed all the harder, kissed me on the lips again, and murmured: 'I'd like not to be ashamed of anything with you.' I defended myself by saying that if we had more complete relations, she'd become more attached to me physically than was sensible, in view of the little that I'd ever be able to give her. But she replied passionately: 'I'm already attached to you.' There's nothing to be done, she wants to sleep with me. We decided that from now on we'd separate work and embraces, and would just do everything as we thought best. Then she became absolutely charming, cuddling against me and asking naive little questions: 'whether I'd ever had physical relations' – I said with Kos. in the past and with you – and why 'a person's less ashamed of doing things than of saying them, though it shouldn't be like that'. And she told me: 'You're the first person I've ever loved' – she'd never before placed that value on the word love. She left – radiant – while I remained behind, most embarrassingly embroiled.

This morning I had lunch with her, after C. Sée, and her face was expressionless; she didn't utter a word throughout the meal, and she was half in tears. Eventually I got out of her that it was because of yesterday. That she thought I didn't care about our tender relations, since I'd suggested renouncing them. And that we'd never be able to 'advance' if we saw so little of each other; or else we could advance in intensity – but then we'd need 'absolutely complete' relations. When I acquiesced, she relaxed and became charming again, saying: 'I'll tell you all my lies – I'll never again be hypocritical with you', etc. She also [said] she'd already kissed someone on the mouth, but without going any further – she didn't say who. I'll have to sleep with her, there's no help for it. I'm quite put out – and pretty well smitten – by this little personage. Well, so what?

Kos. didn't arrive until 9 yesterday, so I had time to bring my diary up to date and write to Bost. She arrived a bit dejected, because Dullin hasn't mentioned anything yet – but apparently he hasn't yet allocated all the parts. We went to eat at Dominique's, then came back to my place. She made conversation with me charmingly – all allurement and assiduity and little attentions. And she really was agreeable, and even at times funny. But she stayed on too late – I was dropping asleep.

I slept well, then went to the post office and on to the Versailles, which I always find charming in the morning – it looks so desolate. I read your notebook, went to school, had lunch with Sorokine, went to Henri IV, worked at the Mahieu – and then wrote this letter.

Till tomorrow, my beloved. I love you so, and would so like to go over again with you all that you talk about in the notebook – and our whole life. I kiss and hug you, dearest little one.

Your charming Beaver

Kos. has found the manuscript – she hasn't given it me, but she does have it.

[Paris]

Friday 15 December [1939]

Most dear little being

My spirits are still quite numbed. It's not so much about 'Emma' – I've reconciled myself to that. Kanapa's coming with me to Megève – that's settled and we've written to book our places at the Idéal-Sport – and I'd be really pleased about it, since he's a good skier, if I weren't so gloomy about Bost. There's really quite a bit of fighting, according to the communiqués. Though I've no delicacy of feeling, I find it hard to just take a train and go off for winter sports, with a young man who isn't Bost; to have that kind of distant yet intimate camaraderie which sports create, with someone other than him. I find it hard – like a parody of myself and a precious past. And I don't like being there, while he's in the mud and perhaps in danger. And I'm afraid, and don't know what to do with myself. But I'll go, almost certainly.

I'm low, too, because I'd so like to do some work – it's going so well and is just a matter of time now. Yet here's Bienenfeld in Paris and insisting on seeing a lot of me, and I don't want brutally to drop Kos. for her during this week, and I've promised Sorokine an evening. I won't go and see the Boxers on Sunday, but even so I shan't get any work done till this week is over. Actually, my sister's apparently not coming to Paris, so there's always that – she writes that the news about Lionel is on the whole better.

Kos. arrived at 8 yesterday, still on edge about not having heard anything. Toulouse had been at the rehearsal, looking quite stunning in her great astrakhan cloak and a Russian-style fur hat. Apparently it's going to have a wonderful cast. Blin's doing Buckingham (Sokoloff's role). He seems to be in love with Kos. At any rate, he's gracefully trying his hand at passion. She still has idyllic relations with Mouloudji, who seems charming to judge from her accounts. She told me a bit about it all, then we went to the Ursulines to see *La Symphonie Burlesque* again – which quite entertained me – and also to see *San Francisco*[227]: it's awful, but the earthquake at the end is 'worth seeing', as my mother says – it's extraordinarily well done and terribly gripping.

We went home, chatted a bit, then I went to sleep.

I worked well at the Dôme, but the Gerassis turned up with their dog – totally obsessed by their dog – and no fun at all. We chatted for a while, then I went to the post office, where I found your letter. How tender and delightful and comforting it was, my dear little one. Come

---

[227]Film by W. S. Van Dyke (1936).

back to me soon and everything will be bearable. Then I worked for another hour at the Biarritz, and Kanapa looked in to settle our plans, and Bienenfeld came by with Lévy. She was maddeningly keyed up and domineering. She'd ordained that I wouldn't go winter sporting now, but at Easter – and Kanapa was furious. She was angry and disappointed that Kos. hadn't left. I'm seeing her this evening until 9.30, and after that Kos. – whom I shan't tell about Bienenfeld being here. If she has work at the Atelier things will turn out fine – and if she leaves it'll be even better.

I'm leaving school now, but have to go to a staff meeting at C. Sée – I find all that a damned nuisance. My love, what a horrible, gloomy letter in exchange for your letters, so tender and agreeable – but with you I don't restrain myself. Come soon, my little one, I do so need you! I feel the loss now I've finished your little notebooks – I loved them so much! All my kisses, o you little thousand Socrates, o lovely little Hippias – I kiss you so tenderly.

Your charming Beaver

Les Vikings
[Paris]

Saturday 16 December [1939]

Most dear little being

No letter from you today – I feel a touch disoriented. Yet I'm in a better mood than the last two days, perhaps simply because I've already worked very well for 3 hours, and because – though I didn't sleep much last night – I'm not yet tired: it's only 4 in the afternoon. Tomorrow I'm sending a little parcel of books. And also 200 F. In a week's time I'll send some more books and money, but I've been hit by a 500 F. bill from the cleaner's. Also, Kos. is staying in Paris, and my private lessons don't begin again till Wednesday. But my budget will be balanced according to plan in the end, with winter sports and taxes paid by the end of the month.

Here's Bost's address: 51st Infantry Regiment
5th Company – Zone 170

I was in the depths of black despair yesterday. I wrote to you, then went by taxi to C. Sée – there was a staff meeting at which my presence had been insisted upon, but when I arrived they'd only reached the second year. I had to wait until 7 – in other words, 2 whole hours.

Luckily I had *Carnets de Moleskine*, which I was precisely wanting to finish off before sending it to you. The second part's quite striking, though the fellow comes over as lifeless and not very likeable. There are some striking things in Giono's preface too – so much so that, in the state of mind I was in, I actually got goose-flesh in spite of the stifling heat. Those violent shivers and crawling skin were something that had never happened to me before. Actually I wasn't too upset to be there, since it brought back countless memories of my student days, when at home or the Sorbonne I used to read or work in the midst of any hubbub. I was totally engrossed in my reading, and when I lifted my eyes and saw all those women it gave me the oddest jolt of astonishment.

They let me go at 7.20 and I took a taxi, knowing what awaited me. I wandered through the darkness of Rue Malebranche, without being able to make out the hotel names. Eventually I chose one more or less at random and went up to room 9, where I found Bienenfeld looking lovely in a blue wrap – but with a 'hardened' expression. I explained how I wasn't to blame, and she melted into agitated passion. Her room is agreeable, in a hotel that couldn't be more seedy and sordid. I went with her to dine at Mirov's, then we went up to her place, after which she accompanied me back to my hotel, still full of passion. She complains that you don't write to her enough, and of having been cut off from you for the last ten days. I do indeed have the impression – although your letters are always so affectionate, my dear little one – that you're far more cut off from the world at Morsbronn than before: far more engulfed in solitude. That doesn't matter between us, since it's solitude *with* me – as the saying goes – and that's how I feel it. But it does strike me as stronger than for a long while. You seem all cocooned in solitude – altogether enclosed with the infernal, felt-haired beast,[228] the warm stove, and your ethical thoughts. Is that just a false impression, or not?

As for me, I soon grew irritated. Too much '*madly* happy' – or: 'I'll tell Sartre how Tito wanted to sleep with me, he'll find it *madly* amusing' – and too much nervous outspokenness. All the same, she was very sweet. But it oppresses me to hear someone say: 'I love you so much – love you both so much', and to see myself landed with so many obligations because of the violence of these declarations.

I went home at 9.30, and knocked at Kos.'s door. Mouloudji was there, extremely agreeable, and greeted me with an odd mixture of shyness and mockery. This was because Kos., pursuing my investigation,

---

[228]The telephone switchboard, as described by Sartre in his letter of 6 December.

had interrogated him minutely about the effect I have on him. He said that I had an interesting face, but that initially he'd found me angular and brusque in my relations and had classified me as one of those women 'who eat only what they need'. Poupette's manner and features used to strike him as more reassuring because she's more like a 'housewife', so a person doesn't feel awkward with her. But then at the Rotonde, when he saw how I was drinking wine and swapping anecdotes, he changed his mind. He likes me now, and even prefers my features to Poupette's – though it's a question more of being interesting than beautiful. He left, and it was at the Rotonde that Kos. told me all this. She still hasn't heard anything, but several parts haven't yet been allocated – including the one Toulouse mentioned. She won't know anything until Tuesday, because rehearsals have been suspended from now till then. I didn't tell her Bienenfeld was here, but said I was going out with the Gerassis this evening. We talked about 'resentment' – she can't get shot of that bit of work and will end up not doing it.

We went home, I did a little (very little) washing and mending, and while doing my nails I began Lewis's *The Monk*, adapted by Artaud, which I'll send you in a week's time – it's very entertaining.

7 hours' sleep. Lycée C. Sée. Good work, across from 71 Rue de Rennes,[229] where I had lunch – a very poor one. Work at the Versailles, after a fruitless visit to the post office – nothing from Bost either. Then I dropped in on Kos. for 20 minutes, and am now writing to you. At 5.30 I'm seeing Sorokine at Les Vikings, to get her to work seriously. Then at 8 Bienenfeld, with whom I'll spend the night.

There you are, my love. Oh! about my novel. I am going to read Fabre-Luce,[230] but have no intention of painting great historical tableaux. I simply want events to be located – but don't have any need of details or subtleties. I've redone the 1st chapter, very well I think, and I'm redoing the second. My little judge, you'll read a big wad of it in January.

Goodbye, most dear little being. My tenderest kisses – I love you, you dear little recluse, o little shrouded star

Your charming Beaver

---

[229]Her mother's address.
[230](André) Alfred Fabre-Luce (1899-): prolific writer on many topics (over 60 titles listed in the British Museum Library catalogue), including before the war *La Ville Ephémère, La Victoire, L'Amour et l'Escorial, Un Fils du Ciel* and *Le Secret de la République*.

It's agreeable – I'm writing from my room and opposite I can hear the piano at the College Inn. Every so often they open the door and a great gust of music assails me – then it's muffled again.

[Paris]

Sunday 17 December [1939]

My love,

I've had two loving letters from you today, which has made me really happy. I've anyway been having an excellent time since I wrote to you. The fact is I've been able to work properly – and if I could do as much every day, I'd be in high fettle every day. You must have been a bit disappointed, because I haven't written all that much about the notebooks. But, my love, you really don't seem sufficiently alien for me to be able to form an objective impression of you – so I was able to judge only the method. As for the ethics, I need more material. In general, I don't at all feel you're making too much fuss about a very small war. It represents a testimony, as you say somewhere, both upon yourself in wartime and upon a moment of your life which is certainly quite specific – and it couldn't be more entertaining. I lent one to the Gerassis, who are revelling in it. Wahl has told me he now has proofs of *L'Imaginaire*, and is informed that it will appear in five months' time – that's all I know. With respect to your hopes regarding Bienenfeld, I think they're fruitless. Unconsummated craving is as fearsome as the other kind, and it binds her tight. So when she sees you again, she'll be utterly smitten again. Especially with sexuality involved, that won't take long. If you want to stop the affair, that may be possible without a *disaster* – but not without a fuss. It would take a lot of toughness, moreover: diminish the passion in your letters, say a cool farewell, etc. – all difficult things. If that would really make you happier, try it. She won't be too seriously hurt, I don't think. But she'll make plenty of pathetic, dreadful scenes. It's your choice.

After writing to you yesterday I hurried down to Les Vikings, where I found Sorokine with a pupil to whom she's imparting my last year's teaching at 15 F. an hour, which allows the said pupil to shine at the Lycée La Fontaine like a brilliant star. The said pupil left, and I sat down next to Sorokine and explained Descartes to her; she's very intelligent when she wants to be and it was interesting. But in a nearby booth there was a fellow 'hurling himself at a poor woman', as Sorokine put it, and showering her with passionate kisses. The woman was young and blonde, and the fellow was Laporte[231] – whom we vulgarly couldn't take our eyes off. Sorokine made me laugh, because she said with a blush that she had a question to ask about a passage in *Quai des Brumes*, which I'd lent her. She twisted and turned and held back, and finally showed me that atrociously purple passage where Mac Orlan compares the prostitute to a source of energy – an electric accumulator concentrating all forces. 'She had wrapped her body in copper wire', he says – or something like that – and Sorokine was convinced this was some frightful obscenity. She asked if it didn't embarrass you to take your books to publishers, seeing that they're so obscene. She confessed to me that her celebrated old scoutmaster had kissed her on the mouth – after two kissing sessions he'd dropped her, however. She was more charming than ever and I'd be happy to see more of her.

After that I sped off to Bienenfeld's, where I found a passionate welcome. We went to dinner at the Knam, we talked, and I made a real effort. Moreover, I was in a good mood and tired at the same time, so that I was entirely myself, unadorned. She always finds me funny at such times – and is quite enchanted. We returned to her place, went to bed and talked a bit, then moved on to embraces. I found it really charming to sleep in her room like that, though I slept quite badly since she shifts around and snores – which is just like her. We woke up at about 8.30, and like a satisfied man I discreetly avoided her caresses. I wanted to have breakfast and work (I feel I can get right into your skin at such moments). We went to the post office to pick up your letters and send off the books and money. Then on to the Mahieu, where we worked side by side. Then we had a slap-up lunch at the Capoulade, and went to the Danton near the Odeon to work some more. I left her at 4.30 and went to a concert with Kos., who was fairly gloomy – still because of the uncertainty regarding the Atelier – but amiable enough all the same. We listened to the 'Eroica' symphony, to a 'Spanish Rhapsody' by Ravel that's a real delight, to a piece by Roussel that we didn't even notice (when I think how you and I went to listen to a whole Roussel concert, my love – how conscientious we were!), and finally to 'The Sorcerer's Apprentice', which I know by heart but which is very agreeable. We came back to eat at Dominique's, then had a drink in the front section of the Dôme – where it was terribly cold. We spotted the Magus in uniform, a red cross on his arm, and exchanged a few affable words: he's gathering health statistics in the Moselle, and I found seeing him quite poetic.

---

[231]Sorbonne philosophy lecturer.

Then I came home at 10.30 to write you this letter. Next I'll get off a note to Bost – but he hasn't written to me for three days. I agree with what you say about his letter, really.

Goodbye, my dear little one. I'll be seeing you in a month, then. I wonder if, upon reflection, it wouldn't be better if you came *without* your frill of whiskers. I so long to see you! I can remember so vividly our last time together, and it quite overwhelms me with love for you and desire. In two months, shall I really be seeing you almost at will, my dear little one? I love you so, care so much about you. My dear love, my life – I kiss you so tenderly, o best and tenderest and most beloved of little ones.

Your Charming Beaver

Wanda hasn't yet written to her sister, who's writing to her for the first time today.

I've given you a poor impression of this agreeable cold Sunday with its hint of snow – a bit disorientated because I didn't wake up at home, well rested after a long lie-in and lots of relaxed work and leisure. The morning was vaguely reminiscent of those Sunday mornings at Rouen, with you. I love you so much.

[Paris]

Monday 18 December [1939]

Most dear little being

[. . .]

I rushed to the post office, where I found two letters from you – dated the 15th and 16th. You're right about how nice it is when they arrive quickly like that. My love, how tender your letters are – they've quite overwhelmed me with happiness. I don't know if it comes from you or from me, but I no longer feel in the least that little cocoon of solitude all round you which I was mentioning two or three days back. On the contrary, you're altogether close and present to me. My love, how well you speak of our love – never have I felt it to be so strong and happy. Oh, yes, we'll have a lovely leave, dear little one, little avid one, little avidly loved one. You'll know by now that Kanapa's coming to Megève with me. Does that satisfy you? I'm going to take my diaries and lots of books, and I think it'll be fairly agreeable. At all events, I'd enjoy it if it weren't for that odd delicacy of feeling with respect to Bost, which makes me vaguely hate Kanapa. I've had an incredibly pleasing, nice and interesting letter from Bost, which confirms what you were saying. I'll send you it once I've reread it properly, and you can send it back to me as you did with the other one – for which I thank you.

[. . .]

Goodbye, my love. I've reread your letters – how I love you, and how strong it makes me that you should love me so well! I'm happy, my love

Your charming Beaver

[Paris]

Wednesday 20 December [1939]

My love

What pleasure your Monday letter gave me! So you'll be here in Paris with me in three weeks' time. Listen, *at all costs* say nothing about it to Bienenfeld – she'll want to see you for *at least* four days. And since her parents will be here, she won't get time off easily, so she'll pester us in snatches every day. That kind of sharing would be even more unbearable than the other. As for Wanda, if you do quarrel with her you'll make up, as once you're here she'll do everything to bring that about. Anyway, once in Paris you'll want to see her – and you'll have to see both of them. So don't mention anything to Bienenfeld, and as for Wanda, handle things as we said. Perhaps on the 8th she'll still be at Laigle – that would be very convenient. I'll write to tell Poupette I'm supposed to be visiting her for a few days, and she should if need be send me a wire I can produce (I'll explain it's to save you from Wanda and Bienenfeld – that'll pose no problem).

[. . .]

I did some work, then went to meet Bienenfeld at the Mahieu. I took the Métro, and from Odéon ran so fast that I fell flat on my face on the stairs. Luckily it was dark, so nobody saw my embarrassment. I didn't want her to be annoyed. When I arrived upstairs at the Mahieu, she was there all charming and not annoyed in the least. She told me how she'd been spending her time, then we went to the Polish tavern – she was full of enthusiasm and happiness. I see my relationship with her as a 'serious affair'. Not exactly a duty, but an affair whose price you know, in which you find a certain charm each time, and which you want as a whole. Something a decent person may count themselves very lucky to have, but which leaves room for lots of immoral desires. She always amuses me by her seriousness. I'd shocked her the day before, because she'd told me I must find it disagreeable when you changed theories in which I'd placed my trust, and I'd answered: 'I change a few too – it adds a bit of variety to one's life and I quite like that.' So she nodded her head and meditated seriously upon her seriousness. She wanted to say goodbye to her father, so she dropped me home by taxi at 8.30. Kos. didn't come till 10.15, which was a godsend. I wrote up my journal carefully and in detail, then corrected two piles of written tests, and despite the ungrateful nature of these pursuits I found that moment of unhoped-for solitude – in my room, in the evening – extremely pleasing.

[. . .]

I met up with Bienenfeld at the Balzar and worked alongside her, then a quick lunch at the Capoulade and another 3 hours at the Mahieu, upstairs. I must take you there – it's extremely pleasing to see the Luxembourg all wintry beneath one. My love! When I think how you're going to see all that again with me! Bienenfeld did something we've often talked about. She told me, with an air of feigned anger and self-importance: 'Sartre wants me to tell him what I think about the Dabit book, so I'm going to have to read all through my little notebook again!' That taste for a tender authority – reflecting one's need for a man, to whom one yields with kind indulgence, and the man plays the game and gives smiling orders (like Jouvet with Gibert) – it's annoying when a woman starts behaving in that way. I'm explaining it badly, because I'm a bit under the weather, but you remember what we said about it.

I worked till my head ached. Bienenfeld finds Chap. 2 overstated and Elizabeth too disagreeable, but I think she's wrong and it was all too low-key for the opening of a novel. She made some correct criticisms of detail, but I'm dying with impatience to show you a big chunk of this final version. I've bought the Fabre Luce, in order to have my conscience with me. I also bought some food for Bost after leaving the Mahieu, and for you *The Revolution of Nihilism*[232] – but I'll send that from Megève, since I want to read it. On Saturday you'll get *The Monk* and I'll pick another two surprises from your list.

---

[232]By Hermann Rauschning (1897-   ), a former Nazi who broke with the party before 1939 and became famous when, on the eve of the war, he published *Hitler Told Me* – an insider's portrait of Hitler's ambitions.

I called in at the post office and found your letter. Bost hadn't written, but he writes dutifully most of the time. He's no longer writing to Kos., in reprisal, but that gives me no pleasure; I don't care either way – I no longer feel that emotional involvement.

After that I met Sorokine from 5.30 to 8, then Kos. from 8 to 11, and now I'm writing to you. Tomorrow I'll tell you all about Sorokine – it was amusing. I'm beginning to feel squeezed. I'd like to press some button that would painlessly inter my serious affair.[233]

Now I'm off to sleep, most dear little beloved being. With you in Paris, how wonderful it'll be! O my beloved, how I feel your love, but how I long to feel yourself in flesh and blood on my arm and experience Paris with you. I love you, my darling. We're as one, o you my other self, my tiny beloved charm

Your charming Beaver

I can see only one advantage to your quarrel with Wanda, and that's the risk that the whole business could come out anyway. My disappearance will coincide with those 5 days of your leave which will be so oddly cancelled – getting the 2 Kos. sisters to swallow that will be the real bitch! The older one's already suspicious. And someone might meet us – in which case you won't appear in a good light.

[Paris]

Thursday 21 December [1939]

My dear, dear love

How sweet your letters are, my little one! Of course I wasn't complaining about them – quite the contrary. What I was saying about them didn't mean that at all; it was just a premonition of what you've now explained. What's more, beware of false simultaneity! The letter where I was saying that referred to earlier letters of yours – it was just an impression which has already vanished long ago. My love – my little caring one – how united I am with you, and what succour I find in you!

I've told you about the evening with Bienenfeld. I'd had to make a big effort to explain some Descartes to Sorokine, so I was in a state of tension – but happy tension, seeing that I'd given an excellent lesson. The result was a nervous overflow of vitality, under orders to be kind

[233]The affair with Bienenfeld, in other words.

but with a certain lack of adjustment. It's for similar reasons, I think, that Kos. is just now more truly *odd* than ever in my eyes – because of her pals presumably. There's a way of being watchful in your casualness, of letting yourself go in a controlled way, of becoming less adjusted without loss of awareness, which works people up in their relations with themselves: false relations with themselves, transposed into social ones. It's a kind of art – with as much bad faith as that of Faulkner or Dos Passos – and which creates ambiguous objects. I felt my behaviour with Bienenfeld was of this kind.* I don't know if you see what I mean, since I'm obviously never like that with you.

[...]

I stopped my letter yesterday to sleep, but now I'm carrying on. So I went to Les Vikings and settled down with Sorokine in a booth at the rear. She had too much of a headache to work, so we spent an absolutely delightful moment just talking. She was all tender and confiding and happy, talking without embarrassment of the time when our relations were 'pure and chaste'. And with all the grace in the world she recounted to me all the little thoughts she has harboured about me since the first day. She even showed me a little diary, dating from the first term of '38, where her own little existence and the dawn of our relations were recorded in snatches. I talked to her about all that too – and she's so pleasing in her anxiety to know me. I read her some passages from my black diary, and as she listened she clasped my hand and plied me with passionate questions about myself. She says: 'I love you' now, and offers me her lips quite naturally, as if it were a lawful romance. She's gauche, but never graceless as Bienenfeld can be. Indeed, there's a quite moving grace in the play of her features and her written language and her speech. She really has a moving little soul – I know none that produces a truer sound. Never the least trace of anything social – no appearance. I've honestly been slow to yield – I'm not getting vainly carried away – but I can't find any fault with her, merely limits. If I were free, I'd surrender myself enthusiastically to this affair. Yesterday I was smitten and she could sense it – it made her really happy. I get on very well with her. I told her lots of things about what tarts and brothels are – all of which she listened to with rapt interest. She's rereading *Intimacy* and is in transports over it this time round. She's sensitive to the style, and was delightedly quoting me expressions of yours that she finds charming. She asked me for explanations of the obscenities in it – but only in my room and with her face turned to the wall. I call her a frightened doe, which drives her wild with rage. It does, all the same, strike me as odd to be passionately loved in this feminine, organic way by two individuals: Bienenfeld, who 'immersed herself' in my face in that photo for a quarter of an hour, and Sorokine. I don't feel myself to be the real object of those passions – they're directed through me towards a dream image. This is especially true of Bienenfeld, for Sorokine has greater stamina, critical sense, curiosity, defences, and deep concern for my inner self. As you used to say of yourself and Wanda, W. loves you because you're you – and it's the same with Sorokine and me. Whereas Bienenfeld – rather like Poupette – loves strangers, endowed with every virtue, whose virtues are necessary to the beauty of *her* love. Sorokine brought me another charming drawing. The Boubou is in transports over her drawings, and finds them full of talent. That amuses me, reminding me of the years when Kos. was still a child – with her grace of language and expression in general, her tyrannical nature, and her enclosed little girl's world. Sorokine lacks 'aristocracy', bodily grace and the Kos. poetry, though. On the other hand, she has the greatest depth of feeling imaginable. She often drives me mad with anger – like this morning, when she refused to understand Descartes – but she never irritates me: all is pure and of good quality. I have the highest esteem for her. As much as for Bost, for example. Bienenfeld's great loss in my mind is a loss of esteem. She has too much, far too much, self-importance; and too much that's social and appearance – a great deal of appearance, of both feeling and thought.

Very well, so I had a delightful time. I like taking that girl out and showing her things – she takes such pleasing advantage of it. But I had to leave her, in order to go and meet Kos. She, at least, isn't a burden to me. It's like a deep, old friendship, presenting itself more or less as what it is – and neither more nor less than the reason why it presents itself. We went to the College Inn. I'd never seen her quite so gloomy, and yet quite amiable – exceptionally so, in fact, and even gay on occasion. These days she's really moving. But the conversation was dismal. Yet that didn't make the whole evening dismal. My work, and Sorokine, had made my day a full one, and I liked the place, and I felt in sympathy with Kos. And then your letters – and Bost's too – bind me solidly to the best part of my life. Yes, my love, my life's a happy one, there's nothing lousy about it – everything's full, precious and solid. It touched me when you said you found our love as moving as the Argentina.[234] That's just how it seems to me. And all the gay friendship, filled with mutual esteem, that exists between Bost and me, and between Bost and us, strikes me likewise as really valid and pleasing – especially

---

[234]'Old brasserie in Rouen which De Beauvoir and Sartre found 'poetic'.

since I find him intensely appealing at present. In that College Inn I was like my heroine, amid lots of fine objects that were real and strong. It was redolent of war – but war-as-refuge, in its other, non-cruel aspect. One nice thing was that the pianist turned up with some friends, in uniform; he played, his friends played the piano too, and they were gay in an appealing way because they expressed it through their craft. When I heard 'The Man I Love', tears almost came to my eyes – that's a tune from our past, my sweet little one. Our affair seems as moving to me as a beautiful novel. I love you, my little one, come quickly!

There you are. I wrote to you when I got home, then slept for 7½ hours and at 8.30 went to the Dôme and worked. Then school. Then lunch with Sorokine, to whom I explained Descartes a bit. But instead of reading him, she tries to reinvent him at every step – so I grew angry, but with a pure anger. Teaching at H.IV, then back to pick up my letters: one from you, two little ones from Bost. And I'm writing from the Versailles. I'll work for two hours, then see Bienenfeld.

Apparently that Rosa Goetschel, who used to write poems and who brought me flowers at my mother's last year, told Sorokine – in reference to me – 'I love her as passionately as if she were a man.'

On the subject of tarts who work in brothels, Sorokine said to me in deep astonishment: 'Poor things! They must be utterly dazed! What interest could anyone take in handling them?' But the pleasing thing was the naive, total sincerity of such a question.

Goodbye, most dear little one, little beloved one.

Send the *Shakespeare* back quickly, and the other books too. You'll get some more on Saturday.

I love you, my beloved. I'm happy. I kiss you most tenderly, little beloved one.

Your charming Beaver

Enclosed: a letter from the Boxer – very touching.

*I wasn't playing on words, and I wasn't 'excited' – a description of myself that I detest.

Le Dôme

Friday 22 December [1939]

My love

Here's a long letter from you, o little most worthy one! Listen, the novel called *L'Eau trouble* by (I think) a certain M. Vaseray began as follows: 'A ray of sunlight caressed the sleeper's cheek.' I was outraged by this, but you maintained that it was permissible. However, that was a development of your own thought, in which you partly had yourself in mind – don't you remember? You were arguing, in a sense, that this was an event existing for consciousness, even if consciousness couldn't for the moment grasp it. But such an argument would have big implications and cannot, I think, be sustained.

I don't know if I should tell you the whole story of my evening yesterday, since – out of solidarity – it'll finish off Bienenfeld in your eyes. I've never felt so chilled by her. Well, I worked at home – putting the final touches to my second chapter – then went to meet her at the Mahieu. She was tired and a bit glum. We had dinner at the little Alsatian restaurant, given over to conversation and explication of Kant. Then we saw *The Petrified Forest* at the Ursulines, which is a marvellous film: Leslie Howard, Bette Davis and Humphrey Bogart are equally marvellous, and the subject is strange and pleasing. I'd like you to see it in January.

We went back to Bienenfeld's place straight away. I'd been tensed up, and remained so throughout the journey: I hate her little jokes and her sprightliness and her gentle authority. She was making travel plans for the 3 of us to visit America, and was picturing us camping out in Arizona. 'But Sartre doesn't like the wild', I told her irritably. 'Oh, he'll like this.' 'No he won't like it', I answered – with an obstinacy matching her own. 'All right, we can leave him in New York with some little American girl, then!' (knowing smile). 'Heh! Heh!' I got out through gritted teeth. We went upstairs, we went to bed, and she stripped naked saying: 'I find it ridiculous, putting on a nightie just to take it off again.' I can't convey to you the reasonable, sedate quality which this little phrase, uttered in this way, imparted to our transports of passion. It reduced me to a state of bleak frigidity – and frigidity gave way to hatred. It was the first time I'd ever felt that: a real hatred of sleeping with a woman I don't love. I articulated it to myself even as she was marvelling at the tender expression on my face. She's all nervous explosions, and the more passion she puts into them the more nervous and clumsy her caresses become. And I was enduring that clumsiness of hers with malicious irony – it couldn't have been more disagreeable. I've got to the point where her every expression, and her voice, and everything she says, all grate on me. She sees nothing of it – she couldn't be happier.

We got up at 8, and at least I slept very well. I went to the Mahieu and worked there for a generous 3 hours, on a crucial conversation at the beginning – quite a difficult one too – between Pierre and Françoise. How impatient I am for your opinion, my dear little one! And then I had lunch at the Biarritz with Kanapa, Lévy and Bienenfeld. Kanapa handed me my ticket and seat reservation: I'm beginning to feel I'm really going – and am terribly pleased about it.

After that, 3 hrs of school. Sorokine picked me up there afterwards, and I called in at the post office – where there was a nice little letter from Bost – and at my place: a note from Merleau-Ponty, who isn't coming on leave till later. Now I have to go and say goodbye to the Gerassis, then see Kos. at 6.30. I still haven't got anything ready for my departure – but I'll do it all tomorrow.

I've already told you I find Bienenfeld rather like Poupette, in the sense that she endows what she loves with an abstract value, but has no real concern for it. I've often mentioned to you her bluntness when I spoke to her about Bost, for example. That goes on. She'll never ask a question about, for example, my real feelings for Kos., or my relations with Sorokine, or what kind of state I'm in regarding your absence. She never for a single instant strives to know me, but takes me for granted – like a mathematical postulate – and builds *her* life upon that. I honestly don't have much feeling left for her. But, my sweet little one, what to advise you? It's impossible, I just don't know. You'll see yourself when you get back.

Goodbye, my love, I'll send you some books tomorrow. I'm pleased to be going to Mont d'Arbois, and shall be sure to tell you all about it. But I'm afraid a host of over-vivid little images of you will come back to haunt me. One – all warm with life – did precisely that yesterday, and it wasn't pleasant. My craving to be with you again is too strong. I love you, my little one – how I'd like to see you again and kiss you, my love!

Your charming Beaver

It's clever of you to say that, while reading your letters, I've been influenced by the viewpoint of your notebooks – I think there's much truth in that. And perhaps my own moroseness formed a little cocoon around me.

I love you, my little one.

Chalet-Hôtel-Restaurant
Idéal-Sport
Megève

Sunday 24 December [1939]

Most dear little being

How pleasant it is to write to you from here. I'm in the lounge of
Chalet Idéal-Sport – which you know so well, my sweet little one. The
sun's setting, and there's a big moon in the sky, and through the window
I can see the snowy mountains and the sky, clear save for a single bar
of ashen cloud. I'm not melancholy – on the contrary, everything here
seems precious to me. It's not yet you, but it's your dear memory that
I've just recovered, as though it had been waiting for me – all embalmed
by the cold – at the top of this little mountain. You've been with me all
day, my love. All these places are full of you and your tenderness, and
when I touch my skis it's as if I were giving you a little kiss. This is my
6th year of winter sports, my love, and the first without you. For five
years we went up and down little slopes together, full of love for one
another – and I can still see you with that little putty-coloured jacket
at Montroc, at Chamonix with your ugly red pullover, and at Megève
with your beautiful white jacket. I'm all melting with tenderness for you,
my love, and with longing to touch your little flesh-and-blood person –
in a fortnight, perhaps. O my little one, I do so want to be with you
again!

[. . .]

Having been unable to write from the day before yesterday till
yesterday, I'm going to tell you everything now. Well, it was Friday. I
went to see the Gerassis, to say goodbye. Only Fernand was there – with
Red-haired Fanny – and our conversation was short and subdued. I
asked Gerassi his opinion on Finland. He told me the White Russians
are delighted with Stalin's policy – saying: 'It's ours, and now it's
reverting to us' – and the Communists and Aragon are delighted too,
claiming the place is being sovietized at full speed, but the true
revolutionaries (among whom he counts himself) are dismayed. He
wasn't willing to say anything about Ehrenburg, and kept sending
anguished winks in my direction because of Fanny – though I didn't
quite understand why. I left him and went home, where I managed to
do a good hour's work, write up my diary in detail and even read the
November issue of *N.R.F.* Kos. didn't arrive till 8.15. In my diary (after
that night with Bienenfeld – it was Thursday, you remember), I was
puzzling over why it should be women rather than men who are clumsy

in localized caresses (since Kos., R.[235] and Bienenfeld have put me through equal tortures). I wonder if it's because – as Gide says in connection with some fellow – they put themselves in your place, but it's always *themselves* they put there. Whereas a man's unable to make this dangerous substitution, so he theorizes the other person quite directly and honestly. There's a little mystery here.

[. . .]

After that I met up with Sorokine, whom I tormented for 5 min. by trying to do some Leibniz with her. But then I yielded – and we chatted, looked at your notebooks, and talked about our feelings. She'd brought me *Intimacy*, so that I could explain the obscenities to her; but there was a fellow who kept staring at us in the most tiresome way, so we went up to my room. There, things were ever so tender but not sensual – chaste kisses, sentimental embraces, protestations and promises – and she was radiant with happiness. She showed me a charming passage she'd written about our relations, where she explained everything she got out of them; and how I got only herself out of them; and how she knew quite well she could be only an infinitesimal fragment of my life; and how her only hopes rested on what she might provide in the way of 'personal charm'. It was lucid, and rational, and altogether pleasing. As I've told you, I like immensely her cast of mind and way of feeling. I like her more and more – and am tempted to let passion flower with her, see more than I should of her, etc. But I don't know if I'll give way.

After that I saw Bienenfeld – all nice and sad – who told me at length about her mood of pathos the night before. I'm more and more indifferent to her moods of pathos, but I'm fond of her little face. I was very tender with her, in spite of everything; but I was scarcely able to prove it to her, since I had to call in at the post office, get dressed, and finish my parcels. No letter from you – I think you must have written to Megève, where there was nothing either this morning, but it'll doubtless be here tomorrow as I told them to forward everything. Write directly to Chalet Idéal-Sport, Mt d'Arbois, Megève, Hte Savoie, up to and including 30 December – then to Paris again.

Bienenfeld accompanied me to the station, where I found Kanapa and an almost empty compartment. We had just a young youth-hosteller with us, who offered me tea and gingerbread. I tenderly bid Bienenfeld farewell, then sat down in my corner opposite Kanapa. We chatted, but he functions poorly in conversation – what a stick he is! I realized then

---

[235]In the corresponding passage from De Beauvoir's *Journal de Guerre* (p.208), the initial is transcribed as P., but it is not clear to whom it refers in either case.

how much tenderness and magic there'd already been in even my most discreet relations with Bost, from the first day I set eyes on him. There's no communication between Kanapa and me — not even the warm companionship conferred by something very pleasant done in common.

[. . .]

When we arrived, we were received with a trace of astonishment: the chalet was reopening that very morning. They got us to choose our rooms — which are charming — then we ate ravenously, and very well. There were lots of people at lunch — local Megève people — but this evening nobody: we're the only guests. You can't imagine how pleasing it is to be alone here in the warm, while an excellent wireless plays Franck's *Nocturne* (the 5th Symphony's over). Straight away after lunch we did two hours' skiing — it's marvellous having this ski-lift just a step away. The ascent's at least twice as long as by cable-car from Megève, and the run back down is wonderfully long and interesting.

We came back inside and here I am. I feel intensely happy: with the skiing, with the solitude — of which I'm going to take good advantage — and with the music. And with yourself, my love, whom I'll see soon, and who are with me meanwhile in all these places to which I'll return with you — my love!

Goodbye, my sweet little one. You're my serenity, and my happiness, and the best of myself. This evening, in this little chalet, I'm more closely united with you than I've ever been. I love you, my little one

Your charming Beaver

[. . .]

Chalet-Hôtel-Restaurant
Idéal-Sport
Megève (Haute-Savoie)

Monday 25 December [1939]

Most dear little being

Like yesterday it's 5 in the afternoon, I've just had tea, the wireless is playing and we're alone in the agreeable, warm lounge. How happy the two of us — *just* the two of us — would be here, my little one! But I'll fix things so it really does happen. Yesterday, after writing to you, I got off a letter to Bost — not as long as yours, but a long one all the same — then finished my detective story and read some more of Kafka's *The*

Trial. On the stroke of 7 they served us dinner – we were alone in the dining-room. A splendid dinner: as much Potage St Germain as we wanted (made with split peas, just as you like it), mountains of Gnocchi alla Romana, an escalope with peas, and a superb crème caramel. I'm going to grow fat for sure, since I'm eating like a horse. We didn't stay up for long, as we were dropping with exhaustion. I read some more of *The Trial*, and finished it in bed at about 9.45. My room was nice and warm, with a hot-water bottle in the bed, and through the window next to the bed – once I'd raised the blind – I could see all the mountains lit up as in broad daylight under a clear, bleak, starless sky, and the moonlight over the snow couldn't have been lovelier. I was comfortable, and blissful, with my heart at peace. I had a little dream about you, of the kind I used to have about Zaza. I was looking at you resentfully, asking you why you'd stopped seeing me, and feeling intensely sad. I also dreamed I was waking up in the morning and all the snow had melted during the night, so nothing could be seen but green meadows – I was beside myself with anger. But in fact when the light woke me just before 7, the snow was there all right. There was a superb sunrise – which I watched from the warmth of my sheet – then I got up quickly, keen to get back to the snow.

[...]

My love, I'm thinking so much about you all these days! I hope those letters will arrive tomorrow. I love you, my dear little one, and constantly yearn to have you with me. And our love – as moving as the old Argentina – is constantly there in my heart. I kiss you with all my Beaver's heart

Your charming Beaver

I've already caught a lot of sun and my face will soon be all tanned. I'm really content, as happy as I can be without you or Bost – and feeling so liberated from my 'charming vermin'.

Chalet-Hôtel-Restaurant
Idéal-Sport
Megève (Haute-Savoie)

Les Arcades
Brasserie at the PLM Coach Station
Megève (Haute-Savoie)

Tuesday 26 December [1939]

Dear little being

I'm starting my letter in a little Megève brasserie where we've never been together – it's just opposite the coaches. It's 11.30 and we're about to go back up to lunch. Kanapa's just ringing his family. I'm still having a prodigiously good time.

[. . .]

At 2.15 we went off to do the St Gervais run. The snow was trampled and again had something of a crust, and Kanapa overtook me cleanly. I came down pretty poorly – lacking the Christie and courage. It should also be said I was in a state of feminine inferiority; I'm feeling so well it's barely noticeable, but it does weaken you all the same. The snow stops half-way between the Bettex and St Gervais, leaving a long stretch you have to go down on foot – which is really tiresome. Next time we'll go only as far as the Bettex. We went back up by the cable-car, which is impressive, and were back at the chalet on the dot of 4.30.

Tea; reading – *Verdun*; then my diaries, which I want to read through again from beginning to end. The first one – on my first month of war – is undoubtedly the best and you'll soon be reading it, my little one. As I was immersed in it the mail arrived – giving me a jolt of pleasure – so I got down to writing to you again. We're no longer alone, unfortunately. There's a woman here now – a schoolmistress of some kind – and a group of young people: not noisy, but chatty, spoiling the atmosphere.

Kanapa's still neuter – nothing of the sex maniac about him! He does often use the word 'bottom', but always with some good excuse – 'I fell on my bottom', 'I've got a bruise on my bottom' – and skiing provides plenty of good opportunities.

Goodbye, my love. This is a wretched letter, but I'm really tired. I kiss you, my dear little one, whom I so long to see again. I love you so.

Your charming Beaver

[Megève]

Wednesday 27 December [1939]

Most dear little being

Here are two letters from you: the one of the 22nd, which did after all arrive dutifully, and the long one of the 24th – which is so long and entertaining and has so gladdened my heart. My love, how well you do love me! You speak to me of 'our' snow, but that's just how I see it; and when this morning I went down the Mont d'Arbois run really well and fast, I turned in thought to you, to give you credit for my success. I'm with you all the time on these slopes, my love. I remember everything so well. Oh! how I'd like to be with you, my little one.

[. . .]

That's all, my love – but I'm going to see you again. I can't wait to show you the beginning of my novel; it's been reworked a lot, I've added lots of stuff, and I think it's good – but I need you to tell me. My little one, my dear little one, I've never loved you more strongly – oh! come quickly. You don't tell me whether I'll be going to spend my holidays at Annecy, as I was hoping. Is that idea of renting a villa going to work out, or not?

Goodbye. I'll write to Bost and Sorokine, then finish off *Verdun*, then sleep.

I kiss you so joyfully, my love

Your charming Beaver

The extract from Bienenfeld's letter doesn't strike me as all that lukewarm, or all that empty. She certainly loves you with all her heart – at least intermittently. She'd told me in an irritating way: 'I've written S. a playful letter' – and I'd foreseen the worst. Nothing suits her worse than playfulness – and the consciousness she has of it. On the other hand, her letter today about the Christmas Eve party with Ramblin and Lévy was quite pleasing. I'm sorry to have put you off her so much, but that's pretty well how I feel myself.

Chalet-Hôtel-Restaurant
Idéal-Sport
Megève (Haute-Savoie)

Friday 29 December [1939]

Most dear little being

I haven't had your little daily greeting today. But that doesn't matter – I'll doubtless get two letters tomorrow.

[. . .]

I was back by quarter to 4, then worked till 7. The new version of Chap. 3 is finished; there's a somewhat philosophical conversation between Pierre and Françoise, but I think it's indispensable. That makes 60 pages of the novel that are in final draft form (subject to your judgement) – it's proving terribly quick to rework, and enjoyable too. I'm hoping by the end of February to have gone back over all last year's work. And there are another 300 pages drafted, which will only need putting into final form.

I've had a tiny note from Bienenfeld, and a tiny one from Bost, written on Monday, when he was frozen stiff from having been on sentry duty for 12 hours. He's hoping to be in a house soon, and doesn't seem to be going to the front. I'm going to write to him for a while now – and to Kos. and Sorokine – but short letters, as I'd like to do a bit more work.

I'm spending fine days, full and poetic, with lots of memories and hopes and plans in my head. I've thought how I'd like to write a big novel covering 30 years of life, to show the whole outline of a life – which is so interesting. It's a vague idea, but I imagine one would have to invent a whole new technique, which could be quite enjoyable.

Goodbye, dear little being, light of my days. I feel I'm on the way towards us – as surely and tranquilly as when you're sliding along, well-balanced, on your skis (the teacher has told me I've a very good downhill stance). We'll soon be together – indeed, I've never really left you, my love. I love you with all my might. Truly, you're everything for me, as I've been repeating to myself again throughout today. My love.

Your charming Beaver

[. . .]

Chalet-hôtel-restaurant
Idéal-Sport
Megève

Brasserie at the Rochebrune
cable-car (lower terminus)

Saturday 30 December [1939] – morning

Most dear little being

I'm beginning my letter early today – it's only 10 in the morning. That's because, as you can see, I'm at the Rochebrune cable-car and there are 100 numbers ahead of me, which means at least half an hour's wait. Do you remember this station crammed with skiers where you always have to queue interminably (and where a pupil with ill-timed zeal had taken your ticket, so I was forced to wait for you all shivering for a quarter of an hour at the top)? It's like that today, jam-packed with people, and I went for a coffee in that buffet place next door where you once had a near-quarrel with Bienenfeld. It's teeming in there, and quite fun.

[. . .]

How happy I am this morning, my love! I've thought at great length about the moment when I'll meet you at the station and we'll set off into Paris. We'll go to the Hôtel Mistral, won't we? How merry we'll be! We're the merry kind, you and I – it's so agreeable. How well we get on, my love! In a week perhaps, I'll be seeing you.

Do tell me *what to tell the Kos. sisters.* It would be so much easier for me not to have to hide – just wonderful! But I don't want to risk problems, or having to see less of you. Decide quickly.

Till this evening, dear little one.

Evening

My love

I've been having a really lovely day. [. . .] Then I got your letter. All right, then, you're not such a bad little one if you sent off the books – that was well done. So I'll inform my sister that I'm supposed to be going on a five-day visit to her, and that she should even send me a wire. And we'll go to the Mistral, my love. I've had some mysterious, lacklustre letters from Bost, who says he can't say anything because of the censors, and who's sometimes doing sentry duty in the ice and sometimes sleeping in Galeries Barbès beds.[236] I don't have any idea

---

[236]Les Galeries Barbès is a Paris department store.

what he's up to, he must be up near the front, and soaking up alcohol all day long – he seems a bit fagged but still alert. A letter from Sorokine, who writes: 'I intend to try and seduce you as thoroughly as possible.' Nothing from Kos. or Bienenfeld. There you are, my little one. We ate very well, and once again I'm getting little snatches of music out of the wireless; but one's constantly being thwarted – it's an instrument that would make a saint swear.

Goodbye, my love, for now. I'm glad you were pleased with the books. I love you, my little one, and I'll send the ink-capsules soon. I kiss you most tenderly, and most happily, my dear little one

Your charming Beaver

[Megève]

Sunday 31 December [1939]

Most dear little being

I'm now spending one of the most poetic evenings of my whole life. Is it Kanapa's absence? It's more a cluster of coincidences. The group of students has vanished too, and some isolated individuals have turned up in their place. So now there are only solitary guests scattered around the two main rooms. A blond man, about whom I know nothing. A divinely handsome skiing instructor, who disembarked yesterday evening. The schoolmistress and a handsome young man whom, to my great astonishment, I found at the schoolmistress's table when I got back just now – they had dinner together. The girls of the household have gone off in beautiful, brand-new ski-clothes, and the chambermaid too – with a scarf on her head – in the company of her husband the cook: they've gone off somewhere or other to see the New Year in. So you really can feel quite intensely that it's New Year's Eve. I've seated myself at a kind of desk in the first room where the wireless is located, and for two hours now I've managed to find good music. But when, by chance, I passed over Gounod's *Ave Maria* and lost it for an instant, in the next room I heard the sound of a violin that was playing it too. It was a musician who showed up here yesterday, declaring that he was capable of doing anything provided he was given board and lodging. He's all dressed in black, with a black tie, a stiff collar, and a frill of beard. He carries parcels, helps with waiting at table, repairs skis, and plays the violin in case of need. Yesterday evening while falling asleep I'd already heard that violin. Just now, he's scraping out gypsy tunes at the request of the schoolmistress (who's forty if she's a day, and you can't conceive how ugly), who must be feeling like a young girl again because of the handsome youth. He's really good-looking – I wonder what he can want with that woman. A moment ago the musician was prowling round the wireless, asking me what kind of music I liked; the teacher was busy repairing a ski; and I felt I was involved in a novel – was myself (without any play-acting on my part, I swear) a character in a novel. An atmospheric novel, of course, that could turn into a detective story or whatever you liked. You can imagine how this little chalet in the snow manages to generate such powerful impressions, on the last evening of the year. The wireless really did compensate me for all my pains this evening – so much so that I've neither read nor worked since 6.30 this evening. I've listened to music by Bach, Beethoven, Ravel, Debussy, Borodin, Lully, etc. There were blank moments, but overall it was wonderfully pleasing. From beginning to end I've been having a splendid day. We left for St Gervais at 8.30, in the most glorious weather you could hope for. The run was hard, but I did it well. We took the ridiculous little train which climbs up to the Col de Voza: just one wooden carriage pushed pantingly by a wheezing engine – it's truly comical. On the train we ate the cold meal I'd brought along. By 11.30 we were at the Col, where we went and had a coffee in that beautiful hotel. How that moved me, my dear little one, to rediscover that place which so enchanted us when we were together. The beautiful hotel was just the same as ever – still just as pleasing, with its bar and the straw mats on the walls. Once we'd drunk our coffees, we left down the Blue Run, which was charming and easy – especially since the snow on it was soft. But I recalled with emotion how we struggled – we two poor little greenhorns, who knew almost nothing – on snow that had crusted over. When the snow's crusted, that run must be of fair to middling difficulty. I rediscovered in detail every turn: the stream near which I fell; a hump I couldn't get down, while you yelled at me from below; the crossing where you bruised your poor little knee. My love, I found you there again with such intensity that I've tears in my eyes as I write this.

[. . .]

After that the evening I've told you about began – and went on till 11. Now it's Monday morning, and I'm finishing off my letter while eating breakfast – it won't go before this afternoon anyway. I slept well and am just off to Rochebrune – feeling full of beans.

No letter from you, so I'm hoping for two today – those of the 27th and 28th. As for the ones of 29th and 30th, if there's anything important in them you must repeat it, because they may go astray: wire post restante if you're arriving by the 6th.

As for me, this evening and tomorrow I'll write a single long letter which I'll post in Paris on Wednesday – that'll give it the best chance of getting there. I'm actually leaving tomorrow – Tuesday – which is the last day when there are adequate trains, but we don't reach Paris until 9. With all the delays, Thursday would be too late. But I'm not letting anyone know about this early return, so I'll have my free Wednesday in Paris – which delights me.

My love, perhaps in a week I'll have you opposite me – I dream of that day and night. I love you, my little one, with all my heart.

Your charming Beaver

🌿 1940

Hôtel-Pension Saint-Antoine
Les Houches (Hte-Savoie)

Tuesday 2 January [1940]

Most dear little being

I wrote to you yesterday morning then, while eating my breakfast. I put the letter into the little tidy which serves the hotel guests as a mail-box, then donned my skis and sped off in magnificent sunlight towards Megève.

[. . .]

In the Café des Houches I read – as I've in fact been doing throughout the past two days – a life of Heinrich Heine published by the *N.R.F.* 3 or 4 years ago, which the Hungarian lent me and which I've really been enjoying. Do you know it? A strange, individualist life, which nevertheless couldn't have been more thoroughly steeped in the social. Rarely has a fellow been more 'situated' than that one. Through him you can trace the whole history of German Jewish immigration a hundred years ago – which is curious to see in the light of today. He knew a host of interesting individuals – Marx, among others, and Lassalle, and Wagner, and G. de Nerval, and hundreds of others. And his destiny was a strange one, and very impressive. I found it altogether gripping. And now, in another café, I'm waiting for the coach that will put me down at St Gervais-Le Fayet. I'll have four hours before my train, which I'll use to get rid of all my correcting for school, so that tomorrow in Paris I'll have a huge day of work – which I covet. If Kos. isn't there I'll go to the cinema in the evening – otherwise probably in the late afternoon. I'm longing to do that – and to get back to Paris. But I'm also dreaming about the start of a new skiing season. I've enjoyed myself tremendously, and I'm genuinely beginning to be able to do a few things. Who knows, perhaps the two of us next winter, my love? I so long to resume my life with you, my little one.

I'm without any letters – but I told them to forward any to Paris. It's because of the New Year, no one at the chalet had any. The last one I got was dated the 26th. Tomorrow in Paris I'll get those of the 31st and 1st, perhaps – which is a happy thought.

Do tell me when you're arriving, my love, so that I can arrange about your suit[237] and rejoice in advance. I'm in such a hurry to see you! I love you passionately, my beloved

Your charming Beaver

[Paris]

Wednesday 3 January [1940]

Most dear little being

This morning I found your letter of 31 December waiting dutifully for me at the post office. But where are those of the 27th-28th-29th-30th? They're adrift somewhere between Megève and Paris, and it annoys me not to have them. I've also had 3 books, but not the *Shakespeare*, you little wretch! I sent you a cable about it. My sweet little one, I'm really embarrassed to be obliged to tell Kos. that you've got her book, especially as last time she asked I told her I'd got it at school. It's going to cause a fuss, and in any case it's very unpleasant. I can't simply buy a new one, since it has her name in it – and she looks on it as the apple of her eye. I implore you to send it off at once if you haven't already done so. Some slight disappointment over the notebooks too – I really should have liked to read them. This day in Paris has been quite disappointing in general, since I was returning with the impression that I was going to 'rediscover' – but rediscover what? – you, of course, and I haven't seen you anywhere, my love. I'm not sad, actually, just a bit dazed from the journey, as is only to be expected.

[...]

We got in at 9. Paris was mild and snow-covered, utterly deserted

---

[237]Sartre kept much of his wardrobe at his mother's flat, where she looked after it.

round the station where I waited almost quarter of an hour for a taxi. I returned to the hotel – no Kos. I unpacked, took my time getting dressed, then called in at the post office, read your letter at the Versailles while eating my breakfast, and sent off your parcel. The notebooks are a bit too big, but I couldn't find anything else with ruled paper. As for the ink, it's superb – best quality and the latest novelty. After that I went to Neuilly to collect your dough, then lunch at my mother's, then to the Dôme where I spent 4 hrs working. I reread my last version of the novel for a while. It has already got to page 80 and I've the impression it has improved a hundred per cent. I found it really well done, and was pleased. But I need your opinion – perhaps you'll find it has become too heavy. After that, I dutifully worked on my Chap. 4 – which needs only a few finishing touches and didn't give me much trouble.

[...]

My father has read your book. He finds it 'well written', but crazy and stupid except for 'The Childhood of a Leader', which he quite likes. But he can't understand how it is that, after starting out on the left, you should become Action Française[238] by the end. He's outraged by the obscenities and by the fact that you dedicated the book to Kos., whom he suspects of being your mistress.

Goodbye, my love. This is a wretched little letter, but I've no strength. Have you sent the books to Bost? I promise them to him daily, poor thing. Send me Rauschning once you've finished it – or bring it with you, there's no hurry. Till tomorrow, my little one – I'm hoping for a big bundle of letters. I miss you. I love you so much, my beloved.

Your charming Beaver

Le Dôme

Paris, Thursday 4 January [1940]

Most dear little being

It's a big occasion today – I've had two letters from you, including one written only *yesterday*. The Megève ones still haven't arrived, which

---

[238]Right-wing political group founded in 1899, and associated with the names of Charles Maurras and Léon Daudet. Monarchist, Catholic and anti-Semitic, it ended in support of the Vichy regime of 1940-44.

annoys me a bit – but less and less so, as I'm back up to date with your life anyway. I'm beginning to hope that the *Shakespeare* may arrive at more or less the same time as Kos., who's turning up tomorrow. Apart from that, my charming vermin are beginning to devour me again, and I'm finding it a bit overwhelming – I *so much* want to work, you can't imagine. To tell the truth for a change, it's Bienenfeld whom I find burdensome. Seeing Sorokine at lunch gave my heart a pleasing little jolt – so much so that I offered her my evening (I'm writing to you while waiting for her). And I quite enjoy the thought of seeing Kos. again tomorrow – she has written me an idyllic little letter. But this afternoon with Bienenfeld was wearisome and insipid. She was harassed because of her family – full of little worries, with nervous outbursts of passion – and I was thoroughly bored. I made my arrangements: two evenings a week, a lunch lasting an hour and a half on Monday, and the same on Friday. Actually, though complaining that we'll hardly ever see one another, she's scarcely disposed to grant me any more.

[. . .]

Back to the post office, where I found your yesterday's letter and a note from Bost dated Monday. I called in at the hotel. Wanda came back this morning, Kos. is coming back tomorrow. Tomorrow I'll also see Merleau-Ponty for a couple of hours, which I'll rather enjoy. And I'll still have a good morning's work, so it all fits in quite well.

I'm now waiting for Sorokine, whom I'll take to a bar. I find you harsh regarding *The Monk*. It's trumpery stuff – but the best kind – and I really enjoyed it. I'm covetous of receiving *Le Diable Amoureux*.[239] Do send those books to that nice little Bost, now that you've got some dough.

Goodbye, my dear little one. I can't wait to know all your little theories, to show you my novel, to talk to you and to kiss you, my little one. I love you so much. It won't be long, my dear, dear love

Your charming Beaver

---

[239]Tale by Jacques Cazotte (1719-92), in which the Devil takes the form of a young woman and wins the love of a Spanish gentleman.

[Paris]

Friday 5 January [1940]

My dear, dear love

It's a big day again today: three letters from you, one from yesterday and two from Megève dated the 27th and 28th – there are only two left for me to recover. I also got three charming little letters from Bost, who's at the front, eating like a prince, idle, and very much enjoying himself. All of this put me in a good mood. My dear little one, are you truly going to come for almost a fortnight? How happy we're going to be! My head's bursting with plans, and these next three weeks are going to proceed gently towards you, through work that delights me at present because I keep thinking how I'm going to show it to you. I love you, my sweet little one. I feel your love around me, so warm, so alive – o little hard one, who for me are more tender than dew. Your letters make me laugh, my love, and your whole little person – it's for good reason that you've founded a comic tradition, o yourself.

I've got things to tell you. Well, Sorokine arrived at the Dôme, all sweet and pleasing. She didn't want to go 'to bars', but had brought her treasure-chest to show me all her secrets. We bought mandarins and went up to my room. There she entrusted her most precious possessions to me: the colonel's letters and her girl friend's, her own little diaries, and diagrams of her 'moods', 'work', and 'daily routine' in the year 1937. These were in red and violet, on a squared background – and superb. In her charming way, she told me a big scandal she'd been involved in when she was sixteen – making me swear not to tell a soul, not even you. For one whole month of her life, she systematically stole with her girl friend from the Uniprix du Printemps store. Neither for fun nor on moral principle, but to earn money. They stole twenty-franc fountain-pens by the dozen, then resold them at school for five francs. They stole wool for pullovers and material for dresses, which their parents reimbursed them for in the belief that they'd bought it legitimately. She actually gave her mother a 50% discount: 'She's so poor, we couldn't charge her the same price as in the department stores', she told me artlessly. The profits went to pay for orgies of roller-coasters and coconuts at the World Exhibition. But then, one day, a fellow in plain clothes showed up in the street behind them and ordered them to follow him: they had their pockets full of fountain-pens. He called a policeman to help him out and, to avoid humiliating the girls too much, they took them to the police-station arm-in-arm like friends. The girls were trembling with fright. They were put in the cells, where a woman was groaning: 'It's a disgrace, I only stole a handbag' – so they took responsibility for the woman's fate: she gave them a *pneu* to post, addressed to a fence friend of hers, to warn him. Meanwhile, the families were being rounded up. Old man Sorokine arrived, and the girl friend's grandfather and grandmother: collapse, sobbing, admonishments from the superintendent, supplications from the parents. The worst thing was that they regarded the parents with suspicion, thinking they'd sent the children out to do the job for them – they'd had 500 F. worth of goods on them. So policemen went off to search the homes of those decent folk, all overcome with shame. Eventually the two thieves were released. 'Last month she was even on the list of merit!' her father was telling the superintendent, to win his sympathy. It's since then that her father has looked upon her as 'the lowest of the low'. Her parents are currently planning to separate, and they're arguing over who'll not have to take her with them.

After that we began to kiss, and without any desire – but from a sense of scruple – I asked her if she wanted us to have 'complete relations', as we'd said. She answered: 'As you like' – so I promptly confined myself to ordinary embraces. After quarter of an hour she started punching the wall, twisting about nervously and half-sobbing into the pillows. Then I told her that for my part I certainly did want more complete relations, but didn't want to do anything that might displease her. 'We mustn't be hypocritical', she moaned. So then I began to undress her a bit, and she said: 'Turn off the light, please.' I told her we could stop right there if she wanted. 'No – but provided the light's turned off.' I turned it off, and a moment later she asked me with the greatest politeness: 'How about you, would you mind undressing?' I took off my blouse and a moment later she said – this time without hypocrisy, but with a taste for plain speaking: 'Very well! All right, we'd better go on to the end while we're about it, but don't turn on the light.' So we undressed and got into bed. I caressed her – intimately, but briefly – then we talked. It was strange and pleasing. Clearly it interested her as an experience more than it gave her pleasure, since she was paralysed by shyness. She asked if I used to sleep like that with you, if it didn't embarrass me, and if you walked round the room naked (I said no). She couldn't be more of a virgin, mistrustful of the male and embarrassed about her body. 'It's ridiculous, the moment when you get undressed or dressed,' she said. There was no question of mad passion – she was mainly happy because it seemed 'really intimate', and she'd like the most complete intimacy. As for me, I was charmed by her – I truly like her a lot. She left me at midnight, with dough for a taxi and quite radiant.

[...]

Goodbye, my little one. I'm going to work really well till your arrival, when you'll see 200 pages of the new version – all last year's work gone over and recast. I'm really happy. Till tomorrow. I love you and am waiting for you, o yourself, my happiness and my life. I kiss you most tenderly, little beloved one.

Your charming Beaver

[Paris]

Saturday 6 January [1940]

Most dear little being

I've had your last little letters from Megève – and a letter written the day before yesterday. How sweet and pleasing they always are, my love, and what a sensible little life you do lead. But heavens! how I'd love to see you and how I am languishing for you! So yesterday I waited for M. Ponty and for Kos., but neither of them turned up – only Wanda, who asked me for dough and whom I invited to go with me to the College Inn at about 9, if her sister didn't arrive. But while waiting I didn't do any work. Just brought my diary up to date – which it really needed – and corrected a sheaf of exercises. I'm going to have two probationers, who'll take that burden off my shoulders for a month. Meanwhile I had dinner Chez Pagès, while reading *Gilles*[240] – which I'm beginning to enjoy less. M. Ponty called in for a couple of minutes to make an appointment with me for today. Then Wanda showed up, with her beautiful black velvet coat and a little blue scarf, perfectly charming. I'd bought some fine cigarettes, she ordered a whisky and I a cocktail, and we chatted with more ease than ever before. I told her lots of gossip and she did the same for me – I find she has a great deal of charm. She's nurturing little dreams about the possible sale of pictures that she might perhaps paint. She'd done a few very poor sketches at [Laigle], but at least she had the urge. She must have told you all about the Lunar Woman and how she wants to become a social celebrity after the war. We came home at 11 and I'd spent a very pleasing moment – I understand perfectly your having tender feelings for that little person. The Kos. sisters 'have class', as our mutual friend [Bienenfeld] says – there's no denying it. I went to bed, read *Gilles* and slept. But not enough: having grown accustomed to long nights, I'm tired this evening.

---

[240]Novel (1939) by the far-right novelist Pierre-Eugène Drieu La Rochelle, who became editor of the *N.R.F.* under Nazi occupation and committed suicide in 1945.

School this morning, then work at the Dôme. I've read through my first 80 pages again, and I really think it's good work – substantial and quite adroit. I can't wait to show you.

Bienenfeld arrived at 12.30 and we had lunch. She was relaxed, so at once I was too – and glad to see her. We talked again about Thursday, working out exactly why things hadn't gone well – it was pleasing and casual.

[. . .]

I went to Les Vikings, where Sorokine tried to sulk because I was 5 min. late, but that didn't last for long. She brought me some hazelnuts and a superb cardboard folder with two pockets, for my papers – I'm really proud of it. We chatted and discussed the *Monadology*.

At 6.30 I dropped in at the hotel, where I found a bundle of letters from you, Bienenfeld and Sorokine – sent back from Megève – and checked that Kos. wasn't there. So I telephoned Bienenfeld, with whom I'm going to spend the evening and whom I'm just now waiting for at the Hoggar, amid the most infernal racket. I haven't yet had the books.

Goodbye, my dear little one, till tomorrow. I see that I have fifteen good days of work ahead of me. This week at least is looking very promising, and I'm terribly pleased about that. I still love you just as ardently, and you're still just as ever-present to me, sweet little beloved being. Goodbye for now

Your charming Beaver

Apparently Gégé's at Castel Novel with stones in her bile duct, terribly ill, and may have to be operated on.

[Paris]

Sunday 7 January [1940]

Most dear little being

I'm feeling jubilant today: I've just worked for almost seven hours non-stop on my novel, and I've reworked twenty-five whole pages – it's splendid. It would go really fast if I worked like this every day. I'm spurred on by your arrival – I'd like to have two hundred pages to show you. Well, I've already got a hundred now. I settled down at the Dôme at 9 on the dot, drank a coffee, ate two currant buns, smoked ten cigarettes and worked for 3½ hours. After that I ate a rumpsteak and potatoes without moving from my seat, while reading *Gilles* which I'm no longer enjoying at all. Then from 1 till 4 I worked again. I've just put away my papers, since I'm intending to go to a concert at 5.30 and I want to get my letters written first, in case Kos. comes back by this evening. Otherwise I'll have a free evening, with the possibility of seeing Bienenfeld – though I don't think I'll avail myself of that. As for Kos., perhaps she came back at midday; but as she hasn't let me know, I shan't call in at the hotel again till 8. Too bad if she grumbles – a whole day of solitude in Paris is so wonderful! I haven't had any letters because it's Sunday, but that doesn't matter – I had three yesterday and I'll get two tomorrow. I feel you so close, my sweet little one, and am altogether united with you.

So yesterday I wrote to you rather hurriedly from the Hoggar. We were upstairs, and could hear the muffled sound of music coming from below. Every so often the magnificent dancing-girls would put in a little appearance. The owner looks fondly upon me and is all smiles and little courtesies. Bienenfeld turned up at 8.30, with her superb coat and a muff slung over her shoulder, and it wasn't unpleasing – humdrum but not tedious. I exerted myself a bit, telling stories – about Sorokine – and discussing Kant. She was really happy. I ate a little Algerian salad, with funny little Algerian sausages[241] all round it, and as I was still hungry I rounded it off with a few cakes from the Alsatian pastry-shop. Bienenfeld confided to me that in her heart of hearts she disapproved of theft – she's terribly steeped in social and Kantian morality. We went back to her place, and though I was dropping asleep we nevertheless spent another hour talking. Then bed, brief and uneventful embraces, and sleep: too short, because I was afraid her mother might roll up in the morning and because I wanted to get some work done. I called back at my hotel – with something of an adultress's guilty conscience – but Kos. hadn't showed up, so there was no need of an alibi. (What a lot of alibis have been consumed since then, alas! – and it's not over.) I'll tell her, actually, that Bienenfeld's in Paris and I'll be spending two evenings with her. After that I came here, and I've nothing – really nothing – more to tell, my dear little one.

[. . .]

There, this time the bottom of the barrel has been reached. I'll just write a little note to Bost, then go off to the concert. I'm really happy,

---

[241]Merguez.

my love – I'm altogether with you and I love you. Come very soon, my little one, we'll be so happy!

Your charming Beaver

'September' is an excellent title.[242]

[Paris]

Monday 8 January [1940]

Little beloved

Two letters today and really big ones – how sweet you are! I love you, my little one, with your sensible little life and your bold thoughts. I'm glad you're finding yourself. I don't know if one should assume oneself as French – I'll think about it between now and tomorrow. Partly yes, of course: it seems to me that to write *Nausea*, in a sense, is to assume yourself as French – didn't we talk about this once Chez Rey? Weren't we saying that one couldn't have the same solidarity with the persecuted Jews of Germany which one would have with the Jews of France, and that the fact of being 'situated' necessarily also included frontiers? I'll think about it (but it seems to me that assuming this no more implies patriotism than assuming the war implies being a warmonger). In this case, it's a matter (or isn't it?) of attaining universal objects, ideas, works, etc. through a singular, historical position. What's now needed is to define the position, and limit it, and see what it commits you to. Talk to me more about this – I find it very interesting. In my little novel, I've devised a conversation in which Pierre assumes himself precisely as French, by refusing the idea of transferring his theatre to America. How impatient I am to read you, and for you to read me, my little one! That's what makes separation most frustrating for me.

You know, the passage you quote from Bienenfeld is highflown and false.[243] She's far from living only for you. She lives to an incredible extent for me, and also for her work and countless little private whims. There's an abstract tension in her relations with you. She calculates – 6 months that I knew him, and 7 months in which I haven't set eyes on him – and it's that representation of your useless love which is present

---

[242]Title considered for a time by Sartre for the future *The Roads to Freedom*.
[243]The passage in question is one of the numerous excisions from De Beauvoir's edition of Sartre's letters.

and painful to her. She's actually intensely happy just now. You shouldn't feel any remorse about not seeing her. It would be dreadful if she were to know, but it's not at all dreadful for her not to see you.

[. . .]

This morning: school; work at the Source for 1½ hrs; pleasant lunch with Bienenfeld – I'm pleased because she's not too clinging. I don't think my charming vermin are going to prevent me working this term. Then school, and on the way out Sorokine, who accompanied me by taxi to the post office and on foot to the Dôme.

[. . .]

Till tomorrow. I haven't yet got the *Shakespeare*, unless it's at the hotel. You'll soon have *Gilles*, which is dreadfully boring and disagreeable.

How sweet you are to write to me so nicely, my love! It's truly wonderful how happy that keeps me. I'm feeling fine – my holiday rested and changed me. I'm now thinking only about working and seeing you soon. I love you, my beloved little one.

Your charming Beaver

[Paris]

Tuesday 9 January 1940

Sweet little being

Do you know what's happening today? I'm 32. But I don't feel too much of an old woman. I'm in the best of health and looking extremely good. I've got all dolled up this evening – wearing my earrings, and a turquoise-blue turban with matching bodice – because I'm going out with the Kos. sisters. We're going to the Comédie Française to see *Right You Are*,[244] because I want to see that Ledoux act, whom everyone praises so highly. I'm waiting for them at present in a little café called Le Dauphin on the theatre square, having arrived early in order to write to you.

[. . .]

This morning – school. Oh! I dreamt I was making another conquest: that brown-haired girl from H. IV who gave me a letter at the beginning

---

[244]*Cosi è se vi pare*, 1917 play by Luigi Pirandello usually translated as *Right You Are If You Think You Are.*

of the year. I was thinking of deceiving Sorokine with her, but after speaking to me she put on a red wig and they warned me she was a shady character. It's full of lessons, but I'm too lazy to draw them – so I'm just giving you the raw material.

At 8, then, I crossed a grey, cold Luxembourg as enchanted as ever with my Tuesday walk. I drank a hot chocolate at the Mahieu, then gave my lesson. I've got two probationers now – real dregs of humanity – and I handed them two bundles of exercises to mark, so that's at least one benefit. Then 2 hrs work at the Mahieu. Brief lunch with Sorokine – charming. She undertook to explain to me why, in my allocation of time, I shouldn't classify friends in order of seniority but of merit – which puts her at the top. 'It's not a matter of squeezing anything out of you', she said slyly. I stood firm. They make me laugh, Bienenfeld and Sorokine, for each in turn explains how ridiculous it is to commit yourself and create duties for yourself, and how she doesn't want me to think I've any duties towards her – and then, at the first opportunity, screams blue murder about my being 5 minutes late, or behindhand with a letter.

[. . .]

Goodbye, dear little loved one, o nice little letter-writer so constant and faithful, little wordsmith, little brainbox. How our tongues will wag before long! I love you with all my might, my sweet little one – I'm waiting for you.

Your charming Beaver

[Paris]

Wednesday 10 January [1940]

Most dear little being

Here's another sweet letter from you in that beautiful South-Sea-Island-blue ink. My little one, how nice it would be if you were here for the Easter holidays in some accessible place! Come soon, my love, I so, so want to see you. Bienenfeld is amazed and shocked that you shouldn't be coming until the end of March. I'd advise you now to furnish her with your story about being withdrawn to the interior – that will console her and provide an explanation.

Yesterday, then, I waited for the Kos. sisters at the little café on Place du Théâtre Français, but they didn't turn up till 7.30. This allowed me to bring my diary up to date. It's merely a summary journal, devoid of interest; but I enjoy keeping it, in order to preserve the detailed outline of a year. They finally bustled in, Wanda placid, Real Kos. nervous and drawn. [. . .] Real Kos. is the more interesting of the two; what she says when telling you something, for example, is always far richer. But Wanda's much more pleasing to experience – she has a somewhat heavy grace, that touches one.

[. . .]

After that I went and worked at the Versailles, alongside Bienenfeld who has read my Chap. 3 and made some slight criticisms – correct ones. I'll touch it up, in order to show you a perfect masterpiece. She was flattered that I should take her seriously. We worked almost without speaking. I went to pick up your letter, began to reply, then went home to see Sorokine. An hour of Leibniz, then tender but superficial embraces, made extremely pleasing by the constant charm of that little person. She found the courage to say: 'I like being in your arms like this' – and a few other sweet nothings, which she drags forth dutifully. She's very happy, by and large. Her own passion's so graceful that it quite reconciles me to passion. She confided lots of little thoughts and feelings concerning me and ended up giving me excellent reports, even with respect to the strength of my will, which does irk her – since she'd like to see more of me – but is also in part what she values about me.

[. . .]

I got myself called a 'crazy old fool' at the Versailles. As usual, there was a gaggle of ill-favoured, housewifely whores grumbling about the work being so hard. 'What I say is, if I don't get a present there's nothing doing', one was declaring in an affronted tone. It was that same one who started grumbling coarsely to her neighbour that I was smoking too much. I just went on smoking one cigarette after another, so she called me a crazy old fool – out loud. I didn't bat an eyelid.

Goodbye, my little one. Sorokine has gone off and now I'm going to see Kos. Till tomorrow. How well you do always write to me, o best of little ones! Your letter was very funny (about Pieter's snores). It'll make a fine volume: 'War Letters'. I love you, and am waiting for you – we'll be so happy, my love!

Your charming Beaver

[Paris]

Thursday 11 January [1940]

Most dear little being

I haven't been able to call in at the post office today, thus depriving myself of a letter – but I'll have two tomorrow, which is a delightful thought. Left to myself and with nothing to reply to you about, I'm very poor in things to tell you – still being studious and dutiful and uneventful. I'm filled with happiness, and serenity, and zeal for work – it's wonderful, the rate I'm keeping up.

[. . .]

This morning I was at the Dôme by 8.30 and worked till 10. Then school, followed by lunch with Sorokine, as angelic as ever. I explained lots of things to her about contraceptives and abortion, which interested her keenly. We parted idyllically – the idyll's now constant. A happy combination of circumstances (Kos. is spending Saturday evening with Wanda and Mouloudji, Bienenfeld's going to the Français with her father to see *Right You Are*) means that I'll be seeing her on Saturday evening and will certainly sleep with her again, an idea that doesn't displease me it must be said – oh! with only the most honourable and affectionate intentions, you understand! After that another two hours of school, work at the Mahieu, then at 5.30 Bienenfeld arrived and we dashed off by taxi to the Opéra-Comique, where we had an excellent ground-floor box. How pleasing Mozart is – it entranced me. In a light comedy with easy music, you no longer feel bothered by sad scenery or by conventions – everything's just a gracious and acceptable game. Moreover, the interpretation was extremely good – genuinely an unalloyed pleasure. After that we went to eat Chez Capoulade, and before going off to sleep (a night of passion, the idea of which I find a bit chilling) we're now writing to you from the Mahieu. This is a wretched letter, with a humdrum flavour to it. But it's my life that's humdrum, not my feelings for you. Just now I was struck by the violent thought that in 10 days I'd be seeing you – and my eyes were starting from their sockets! My sweet little one. [. . .]

We're being chucked out – they're upturning the chairs and switching off all the lights. Goodbye, my love, for now. I love you so much.

Your charming Beaver

[Paris]

Friday 12 January [1940]

Most dear little being

I've worked flat out again today. That means the first 160 pages are now finished, and I've drawn up a big plan for recasting and fleshing out the next 50 – so you'll have something to read. But I'll tell you everything in order. Well, yesterday at 11 we went home to Bienenfeld's place. Embraces. If I'm to tell you everything, in addition to the usual rufous odour of her body she had a pungent fecal odour which made things pretty unpleasant. So far as friendship with her goes, no problem – but our physical relations couldn't be more distasteful to me. We talked a bit in bed, and she said she often felt she was shocking me when she made jokes. I said that was true, but perhaps it simply meant I was excessively thin-skinned. She excused herself by claiming you were coarser than she was – but that's not true. Not only are yourself never 'out of place', you've a very keen sense of when other people are. On your better days this shocks you, while on your worse you derive a sadistic pleasure from it. But it no more passes over your head than it does over mine. She says she often herself feels she shouldn't have said something – whether too vapid or too heavy – but the fact is she shouldn't even think it. She's always swamped by herself, and as she justly and sadly concluded: 'I'm not authentic.' [. . .]

I must report to you a charming sally by that altogether authentic person, Sorokine. You know she forgives me my literary activities, but finds them utterly derisory. Yesterday she said to me: 'So, when you've finished your novel you'll start another one, then you'll be hurrying to finish that one so you can begin yet another!' That made her laugh. I told her: 'You too – you study a page of Leibniz so you can move on to the next, and so on!' She couldn't contain herself at this: 'It's not the same! With you, you *invent* things so you can write them down afterwards!' – that struck her as the absolute limit. It filled me with an immense liking for her, of the same kind I sometimes feel for Bost.

[. . .]

You don't say anything about my evening with Wanda at the College Inn. Hasn't she written to you about it? Tell me what she says about me, and some more about her too – she interests me. Have I told you I want to take the two Kos. sisters out with Mouloudji one of these days?

I'm going to write a short letter to Bost – short, both because I've nothing to recount and because contact does, after all, get lost with a fellow who has frozen feet all the time and survives only through big doses of alcohol. He's ever so decent – and I'm not like Kos., I retain the most powerful and vivid feelings for him – but I don't much want to tell him things or, above all, go into too much trivial detail. I wonder how it would be if *you* were in the same situation. As things are, I feel you precisely within arm's reach.

Goodbye, my little one – my little so-modest one. I shan't exhort you to climb back on your pinnacle, since you've returned there all on your own. I love you so much, my love. I'm all outstretched towards your arrival. I kiss you most tenderly.

Your charming Beaver

Do send the books to Bost, wretched egoist – little not-nice-at-all! And send me back his long letter.

Envelope
F.M.
Private Sartre
Observation Post
E.M.A.D.[245]
Zone 108*

[Paris]

Saturday 13 January [1940]

Most dear little being

I've just found your day before yesterday's letter, with the description of those Uncle Jules stories.[246] I can scarcely have any opinion, my sweet little one. It somewhat disconcerts me, that whole idea of a 'genre' – and especially the idea of illustrating your arguments by a story. On the other hand, I really like the idea of little, free-wheeling essays in which you say whatever you've got to say on all sorts of topics. But, as you say, work away for twenty (?) days without bothering about me – then

---

*Letters 12 to 17 January 1940 and 19 January to 23 March 1940 addressed as above.
[245]*État-Major d'Artillerie de Division* (Artillery H.Q.)
[246]For two or three days, Sartre entertained the idea of using the framework of stories told by a fictional uncle to his nephew as a vehicle for a witty examination of literary genres which these stories would illustrate. But he tore up the six pages he actually wrote.

I'li see it all when you come. Are you coming so late then? That really annoys me – first because I can't wait to see you, and secondly because it's going to fall at the same time as Bost, which will work out badly (so far as Bost's concerned, since so far as you're concerned, it won't change anything). Well, we shall see. Do come, that's what matters. If you're going to Annecy before Easter, I thought we shouldn't tell anyone – and especially not Bienenfeld – that you can be visited, otherwise she'll demand half the Easter holidays. Do take care. You know, she was quite downcast at not getting a letter for two days. She ascribed it to the mails, but it left a real gap for her.

Assuming yourself as a Jew doesn't, of course, mean wanting rights *as a Jew*. It's absurd to think that, otherwise assuming your situation as a French person would be tantamount to chauvinism. It's the second interpretation that's right. We never discussed this with Bienenfeld.[247]

[. . .]

Goodbye, joy of my life, little pure-gold one, little beloved. My life's full but terribly barren, with abrupt fissurations of pain (more for Bost than for you, actually – you seem so close, not really lost at all). It's you, and the way I miss you, that creates this barrenness of my whole being. Come back soon, little dew – it's only in the instant when I read your letters that I grow soft.

Come quickly and clasp me in your little arms, and kiss me, and give me back a true Beaver's heart. My love.

Your charming Beaver

[Paris]

Sunday 14 January [1940]

My sweet little one

How dutiful my life continues to be! That's almost another 6 hrs work today. I was at the Dôme and didn't leave till 4.30, my only distraction having been a handshake from Gerassi, who wants to invite me to a tête-à-tête dinner – doubtless so he can have a discussion with me about the Baba. Oh yes, there was the additional distraction of a rumpsteak and fried potatoes, washed down with wine and with

---

[247]Another reference to a censored passage in Sartre's published letters.

pudding to follow. While eating this I finished *Vorge contre Quinette*,[248] which is very poor. The character of Quinette is ever so slightly entertaining, in a facile way, but the rest's odious – especially Vorge. So you're going to get a bunch of bad books, but it's your own fault.

There was a bit of movement, however, before and after this studious day. First, yesterday evening after writing to you I went to buy some envelopes so I could post my letter, and on leaving the stationery shop on Boulevard Montparnasse I found Sorokine standing outside the door, waiting for me reproachfully: she'd been coming down from the Métro and seen me go in. She had a little scarf round her face and looked quite charming. We went up to my room and there realized – or rather I realized, with horror – that I'd forgotten my black notebook at the Coupole. I was scared stiff it might fall into someone's hands, so rushed over there – luckily I found it again. We came back, sat down side by side, and after 10 min. of conversation got down to kisses. After ¼ hr of kisses we were in bed – first having modestly switched off the lights. I find it all a bit like an 'initiation', which would bother me if I weren't momentarily smitten by that little person with all her charm. But it's really momentary. With her, I'm not capable even of that semblance of passion I managed to feel for Bienenfeld, on one or two occasions when she kicked up a fuss about wanting physical relations. Yet it's a violent affection I feel in her case, because I find her so perfect and charming. She was relaxed this time, all calm and happy and tender, without any tiresome effusion of passion. There were embraces – one-sided. Then she said we had to turn on the lights, so she could read me her diaries – and she read me some charming little passages on the education of her will. But we didn't get far – having remained in bed and unclad – and the embraces started up again, this time with reciprocity. It's certainly not what it was with Kos. But I've a very keen taste for her body, and find these moments extremely pleasing – especially her expressions, which are ever so moving – and her tenderness, all trustful but without surrender. She asked me what was the worst thing that could be done between women, and I told her the story of Toulouse and Zina.[249] She also asked me if we were criminals, and if we'd be put in prison if we were discovered like that. I said no – and she was sorry: she'd found the idea delightful. She went at a quarter to midnight, leaving me in bed – and forgetting her watch, her comb and her

---

[248] Novel (1939) by Jules Romains.

[249] For Zina, the gypsy girl adopted by Toulouse's mother as a companion for her only daughter and who became her accomplice (in forays into prostitution) and willing slave, see *The Prime of Life*, pp.66-9.

spectacles. Kos. told me she ran into her downstairs, calling with some acerbity for the street-door to be released. Kos. helped her open the door – and S. looked at her like a cat ready to spring. Kos. has taken her to her heart – in part sincerely, in part against Bienenfeld.

[. . .]

I'm not as dried out as all that. This afternoon, while working, I was assailed by the tenderest, most heartrending feelings of regret at the thought of days spent travelling with you – directed first at you, but then also at the charm of those days and places. I saw again our ascent of Vesuvius – do you remember, my love? Our journeys were always full of adventure – how pleasant it was! And now a little open-air dance-floor has just come back to me – Les Oranges, or something of that sort – above the Bay of Naples facing Vesuvius, one night. My sweet little one, shall we have that again?

How happy I've been with you! I love you, my little one – come back to me!

Your charming Beaver

[Paris]

Monday 15 January [1940]

Most dear little being

I've just had two letters from you, so sweet that they filled me with poetry, joy and warmth. O my little one, you're not a little dead person for me – you're so much alive, you're all my life. So when your letters don't come and I can no longer feel you, I cease to be anything but a poor, stubborn lichen. How cheerful and lively you seem, little being! Oh! how I'd love to eat omelettes with you (but why at the Relais de la Belle Aurore, my love? – it's no good). I'm glad you've abandoned those Uncle Jules stories – the truth is I was a bit suspicious of them, as I told you. I'm also a bit wary of symbols: couldn't you create a dictator of freedom who's not Prometheus, and at a time slightly in the future rather than in the past? But I like the idea of you writing a stage play.

What am I to tell you? There isn't much. Yesterday evening I wrote to Bost, then read a bit of Romains – La Douceur de Vie – which looks like being very boring, while eating some dates I'd bought which kept sticking to my fingers. I dreamt I was fighting in the war and weeping hot tears for my lost youth. This was because of something at the cinema about cannon and trenches which had made an impression on me. Those cannon, which seem so technical and civilized and so noble in the realm of machines – it's strange to think how they're just for destroying poor fragile little bodies. Oh! concrete too, of course – but only because of the body hidden within. I found it truly shattering.

This morning, Lycée C. Sée. Then I went to Café La Sorbonne, where Bienenfeld was. She'd indulged in a bit of pathos the evening before – just to keep her hand in – and explained to me how I loved her less than you (I make no protest, I'm perfectly happy for it to be admitted), and how the worst was that I didn't *want* to love her as much. I got off with mere bruises (verbal ones, of course), but it makes me laugh that she should think I need to hold myself in check. I was cold, cold, cold – more and more so – to the point of feeling a specific irritation with every word and every gesture, almost like with Poupette, which is rather dreadful. Thank heavens, it's quite impossible for us to see each other more than two evenings a week. I worked for almost 2½ hrs; ate some sauerkraut while looking at a copy of the *N.R.F.* I'd stolen from school, in which there was nothing at all; then went to school, where I made my pupils laugh as usual – I quite like that class at H. IV.

[...]

Goodbye, sweet little one. How do you manage to write me such tender, immediate letters? I feel my own are dry as dust. Yet this evening there's nothing arid about the way I miss you; your sentences and your very writing is so tangible, so much you, that I feel as though I'd just seen you. I love you, little one – so alive and so lively.

How did you explain to Wanda that your leave only lasts 5 days? On Wednesday I'm seeing your mother, and she'll leave your clothes at my place – she has sent me a note.

How sweet you are, my dear little one, to have restarted the letter for me that had wine spilt on it!

Little Bost has received your books safely. He's beside himself with fury because – thanks to the thaw – he hasn't been relieved, so he has stayed at the front for 25 days instead of 10. He has been very downcast and glum, because it was so cold, but he says that in a certain sense it's better than being in the rear, because they leave you alone – it's just sentry duty that's killing.

Goodbye for now, little beloved one. I kiss you so hard, hard, hard! I'm nothing but love for you.

Your charming Beaver

[Paris]

Tuesday 16 January [1940]

My sweet little one

How well I can picture you, gnawing your little fists and frantically racking your little brains in search of a subject! The Assistants must be terrified.[250] Wouldn't I just like to talk to you about all that! But it seems we'll have to wait such a long time still. My sweet little one, how bored I am! For the first time for ages, yesterday in bed I started weeping like an idiot while rereading your little letters. I looked at your photographs, saw myself back with you in the pine-wood at Juan-les-Pins – and when you were teaching me to swim, little being – and I was overwhelmed by a desolation of boredom. It wasn't sadness. I feel you so close – and am sure you must feel my tenderness for you, as I feel yours – so nothing's really lost. But how empty things are without you! I swear I'll die of it eventually. Can't you find some way of sending me your notebooks? Or the novel? In spite of your sweet letters, I so need your presence to grow a bit more substantial.

[. . .]

Goodbye, my little one, little loved one, little tear-jerker. Oh! you're no little fossil, my love, I can feel you all alive – which makes me laugh when I read your letters. I love you.

Your charming Beaver

[Paris]

Wednesday 17 January [1940]

Most dear little being

I'm full of excitement, because this new chapter I'm inserting into my novel (in the first part, which you know) is going marvellously, and I've made lots of happy innovations. I really think you'll heap me with praises when you read my 250 pages (for there'll be at least 250, o little so-tardy one). At this rate, if I work during the summer holidays the whole thing will be finished in October. That would make me incredibly happy.

[. . .]

---

[250]Sartre's nickname for the other soldiers in his unit, drawn from Kafka's *The Castle*.

I made my escape and arrived at the Brasserie Lutétia, where your mother had been churlish enough to fix for us to meet. I worked there for a good hour and started this letter, but then your mother arrived – with a somewhat ravaged expression, poor woman. Not seeing you has cast her into a depression and she's eating her heart out. She's very decent: she's asking only for the lunches I promised her, and an afternoon when she'll take us to the cinema. She claims you're keen to change clothes at their place. So if you arrive in the evening, does that mean you'll be gallivanting around as a soldier? Well, after all, you see so many of them that no one even notices – and you can go anywhere in the hero's uniform.

There – she has just left, after her very punctual little hour.. As for me, I've finished this letter and I'm leaving too, to pick up your letter from the post office. I'll add a note to tell you if it was there all right.

There was nothing! How's this? I hope you're not going to play the night observation trick on me?[251] But I think I'll get two tomorrow, so 'I'm not pathetic' – as Bienenfeld would say heroically. Now I'm off to see Sorokine. I'll have a little half-hour to write to Bost – then I'll see Bienenfeld.

Goodbye, o little so-awaited and so-desired one. Do hurry up and become a little welcome one! – so that in our correspondence there'll be one of those gaps which deceive the benevolent reader, who can't help thinking there's some quarrel or cooling of relations. My whole being's directed towards your arrival. I love you with all my might, my love. What omelettes we'll eat! I kiss you, my sweet little one

Your charming Beaver

[Paris]

Thursday 18 January [1940]

My sweet little one

Your letter was there this morning, as good as gold – they'd even put it on one side for me. I find it very wise of you to be doing so much philosophy, little wise one – and I approve wholeheartedly all your activities and your whole little person. Except that, like a fool, you

---

[251]Sartre used to claim tiredness, caused by fictional 'night observation' duties, as an excuse for not having written sooner to tiresome correspondents.

always look at the last page of detective stories. Tomorrow morning I'll send the books.

[. . .]

Bienenfeld danced – to show me how well she dances, and to outdo the Kos. sisters. She dances correctly but lifelessly, like a well brought up and very nervous little girl. We chatted affectionately, but simultaneously with this letter you're bound to receive a long philosophical epistle, since I maliciously threw her mind into turmoil. She was talking to me about Kos., and how angry it had made her that I should be giving her only 2 evenings (though her parents weren't coming back), in comparison with 5 for Kos. I trotted out the habitual refrain: duty, pity, desire for good relations. One thing leading to another, she said that this was 'unfair', that the Kos. sisters didn't 'deserve' it, and that these were taboos untouched by any ethical considerations. I then expounded to her our old (old but still true) idea of ethics without deserts – of grace, and the gift – and she was thunderstruck. 'Then, just as Elizabeth says in your novel, it's not any *use* being ethical!' And she admitted, quite unabashed, that she was ethical only in order to win my esteem. I told her that her ethical concerns delighted me, but didn't actually alter anything in my feelings for her – so she's now rather up against it. But that ethical scholasticism of hers is irritating. She didn't understand at all, when I told her morality was above all an existential stance. Indeed, in the whole world she's the being most devoid of any existential feeling. That's what makes her into nothing but a little intelligent monkey – and what's separating us more and more. She doesn't in the least live *her* situation in the world. Almost as much as Pieter, she's the *das Man* and nothing else.[252] But I couldn't explain properly, and got into a muddle – because a clear explanation would involve a terrible condemnation of her character. Actually, I'd really like to go more deeply into these ethical questions with you. But I'm sure you're in agreement about rejecting that idea of a morality granted to acts *from outside*, through imitation of a norm. She's quite incapable of seeing that being ethical is a matter of *being*. That you can't just 'do something rotten' with a pretty pout, telling oneself: 'After all, why not?' Nor can you be the least bit moral, when you're working for your own profit.

We spoke of almost nothing else, and at about 11 we left. She came up to kiss me for a while, then left in a taxi. [. . .] I met up with Bienenfeld again at the Mahieu and we worked side by side. See how little Heidegger's definition of metaphysics applies to her! She hadn't

---

[252]Heidegger's concept of *das Man* is usually rendered as 'the "they"'.

taken the time to think again about our conversation the evening before, even though she considered it of prime importance. That seems odd to me. I'd have racked my brains over it – as any well-born person would. But for her *there's no issue*. That's the worst thing. She's ensconced among people and ideas, with clear orders to purchase good securities and speculate adroitly – and that's absolutely all.

We were chucked out because the place was too crowded, so I went home to do an hour's work, and sleep, and write to Bost and you. I'm now seeing Kos. this evening.

Goodbye, dear little beloved one, little close-at-hand one, little oh-so-close one! I squeeze you so hard in my arms, my little one – how I am waiting for you!

Your charming Beaver

[Paris]

Friday 19 January [1940]

My dear little one

You've written to me so dutifully, my love, such a long letter! How seductive it sounds, that theory of Nothingness which solves every problem! So you're a truly great philosopher, are you then, little brainbox? Listen, I find your decision to recast the novel extremely sensible. Would you like the following: for me to tell That Lady to send the manuscript by registered post to Poupette, who'll type it? I really don't think there's anything to fear if it's registered. She'd make five copies – she's got a typewriter and time on her hands. But if you've got to rework it from beginning to end perhaps that would really be just wasted labour, and you might as well take it with you when you move to the rear, which seems to be pretty certain. It's as you like. I can't see any advantage in having it typed here, since it would cost between 500 and 1000 F., while the cost of a registered parcel is much the same La Pouèze-Paris or La Pouèze-La Grillère. I'll write as soon as I get your answer.

[. . .]

In connection with the corrida with Bienenfeld of which an account follows, I thought of how you once told me at St-Germain-les-Belles: 'I won't give "myself", but I'll give you lots of presents' – and you wrote me the same thing. Yet ultimately you converted your whole self into currency and gave me all that it's possible to give someone, my dear love. It's still the case that love's no symbiosis – but we'll weep over that some other day. 'That's what really devastates me', Bienenfeld told me, her teeth chattering.

At midday, you see, I arrived at La Sorbonne to find her wearing a scowl. She handed me a paper – containing some drivel about our ethical conversation of the other day – after which there was a formal 'address':

> You don't give yourself, you take.
> It's *false* that I'm your life – your life is a mosaic.
> For me, though, you are my life – I'm all yours.

And she explained to me that the night before in bed she'd thought (one thing leading to another) how I was at the centre of my own life – and had hated me for it. That she still hated me. And that she shouldn't have come. I first pointed out that you exist for her, which – as she now keeps us entirely separate – makes a mosaic in two colours. Also, that she's concerned about her parents, her work, etc., that nobody *is* anybody else's life, of course, but you build things together, etc., that giving and taking are strange words – and giving yourself is the best way of taking. Something which I didn't say to her was that I'd just as soon she didn't give me all the time she takes from me. She explained, in a woolly way, that for the first time yesterday she'd tried to look at the affair from my viewpoint: but then I was at the centre and all the people in my life were there too – whereas normally whenever she thought about me she'd deliberately wipe them out – and it was horrible. She was really trembling. Perhaps I've a heart of stone, but I wasn't moved in the least. I think it was her own fault – anyway placing yourself in the other person's shoes is elementary. My God! at the start of our own love affair I always tried to understand how I was placing myself in your life, from your point of view. And how, if I loved you more than you loved me, this meant I found more riches in you and was the more advantaged – in view of what I was receiving, and also by the very plenitude of my feelings. If, in love, there are things you find metaphysically painful, I can understand that. But you have to digest it in the same way as all the other things you have to digest about the human condition, telling your friends about it but not making it into a personal grievance. I find those alternations between dogged optimism and ill-considered lapses into tragedy frankly odious, in all objectivity.

The most concrete element in all this, I think, is her jealousy with regard to Kos.

She unburdened herself of this over lunch, then accompanied me to H. IV, all shivering with cold and nerves. There'll be more of the same tomorrow. I quite understand it all has to do with a certain sadistic wretch, but it still inspires me with as much repugnance as a scallop![253] The story about 'Sartre not wearing underpants' is quite true – that's when she started thinking about the coarseness of her jokes. But I'm so used to her out-of-place tone, that this shocked me no worse than the rest.

[. . .]

My sweet little one, goodbye, till tomorrow. On Sunday you'll get the sequel of the Bienenfeld story. I think you find me a bit mean to her, which is possible. I'll see tomorrow evening whether I should be nice – but she does get on my nerves.

I love you so much, dear little being.

Your charming Beaver

Le Dôme
[Paris]

Saturday 20 January [1940]

My dear little one

I had a little disappointment this morning, in that I didn't get a letter from you. I'll go back after 4, but it means there's a day's delay now. How cold it is! – we're quite numb. Outside it's dreadful, we shiver in the hotel and the Dôme's positively unendurable. I did stay there from 11 to 1, but for lunch I fled to the Coupole where I am now. I'll try to stay and work here this afternoon, where at least it's bearable.

[. . .]

I returned to my room and at 8, just as I was wondering if she were sulking and not going to come, Bienenfeld turned up with a little scarf on her head like at winter sports, all smiles and full of charm. I felt one weight lift from my mind, despite everything. She'd brought along some records, so we spent an hour listening to a pretty uninteresting Schubert trio, a rather beautiful Chopin ballade, and the beginning of Beethoven's 16th string quartet – which is superb. I graciously took both gramophone and records up to Kos., then – since there was no room at the Dôme or the Coupole – we went for a steak at the Sélect, where

---

[253]Shellfish (like butter and cheese) were among a number of foods which De Beauvoir viewed with horror.

Bienenfeld was as charming as she'd been odious yesterday. She can be really moving the day after one of her frenzies – so here I am, more attached to her than for weeks past. She explained how her gloom of two days ago had involved a certain imitation of the Kos. gloom. Also, how yesterday she'd deliberately prolonged her frenzy in order to make an impression on me, – even though she'd in fact come through it. We went over one point after another, and I explained everything to her on the basis of phenomenology. She understood everything, saying that naively she had a childish ideal of a Prince Charming, and of a life submerged in that of a Prince Charming. It's comical, this kind of gap between a thought that's almost mature and an infantile sensibility. Truly, in her perfect sincerity and simplicity (uncomplicated by reflection), she was altogether touching – and I was altogether tender and convincing. She told me, what's more, that even if her frenzy had been warranted and she held only the tiniest place in my life, though she'd certainly be desperately unhappy she'd hang on all the same. Also that – albeit believing her life to be all screwed up – she'd entirely forgotten to think about you, or have recourse to you (which proves nothing so far as you're concerned, as I can well imagine her doing just the same thing with our roles reversed). We talked about all this till they chucked us out. She related it to her mother's frenzies – correctly, I think. She came up with me for 20 minutes and we kissed, now I'm writing to you – so sleepy I'm ready to drop. Goodnight, my little one, I'm going to sleep. I kiss you with all my might, most dear little beloved.

Your charming Beaver

Bost has sent Kos. some striking little photos, where he can be seen in a huge hole in the snow from which only his shoulders protrude. That's the hole where he has to stand for 14 hours. But that's over – he hasn't been relieved, but he's back in the dug-out. He says the splendid thing about the front is that, sentry-duty apart, they leave you in peace. He seems quite lively and alert again.

Bienenfeld has charged me to tell you she forgot to write to you because she was working so hard, and apologizes profusely.

[Paris]

Sunday 21 January [1940]

Most dear little being

Well, I've been properly punished this morning for having been lazy yesterday evening! When I reached the post office I found all the counters closed – so I'm all solitary and abandoned. But I'll be there at 8 tomorrow morning and will read your letters while I eat my breakfast, before going to school. I love you so much, my little one! Just now Gégé took an old photo of you out of her bag, in which you were all thin and pleasing, and it gave me quite a jolt – I've almost got tears in my eyes at the memory. O dear little flesh-and-blood presence, how I desire you!

This time I've really very little to tell. After finishing my letter yesterday evening, I flung myself into bed utterly exhausted and woke with a start when my alarm went off at 8 – but I got up dutifully. The weather was milder in Paris, and it was snowing which was wonderfully poetic and pleasing.

[. . .]

It has occurred to me that it would be a terribly good idea if you were to come on about 6 February, since it'll be Shrovetide and I'll have a good excuse for pretending to go off on a visit to Poupette. But you can't choose, of course. Oh, how I long to see you! I've been in anguish for the past hour thinking about your life, with which you content yourself so well but where you're alone, my little one, and so devoid of everything – you who loved few things but loved them so intensely! Little all-alive, all-gay, all-warm, who've been embalmed like a little mummy. My love, we'll see a few things – we'll make a beautiful leave for you! I love you, my beloved, so very, very much, so tenderly – for what you are for me, and simply for what you are, my sweet little one.

Your charming Beaver

[Paris]

Monday 22 January [1940]

My sweet little one

At 8 this morning there were no letters. The big mail bag was there, but still unopened. Luckily, when I returned after school they were both there dutifully – the one of the 17th and the one of the 18th. How postponed leave was going to cause me. But I knew from the papers, and from people, that the English had already stopped having any, and everyone was saying they were going to do the same thing with the French – even though nobody seemed to regard this as absolutely definite. Moreover, I'm made of steel now. What's more, I think it's more annoying to be the person who doesn't go on leave than the person who can't see anyone arriving. I was wrought up about my trip to see Emma, because it was I who was active. Here, I'm wholly inert. So inert that this date of 1 February which you set as the final limit doesn't affect me – even though it's only eight days away. It remains something purely unreal. I haven't been rejoicing at all. On the contrary, I'm feeling vaguely off balance today, for the first time for ages. Probably because I've finished an important chapter; because I've got to fix up another one, which isn't too good; and because I've nevertheless been disconnected from my work by the idea of your arrival, without being connected to that arrival itself. My thoughts no longer know which way to turn.

[. . .]

I worked for over two hours, but with no taste for it. Perhaps it's because the chapter's no good (the one at the Flea Market, between Françoise and Gerbert). I'm writing to you, then I'm going to write a letter to Bost, who still doesn't know anything definite about his leave. But listen, since the Kos. sisters don't think you can tell when a soldier on leave is going to arrive – to within a few days – you can turn up more or less unexpectedly. He too can turn up with a certain lag – it'll be easy to arrange.

I'm going to meet Kos. at the Deux Magots, then we'll go to a cinema in Rue Récamier of which Gégé has spoken highly to me. I'm glad to be going to the cinema, off balance as I am. Goodbye, my sweet little one. Till tomorrow. I'll see you soon. I need you so much!

Your charming Beaver

[Paris]

Tuesday 23 January [1940]

My sweet little one

So it's true, you're going to come! I've just had your letter, and it has put me in such a fever I'm afraid I shan't be able to work all day – or perhaps all week. It's a kind of dread I'm feeling, not at all agreeable, with a nervous desire to weep. But I think in a day or two – certainty aiding – it'll become stabilized as happiness.

In a week at the latest – my love! Listen, Little Bost isn't even talking about coming, and in any case I can arrange things with him on the spot. I'll go, with or without you, and pick him up at the station when he arrives. So tell Wanda, as arranged, that you're arriving six days later. Tell her *as soon as possible*, so that I can explain my departure to my sister's before your arrival. As for your civilian clothes, your mother's trying to keep them – so write to her. I'll write to her myself – under Eugénie's name[254] – pleading with her to drop them off at the Hôtel Mistral or my place. I pressed her about it but she dug her heels in, claiming you were in agreement. I'll tell her you're arriving the day after and we want a long time just on our own, my little one. Oh! I'm only now starting to feel how thirsty I've been to see you – I can't bear it, I want you so! If you arrive on Thursday the 1st, I'll miss the Friday at H. IV and the Saturday at C.Sée, which makes only one day at each place and leaves me all yours for 3 days, with no school. By 4.30 at the latest, on whatever day it may be, I'll be in that gloomy café at the Gare de l'Est where we often used to go in Laon days, *on the right* when you leave the station, all in black panelling with a downstairs room – do you know the one? It must be the third café down – on the corner of the Boulevard, I think, before you cross over. Tell me if you remember it, my little one, and whether it suits you? We used to like it a lot.

I've begun to have dreams about your arrival. Last night, by one of those childish transpositions I've already discussed with you, I dreamt I'd gone back – as in the last war – to see my father (when he was a zouave) at Villetaneuse near St Denis. It was actually a memory of that road where my mother and I met him. And I encountered my father again with a joy that left me bewildered, since I could vaguely recall that I didn't love him at all and he was old and senile, but while I was puzzling over whom it was I loved in that way, you came along – and that woke me up.

[. . .]

I love you, and I'm pining for you. I felt like crying with desire while listening to Bach just now – and I still do. Oh, may my life with you be restored to me, my little one! Do come! I'm so waiting for you, my love.

Your charming Beaver

---

[254]Eugénie was Sartre's mother's housekeeper: his stepfather would not insist on being shown a letter addressed to her.

I've been reading *The Castle* for a while, and find it wonderful – better than *The Trial*, but desperately gloomy.

[Paris]

Wednesday 24th January [1940]

Most dear little being

I've had two letters from you today, my love. They haven't given me certainty, but what is certain anyway is that by the 10th at the latest you'll be here – and I'm beginning to feel like celebrating. I'm beginning really to *believe* it. Little Bost has written me two very cheerful letters too, and it seems certain he'll arrive before the 10th. It would be perfect if he came just a few days after you. I've warned him he'll have to see me while you're seeing Wanda.

[. . .]

I went back to the Dôme, worked for 2½ hrs and wrote to Bost for ½ hr, then came home to meet Sorokine. She quite overwhelmed me. I find her love for me so poignant, and feel I could love her really a lot if I had more time to give her. She'd been nervy these past few days, and today she wanted an afternoon of embraces. But precisely I wasn't in a fit state – which I explained, as discreetly as I could, after our first kisses – so we just stayed tenderly intertwined, with impure kisses but nothing more. She explained, very touchingly, how she depended on me; and how I was everything for her; and how little she saw of me; and how she wasn't hoping for the impossible, namely that I should ever care passionately for her, but would merely like to be sure that if she disappeared from my life it wouldn't be altogether a matter of indifference to me – though she often wasn't sure even about that. It wasn't in the least pathetic or reproachful, and every so often after a struggle she'd say, with a great gulp, as though it were a malediction: 'I love you so much, so very much . . . it's such a burden, like a tension that never lets up for an instant.' After that we went back to embraces, and she grew languid and melting till I was obliged to ravish her after all. It was comical how she grew calm in an instant – all gay tenderness and truly charming. I very much like, for instance, the way in which she takes my head in her hands, caresses it tenderly, and says laughingly: 'And there's a brain in there!' then proudly: 'I know what it's like: there's a bulb, and it's yellow and red . . . ' and she describes it, then in a slightly shocked tone: 'and that's you'. I'm never bored for a moment with her, she's all inventiveness – in feeling as in thought. I find her endlessly graceful of mind – she's really got something. I was in turmoil when she left, and still am.

I passed from her hands into Bienenfeld's. No aftermath of a frenzy this time, but tranquil tedium – nothing really irritating, but terribly humdrum. The truth was, moreover, that a heart pretty much replete with Sorokine's features was left untouched by that sharp little face. We ate at the Nordland where we talked about food, then talked about politics at the Dôme. She honestly offers me nothing, whereas the other one gives me what used to be precious about Kos. – in a more facile way this time, but also more pleasing. Namely, a new perception of the world, a world rethought in an absolutely unexpected way by an original little consciousness. But Bienenfeld was extremely pleased with me and everything passed off as well as could be.

She has just left me, it's almost midnight, I've written to you – and now I'm going to read *The Castle* for a while, then sleep. Have I told you that, on a second reading, *The Castle* strikes me as far better conceived than *The Trial*? Yesterday evening as I was going to bed, it made me quite sick of writing: I've the feeling it's pointless to write, if one can't strike a novel and disturbing note – like Kafka and you.

My sweet little one, I'm going to reread your letters now. I love you so, and feel your love so strongly. In a week, shall I really fall asleep in your little arms? We're going to be so happy, my little one. I love you – and am waiting for you.

Your charming Beaver

[. . .]

[Paris]

Thursday 25 January [1940]

Most dear little being

Yes, you do indeed seem busy from your letters, my little one. But how pleasing it is, I can now feel really strongly how – in a week, at this hour – I'll be holding your little arm. [. . .] At the post office I found two charming letters from Bost, which nonetheless cast me into gloom. For he mentions comrades of his – belonging to commando units – who have taken hard knocks and won medals. What exactly is a commando unit? It could just as easily have been him. I felt a retrospective fear that quite upset me. What's more, spring's approaching, the papers are full of alarming rumours, and I view this leave – not yours, thank Heavens, but his – like the last interview with his family granted to a condemned man. When he writes so nicely it revives my feelings for him – and my fears too. Also, I was still only half believing in your leave and then your letter wasn't there. So I went and sat down at the Dupont in the deepest despair. But I'd brought a lovely notebook just like yours in which to record my history, so I spent almost an hour bringing my little journal up to date, while drinking a cup of chocolate and listening to the music on the wireless – which seemed fit to chill the soul. I was caught up in the war again, and it seemed dreadful. But afterwards that passed and now, on the contrary, I'm feverishly happy – so happy I could cry. I think about how I'm going to see you – really and truly – and it's almost unbearable, though I know perfectly well how easy it will be to meet again, like last time – my love.

[. . .]

I'm going out with Kos. now. I think my cold and fatigue will all be gone by next Thursday, and you'll have a beautiful Beaver. At any rate, one who'll be so happy to see you, my dear, dear love. How I do need you!

Your charming Beaver

[. . .]

Here the first gap occurs in the daily correspondence De Beauvoir had kept up with Sartre since his call-up five months earlier. She stopped writing (a bit early, Sartre complained) in the belief that his leave would begin on 1 February. The letter which follows was written on the new assumption that there would be a two-week postponement. In fact he arrived in Paris on 4 February, staying until 15 February (the day before Bost in turn arrived in Paris). Although De Beauvoir started writing daily again as soon as Sartre left Paris – and we know her letters arrived safely – those for the last week in February must subsequently have been mislaid.

Le Dôme
[Paris]

Saturday 3 February [1940]

My love

Don't worry too much about me. Yes, it's a disappointment. But I hadn't yet believed in your arrival enough to feel real joy, so I'm in just the same state as yesterday – less tense, if anything, because I know how things stand. What's more, gradually – through raw nerves and delays – that leave of yours is starting to tend towards reality. It's beginning to seem almost certain – distant, but almost certain. Just imagine, yesterday – with no letter and no cable – at 5 in the afternoon on the off chance I went to the café at the Gare de l'Est. And I had the impression that this whole business, indeed almost your very existence, were the product of mythomania – something I'd simply invented on my own – and there was nothing to it all but imaginary certainties. Only I was agitated at the thought that you might come and miss me, so I called in at the Hôtel Mistral and left a note for you. I was in a state of dark, uncertain passion far more painful than this morning's cool boredom. Alas! my love, what rends my heart is the fact of having spent a week without writing to you. In a moment I'll send off the money and books, but first I'm writing you a long letter, my little one. I love you so much, and so tenderly, my dear love. It's stupid of me to have stopped writing. It was less out of any certainty, than a kind of conjuration – making an act of belief that would actually make it all real. But now I'm biting my nails over it. Poor, dear little man, I can't wait for you to get this note and feel once more that your Beaver's there with you in your life.

Listen: Little Bost says he's arriving on about Wednesday, and he'll go for two days to Taverny, so he'll probably see me on about Friday – but that's not certain. I'd much rather see him at the beginning of his leave – I'd find it disagreeable for him to see Kos. before me. But, of course, I also want to see you for at least two days before relinquishing you to Wanda. If really necessary, I'd put up with 2 days (on the sly) – 3 days for Wanda – then 2 days (official) and another 4 days on the sly. But between this 2-3-6 arrangement and the other 6-3-2 one, there'd be a 4-day lag so far as Wanda's concerned, which could be awkward. Can you leave things vague with her? As for me, I'll *wire* as soon as I know exactly how everything's working out with Bost. But try to persuade Wanda that there's a wide margin of uncertainty.

My love, the one thing that's certain – as you explain so sensibly – is that I'm going to see you.

Luckily I've been keeping my little notebook up dutifully this week, in the hope of showing it to you. So I'll more or less copy it out, as we're back to writing.

Well, I wrote to you on Saturday evening, after seeing Sorokine. I went to bed and slept very badly. I had a dreadful nightmare, in which I saw you but without feeling any tenderness for you, given that you were simultaneously Dullin, another actor from the Atelier, and one of the girls I'm teaching this year. I was saying – quite angrily – that if they kept changing him like that, then of course I couldn't keep my love for him. I thought it was the rule and in time love would return – but I wasn't best pleased.

[. . .]

I'll tell you tomorrow how we went to the Jockey, and about my Thursday evening with Bienenfeld, to whom I spoke words of wisdom, I think, justifying to her (quite sincerely) her inauthenticity. I'll explain it all to you, but I'm stopping for now as my arm's hurting and I want to do some work.

I'm quite serene, though tears do prick my eyes at times. I'm a bit scared of these periods of leave: it's funny to have to live again when one was sleeping so peacefully. I'm satisfied with Bost. He writes tenderly, and will see me first and for quite a while, I think. But I'm fearful of any passion, all the same. And as for you, my love – I'm already fearful of your departure. That's another reason why I'm rather indifferent to the delay, since it also delays that separation after which we'll have nothing left but hope.

I need you, my love

Your Beaver

Café-Restaurant de Versailles
3 Place de Rennes
Paris VI

Paris, Friday [16 February 1940]

Most dear little being

I thought it was charming, the way the men queued up to take their turns at the carriage-door and kiss their good ladies. So I squeezed your little hand one last time and vaguely made out your face, then the train left and it was like a physical wrench. At that moment I thought I was really going to collapse or something – but no, I was very sensible. I left that icy station at a run, and took a taxi which set me down first at the post office – where there was nothing from Bost – then at school, where I delivered my lessons dutifully. I wasn't too exhausted. Sorokine was there on the way out: she was wearing a little tartan hood on her head, and lipstick, and was altogether pleasing. We've never got on better. We went and ate in that blue brasserie which you now know, and I told her lots of little stories about both you and me which made her laugh till the tears came to her eyes – and quite entranced her. I did another two hours at H.IV, or rather I got my pupils talking for two hours, which suited me fine since I had a sore throat and a touch of mental frailty. Sorokine kept me company again as far as the Place de la Sorbonne, when I went to meet Bienenfeld at La Sorbonne: she was in one of the booths, smiling but with a mistrustful look. I began scolding her – now nicely, now harshly – but she was already unresisting, quite ashamed to have written as she had. I took her to the Hoggar, where we talked till 7 p.m. – about our relations, of course. I explained to her firmly once again that I'd never see any more of her; that she'd always known my life was encumbered; that anyway I had a need for solitude, with only a very modest need to see people; and that she lived only to love and be loved, but that wasn't right. I moved skilfully on to the solitude in which you're currently immersed, and which your letters describe – something that makes me a bit gloomy, but that I well understand. She sighed, saying it was sad for her not to have the same character as us. It must be said she was moving: all restrained, serious, attentive and silent, smiling at me every so often – and every so often restraining her tears. What's more she was beautiful yesterday. It struck me as rotten, thinking of the blow that was about to fall on her head.[255] Yet I've the impression it's still possible she won't be too, too upset. For my own part I felt tenderness for her once again yesterday, and I'm going to try to be nice. She irritated me only once – with her talk about 'life in common': she reproached me with not having a life in common with her, and particularly with not having introduced her to the 'people I know'. I find that comical, social, and stupid – and didn't shrink from telling her so.

[...]

Kos. is still very low. She no longer goes to the Atelier, and she too is without news of Bost. She also expects him to stay for ages at Taverny – which suits very well. With me she was tenderer than ever, giving me dressing tips and – for a joke – amusing herself by giving them with

---

[255] A reference to Sartre's intention to write imminently breaking off relations with her.

excessive authority: 'Full of kind feelings towards you as I am, I must now speak to you quite crossly' – that kind of thing. It has never been so purely idyllic. She grew sentimental about my youth, and told me she found my walking trips ever so pleasing and 'adventurous'. I wonder if there isn't some reaction against Wanda's ill will, and if she's not seeking to form a couple with me against Wanda and you – for that kind of adoption of me had never been so insistent as yesterday.

[...]

I came here to the Versailles to have breakfast and write to you. Then I'll go to the hairdresser's and do the shopping, which I'll finish off this afternoon. I've had a letter from Poupette, who says that Gerassi has some suspicions regarding your leave. I'll write to him as soon as I know the score about Bost.

My sweet little one, I'm not at all sad – as you can see. Your leave has closed in on itself again and I'm recovering my wartime existence – with your visit in its proper place in that existence, like something that couldn't be other than what it was. I feel such total peace of mind that I don't even need to throw myself into my work. I'm waiting for Bost with immense calm, and can contemplate his days with Kos. without the least concern – especially since Kos. is being so nice at present. As always you've given me back the sense of my life and happiness. Instead of being bogged down in the sequence of days, or even in the war, I see everything on a large scale now – in the whole context of the world and my existence – and I'm altogether immersed in the happiness I derive from seeing you. Nothing else counts. I have *you* – little all-precious one, little beloved one – as much today as the day before yesterday when I could see you, and I'll have you till the day you die. After that, nothing of all that may happen to me really has any importance. Not only am I not sad, I'm even deeply happy and secure. Even the tenderest memories – of all your dear expressions, or your little arms cradling the pillow in the morning – aren't painful to me. I feel myself all enfolded and sustained by your love. My beloved, we had a beautiful leave and how intense that last evening was! Goodbye, my sweet little one. This is now the eleventh year of happiness you've given me. I'm still with you, just like the day before yesterday in the evening, when you were kissing that old warhorse's cheek of mine and I was hugging you so tight.

I love you more than ever.

Your charming Beaver

Café de Flore
172 Bd St-Germain
Paris

Sunday [18 February 1940]

Dear little being

I'm really angry. Yesterday I wrote you a little letter – little, but pretty significant all the same actually – and I've lost it in some café. It's possible someone will have mailed it to you, since it was already in its envelope, but that's far from certain. So I'm going to tell you everything all over again. You should first know – since I'm itching to tell you – that Bost and I spent a long while yesterday evening reading the chapter at the Sumatra,[256] and were quite staggered by it. Bost said he'd never read anything more moving, that one couldn't restrain one's tears, and that he'd seen nothing comparable in Stendhal or Dostoievsky. He remained in a daze of admiration and a whirl of emotion almost all evening. As for me, I knew it already but still found it shattering all over again – it's truly a work of *great beauty*, my little one. I'm spending quite a pleasing time – potent as can be – with Little Bost. He deserves all the esteem and tenderness in the world. He couldn't be more charming, and though we talk non-stop from morning to night we'll never get to the end of what we have to say to one another. He's really taken with the idea that you want to go in for politics later on – and really attracted too – asking me for countless explanations of what you think. In a sense, if all this is going to be over in two years, the idea that he'll have lived through it interests him. But at moments – albeit very brief – he also becomes depressed at the thought of how hard it's still going to be to get through. Indeed, if you take it detail by detail, that existence of his does seem pretty abominable, with those huge bouts of drinking – great abysses of self-abasement and degradation – which are often the only possible defence. He has told me that some fellow once remained flat out for 68 hrs in a barn – and he has done so for almost as long – from cold, disgust, dejection, and the impossibility of finding any place to rest your bones. It's the return from the front to the rear that seems to have been terrible, because of the bitter cold, impossible grub, and lamentable organization.

But I'll go back over everything in order since Friday morning. [. . .] As I was ending my lesson, a good lady in black approached mysteriously and, with a sinister look, told me: 'There's a M. Bost waiting for you downstairs in the visitors' room.' My hands started to tremble and my heart to thump, and I had the greatest difficulty in

---

[256]Chapter in *The Age of Reason*, which Sartre was just completing.

continuing on the subject of sociology – that last quarter of an hour passing in the strangest agony of impatience. I rushed down – and there, all solitary amid the green settees and mirrors of a vast visitors' room, I found Little Bost waiting for me. He was so exactly himself that I was scarcely surprised at seeing him – and he too, I think, rediscovered me at once. He seemed quite genuinely moved, but things were easy and charming from the start. The weather was superb, by chance, so we set off towards the Seine embankment, then on to Bastille, République, the Canal St Martin, Jaurès and the Gare de l'Est. He barely looked about him, just talked and talked endlessly. He had a great deal to get off his chest and it was terribly interesting, even though I knew the essential part from his letters and diaries. We went to the black café at the Gare de l'Est – where I met you, my little one – and talked on for a long while. At some point I phoned to tell Kos. that Poupette had just got in, but she didn't sound best pleased – her voice was extremely cool. [. . .]

We went and slept at the Hôtel Oriental on Place Denfert-Rochereau, over the green café with the same name. It's pretty sumptuous – lift, and fine, warm rooms with velvet drapes and a pink counterpane. We spent an altogether tender and passionate night, as was fitting, but I slept very badly because of the stifling heat – and also, I think, because my nerves were overwrought.

[. . .]

Bost read long extracts of your Notebook XI in wild exhilaration. He wonders if you realize how comic you are. I explained the Wanda and Bienenfeld situations to him, and to my great surprise he insinuated that if she were being dropped anyway, I too should drop her.[257] From the standpoint of principle he finds us infamous – but his heart's with us. I delighted him with the information that Sorokine shakes her fist at me and even beats me – he wants to offer her a strap.

[. . .]

We went to the Nox, sat down at a table and talked – gently, so gently. He was truly moving: seeking in you, and me, hopes for later on; talking about his comrades – and about himself and his moods out there, his regrets and his joys – by fits and starts, without the volubility of the previous day, but drawing things from his innermost depths. I was moved to tears (actually shedding a couple) and was feverish – I'd drunk a lot of toddies and other alcohol – but I didn't lapse into pathos.

---

[257]Sartre was planning to break off relations with Bienenfeld.

There's one thing of which I'm now sure, which is that Bost forms part of my future in an absolutely certain – even essential – way. I felt such 'remorse' because of him, that I want a postwar existence with him – and partly *for* him. I'd like us to be able to help the fellows returning from the war at the age of 25 *not to become* like Brice Parain.[258] We stayed there for two jam-packed, potent hours. It was the same place as in the old days – same hostesses, same gypsy – but the meaning was entirely altered, because you had an intense feeling of the war outside and the provisional, facticious nature of the intoxication people were coming there in search of. We went to spend the night at that hotel near the Bd St Michel where we often used to go in the old days, and this time I slept well.

[. . .]

Meanwhile, I've written this letter and am now going to mail it, then I'll go to the Source to meet Bost. He may now spend quite a while away from the front, in Marne or Oise, in which case it would be possible for me to go and visit him there.

My little one, tomorrow I'll have some news from you. Yesterday morning, when I called in at about 1 p.m., there wasn't anything yet. I was telling you yesterday how I've kept the memory of how you last looked – with your forage-cap and glasses, in the shadows of the compartment behind the other fellows, smiling at me so tenderly. My little all-beloved, I'm with you utterly and surrounded by you and protected from everything, even from the sadness my dear images of you might hold. I love you. I cover your sweet little face with kisses – my love

Your charming Beaver

[Paris]

Monday 19 February [1940]

My sweet little one, my love

Just now I got three letters from you – and it's I who am racked by remorse because I've written so poorly since Thursday, especially with

---

[258]Brice Parain (1897-1971), decorated in World War I, completed his studies thereafter and was a communist from the mid twenties until 1933, helping to found *La Revue Marxiste* to which Nizan was a principal contributor. From 1927 until 1961 he held an influential position in the publishing house Gallimard, in which capacity he dealt with both De Beauvoir and Sartre from the start of their authorial careers.

that letter which got lost. O my little one, how sweet and tender you are, and how potent it is to feel how you love me. I feel quite overwhelmed by happiness this evening because of those letters. What's more, I'll perhaps be seeing you in a month. I love you so much, my love.

So I went off yesterday evening to meet Bost at the Source. [. . .] It was a truly beautiful evening. Truly (apart from times with yourself) I've never experienced anything so potent and rich in my entire life. You'd sensibly told me that — regarding the pleasure of this leave — I should make allowance for what Little Bost would be. And he has been beyond all that I hoped for: in himself, in how he felt things and talked about them, and also in his relations with me. I honestly felt there was no comparison between the ways in which he cares for Kos. or for me — and felt, too, how I was essential to him. He was charmingly tender and I felt altogether united with him. We went and slept at the hotel on that square with the flights of stairs, opposite the one where you once went with Wanda. The good lady was quite touched when she recognized us.

[. . .]

I left Bost outside his brother's place. He'll see me again at length one afternoon before his departure. I'm not sad about leaving him. I came here (to my place) to reread your letters, over which I've shed a few tears, and to write to you. I'm half-dead from lack of sleep, but without being overwrought. On the contrary, sleepiness anaesthetizes regrets and feelings, and I'm literally thinking only of the moment when I'll be able to stretch out between the sheets and sleep. I'll have to spend the evening with Bienenfeld between now and then, but luckily I shan't have to make any great efforts. I think I'm going to grab half an hour's sleep before going off to meet her.

Here's another wretched letter — I'm ashamed — yours are so tender and altogether rich, my love. You seem all pathetic to me, as you were in the train — and in your hutments. I so hope you'll find a nice little *querencia*, my little one, and that you'll get back to your beautiful novel.

Goodbye, tomorrow I'll write better, but I haven't got all that much to tell. I'm not at all upset. On the contrary, this affair with Bost now seems cleansed of all the old slag and brought back to what's essential and pleasing about it. Now I'm going to eke out a week of 'atonement' with Poupette, Bienenfeld and Sorokine — then it'll be back to dutiful work for twenty days — then the holidays.

As these leave periods come to an end, it seems really strange to be finding myself alive and all happy. I love you, my beloved. If I gazed at you lovingly when the train left, then remember that expression and think how, at this very moment, my face is just as full of passion.

Your charming Beaver

[Paris]

Tuesday 27 February [1940]

My sweet little one

[. . .]

My dear, dear little beloved being, I had a sweet letter from you today and felt a bit sad at the thought of the harsh letter I wrote you yesterday, and Bienenfeld's letter which I posted along with it. I love you so much – how disagreeable all those rebukes heaped on your head must have been for you! But, my love, you really did go too far with Bienenfeld. A bit more consideration was needed – that girl's no Gibert. I went to the Hoggar yesterday, bearing your two letters and feeling pretty anxious. She showed up, tragic and beautiful, with a kind of necessity for which I was grateful to her. She was wearing her dark red dress, and a very pretty black hat with a net, which gave her a fateful look – the look of a woman still young but already marked by life. She read your letters, she restrained herself with astounding guts – but she was transfigured by anger. And honestly, I don't know what got into your head. That letter, with its moral exhortations and protestations of esteem, was quite unacceptable. I'll tell you quite bluntly what it reminded me of – the Scoutmaster gazing into Sorokine's eyes and saying: 'Now you must follow your own path without me, all by yourself.' Bienenfeld felt it that way, and tore every sentence apart with gusto. And she was humiliated that you didn't even take the trouble to explain things to her properly. Humiliated and disgusted by the passionate letters you were writing her only a fortnight earlier. I found it desperately unpleasant. I wasn't at heart in sympathy with her, but I found her estimable in her attitude that evening, and scathing, and right. She's not an idiot, and you didn't take that sufficiently into account. It's quite true that your letter was indefensible. She knows there's a lie somewhere and is wondering what the truth is – she's not without her suspicions even with respect to me. I still think scorn will help her to pick herself up and survive it – but she's taking it hard.

[. . .]

I'm going to bed now, my little one, since I'm dropping asleep. My beloved, whom I love so much, I'd have liked to talk all this over with you instead of writing about it. I'm afraid my letters may seem too condemnatory – and I'm incapable of really condemning you, I find it so abstract. I love you, my dear little one, and am so happy when I think about seeing you again in 6 weeks. The arrangement you propose is perfect: no one will suspect a thing and we'll see as much of each other as possible. My love, I so long to have you beside me once more! I love you most passionately – little face gazing fiercely at me from the wall opposite. Goodnight, my sweet little one – so tenderly loved.

Your charming Beaver

Le Dôme
[Paris]

Thursday 29 February [1940]

My sweet little one

No letter from you. That means they gave you your jab on Tuesday and you were all feverish. It's a very good thing you've taken a bed at the hotel, but why don't you take one for the month, so that you'll have a genuine little *querencia*? The food's good there. I'm a bit distraught without my letter.

I did get a very amiable one from Little Bost. He says a safe-conduct is needed to go and see him – but it must be easy to obtain, so near to Paris. I'll go and find out tomorow. He seems a bit gloomy about being back, but nothing to worry about.

[. . .]

Bienenfeld arrived a bit later, very glum. But I think she's gradually recovering and it's something she'll absorb quite quickly. She talked about it to Lévy all yesterday evening, of course, displaying your letter – in which Lévy detected a certain sadism. I'm still just as cool about her, and that won't change.

[. . .]

There, my love. It's a fortnight now since the train carried your little face away. I've become once again just as before, but happier because you're going to come again soon, and I touched you – you're even more present to me than in the month of January. I love you so much. In six weeks' time I'll once again be in the black café near the Gare de l'Est, with my heart pounding, and see you arrive. I love you, and kiss you with all my Beaver's heart.

Your charming Beaver

[Paris]

Friday 1 March [1940]

Most dear little being

That's what I call letters! I've just received your Tuesday letter, when you had your jab – the censors had opened and resealed it – and along with it the enormous missive of the following day. That one was so thick it had come open all on its own, but there was nothing missing there either. My little one, I'm *absolutely* convinced by what you tell me. The only thing I still reproach you with is having dispatched Bienenfeld a bit summarily – but that's unimportant. Especially as she's already well on the way to recovery. She was quite sprightly this morning at lunch, so I asked her: 'You're looking very cheerful, how come?' and she told me: 'I had trouble removing Sartre from my life, but now he's removed.' Didn't take long, did it? It's comical how that girl goes completely off the deep end in words, then finds joy and comfort in the same way. Constructing relations and splitting up cast her into states of ecstasy or despair, like with mad people. I asked her if her calm came from the fact she didn't see things as final; but she told me that, on the contrary, she no longer had any thought of being able to love you now. Of course, it's not over that easily – she'll have twitches – but it's strange, all the same. What I find irritating and embarrassing is her determination to mix me up with herself. She asks me for confidences – if I still love you, why I write to you, etc. I'm afraid she may want to continue writing to you, because I write to you – and on the pretext that she's now sufficiently detached from you for that. I'll end up having to tell her that I've stopped writing – but really, I'm not going to spend the rest of my life hiding my relations with you from her! Do advise me. At least she's not shocked by the idea of my going to see you, and if I go and see Bost I'd quite like to say it's you I'm with. What do you think? She was gloomy again at 5, but that's because she'd seen Wahl, because her essay on truth wasn't going well, and because she was puzzling over truth in general and the meaning of life, saying she no longer knew what to think about anything. All of this struck me as really pretty empty, and I still feel very cool about her.

[. . .]

I went to meet up with Bienenfeld again at the Mt St Michel, which was very elegant and rather dashing. They tried to dump us at an impossible table, so we swept out – leaving two francs for the bread we'd started nibbling. We went to the Capoulade, where we ate and talked. She was really nice with me – seeking intimacy. She made a criticism of my novel which rather rankled, because it's fair: which is that it lacks the gratuitousness you find in Hemingway, so that everything's always there *for* something. That's what you were saying to me, but as a compliment – and it's indeed what I wanted, but obviously it loses in charm what it gains in solidity. She also says that in my work – like in yours – there's too much thought, whereas the pleasing thing about American novels is the absence of thought. That's true too. But you shouldn't make a dogma out of the American novel either, or try to do that at all costs if the things you've got to say are different. That's where she was talking drivel, when she said it was all a matter of style and method. But it certainly does represent a genre of novel – while other genres can still be more attractive and have other qualities. What do you think?

[. . .]

I've just come in, written to Bost, finished off this letter to you, and am now off to sleep – it's almost 12.30. My little one, I've read your letter once again and am absolutely convinced. I'm satisfied with all your resolutions – I who precisely was condemning your suspect generosity. I think you're right, and a clean sweep has now been made. I approve of you wholeheartedly. We'll talk about all this in a month's time, my love. I'll be seeing you just after the Easter holidays – how splendid that will be! I love you, my beloved, and kiss you so passionately – o little totally-refurbished one, little pure one.

Your charming Beaver

[Paris]

Saturday 2 March [1940]

Most dear little being

I'm a bit upset by your letter, even though you've told me not to let it disturb me. O my beloved, I love you so intensely and do so wish I could hug you tight and see your little face and speak to you. When I think how worried you were the day before yesterday, because of me and my feelings for – or rather judgements on – you, and when I picture the strange state in which you found yourself, I weep with impatience to see you. It's as though I were seeing you through a transparent but deceptive glass: I'm borne towards you, you're so close, I feel as if I'm about to touch you, but then – no, there's this obstacle, I have to write, and the letters take two days to arrive, and the reply takes another two days, and letters are anyway too short. I picture you turning them inside out in annoyance as you do with me, when you question me about some story I've been told about in a couple of words, but of which you want to extract an hour-long account from me. And the letter's just like me – all stubborn, saying just what has been put into it. My dear little one, I want to see you – and never have I felt such tenderness for you. How can you imagine, sweet little being, that I don't think you utterly honest and pure with me? There's no more bracketing off and never will be, my love. Your words and smiles aren't signs – I believe in them as totally as it's possible to believe in anything. My love, I think you were right to break with Bienenfeld. I think only well of you. It's true I found it unpleasant, for the reason you mention – that sentence to W.: 'I'd trample the whole world underfoot'[259] – but I'm over that. And you must have been out of your mind, my little one, to believe that could prevent me from writing to you. It's annoying because tomorrow's Sunday – a letterless day – so I'll have to wait for Monday to know if you've had my letter, if you've emerged from that strange state, and if you've recovered your peace of mind. My love, it so touches me – you can't imagine how much – that you should care as you do about my letters, and my judgements. I feel so intensely how you care for me, and am so happy about the fact that you're with me. It's the eleventh year of happiness you've given me, my little one, and never has our love been stronger or purer. I love you – quite passionately. I'd like you to be all imbued with it and see how beautiful you are in my heart, dear little image.

[. . .]

At 7.30 I left and went to meet Bienenfeld at the Ternes Dupont, before going to a concert at the Salle Pleyel. She was under the weather.

---

[259]In his letter of 28 February, Sartre had apologized to De Beauvoir for the protestations of exclusive passion he felt obliged to make to Wanda in order to keep her calm. He wrote: 'There's something ignoble about my relations with Wanda. It's ignoble that I should be obliged to tell her that I no longer love you, ignoble that I should feel I have to write to her: "I'd trample the whole world under foot (even the Beaver, despite my mysticism)" . . . but . . . whoever wants the end, must want the means.'

She has done with you, but the meaning of life's bothering her and she no longer knows whom she cares for – even I myself am 'tossed to and fro' in her heart. You were right, that rupture's introducing a certain coolness between her and me too – and that opens up prospects of freedom for me, since she's soon going to need a man. She's already talking about getting drunk, soon she'll be looking for adventure, then another love – and I'll be delivered. She's not by any means so groggy as all that – she's now concerned only with what attitude to take, what I think of her, etc. She's not gay, of course, but she seems even more resilient than I thought. I definitely don't find her very appealing – it's over.

[. ..]

Goodbye, my love. I'll write at length again tomorrow. I love you passionately.

Your charming Beaver

[Café Perrier,
Rue de la Boétie, Paris VII]

Sunday 3 March [1940]

Most dear little being

[. . .]

I'm not sure whether or not you should write to Bienenfeld. You could write and tell her you find writing pointless – or write her stilted letters at extremely infrequent intervals. I don't at all think she's clinging on to you – indeed, I've been quite surprised by it. I think she'd like you not to disappear from her life – her inclination being to hang on to everything – but she's a bit self-critical about it. I'll keep you well posted. In the light of her letters and my own, I'd like you to write to me at length about what you think of her attitude.

[. . .]

Returning home, I arrived before 8 and, as Kos. didn't turn up till 8.30, was able to get on with some correcting of pupils' work. I don't think I'm going to continue my journal – it's too far behind and I keep it up only out of habit. It no longer interests me, and I'd rather keep all my time for letters – you're already finding mine too short. Kos. eventually showed up, terribly tired and gloomy, and we spent two wretched hours at the Dôme – which was her fault, since she was utterly down in the dumps. I came home at 11 – which is now – and am going to bed, as I'm too tired. I'm reading an enjoyable detective story, which I'll be sending you pretty soon.[. . .]

Goodbye, beloved little being. I love you with all my might. Come back to me soon, my love

Your charming Beaver

[Paris]

Monday 4 March [1940]

Most dear little being

What a joy it is to receive such long letters! I've had two today and am so happy. My love, how splendid it would be if you spent all summer in the rear! I'll be free by the month of June this year, you know, and provided I just pop back to Paris for the prize-giving and the baccalaureat orals, I'll be able to instal myself close by you. [. . .]

As for Bienenfeld, I subscribe wholeheartedly to everything you say, as you must have seen from my last letters. Why doesn't she hold any appeal for me? Probably – although I felt she deserved respect for the way she took things – because of that hollow, cold side she has, despite the outbursts of passion. You've seen through me: it's quite true that, in experiencing this rupture along with her, willy-nilly I did rather take her side. I never blamed you for making the break, since after all that's what I'd advised you to do. But I blamed us – myself as much as you, actually – in the past, in the future, in the absolute: the way we treat people. I felt it was unacceptable that we'd managed to make her suffer so much. In fact, though, she isn't suffering all that much, so I feel much calmer about things. It's quite true what people say, that one soon resigns oneself to other people's troubles.

So I finished my letters yesterday evening and went to bed. I slept sparingly (for a little over 7 hours) but very well, and woke up fresh and cheerful, with one good day behind me and another ahead of me, with letters in prospect, my work, and – further away on the horizon – the Easter holidays with Bost and your leave. Now I'll be prolonging that by a summer spent with you – how splendid that would be! We'd look out for a convenient little *querencia,* we'd get hold of lots of books, we'd talk and work and I'd manage to find some way of gadding about a bit – and we'd be so united and happy, my love! It would remind me of our holidays at Ste Radegonde,[260] do you recall? That's already an age ago, but it warms my heart whenever I remember it. We were reading *Point Counterpoint* at the time, and you were working on *La Légende de la Vérité*.[261] We didn't have any money, but you could picnic in the woods for ten francs. Do you recall the little pilgrimage we made to Tours? That was only two years ago. We really loved each other there too. Alas! if you were to abandon me – from authenticity or any other whim[262] – there's no doubt about it, I shouldn't endure the blow with as much dignity as Bienenfeld. I can't imagine what would become of me, the world would crumble beneath my feet. [. . .] I think you should write to her once at least – to answer her, and to say that you find writing pointless – since she told me sadly: 'He's hostile.' She still goes to the post office to look for your letters, which I find pitiful.

[. . .]

My detective story's still very enjoyable, and I'll send it to you. Now I'm going to write to Bost, then I'll meet Kos. and spend the evening with her. I'm ashamed of these letters, so much shorter than yours, but it's also the case that I don't have such moral and sentimental tempests. My life's uneventful and subdued, albeit illuminated by the satisfaction of good work done and all those pleasing hopes on the horizon. My little one, how splendid it would be to live with you, even in the wretchedest hole in all flea-ridden Champagne! Goodbye, dear, dear little being. You're my life. I love you

Your charming Beaver

[Paris]

Saturday 9 March [1940]

Most dear little being

I'm writing to you again from that little Café Perrier, since I'm off to another concert at the Salle Gaveau. It's piano this time, with a lovely

---

[260]In August 1930, during Sartre's military service.
[261]Philosophical work, begun while Sartre was doing his military service and written in the form of a story, on the model of Nietzsche. It was rejected for publication, despite Nizan's sponsorship (apart from an extract that appeared in the journal *Bifur*).
[262]Pretext used by Sartre to justify his break with Bienenfeld.

programme: lots of Bach, some Mussorgsky, and a tiny bit of Liszt. Tomorrow I'm going to the Conservatoire again, so I'll have had plenty of music this week. On the other hand, I've absolutely stopped reading – I haven't even finished *48* yet. Since you left I've just read a detective story and two issues of the *N.R.F.*. I quite like the Saroyan story in the last number, though it's a genre which can also seem a bit stereotyped.

I haven't yet had your letter, but hope to find it at home when I get back, and I'll answer before going to sleep. Let me repeat, do write to me at home from now on – since the Kos. sisters have stopped coming here – and do send me some books, my sweet little one.

[. . .]

It's after 12.30, and I'm going to write a note to Little Bost – but a very short one, I think – then go to sleep.

Goodbye, my love. If you've been clever enough to write to me at home, I'll have a letter tomorrow. I love you so intensely, my dear little one – you haven't forgotten, have you? Your little letters are so sweet. How happy we'll be in three weeks' time! How we'll talk! And I'll once again see you wake up beside me with your little arms cradling the pillow. I love you

Your charming Beaver

[Paris]

Sunday 10 March [1940]

My sweet little one

What a tender little spring evening this is! It fills your heart with sweet melancholy. I've just come out of the concert and I'm at the Café de la Poste Montmartre. I'm meeting Kos. at the Touraine in half an hour, and I'd really like to stroll through the streets of the Butte and take advantage of this lovely evening. Lots of little memories have come to moisten my eyes during today. How I'd love to stroll through the streets, on an evening just like this, clasping your little arm. But that'll come, my little one, and before very long. I'm beginning to miss you again, miss you dreadfully, o yourself – joy and salt and happiness of my life.

[. . .]

I got down to work. I was writing a rather hard scene, and racked my brains over it all day. I don't know if it's all right, but I'll have another look tomorrow. Barely pausing to snatch a bite, I went at it so hard that my head was throbbing. Bienenfeld came and worked alongside me, elegant and rather beautiful, but with the most appalling dumb-show of sidelong glances, discreet mysterious smiles, hesitations, etc. – all in order to ask me passionately on a Métro platform whether I still loved her just as much. Really, what gets into her? Does she imagine I could just say no and be done with it? I've already told you how stupid and blameworthy I find that method. So I said yes – without too much warmth – and she clasped my hands reverently. But she admits she no longer feels any great surges of passion for me. She's getting over it so far as you're concerned, but there's still just a little painful flare-up every so often – and a feeling of disenchantment. She's prophesying doom like a Cassandra (what's new?) and hesitating between the concentration camp and suicide, with a preference for suicide: she calls this sensing her destiny. I've been delighted about your rupture, since on my own I find I've incredibly much more freedom where she's concerned. For example: (after the war) no more Bienenfeld at winter sports – the two of us will go on our own to that little Chalet Idéal-Sport. Moreover, the road's open for her to love someone else and detach herself tearfully from me.

After that I rushed over here by taxi, so as to have time to write to you. This is a very humdrum letter, my dear little one, but my heart's not dusty, as you well know, and I love you – o dear little one, so full of life. It quite wrings my heart to think of you in that dismal hut, in your exile, and none too cheerful yourself.

Do send the books to me and to Bost too.

You'll now get two letters on Tuesday and none on Wednesday, but too bad! – I'm still going to post this one straight away. Goodbye, my beloved, I love you.

Your charming Beaver

[Paris]

Monday 11 [March 1940]

My sweet little one

I'm going to write you a first little letter before Bienenfeld arrives, then I'll write again this evening before going to bed. But I must tell you straight away that from Saturday I'll be at Nettancourt (Meuse).[263] So write to: Poste Restante, Nettancourt, Meuse. *Wednesday's* letter is the last you should send me in Paris (the letter *written* on Wednesday and sent as usual: that's how they arrive — in a day — if I understand right, so that I get them two days after the date of *the letter*, which is what you haven't understood this time). My little one, how happy I am about all the things you tell me, o little busy one! I'm pretty busy myself this evening, and so happy. So you'll be moving back? We'll go and eat at Soleil d'Or, at that nice little St-Cyr.[264] But I'm wondering, of course — being what they call the worrying kind — how we'll manage to hide from Kos. the fact of my spending so many evenings with you. For if you tell Wanda, she'll undoubtedly make a fuss. If I don't tell Kos., what can I come up with instead that won't stick out like a sore thumb? Well, if it's in June or thereabouts that'll be easier, as I shan't have school any more and can organize my time far more easily. But how glad I am, my little one! I'll be spending my holidays with you, then? Perhaps I'll live actually at St-Cyr. I can work as I please, eat at the Soleil d'Or — like that lady-boarder we used to see there, in the days of your military service — and every so often we'd go to Paris and celebrate. At any rate, no more separations!

If you come on the 26th, I'd infinitely rather you saw Wanda first. I reckon you'd join me on the morning of the 30th — which would make three days and four evenings for Wanda like last time — wouldn't you? That would be perfect. We'd have the whole of Saturday and Sunday, when there's no school. My little one, in 3 weeks' time at this hour, I'll be having dinner with you — and perhaps precisely at Lipp's, which is where I'm writing from. I love you.

I thoroughly approve of your letter to Bienenfeld, which I'll give her in ¼ of an hour. [. . .]

I shan't spend any money while I'm with Bost, since I shan't even eat lunch in the middle of the day — I'll tighten my belt. I'm really pleased to be going off to see him. I'm going to work hard down there, so I'll

---

[263]Close to where Bost was stationed.

[264]Sartre was expecting his unit to be transferred imminently to the rear, and held in reserve near St-Cyr where he had begun his military service in November 1929.

have a hundred little pages to show you after all. I've just been given my pass.

Goodbye, my little one. Tonight I'll tell you what I've been doing since yesterday. There are one or two tiny things that will make you laugh. I love you – with busy, contented kisses. Goodbye for now, my little one.

Your charming Beaver

[Paris]

Tuesday [12 March 1940]

Most dear little being

I've been a very unworthy morganatic spouse. Bienenfeld left me so late that I couldn't write to you last night, but just fell asleep. I'm going to write you a huge letter now, though, and have taken measures to have all the time I need for it.

Do you know where I'm writing from, with this lovely green ink – a capsule of which I've just stolen? From Dullin's private office, where Toulouse ensconced me while she's busy in the prop-room. I can see that little Rue d'Orsel through the window, and enjoy being here at the heart of the Atelier: in that converted box at the top of the stairs – do you know it? I'll first tell you about yesterday evening, since you may be a bit anxious about it. I met Bienenfeld at 8 and at once informed her that I had a letter, which she might or might not be pleased with. We talked for a while and I began eating, then a moment later she asked me for it. She read it through, and at this first reading – without actually reacting against anything – found it disagreeable. She then reread it, however, and was more or less soothed. She said that one of the hardest things at this time had been precisely being left without a letter – in a vague uncertainty that was like being enmired in gloom – but that things would go better now. We left Lipp's fairly soon and, as it was a mild, star-spangled night, went as far as the Seine. Twelve searchlights were criss-crossing in the sky and the scene was really beautiful. The guns fired twice, then it was all over. We came back and sat in the front part of the Flore, not far from Sonia. The Flore was full, and I saw Gégé who fixed an appointment with me for tomorrow (which is good, since I can put the squeeze on her too). Adamov was there, and Chonez, and Fargue, and all the usual gang including lots of pleasing, pretty women. We stayed there till 11.30, shivering just the tiniest bit, and I felt myself more in sympathy with Bienenfeld than for a long while. She was rational and calm and straightforward. She did weep a bit, not because you said this or that to her, but because it was a letter from you – and that simple reaction seemed rather touching after all her metaphysics. She said, too, that she'd thought she'd removed you from her life – because you were far away, there weren't any letters and everything seemed easy – but in fact at the first letter she'd found herself all cut up again. But this was said perfectly calmly. She said that actually, out of your entire past, it was only she with whom you'd severed relations. Also that she quite understood, she was too little; and that this was what used to torment her, when you'd tell her about your life or write your notebooks and she'd always have the impression that it was against her; that she wouldn't be able to catch you up; and that she'd spent last year waiting and thinking about the perfect happiness she'd share with you in the future, but she'd been wrong not to feel her age – and she did feel it now. And she said that, in a sense, the path taken by this affair struck her as *necessary*; and it was this, above all, which poured some balm onto her wounded heart – but a bitter balm, since she felt it was rotten for her all the same. She feels astonished by the crazy speed of her affair with you, and at having fallen for you so quickly. I told her it all seemed rather artificial – love grown in an incubator – but she protested a bit, saying that it still wouldn't go away so easily. That made me laugh, since it has almost gone away in 3 weeks – proving, on the contrary, quite incredibly easy. She says she finds it strange to think that you've been 'an episode in her life', but she's beginning to contemplate that idea even so. I asked her whether a rupture with me would have hurt her more or less, and she reassuringly answered: 'the same' – which does indeed reassure me, since I'll be able to break off when my day comes without wrecking her life. It's funny how she's scared of things in advance – quite frantically so – but then absorbs them. She's scared of herself in a way: scared precisely of her life being reconstructed in a different way – scared of the future she knows she'd like to have. We talked about her. She admitted she'd been 'intoxicated' last year. She made me laugh when I told her she didn't like things but people and she protested, saying she was so sensitive to atmospheres that on Sunday – for 5 minutes – she'd *regretted* resuming work. She said that if she'd really cared about that affair with you, she wouldn't have resumed work – and though she was too rational for that, of course, it was what she'd *wanted*. That really sums her up, don't you think? I found her helpless and pitiful, but I can't contemplate spending a week on my own with her.

[. . .]

I love you, my little one, and have felt it really strongly these past days, with a combination of joy and suffering. I feel it as more of a separation than last time, perhaps because you yourself feel alone – and that rather distresses me. I need you. In 18 days' time I'll be seeing you, my little one. I feel a certain regret and remorse not to be coming straight away, but it would be silly to lose 3 days of Bost and have to spend 3 days in Paris – with you there but without my being able to see you. This way I'll arrive, pick you up and not let you go again. Why did you tell your family about this leave? Write to Nettancourt (Meuse), poste restante. I love you, my beloved.

Your charming Beaver

Brasserie at the Hotel Lutétia
Square du Bon Marché
[Paris]

Wednesday [13 March 1940]

Most dear little being

I'm very annoyed and jolly dismal. I've just received a note from Bost – in utter despair – telling me they're moving him somewhere 20 km away, this week. That doesn't make it impossible to go and see him, of course, but it'll delay things a lot, since he doesn't know exactly either where or when he's going, or whether he'll find another room for me to stay in. I think I'll be able to manage to get my pass altered, but suddenly nothing's certain any more and it's one of those things that plunge you into gloom. As I've told you, moreover, I'm finding everything dreary in general since the leave periods ended, especially these days – so I was just carelessly letting things drift, shoulders hunched and eyes fixed on that Saturday which seemed to set the limit on my present life. But that limit's now receding – so here I am, suddenly plunged into dreariness until Heaven knows when. I'll doubtless get another letter at 5, so I'll add a note to tell you how things stand. Meanwhile, write to Paris, poste restante, because I'll have the mail forwarded but don't want to tell the hotel where I'm going.

The weather's fine this afternoon. I wouldn't care a hang for anything else, if I thought you'd appear – with your busy step, and your smile that has just come back to me so vividly – and lead me through the streets on your little arm. I love you, my little one – but, as I was telling you yesterday, with a touch of distress: with need and urgency. I love you, and in a fortnight I'll see you. My love.

Your charming Beaver

[Paris]

Thursday 14 March [1940]

Most dear little being

No letter from you this evening – I'm a bit disappointed and need two tomorrow. But yesterday I got your lovely typed letter: how clever you are then, my little one, and how you did surprise me! I'd no idea you'd be able to type so beautifully – there are hardly any mistakes and it all hangs together very well. My sweet little one, in two weeks now it'll be the 28th and I'll be on the point of seeing you – or more or less so. You'll be in Paris, at any rate, and only my ill nature will be preventing me from seeing you. My love, we'll be as happy as last time in that little Hôtel Mistral. I love you so much, little man.

I'm far less nervy than yesterday. I've had some more reassuring letters from Bost. First, he may not be moving – and in any case he won't move far. I'll go to Vitry-le François on Sunday anyway, since he'll definitely be able to spend the day there and make plans with me. Keep writing poste restante to Paris – I'll have everything forwarded and give you another address as soon as I'm settled.

After taking my leave of you yesterday I caught the S, which conveyed me to Place Médicis. I spotted Sorokine, who had a wild look and – uninvited – was keeping watch on the gate to the Luxembourg through which she expected to see me arrive. She was quite surprised when I touched her on the shoulder, but accompanied me to the staff meeting at school. I was expecting to get off with 10 min. but actually spent ¾ hr there – though I did manage to correct a pile of essays, so it wasn't time wasted. I met her again in front of the Mahieu, looking grim and already convinced that I'd gone away on purpose to spite her. I took her with me by taxi to the post office, where I found Bost's second letter. I was terribly put out and tense – as I warned her, with profuse apologies – but did my best to be nice. It went pretty well, we talked a bit about my novel and about her. We kissed, but I warned her that she'd have to leave just before eight, so that I could finish some letters – though I'd make up the lost time to her with interest, through an extra hour. But she still pulled a long face and began to wrangle, so I said irritably I couldn't comprehend what pleasure she could take in staying, when I wanted her to leave. At this she went with dignity to collect her coat and proceeded out of the door, but she couldn't even bring herself to go as far as the stairs. Instead, she waited openly for me to bid her come back – and when I said nothing returned of her own accord. She let out a stream of apologies, so did I, and we parted tenderly.

[...]

Then Lycée C. Sée. Lunch with Sorokine, who was charming because she'd decided to give me back my freedom. But she was also scared stiff I might not use it properly, and as soon as I made any plans her face expressed the wildest panic. I told her I'd just as soon she took my freedom away again – and now she's all anxious, since she can't resolve the following dilemma: either she *exacts* promises, and then feels I'm keeping them out of duty; or else she doesn't demand anything, but then she's consumed by fear. She was charming, and made me read her views on *Grand Meaulnes* which she regards as an odious book, hating the hero because he must be so boring – which is astute. Also, her views on 'the opacity of fictional characters' – where she was saying some really intelligent things. She's estimable and pleasing.

[. . .]

I had a talk with C. Audry. Apparently Wahl's maintaining that *L'Imaginaire* can appear as a thesis even after its publication, and that there has been a precedent with some other fellow who'd been called up. Perhaps that's the explanation of the little mystery.[265] She's still as hilarious as ever. Her husband, not finding her sufficiently affectionate, is sending her to a psychoanalyst who claims to practise existential psychoanalysis – though he's actually just an Adlerian. This fellow explains to her that she's a sphinx, who enjoys asking men impossible questions in order subsequently to drive them away (there's some truth in this, she says); also that she has a dreadful instinct for domination – proved by the fact that one of her childhood memories is a spider in its web; also that her cerebrality kills her sexuality. She's no longer getting on with Minder at all, and is thinking of leaving him. There aren't any scenes, it's more of a dreary business – long evenings without a word, desperate boredom. She explains quite seriously how they don't like Breughel in the same way.

After that, I came back to write to you. I'm expecting Bienenfeld at my place, but I shan't be up to indulging in any reprehensible embraces – I'll feign some feminine ailment.

My dear little one, my love, I'm really hoping for some letters from you. I'd love you to type one from time to time – it's a beautiful sight. I'm all imbued with tenderness for your little flesh-and-blood person and your dear face. Goodbye for now, little all-beloved.

Your charming Beaver

---

[265]That is to say, the mystery of Paulhan's attitude: Jean Paulhan (editor of the *N.R.F.* from 1925 to 1940), though seemingly favourable to the idea of turning *L'Imaginaire* into a thesis, had 'forgotten' to let Sartre know about it in time.

[Paris]

Saturday 16 March [1940]

First read Part 2

My sweet little one

I'm jolly glum today – not gloomy, more depressed. It has a lot to do with lack of sleep – since I haven't slept enough for two nights now – and even more to do with the annoyance of waiting. In a little while, there'll doubtless be a letter and I'll be able to make a firm decision for tomorrow, but it's a nerve-racking situation. What saves me from gloom is the certainty of seeing you in a fortnight: that's now the pole towards which I'm oriented, so that the fortnight itself will at worst be only a great blank, terminated at the far end by that happiness. This is what stops me feeling enmired. Afterwards there'll be your constant presence – and I'll know peace of mind, my little one. Luckily, too, I'm quite taken up by my work, which is altogether easy and charming and productive now that I have this prepared canvas. That too gives these holidays a meaning. There'll be 50 new pages, at the very least.

There's still one shadow, which is dough. Not yours, mine – since the Kos. sisters have taken the lot off me, or almost. They've spent almost as much as in a full month. And I've still got to pay 100 F. for typing paper and 100 F. for books for you, so that with 100 F. travel expenses I'll be left with just 300 F. to live on. So I'll have to appeal to That Lady. I'll ask for 500 F., and send you a bit of that. But where shall I ask for it to be sent? I don't know where I'm going. It's the same with your letters: I'm certain to have problems and not get them all – it's hateful.

[. . .]

I find it altogether poetic to think that you've gone back to your old quarters,[266] and it's there no doubt that you'll receive this letter.

Goodbye for now, my sweet little all-beloved.

Part 2

My sweet little one – here I am, as happy as can be! By some miracle or other I've had two letters from Bost dated Friday, and I can go to the very spot where he is – and has found a lodging. I'm really pleased, and am leaving tomorrow morning. Write and send the books to Charmont, Poste Restante, Marne. I've told them to forward your other letters, so I'll have them on Tuesday, I think. My love, you've written

---

[266] At Brumath.

me such a sweet, entertaining long letter – o little busybody, with your spilt beer-bottles! I'll come back to it tomorrow. I'll write on the train and in buffets – and from Charmont itself – and tell you all about how we're fixed up. I'm delighted.

I've sent you the books. I've been a bit stingy because I'm so hard up, but I think there'll be plenty. I'd really love to reread the whole first part of your novel. Till tomorrow. Your letter genuinely moved me – you love me so well, my little one, and in a way that brings you to me. I kiss you quite passionately.

Your charming Beaver

I'm not too sure what's up with Wanda. She was flourishing yesterday, but the other day Kos. told me – in a voice of such deep conviction that I was astounded – 'She's not happy at present.' Keep me informed.

In a fortnight, at this hour, I'll be on your arm. I love you with a grand passion, my beloved.

Café de l'Industrie
Saint-Dizier (Haute-Marne)

St Dizier, Sunday 17 March [1940]

My sweet little beloved one

What has happened is the last straw – *I've taken the wrong train!* I arrived at the Gare de l'Est with my mind still clouded with sleep, and fixed on the idea that I was going to take the same little 7.50 train that had taken you to Nancy – and that I took subsequently myself, when I went to see Emma. I knew the platform, I walked towards it like a blind woman, I barely glanced at the destination board saying 7.50 with a list of places in the Est, and I found a seat. Then, just as the train was starting to move, I saw another train next to ours that was leaving at the same time – and carrying a sign saying Nancy. My heart in my mouth, I questioned my travelling companions in horror. They confirmed me in my despair: we were speeding towards Troyes and Chaumont, 100 km away from the other line. I was in the wildest panic and on the verge of tears, especially since I had no means of warning Bost.

[...]

I spent the first hours of the journey in the restaurant-car, where I brooded darkly while trying to read the last 'Empreinte', *Is it Possible?* – but it's a frightful let-down, all just a dream. I got into a fight with the ticket-inspector, who wanted me to catch a stopping-train from Troyes that would have taken 7 hours. Instead I went to Chaumont, from where a stopping-train carried me in 1½ hrs to this frightful St Dizier. I'm now going to write to Bienenfeld, but am incapable of injecting any passion into the letter. I'll enjoy writing to Sorokine a bit more. If I find any paper without a heading, I'll do Kos. and Poupette too. That's all, my little one – tomorrow you'll get the continuation of these misadventures. I've reread your pleasing, tender letter again – and I love you, my little one. It's true that I'm very sensitive at the moment, and those little images of you often bring tears to my eyes. In a fortnight we'll be together, my love. I need you so much. I love you so intensely, my little one – can you still feel that, through all these nervy letters? I kiss your beloved little face.

Your charming Beaver

[Charmont (Marne)]

Monday 18 March [1940]

Most dear little being

You should first know, just to reassure you, that my ills have come to an end. It's 9 p.m. and I'm writing from Emma's, [267] so I did finally find her. But Heavens! they weren't to be sneezed at, and yesterday evening at the least provocation I'd have fallen into hysterics. That was quite an escapade, my little one!

[...]

So here I am, ensconced in a room of no great charm but quite spacious, with a huge bed, a tiny dressing-table, and a big round table on which I've already spread out my books and papers. There's a kitchen and dining-room next door, with a stove that provides a bit of warmth and where the good lady and Emma do the cooking. On the other side there's a minute room where the old lady sleeps, so she has to cross ours when she gets up in the morning or goes to bed at night – but that's a minor inconvenience. Anyway she's going off for two days. Emma feels quite hunted, of course. She won't let me poke my

---

[267] 'Emma' is here Bost, of course.

nose outside – though when the weather's fine I'll slip out into the countryside all the same. She does all the shopping herself and won't even allow me to lean out of the window, since it looks onto the street. Actually, the country looks rather bleak anyway so far as walking's concerned, and what with all my books and my novel I'm quite tempted by this detainee's existence – and am enjoying it too. Emma left me at 8 and came back at 9, then again at 10.15 to return at 11 with all the shopping done – her work doesn't take up too much of her time.

Apparently it would be better if you were to write c/o Madame Barreau – Rue Basse – Charmont (CHARMONT), Marne, and mark it F.M. with a little circle round it – that way I wouldn't have to call in at the Poste Restante. But I'll call in there anyway till Thursday.

Goodbye, my little one. I'll tell you in detail all about my life here, which is going to be really nice and peaceful now. I'm going to have a good holiday and in 12 days I'll be seeing you, my love. I'm so happy, we shan't be separated much from now on. Goodbye, little being, my little all. I kiss you quite passionately.

Your charming Beaver

[Nettancourt (Meuse)]

Tuesday 19 March [1940]

1. The first part of this letter was written while waiting for the gendarmes – and in distress
2. The situation is now brighter – and almost satisfactory
3. Even very satisfactory

My sweet little one

I'm on a losing streak! I feel gloomy and sick at heart, and don't yet know how it's going to pan out – I still have a very faint hope, but a dirty trick has been played on me. I'll tell you all about it, but in a novelistic rather than an explanatory mode, since events unfolded in a way that was as novelistic as it was brutal. Let me first tell you, however, that the certainty of seeing you in 8 or 10 days has been of indescribable assistance – and is helping me to endure my very bitter disappointment pretty cheerfully.

Well, yesterday when I wrote to you at about 11 everything was fine. Little Bost arrived – altogether amiable – a bottle of Moulin à Vent in his arms; rillettes, eggs and sardines in his pockets. We cut some wood, made a fire in the kitchen and had a merry lunch in the dining-room. In actual fact, you see, for 4.50 F. a day we'd got a bedroom plus kitchen and dining-room. We made plans for these ten days of conjugal life – and were thinking even of giving an at-home or two, with boozing. We parted, and I decided to go for a country walk. I left in bright sunlight – clutching the beautiful Pléiade *Shakespeare* – but did a bare 3 kilometers. Viewed on foot, that countryside's decidedly short of appeal, so I resolved to stop and find a suitable spot for siesta and reading. Spotting a little lake where two soldiers were boating, I slipped along the verge through a marshy wood, sinking up to my ankles in the mud, till I found a little dry spot. There I rolled my coat into a ball for a pillow and began to doze, while making plans for walks, reading and work during the following days. My spirits were buoyant – it was my first moment of security and happiness. But that wasn't to last for long.

I'd been there for 5 min. when two glossy young officers appeared along the muddy path. They passed me, then – as though thinking better of it – retraced their steps. One asked me: 'Have you got your papers?' I took out my pass, pretty cheerfully. 'It's not stamped – you're supposed to have it stamped on arrival.' I said I thought I had 24 hrs to do it in, but they shook their heads and said I'd better return at once with them. A car was waiting where the path began and I climbed in. They asked me carelessly if I had a husband or boy friend here, and I said no, I was visiting an old aunt – and gave her name. I was feeling a bit uneasy. They showed me into the commandant's office and sent someone to fetch him *urgently* – which was very odd. I stayed there with the officers and tried to brazen it out, speaking of the region as if I knew it well. They replied politely. Then the commandant came in. I began my story: 'I'm staying with a cousin . . .'. 'No point in lying, you haven't got any relative here – you saw the woman in question for the first time in your life at 7.15 this morning.' He outlined everything I'd done since the evening before at Nettancourt. 'You came here to see a soldier. We know his name – he's the one who rented the room.' I said this was quite true, but it wasn't really a hanging offence; that hundreds of other women were doing the same thing and the authorities closed their eyes to it. 'We may close our eyes, but not if you oblige us to open them. The higher authorities are very careful, so we've even searched your room.' Giving a start of amazement, I cited my appointment to C. Sée, declaring that I wasn't in any way an unworthy citizen of France, otherwise I shouldn't have been promoted. He relaxed somewhat, and told me: 'From the civilian point of view, I congratulate you. But from the military point of view that means nothing. We've found your writings.' I smiled again, very urbanely. 'Oh, so what have you read, then?' 'September and October – you've even got considerable talent.' I realized he was talking about your notebooks and my own, and that I was now deep in the mire – since there are all kinds of stuff in them, and I couldn't tell what had caused all this or anything. I asked what they were going to do with me. Reply: send me back to Paris immediately. My insides quaked at this news (though externally I held up very well the whole time), and as I was left alone with him for a couple of minutes, I pleaded despicably: '24 hrs, at least! Just because I've got myself caught is no good reason, when so many others are swanning around in broad daylight.' But he was inflexible: 'You shouldn't have got yourself caught. Who ever heard of turning up with a huge suitcase and depositing it at the left-luggage office! And then there's the War, and France, etc. etc.' I found the idea appalling of leaving under police escort, without having seen Bost again. Yes, in my tired state after the previous day's journey, truly appalling. I'm sure you can imagine what it was like: all that intent will, then that brief oasis of one morning – and then that brutal wrench. I've never had an experience like it, never felt such despair or indignation.

So I pleaded. But he told me: 'It's now in the hands of the higher authorities.' 'Might I see them?' 'You'll see them.' 'Shall I have a chance?' He shrugged his shoulders: 'Who knows?' and left me – while he went for lunch – under the guard of a young sergeant who looked askance at me, firmly resolved not to let himself be seduced by the suspect. I waited for a long while, in a very low state, and then the door opened to admit a young, handsome, smiling, fair-haired lieutenant – divinely handsome and incredibly urbane – who said to me: 'You're Mlle de Beauvoir, aren't you? We've met, actually – in Marseilles, at Mme Chazotte's. And then in Caen you invigilated my philosophy baccalaureat – and even gave me a zero.[268] I heard your name by chance and interceded on your behalf with the commandant.' The commandant came back in and told me: 'Very well! We'll grant you 24 hrs, that's all we can do. These gentlemen will go and search your room, and tomorrow you'll be taken to the police-station.' I felt a spurt of joy beneath my misery – this was already far better than nothing. I went out escorted by 2 lieutenants – one who'd picked me up and who's called J., the other whom I'd made mincemeat of in Caen and who's called C. C. told me the whole story. It was your black notebooks that

---

[268]De Beauvoir taught at Marseilles in 1931-2; in July 1934 she went to Caen as an examiner in the baccalaureat (see *The Prime of Life*, p.190), where many of the candidates came from the Military Academy at La Flèche.

were at the root of the whole thing. I'd brought them along with my own for Bost, and there were also some pupils' essays and a heap of wretched forms. The station clerk opened it all up last night and thought: 'They're communist tracts!' So he alerted the gendarmes, they followed my trail, and this morning everyone in Ch.[armont] was in a high old state, thinking there was a dangerous propagandist loose in the village. They organized a hunt for me, and while I was off walking a car sped after me and quickly ran me to ground. In the meantime, they were carrying out a preliminary search of my room. They took several of your notebooks to the colonel's HQ, and the commandant called for Lieutenant C., telling him: 'It's German or Czech, see if you can make head or tail of it.' C. opened the notebook, read: 'Jules Romains, *Verdun: the Prelude*', then began reading your poor little notebooks. They began to realize they'd made a blunder, but my case remained parlous. They summoned my landlady, who said my room had been reserved by a soldier and told them who he was.

When I arrived back, I found the woman looking very scared and mistrustful. I spent an hour prostrate on my bed, after which the lieutenants came back, as affable as could be. C., who lived just opposite me, invited me over for a brandy at his place. Man to man, they considered the chances of the captain of gendarmes not cancelling my safe-conduct. Then they came back to search my room. They leafed through your notebooks, making comments – and proud of finding themselves in a position to despise the intelligentsia. C. asked me severely how a person could accept being just a meteorologist, instead of waging war properly. They inspected my own notebooks and my novel – politely, but with an intolerably superior attitude that I was obliged to endure. They left in sportive mood, promising themselves to take me next day to the gendarmerie and explain everything to the captain.

I flung myself on my bed. I was deeply and painfully *humiliated*. I depended upon those people – and not just as pieces of machinery but on their consciousnesses, which I was flattering and bowing and scraping to, because in their hands they held something about which I cared so much. I understood and felt lots of things that I don't have time to elaborate here, about humiliation and despair – and the absence of freedom. In the depressed state I was in, all this was magnified – becoming vast and overwhelming. I remained motionless for over two hours, crushed by my feeling of utter gloom – though this kind of *full* gloom is ultimately less painful than gloom due to emptiness. In any case, you reach a point of such nervous exhaustion that you can eventually endure anything.

At this point Bost turned up, carrying a bottle of Barsac and all smiles. He knew nothing. I told him what had happened, but for quite a while – until tears came to my eyes – he thought I was just teasing him. Then he was horror-struck, and touched me both by his despair and by his subsequent indifference to any punishment, if only I could fix things so as to stay on. He was summoned to see that Lieutenant M. he talks so much about, with whom he had the following exchange:

– 'This morning, when I met you, I asked you where you'd been and you told me: "To post a letter". Was that true?'

– 'No, sir.'

– 'You'd just been seeing her?'

– 'Yes, sir.' He smiled. 'She's not the first woman to have come here.'

– 'No, but she's the first to get herself caught.'

He returned, after first begging some fellows to stand in for him next day at the range. We were pretty distraught for a time, and I even had a fit of sobbing – I was at the end of my tether. Again we didn't eat, but went to bed very early and set the alarm for 6: we were already in bed by 9 and tried to get to sleep at about 11 – and I did in fact manage to sleep, without too much inner turmoil.

From 6 to 8, we stayed in bed and talked, with heavy hearts. Then Bost came back again from 8.30 to 10 and from 11 to 1, but we still didn't eat – or just some sardines and chocolate, washed down with Moulin à Vent. I don't know why, but our hopes were reviving somewhat and we chatted almost cheerfully. We were pretty pleased to have seen each other at any rate for those 24 hrs – there was that at least. Bost went off, and I wrote the first part of this letter. I was waiting for the lieutenants in much the same mood in which a person awaits gaolers taking him before a judge – I wasn't feeling too bright. B. came back again for a moment, then the lieutenants arrived. J. was to conduct me on his own to Seunaize, 15 km away, to see the captain of gendarmes. He was slightly encouraging – but not over much – so I set off in the military vehicle with him and two soldiers, feeling pretty desperate. We drove through the countryside, arrived at the gendarmerie headquarters and waited for the captain. I'd lost all hope. The captain arrived – a splendid man with wavy blond hair, dark eyes and a swarthy complexion – and the sight of him restored a bit of vigour to my spirits. The lieutenant was closeted with him to plead my cause, while I discussed with the gendarmes. Then they brought me back in to face the captain alone. I allowed my eyes to brim over with tears that were in any case not far away, since I felt that an attitude of weakness and despair was good policy. I also made good play with a strangled voice. The fellow explained to me the reasons for their suspicion almost apologetically, then hesitated, before eventually authorizing me to remain in Nettancourt – for which he even gave me a stamp, which beats all!

I've now just found a taxi and am leaving for Nettancourt. All I now hope is that they'll agree to put me up. I know there's room in the hotel, but what if they think I'm a spy? I'll show my papers and have another go at winning them over.

That's all – till tomorrow, my little one, my taxi's waiting. I love you with all my might.

Your charming Beaver

My love, I think I'm finally at peace. I've found a room for this evening at the hotel and a definitive private lodging from tomorrow. The lieutenant of whom I was brazen enough to make the request has promised to inform B.; and although I'm not sure whether that'll be done quickly enough for me to see him today, I'll certainly do so tomorrow – and we'd anyway arranged that he'd call in here tomorrow. The only problem is that the place is outside the area of his billet – but apparently there's almost no chance of his being nabbed. I'm going to try and get your letters forwarded to me, and also the money I requested from That Lady. We've already had some money problems, as we needed some for taxi expenses and hadn't got a bean, but B. eventually managed to borrow what we needed. I must either retrieve what was sent to Ch. or else have some more sent.

Goodbye for now, my little one. Write to Poste Restante, Nettancourt, Meuse – we're back to there. I feel as though I'd lived through a week in these past three days. And all I've eaten since Saturday evening is: three cakes (Sunday), 3 eggs and three sardines (Monday), 2 sardines and a packet of petits-beurre (today). Now I'm going to buy myself something for dinner. The good lady of the house is going to cook for me, which will be perfect. I'm not sure whether I've told you the whole story properly. So far as yesterday's concerned, you must situate it all in a *black* state of depression and nervousness that made me feel the war, fascism, the concentration camps, as violently as Bienenfeld does – but in a more intimate way, I think. You know: a nature that, once grasped, needs only to be extended for it to attain full dimensions.

My love, you've been my only comfort all this time. I love you and kiss you most tenderly.

Your charming Beaver

[Nettancourt (Meuse)]

Thursday 21 March [1940]

My sweet little one

It's only 8 in the morning, and I'm too wide awake to go back to sleep but still too sleepy to work, so I'll start a letter to you. I wanted to do so anyway, since my heart's swelling with love for you and I felt disturbed last night at the thought that, in those last agitated letters of mine, I can't have told you sufficiently how much I love you. My beloved. In a week, my sweet little one, I'll be within two days of taking your little arm and giving you a big, big kiss. What a lot of things we'll have to say to each other, my love, and how happy we'll be!

[. . .]

We looked to see whether the coast was clear and B. left. I went back up to my room, slipped back into bed, and am now feeling as happy as can be. I've read a bit more of *Fear and Trembling*: it's badly constructed and long-winded, but that fellow did realize what an existential ethics was — and you can already sense there what Kafka owes to him. I'll read the other one too, since he interests me more than I expected.

But now I'm going to try and get down to some work, despite everything. It's a delight to have a blank day ahead of me, like a day of sickness without being sick. Goodbye for now, my sweet little one. I'm quite melting with affection for you, and moved at the thought of getting your letters — as though I were going to see you in the flesh. I love you.

Hullo again, my love. It's 4 and I'm just off to the post office. I've spent an excellent day. The good lady departed and here I am on my own, like the owner of this big house. I've installed myself in the kitchen where there's a vast table, and since 9 this morning I've done barely anything but work. Someone sold me some eggs on the doorstep, so I put three of them to boil on the range — which was blazing away behind my back and has kept me nice and warm. This evening B. will relight the fire and make us a proper dinner with steaks. I'm going to do the shopping, keeping close to the walls. This afternoon was really delightful in this lovely warm, bright kitchen. There are cats in one corner, hens and a lamb in the courtyard, so it's all still full of life — this house where there's no human being but me.

I'm a bit uneasy about going out — I hope nothing will happen to me. It's going to the post office that's furthest — but I do so want your letters.

Goodbye, little beloved. I hug and kiss you. I'm happy to think my adventures have given you some entertainment. I love you, my dear little one.

Your charming Beaver

I love you – and while writing your address was seized by a passionate desire to tell you so, loudly, loudly, loudly, my little one.

[Nettancourt (Meuse)]

Friday 22 March [1940]

My dear, dear love

How I was longing to get some letters from you! And here at last are two of them, somewhat old – they're from last Friday and Saturday – but even so it's your little writing and your affection that are restored to me: my heart was bursting all morning. My love, I'm so grieved to have made you postpone your leave. I find it rather disturbing to be so far away from you, in terms of power to communicate. All you have to do now is wire NETTANCOURT – MEUSE (Poste Restante) and I could certainly be in Paris the day after you send the cable, if need be. I'd never get over it if I missed you, even for only a day. I need you, my little one. My being so happy here now is all to no avail – a mixture of need and anguish is fixed there inside me. I love you, my beloved.

I've also had the money from That Lady, so I'm altogether contented now. There remains just the tiniest blur of insecurity, connected with Bost's visits and my healthy fear of the gendarmes.

[. . .]

I'll add just a word. I feel a vague remorse with respect to you. I delayed your leave, my little one, and though I know you don't hold it against me that does distress me. I don't like sacrificing the least thing about you to anything else at all, so I'm on the verge of nervous tears. I always feel I'm not nice enough to you, whatever I do. That's because you're so terribly nice yourself, my love – terribly, terribly.

I approve *with all my heart* – and both hands too – the plan for a prologue.[269] That'll be so moving and agreeable.

You'll have to see Bienenfeld for 2 hrs *but no more* while I'm at

---

[269]A plan, later abandoned by Sartre, for a prologue to *The Age of Reason* showing Ivitch, Mathieu and Marcelle ten years before the events in the novel.

school. Wanda certainly wasn't pregnant — but why the devil was she so unhappy? She left last Sunday for Laigle, but you must know that by now.

Goodbye, my love.

My sweet little one. It's now 4.30 in the afternoon. I've been working the whole time, stopping only to smoke cigarettes and put coal into this stove that's blazing away behind my back. I lunched off biscuits and apple jam, but am hoping to eat properly this evening.

I've reread your letters, and rather than rending my heart they made me happy. You love me so nicely, my little one, and make me feel it so clearly! How I'd love to hug you in my arms — but that'll come, in a week. My love, I'm so afraid you may think my heart's dry as dust, when in fact it's bursting with life, you know. I love you, my little one, quite violently — with need, and with all the tenderness in the world. I'd like to hold you in my hands.

Your charming Beaver

[Nettancourt (Meuse)]

Saturday 23 March [1940]

My sweet little one

I'd be spending a good day today, if I weren't so disappointed at not having a letter from you. But perhaps at 5 Bost will bring me one from Charmont. I'm hoping the old woman will hand him the one I told you to write addressed to him — although she did make a great fuss yesterday when he went to pick up his things, on the pretext that we weren't married and had caused problems for her. At the post office, in any case, nothing had been forwarded. I also realize that I don't know where to write to you. You'll have left on leave by the time this letter arrives. Being cut off from you like this weighs upon me and makes me nervy. I'm scared Heaven knows what may happen, and couldn't feel more ill at ease. However, I think you'd wire if you needed to. I've had a note from That Lady, who kindly forwarded on to me a very kind note from Kos. — that was the entirety of my mail.

[. . .]

I called in at the post office and bought some cigarettes. I also jubilantly bought 4 enormous steaks, since this evening we're intending to eat two each. I was at work by about 10.30, but it didn't go all that well. I ruminated a bit, and was vaguely sick of my opus – from over-saturation. What's more, this is the phase when you stop inventing anything – when you exploit earlier inventions without feeling anything – and that seems sterile. So, because I was getting bogged down, I simply changed chapters and began one about Gerbert, which I'm quite enjoying. That's the lot – that's where I've got to. I'm going to write to Sorokine, and to Kos., powder my nose a bit, then go back to my book for a while. I'm delighted with Little B. and glad to be here, but I miss you too much. If only I'd got your letters! I'm still under the effect of having made you postpone your leave. It's a disquiet that will pass only when I've kissed you, my love, as I so long to do! I've also been upset by rereading all your last letters – you're so, so nice to me, my little one! I so long to have your love back, in flesh and blood. I love you, with a passionate need, my love.

Your charming Beaver

LETTERS

JULY 1940 – MARCH 1941
Sartre Prisoner

At this point, the surviving correspondence is interrupted on De Beauvoir's side for almost four months. From 27 March until 9 April, Sartre was on leave in Paris. From 10 April until 10 June, the correspondence did continue (see Lettres au Castor, vol.2*), but De Beauvoir's letters have apparently been lost. On 10 June De Beauvoir left Paris for La Pouèze, returning only on 21 June after the Armistice. In mid June Sartre was taken prisoner, following the collapse of the French armies, and for a further three weeks De Beauvoir remained without news of him. On 11 July she received a pencilled note confirming that he was alive and a prisoner of war, but then heard nothing more till mid October – although she herself continued writing throughout July.*

[Paris]

11 July [1940], morning

My love

I'm so moved to have word of you. I looked stupidly at that pencil-written note without believing in it. I'd been expecting, at best, one of these days to receive a printed card. You tell me almost nothing, but it's a living word. And you speak of being back before the end of the month – is that possible? I knew with total inner certainty from the outset that you were a prisoner. That filled me with distress, above all because I pictured you not having any news and could well imagine your pent-up fury. Moreover, I was afraid I wouldn't be able to see you again before peace was signed – and so unhappy at not being able to write to you.

You should first know that I'm doing fine. The Kos. sisters are safe and sound at Laigle (that's actually all I know). Bost was at Carpentras ten days ago well on the way to recovery.[270]

My only worry was you, and since you're in good condition we can all be said to have been really lucky, my little one, to end up all right.

---

[270]Bost had been seriously wounded on 23 May and evacuated to the vicinity of Beaune, then on to Carpentras, near Avignon.

I've kept a detailed diary, you know, of everything that has happened to me over the past month. It's like a long letter addressed to you. I'm not going to copy it all out, since in spite of everything I'm too unsure about whether my letter's going to get through, but I'll go on keeping it. My love, am I truly going to see you again?

I don't know which was the last letter you had from me. On Monday 10 June I wrote to you that I was leaving Paris with the Bienenfelds. I had an excellent journey and arrived on the Tuesday evening at La Pouèze. I stayed there till 28 June, in an extremely sombre state as you can imagine – those were among the worst days of my life. The last letter I'd had from you was dated 8 June. I got another one, dated the 9th, in Paris a week ago – but for the rest, absolute silence. I lived for a fortnight off reading, the wireless and black despair – surrounded, as always at That Lady's, by all kinds of people and farcical events. On 28 June I resolved to return to Paris, with some people who had a car – but who'd omitted to mention that they didn't have any petrol. It was a crazy venture. I ditched them on the second day and got back on a German lorry, and then in a Red Cross car. In Paris I met up with my parents and Sorokine. I've installed myself at my grandmother's, but receive my mail at Rue Vavin. I've been given 10 hours teaching at Duruy, which isn't unwelcome. And I've learnt to ride a bicycle. I managed on my own straight off and for the past 5 days I've begun going for long rides all over Paris. I'm reading Hegel for three hours a day at the Nationale, in the hope of understanding him and presenting you with a huge exposition of his thought.

Your parents have left Paris – I'm not sure where for. In the past week I've begun receiving letters and have had news of Kos., of Bost, and of Bienenfeld – who's in Quimper – so it has been far less painful than before. Regarding you, my life was hanging on one question: how long will the prisoners be kept? Whence alternating moments of hope and despair, with despair predominating. But I'm very patient and, as at the outset of the war, too involved to be unhappy.

I don't dare write too long a letter, for fear of wearying the censors. I'm going to write a card at the same time, which will perhaps arrive faster. This letter is empty and I've so much to tell you. But I'm sending it as it is, and will write another later. I'd never before tested to this degree how I truly love you more than myself.

You're everything to me.

Your charming Beaver

[Transit P.O.W. Camp No. 1,
9th Company – Baccarat]

[Paris]

11 July [1940], afternoon

My love

I've just been to the post office and they assure me it's permitted to write to prisoners, and specifically to those in Meurthe-et-Moselle. So I'm going to fill out this morning's letter a bit. Alas!, my love, it's not permitted to send parcels. As soon as it's allowed, you'll have plenty of sausages and sweetmeats of every kind. But perhaps you'll be here first – am I really going to see your face again, my love? For a month now my life has been reduced to that one wish. There's truly nothing in the world I wasn't ready to renounce, if we were only allowed to be together once more. During this whole month, I've existed only with you and for you – and it's through you that I've experienced all my agonies. How I'd like to know what you're thinking and feeling! It has been brought home to me that I'll always be happy so long as it's possible for you to be happy. It's for your happiness and your fate that I've suffered and trembled. And today I've recovered my serenity, because your little pencilled note however terse it may have been – that specific sign of your existence – has restored to me a clear view of what you are. At all events, your fate will have a meaning and your stubborn little consciousness manage to secure some joy. When I left Paris on 10 June, my love, I knew you'd be taken prisoner – and in a sense it was painful to me. In another sense, however, that was just the fate which suited you, little being, and That Lady and I laughed about it, imagining you using your knowledge of the German language to converse with your gaolers. I can picture you so well, with a shaven head, saying 'Ja' with a nice smile just as you used to in Berlin, as blond and Germanic in appearance as the Germans guarding you, and finding satisfaction – I'm sure – in speaking with your purest accent. I can also picture your authentic little soul struggling against the contortions of stoicism, and against any sea-elephantine bouts of nausea.[271] My dear little one – how tenderly I do love you! Will you be able to write longer letters? Can you keep a diary? Haven't you lost the drafts for your novel? How I'd like to know all that! My love, in three weeks' time perhaps I'll have your little arm tucked in mine and we'll be walking on the streets of Paris – won't we? Is that possible? What a song and dance we'll make about it! How I'd like to know how you envisage your future – and what it

---

[271]Allusion to a game dating from the early years of their relationship (see *The Prime of life*, p.19), in which Sartre would imitate the wretched-looking sea-elephant they had seen in a zoo at Vincennes – thus ridding himself of the contingency of a bad mood by assuming it, as a temporary disguise to be discarded at will.

will be. I think you must have had moments of really black despair, my love – the idea has often tormented me. How hard this total separation was! Yet, in a sense, I never felt totally separated from you, for I think I can picture clearly enough how you've lived and thought throughout this month – it must have resembled what I experienced myself. There were countless moments when I felt myself to be in perfect, assured and tranquil unity with yourself.

I'm now feverish and impatient, my love, and can't write an orderly letter. I'm writing to you from that little Café Delcour, where we once discussed blame and responsibilities. It's open to a bright, sunny street and people are passing by. Paris is still itself. We're properly fed – to tell the truth I don't even notice any restrictions. It's mainly a matter of queuing up for things, and I don't do that. Lots of people have already come back. There's very little traffic – neither taxis nor buses – but the Métros are running. There's a superabundance of bicycles on the streets. You'll laugh when you see me – but riding round Paris on a bicycle is a real delight. The Flore is closed, but the Dôme's open and I always stop there for quite a while. There are hardly any cinemas left, but the libraries open in the afternoon: the Sorbonne, the Ste-Geneviève, the Nationale. You know, Hegel's horribly difficult, but also extremely interesting. You must know him – it's akin to your own philosophy of nothingness. I'm enjoying reading him and thinking precisely about expounding him to you.

Is it true you're going to come back? You're 35 and an auxiliary – which must be good reasons why you should be demobilized – but I don't dare hope too much. Well, sooner or later I'll have you back, just as you always were, but enriched by new treasures of experience and assuredly further improved.

You'll see, when I tell you everything in detail, that I've been extremely sensible and well-behaved all this month. It was actually a great help to me to go to La Pouèze – I was extraordinarily lucky. I can't imagine a better haven in such circumstances. That Lady was an absolute treasure. I'm going to send her news of you right away, since she was quite anxious about you. Nothing's known about Guille, who must have been taken prisoner too.

I've so many things to tell you that I don't know where to start. When I think that these letters will be your first contact with the rest of the world, I'd like to include everything that may interest you. At the same time, though, nothing strikes me as essential enough. From tomorrow on, I'll try to write to you day by day as before, and at the same time summarize for you the month that has gone by. By and large, as I've already told you, I've found everything so interesting that my life has endowed me with an amazing plenitude – there were at most three or four empty days at La Pouèze. For the remainder, there was either plenitude in the object – as on my return journey, for example – or plenitude of anguish and fatigue. And always the impression of an immense collective adventure, which still grips me even now. I imagine things were much the same for you – albeit harsher. I imagine, too, that this very harshness didn't displease you all that much. Perhaps that's just optimism – but you're an invitation to optimism, my love. I'd so like to know the truth of it. There were moments when I imagined your fate in the blackest terms, and then I was utterly downcast. All things considered, however, I'd wager that through anguish, gloom and misfortune, you've managed to remain just the same as you've always been.

My little one, I'm going to go for a walk and think about you. I'm too wrought up to write. Perhaps during the evening I'll begin a narrative letter, that I'll continue tomorrow – and that will partly reproduce my diary. Finally, you should know that I've had just one postcard from the Kos. sisters, saying that they almost left for Bordeaux but in fact have remained at Laigle, where all is calm once more. I've had a shoal of letters from Bost, the last dated 28 June: he'd been evacuated to Avignon, then to Carpentras – and was still very tired. I think he'll be sent back to his family very shortly. Bienenfeld's still in Quimper, I think. That's everything about people.

My little one, I've really undergone the most complete and varied test of my love for you. There's enough to satisfy a heart. You suddenly seem so close that it brings tears to my eyes, just as, when I was leaving Paris on that fateful 10 June, I felt as though I were being wrenched away for the last time from yourself in the flesh. Between the two, I've thought of you almost always as yourself, separated from me – but also as the essential, undefined condition of my own life. But when I climbed into M. Bienenfeld's car, I lost the sweetness of our love – all concrete, and tender, and full, as it is in your presence (I pictured you in summer clothes, walking down the street and smiling at me in the distance) – and it's only now that I'm recovering it. My love. I'll recover you – concretely – on a street corner, with your face, your smiles, your little body and your determined step. I love you, my sweet little one.

Your charming Beaver

[Paris]

Thursday 11 July [1940]

My love

I've already written you two letters in the course of today, but I'm afraid they may not arrive – because I fear I may have forgotten '9th Company' in the address – which would be stupid. Perhaps you'll get them all the same, though, if you warn the Mails Orderly. I've no real idea what a prisoner-of-war camp is like. *Paris-Soir* carried a lengthy description of the one at Pithiviers, but it still didn't tell one all that much. It was stated in the article that visits are allowed, so as soon as I had your address I promptly had a moment of hope – but then I called in at the Gare de l'Est and there are no trains. So I'll have to wait for you. Perhaps you'll be able to write in a regular fashion now – that would change my life so much. At any rate, it's already changed entirely by virtue of the fact that I've had that little note. Since this morning I haven't stopped turning the envelope in my fingers. It's strange and looks almost pathetic – with its pencilled writing, and the postmark, and the big stamp of the Paris military command. When I found it this morning, for a long while I remained unable to believe my eyes – and I still look at this little scrap of torn paper with a somewhat fearful amazement. I'd so like some details, my love – and for a genuine correspondence to be possible!

I'll now embark on a detailed account of my own life. I'll start with my return to Paris, because everything before that already seems very ancient – so although I'll be returning to it, I'll leave that for later – I'll start with what's most alive. Well, I arrived back on 29 June in the evening. I'd left La Pouèze like a whirlwind, as soon as I'd thought – foolishly, in fact – that perhaps you were already there in Paris and waiting for me. I spent two days on the journey – it was very interesting, and I'll tell you all about it shortly – and was worn out, though also overcome by emotion, when I arrived at Rue Vavin. The good lady raised her arms to the sky when she saw me, and handed me a letter from you – dated 9 June – in which you seemed to be hale and hearty. I sobbed my heart out, of course, when I received it, both because of the letter itself and also because of my intense disappointment, for there was no note saying you were in Paris and I felt horribly lost and lonely. I had a good cry in my hotel room, then went out – since I wanted to go to the post office to ring your parents, and to call on the Bosts – but on the way I met my father sitting outside at the Daumesnil. He offered me a beer and a ham sandwich, which I really did need. I then left him and walked to St Germain-des-Prés, where I saw that the Flore was closed – which wrung my heart. But the Deux Magots was open, and

I telephoned from there – to no avail, in fact – then went up to see my mother, who burst into tears at the sight of me. I had dinner there, but was chucked out promptly at 9.30, with an admonition to hurry home. Now I've grown quite accustomed to it, but that first evening it made a strange impression on me when – at a quarter to ten – I heard the loudspeaker giving a first warning, and again at 10 its imperious voice (curfew's at 11 now, in fact, which leaves a greater margin). That evening I was low as could be: feverish, exhausted, and separated from you for Heaven knows how long. Luckily I found a detective story of sorts, which filled my mind till sleep came.

I woke up much less downcast. The weather was mild, and Paris – which the evening before had seemed like a vague, gloomy 'somewhere on the planet' – had recovered its individuality. I bought *Le Matin*, the sole survivor along with *Paris Soir* of the former newspapers (the choice is a happy one I find, don't you agree?[272]). I sat down at the Dôme and rediscovered my place near the front, my coffee, and my 'Swiss pastries' with raisins, just as they'd been a month before. I began writing in a big notebook that I'd just bought, and at about 10 set off across Paris. I called on your mother (hoping for news of you), but she wasn't in; on C. Audry; on Sorokine – but saw only her mother. I tried in vain to ring Taverny. Passy was utterly empty. In a sense, that emptiness, that fine weather and that despair in my heart recalled the month of September – but there were countless differences in the situation and my way of feeling it. I returned towards the Latin Quarter, noting with satisfaction a great abundance of fruit, and of food shops generally, in the streets of Paris. Arriving in the Latin Quarter, I first installed myself at the Mahieu, then went to read at the Dôme – where I stayed until 6. The dominating theme of people's conversations on the Métro, in cafés, on doorsteps, was – and has remained to this day – 'Do you have any news?' The washroom ladies at the Dôme, and at the Trois Mousquetaires too, asked after you, my love. All the women everywhere were complaining about not knowing anything. And the big question, the all-consuming question, was: 'Will they keep the prisoners-of-war, or won't they?' For the Armistice terms are clear regarding those in Germany, who have to remain there till the end of the War; but regarding those in France, everything's vague – so every kind of hypothesis was rife. I

---

[272]*Le Matin* (founded 1884) made its reputation as a newspaper of moral campaigns and noble causes, but was owned by an archetypal press baron himself involved in all kinds of shady deals. *Paris Soir* (founded 1931) was the first successful popular newspaper of the modern kind in France, combining photographs, sport, crime, advertising, etc. with some serious journalism.

myself oscillated daily between one indication and another, my days serene or desolate depending on whether I thought I'd see you within a month or only when peace was signed. I can assure you it was astonishing: morning, noon and night that same litany everywhere – 'It's hard, being without news.' In the popular neighbourhoods, this was mingled with another refrain: 'If people had only known, they'd have stayed – they'd never have left!'

At about 6 I felt like talking to someone, so I called in at Avenue d'Orléans to see whether Zebuth had come back.[273] She'd been at La Pouèze with me and had been really kind and nice, telling me to come and see her as soon as I arrived – so I did. I found her in her confectionery shop, which she'd just reopened. She'd just arrived, having had an excellent journey (in the company of 'someone completely different' whom I'd met at La Pouèze, and who's very nice), leaving in the morning with petrol and reaching Paris without mishap. We chatted a bit, she lent me a few books, then I went and had dinner with my parents. When I got back home to Rue Vavin, I found Sorokine – who'd been waiting for me for almost three hours, and whom I had to keep there for the night. I was rather pleased to see her again. She'd tried to join me by bicycle, but had started out too late and been caught by the Germans, who put her in a lorry with her bicycle and sent her home again. She was so happy to meet up with me, and described to me in such terms her sorrows during the previous two weeks, that I was really moved. Only she at once annoyed me and appeared clinging by deciding to move in with me for a few days, and by declaring in a peremptory tone of voice that I was going to be happy and forget all my troubles, now that I'd found her again. She slept in my room, which – combined with my overwrought state – meant that I barely closed my eyes.

The next day, more from a frantic need for activity than from hope, I decided to go to Taverny for some news of Bost. I was afraid he'd remained in Beaune and been taken prisoner too. Actually, I didn't really believe it – but I wanted to go to Taverny and find out. I also had some vague idea that he'd been discharged and sent home to recuperate. The project appealed to me because I had to do it on foot and it was a real expedition. The day began with a little drama, because Sorokine demanded to go with me. She wanted to take me sitting on the luggage-rack of her bicycle. But she also wanted to go and warn her mother, so she first took me to Pte de St Cloud – whereas I wanted to leave on the other side of Paris, by the Pte de la Chapelle. This little trip was tiring,

---

[273]A cousin of the Morels.

and also persuasive – the bicycle was impracticable. Then she declared that she'd go with me on foot, and began pawing the ground – yet she was already complaining of a pain in her back. Into the bargain, while I was pushing her bicycle a parcel of provisions I was carrying slipped from my hands and something broke. That drove me really mad – I was trembling with rage. You'd laugh at me when I'm like that – which often happens to me with Sorokine (just with her) and is a sign of the nervous state I'm in at present: a nervousness I don't feel when I'm alone, but which emerges as soon as she irritates me. I break things, I tremble, my voice becomes toneless – and once I almost slapped her. This time it wasn't so violent – but sharp enough, even so, to scare her. Keeping mum, she merely accompanied me by Métro to the Pte de la Chapelle. As we'd left at 6 in the morning, it was despite everything still only 8 when I found myself confronted by the huge, arrow-straight, grey avenue leading towards Saint-Denis.

My love, I'm tired of writing. I'll go on tomorrow. In my other letters I explained to you at length the state of my heart, but basically you know that. All the same, do put in a claim if you can – I think 9th Company was left off the address. Starting to write to you again seemed strange at first, but now it has become natural to me once more and every day I'll write you a long letter. For the first time in ages I've had a moment of true, full happiness today: life's beginning to be rebuilt, we'll be reunited, and I'm as sure of you as of myself. We'll be happy. We'll work. We'll think. We'll talk. All that's needed is a little patience.

My dear little one, how close you are to me, how living you are, how I love you! – you who are the necessary and the superfluous to me (the perfect synthesis of the universal and the particular, towards which the unhappy consciousness aspires according to Hegel and Monsieur Wahl). My love, I'll see your dear expressions once more. I'll kiss you. I'll hold your arm. Come back to me quickly.

Your charming Beaver

[Paris]

Friday 12 July [1940]

My sweet little one

How pleasing I find it to be able to write to you once more! It's 9.30 in the morning, today there's no school, I'm totally free. I've just had my breakfast at the Dôme. The weather's grey and even rather chilly. I started reading your *L'Imaginaire* – I've just reread the whole section on 'The Certain', and will shortly be tackling 'The Probable'. There were tears of affection in my eyes when I encountered the drawing of the little man running – I've become quite weepy again since yesterday, with a little blur of emotion continually rimming my eyelids. My little one, I no longer think of anything but your little living silhouette that I'm going to see again. How I long to know what's going on in your little head! How I hope it's not too gloomy!

Speaking of *L'Imaginaire*, have you heard that it was a big success in both Paris and the provinces? That the students were fighting over it?

I'll tell you how I've been living, starting from where I left off yesterday. This is my fourth letter, not counting the postcard. I hope you've had them all, even though I forgot to put 9th Company on the first two. I can't wait to get a letter from you, telling me that you've had mine. Then contact will truly have been restored. And after that you'll come, my love.

So, on 1 July – which was a Monday – I found myself at 8 in the morning at the Porte de la Chapelle. I wanted to go to Taverny. There was a group of refugees waiting for lorries at the Métro exit, and lots of others on bicycles or walking, laden with baggage, starting up the broad avenue. I strode off, not thinking much about anything. At that time I'd had no news at all of the Kos. sisters, Bost or you – and my life was extremely unsettled. So I was happy to have to provide some motivated physical effort. I crossed St Denis and Épinay, then followed the banks of the Seine. I don't know the outer suburbs at all well, so was interested in seeing them. Moreover, they had a kind of historic character, since that was the way the Germans had come a few days earlier, it was the way the tide of refugees from the Nord had flowed, and it was still full of refugees returning. All along the way, you continually heard the same refrain: '500 km. on foot, 300 km. by bicycle, so exhausted ... we've come from Montauban, we've come from Toulouse ... oh! if we'd only known, we'd never have left.' People would recognize each other and pause on their way. A cyclist dismounted in front of a group of pedestrians laden with parcels: 'Hey! your mother has been back three days already,' etc. etc. The mails were not yet functioning at all, and even from Paris to the outer suburbs people felt miles away from one another – totally separated. Other people were asking for news of the house towards which they were making their way: 'Nothing has been damaged, eh?' and so on.

I walked a long way – especially since I stupidly veered off towards Argenteuil, which meant I made a 4-km. loop. That was where I encountered garden suburbs. It was a fine day, I ate petits-beurre as I walked, and I stopped for quarter of an hour in a bistro to drink lemonade and write a note to Bost. A woman was talking about her husband, who was in captivity but she didn't know where, while two others were entreating some fellow to sell them some potatoes – but he was refusing stubbornly (they were in terribly short supply 10 days ago). I continued on my way, following the line of the railway. There were gardens full of gooseberry bushes – separated by meadows, and by wheatfields sprinkled with poppies – and a blazing sun. The odd thing was that gardens and countryside alike were alive and blooming, but the houses were dead. Every now and again, on the door of one of these sleeping villas, you could read a notice saying: 'House inhabited' – or, more often, '*Bewohnt*'.

I arrived at the Vaucelles station, which couldn't have been deader. What with all those cafés now closed, it seemed strange to recall that rainy day when I'd been there with Bost and it had all been swarming with people. I passed by the Pastor's house.[274] Its windows were wide open and on the gate hung the sign: '*Bewohnt*'. (Bost has since written and told me how the Pastor, in some extremely heroic letters, had expressed his determination not to leave, whereas the Pastoress was simply dying to go and join her children at Laval.) I didn't dare go in right away, but walked on to a café to wash and tidy up a bit, then wrote up my diary for an hour (which I'm partly copying out here for you) while finishing off my petits-beurre. After that, pretty intimidated by the idea of confronting the Pastoress, I nevertheless bravely proceeded to the house. Alas!, my poor, dear little husband, you're going to be disappointed if you were licking your lips over the idea of that interview, since neither the Pastoress nor the Pastor were there: they'd left for Paris to see one of their daughters, and I found only an old housekeeper. At least I found out that Bost was not yet back. I set off again along a wide, tarred road bathed in sunlight, proud of myself because I'd done 25 km. in one go, in indifferent shoes, and was still setting off again cheerfully. All the same, I was hot and kept a weather eye open for cars. Two zoomed rudely straight past me, but the third – a little old crock with an open roof – stopped. The fellow eagerly told me to get in, because after doing 700 km. on a motorbike he'd 'understood' and was only too happy to give someone a helping hand. Yet one more person who told me: 'Oh, if I'd only known!' He'd evacuated himself and his wife on the bike, and had returned from Montauban in the same way. The poor woman, who had a crooked

---

[274]The Pastor and the Pastoress: nicknames for Bost's parents.

spine, had been shaken about terribly. As for him: 'I can tell you, Madame – since you're getting on in years – that down there round my privates, I'm in the most frightful pain!' It seems that in those departments that hadn't been occupied, the prefects were at that time forbidding people to leave their department (on the pretext of famine in Paris). On the one hand, people were being advised to return home, while on the other gendarmes were posted on the borders between departments. People waited till night fell and the gendarmes left, then passed through all the same. He took me back all along the Seine. We passed by the Île de la Grande Jatte – which struck me as incredibly poetic, since it had always been a legendary place for me that I'd never imagined materially existing somewhere. There were people boating and bathing, so that it had a strange holiday atmosphere. Moreover the season, people's nonchalance, and the low value of time – all that gives the days a gratuitous air, rather charming but rather disturbing. Near a bridge, when the car came to a halt near a German lorry, a solid object struck me: a bar of chocolate thrown me by a German soldier. I alighted at the Neuilly bridge, where I made the painful discovery that I was completely stiff. I took the Métro, called in at the Dôme to write up my diary, then returned to the hotel in Rue Vavin to sleep a bit. It was precisely then that I found an old letter from Bost – sent from Avignon – which wholly reassured me about his fate. I slept for a while, but at 6 Sorokine arrived in floods of tears because her mother had turned her out. First of all, as you'll recall, she'd spent the previous night at my place, and then she'd told her mother she wanted to stay with me for a few days. Whereupon her mother – delighted, since she's penniless – declared that this was perfect and I could simply keep her. The daughter said, between sobs, that she'd never again set foot in her mother's house. As for me, I explained that I couldn't maintain her – but we ended up with a compromise. I promised her 500 F. a month for three months, which is enough for her to live on in Paris or at La Pouèze, and she'll go back to her mother's in October. To offset this, I decided to live at my grandmother's, for part of the time to eat there, and to have almost all my dinners at my parents' place. In that way, I scarcely spend more than 20 F. a day on myself. Besides, I can tell you right away (you'll see by and by) that money doesn't bother me. We'll get our *June* salaries for sure towards the end of this month, and the July ones probably a bit later – we'll even have money left over. I had 1,000 F. in hand when I returned to Paris, since I hadn't spent anything at That Lady's, and if it takes me 1,000 to get through the month that will be the absolute maximum. I wondered anxiously if you'd actually received that money order. I think you must have, but I was very worried, since you'd certainly have found it useful to have a bit of cash on you. My God! how I'd like a real letter with some real news!

Anyway, I calmed Sorokine down and she told me lots of amusing stories about her life in Paris during my absence. For 8 days she earned her living peddling newspapers – she says you can make 45 F. a day, but only by flogging yourself to death – but then they prevented her from continuing since she didn't have a work permit. She's really wondering what her future's going to be, and it doesn't in fact look any too bright. She also told me how, for two days after my departure, Paris had been black with soot, because fuel trains were burning everywhere and belching out thick clouds of smoke – Zebuth had told me about this too. The Parisians all looked like chimney-sweeps, and apparently it was strange: a certain quality of the light that made you think of fine weather, combined with a black ceiling overhead.

I went and had dinner with my parents. The difficulties of finding provisions were the main subject of conversation, of course – it was harder than it is now. After that I went home, where I found Sorokine. We divided the beds – to give ourselves one each – and after an hour of tender conversation fell asleep.

[. . .]

My little one, I'll go on in full detail this evening or tomorrow – I enjoy telling you it all. As for today, it's already noon and I've spent all morning reading *L'Imaginaire* and writing to you. I'll call in and see whether there's a letter from you. If not, I'll mail this letter as it is. Goodbye, my love. Here I am now, as close to you as can be. I'm so happy about it. I love you and am waiting for you, my love.

Your charming Beaver

[Paris]

Saturday 13 July [1940]

My sweet little one

It's 5.30 and I've nothing to do till this evening except write to you. Only I'm rather afraid these letters may not be reaching you (this is the fifth), which paralyses me somewhat. I haven't had any news, of course, since your pencilled note. I had some vague hope this morning – now I've transferred it to tomorrow. How happy I'll be when I have a real letter, my love.

I've had some more detailed news from Kos. She says that Laigle hasn't suffered all that much. There were a few bombs, but really only one family was devastated. All the locals had left, and they themselves stayed only because, as usual, Mme Kos. felt ill enough to be at death's door. She's going to come to Paris any day now – but I'll keep her for only three or four days. Bienenfeld has written to say she's coming back too, but it's not certain that she'll stay.

I'm first going to tell you about the past two days. As you'll see, my life is calm and even melancholy, with dull throbbings of desire whenever I think how you're there in flesh and blood in a particular spot in France, and that a train – and permission to board it – would be enough to bring you back here in five hours. My love, I don't know if you can feel the need that I have of you. I've borne it with all the patience I could muster, but now that I'm relaxed – because I'm no longer worried – it utterly suffocates me.

So yesterday I spent the morning reading *L'Imaginaire* and writing to you. I walked to the Latin Quarter, then over towards the Seine and on to the Palais Royal. I went to eat at the Fleur de Lys – near the Bib. Nationale – where the Llama used to take me on days of particular jollity. Then I read Hegel from 2 to 5 at the Nationale. I'm beginning to understand – it's at once interesting and irritating. I'm now on the *Phenomenology of Mind*, after which I'll move on to the *Logic*. Reflecting on him and Husserl, I've realized I'd forgotten a great deal of Husserl – so you can explain him to me again, while I'll expound Hegel to you.

After that, I went to pick up my case at the Gare de Lyon. I found my papers and clothes all right, and took them home – where I proceeded to make a few sartorial adjustments, then went off to meet Sorokine at the Dôme. It was a dreary occasion, since the evening before we'd had a big scene. I'll tell you all about it at the right time, but I find such scenes so tedious that the very idea of telling you about them bores me stiff. After that, at 8.30, I went up to my parents' place to take simultaneous advantage of dinner and the concert, which was excellent (there's a concert every evening now on the wireless): some very pleasing early music, some Bach, and some Debussy. Then I walked home with Sorokine and went to bed.

This morning, school from 9 to midday, then lunch and total reconciliation with Sorokine. Hegel from 2 to 5, and now I'm back here again. It's raining. I'm deeply and intimately bored, and think *you* must be intolerably bored. Are you with Pieter? You surely can't read, or even write if you've only a pencil. Did you manage to save your drafts? My love, I've shed as many tears over Mathieu[275] as over you yourself – nothing has been more painful to me than the uncertainty of his fate. Truly, my sole concern has been to ascertain what will become of your life.

I'm going to go on with my story – I'd reached Thursday 4 July. I had school from 9 to 11, then went to the Deux Magots and sat outside reading *Gone with the Wind*, which Zebuth had lent me. It's less boring than I'd thought, but less enjoyable than people say. I had lunch with the family, where I ate beef for the first time in ages. I went back to the Deux Magots, to read and write to Kos., then for an hour went bicycling – with enjoyment, weariness and skill. After that I read a newspaper at the Dôme, from which I got the idea that prisoners-of-war weren't going to be released. This put me in a black mood, so that when Sorokine came along at 7 and I thought how I was going to spend 4 hours with her, I started to hate her. We left on foot for the Palais Royal, where I had the vague intention of looking at the prisoner-of-war lists – the idea being to beguile my uncertainty. We quarrelled vaguely, because she wanted me to take various steps to get hold of a bicycle and I didn't want to. Then we saw that the place where they kept the lists was closed (apparently there are not many names posted, and queues of 600 people), so we left – she dragging her feet, I striding out – which opened up huge distances between us. We met up again all the same near the Café de la Paix, where in a hate-filled silence we ate delicious pineapple sorbets. It was full of very smart Germans – but, apart from that, deserted and gloomy.

We returned via the Tuileries and there – at the sight of an old madwoman, wracked by nervous twitches, dropping her knickers behind a tree with a hunted look – we laughed and made up.

I came back to settle in at my grandmother's – where we had dinner, gorging ourselves with sausage – then went off to bed, read a detective story for a while, and slept for almost 11 hours. I dreamt about you: you were dressed as a soldier and you were a murderer and wanted to strangle me. After that you calmed down, and I was kissing you and caressing your hair. But then, while still dreaming, I started up in fury at my dream – finding it out of place and painful – and woke up on the spot. It was already 11 o'clock. I went to do some shopping with Sorokine, since at that time she liked to think she could prepare my meals – and was determined to do so. She boiled some rice, but spilt

---

[275]Mathieu: main character in Sartre's *The Age of Reason*.

almost all of it on the floor as soon as it was cooked. Then we went to the Sorbonne library, where I read an interesting big book on Debussy. The idiotic thing is that the libraries are open only from 2 to 5, otherwise I'd have educated myself about both Hegel and music, whereas I had to choose. Then I came and sat down at the Dôme, where the waiter expelled me from the interior to an outside table, saying they no longer accepted unaccompanied women. Actually, they accept them perfectly well – but the fact was, he'd taken me for a tart. During the first days the Dôme had reassumed its brothel-like aspect of yore, with all the tarts in the most prominent places. Then they'd been relegated to the rear. And after that they'd stopped coming, because they were looking for German clients. There'd been crowds of Germans at the Dôme those first days, you see, but now there are a certain number of cafés – the Dôme, the Deux Magots, some of the Dupont chain – which have signs forbidding Germans from entering. The managers are very unhappy about this, and nobody knows where the ban originated. Anyway, I sat down outside, had a bite to eat, then went home. Sorokine dropped in from 9 to 10, then I went to bed.

I woke up with a thick head and feeling really low. I set off down Rue Froidevaux, which always wrings my heart because it's one of my last memories of you and your leave, when we walked down that street and I was telling you that what I found with you was the totality of the world. (This next time it'll be different. I really have the impression – in my solitude – of being in contact with the totality of the world. So it's just your individual experience that I'm awaiting so impatiently.) I drank a melancholy coffee at the Trois Mousquetaires, then went on as far as Duruy, where I taught for two hours. After that I read at the Deux Magots, then had lunch with my family. There was a first postcard from Kos., and a long letter from Poupette in Portugal. Those were the first fresh letters anyone had received for ages, and they gave me as much pleasure as a first escape from prison. I walked to the Nationale, and that was when I began to decipher Hegel's *Phenomenology* – with the help of Wahl's book and some English commentators. But it's discouraging, since each of them makes clear at length how he understands nothing. I found it agreeable to be back there – it reminded me of the time long ago when I was preparing for my *agrégation*. Also, it restored my equanimity to rediscover philosophy and books – all those things which are truly real, and so solid, and which we'll never be without. I went back to Rue Vavin, read, then saw Sorokine, whom I forced to practise her maths – which I quite enjoyed – then took home for some pâté and conversation. I told her stories, and we exchanged innumerable marks of affection – it made a pretty agreeable evening.

Goodnight, my sweet little one. At 7 I left the Dôme and went to say hello to Zebuth, who kept me to dinner. Her fellow was there, we talked, it was neither enjoyable nor boring – but I was gripped by an intense sadness. It's raining. What's rain like in a prisoner-of-war camp? It must be gloomy. Today I'm less optimistic about you than the day before yesterday, I think you must be so bored that it makes me want to cry. If only my letters reach you, my love! That would connect you to the world a bit. If I were sure you got my letters, I'd write morning, noon and night. I'm going off to the Red Cross to see whether I might by any chance be able to send you a parcel. If that is possible, I'll put in everything that's allowed – books and food. I'll also ask if I can send money. I recall your first letter from a barracks in Nancy, when you wrote to me that you felt 'absurd and tiny', sitting in a corner on a wooden box. That's how I picture you. And I'm wracked by grief and love for you – I can't bear you to be unhappy. And there are assuredly moments when the days must seem so long to you. O my little one, you'll see how nice I'll be when you're back with me again. I'll try to be really very nice. And what a welcome I'll give you, my love! – as good a one as the flies at Ouarzazate (it was Ouarzazate, wasn't it?). [276] I'm all weighed down with tender memories, and images of you, and a love that's utterly humble and straightforward. If I could only be with you – exactly where you are, sharing your lot – that would be happiness indeed! My heart's no dry bone, my love, since you're alive within it. This evening of all evenings, you're altogether present to me. And since you sometimes feel yourself all perfumed, it's that very perfume of yourself that I feel in me. Goodbye, my love. I kiss you passionately.

Your charming Beaver

[Paris]

Sunday 14 July [1940]

My love

It's fine and cool this morning. It gives me a strange feeling to write this date: 14 July. In other years that meant going off on holiday – a long time to be spent entirely with each other, seeing the world. Sometimes it would mean long, agreeable walks through a festive Paris. But today it's out of season, since there's not even summer weather: the

---

[276]Visited during a trip to Morocco in the summer of 1938 (see *The Prime of Life*, pp.333-4).

weather being so ill-defined, it has no place in the year. I'd thought of going off on a long bicycle trip, but I'm too spineless – all I want to do is let myself gently stagnate. I slept late, came here to eat my breakfast, and am going to write to you, read the rest of your *Imaginaire*, and draft some notes on Hegel. How I long to see you! Above all, I'm so impatient for that happiness which has once again become certain for me – and almost close at hand: your presence beside me, my dear little being.

I'm going to finish telling you about my life in Paris. That way, if you put my letters end to end, you'll have a detailed history of my life over this past fortnight. I'd reached last Sunday. I rose as late as possible – at about 9.30 – since the moment of waking is always among the most painful. Then I accompanied Sorokine down for a cup of coffee on the Avenue d'Orléans. Next, I went and picked up her bicycle. It was only the third day I'd been riding, yet I was perfectly able to go for a real ride – first to the Parc de Montsouris and back, then to the Closerie des Lilas and back. Once I ran into a dog, and another time into two good ladies – who were very indignant about it – but for the most part it was a glorious performance. On Boulevard Raspail I passed some armoured cars laden with Germans, all in black. They were tank crews, I think, with their black uniforms, big berets and death's-head insignia. I sat down at the Dôme and read some selected passages from Hegel. I found one sentence that would do marvellously as an epigraph for my novel:

'In so far as it is the Other who acts, every consciousness pursues the death of the other . . . The relation between the two self-consciousnesses is thus determined as follows: they test themselves and each other by a struggle to the death. They cannot avoid this struggle, *since they are forced to raise this certainty of self to the level of truth.*

'Every self-consciousness must pursue the death of the other . . . The essence of the other appears to it as an other, as external, and it has to transcend that externality.'

I suddenly experienced a brief moment of intellectual ardour. I felt like doing some philosophy, talking to you, taking up my novel again. But I'm too undecided to get back to the novel – I shan't be able to touch it before seeing you again. I had lunch, wrote to Kos., made up my diary, read, and at 5 went for a really long bicycle ride. I called in at Rue de Charenton and saw that the people who had my suitcase were back[277] – but they weren't in just then, so I returned home empty-

---

[277]As recounted in the letter of 11 July (morning) above, De Beauvoir had set out from La Pouèze by car; when the car ran out of petrol and she struck out on her own, her suitcase had remained with the car's owners.

handed. I did two hours' cycling, but since this was on very badly paved roads, where I was jolted dreadfully. I returned home very tired. Moreover, I'm in a constant state of nervousness – which is necessarily reduced when I'm alone, but which Sorokine's presence readily exacerbates to the highest degree. This brought about a violent and farcical scene. When I turned up, I found Sorokine busy making fried potatoes – and also a packet of letters forwarded on from La Pouèze by That Lady: they were six fairly recent letters from Bost (up to 18 June). At first I felt violently disappointed at not finding anything from you, but then Bost's letters themselves brought tears to my eyes and wrung my heart, and I'd have liked to be alone to brood over my sorrows. Instead of that, I knew Sorokine was expecting to have a good time, with a person of amiable disposition, full of interesting ideas and entertaining stories. I found having this role to play for 4 hours hateful. She sensed that. She resented my having received so many letters, and wore a sulky expression as we ate our fried potatoes. As for me, I resented her asking me nothing about those letters – never being interested, for a single second, in my life for myself. An hour went by in dreary politeness. Then we moved from the kitchen to a bedroom, where I began – at her bidding – to explain Valéry's *Eupalinos*. She at once started grumbling about how she didn't understand, so for an hour I explained to her – in a harsh, spiteful tone of voice – while she listened in fury. There were another two hours to get through and they seemed endless to me. To create a diversion I wanted to reread a letter I'd written her from La Pouèze, which was lying around there. She tried to stop me – out of pure spirit of contrariness – and I was shaken by a black rage which led me to tear the letter to shreds. This was followed first by sulking, then by a vague reconciliation. After that, I obligingly set about finding subjects of conversation, but she let them all drop, seizing my hands and rubbing her head on my shoulder – which I found detestable. I was increasingly choking with anger. Eventually she declared that she didn't want to talk as long as I just sat in my armchair like that. Then I exploded – reviling her stupidly. She left the room, while I took a detective story and read – which calmed my spirit. At about quarter to eleven I went to look for her, in order to send her home. At first I didn't find her, calling and searching for her in vain. But eventually I discovered her at the back of the kitchen, crouching beside the meat-safe with a look of fury. I told her to leave, but she said she wouldn't – and when I tried to shake her, she pummelled me with her fists. I nevertheless dragged her as far as the front door, dinning it into her ears that if she didn't leave I wouldn't see her for a week. That intimidated her, so she went out through the door, yelling that she'd remain on the stairs. I slammed the door in her face. I went to bed and, of course, a quarter of an hour later the doorbell rang. I went to open the door, trembling with rage – I wanted to be alone, have some peace, and sleep. I frankly hated her. She wanted to 'talk', but I refused angrily and threw her a mattress, a pillow and some blankets – so that she could make herself comfortable on the floor – then with dignity returned to my detective story. She quietened down then, and dragged her bedding off to the corridor. I read for a while, then fell asleep – and awoke with restored equanimity and even affection, when I recalled how the evening before she'd had great black streaks on her face, from attempting to sleep on the doormat. Moreover – although I find her tyrannical, indiscreet and unbearable in the same way that a stubborn child can be – in the scene in question, a good share of the fault had been on my side. Accordingly, I greeted her in the morning with smiles, to which she responded likewise with smiles; we took breakfast together; and after school I met her for lunch at the Milk Bar, to begin one of those grand explanations in depth which are the joy of her life. They're just like the confessions of depressives, who go round in circles while every time believing they're yielding up the innermost depths of their souls – but, after all, it does help to pass the time. She was quite overwhelmed when she grasped what all the trouble had been about – and admitted she'd never regarded me as anything other than an object to exploit. She accompanied me to the Nationale, where I read Hegel. Then, from 5 to 7, I went for a long bicycle ride – over towards the Rue des Francs-Bourgeois – and began to find traipsing round Paris on a bicycle absolutely delightful. After that, I went to finish off my detective story over a glass of sherry at the Deux Magots. I dined at home, then saw Sorokine again for a while – we had a drink together on the Avenue d'Orléans.

11 o'clock. I've just called in at the hotel to see if there were any letters for me – but there weren't. The good lady told me they'd taken the poor hermaphrodite away in handcuffs some two months earlier: she's in a camp at St Germain-les-Belles, and the good lady read me a pitiful letter in which she complains of her troubles and asks for a bit of money.

[...]

After that it was Thursday. I went to school – in a state of dreary dejection, as usual. I called in at the hotel, and that's when I had your note, my love. I was quite overcome by it. It was strange, because it represented so many things, yet at the same time it was nothing. I turned it vainly between my fingers: nothing changed around me, and I didn't see you appear at the end of the street. I began writing you a first letter, but then Sorokine came to have lunch with me at the Dôme. She demanded that I show her a letter from Bienenfeld, but as they were all too passionate I refused. Then she had the sulks for quite a while, while I picked up a book. She pinched me till the blood came, and I responded with a little slap – which so outraged her that she swept out and I didn't see her for the rest of the day. That suited me very well, since I wanted to remain alone with you. I wrote to you, went to the Rue du Louvre[278] – where I ascertained that I had the right to write to you – then wrote a second letter at the Café Delcour. After that, I went for a long walk through Paris – Rue du Faubourg St Denis, Boulevard Sébastopol, the boulevards, the Champs-Élysées – it was all teeming with people and overflowing with provisions. I was happy and felt that life was going to be reborn. That evening I had dinner with my parents, and listened to a good concert – Schumann, Beethoven, Rimsky-Korsakov's *Golden Cockerel*, *Firebird* – then returned home at 10.30, sure that I'd find Sorokine there and determined to get shot of any explanation in a quarter of an hour. But like a madwoman, after waiting a long time for me she'd decided to wash her hair – and met me with her hair all soapy and her soul in fury.

She didn't want to go home, of course. I wasn't angry, but I was determined not to let her tyrannize me, so – amid complaints, blows, clinches and threats – I eventually threw her out. But at 11 she began ringing the bell again – she'd been waiting on the stairs. I let her languish there for half an hour – I was reading – then opened the door, threw the mattress and blankets into the corridor for her, and in a few choice words gave her a piece of my mind. Then I closed the door again and went to sleep – though very poorly. Apparently, all night long she never stopped pacing up and down the flat in a towering rage. At 7 in the morning she knocked at my door, in order to wake me up and have a reconciliation. Since I was firmly asleep, this outraged me – and I spoke to her in such terms that she was terrified and made herself scarce. After that, I went back to sleep – and I've already told you about my day of reading, letters to yourself, walking, and Hegel. I didn't see her till evening, subdued and melancholy. But yesterday we made up altogether, at lunch and in the evening, and now all will be idyllic until the next crisis. I think I've intimidated her so much that she won't start that kind of violent scene again. It's entertaining from afar but pretty odious close up, especially when it becomes regular and mechanical. Apart from that, she can be charming.

---

[278]Central Post Office.

There you are, my little one! I'm now writing to you from the Deux Magots, having come down here in the course of this letter just in order to move around a bit. I find it very hard to stay put. Now that I'm expecting you, the days drag terribly. I phoned Toulouse – she has been in Paris since Tuesday – and am going to see her shortly, which will provide a resource. I'm enormously glad to be seeing her – I have such a need to talk! She returned with what she could carry on her back, and is rather worried she may have lost all her papers and precious notes, which she sent off as registered luggage. I'll tell you everything properly tomorrow.

But have you had these letters? How hard it is, not knowing anything more about you! I can't stop fretting, my love. Every time I get bored, it's like experiencing the same boredom you must feel yourself – and that wrings my heart. Everything about you comes back to me – your gestures, your expressions, your voice, your words – o delectable little being, who from your head to your feet are made to gladden the heart. Moreover, I'm no longer as rational as before – I count the hours and can't stay still in one place. I've never known anything like this time, which is now pure waiting – and so very long! Honestly, I'm waiting, and measuring the moments, as though you were going to arrive this very evening. I'm waiting as one does when there are only a few hours left to while away, yet I know I'll have to start again tomorrow – and again after that – and again for day after day. My love, I live absolutely for you alone now. I kiss you, my sweet little one. I'd like to hug your little person tight, so tight, and keep it for ever.

Your charming Beaver

[Paris]

Tuesday 16 July [1940]

My love

I've just received from La Pouèze a mysterious little note dated 28 June, in which you inform me you're well. And I've also been forwarded a long letter dated 9 June, which is old but as you can imagine very apposite, since in it you envisage precisely the present situation – and with optimism, I must say. That's exactly what I think about you: that you and I shall always be able to find a joy in looking, understanding and, if need be, living anew. My love, I felt that – through that old letter – you were speaking to me in the present. You know you won't find me moaning but, on the contrary, full of experience and reason, and full of enthusiasm to make a new start with you. Only I'm waiting for you to clarify what I think – everything's still confused. How I wish we could talk! I'm full of rather aggressive optimism this evening, because I've seen B. again and she has the gift of reinvigorating me by the very excess of her despair – though it's true her situation isn't the same as mine.

I've had some fresh news of Bost – dating from 8 July. It seems certain that your notebooks are safe – which is well done, after all.[279] He's cured and off to Marseilles for 10 days, after which he'll doubtless be sent to some depot.

Oh! I don't know why, but this evening I feel I'm really going to see you again, my little one. I'll be happy again, since happiness is you. How we'll talk! How I'll gaze at you! How I'll listen to you and kiss you, my love!

Yesterday evening, by contrast, I was really dismal. After writing to you, I drafted some notes on Hegel, then went to listen to some Debussy at my parents' place: some piano music, and a curious sonata for flute, harp and viola – which is beautiful and pleasing. They kept me for a meal, then I went to the Dôme to finish my notes on Hegel (or continue them, at least), and Sorokine came along at about 10. We talked and then I took her home with me, where we talked tenderly till midnight.

This morning I went to school by bicycle, like a real lusty wench. Two hours of lessons. Then – by bicycle again – I went over to Rue François-Ier, to the Red Cross, to ask whether I could send you parcels. They told me no, but that on the other hand there was every chance you'd receive my letters. I went to the Nationale, ate in a little milk bar, and between 12.30 and 5 finished a book on Debussy and almost finished Hegel's *Phenomenology* – tomorrow it'll be over and done with. After that I returned by bicycle to the Dôme where I found Sorokine, who told me B. was there, hunting for me all over the neighbourhood. S. had sent her to my grandmother's in order to get rid of her, but for my part I wanted to see B. – for the sake of something new. So I spent some time trying to find her, eventually meeting up with her at the Dôme. We talked for two hours, but it wasn't very interesting. I was disappointed – just as I've explained to you I used to be every time I found myself with anyone other than you. Then, at 7.30, I went to my parents' flat to listen to Ravel's *Quartet*. I found 12 letters, including the two from

---

[279]For the uncertainty concerning the number and fate of those of Sartre's war diaries that had been lent to Bost, only to go astray after he was wounded and while he was being evacuated by train to Beaune, see Sartre, *War Diaries*, London 1984, p. xv. However, if what De Beauvoir reports here is true, then it must be concluded that the disappearance of any notebooks in Bost's possession can only have occurred at some later date.

you I've mentioned, four from Bost, the same number from Kos., one from Sorokine, one from Poupette, and some cables from Bienenfeld. I began reading all this, listened to the wireless, then went down to write to you for a while in a café. Now I'm going back up to have dinner with my parents, while listening to a Mozart festival. I'll go on with the letter this evening.

I love you passionately, and feel so close to you – altogether with you. We're as one, my love, truly as one.

My sweet little one

It's 10 p.m. now, and I'm at the Dôme. Blin's sitting outside with his good lady. I listened for an hour to some very fine Mozart pieces, then walked over here sunk in thought about you. I'm happy this evening. For the first time, I can look ahead with a kind of assurance – and think of your little person with all the tenderness in the world, without at once turning to mush inside. My love, it's your voice reaching me across time which has worked this miracle. Out there you're a tiny prisoner, all lost among thousands of others, but in my heart you're gentle light, and truth, and joy. O my little one who, in former times, used to wish to have a necessary face, it's a pity authenticity has caused you to lose that desire. For you'd be quite moved to see your lovely little face wearing a halo, so romantic and pure – and *true*, my love, that's the real miracle. My little one, I wish I could somehow be present to you in the same way that you're present to me, and wish you could feel a true, solid Beaver beside you – at this war's end, where you'd arranged to meet – eager to be with you again and follow you wherever you please. I love you, my beloved. This evening I'm thinking emotionally about you as a *new adventure*, as well as a past. It's myself I'll be rediscovering when I rediscover you – yet it's an unknown, unexpected person, which gives me a strange, dizzying elation. Yes, o little yourself – doubtless all dirty and bored and perhaps quite dismal – for me you're everything that's brilliant and alluring and infinitely precious.

Till tomorrow, my little one, my love, my dear past and my beautiful, eagerly awaited future. I hug you to me with such passion and joy!

Your charming Beaver

[Paris]

Friday [19 July 1940]

Most dear little being

I haven't written for two days now. This was partly because I was caught first by Bienenfeld, then by Kos., and they don't leave me alone for a moment. It was also because I don't quite have the stomach – I still haven't any fresh sign of life from you, and am really afraid these letters aren't getting through. What's more, the essential thing I'd have to tell you is too difficult to write. I so wish we could talk. I thought for a long while the other day about Bienenfeld, whose determinedly desperate reactions irritate me, in connection with the individual's relation to the historical world: how it's an absurdity to speak of one epoch being more comfortable and agreeable to live in than another, from the standpoint of the mind. Everything obviously depends upon what you expect of the mind – what you want and hope from it. But, after all, expression as expression isn't an end in itself. For me, at least, when I express something it's largely a matter of particularizing the universal; of putting my singular mark on a thought seeking to rejoin the universal. But what if the universal is realized in a moment precluding individual expression? Is there not a contradiction in suffering from this? Can you ask the universal to be such as to allow individual comfort and happiness if, precisely, this happiness is merely a way of entering into contact with the totality? I don't know if I'm expressing myself well, but this strikes me as brilliant. I was also struck, when thinking about it, by how correct that Hegelian idea was of enveloping the totality in our individual becoming. For when you're concerned to create a work, you certainly do look upon it as itself a moment of the total becoming – in which the whole past culminates, and which is effectively linked to the whole future. I recall a conversation at the Louis XIV – designed to find out whether we did or did not think within the limits of a human life – in which we were wondering what meaning the viewpoint of universal life had: a viewpoint that excluded the limitation of death and the being-to-die character of life. It seemed to us then that such a viewpoint reduced everything to a kind of absurd indifference. But I no longer believe that. Basically, such a viewpoint is *real*. And the combined influences of Hegel and events have caused me to adopt from within – for the first time in my life – this attitude, not too far away from Spinozism, that always used to be so alien to me. It's far more accessible and obvious through Hegel, of course, than through Spinoza. Thus I'm living not exactly cocooned in philosophical optimism – for my ideas aren't clear enough – but at least on a philosophical plane such that optimism is possible.

I so wish we could make a comparison between your ideas on nothingness, the in-itself, and the for-itself, and the ideas of Hegel. For there are many analogies – although Hegel turns into joy that which for you is instead gloomy and despairing. It seems to me that both are true, and I'd like to find a point of equilibrium.

There you are, my sweet little one: so that I don't forget it, a basis of present reflections for me, and for us a point of departure for future conversations. When? I'm in such a hurry. I'm torn apart and in suspense.

As for my life, here it is: I wrote to you on Tuesday evening, I think, and posted the letter on Wednesday morning. It was raining. I went to work on Hegel at the Nationale till 5 – having spent the morning at the Dôme drafting my notes on him. At 5 I went to meet Bienenfeld at the Trocadero. We walked to St Germain-des-Prés, had dinner in a little restaurant called Le Casque in Rue Bonaparte, then had a drink outside at the Deux Magots. As usual, she was torn between specific individual anxieties and great, vague appearances – and I shook her a bit. I'm as indifferent to her as ever. To be precise, I no longer find the least thing interesting about her in any respect. After that I went and met Sorokine at the Dôme, brought her home with me, and we finished the evening affectionately. I tried to explain to her that she ought to resign herself from now on to seeing less of me – but that will be hard. Yesterday evening I went to school by bicycle. I came back in driving rain and called in at the hotel: no word from you yet – but, on the other hand, a note from Kos. who'd slept there. They called her and she came down, pleasing in a fine new raincoat with a red scarf on her head.

[...]

My dear little one, Kos. is ready. I'm going to keep her only for a few days. I'll call in at the hotel shortly, to see if there's anything from you. I didn't mention, of course, that there was any hope of your returning imminently – there'll be plenty of time to talk about it once you're there. O my love, I can't wait to see you! I live in chaos, so long as you aren't here with me to order it. I want only an order that's common to us – and my very thoughts are adorned with question-marks. If only you could write to me, my love! Have you got my letters?

Goodbye, little beloved, most dear little being – o yourself, my life, my other self.

Your charming Beaver

[Paris]

Wednesday [24 July 1940]

My love

I'm rather discouraged. Here's the end of the month drawing near, but there's no sign of you. I wonder if my letters reach you, and am so sure they don't that writing fills me with repugnance. How I'd love to see you! I dream of you every night, but always in a nightmare atmosphere. And waking up is so painful: I wonder vaguely in my sleep why there's such an impression of sadness linked to your person, then find that it's because you're quite out of reach, my love. I love you. Lots and lots of heartrending memories come back to me, and I'm amazed at all the virtues adorning you in my remembrance. Yet I know when I see you I'll be even more amazed, to find you more delectable than all my memories. My sweet little one, I can't help weeping this morning as I write to you. I so want to see you smile at me and to touch your little arm – to be folded in your arms, my love! Dear little being, dear face, how nice you were with me! – you were the nicest – how precious you were! Oh! I miss you, I pine for you, the world's empty – how hollow people are, how flat the days! I feel deeply lonely – I can't exchange a single word of what I really think with anyone but myself. I do nothing from dawn to dusk but wait for you and count the days.

These past few days form a great, shapeless mass behind me – I'm not quite sure when I last wrote to you. Kos. was in Paris, she's still here and we trail around together all day long. I think she's leaving tomorrow. She's dismal, tired and spineless, and also obstinate and stupid so far as current events are concerned – it's just like hearing her father speak – yet she's keen to talk about them. I find her so superficial, I no longer have any wish to open my mouth in her presence. She has rarely been lower in my esteem, and I'm bored in her company. It's raining, which adds nothing to the charm of her stay. We trail round to the Dôme or the Deux Magots. On Sunday we went to a concert in the Salle Gaveau. It was odd to see that crowd – two thirds French, one third Germans – filling the hall, for a programme made up of the most timeworn old standbys: *5th Symphony, Afternoon of a Faun, Damnation of Faust.* You get the impression people are greedy for any kind of distraction. On the other hand, we went twice to the cinema – to see *Tempête sur l'Asie*[280] in the Latin Quarter and a fairly entertaining German film, *The Tiger Woman,* on the Champs-Élysées – and the auditorium was empty both times. As another distraction, we spent one afternoon in Place du Tertre watching the Germans troop past to take

_____

[280]Directed by Richard Oswald (1939).

photographs of the Sacré-Coeur. And on Monday we went to dinner with Toulouse. She was all in white, with a long dress, a burnous and long tresses – she looked like a Valkyrie. She was enthusiastically making plans for the future, since she thinks the moment of her glory – and the flowering of her genius – has finally come. They're hoping to play her version of *Plutus* in the Arènes de Lutèce in September, and she's adapting Aristophanes's *Knights* too, which is a satire against demagogy. She's also hoping to act in her own play this winter. She seems to hold Dullin wholly in the palm of her hand. She was eager to get me (and you by proxy) to share her point of view. For my part, I was bored to death and thought of you with a heavy heart.

Meanwhile, I've seen a bit of Bienenfeld, though not much – which she complains of, albeit very mildly. She's nice at present, and has a human intelligence compared with Kos. I've also seen Sorokine – there were two very pleasant evenings on Friday and Saturday, since in order to let Kos. have a good sleep I went and met S. at the hotel, which made her very touched and happy. But then she was gripped by fury because I was seeing Kos., so on Monday we quarrelled for an hour – and this morning, when I opened the door to go and see her, I found her crouched sobbing on the landing. She'd spent the night there wallowing in jealousy and rage. I first berated then consoled her, and we parted on so-so terms.

There! Tomorrow I'm going to get back to Hegel and the bicycle. I'm glad Kos. is leaving, because I'm a bit sick of her. I'm going to take up my diary again for a while, so as to bring you properly up to date on my life and little private troubles when you get back, o little eagerly awaited one. My little one, we love one another so much – how marvellous it will be for both of us to recover each its other self, to recast our lives together, to recreate a common past out of all these times, my dear little one!

Apparently it's going to be possible to send parcels – I'll put in all the books I can and some food.

I've got your dough – and will keep it for you carefully. I found them strangely curt at your bursary, which intrigued me. I find people pretty sickening: Kos., Toulouse, Dullin. I caught sight of the Lunar Woman, back from exile and unbearable. Kos. and I were determinedly rude to her.

Goodbye. My love. If only I believed these letters arrived! I'm still basically in good heart, but yearn most agonizingly to see you – nothing counts but that. You're so present to me, almost physically, little being, most dear little being. I'm all melting with affection for you. My love.

Your charming Beaver

[Paris]

Monday 29 July [1940]

My love

Exactly like the day before yesterday, I'm writing to you from that table overlooking the front part of the Dôme. It's 10 in the morning, the weather's fine and there are crowds of people at the crossroads. We've just seen a long procession of Germans pass down Boulevard Raspail on bicycles. Inside the Dôme they're washing the floor, so there's a strong smell of soapsuds. I have Faulkner's latest novel with me,[281] and will read it once I've written to you. Then I'll go off to work on Hegel, see your mother, and read a bit more – after which I'll go and have dinner at my parents' place, while listening to a Wagner festival on the wireless. I'm telling you all this because my whole programme for the day is present, here in this morning hour. Loads of German lorries are going past, and loads of cars still full of returning refugees.

Anyway, it was Saturday when I wrote to you, after which I went to the Nationale – where I made considerable progress with Hegel's *Logic*. I've done one part out of three – and am no longer finding it too tedious. Then, at 5, I went out with Sorokine. Since we hadn't had any lunch, we bought rillettes, onion tarts and raspberry tarts and went to eat them all in a little café, talking the while about my novel – which she's busy reading in minute detail. She kept me company to the Métro station at Passy. She radiated contentment – because she's delighted with me in general – and was charming. I went to the *tabac* on the Quai de Passy – to write a little letter to Bost – then climbed up to the room that Bienenfeld has fixed up for herself on the 6th floor of her building: it's quite pleasing, with a wide view over the roofs. Lévy and Ramblin were there. I ate a fruit salad – made out of blackcurrants and gooseberries, sprinkled with wine – then we listened to some records. (For the past 5 minutes there has been a long, silent parade of German infantry down Bd Montparnasse – with lorries and field-kitchens, a veritable army – and pedestrians and cars are at a standstill.)

So we listened to a lot of Bach and a bit of jazz. During the jazz, Ramblin and Bienenfeld jigged about on their chairs to mark the rhythm – it was mildly ridiculous. Then the two men went off, while I stayed for the night. There was an hour of tenderness and passion, alas! – after which I went to sleep on the couch, in a sleeping-bag smelling of rubber, while Bienenfeld went downstairs to the flat. We'd decided on a long bicycle-ride next day – I on her beautiful, brand-new red bicycle, she

---

[281]Probably *The Wild Palms* (1939).

on a bicycle belonging to her sister. We left at 8, and you should know that we actually did 75 km. in the course of that day! Bienenfeld was tired, but I wasn't in the least. We went first to Maisons-Laffitte: it's agreeable because, as the bridge has been blown up, you have to cross the Seine in a small boat. Next we went for a ride through the forest of St Germain, before returning to St Germain itself where we had lunch. In the afternoon we climbed into the Bois de Ville-d'Avray, crossed the Bois de Fausses-Reposes — where we used to go in the old days by car, with Guille and That Lady — then returned home via St-Cloud. Bienenfeld grumbled a bit — because she had dreams of sitting holding hands in glades, whereas I wanted only to eat up the kilometers on my bicycle. It's a new joy in life that I've discovered and, instead of wishing for a car, my desires will henceforth be limited to a bicycle of my own.

We arrived at the Salle Pleyel just in time for the concert. I was supposed to meet Sorokine there — and did indeed meet her, but she was wearing a sullen look because I'd been out riding all day with my red-haired friend. We exchanged a few cool words, then listened to the concert. A certain Cécile Borgman had organized it, and I think that must have been the only way she could find an audience for her own voice — the whole hall was laughing at her. There was some Schumann and some Lully — an agreeable programme, but none too well executed. After that, there was an unfortunate mishap. I was supposed to take Bienenfeld's bicycle back to her on foot, accompanied by Sorokine; but when I went to unlock the bicycle, I realized that Bienenfeld had given me the wrong key — so we had to carry the disabled bicycle, which was an arduous business. Sorokine complained bitterly. We toted the wretched object as far as the Étoile. People were looking at us askance, since we must have looked like two looters — a crazy amount of bicycles are being stolen these days. So we then ensconced ourselves in a café on Avenue Wagram, and I phoned Bienenfeld to bring me the right key. The café was full of Germans, and four good ladies in long silver dresses were playing the [. . .] Symphony — just the sort of good ladies whom you find so amusing: bespectacled like piano teachers, but all powdered and curled and in shiny dresses. At 8.30 B. finally turned up and liberated us from the bicycle. After that, I walked with Sorokine to Montparnasse and we had dinner at the Dôme. The sculptor[282] is hovering round her a lot, but he has disappointed her enormously by the absurdity of his ideas and his unjustified intellectual pretensions. She decided to drink a Pernod, which made her half-tipsy — and she was full

---

[282]Alberto Giacometti, whose acquaintance De Beauvoir and Sartre were to make — precisely through Sorokine — only in the spring of 1941 (see *The Prime of Life*, pp.486-9).

of delight at being tipsy and agreeable. In the meantime, we made peace spectacularly. We went home to my place, spent a tender while, then I slept till 8 and she accompanied me to school. It's the *bac* exam today, and I wanted to know if I'd have anything to do – but they left me in peace. In theory lessons don't end till 8 August, but I don't think I have a single pupil left.

That's all, my little one. I've rather given up expecting you hourly. I fear I may still have a lot of days to spend without you. If I only knew you weren't too bored! Once again, I feel that when I see you I'll faint with joy. I know I shan't really – but the idea of seeing you so overwhelms me that it's genuinely almost unbearable. My sweet little one, I'm living with my heart outstretched towards that corner of Meurthe-et-Moselle where it's forbidden to go, but whence you'll one day emerge. I love you, my beloved.

Your charming Beaver

A further two-and-a-half-month break in the correspondence occurs at this point. Although Sartre was receiving her letters, De Beauvoir heard nothing from him after the pencilled note which arrived on 11 July (aside from a couple of delayed items written earlier). In mid August, Sartre was moved from captivity in Lorraine to a prisoner-of-war camp near Trier in Germany. Only in mid October did correspondence become possible again – at least on De Beauvoir's side – on official forms. (See The Prime of Life, *p.462.)*

[Paris]

17 October [1940]

My love

How hard it has been to spend these last two months without a sign of life from you – without even an address. Now, once again, I know you're alive somewhere in flesh and blood; and I'll see you again; and, even if we have to wait some more, we'll still have a long life ahead of us, to love one another and be happy – my dear little one. I feel full of courage. I know you are too, and that sustains me. Apparently, one mustn't write too much.[283] So I won't tell you all about the last two months. Apart from a gloomy fortnight when Olga was ill and I was alone with her in Paris, they were entirely agreeable: I spent 10 days at Montpellier with Bost,[284] bicycled round Brittany for a week with Bianca Bienenfeld, bicycled round Paris alone or with Sorokine. I read American novels, etc. Now Bost's in Paris, I see a lot of him and very agreeably. I have a preparatory class for the École – just 9 hours' teaching. I've got down to my novel again and it's going marvellously. Things couldn't be better for me. I love you more passionately – and more exclusively – than ever.

Your charming Beaver

Envelope
KRIEGSGEFANGENPOST
Prisoners of War
Sartre Jean-Paul
Sanität Stalag XII-D
Mle 10788
Kranken-Revier
Deutschland
Sender: De Beauvoir Simone
        21 Rue Vavin Paris

[Paris – official form]

18 October [1940]

My sweet little one

I told you in my last letter that all was well with me: school, work, relations with Bost, Sorokine, Olga. I've more or less broken with Bianca. There were tears (I told her all about Bost), but she's having an idyll with Ramblin, so that's working out. Olga has a part with Dullin: the little bathing-girl in *Plutus*. Yesterday was the premiere, all's going well and she's earning some dough. I've seen everybody again. Zuorro – who spent the whole war in Algeria and is blooming – I see him often and find him entertaining. Guille just missed being taken prisoner – he's in Paris and expecting a kid. Nizan has disappeared, the Lunar Man is

---

[283]De Beauvoir had received some news (reassuring) of Sartre from a recently repatriated fellow-prisoner: see *The Prime of Life*, pp.466-8.
[284]He was completing his convalescence there: see *The Prime of Life*, p.466 (where De Beauvoir, of course, makes no mention of her visit).

a P.O.W., Pierre Bost too. Merleau-Ponty got off with pneumonia – he has recovered now. Gégé has started work again. Denonain is a P.O.W. That Lady's still at La Pouèze. I've seen Brice Parain – very amiable: the *N.R.F.* is publishing a few books, but gradually. People, concerts, lots of work – it's a decent life, as you can see. We've made hundreds of applications on your behalf. I've some slight hope. I've seen the Boxer, quite charming, and also Seltzer: their enthusiasm for you is very touching. I'll write again in a few days. My whole life is nothing but waiting for your return.

Your charming Beaver

[Paris – Official Form]

19 October [1940]

My love

It's such a fine autumn in Paris at present that my heart's in utter turmoil. I'm at the back of the Deux Magots and working – it's 2 o'clock. This morning I rose early, it was still a bit dark when I met Bost at the counter in the Rotonde where we ate breakfast together, then I walked to his school with him. He's a teaching supervisor (in philosophy, to his despair) at a school in Rue Denfert, at 1,500 F. a month – it's a pretty cushy job. He met up with me again at the Mahieu, we went for a walk, then I worked at the Mahieu from 10 to midday. I had lunch with my parents. I'm planning to work till 5, then go to a concert with Sorokine. After that, I'll spend the evening round the Théatre de Paris (Théatre Dullin currently) with Olga.

There you have a typical day – I spend lots just like it. I'm working extremely well. But, my dear little one, my whole life is as though 'bracketed off' – it's not valid, it doesn't count. How curt these little letters are, when I'm suffocating with things to tell you – suffocating with love and need for you.

I forgot to tell you that W.'s in Paris – she must have written to you. Maheu's in Toulouse, where Merleau-Ponty bumped into him. How quickly I'd leave Paris and everybody and even my work, in order to rush to your side and share your life, if the choice were left to me, my love.

(Address as letter 17 October 1940 above)

[Paris – Official Form]

Monday 29 October [1940]

My sweet little one

How my life has changed since I had your letter![285] Moreover, I'm beginning to have some hope of actually seeing you again soon – lots of reassuring rumours are going round. I'm living with you once more, you're all alive. I feel almost happy. I've still the same little pattern of life. On Thursday I made Mouloudji practise his geometry a bit. He told me some entertaining stories about Savin and Delarue, who have taken him in hand entirely and don't much like us. I had lunch with the Ziuthre,[286] and found him as entertaining as ever. Then I worked and in the evening went to a fine concert with Bianca. Evenings with her are painful, because she keeps sobbing at the idea of going away – she's leaving in a month's time. On Friday it was again work, school, concert, then 2 hours with Sorokine and the same amount with Olga. It's all idyllic with Sorokine, though interrupted by jealousies and bad moods – but we no longer come to blows. Olga's as dismal as ever – the play isn't going very well. Everybody strikes me as rather wretched. There's only you, prisoner though you may be, who seem solid and give me a taste for life. It's precious, my dear little one, to feel that for you and me, in the worst circumstances, the world remains interesting and strong and our lives full. I'm serene. I know that I'll be marvellously happy again. I love you, my dear happiness, and my lovely little absolute.

Your charming Beaver

[Paris]

Tuesday 29 October [1940]

My dear little one

I've written you lots of little letters, in a very careful handwriting so that the censors don't take umbrage. But what I'd give to know you received them! They're so curt anyway, those little notes, when I've so many things to tell you, so many others to discuss with you. But I'm starting to hope it won't be long. Perhaps a month from now you'll be

---

[285]De Beauvoir had been panic-stricken when she misinterpreted Sartre's address 'Kranken-Revier' (infirmary) as meaning that he was sick and perhaps dying of typhus (see *The Prime of Life*, p.470), whereas he had taken up residence in the infirmary simply because it offered more comfortable accommodation.

[286]Another nickname for Marc Zuore.

sitting beside me, on one of these benches, just the same as ever, jaunty and full of experience. I still recall sitting outside the Café Victor in Rouen, when you so longed for some extra-sentimental experience – like crossing the Sahara in a half-track. Well, now you've really had one. And may the Heavens presently grant you the life of Tennyson[287] at my side for a long while – that's my dearest wish. As I've already told you, I find the idea of your return infinitely romantic. Apart from your mother, we won't tell anyone for as long as possible, will we? I have such need of you, my little one. It's going to be so amazing to find myself happy like in the old days. And I'm so eager to know everything that has gone on in that dear, industrious head of yours. You'll be the same, but where will you be in your thoughts? For the first time I'll be finding myself confronted by fine, brand-new theories that won't have been tried out on me, and that I shan't have fought against step by step. Seven months that I haven't seen you, my little one![288] Yet, in a sense, it's as though I'd left you only yesterday. I feel I'm going to recover myself in recovering you. There are so many things in me that are of no use, finding no purchase, when you're not there. But now once again – as in Rue Froidevaux on one fine day of your leave – the world will become all wide and rich. Come quickly, I'm waiting so eagerly for you!

It's winter now in Paris. It's quite dark when you get up in the mornings, and very cold till the day takes the edge off it – a cold that fills me with poetic feelings because it recalls Brumath and our little lunches at the Rose. For my part, I'm leading a model life of Tennyson. I've finished the last chapter of the novel, and am working back over it. There are just 3 linking chapters left, then it'll all be finished – and perhaps I'll have your advice when it comes to working over the whole thing. I'm teaching Kant to my pupils, and am accordingly studying him in some depth, thanks to an excellent book full of texts taken from his posthumous work. It's very interesting, I'll instruct you in that as well as Hegel. 9 hours of teaching is nothing at all. I sleep my fill, see my friends more than my fill, go to heaps of concerts, and have leisure coming out of my ears! On Sunday I met Wanda instead of her sister at the concert, and she was quite angelically amiable to me, even taking my arm on the way out. She looked dreadful when she arrived in Paris, but has become pretty again. She doesn't do a thing, but has lots of

---

[287]See Sartre, *War Diaries*, p.87: 'I particularly detested Tennyson, because that English writer – of whom I hadn't read a single line – had, according to reliable reports, lived in conformity with my sermons: he had written, and nothing had ever happened to him. I used to say furiously to the Beaver: "I certainly don't want to have a life like Tennyson's".'
[288]Since Sartre's second period of leave, that is to say.

plans, seeing that Delarue has taken her in hand with the idea of making her do history of art and decoration – she seems more or less blooming. I've already told you that Bianca's weeping all over the shop, because she's getting married and leaving Paris. She's willing, but upset – which I can understand, especially as she was starting to be seriously keen on Ramblin, who gave her every satisfaction to be wished for. Olga and Bost are together all right, but in a mild, dismal sort of way, since both are in a morose state of mind and reproaching one another. They all follow their little daily routines and all find each other somewhat damaged and wretched – which they all are, moreover. I feel incredibly alive compared with them. Apparently, That Lady's arriving this evening and Zuorro's putting her up in his studio. I'm glad to be seeing her again and delighted to be able to give her news of you. You know, it's agreeable the number of people for whom you're by no means a little dead man, to be contemplated with an old ossified heart. You'll see what a fuss will be made of you, my little one.

Have I told you that the last time I saw Toulouse and Dullin we had a real shouting match, for the same reasons as ever – though at the same time they're quite besotted with friendly feelings for you! *Plutus* is on its last legs – and deserves to be. Try to let me know which were the last letters you had from me at Baccarat – and my lovely parcel, did you receive that? Do you feel me as close as I feel you, o you my other self?

Your charming Beaver

[Paris – Official Form]

9 November [1940]

My love

I haven't written for a while, because I'm really afraid you're not receiving my letters – which is discouraging. But I've had news of you. Your mother showed me the note she has received from you and it quite overwhelmed me, my little one – I remained dazed by emotion for two days. I'm picking myself up, but how I do miss you! The main thing I've done during all these past days is to work a lot. I've seen Bost in the evenings, a bit of Kos., a bit of That Lady and a bit of Sorokine, whose idyll with a dark-haired Nietzschean student is advancing apace – though she loves me none the less for it. I took her yesterday evening to the Atelier, to see *Le Bal des Voleurs*,[289] which we both found

---

[289]By Jean Anouilh.

disappointing. I haven't seen anything of Bianca, who wrote me a long, pathetic letter. I'm feeling the effects of a possible reconciliation – but don't really think, all the same, that there'll be one. My work's taking giant steps forward. I've also started reading again – about music and about the Middle Ages. There's a real autumn cold snap in Paris just now, but for the moment the cafés and hotels are still very well heated. My life seems so devoid of importance that if I don't make it my duty to tell you all about everything, nothing seems interesting to me any longer. Dullin's company have suggested to Wanda that she do some theatrical scenery – as a job – but she's so lazy she's going to let the chance slip. Kos. is finishing on Sunday and in despair. Everybody's pretty dismal. In general, I feel cheerful by comparison – but I'm fretting a bit: your absence is very hard, my little one. I know we're together in the world for ever, but all that specific happiness your smiles used to give me – oh! it's no use looking at photos of you or rereading your books and your letters, when I try to revive it I feel like a table-turner calling up a spirit. How I love you! How I miss you!

Your charming Beaver

[Paris – Official Form]

NO LONG LETTERS
VERY LEGIBLE HANDWRITING

14 November [1940]

My love

More and more, I've no heart to write to you – I've a feeling you haven't been getting my letters. What's more, nothing in my life seems to count for me, except this need I have for you. Everything's fine with me – I have time, I eat, I sleep, I read, the work's going well, I enjoy my teaching, Kos. isn't a burden to me, there are good concerts, Bost isn't getting on too well with Kos. but he's charming with me. I've got rid of Bianca and still find Sorokine amusing (she has slept with her young man, who actually seems as intelligent and nice as can be). I'm still listening to a lot of music, I see a bit of Zuorro and quite a lot of That Lady: I dined alone with her yesterday, off a delicious chicken from La Pouèze. But all of this is against a background of emptiness, and every so often I take my head in my hands and wonder how I manage to get through my days so well. It's dead time, nothing counts. And with streaming eyes I recall a miraculous age when my heart was always full, my hours too short, my thoughts at once alive yet always too poor – since there was you to lay hold of them and return them to me all enriched. It's not that I feel diminished within myself – but all my resources seem useless to me, it's sterile, it's not worth anything, if you're not there to give a meaning to the world. Then too I recall your love: it was there all the time around me – so warm, so present, so full! On this bench at the Dôme you've sat beside me, in flesh and blood. You won't have changed, nor will your love, nor mine – but how long this silence is, my little one! All that I can have of life without you, I have – but it's nothing. I already knew that, when you were here – you're everything to me. I know it still better now, and find it both cruel and sweet.

Your charming Beaver

[Paris – Official Form]

18 November [1940]

My love

Three days ago I had a letter from you, dated 15 June. It was like a voice from beyond the grave and quite shattered me. How I'd like to know what's becoming of you at this moment – I'm fretting. Today it's rainy and grey in Paris, and I'm in very low spirits. My life is still comfortable enough, but I miss you too much. Delarue has been put in charge of the N.R.F.'s theatre criticism, and claims they'd like you as editor of the journal. Perhaps they'll manage to get you brought back for that purpose, but I no longer dare hope for anything. My life has gone on – all the same and not too gloomy. Yesterday evening Bost and I met his friend Amsellem, who's a prisoner on parole – which is a very pleasant situation. Bost was in seventh heaven at meeting up with him again, which inevitably threw Kos. into paroxysms of fury, since her jealousy's unrelenting. It seems that my break with Bianca is definitive, and I no longer hear anything of her. Sorokine has had lots of problems with her mother – who wanted to lock her up at home – so she ended up inventing an engagement with the little boy friend she's fond of, who seems very nice. But I haven't seen much of her this week, on account of these maternal squabbles. I've seen a bit of That Lady, who's leaving Paris at the end of this week. On my behalf, she has instructed Marcelle Jeannel, who lives in Lyons, to send you two parcels of food and tobacco every week – how I hope you'll receive them! How I hope, too, that you're getting my letters – that would restore some meaning to my life. But I'm discouraged. I'm working, and that's going ahead well. I've listened to some superb concerts: Chopin, Schumann, and above all yesterday a superb Bach concert. I've also been to see a Spanish dancer at the Salle Pleyel. I'm reading a bit – I've gone back to mediaeval history – but now the libraries are all closed. The *N.R.F.* sends me free copies of this year's new publications, but there's nothing good. Wanda's well, leading a quiet life with no escapades, but doing sod all. Her sister's now doing sod all too. Goodbye, my little one – my heart's so heavy, I can't bear living without you any longer.

Your charming Beaver

[Paris – Official Form]

29 November [1940]

My love

I haven't written for a long while, I'm so convinced my letters aren't getting through. I receive absolutely nothing – you've plunged into darkness. But I know you'll reappear one fine day, just the same as ever, and then there'll be happiness again. I live with my eyes fixed on that moment – I live for that moment alone. I'm working a lot, thinking about the day when you'll be beside me reading my novel, which will be almost finished when I submit it to you. This work is my greatest joy: it's the only true link between my past and my future, the only tangible link between you and me. For the rest, I have an apparently full existence – and it's still all roses with Bost, Olga and Sorokine. I've seen a lot of That Lady, who's now about to return to La Pouèze; a bit of Zuorro, who's swooning with ardour; nothing at all of Guille, who's bleakly preparing to become a father. Apparently the Llama's teaching in Fez. They gave a reading from your works the other day at the Café de Versailles – so the world isn't forgetting you. It's even extraordinary, my little one, how strongly present you are in lots of people's hearts. As for me, I'm at times very unhappy – I want to see you so much. But then, at others, I've all the courage in the world – because despite everything we remain inseparable, we're still together in the world, and I know that I'll clasp you in my arms again. If only I had a letter from time to time, in order to be really easy as to your health and peace of mind. My love, if our love has been reinforced by every ordeal, it's now harder than diamond. Do keep me with you, my little one, as I keep you – all intertwined with my life. I kiss you passionately.

Your charming Beaver

[Paris – Official Form]

10 December [1940]

My love

It's quite a time since I wrote. I still haven't had any letter from you, you see, and that disheartens me. All I've had is a note dated 26 October, which is already old. Luckily your mother has given me more detailed news of you. I'm still living in the same old way, just waiting. I think only of the day when I'll see you again. It's for that moment that I'm working dutifully on my novel. It's finished, and I'm polishing the first part – but there'll still be lots of work to be done on the second. Everything else just helps pass the time. But the time does pass, anyway. I have moments of dejection, when it's unbearable to me to be separated from you like this – and there's not a night that I don't have nightmares on your account – but by and large my days are pleasant. I'm often at the Dôme by 8 in the morning, in pitch darkness – which strikes me as very poetic. I see a lot of Bost, listen to a lot of music. I've had to take up with Bianca again, but its only limping along. Olga's in the process of leaving Dullin's workshop. Wanda's still hanging round doing nothing and seeing nobody. I've seen a lot of That Lady, who has been making a long stay in Paris but is leaving again at any moment. Life in Paris is lively, apart from the evening. The *N.R.F.* is coming out again, edited by Drieu and with Gide, Fabre-Luce and Giono writing for it. The populists have given a reading of 'The Wall' at the Café de Versailles – as I told you, people aren't forgetting you.[290] I'd so like to know how you're living! If at least I had letters from you regularly! – but perhaps the mail will work better from January on. What a lot of little stories I'll have to tell you, my little one. You know that Maheu's teaching in Fez? That Guille's expecting a child (without enthusiasm, but the Bel Eute is radiant)? My sweet little one, you haven't left my life. Nothing has any meaning except through you. I'm hoping you haven't too much lost me – hoping you continue to feel inseparable from

---

[290]'The Wall' was one of the stories in the collection of the same name (*Le Mur*, 1939), entitled *Intimacy* in English translation. The Populists, in inter-war French culture, held that literature should be written for the people and about the people.

myself, in that strange existence of yours. How I love you! It's impossible to love anyone more intensely than I love you, after these eleven years of common life. I kiss you passionately, my love.

Your charming Beaver

[Paris – Official Form]

Saturday 14 December [1940]

My dear, dear love

At last, a letter from you – and one that tells me you're receiving mine![291] How I regret not having written every day, my sweet little one! – but I was in despair. I'll do so now. It changes my whole life – the idea that, as in the old days, you'll know everything that happens to me. I was so scared, my little one, that in spite of everything you might be unhappy. I know quite well you're rock hard – but you're also a 'sensitive soul', and the slightest pang of your heart throws my own heart into turmoil. Of course I'm not bored from a sense of duty, my dear little one. On the contrary, I hate being unhappy and since June have never ceased to flee unhappiness, often successfully. My life's full – with people, work, and music. But at times I have so painful a craving to see you that I'm unhappy despite myself. The fact is that I love you, my little one – you and nothing else – with your dear face that I no longer see, and your tiny person, and your tenderness, and all our happiness. Usually I tell myself wisely that nothing of all this has been lost – and live in waiting. But at times one gets tired of waiting. One wants plenitude – and it's you alone who can give me it. But, as you say, I shall have you back, my love, and for always – and we still have a life ahead of us. Above all, don't worry about me. Especially now that I have this letter, I'll have peace of mind. I'm living more or less like last year and, in the last resort, that's much closer to happiness than to unhappiness: it's a kind of happiness in abeyance. Starting from tomorrow, every day I'll tell you everything in detail. Have you received any parcels? The N.R.F.'s concerning itself with you and others – so who knows? The N.R.F. has reappeared, edited by Drieu, with articles by Fabre-Luce, Gide, Giono, a story by Marcel Aymé . . . as a whole it's

[291]As De Beauvoir reported in her letter of 10 December, she had received nothing from Sartre since a note written on 26 October, until she now received his letter dated 10 December. It is not clear from the *Lettres au Castor* whether Sartre had been unable to write, or his letters had gone astray.

not brilliant. They're giving me free copies of their books, which are miserable. I'm not reading much, but I've studied Kant thoroughly and am beginning to know something about music. I'm pleased with my novel: in three months it'll be finished, and the only thing missing will be your criticisms. My love, how happy I am to be able to write to you! In itself my life is pleasant, if only I can think about yours with satisfaction – which I'm now going to do. But how I do love you, my little one, and how inseparable I am from you! Do keep me with you.

Your charming Beaver

[Paris – Official Form]

[14 December 1940]

My love

I'm at once writing you a second letter, since you're receiving them so well. I'm going to get down to telling you about my days. I'm at the back of the Sélect, next to a tableful of rather pleasing young German women, who give the place an odd little exotic air. It's Saturday and 2 o'clock in the afternoon. Outside the weather's dry and biting, like at winter sports, and sunlight's flooding into the café. This morning I got up at 7.30 and left home in pitch darkness. It's amazing that morning gloom – so lively, with all those vehicles of which you can see only the lights, and hurrying shadows, and draught-proofed cafés. I went off to take the Métro and meet Bianca at Le Passy, in order to go with her to the Conservatoire rehearsal. As I've told you, we broke off, then made up again – and it's just limping along. But we're dragging it out, because she's going to be married in a fortnight and follow her husband to America. We probably shan't ever see each other again, and that solves the problem. Lamblin's in despair as usual. All things considered he isn't exactly impotent, only his parents neglected to have him circumcised and that's the key to the mystery. They're all very happy because the German authorities have been merciful and the University's reopening on 20 December.[292] I'll be able to return to the library and resume my studies on the Middle Ages. Anyway, we went to that concert – in the first row of the stalls. They were playing Bach, it was first-class, and Charles Munch was a joy to behold – tapping his foot, singing, and

---

[292]The Sorbonne had been closed by the Germans following a student demonstration on the Champs–Élysées on 11 November 1940.

calling on one performer after another. I was in seventh heaven. After that I took the Métro to St Michel and met Bost for dinner. He told me how Kos. had informed Dullin yesterday that she was attending drama classes under Rouleau, Bertheau and Barrault. Dullin sank back onto a couch, then chucked her out – both her and Keshelevich. Everything's going kaputt for him, and it serves him right. Kos. is nervous, but I think she did the right thing – she was mouldering away in that dump. Have I told you I'm having quite a lot to do with Mouloudji, who's writing some really pleasing things and interests me? Sorokine's worried about it (wrongly) – I must tell you about her too. I'm full of stories and you'll know them all. I love you. I'm happy, because of your letter, as I hadn't been for ages. My love.

Your charming Beaver

[Paris – Official Form]

Sunday 15 December [1940]

Most dear little being

How it delights me to write to you, now that I know my letters are getting through. I'm going to tell you everything. Well, yesterday I found your little letter, which filled my heart with joy: I'd like some details of this new theatrical art and your work.[293] I think it's a new string to your bow for good now, and that you'll be working relentlessly for the theatre on your return. I wrote to you from the Sélect, then worked. I'm redoing the first part, livening up the character and life of Françoise – which is easy – and trying to establish Pierre better, which by contrast is very hard.

[. . .]

Since yesterday, I've been happy. I love you passionately.

Your charming Beaver

---

[293]Sartre had informed her that he was writing a play (*Bariona*) as a Christmas entertainment in his prison camp.

[Paris – Official Form]

[16 December 1940] – Monday

My love

I'm going to tell you about my evening with Sorokine. You should first know that she has left her mother's, shamefully driven out amid frightful scenes because the bitch was no longer willing to support her – she even stole a bracelet from her. Sor. counter-attacked by stealing soap to the value of 350 F. and an electric fire. The Russian colony has been thrown into turmoil by all this. Sorokine accordingly has to live off a few lessons, some meagre assistance on my part, and the help of the fellow of whom she has made a conquest. He's a young philosophy student of 21, fairly good-looking, very intelligent, a bit too austere, who at 17 had an amazing three-way affair with a homosexual and a woman – who was none other than our friend Claudine Chonez, which I found prodigiously amusing. There are lots of hilarious details (I was shown textual proof). This fellow has installed Sor. in a kind of lodging-house, where he himself lives, on Bd Port Royal. She took me to her room, where we ate sardines and jam and talked – she was terribly nice and engaging. The situation, in broad terms, is that the fellow is madly jealous of me. She, on the other hand, persists in loving me – although she does want to avoid losing him, and even (for material reasons) to marry him. My inclination's to push her into his arms, but she won't listen to a word. Oh! I'd like to tell you everything in detail – but I'll try gradually. Tell me what you'd most like me to write about – it's so annoying having to choose, when I've such a lot to tell you. I live with you all the time – you're my sole reason for living and I don't leave you. I love you, my little one.

Your charming Beaver

Envelope
KRIEGSGEFANGENENPOST – Prisoners of War
Vor- und Zuname: Sartre Jean-Paul
Gefangenennummer: Mle 10788
Lager-Bezeichnung: Stalag XII-D
Sender: De Beauvoir Simone
        21 Rue Vavin Paris

[Paris – Official Form]

Wednesday 18 December [1940]

Dear little being

I was really moved just now because I met the chambermaid from the Hôtel Mistral, who stopped me in Rue Vavin and asked me effusively for news of you. It reminded me of that happy past of ours, my love – we'll go back there, won't we? Her husband's a prisoner too. During the day I also met old man Gerassi, who gave me news of Fernand and Stépha: they're in New York with the kid and very happy. I had a studious day: from 8 to 11 working at the Dôme; 1 hour's teaching; lunch with Bost in a pleasant bistro opposite your grandmother's place – hardly anybody goes there except labourers and there's a big stove in the middle of the room. After that, I listened to Bach records for an hour in Bd St Michel, and since 3 I've been working at the Dôme – it's 6 now and I'm going to work on. You run into Merleau-Ponty almost every morning at the Dôme – he's now married to that young Jolibois woman. I was the one who made the marriage – did I tell you about it? She was expecting a baby again, and didn't want any other solution. She was very nice, moreover, explaining to me how she wanted the marriage personally, but didn't want to impose it on him. And he was sickening, going on about how – even when they were living apart – he was afraid of any least hint of a responsibility. What's more – objecting to that little 'contortion' men perform when they don't want a child – he left her to take care of all the risks on her own, so regarded it as her own fault if things turned out badly. They're living in separate Montparnasse hotels and maintaining polite relations.

Goodbye, my little one, how I'd love to tell you everything in more detail. You're with me all day long. I love you.

Your charming Beaver

[Paris – Official Form]

Saturday 21 December [1940]

My love

So here I am on holiday, with Paris enjoying the most superb cold, dry, ski-ing weather. I've got hold of heaps of books by Kierkegaard and Scheler, and also some books on music, and I'm going to listen to heaps of concerts – so I feel I've got a good holiday ahead of me. So they're going to stage your Christmas mystery-play, are they? – in fact,

they'll already have done so by the time you get this note – but I shan't
see it. It does make me bitter at times – even if I think you're at peace
– to think of you without me. I'd give all the amenities of my life, and
accept all the hardships of yours, in order to live beside you – even if I
were only to see you for a few hours each week. You're more precious
to me than the rest of the world put together. I love you solely, my sweet
little one. My days oscillate, you see, between a tranquil satisfaction
(because they're very full and pleasant) and an all-consuming regret
because you alone count in my eyes. When I think that I've had you to
myself for days and weeks! That we used to talk for hours on end, and
I used to see your face! Praise be to Heaven, I've never been lightminded: I've always understood what a miracle it was that you should
be granted me, and in 11 years I don't think I've wasted a minute of
your presence. I try not to think too much about all I'm lacking through
your absence. As soon as I feel it, though – as at this moment – as soon
as I see your face again too much, it's unbearable. I love you
passionately, my little one – and I'd like you to feel it. It's not just a
tranquil fidelity that welds me to you. When I think about you, it's as
burning within me as if you were there – and I think about you all the
time. Since getting your note, I've not been sad any more. But at times
I literally choke with the need to see you – it shakes me to the core. Do
keep me with you, my little one. I wrote to yesterday morning. It was
the day the University was reopening and there was a rush at the
Sorbonne library. It was really agreeable seeing the Latin Quarter come
back to life. I went to hunt for books and met lots of former pupils. I
read a book about Bach at the Mahieu, had lunch with Bost, read some
more, went to school, finished revising the first part of my novel, then
spent the evening with Sorokine – whom I kept to sleep at my place,
which put her in seventh heaven. This morning I went to a concert at
the Conservatoire, then had lunch with Bost. I'll tell you all about it.
But I felt my need of you so intensely that I haven't been able to talk
about anything else. You're everything to me.

Your charming Beaver

[Paris – Official Form]

Monday 23 December [1940]

My love

It's very cold this morning throughout Paris and particularly in the
Dôme. Merleau-Ponty's here, a few steps away, busy reading my novel.

I had dinner with him yesterday (we ate at the Crêperie Bretonne and had a drink at Les Vikings), but I didn't find him much fun. He thinks C. Gibert's pregnant – it's an epidemic. Actually, he congratulates himself on not having been changed by marriage. You have no more ardent fan: he reads your philosophical works to his pupils and tells them stories about you. Apparently he spends his life preparing his lectures. Before seeing him, I'd been to listen to Beethoven's *Missa Solemnis*, which is superb. This morning I saw Sorokine, still tender and charming, who told me about a dreadful 17-hour quarrel with her young man. What it boils down to is that he realizes she doesn't love him – which she barely troubles to hide from him – and hates me. However, he loves her too much to break off, so I wonder how it's going to end. She left at 10 and I'm busy reading Kierkegaard, and Wahl's essays on him – it really interests me and I'm glad to have got down to reading again. I was expecting Bost, but there's no sign of him: he must be having another scene with Kos. She's continually mistaking nervous fits for material disorders, and he's pretty fed up with it. She's becoming a nasty piece of work, though she makes amends by turning on the cheap charm. I think she's off to Laigle tomorrow. Goodbye, my dear little one. How I long for a letter from you! I often see again, in its entirety, your little person – body and soul – and am moved to tears by it. I love you, my beloved.

Your charming Beaver

[Paris – Official Form]

Wednesday 25 December [1940]

My love

Here's my second Christmas without you – and sadder than the other one, since I don't know when I'll see you again. From time to time I'm filled with dread – it's especially hard at night. I love you so, my little one, I remember your dear expressions so well and miss you so desperately. It's 3 in the afternoon and I'm at the Flore. There's all the usual crowd and it's packed and warm. Outside the weather's beautifully cold and dry, and Paris has a deserted, country look. I feel comfortable because I'm going to spend quite a while reading Kierkegaard, then I'll go to the concert, and then at 8 I'll meet up with Bost.

It was a strange Christmas Eve, and pretty lugubrious. The cafés stayed open till 2.30, and were fairly full but not very lively. Outside it was pitch dark and, since neither Métro nor taxis function after midnight, people had to go home on foot. Moreover, Boulevards St Michel and St Germain were utterly deserted. I met Bost at 10.30 at the Deux Magots, and we went off to the Capoulade. On our way we met a woman asking, with some anguish, if Concorde was still a long way off. She was going to Miromesnil – and God knows where she came from. We spent the time conversing – we were glad to be together and it was pleasant. We took a room for the week in a neighbourhood hotel. This morning we got up late, and had something to drink and a sandwich at the Mahieu and the D'Harcourt. Now B.'s off to celebrate Christmas with his family and I've come here.

My little one, I've a good life but I'm in real distress. I'd so hoped you'd be restored to me at Christmas. I dreamt last night that you were forgetting me – and it was dreadful. But I know it's false.

Your charming Beaver

[Paris – Official Form]

Thursday 26 December [1940]

My love

Your letter has just arrived, exactly like a beautiful Christmas present. My sweet little one, I so needed to feel I was still really present to you. I found all of you – with such emotion – through your spidery scrawl, dear, dear little being. Yesterday, after writing to you, I read *The Concept of Dread*[294] at the Café de Flore, then went to the Châtelet to listen to a superb Bach *Magnificat*, some fairly agreeable Berlioz, and a bad rendering of Franck's *Beatitude*. I called in at my hotel and that's when I found your letter in my pigeonhole – and pounced upon it. I'd had something of a presentiment that it was going to be there.

[. . .]

Goodbye my love. I love you with all my might.

Your charming Beaver

---

[294]By Sören Kierkegaard.

[Paris – Official Form]

Saturday 28 December [1940]

My love

I'm continuing to permit myself a lazy existence. Yesterday afternoon I went to the Ursulines with Bost and saw *Carnet de Bal* – seeing Harry Baur made me laugh, because I recalled your imitations.[295] Apart from that and Jouvet, there's hardly any entertainment to be found. After that we went and drank mulled wine at the Capoulade, and by 7 rushed off to the Petit St Benoît, where there was nothing to eat except leeks and tripe – which was a disappointment, since in an exaggerated excess of thrift we hadn't had any lunch. (I find it ironical to be speaking to you about food shortages.)

[. . .]

Goodbye, my dear little one. I wish I could write to you at greater length, with copious preambles. I'm no longer so sad, since I've had your letters. I love you and kiss you passionately.

Your charming Beaver

[Paris – Official Form]

Tuesday 31 December [1940]

My love

I've just seen your mother and am really moved, because she has seen some fellow from your camp who was set free, and he has given her news of you. To think that people have the luck to have you all alive to themselves! I wouldn't be one to choose freedom, in such circumstances. How I long to have you back, dear little being, salt of the earth! I miss you. On the other hand, I'm continuing to spend an excellent holiday season with Bost. On Sunday afternoon we went to an excellent Ravel festival at the Salle Pleyel, returned home to eat pâté and turkey sent by Kos. in our room, then went for a drink at the Balzar (in the morning I'd seen Bienenfeld for two hours – she's going to marry Lamblin finally – and then had lunch with Bost at St Germain-des-Prés, before going on to the Flore). Yesterday morning I saw Sorokine at the Mahieu. She's more and more sickened by her young man, and they

---

[295]*Carnet de Bal:* 1937 film directed by Julien Duvivier. Harry Baur (1880-1943) was one of the best known French actors of the 1930s.

weave lots of ethical and psychological complications around the simple fact that she doesn't love him while he loves her. With me, things are working out wonderfully well and it's a real success. She has realized she'd never be able to build her life with me – and doesn't hold it against me or suffer from it – yet she continues to care about me in the pleasantest possible way. Our relations are still interspersed with storms over such matters as soap she won't give me, or cakes of mine she wants to eat up, or because she suddenly takes it into her head to be jealous of Mouloudji. But we no longer come to blows and by and large there's perfect harmony.

Goodbye, my little one, I'll tell you the rest in my next letter. I love you – with need, tenderness and passion.

Your charming Beaver

[Paris – Official Form]

Tuesday 31 December [1940]

Dear little being

Yesterday morning, then, I saw Sorokine and after that went to wait for Bost at the Flore, where I spotted Bienenfeld – who now permanently has quivering nostrils, difficulty in breathing, and anguish of spirit. Her father was conferring with M. Lamblin: she knows she's getting married in a fortnight, but doesn't know to whom – Lamblin or the American? It's a pitiful situation, yet one with which I can summon up no sympathy.

[...]

I lunched with Bost, saw your mother, and here I am at the Dôme – which has just been provided with an appallingly noisy 'pick-up' that reduces me to despair.

Here's the last day of a year in which we've been well and truly separated, my love. Perhaps this next year will be the one in which we recover one another for ever. Be patient, above all, and leave everything to Providence.[296] I love you, my little one.

Your charming Beaver

---

[296]De Beauvoir was worried that Sartre might attempt to escape.

✿ 1941

[Paris – Official Form]

Wednesday 1 January [1941]

My heart's so full this evening I'm on the verge of tears. It has been snowing over Paris since morning and, as there are no taxis or other vehicles, the snow has remained on the streets. Everything's as white and silent as in the middle of the countryside, with a grey winter-sports sky. I'm thinking about you. I always think about you, but this evening it's through so many dear memories and such yearnings that it's suffocating me. When shall I see you again, my sweet little one? I could wait for you for years, allowing the time to slide by like this indefinitely, but they'd be that many years of my life stolen from me – and my life's none too long any more for all the love I have for you. I wrote to you yesterday from the Dôme, then in the evening went with Bost to see *L'Avare*.[297] The theatre was half empty, which is unfair because Dullin's literally miraculous: even smaller than in real life, all old, dirty and patched – never, by a long chalk, have I seen him act so well. It was New Year's Eve and we went to the Capoulade – which was dismal. At midnight, they switched off the lights and gave twelve gong-strokes. My heart was full there too. We dragged on till about 2 in the morning, pretty much in silence. I couldn't get on better with Bost – yet how alone I always am in his company! How alone I am, wherever you're not present! This evening I have violent memories of how happy I've been. I'll have you back one day, my dear happiness, my life. I clasp you passionately in my arms.

Your charming Beaver

[Paris – Official Form]

Wednesday [1 January 1941]

My dear little one

I'm a bit troubled this evening. Wanda's at Laigle, and this afternoon I entered her room with Bost and saw in her diary that – despite excellent feelings for you – she was intensely annoyed by having twice received news of you from me. This is how it had occurred. I don't know if I've told that, when I got your address, I was utterly devastated by

---

[297]By Molière (see *The Prime of Life*, p.475).

the words 'Kranken-Revier'.[298] I knew nothing about you and thought you must be dying. I spent a dreadful evening. I'd arranged to meet Kos. at the Atelier, so got Tyssen to translate the address for me – and burst into tears virtually on the spot. In the course of the evening W. saw me with 'dragonfly eyes' (as she put it) and was sickened by it. Later on – thinking she must be worried – on receipt of your 1st letter I said you were charging me with giving news of you to everybody and left a little reassuring note for her. Subsequently, when your mother had a letter from you, I copied it out and read it out to Wanda (telling her clearly that it was to your mother). Anyway, as 50 people have asked me for news of you and I was providing them, it couldn't fail to get back to Wanda's ears. I'd find it unbearable if you were to think I'd acted thoughtlessly, my little one – I've mentioned only *one* letter to me and one to your mother. Incidentally, Gégé's offering W. the chance of joining the firm of Kientz: for 4 hours' work each afternoon, she'd learn the job and earn 600 F. I wish she'd accept, so she'd at least have a job in hand. She has a truly wretched life. She hates me, though – that's why I've given up bothering about her.

Goodbye, my love. How I yearn to speak to you, and touch you. How hard these layers of silence are! I kiss you most passionately.

Your charming Beaver

[Paris – Official Form]

Thursday 2 January [1941]

My dear love

My soul's still wracked with longing to see you. I wrote to you yesterday from the Flore, then dined with my parents and met Bost at the 2 Magots. He was tired and in low spirits, because the idea of teaching again makes him literally ill. We went home to bed very early, in a little prostitutes' hotel in Rue St André des Arts. This morning I'd arranged to meet Bianca at the Dôme, and I found her at 9.30 looking radiant because she's staying in Paris after all and marrying Lamblin in a month's time.

[. . .]

I feel terribly melancholy. When shall I see you again? – that's all I

---

[298]Infirmary: see note 285 above.

wonder from dawn to dusk. Goodbye, my love – how impatiently I'm waiting for your next letter! I kiss you most passionately.

Your charming Beaver

[Paris – Official Form]

Friday 3 January [1941]

My dear little one

So the holiday season's over now, but I'm prolonging it a bit – I won't get down to work till Monday. Well, last night we came home early and I was able to assess how painful the wretched Bost finds having to give lessons. From 5 in the morning on, he could no longer sleep – but was turning on the light with a jerk every half-hour, to see what time it was. As a result I slept very badly. I rose to find an icy-cold day. They can't manage to clear the Paris streets of snow, and though in places it's white and poetic, in others it's just slush. I went to the Dôme and met Sorokine – more affecting than ever. I've told you – I think? – how touching I found her, when she was explaining how she'd realized she had her own life outside me, without for all that ceasing to love me. She's now devoid of jealousy, no longer demanding, and quite movingly generous and affectionate. I love her more and more. She had a delightful face, roughened and reddened by the cold. She has written to her young man, explaining that she can't love him but offering him friendship. He has answered in low-key fashion – and showering me with compliments – but pretending to confuse the proposed friendship with true love. His letters aren't nice. I took Sorokine on some errands: to make my tax declaration, which was shamefully late, and to collect some dough. Then we had lunch and from 1 to 3 I did some Kant and Kierkegaard before going off to school. My little one, I'm living in dread again. I'd fixed on the hope of seeing you back for Christmas, and now I no longer dare hope for anything. How painful I find it, too, no longer to know your moods and thoughts in detail. I miss you so, dear little flesh-and-blood person living elsewhere – and whom I'd so like to see safely back. I love you more than ever.

Your charming Beaver

[Paris – Official Form]

Sunday 5 January [1941]

My love

I'm writing to you from the Dôme. It's one o'clock and the place is full of people eating. The weather's none too warm. I wonder anxiously whether you're not dying of cold. There are so many things I'd like to know about you. Do you have papers there? Wireless? What's the situation with your writings? Aren't you interested in anything except the theatre any more? And also: how do you feel about these letters? Are you still interested in what's going on in our little world, or is it merely like watching a film? As for me, after writing to you I went yesterday to a concert at the Atelier. They were playing Franck's *Quintet*, which I was hearing for the third time and which is splendid. I was very amused, because I found myself sitting next to Magali and Eloy de Staecklin, and she was complaining bitterly that he'd taken poor seats – while he was too mean to admit the fact. They had a real shouting-match, but eventually moved down to the stalls. After that, I went to meet Sorokine in a little café near the Arts et Metiers that's a genuine brothel.[299] As a rule they don't serve unaccompanied women – to the point where Wanda and Sorokine (in the days when they used to frequent each other's company) once got themselves chucked out – but they let me stay all the same. There were only tarts there, and an exotic clientele, and a mechanical piano in lieu of a phonograph. It was crowded and warm. Sorokine was distressed because her young man was returning home that very night, so she couldn't avoid giving her evening up to him. I was a bit disappointed – I'd liked the idea of spending 24 hours with her – but, urging her warmly to postpone that for a few days, I telephoned M. Ponty instead, met up with him at the Dôme, and spent the evening with him. He paid me vast compliments on my novel (the 1st part), telling me it was 'great': in spite of everything, that really did encourage me. He also told me how he'd slept with Piquard (his former pupil – a girl friend of Bienenfeld's and one of my probationers). He took her home and kissed her, and she promptly said: 'I love you.' He answered (approximately): 'Oh, don't mention it' – and upended her. Afterwards he thought she was pregnant, but it was a false alarm. She threatened sentimental complications, but he more or less broke it off almost at once. He seeks erotic conversation

---

[299]Arts et Metiers: the École Nationale des Arts et Metiers, in Boulevard de l'Hôpital near Place d'Italie.

with me – just like the old headmaster[300] – and I find him nauseating. Apart from that, Kos. hasn't come back – since the trains are blocked by snow. Goodbye, my dear, dear love. I'm joined to you in passion.

Your charming Beaver

Envelope
KRIEGSGEFANGENENPOST
Sartre Jean-Paul
GEFANGENENNUMMER (Prisoner number) 10788
Lager-Bezeichnung (Camp name) STALAG XII-D
DEUTSCHLAND (Germany)

[Paris – Official Form)

Tuesday 7 January [1941]

My love

I'm still very glum – perhaps when I get back to work again it'll be better, but I feel slack after this fortnight on holiday – and the weather's cold and grey and dismal. [. . .] This morning I went to school, then installed myself at the Dôme and worked like a dream from midday till 4. I'm redoing the second part and think everything will be finished by Easter. My heart's breaking all the time as I work, because it involves our past and yourself, my sweet little one. Yesterday, too, I had tears in my eyes as I read an article on Heidegger – and recalled that journey through Provence when you were explaining it to me. My little one, I feel like weeping all the time these days. I love you so, with such a yearning for your face and your affection. Intellectual solitude's no burden to me, nor the fact of being alone in general. It's *you* I miss, your smiles, the little nape of your neck that I remember so well, and all that warmth one feels in your presence. My love. I ended the day at Merleau-Ponty's, alone in his cosy room listening to some splendid Franck and some Bach. I listened for 3½ hours without feeling tired, then met Kos. at the Dôme – she'd arrived on Monday by roundabout ways. She was thoroughly amiable and pleasant, and we spent a very

---

[300]In October 1930, when De Beauvoir was thinking of finding a job in journalism in order to avoid having to teach in the provinces, she met a couple who might help her. The husband – a sixty-year-old lycée headmaster – showed rather too lively an interest in her: 'he would promise me a lot of useful introductions and talk to me about Life, with an eager emphasis on its more libidinous aspects' (*The Prime of Life*, pp.52-3).

good evening. Goodbye, my dear, dear love. I'm wasting away with longing to see you. Do think about me.

Your charming Beaver

[Paris – Official Form]

Wednesday 8 January [1941]

My love

So yesterday evening I slipped on ski-trousers and pullover and went to bed, where I read Eddington on modern science – it was mildly entertaining, even though he's so stupid.[301] Then I went to sleep. I'd promised Sorokine to spend 24 hours with her, and she came and woke me up at 8 in the morning. We spent a very agreeable day. [. . .] We came home to stuff ourselves with pâté and chocolate, talk and sleep.

Thursday

My love. I'm having trouble writing to you – I'm more disoriented and tragic than for a long while. First, it's apparently the last day one can write freely. Also, I want to see you too much. Yesterday evening I was recalling ballets I'd seen with you at the Opéra and I felt like weeping. I'm constantly coming up against memories that rend me apart. Also, I've just read the latest N.R.F. and it's so stupid and contemptible that I was shattered by it. Yesterday I was telling you that intellectual solitude didn't bother me much. But when it takes on cosmic proportions it shatters me – and Hegel, who was such a comfort to me last August, no longer consoles me. There's not so much of my life left that I can calmly accept sacrificing years of it – and years without you (or months, or weeks) are a meaningless measure.

If this is my last letter for a long while, I wouldn't all the same like to leave you on a falsely gloomy note. Like you, I too have the hope that every ordeal is a step forward; and I feel this year just over has well and truly delivered me from a rationalist false optimism. I think I've internalized myself, and made myself more authentic than in former days – I truly believe this is no illusion. But whether I'm depressed or of good heart, the fact remains that one thing alone counts for me: to see you again, and to recover your thought, your reality, your presence

---

[301]One of Sir Arthur Eddington's popular works, probably *The Nature of the Physical World* (1935).

– and also your love and your expressions. You're everything to me, for always.

Your charming Beaver

[Paris – Official Form]

Monday 20 January [1941]

My love

I stopped writing to you, because they claimed letters were no longer being accepted – but apparently they are. Apart from that, I've been so seared by grief during the past 10 days that I've scarcely had any desire any longer to write. I have constant nightmares about you: you come back (since I think it's impossible directly to dream an absence), but you don't love me any more and I'm filled with despair. At times, not knowing when I'll see you again has me literally fighting for breath. Today I feel better, because on Saturday I saw your mother and she gave me news of you. I'm so pleased the performance was a splendid success! So pleased to think that your life over there retains a meaning, and that you're interested in it! [. . .] As for me, my love, my joy hangs upon you. I knew very well that I loved you, but I love you even more than I knew.

Your charming Beaver

[Paris – Official Form]

Tuesday 21 January [1941]

My love

It's raining, and the weather today is damp and gloomy. I've given myself two days' leave on the pretext of flu.

[. . .]

I spent almost 6 hours working away at the back of the Dôme, interrupted only by a brief conversation with the Lunar Woman, who's the same as ever though pregnant. The Lunar Man will be really amazed if he finds a brat when he gets back. Apparently, some fellows from your camp are going to be set free. I'm going crazy with impatience waiting for someone to turn up who can give me news of you. My love, I live only in the past and the future. I do nothing but wait for you.

Your charming Beaver

[Paris – Official Form]

Wednesday 22 January [1941]

My sweet little one

Well, I spent a studious day yesterday, then went to Kos.'s for dinner.

[. . .]

The other day I caught sight of Gibert, who seems to have given up acting. She's even preparing to take an *agrégation* in philosophy: she wanted to do her probation under me, which would have made me laugh, but I don't think it'll happen. I came home at 10.30 and read in bed – some detective stories and pornographic books that Sorokine passed on to me – but that kind of literature is disappointingly monotonous. Then I came back to work at the Dôme. I have an hour's teaching to do, then I'll have lunch with Bost and work again. Goodbye, my love – I so long for some letters and news! I'll send you Hegel's *Phenomenology* in the next parcel, so you'll be able to improve your education. Goodbye, little best beloved, my dear love, my life.

Your charming Beaver

[Paris – Official Form]

Thursday 23 January [1941]

My love

I'm upstairs at the Flore and it's 7 in the evening. It's agreeable, because you can hear all the people swarming beneath you, yet you're totally peaceful – between two tables occupied by chess players. I've regained all my peace of mind, since I had news of you and began writing to you again. This morning I sent you 1,000 F. and hope you'll receive them safely – I'll send some more each month. Yesterday I worked well in the morning, went to school, had lunch with Bost, wasted an hour at the Sorbonne collecting a few books, then saw Bost again for 2 hours – after which I inspected my books at the Mahieu.

I've read Scheler's *Ressentiment*,[302] which I found very weak. I'm dying to do some real philosophy – there's heaps of stuff I've now assimilated – but by God! how I long for some solid discussions! How I yearn to talk to you! If I were condemned for long never to talk, I'd end up *writing* philosophy, from the need to express myself. I got down to Hegel again with my pupils this morning, and I find him interesting, even though I've become a bit repelled by his system.[303] At this moment, I feel my metaphysical situation as acutely as I used to during my youth – probably out of loneliness – and it's the only true wealth of my life. On the other hand, my work is going well and books and music still interest me. But the whole of our little world is really rather small. You know, you aren't characterized by 'ressentiment' – even though you've claimed to be – you're precisely in the camp of what Simmel and Scheler call 'genius', which is just the opposite. My beloved, I love you. I long to talk to you – as intensely as I long to kiss you.

Your charming Beaver

[Paris – Official Form]

Sunday 26 January [1941]

My love

[. . .]

Yesterday, after leaving Kos. at 10, I met up with Bost. We talked late into the night – till 2 – and got up only just in time to go and have lunch at the Capoulade. We talked some more in the afternoon – at table, and then strolling around a bit – he's very agreeable during the genuine conversations I sometimes have with him. I've got something of an itch to write some philosophy – my head's bursting with ideas.

My little one, the more I see people, the more I marvel at all that makes you so different from anyone else. I'm for ever rediscovering – with the bitterest sorrow – one or other of your virtues and being moved to tears by it. I love you, with passion, my little one. I cover your dear face with kisses.

Your charming Beaver

---

[302]Max Scheler (1874-1928), German philosopher, author of phenomenological and ethical works, often seen as one of the founders of existentialism.
[303]The evolution of De Beauvoir's attitude to Hegel is explained in *The Prime of Life*, pp.568-9.

[Paris – Official Form]

Monday 27 January [1941]

My dear little one

Here's another peaceful day well spent. I spent the morning with Bost, worked for 2 hours, went to school, then saw Bienenfeld for a while. Mouloudji joined us, which bothered her but not me – since he interests me more than she does. Then I had dinner with Kos. at the Milk Bar. You can see how my weeks are made up – as regular as the rules on music-paper. I'm up at about 8, then my day's spent in school, work, and conversation with Bost. I always have lunch with him, except on Thursday when I go to my parents. I see Sorokine twice for 2 hours, and the same with Bienenfeld. As for the evenings, I see Kos. one evening out of two, usually in her room where she cooks a bit for me. I go home early and read for a good hour in bed. On two evenings I see Sorokine at her place. She cooks pasta for me and I stay overnight – they're always agreeable evenings. Once a week, I'm bored with Bienenfeld. And finally, every Saturday I meet up with Bost at about 8 and stay with him until the Sunday concert. There are few unexpected events: a concert here and there, an hour with Mouloudji, a meal with Zuorro or Merleau-Ponty. Things really couldn't be arranged better – I've lots of time for everything without being too much on my own. It's decent, for a temporary life. But there are moments when I'm quite consumed by the longing to recover my true life, which was so full, so rich, so gay – because it was you, my love. I love you without respite. I'm waiting for you constantly.

Your charming Beaver

[Paris – Official Form]

Thursday 30 January [1941]

My sweet little one

I saw your mother yesterday at the Bon Marché and gave her news of you, then went and worked at the Dôme till evening, when I had dinner with Kos. [...] Bienenfeld has written me another little impassioned, desolate letter, but it left me cold. I hope that marriage, and above all the honeymoon, will calm her down. Goodbye, my dear, dear love. You've been ever present to me since I had your letter. I have peace of mind again, and sleep without nightmares. I love you, and kiss you passionately.

Your charming Beaver

[Paris – Official Form]

Friday 31 January [1941]

Dear little being

I blew in to the Dôme at 8.30, all agog at the idea of reading *Perry Mason and the Lame Canary*, which the N.R.R. had sent me yesterday along with M. Aymé's *La Belle Image* and a book by Bosco.[304] But then who should show up but M. Ponty, and I can't decently take out a detective story under his very nose.

[. . .]

I worked for another hour at the Bonaparte, before meeting up at the Flore with Bienenfeld – full of passion, alas! Goodbye, my love. I remember everything about you. I kiss you passionately.

Your charming Beaver

[Paris – Official Form]

21 February [1941]

My dear love

I was returning to the hotel with my heart full of you when I found your letter. Alas! my sweet little one, since 1 February they've returned all the letters I'd tried to write you. Send me as many as possible of these answer sheets – that's all they'll accept now. Your two last little letters had filled my heart with joy, and I've lived all month on the hope they gave me. This one leaves me more gloomy. How I long to see your friend and know something about you![305] I live – but I'm mutilated. I've almost finished my novel, and I think this second part's very good. I read Hegel and listen to music. Bianca's married and has left on her honeymoon with Lamblin: it's only half working. C. Audry's going to be a mother, Guille's a father, I've seen Dullin – who's taking up your case – and I'm going to see Toulouse again. Magnane has been published in the N.R.F. – his novel's dreadful. The Boxer has written a poem about you, which is pitiful in more than one sense. He thinks like Toulouse, which is sad. I've dreamt hundreds of times that you were returning – I didn't go away for the Shrovetide holiday, so that I could wait for you. I scan every street corner for you. I live only for the moment when I set eyes

---

[304]Henri Bosco (1889-1976), regional novelist whose works were set in Provence.
[305]Sartre had announced that a medical orderly repatriated from his camp would be visiting De Beauvoir soon.

on you again. Goodbye, my love, sweet little beloved. I kiss you so passionately.

Your charming Beaver

[Paris – Official Form]

14 March [1941]

My dear love

I'm still living in expectation. I haven't seen your friend yet. Paris hasn't forgotten you – there are paragraphs about you here and there. *La Gerbe* was saying the other day: 'We're informed that M. Sartre is working on a novel called *The Age of Reason* – let's hope he reaches it himself.' Nothing new happens to me. Spring's definitely here – I've changed my heavy shoes for lovely light ones. There has been a splendid moonlight these past few days, and I've strolled along Avenue de Maine with a great longing to relive such nights with you, my love. I'm working. I've finished everything and am polishing up the fine points – but what a need I have of your judgement! Alone in front of my text, I get to feel pretty sick of it in the long run. I've been to the theatre. I saw *Britannicus*, preceded by a shameless spoken prelude by Cocteau, but with Marais who was excellent.[306] I saw *La Main Passe!*, a light comedy by Feydeau staged by Marchat and mildly funny. Wanda's painting me. We have very polite relations at present, though she has given me a face shaped like a gourd. Kos. is playing half a giraffe at the Français in Obey's *Noë*, and a 3rd tart in a play by Rouleau.[307] Bost's advancing in Grémillon's favours, and I'm helping him work on scripts. Sorokine and I have had a screaming quarrel, in which I almost collapsed from fury – but in general it's idyllic. I'm living gently in the midst of this whole little world – and waiting for you with passion, my love.[308]

Your charming Beaver

---

[306]In the production in question (at the Bouffes-Parisiens) of Racine's *Britannicus*, Jean Marais played the part of Nero.
[307]Andre Obey's *Noë* was written in 1931; Raymond Rouleau was an actor-director, who collaborated with Badel at the Théâtre du Vieux Colombier.
[308]Sartre returned to Paris at the end of March 1941 (see *The Prime of Life*, pp.478 ff.).

Envelope
KRIEGSGEFANGENENPOST – Prisoners of War
Sartre Jean-Paul
Prisoner number 10788
Lager-Bezeichnung: Stalag XII-D
Sender: S. de Beauvoir
      Lycée C. Sée
      11 Rue Léon Lhermitte

LETTERS

July 1943 – February 1946
Before Liberation and After

❧ 1943

[Roanne, Loire]

Thursday 1 July [1943]

My dear little one

I'm horribly disappointed, because my bicycle hasn't arrived yet. It really wasn't worth the trouble of being in such a rush. I feel quite absurd to be kicking my heels in Roanne, at 8 in the morning, with nothing to do. It would be rather poetic, if only I didn't dread having to stay here for two or three days, or a week . . . or indefinitely. I'm writing to you from the little café where we ended up that morning before we went to see Abbé Perrin.[309] The weather's superb, and if I were only sure of having the bike at 4, I'd enjoy revisiting all those places where we roamed so painfully with our ailing bicycles. It's all very familiar to me, even though the time of year's quite different.

So I finished my move yesterday evening,[310] then ate some fried potatoes before going off to catch my train. My dear little one, do at all costs reserve your seat, since those corridors are quite frightful! People were standing in the wc's and on the steps; and at the stops women were in tears on the platform, because they couldn't manage to get onto the train and had to pick up their bags and go home. You had to alight via the windows – it was dreadful. Luckily I had my seat. I slept badly, but the journey struck me as poetic because I saw myself on arrival mounting my bicycle and speeding off into the countryside. I was very much diverted because my three companions on the right, two men and a frightful woman, started chatting – after first taking out their books – and I caught the word 'flies': I thought how your damn play decidedly was pursuing me everywhere.[311] They drew a parallel between *The Stranger* and *Nausea*[312] – to Camus's advantage – because

---

[309]One of Sartre's companions in captivity, whom they went to visit in the summer of 1941 (see *The Prime of Life*, p.490).
[310]She was moving from the squalid Hôtel d'Aubusson in Rue Dauphine to the Hôtel de la Louisiane in Rue de Seine, where she was to remain until she obtained her first real apartment in Rue de la Bûcherie, in October 1948.
[311]*The Flies* had had its premiere in June 1943.
[312]Camus's *The Stranger* had been published in 1942, Sartre's *Nausea* in 1938.

they found *Nausea* boring in spite of fine passages. But then the moving spirit declared that there'd been good things in *The Flies* all the same; that it was odd it hadn't been a hit; that he'd heard from Alquié you were disturbed because Valéry didn't like it; and that for his own part, despite everything, he couldn't call it utterly without interest. After that they talked about something else. As for me, I read a bit of the Saroyan,[313] which isn't very good but quite agreeable, then tried to sleep. By 4.30 I was at Roanne. I dozed for three quarters of an hour in the waiting-room, and at dawn went off to collect the bike: no bike. Then I took a room and slept till 8, washed, and had a cup of white coffee before going back to the station: still no bike! I'll have to go back at 4, 8 and 8.20 – it reminds me of the time those damned bicycles wouldn't arrive at Pau.[314] Luckily I'm certain of a room for this evening, as it's apparently hard to find one. I bumped into a group of actors on tour, wandering sadly in search of lodgings without success. They struck me as poetic in this dismal province.

There. I'm going to write letters and read. I'll tell you this evening whether the bike's there or not. I'm hoping for lengthy news at Ambert – but I don't feel at all separated from you. I was telling myself last night that I've never been so happy in my life as at this moment, and it's yourself who's my happiness. Goodbye, my very dear love.

Your charming Beaver

[. . .]

Monsieur Sartre
Poste Restante, Office 43
Rue Littré
Paris 6

[Thiers, Puy-de-Dôme]

Monday 5 July [1943]

My dear little one
I'm writing to you from the terrace of a superb restaurant in Thiers, on a charming square with a big view over the plain below me. This

---

[313]William Saroyan (1908-81) had published a number of short story collections by this date, including *The Daring Young Man on the Flying Trapeze* in 1934, and *My Name is Aram* in 1940.
[314]In the summer of 1942 (see *The Prime of Life*, p.521).

Thiers is a very agreeable town, and I've just done fifteen kilometers downhill to get here. Well, I joyfully took to my bicycle again yesterday morning. I rose at first light and by 6 was leaving Roanne. It would break my heart to lose the morning hours – or the evening ones either – since they're the most agreeable; so I scarcely sleep more than seven hours each night, but take a siesta during those stupid, dull afternoon hours. I spent the morning winding along the gorges of the Loire, on a little road that was very stony but also very pretty. Then I took to the mountains again and stopped in a village, where I ate meat for the first time in a week: leg of lamb – preceded by a fine fish – and fine, plump potatoes, with a vanilla ice to finish off. There's really no problem about food, and so far I've had no trouble finding a bed. But then I realized to my fury that Sor. had given me a rotten inner tube, which was totally deflated after 40 km. and impossible to blow up again. Luckily I had a spare one, though, which a mechanic put on for me and which seems all right. Couldn't you perhaps get one in Paris? They cost 250 F. and it's stupid to spoil our trip for that sum. If you could call in and ask the little garage-owner at Avenue du Parc Montsouris – on behalf of M. Francoeur[315] – he has some at that price. Or else if Bost agreed to lend us one, it's a 'half-balloon' we need and we'd send it back to him in September. It's stupid if you have a breakdown. After lunch I took my siesta and read *Julius Caesar* – which wasn't very interesting – on a little green with a big view over the plain. Then, at about 5, I left and climbed higher into the mountains. I wrote letters and had a decent dinner with a mutton chop in a little holiday village, then did another 15 km – the most agreeable of all – as the sun went down. After finding a room I went out into a field until dark, quite blissful, to contemplate the landscape. It's a bit like a more mountainous version of the country round Usson – and very pretty.

This morning I was once again on the road by 6. Scaling on my way a large boulder carrying a direction-finder, I breakfasted off bread and saveloy, struggled over some steep passes, and stopped in a hamlet at the foot of a mountain I wanted to climb. For lunch I finished off my saveloy – a big lump – with bread and some sugar. I slept for two hours in a meadow, did 4 km. right to the foot of the mountain, but then a superb and terrifying storm broke – just as I was coming to a shed. Hail and lightning above a great landscape of mountains black with pines – it was very beautiful. In my shed I read the book about Charlemagne's empire and by 5 it was fine again, the air full of rain smells. I wasn't

---

[315] A distant relation of Bost.

able to climb my mountain, but I was quite happy all the same and made my descent to this place through lovely scenery. I'm going to have dinner, then go to Noirétable to spend the night – unless the storm breaks out again, since the sky's black. Then I'm not too sure what will become of me, since it seems to be hard to find a place to sleep here. I have only one problem and that's the luggage, which falls off three times a day. Bring only what you can carry yourself, and please ask Bost to lend you something practical. My little one, every so often I tell myself how in ten days' time I'll be seeing your little back on the road in front of me, and it makes my heart burst with joy. My love, we'll have a really good time. How I do love you.

Your charming Beaver

❦ 1944

[Morzine, Haute-Savoie]

Wednesday [20 January 1944]

Most dear little being

Here I am, dead beat and very happy. I already have a big day behind me and have been having a fantastically enjoyable time. I'll tell you all about it in the proper order. First, on Monday I went to the radio[316] – perhaps Kos. has told you about it – it was great fun seeing a broadcast, and the really interesting thing is that Jacques Armand has suggested I become a radio producer. He'll teach me the job, and then I'll produce my own programmes myself. That would surely bring in quite a bit, and if it takes a lot of time I'll leave more of the other work to Bost. He was cool about Kos., because after seeing her as Electra he doesn't regard her as exactly a cheerful actress.[317] After that I had dinner with my mother, which passed off without incident, then went off to meet Bost at the station buffet. But then we had a few difficulties, because they didn't accept skis on the train, so we had to register them; our tickets, however, were for Thonon while we wanted to send the skis to Cluses – which proved impossible. The end result is that they're stuck at

---

[316]After her removal from the roll of the University, which meant automatic dismissal from her teaching post, in June 1943 (as the result of being accused by Sorokine's mother of corruption of a minor, in revenge for her refusal to help break Sorokine's relationship with Bourla – see note 318 below), De Beauvoir began working for radio as a features producer, making a series of programmes reconstructing traditional festivals from the Middle Ages to the present (see *The Prime of Life*, p.540).

[317]Olga had played the part of Electra in Dullin's production of *The Flies* at the Théâtre Sarah Bernhardt: see *The Prime of Life*, pp.538-9.

Annemasse, from where I hope they'll send them on to us. Apart from that, we had a very good journey and I slept till morning. The weather was very grey during the last part of the journey, and also at Cluses where we got out – it looked really dismal. The train was full of the most opulent skiers: fur coats and sheepskin jackets. The first places to be booked in these particular trains are the sleeping berths, then the first-class seats, and lastly the third-class. So we had 4 moneybags with us, who were travelling third because there were no sleeping berths – they were revolting. The people in the coach were revolting too. It was a dreadful coach: we waited to get off from 12.30 to 1.30, and after that we had a 4-hour journey. But Bost had a seat – with me on his knees – and it was a front one and the road was pretty, so it wasn't unpleasant. Especially as we had the pleasure of gradually seeing the sky turn clear blue. Then, in a village 5 km away from Morzine, we saw the first slopes with their skiers and were really greedy for the next day to come. At Morzine, we at once found beds at the Soleil Levant. It's a decent hotel, the same type as those ones at Argentières or Megève, quite warm, and you can eat very decently there, with white coffee in the morning and English tea for 10 F. We settled ourselves in, then took a stroll round the village – which is tiny and absolutely empty. We bought a few cakes, which are neither very expensive nor very good; we shan't be ruining ourselves on food, since the meals with a bit of extra bread will be plenty for us. After dinner I read *La Société Française au XVIIIme* for a while – it's very enjoyable – and by 9 in the evening we were asleep in beautifully soft, warm beds.

This morning we rose at 7.30. By 8 there was already a blue sky and blazing sun, and we went to practise near the cable-car. I was scared to death at first, but it came back gradually. At about 10, the cable-car took us up to Plenay at 1600 m. There's a superb view up there and a scorching sun. We were in seventh heaven. However, a big disappointment awaited us. It hasn't snowed for ages and the runs are iced over. Except for very expert types who go down the Olympic Run in 3 minutes, nobody attempts them, so that the cable-cars going down at 5 are jam-packed. It's like at Chamonix – and really depressing. We're calling fervently for snow. We tried taking Run 19 – the one for beginners where Bourla[318] took Sorokine – but after a few snowfields where going down was easy it became impassable, so we climbed back up feeling foolish. We missed the noon cable-car by a whisker, so had

---

[318]Bourla was a young Spanish Jew, a former pupil of Sartre's at the Lycée Pasteur, who had been living with Sorokine since 1942. He was arrested and killed by the Nazis in the spring of 1944 (see *The Prime of Life*, pp.528 and 577-8).

lunch in the hotel up on top: a fantastically beautiful hotel – rather like that one on the Col de Voza – but where board and lodging costs 250 F., alas! We had a very good lunch, played a few games of backgammon, then spent the afternoon getting all worked up. Bost's appalled and thinks we're useless, but I think it wasn't so bad for the first day. Tomorrow we're taking a private lesson, then we'll try and join a class. We've just come in and had a cup of tea. I think it'll all go swimmingly so far as money's concerned, even though the lessons are so dear (160 F. for two). If we can take suitable classes instead of private lessons, then we're saved. Morzine itself's a bit shut in – not very sunny and with no beautiful ski slopes – but up on top it's superb. Everything would be perfect if it would only snow, because if we can't do any runs things will be much less fun.

There, my dear little one. I'll write again in two days' time. Do write too. It's obvious I shan't do any work here. It's not that I'm very exhausted, but I totally lack any desire. Anyway, we get in at 5.30 and have dinner at 7, so the time's all chopped up.

Goodbye, my dear love. This is a really lovely present you've given me. I'm so happy and love you with all my might.

Your Beaver

M. Sartre
Hotel de la Louisiane
60 Rue de Seine
Paris 6

[Morzine, Haute-Savoie]

Saturday [23 January 1944]

Most dear little being

I'm enjoying myself more and more. I'm fantastically happy to be here. I'm eating well and sleep ten hours a night, to the point where this morning I woke up at 7 gorged with sleep and read in bed. Bost's a good companion and the weather's wonderful, with a magnificent sun.

[...]

I've read the *D'Holbach* with some enjoyment, but that poor Naville's[319] an idiot – like d'Holbach himself. You have a set of people

---

[319]Pierre Naville (1904-   ), sociologist and political writer, had published his *Paul Thiry d'Holbach et la Philosophie Scientifique au XVIIIe Siècle* in 1943.

there who thought they were wildly modern, but who seem more outdated than the alchemists of the Middle Ages. I was outraged at several points, especially by that poor wretch Naville, who hasn't a clue about anything. I'm finding the War of Secession incredibly interesting. There you are, my dear little one, I dream of nothing any more except uphill and downhill christies – and I'd give the Prix Renaudot to be able to do a downhill christie. It seems almost strange to me to think how at the same time our life in Paris is continuing through you. The other night I dreamed, to my great distress, that I was no longer myself: I could no longer manage to recognize myself, because my life was devoid of you. I'm wonderfully well off for money, especially as we don't splash out on anything – neither cakes nor brioches, just tea at 6, and in the morning after skiing a white wine in the sun at a little bar beside the run. We're as happy as it's possible to be. Next year, do come, my dear love, I'd so like to see your diligent little blue silhouette on the slopes. I love you with all my might. I'll be quite overcome when I see you again. I kiss and hug you with all my might, my dear little absolute, happiness of my life, my other self.

Your charming Beaver

[. . .]

[Morzine, Haute-Savoie]

Wednesday [27 January 1944]

Most dear little being

The hotel's in turmoil, and Bost and I are as excited as the rest. An hour ago, at 6.30 in the evening, three fellows from the Maquis came into the hotel with pistols in their hands, asking for a certain Odette – a smart, disagreeable young holidaymaker who eats at the table next to ours, and who was apparently a member of the Gestapo. They grabbed a poor silly young girl who'd struck up a friendship with Odette in the last few days, they made her go up to her room, they examined her papers – very politely – then they came back down to the foyer again, where they drank an apéritif while awaiting Odette. The landlord insisted on offering them the apéritif gratis – all the people in the hotel were full of sympathy for them and they've now gone to wait for Odette outside the door. Dinner's now over, but she hasn't come back. It was a strange dinner, with all eyes fixed upon that empty table. Apparently everyone in the hotel knew what the girl was up to, as she has already informed on a lot of fellows. We'd noticed how sociable she was with everybody, but it seemed like mere casual flirting. Apart from that, she went to church and looked like a girl from a respectable family. They said they were going to shoot her, and no one – not even her girl friend of a week's standing – voiced the idea of warning her. Spread this story around, because I'm too lazy to write it all over again to Sorokine.

This afternoon I also saw two Teutons in uniform, solemnly practising their skiing on the slopes – it was quite as surprising as a Moslem woman on a bicycle.

Apart from this, I've really nothing to tell. Yesterday I had your Wednesday letter and that cheered me up for the whole day. It was snowing and I've got a frightful cold, so I stayed in bed reading all morning. Luckily in the afternoon the snow stopped falling, and we were able to make two descents on marvellously soft runs. This morning there was no sun, but splendid snow, and we made 5 descents in the course of the day, including the Olympic Run twice. Bost's beginning to ski really well. As for me, I manage well enough for it to be enjoyable. Taking everything into account (and it is in fact precisely a question of accounts), we're leaving on *Tuesday*. So I'll be in Paris on *Wednesday morning*. I'll be at the Flore at midday, and if you can miss school I'll certainly be at the hotel at 8 in the morning. At any rate, leave me a note at the hotel and keep a long day free for me. I'm so happy to be seeing you again that I'm not even sad not to be staying till Thursday.

I had a letter from Sorokine, who loathes *The Blood of Others*[320] but for very silly reasons – essentially because it bores her. This is my last letter, and I'm going to give it to some people who are going back to Paris tomorrow. I hope you'll get it quite quickly. Till Wednesday, my love. I love you so intensely. I really want to see you again.

Your charming Beaver

[Morzine, Haute-Savoie]

Friday [29 January 1944]

Most dear little being

Well, after taking everything into account again, we're not leaving till Thursday – especially since I foolishly strained my knee yesterday during my last descent. I had to rest today and probably won't be skiing

---

[320]Written between 1941 and 1943, De Beauvoir's novel was to be published only in 1945 when wartime censorship ended.

tomorrow either, so I'd like to make up for that a bit. It's on Friday morning, then, that we'll be meeting – and this time it's final. This is the letter that counts, even if you receive it before the other one.

I told you about Wednesday evening's adventure. The girl didn't return and there can be no doubt of her fate. For two meals her table remained empty – with a bottle of Phosphatine awaiting her – but then they replaced her with a bearded gentleman and nobody speaks of her any longer. But that wasn't all. Yesterday morning the whole resort was in turmoil because the maquisards, coming as they did on Wednesday in a van, had cut the telephone line and burgled the big ski store where we usually leave our own skis to be waxed in the morning. Luckily we'd brought ours in, but there were at least fifty skiers who'd been robbed and they'd taken all the store owners' money. Actually, the people didn't really hold it against them – except for the boss's wife, who'd been gagged and terrorized. The others, the winter visitors, are so rich that a pair of skis more or less doesn't matter to them. I didn't ski well yesterday. I was tired, and the snow was dreadfully bad – heavy and wet. In the afternoon, there was the lady champion of France giving an exhibition. She was agreeable to watch, and all the instructors showed off afterwards with slaloms and dangerous jumps, amid hurrahs and boos. It's just like one big family: everybody knows each other, watches each other work, and gives each other advice – it's not unpleasant. In the evening I wanted to do a run all the same, but in that soft snow I had an idiotic fall. I was able to finish the run, however, and even go to the post office, where I got your letter. I *truly* did write to Youki, my dear little one. Moreover, I'm *outraged* that they should allow themselves to demand another two scripts from you. Bost is outraged too – but at you: he says you let yourself be treated like a doormat. In the evening my knee swelled up like a melon, so I had to stay in bed this morning. My window was open over a great snowy landscape and I could feel the sun burning me. I wasn't too glum, because the snow today was frozen and it wasn't possible to go down any of the runs. A masseur gave me a vigorous massage, and by the afternoon I was able to walk – now it hardly hurts at all. Apparently there were 15 sprains or strains yesterday alone, not to mention the other days.

Goodbye, my love – if you were here I'd be so very happy. Till Friday. I kiss you with all my might.

Your charming Beaver

🦋 1945

[Vichy]

Thursday 26 July [1945]

My dear love

You should know at once that I've lost nothing of my youth, and that you've presented me with a very fine bike. I've just spent a splendidly agreeable week. So agreeable, in fact, that today – in this big Vichy café where I've ended up – I feel a certain vague melancholy.

Well, I caught my train last Wednesday morning, had no trouble finding a seat and made an uneventful journey by that little stopping train as far as Tours, where I arrived exactly on time: at 1.30. There, everything started off well. My bicycle was waiting obediently for me at the station, and so was Vitold – with his new Portuguese shirt,[321] an eight-day beard that made him look like a true half-starved Russian, and a broad smile. He took me to lunch – a very bad one – and didn't seem too bothered by the idea that Badel[322] wasn't planning to audition until 15 October. On the other hand, he was shattered by the fact that within the space of two days he'd lost a superb trench-coat and a pair of sandals; also by the fact that his inner tube was riddled with punctures. We wandered all round Tours, in overpowering heat, trying to get the wretched object repaired. Tours was even more gloomy than on that day we went there with Bost.[323] But I was poetic, because Tours is full of tender memories connected with you, and because I was glad to have met up with Vitold again – he has a certain 'presence', as people say, which charms me at once. So we wandered about till 7, when I suggested going to St Avertin. He took me there on the luggage-rack of my bicycle. We had dinner at the water's edge, did some drinking, and went boating on the Cher – it was charming. Next morning his tyre had been repaired, so we left for Loches, then proceeded to the banks of the Creuse and the Plateau de Millevaches – all very pretty scenery. On the Plateau de Millevaches, Vitold had a lengthy bout of irresoluteness, lasting for more than two hours, the outcome of which – after a plethora of cables and letters – was a decision to go to Vichy and see his mother. So we

---

[321]From 27 February until the beginning of April in this same year of 1945, De Beauvoir had visited Spain and Portugal, from where she had brought presents for all those near and dear to her. Relatively untouched by the War, Portugal (where Poupette and Lionel were living) struck her as a land of plenty: see *Force of Circumstance*, pp.25-8.

[322]Manager of the Vieux Colombier theatre, who had promised to stage De Beauvoir's *Useless Mouths*. In the event this plan fell through, and the play was put on at the Théâtre des Carrefours in November 1945, in Michel Vitold's production.

[323]On a bicycle trip in the summer of 1942.

planned a route accordingly – pretty much the same one you and I followed, that time we had to get from the Limousin to the Massif Central. Altogether, we rode like that for a week. He's a splendid travelling companion, is Vitold. In the first place, he's an ace cyclist: he can do 250 km. in a day and climb any hill at 15 km. an hour, so he never gets tired of riding and gives me a shove on the hills. What's more, he has the patience of an angel, and he repairs everything skilfully and with a smile. We'd usually rise late, ride a bit in the morning, lunch as well as we could – never very well, but never very badly, with plenty of wine which is never in short supply in these parts – then we'd go bathing and sunbathing by the side of some stream, chat till evening, and get some more riding in before (and sometimes after) dinner. Then we'd spend charming evenings drinking and chatting. Once we slept outdoors, to indulge a whim on the part of Vitold who wanted to sample the open-air life, but we were rather cold. Another time we slept on benches in a café. The rest of the time we had rooms with twin beds, or a double bed – honi soit qui mal y pense. I spent an enjoyable time with him. He has a thoroughly agreeable way of appreciating people and things; of loving life and loving himself. He adores himself – he's a true Russian – and I used to find it charming to look at him looking at himself anxiously in mirrors, to see whether he'd put on weight. Yesterday evening at Riom we spent a very poetic evening, because a film club was putting on a festival of American comedies: there was Charlie Chaplin in the army, a Harold Lloyd, a quite charming old Laurel (without Hardy), and some cartoons: coming across this was quite a surprise. And then this morning we lit out for Vichy. He's staying there until the morning of the day after tomorrow, and I'm going to stay there too in order to work on my play, about which he has made a lot of very pertinent comments and which I must get into shape before we separate. So I'm going to spend this afternoon and the whole day tomorrow working in this ridiculous town. Then he'll go back to Paris, to get ready for the rehearsals; he's not likely to get started before the 5th or 6th, so I'll return on the *morning of the 8th*, as agreed, in order to see you. I haven't yet decided where to spend those two solitary days. I'll add a P.S. to tell you where to write to me, as soon as I've made my plans. I've easily found places to eat and sleep here, and the cafés have good drinks – but how dreary and ugly it is! Incidentally, Vitold told me (don't repeat this to your mother[324]) how he once worked for a Vichy druggist and, one year when the Célestins spring had dried up,

---

[324]Sartre's mother often took the waters at Vichy.

he used to go after dark with a tarpaulin-covered lorry and pour tons and tons of acid into the spring. I realize now that a glass of water may be enough to polish a man off, the day some druggist has overdone things a bit.

My own little one, I'm really bothered by having no news of you – either I'll go to Limoges after all, or I'll have the letter forwarded. Did you have an enjoyable time too in the Midi?[325] You're still there as I write, but I can't picture your life at all. I'd so like to spend a long while alone with you, and do agreeable things with you. I thought of you with love on the roads. There are lots of places I passed through which we'd passed through together, and I was really moved by seeing them again.

Goodbye, my dear love. I'll go and wander round this filthy town a bit more, then work. I'm rather distraught, because something that was very agreeable is coming to an end. Also (making all due allowances) Vichy really is – like Washington[326] – the ideal kind of gloomy town for such little travails of the heart.

I'll add a P.S. this evening. I hug and kiss you.

Your charming Beaver

Having found guidebooks and maps, I've taken some decisions. I'll be at *St Étienne* on the 30th, and return there 4 or 5 days later. Write me a little letter there.

27 July [1945]

I'm adding a little postscript, since I didn't mail the letter yesterday. I feel very sprightly today, for – as I have a well-formed character – I find it enjoyable now to set off on a little journey all alone. Yesterday I found some guidebooks and maps, and I worked out a route in the direction of the Cévennes. Yesterday afternoon I worked. And after dinner I went with Vitold to one of the bistros on the banks of the Allier. We spent a delightful evening – I really like him very much, he touches me. There were lights under the green canopy and boats on the water, I wonder if you used to frequent that kind of place when you were in Vichy? I dined badly and slept well in the bleak hotel I managed to pick out near the station. And I've worked all day. I finished everything I meant to finish.

---

[325]Sartre was on holiday there with his mother – who had been a widow since winter.
[326]De Beauvoir was here going by Sartre's own account of Washington, which he had visited during a first trip to the United States with a group of French journalists in January 1945.

Then I wrote a few letters. I'm going to see Vitold again in a little while, to bid him farewell. But now I'm pleased to be on my own again. I want to read and work a bit – perhaps dream about another play, for example. Goodbye, my dear love. In about ten days I'll be seeing you again. I'll kiss you properly. When I woke this morning, after a night's sleep without thinking of you, I suddenly remembered that you existed and joy flooded into my heart.

Your charming Beaver

[Paris]
Thursday evening 13 December [1945]
Dearest little one,

It seems funny to be writing to you. It's almost like a play in which I can't quite believe – because you're still so close, barely 5 hours away from me, and I could easily imagine you coming back in an hour or so and slipping into the bed in your little blue pyjamas. But then, nothing of the kind: I'll remain on my own here with the footwarmer, while you're already two months distant – it's hard to contemplate.[327] If you came back in an hour, I'd tell you about my evening – and that's why I'm writing so quickly. I'm a bit upset, and I don't want to go up and see Sorokine[328] or sleep, just to talk to you. I'm upset about Bianca Bienenfeld. I took her to the Golfe-Juan – Badel was there with Gaby Sylvia at one table, the fair Sumerville with Arbessier at the table opposite – and we stayed there talking till midnight. She moved me – and filled me with remorse – because she's suffering from an intense and dreadful attack of neurasthenia, and it's our fault I think. It's the very indirect, but profound, after-shock of the business between her and us. She's the only person to whom we've really done harm, but we have harmed her. What's very interesting is the fact that her attack has a multiple significance. It's the metaphysical drama of *Being and Nothingness*:[329] an intense awareness of nothingness, the mirage of the For-others, the fascination of the objective, and the knowledge of

---

[327]Sartre was about to set off to the United States again, this time aboard a Liberty Ship.
[328]Sorokine was now living in the same hotel as De Beauvoir – the Hôtel de la Louisiane – and was engaged to an American G.I., Ivan Moffat, whom she was preparing to join in California.
[329]*Being and Nothingness*, begun during Sartre's captivity and completed in November 1942, had been published in 1943.

subjectivity and its gratuitousness. And it's also, psychologically, Bienenfeld's reflection upon what might be called her character: her masochism (which she discovered with horror while reading *Being and Nothingness*); her assertive, harsh, almost unattractive side, of which she's clearly aware. It's also her situation: married, tied down, settled into the tedium of adult life with a delayed-action crisis of youth; her situation as a student, in contradiction with her settled existence; her lack of either an adult project or an adolescent one. And then, there's a physiological dimension: headaches, fatigue, etc. She weeps all the time – she wept three times during the dinner, and she weeps at home when she has to read a book or go to the kitchen to eat. Out of all this, what's primary? In any case, it takes the form of a comparison with us: nothingness in relation to us; need of me, of a prop, etc. She's terribly unhappy, and extremely lucid without her lucidity getting her anywhere. At times, she really looked quite mad – bottling things up, anxious, but with moments of repressed tenderness and mute appeals that tore at my heartstrings. It's important to see a lot of her, and I'm going to try because I'm filled with remorse. I'm describing this to you very badly, but I know you'd have been very upset and full of sympathy for her, because she was moving and even pathetic that evening, thanks to that rationalism and taste for seriousness that suddenly assumed the mask of madness, that complete and painful authenticity under the guise of the inauthentic. And then, that kind of reasonable, controlled, intelligent psychosis is far more appealing – and almost contagious – than the gross excesses of someone like Violette Leduc,[330] or of Russian women in general. It strikes me as more serious too, and I'm worried. I don't think she'll go mad. But I am afraid of her growing resigned. On the other hand, if she saves herself by relapsing into inauthenticity, that's lousy. In the end, I came home almost thinking how I was going to talk to you about it all – and even now I can scarcely believe that it's all going to be engulfed; that I'm going to start living things that will be engulfed without being shared with you. Goodbye, little one, dear beloved little one. You're in the train, and you're dozing at Wanda's side. As for me, I'm going to sleep. I haven't begun to be separated from you, and even as I write this letter I don't yet believe it.

---

[330]De Beauvoir had met the novelist Violette Leduc through a mutual friend in a cinema queue in the autumn of 1945 (see *Force of Circumstance*, p.19) and was to befriend (and sometimes support) her until the publication of *La Bâtarde* in 1964 brought her success. Leduc left Paris for good a year later, and died of cancer in 1972.

Saturday morning

Dearest little one. Now I've really begun to feel your departure. It's especially in the morning on waking that it causes me a little anguish. After that, the days are full and pleasant, especially as Charles V[331] is at last beginning to yield. I've done all those little things for you, and I'm waiting for Rouleau's answer.[332] I'm pleased because Sorokine has seen a doctor, who told her everything was going just fine.[333] So I'll be able to go off with an easy mind – but nothing new for the time being on that front.[334] Yesterday morning I worked at the Flore, had lunch with mother, saw Sorokine, and worked at the Pont Royal – which was ever so comfortable. Then I went to the *Temps Modernes*,[335] where there was a mad rush on. I dealt with all the visitors, and in the evening dined with Bost at the Golfe-Juan. We had a long explanation (in which, of course, he didn't explain anything at all): I told him at length all about his behaviour in general and towards me in particular. He was devastated – but in a way pleased, because it was a proof of affection on my part. He maintains that what weighs upon him is to a great extent the same thing that weighs on Sorokine or Poupette. He doesn't have the impression he's got any real place in a life where you are. He even went so far as to chuck away letters he wrote to me on the boat – as being pointless. That doesn't explain everything, though. All in all he was full of good will and very sweet, and I'm glad we had a talk, though it doesn't change anything. This morning I worked and finished correcting your lecture[336] at the Flore. I'm expecting Vitold for lunch. You must be on the open sea by now. That means you haven't yet abandoned me entirely – I can still feel you half in France, even though the other half is turned towards America. When you're there, I think I'll be in Tunis, so it will be less painful to let you go. There you are, little one. It's mild, grey and dreary and I don't feel bad at all. I

---

[331]One of the protagonists of *All Men Are Mortal*.

[332]Raymond Rouleau, actor-director, had produced Sartre's *Huis Clos* (translated into English as *No Exit*) at the Vieux Colombier in June 1944. The reference here is to the beginning of laborious negotiations for the staging of Sartre's new play, *Men Without Shadows*, in the course of which first Rouleau, then Hébertot, then Beer were to withdraw.

[333]She was pregnant.

[334]The Alliance Française had invited De Beauvoir to give some lectures at Tunis and Algiers, but it was still very hard at this time to get a berth on a boat or plane.

[335]The journal *Les Temps Modernes* had been launched by Sartre in October 1945, with Aron, De Beauvoir, Michel Leiris, Merleau-Ponty, Albert Ollivier and Paulhan on the editorial board.

[336]'Existentialism and Humanism'.

telephoned to Aron,[337] who greeted my request with a degree of favour. I'll keep you posted. Blanket of silence about you in the weeklies these past couple of days – just a report on my lecture with a caricature (in *Terre des Hommes*),[338] and a nice interview by Beaufret on existentialism in *Le Monde*. I'll be sure to keep everything for you.

Wednesday

Dearest little one, my love. Now I do feel that you've left. Yet I'm just as much united with you as when you were here – I haven't lost you at all. Beside my bed I've two photos of you: one with snow on your shoulders, and the other that I like so much where you're all tousled in the aeroplane.[339] I find you there each time I wake up, so I start the day with you. Today I'm at the Pont Royal – it's 2 o'clock and very peaceful. I feel very happy. I think about your beloved self, the work's going well, I'm working a lot and will soon have finished Charles V – and I spent a marvellous evening with Camus. I say marvellous because, as I like him enormously, it bowled me over that he should be so affectionate, and that we should be so intimate and talk so easily. We had dinner Chez Lipp, drank at the Pont Royal, then took a bottle of champagne to the Louisiane and drank it till 3 in the morning. He talked a lot about himself – private life and literary life – in a way that touched me. And it made me want to write good things – it gave me a great thirst for life – that one can be such good friends with somebody for whom the same things count as for you. If everything works out well, we'll go and spend a fortnight winter-sporting in February – he seemed really to like the idea too.

Apart from that, on Saturday evening I saw Bost, for Sunday lunch your mother, and on Monday for two hours Violette Leduc – with whom things started off worldly and almost gay, only to end up in disaster. When she was leaving me at Place Pigalle, I thought she was

---

[337]Raymond Aron, a friend of Sartre since their days at the École Normale Supérieure and instrumental in steering him first towards meteorology for his military service, later towards phenomenology (and in helping him to spend a year in Berlin to study it in 1933-4), joined the editorial committee of *Les Temps Modernes* from the start, but was to resign less than a year later over differences on the Cold War.

[338]A lecture on the novel and metaphysics, first delivered in February 1945 to the students of the Catholic philosopher Gabriel Marcel and to be given on this occasion at the Club Maintenant. It was to be the basis for her April 1946 essay 'Littérature et métaphysique' in *Les Temps Modernes*. *Terre des Hommes*, a weekly founded by Herbart, lasted only a few months.

[339]The military plane that took Sartre to the United States on his first visit in January 1945.

about to pass out and she really did look crazy. She telephoned Nathalie Sarraute,[340] who couldn't face seeing her. On Monday evening I went with Bost to a dress rehearsal of *The Brothers Karamazov*. I really put my foot in it by saying to Mayenne Daste: 'This adaptation's appalling.'[341] Poor Oettly's beneath contempt – he plays Father Karamazov as M. Perrichon[342] – and Davy's unbearable. Casarès wonderful, Dufilho good, Vitold excellent – we congratulated him warmly and he was really pleased.

Yesterday I had lunch with Merleau-Ponty and on Monday with Genet.[343] Genet was very nice, no problems. M.Ponty told me that Magny's nursing a big grudge against us, because of the article – and because of the party as well. Apparently, an anonymous cyclist who just missed knocking Beaufret down in the street shouted at him: 'Hey! Clear off! Existentialist!', and on the radio even sports programmes start off with jokes about existentialism. However, nothing new about you or me in the weeklies.

The journal's going well – we've got the Russian article, Sarraute's translating the document, Hadjibelli[344] has given us a schizophrenic's diary, Beaufret and Mounin will be happy to contribute columns. Even No. 6 is almost under way. I'd like to do an editorial in No. 6 on objectivity. What do you think? Apparently my editorial in No. 3 has gone down very well, so M.Ponty and Camus tell me. Camus is asking me to do the essay on action I spoke to you about, for his series.[345] It would be put out along with some articles by me, by him perhaps, and by you if you like, on the subject of existentialism. I'm very much tempted, I could probably get down to it on holiday.

Practical matters: from Maurienne, I'll get either all the money or 100,000 F., with which I'll get by – so that's o.k.

About the play:[346] if you want the Ambassadeurs, Certes has written to tell me you'll have to see Bernstein.[347] Bernstein's in America.

---

[340]The novelist Nathalie Sarraute, a Russian Jew settled in Paris whose first book *Tropismes* had appeared in 1939, offered her services to *Les Temps Modernes* – as a writer and translator from Russian – shortly after it was launched. Sartre directed her to De Beauvoir, but the two women did not hit it off and Sarraute later claimed that De Beauvoir had seen her as a potential rival for Sartre's affections, to be headed off.

[341]The adaptation was by Dasté's father, Jacques Copeau.

[342]M. Perrichon: protagonist of a farcical comedy by Eugène Labiche (1860).

[343]The poet and prose writer Jean Genet became a friend of De Beauvoir and Sartre in May 1944 (see *The Prime of Life*, pp.579-81).

[344]A former pupil of Sartre.

[345]Camus edited a series of his own called *Esprit* for the publisher Gallimard.

[346]*Men Without Shadows.*

[347]Henry Bernstein (1876-1953) was a major playwright of the day in France.

Rouleau wrote to me saying he'd reply, but he hasn't done so. Hébertot doesn't want Vitold. I'll see to everything as best I can before leaving, and I'll also hand over anything I haven't concluded to Bost. As for getting four new copies typed out, that's difficult – it's impossible to find anything before Christmas.

Goodbye, dearest little love. This evening I'll add a P.S. to tell you whether I'm leaving or not, which is still hanging in the balance. I think you'll find this letter on your arrival. Write to me, my love, I want to remain closely united with you. I'm very happy with our life and with you. I want you to have a good stay over there. Think of me with satisfaction, as I think of you. I hug you tight, tight, in my arms and kiss your dear little face, which is there, all warm, in my heart. I love you, my little one.

Your charming Beaver

There. I'm very disappointed, as I shan't be leaving for Tunis till the beginning of January. Before the 15th, but I'm not sure exactly when – so write to me in Paris anyway. I'll probably leave for winter sports on Saturday evening, probably to Megève. I'm very pleased about that, and somewhat consoled.

Goodbye, my love.

[Megève]

Thursday 27 December [1945]

Dearest little yourself,

I wonder when you'll get this letter. New York seems such a long way away from here, yet I'd really like to feel I was talking to you and you could hear me. I think about you so intensely here: about you who left me a fortnight ago already, whom I shan't see for six weeks, and who's arriving in America where you have a quite alien life; and about you who used to ski with me in the old days, on these very slopes, in a little blue suit that I can still see as if it were yesterday. I'd so like to think that we'll come back here together some day, just the two of us on our own and perfectly happy. You know I wouldn't make you ski all day long, and that it's a fantastic place for working. I'm delighted to be here, I'm having one of the best times I've had this year, except that you're not with me.

[. . .]

Six years ago I was writing to you from here and it was wartime. It seems strange to remember that. In a sense, it seems much longer to me than six years. I feel somehow beyond all that, as though in a second life. I no longer really recognize either myself or the old world. Yet there are the memories – the memories with yourself, in that former life. But they have a strange effect, rather harrowing, because they're so little related to the present.

Goodbye, dearest love. I don't know where to tell you to write to me. To Paris perhaps, from where everything will be forwarded. I'll send a wire to the consulate as soon as I know that I'm leaving for Tunis. Be happy over there, and come back to me soon. You and I are as one, and I kiss you with all my might.

Your charming Beaver

🦫 1946

[Paris]

18 January [1946]

Most dear little being

Here I am back in Paris since this morning, having missed a first plane for Tunisia and anxious to catch the second if possible. I was terribly upset to be leaving the Idéal-Sport, the day before yesterday in the evening when I found the cable summoning me back. I felt a real little pang in my heart. But with my vice of always being satisfied, this morning I'm enjoying sitting at the Flore, with Begbeider and Erval and others prowling in the vicinity. I was above all happy to find a letter from you. There's only one as yet, but that's to be expected – apparently they take ten days to arrive. What an abrupt change of life! Yesterday at this hour I was still on my skis and making my descent towards Megève. Now I'm in town clothes, I've just had my hair done, and what's more I'm stunningly handsome because I've a magnificent complexion, all tanned and with my face all relaxed – which is quite out of keeping in Paris. Paris is icy, the hotel has no heating and apparently there's absolutely nothing to eat here. I certainly won't stay. If things don't work out for Tunisia, I'll go off again to the Mont d'Arbois.

I can't quite remember when I last wrote to you, a week ago probably. Life went on being wonderful there. I saw quite a lot of that little

Lefèvre-Pontalis.[348] He'd be quite overcome with emotion and gratitude each time I showed up to have lunch with them, and I used to get him to go up so we could ski together. We were planning to come back together on Saturday, and he was taking ski lessons in order to make a respectable descent towards St Gervais with me. He was frightfully disappointed when he saw me decamp yesterday. His wife looks like a fat sow and he's bored with her. I saw Salacrou[349] too, who's an old habitué of the Idéal-Sport. We had lunch together yesterday, just before I left. He's like a doddering old fool. On one of his first ski runs he fell on his 'liver', and now he has himself accompanied everywhere by a teacher. He's so cowardly that he's not going to Greece, where he has been invited, because he's scared of boarding a French plane. In my case, I'm at least going to board one – and I'm even choosing the plane rather than the boat – though I'll undoubtedly be scared on the way.[350]

So now you know what kind of life I led. Kos. decided to get onto her skis, and twice over she went down the Mont d'Arbois, escorted by Bost, quite slowly but almost without falling – she was beginning to enjoy it and was in a far better mood. But poor Bost told me that his life was really utterly, if not ruined, at least crushed by that existence with Kos., and that he didn't feel at all happy. And seeing them living side by side, I can understand him. I find her quite terrifying – and the nicer she's being, the more quietly terrifying she becomes. Wanda went on with her little old lady's life, with a few hours of skiing every now and then. She too would make her run without falling too much – but it would take her an hour and a half. Bost and I had a splendid day on Tuesday – we went to the Col de Voza. In other words, very early in the morning we made a run down to St Gervais, then took a little local train up to the pass. After that we skied down to Les Houches, on that run where you wrecked your knee. I was quite overcome remembering how we were two poor little beginners on that icy run. It was pretty hard on Tuesday, and Bost couldn't get over our courage. My little one, I'd so like to go off alone with you again – skiing, travelling, or anywhere – I feel quite bursting with tenderness for you. After that, Bost and I had lunch in one of the beautiful hotels at the pass – which we'd regained by cable-car – then we skied down to St Gervais through magnificent fields of fresh snow. There was bright sunlight and in the evening an extraordinary moonlight, with a literally violet sky and green mountains. It was when we reached home that I found the telegram

---

[348] A former pupil of Sartre and friend of Bourla, a psychoanalyst.
[349] Armand Salacrou (1899-1989), one of the main French playwrights of the day.
[350] De Beauvoir had never previously travelled by plane.

summoning me back to Paris, if I didn't want to miss the second plane. I was very upset that evening – by my grief at leaving, my hope of Tunisia, and my fear it might fall through. I had to drink a lot of little shots of marc to drown my joy and my sorrow – the hotel had some fantastic marcs and kirsches. Yesterday I made one last melancholy run, then had lunch with Salacrou, who told me how at his dress-rehearsal Toulouse threw up in Dullin's box, and all Dullin could think about was how to prevent the people who'd come to congratulate him from coming in. Salacrou's entertaining for an hour, albeit instantly unlikeable. After that, Bost and Kos. accompanied me to the cable-car and I plunged with sinking heart into the valley. A taxi took me to Le Fayet, where I got a nice corner seat with no trouble. I slept all night, alighted at 7 in the morning, spent some time with Sorokine – who seems in a good state – then went first to the hairdresser and afterwards to the Flore, where I'm now writing to you and where everybody, of course, began talking to me about the journal and countless other things. Nothing new in the weeklies. I'd promised Merleau-Ponty an editorial for No. 6, but I feel empty, incapable of thinking or writing the tiniest article. The novel is going all right because it's non-topical, and can be written in the wilds, but philosophical discussions, polemics and so on really go clean out of my mind there. I don't know how I'll manage to get back into the swing of things for at least a week.

My little one, I was amazingly pleased to get your letter. I think the absence of your article will be catastrophic for the journal, but I do understand how you weren't able to write anything on that boat. Really, you're a horrible termite, a lobster, an absurd insect! Have you at least written to J. Audry? You really must, otherwise you're an ugly brute – don't forget to do it!

I've also read a well-disposed article on you by M. André Lévy in *Elle*; and I've seen a few items, and a few cartoons and photos, on you and me. But nothing of significance.

Did you know I'm really rather famous too? The good lady from the Idéal-Sport asked Kos.: 'Is she very well known, that Mlle de Beauvoir? Customers keep coming and asking me if that's really her. It's the same as with M. Salacrou . . .'

You should know that Rouleau no longer controls the Oeuvre. Beer[351] has won his lawsuit, and has already asked me whether I have any manuscripts by you or by me. Moreover, Vitold told me on the telephone that he'd started negotiations with Beer – I'm seeing him

---

[351]Lucien Beer, manager of the Théâtre de l'Oeuvre.

shortly (Vitold) and then I'll have more details. I think it's going to work out. I'll tell you in a P.S.

Do you know what Badel did? As Vilar[352] didn't want *Murder*[353] to be revived in place of *Voices*, Badel revived it without mentioning the producer. Vilar sued him for theft of his production. And Rouleau has promised to give Badel the production of *The Petrified Forest*.[354]

No Exit[355] has been sold to an Italian cinema company – a cheque awaits you. There wasn't much mail for you, and not much of interest. I'll call in at the journal shortly and give you any news.

19 January

I haven't seen Beer yet – I'm seeing him this evening. Apparently he likes the play and is especially impressed by Vitold, who's recommending it to him. Rouleau doesn't like it, finding it 'impossible to act'. I'll tell you the result of the interview this evening. I spent the day at the journal. Things are going all right – Merleau-Ponty has been incredibly energetic and we've got lots of texts. Literature's beginning to be in rather short supply, and after No. 7 we'll have to take stock, but documents and reports are flooding in. We've finally received the 'St Just', and an article by Paulhan on language, the article on Russian criticism, etc. You've got some quite amusing mail at the journal, and so have I. I answered the most urgent things and am keeping everything carefully.

My first day in Paris made a strange impression on me. I saw Vitold, who was angelically nice and so happy to see me that I felt quite touched. I'm having lunch with him this morning – he has broken with Loleh, or rather she has with him, and he's quite distraught. I saw Sorokine, who was very sweet and looking well. She'll go off at the beginning of February if I can find 40,000 F. between now and Monday (I've lent Bost 40,000, and although you have a pile of cheques, they're impossible to cash in your absence). So I'm looking for the 40,000 F. – and I'll find them, because she really wants to leave and I want her to leave too (she'll pay it back from America anyway, since Moffat earns lots of money; he simply can't send any that quickly). I briefly saw Leiris and the good sculptor,[356] Scipion,[357] Astruc,[358] and above all Merleau-

---

[352]Jean Vilar (1912-71), actor and theatrical producer, a former pupil of Dullin.
[353]T.S. Eliot's *Murder in the Cathedral*.
[354]By Robert Sherwood (1935).
[355]See note 332 above.
[356]Giacometti (see note 282 above).
[357]A satirist friend of Bost.
[358]Alexandre Astruc (1923-   ), the film director, who also scripted Sartre's *La Putain Respectueuse*.

Ponty at length at the journal – which I left carrying a huge pile of manuscripts that I've conscientiously read and filed this morning. I'll do the page make-up of No. 5 before I leave, and No. 6 when I get back. I've been caught up again somewhat by the journal, your play, and the spirit of enterprise – but I'm simultaneously thinking of leaving in three days' time. I don't feel settled. I'd really like to live like that: 4 or 5 days a month of fast work and seeing people in Paris, then rest and withdrawal and real work.

I've just caught sight of Claude Roy:[359] apparently he's becoming an existentialist and his wife is reading *Being and Nothingness* admiringly.

Evening

I've just seen Beer. Things aren't going well, because Rouleau's a swine. To annoy Beer – and probably Vitold too – because he's angry that you haven't entrusted the production to him (I presume), he's *against* Beer putting the play on. And as he still has rights over the theatre (the lawsuit hasn't been completely settled yet, and there's a sequestration order or something), nothing can be done against him. He finds the play too hard. Beer says he might perhaps give way if the torture scene was cut out, but even that's not certain. Now, it's possible that in a month Beer will have won his lawsuit, and then he'll take the play at once – he's delighted with the play and at working with Vitold. It's also possible that if you yourself see Rouleau, he won't dare prevent you from being staged at the Oeuvre. But what's a pity is the fact that, in the absence of a firm reply, Cuny's going to agree to act in *Of Mice and Men*[360] for Hébertot in April – in other words, drop your play. Moreover, everyone tells me Bernstein won't let you have the Ambassadeurs; and Nagel hasn't found a theatre – the St Georges isn't available. The only thing left to do is await your return and try to persuade Rouleau. I'm sorry it isn't working out better. Old Beer seems very nice, and is opening the doors of his theatre to me, since he liked *Useless Mouths* a lot.[361] I worked on the journal with Merleau-Ponty – it really does seem to be going well.

---

[359]Claude Roy (1915-   ), pseudonym of C. Orland, poet and prolific essayist – on travel, love, painting, theatre, music, etc. – who at this time was a Communist. Always maintaining friendly relations with De Beauvoir and Sartre, he was the lover of Évelyne Rey before her relationship with Sartre (see note 517 below).
[360]Adaptation of John Steinbeck's novel (1937).
[361]Written in the autumn of 1942, De Beauvoir's *Useless Mouths* had been staged (by Vitold) only in December 1945.

Here's a little cartoon that Pascal gave me proudly this morning. It's still going on, as you can see.

I learn that you gave a lecture in New York which made a big splash. I'd like to know more about it.

Goodbye, little best beloved. Write to me. I feel very close to you in all these activities, and each is a little act of love. I kiss and hug you, and hug you . . .

Your charming Beaver

[Paris]

Thursday 25 January [1946]

Most dear little one, my love

No letter from you! I can't believe that you can be such a bad little one, you who are such a nice yourself, and I hope to find something at Tunis – I'll rush to the post office tomorrow. I'm writing this with jubilation, since I'm beginning to believe I really am leaving this evening. There have been a whole load of setbacks – plane cancelled, papers lost, etc. – but finally I have to take the train to Marseilles at 7, get off at Pas-des-Lanciers, and embark on a civilian plane – which is pleasanter and less dangerous than the military ones. I'll stay there for a month even if you come back earlier, because I do after all want to take advantage of this trip. Good things are happening to me. *Useless Mouths* is being staged in Prague in May, and I'm going to be invited there; given the friendship the Czechs have for us, I hope we'll go together. And then the Alliance Française has *promised* to send me to America and *Mexico* for at least three months, as soon as October comes. My heart beats faster at the thought. What's more we've just had 300,000 F. out of the blue – Nagel has sold *No Exit* to an Italian firm. It's better not even to think of the taxes you'll have to pay on it, but I managed at least to extract the 50,000 F. I needed to put aside in case Sorokine leaves. That doesn't seem really to be working out, but she's gentle and nice and she's blooming – as is the child.

Regarding yourself, you can't imagine the exertions I'm making. I've seen Beer three times, and Cuny too. Yesterday I saw Beer with Vitold: he was no longer talking about Rouleau's opposition (he's an old liar, and none too nice himself), and was willing to stage the play. If he does so, however, it would have to be put on in April, which would make it necessary to begin rehearsals at the beginning of February. But Vitold can't work for more than ten days without you, so that your return is necessary by 15 February at the latest. And just when that seemed more or less fixed – a coup de théâtre! He comes out with the name of an actress he has in mind for the role of Lucie (though he'd been told about Wanda). We argued, and now the matter's pending, and I don't know whether he'll accept it with Wanda or whether he'll refuse. Hébertot suggests putting on the play, but alternating it with *Of Mice and Men* – which is unacceptable. Another problem is that Vitold probably won't be free to *act* in April, because of *Karamazov*. All in all, it's hardly possible to decide anything before your return. I think that in September you could place the play at will, but with April there are a great many problems. Chauffard[362] has read it and finds it *excellent*. Like Bost, Lefèvre-Pontalis and myself, however, he finds that the relationship to the Cause – the fine balance between the gratuitous and the objective – is not brought out properly, either at the beginning or in the final scene (which Vitold also thinks doesn't quite come off, and I think that's true). Chauffard thinks it will cause a scandal. At all events, it's important that you should have weighed up carefully the meaning of any such scandal, so that it isn't based on misunderstandings. Vitold is also afraid that the choice of Caussimon may accentuate the Grand Guignol aspect:[363] he'd like the militiamen to have perfectly normal faces – which strikes me as correct. Judging by such conversation as I've had with Cuny, he struck me as a prize booby, and thoroughly disagreeable in his solemn pretentiousness.

Long and very funny article by Scipion in *Action* about the Flore – the waiters are very agitated. Features on existentialism pretty well everywhere. Always photographs, interviews, and so on. I refuse everything, but one American journalist did nevertheless take my photo just now in the Flore.

The 4th issue of *T.M.* is finally printed, but not yet distributed. I think No.s 5 and 6 will be very good. Merleau-Ponty has asked me for an editorial for 6, and I've done a little article – definitely more interesting than my lecture – on 'Metaphysics and the Novel'[364]; but it's not finished and I'll have to complete it in Tunis. I've had a lot of trouble with that Gorrély, from whom you'd imprudently commissioned a huge article on Russian literature (objective criticism). He has handed me 50 pages devoid of interest and is promising another 50. I refused as best I could, by saying it was necessary to wait for your return before a

---

[362] Actor and playwright, a former pupil of Sartre.
[363] Grand Guignol: exaggerated acting of the kind seen at the Théâtre du Grand Guignol in Paris, specializing in crude representations of horror and violence.
[364] See note 338 above.

decision could be made. You'll have to sort things out yourself – he was already furious. Apart from that, we've lots of good texts – it's going fine. Kanapa has done an article in which he attacks you on the plane of philosophy of history. Actually, it's mainly me he's attacking, and in Tunis I want to write a long article about an ethics of finitude: about action and finitude, against their myth of the future and progress. I've recovered a great deal of intellectual vivacity since I've been here. It's funny – it'll all probably melt away again in the sun. But I'm glad to be leaving. Paris exudes the most unbearable tedium. It's not light till 9, and there's no electricity; all the bars close at 10; the people are dismal; and it's cold. When I get back, you'll be there and that will change everything – but at least I shan't have spent this month here.

Now that I'm leaving, I actually find that this week in Paris hasn't been unpleasant. Unfortunately, I've barely seen Camus. I did see the Sculptor, dejected because Isabelle has run off with Leibowitz (!),[365] who has cleared out the family coffers. Saw the Leirises, sweet but boring. Maheu, very affectionate and nice, who has again promised some articles. Above all I've seen Merleau-Ponty, because we were working together at the journal. I spent one gloomy evening with Bienenfeld. She's having herself psychoanalysed by Paule, and says that it's horribly unpleasant, which proves that it's pretty serious. She was furious because I hadn't written to her from Megève (partly because, in the constant belief that I was going back next day, I wasn't writing to anyone). She was very hostile, and attacked you with malevolent, stupid vehemence. I think she's going to join the Communist Party, and that's the best thing for her to do.

There was a reading of Tzara's *La Fuite* at the Vieux Colombier. Done before an audience of 'Seated Ones'[366] all wearing decorations, it was a disaster: deathly boredom and sniggers. I didn't go, naturally – but Giacometti told me all about it. Even Leiris was shaken by it, and thought the play was bad. I congratulated myself on my firmness of judgement, and find the end of the Leiris episode pretty juicy.[367]

My little one, write to me at Tunis poste restante. I'll get the letters forwarded on. And *cable me* as soon as you know more or less the date of your return. I'll make my arrangements accordingly. If you return

---

[365]René Leibowitz, a musicologist and composer, whom she had known since 1945 and to whose book *L'Artiste et sa Conscience* Sartre wrote a preface in 1950.
[366]Allusion to the poem *Les Assis* by Rimbaud.
[367]Michel Leiris, the surrealist writer, had been a friend of De Beauvoir and Sartre since 1943 (see *The Prime of Life*, pp.559-60), and was on the first editorial committee of *Les Temps Modernes*. On tension between him and De Beauvoir, see *Force of Circumstance*, p.47: 'Leiris was in charge of poetry, and our tastes rarely coincided.'

before me, remember that Bost owes us 40,000 F. and M.Ponty 10,000, and Nagel's holding 250,000 F. at your disposition – and that's not counting a cheque at your mother's and another at Zette's.[368] You won't be poor. Try to keep a long time reserved *for me* at the beginning of March – I'd so like to be alone with you, either at La Pouèze or anywhere else. I'm always anxious, even before trips I enjoy – I wouldn't like life to separate us. My dear love, my sweet little one, do whatever you think best – bearing in mind how much I love you. I kiss you most passionately – I'll write from Tunis.

Your charming Beaver

[Tunis]

13 February [1946]

Most dear little being

No letter at Tunis. I know nothing of you since you set foot in America. I don't hold it against you, since 15 years' experience have taught me that you're an unblemished marvel and always do whatever's best – there must have been hitches and some misunderstanding. But it was a little black spot, the only one on this journey. For my own part I haven't written, since I didn't know where to reach you. This is just a brief note in case you return to Paris before me. First, you should know that I'm thinking of you with love. I have plenty of time for thinking and always contemplate your little image with the same joy. After that, you should know that I'll be in Paris on *the 25th*. If there's a delay of a day or two, I'll cable. I'll be returning by plane from Algiers, almost certainly. Arrange things cleverly so that I can get my hands on you as soon as I arrive, since I'll be dying of impatience. Also I hope to find a letter or telegram at Algiers (poste restante) when I get there on 22 or 23 February – otherwise I'll be in a state during the last days of my stay, and my return will be spoilt. Make me some little sign quickly. My love, I'll have a million things to tell you, particularly about the wild success of existentialism – people fought with their bare hands to get into my lectures. I've had a splendid trip. I was entranced by the plane,[369] and the people who received me at Tunis were really very nice.

---

[368] Zette Leiris, Michel's wife, who ran a modern art gallery.
[369] This had been her first flight, and she had been allowed to spend it in the cockpit with the pilots.

I was able to see lots of very beautiful things. And now here I am on the edge of the desert and I have ten days ahead of me before getting back to Algiers, in which to traipse around the Algerian South. I'm in absolute seventh heaven. Only I'm a bit distraught every night to feel that I'm cut off from you. A swift word, my dear little one, my love. Don't forget me. Don't forget how passionately I love you. I kiss you with all my might — and for a long, long time.

Your charming Beaver

LETTERS
JANUARY 1947 – OCTOBER 1951
America

<h1 style="text-align:center">🎇 1947</h1>

Newfoundland
Air France
New York – Paris – New York

Saturday 6 p.m. (Paris Time) [25 January 1947]

My dear love,

I'm so happy – and also so moved – to be here, since I know that you were here:[370] it's the big foyer-cum-bar-cum-waiting-room of the French and American airlines. I've just eaten at the hotel where you too ate and slept. I find your tracks everywhere and that's another way of feeling how tightly joined we are.

Well, after phoning you I sat down at the bar and downed a couple of brandies while finishing reading Maurice Sachs.[371] I felt very nervous, even though everything around me was calm – quite different from the previous day.[372] At 11 they called all passengers for New York. 'Air France wishes you a safe flight', the loudspeaker intoned solemnly. I was feeling more and more excited and when I saw the huge plane, as imposing as a ship, my heart missed a beat. I climbed aboard and settled into my seat. We were lost, just ten passengers in that big cargo-plane with its 40 seats: apparently they're carrying too heavy a load of mail and goods to take any more. I also learned from the stewardess that it wasn't at all due to bad weather that we didn't leave yesterday – it was the plane that was out of order. As for the weather, it was probably as fine on Thursday as on Friday. They'd told me the weather would be good – which made me feel quite relaxed during the final preparations – and they weren't deceiving me. The journey has been wonderful so far. First there was that take-off in the dark, which I found truly splendid: you have the impression you're falling into the sky, into the darkness, and all the lights of Paris were shining while above them flashed the reds and greens of the runway beacons. It was like a *festival*

---

[370]In January 1945.
[371]Maurice Sachs, writer of memoirs of the interwar period, plays, novels and essays – a friend of Violette Leduc and contributor to *Les Temps Modernes*.
[372]The flight had been postponed at the last moment.

in the sense in which Genet understands festivals – a festival of man and nature together – and also something at once non-human and against nature. I knew we were to fly via the Azores and Newfoundland, and it struck me as very mysterious and poetic to be combining South and North in this way, and the memory of your two journeys into a single one. A strange night then began, a night of the kind you've known too, which began at 11 o'clock in Paris, resumed at 3 in the Azores – though on my watch it was 6.30 – and ended in a magnificent sunrise lasting two hours over a sea of cloud, at an hour which no longer had a name in any language: 10 o'clock in Paris, 2 in New York – but where was I? The sky was wonderfully clear, though I could vaguely discern the carpet of cloud. I slept, or rather dozed, a bit till the Azores amid joy, love for you, and a vague fear that was very poetic. As soon as you're in that civilized plane where they serve you little brandies and so on, you no longer think of a possible accident, just as in daily life you no longer think of death. But every so often you're struck by the obvious fact that you're mortal, the plane can crumble, and your passage through the air is almost supernatural – disquieting. It's the contrast, I think, which makes such an impact. You know the stop-over at the Azores – a night landing's wonderful and the air was so mild. In the restaurant, I was amused to see black Portuguese in trilby hats just as I'd known them in Lisbon – and also the lightweight furniture and bright fabrics of those hot countries and, in a shop, souvenirs from Madeira. We were served fried eggs and white coffee. I poked my nose outside, but there was nothing to see except the airport lights – so I went back inside to read Koestler's *Arrival and Departure*, which is very bad. From the Azores to Newfoundland is 9 hours. I slept, and then saw the day break. I was overwhelmed by that landscape of clouds – just like the North Pole or the Moon – and found it fantastically beautiful. We flew all the time at 4,000 metres, which gives one a bit of a headache, especially as the heat is stifling. But not a tremor. I slept; I read (you can read perfectly well in a plane, what on earth's Bost talking about?); they served us a little cold meal with champagne – and when I'd drunk my two quarter-bottles of champagne I felt at the peak of happiness. You were as close to me as if you'd touched me. I really feel I shan't be separated from you for an instant – nothing can separate us. In order to land we had to go down through layers upon layers of cloud, then suddenly – at barely 300m. – Newfoundland came into sight: white and black, harsh, and very beautiful. We circled and wobbled a great deal, and I felt a bit queasy on the way down. I nevertheless managed to do justice to the meal, poor though it was. I sampled a 'fruit-pilly' which was already pure America. But now I've had a brandy and feel sprightly again, just a bit soporific. Apparently it will take 5 hours to get to New York, because the winds are against us. So I shan't be there till 7 in the evening (New York time) and shan't see much – especially as I'll be longing to sleep. But tomorrow everything will begin. I can't yet grasp it. I'm still immersed in the journey, and would like the final take-off to be over so that there's no further apprehension. I'm stopping because we're about to leave. Do you remember that hall where I'm writing to you, with its pale blue walls? You're so present to me there. Goodbye, my love. This evening I'll send a cable, and tomorrow or Monday another letter. This trip has been wonderful – it was really worth paying a bit. Also, I really loved our little evening yesterday. I love you with all my might – you've been so nice, so warm, I have such trust in you, my heart, my dear heart. I hold you tight, as I do in the morning. Near or far, I'm all yours.

Your charming Beaver

Kisses to Bost. Tell him I'm really thinking about him.

Hotel Lincoln
44th Street
8th Avenue

Sunday 26 January [1947]

My love

It's 5 in the afternoon and I'm very sleepy – I scarcely slept yesterday from jubilation. But I want to write to you, because I feel so close to you through this New York where I find you everywhere. You'd told me all about it, of course, but it's a thousand times more wonderful than what I'd imagined and I've been put in such a whirl that I wonder how I'll ever manage to prepare a lecture and deliver it the day after tomorrow. I think it's partly because I *recognise* New York, just as you and Bost described it to me, that I feel so well here. As soon as I arrived here, it seemed like a country that belonged to me.

Well, I wrote to you yesterday from the airport in Newfoundland. We set off again, and then I did find the time dragging somewhat. It was foggy, so one was obliged to either read or sleep, and I had a bit of a headache. But the first miraculous effect came at sunset, when the fog gave way to a landscape of cloud, sea and land – it was the American coast, with a marvellously clear sky and extravagant clouds pierced by blue water and flat ground. I slept a little longer, and when I opened my eyes my heart leapt. Did you see the same thing? No more cloud, just a vast black material as far as the eye could see, and against its background girandoles of light of every hue. It was extraordinary, that discovery of America through stars and chains of glittering sequins. They told me it was Boston. Afterwards there were still other lights, and after that the most intense emotion of my travelling life: as far as the eye could see, red, blue and green, motionless or scintillating – the lights of New York. They looked just like jewels or boiled sweets: something to take – whether for eating or adornment – and at all events to hold in your own hands. Nothing can be more extraordinary than a beautiful arrival. For a moment the plane circled before touching down, and as at every landing I felt a hint of fear. Generally I disregard it, telling myself that whatever has to happen will happen. But this time I felt a passionate dread: I told myself I didn't want on any account to die having seen what I was seeing, but not having touched it – upon which the plane touched down obediently. They inspected my teeth and eyes, asked for 8 dollars, and kept me waiting for an hour in overheated corridors; but then I was happily surprised to find a good lady from the Cultural Section, Denise Perrier – the mother of a former pupil of mine, moreover – who'd come to pick me up by car. She asked a fellow from Air France to find me a room, and he gave me a note for the Hotel Lincoln. Fresh delight. The weather was as mild as during a Midi winter, very different from Paris, and you could almost taste its aroma. She took me by car along the East River and into the heart of New York – and even into Central Park to view the extraordinary skyscrapers. I was dazzled once more. What most struck me was the silence of those teeming streets, the buses gliding silently along – no horns – and the people scarcely talking or laughing. It's surprising set beside Paris or Madrid – you'd almost think yourself at Leysin.[373] Or rather, it's like a silent film – you have your eyes full and your ears empty. It was pleasing as a first impression. At the hotel, another piece of luck: the porter said they'd keep me 'indefinitely', and the room costs only $3. It's a vast building with 30 floors, between 44th and 45th and 8th Avenue – i.e. bang in the middle of town. My room's ghastly, but decent, with a bathroom and fairly quiet. The good lady took me off to eat lobster in a scarlet cavern of Hell with gold-leaved palm trees, which absolutely bowled me over. I've realized that Bost and you weren't lying about the

---

[373]In March 1946, Olga had gone down with a serious lung illness, and after initial treatment (a pneumothorax) at the Beaujon hospital was sent to a clinic at Leysin in Switzerland, where De Beauvoir had visited her prior to her departure for the United States. Her illness was to keep Olga off the stage until 1950.

martinis: they bear no relation – it's like night and day. I've accordingly promised myself to put plenty of them away. She left me at 10 and I walked like a zombie down 42nd St., Broadway, etc. – still amid that same silence. The shops are dreadful, but funny. I adore drugstores. I find you gave me a very good description of the poetry of comfort here – it's fantastic. Having everything you need to live and enjoy yourself right there in your hotel – detective stories as well as a toothbrush – is a joy I hope I shan't tire of too quickly. I got in at midnight, utterly exhausted, but so keyed up that at 5 I woke up thinking in my sleep: 'Something's happening to me . . . What's happening to me?' – and was scarcely able to get back to sleep again. The good lady has asked me to dinner, but I didn't want to phone anyone – I wanted a day just to myself. And I was right. I rose at 8, took a shower, and by 9 I was on the street. It was lovely it being Sunday: all the 'natural' side of New York – all the cliffs, canyons, sky, sea, horizons – stood out more dramatically. I walked the whole length of Broadway, and found that this city has a beauty and grandeur resembling that of mountains. At the same time, it's so much a city that you no longer have any desire to visit another after this. The sky was one of those skies you told me about, and everything lay deserted and silent. I saw Wall Street and the Battery, and took the boat to the Statue of Liberty; I didn't go right up to it, I just wanted the view of arriving in New York by the Battery – and it really is an extraordinary view. I walked around in this way for almost 3 hours, quite beside myself. I had lunch for $1.50 at the corner of *Beaver* Street and Broad Street – not too bad. I liked the white coffee and the big raisin pastries they serve with it for breakfast in the cafeterias. I find there's hardly any problem with food here. You can eat anything, anywhere, very quickly – I like that. After lunch I went over towards the Bowery, and that staggered me even more than what I'd seen in the morning. I saw the Chinese streets, the Jewish streets, Chatham Square, etc., and find the unity of Wall Street and Chatham Square (I mean the fact that they comprise a single ensemble, a single city) something quite extraordinary. I was so dazed by looking at things that I had to stop. I went to a Greenwich cinema (Greenwich is the only thing I haven't found very fantastic, but I'll have to see it by night) and saw *Journey into Fear*,[374] which is enjoyable. Then I took the bus back up 5th Av., and came to my room to write to you. It's 5.30. In an hour the lady's coming, but I don't care if I'm bored at her place – I'm too exhausted anyway to go out properly. I'll have to go to bed early. I'm

---

[374]1942 film co-directed (with Norman Foster) by Orson Welles.

telling you everything in detail, because I know it will conjure up very clear images for you, and that you like all that. What amazed me was how accurate everything Bost and you had told me was: the drunks on the Bowery pavements, the sky, the street horizon, everything. Only I don't feel in the least terrorized. On the contrary, I'd like to remain for a time without knowing anyone here, just because this city so warms my heart. You feel free here. Nobody looks at you, even at the hotel it's impersonal – and that's pleasant. However, tomorrow I'll make some telephone calls. The only trouble is that I'm really going to [be] penniless. I don't know how they went about it, but I've got very few lectures – none in the South, despite what Soupault said[375] – and the dates are so damn stupidly arranged that there are some I'll be absolutely unable to give if I want to spend any time at all in California.[376] I've cabled Soupault about this and am writing to him. Mme Perrier says it's outrageous that they haven't financed this trip for me – Lévi-Strauss[377] was sure they'd do so. Since Joxe[378] is coming in the next few days, they're going to speak to him about it. At all events, don't worry, I'll manage. She says there are already heaps of people telephoning her in order to see me. I'm going to try and see the Saunders woman[379] as soon as possible, and Dolores,[380] to find out how much I can be sure of. At any rate, I'll easily be able to live on $12 a day in New York, and if I can't buy myself anything, who cares? I just want to be able to travel round a bit, and see New Orleans. But even if I were to see only New York, I'd be in seventh heaven. Well, the harsh side of this city doubtless reveals itself a bit later on, and the weather can change too – the kind we've been having yesterday and today is apparently unusual for this time of year.

---

[375]Philippe Soupault (1897-), founded the review *Littérature* – organ of the Dada movement – with Louis Aragon and André Breton, collaborated with Breton on *Les Champs Magnétiques*, and was one of the main leaders of the surrealist movement of the 1920s. It was he who had organized an invitation for De Beauvoir – whom he had first met at the Flore in May 1946 – to speak at various universities in the United States, thus making her present trip financially possible.

[376]Where Sorokine had lived since February 1946 with her husband Ivan Moffat.

[377]'They' here refers to the French Institute in the United States. De Beauvoir had known the anthropologist Claude Lévi-Strauss (incidentally a cousin of Sartre) since they had done their teaching practice together in 1930. He had emigrated to the United States when the war broke out, and was at this time working in the Cultural Relations section of the French Institute.

[378]Joxe was the French minister of culture at this time.

[379]Marion Saunders, a literary agent.

[380]Dolores Vanetti Ehrenreich, with whom Sartre had begun an affair on his first trip to the United States which was to last for five years. The first issue of *Les Temps Modernes* was dedicated to her. Married to a wealthy American doctor, she had worked for the Office of War Information giving French-language broadcasts.

Farewell, my love. It hasn't yet sunk in that I shan't see you for another 3 months – you seem so close to me. How I'd like to be with you some day in this city! I've never stopped thinking about you as I walk round – it was as though you were still speaking to me. I feel very intensely that when we see each other again, it will be as though we'd left each other just the day before – so it really does seem as if it were tomorrow that I'll be seeing you again.

I kiss and hug you, as joyfully as can be.

Your charming Beaver

Envelope:
M. Sartre
42 rue Bonaparte[381]
Paris 6, France. AIR MAIL

[New York]

Thursday 30 January [1947]

My most dear love

I was very foolish to think I'd be separated from you here – it's just the opposite. It's as if I were remaking this journey with you: I find your tracks everywhere and it pleases me enormously. For example, this morning I came to the Bristol to see if there was any mail for me, and at once settled myself down in the lobby to write to you – I can picture you vividly here. I have so many things to tell you, my dear little yourself, that I don't know how I'll get to the end of them. Well, I'll make a start anyway.

It was Sunday afternoon, then, and I was still dazed with travelling and walking. There was a good lady from the Cultural Section, the Perrier woman I've told you about, who came to pick me up for dinner at her home. In her apartment I found an old French professor from Harvard, quite vile, who cooked for me and flattered me and who I later learned was one of those who wanted to stop me coming, out of hatred for existentialism. To cap it all, I'd once given him a bad mark for a piece of homework on *Polyeucte*,[382] presented under the name of the little Perrier girl when she was a pupil at Molière.[383] So he was very

---

[381]Sartre moved into his mother's apartment at this address in July 1946, and remained there until it was bombed by the O.A.S. in 1962.
[382]A play by Corneille.
[383]The Lycée Molière, see note 75 above.

friendly, as was she, but I soon came to blows with her over psychoanalysis – which she's mad keen on – and more seriously with both of them regarding the Negro question, because they wanted to get me to swear never to write a line on the matter. They took me home to bed quite beside myself with mingled rage and sleepiness. I was hoping to sleep late, but was on my feet again by 7.30. I can't get a good night's sleep here, it's the anxiety and over-excitement – and perhaps that six-hour lag also plays some part.

On Monday morning I went to take my orange juice and white coffee with big round cakes in the cafeteria opposite. I take that every morning, and it's a breakfast that suits me very well. Then: hairdresser's (which I was badly in need of); visit to the Cultural Section, to discuss my programme of lectures; and lunch with Marion Saunders. She's a real old horror. She gave me $200, and rang Gallimard[384] so that I could get the other $120. She took me for an excellent lunch at a very chic American restaurant – the 'Old Town' or something like that. Talking of which, food is one of the only things about which you misled me. I find these plain dishes easy on the stomach, and like the fact that for lunch you can just hurriedly wolf down anything you please. Anyway, the Saunders woman kept giving vent to great diatribes against Camus,[385] and exhorting me to take her on as my literary agent. I refused politely, but have since learnt that she's working surreptitiously. Actually, I must ring her. It was still a fantastically fine day. I went to visit Central Station, then retraced my steps towards 58th St. in order to take Walk No. 3 as recommended in my little notebook.[386] I took the East River embankment and continued from Queens[boro] Bridge to Brooklyn Bridge. At the outset it was hard to find your way as a pedestrian, but I managed and it was one of the most beautiful outings of my life. God, I do love New York! It was so mild that by the river's edge there were children sitting, and Negroes, and lots of peaceful people. My eyes and my heart were full of them. And there was also an astonishing and delicious aroma of sea and spices. I arrived at Brooklyn Bridge at sunset. Through the wire lattice-work you could see the Battery and the red sky, and the gulls on the water – I could have wept. I took the elevated train to get back – I had an appointment at the Plaza with the Macht woman.[387] With a foretaste of reluctance, I first took

---

[384]The Éditions Gallimard, De Beauvoir's publisher.

[385]Camus had visited the United States the previous year.

[386]The back portion of De Beauvoir's diary for 1947 is full of addresses of bars and restaurants written in Sartre's handwriting, itineraries recommended by him, and information provided by Bost who had also recently visited the United States.

[387]Another literary agent.

an express that carried me in one fell swoop to 105th St. Then, after returning, I went to wait at the Savoy-Plaza. However, I did eventually realize my error and crossed the street, where I saw that dreadful lump of a girl in person. She conducted me into the 'Oak Room', saying it was one of your favourite spots. It really touched me to think of you in those surroundings you so loved. We drank martinis, while she gazed into my eyes and talked of Dolores – in tones of the utmost loathing – and of you, in tones of the utmost self-importance. She really is the most filthy bitch! She insinuated that if she'd given Dolores the cheque, Dolores would have kept it for herself. What it comes down to is that she refused to give me it via her, but instead sent it to you (as you know). A priori, I said everything nice I could about D., just to infuriate her. And as I was precisely about to ring Dolores, she followed me – confessing impudently that she was burning with curiosity – and I had to shut the door of the booth in her face.

After leaving her, dinner at Lévi-Strauss's. Well, you know him. But what a lovely view from his window over the lights of New York! And his wife, though awfully pregnant, is quite nice and quite lively. He told me that everybody – including Joxe – had been lukewarm about this trip, and that an existentialist *woman* was more than they could tolerate. But he said he'd arrange for me to get at least my travel paid, which would make a huge difference. I can tell you at once that things are going to work out very well, in terms of both cash and general organization. I'm very pleased. At 10, I pretended to be tired – they were both yawning anyway. I met D. at the Sherry-Netherland, I imagine she'll tell you about it. I found her exactly as I'd imagined. I like her a lot, and was very happy because I understood your feelings – I could appreciate them, and honoured you for having them – and at the same time didn't feel the least bit embarrassed. She drank one whisky after another, and this was reflected in a certain nervousness, a certain volubility, and some classic crazy behaviour. She took me to see the Pink Elephant bar – which quite overwhelmed me – and then on to another bar on Broadway, where we stayed till 3 in the morning. She was fantastically moving – very scared at the idea of that trip.[388]

My love, I'm stopping, precisely because I'm just off to say my farewells to Dolores. I'll tell you the rest this evening or tomorrow. Know only that I'm still in seventh heaven. I'll be staying roughly till 13 February in New York, at the Hotel Lincoln; then on the *24th* I'll be at 411 South Barrington Avenue, Westwood 24, Los Angeles. Do

---

[388]Dolores was on the point of leaving for Paris, where she was to spend the first of several lengthy stays with Sartre.

write. Send the cheque back to me as quickly as possible, I'll need it in California. My love, you're everywhere with me. I think one of the pleasures of New York is the fact that I find you everywhere here and love it with you. Till this evening or tomorrow. I've still lots of things to tell you. Tell Bost that I'm thinking all the time about him too and send him a big kiss. I cover you with tender kisses.

Your charming Beaver

(Address as letter 26 January 1947)

[New York]

Friday [31 January 1947]

My dear love

I must finish yesterday's letter for you. I'd like to tell you everything in such detail that I'm afraid I'll never get to the end of it. Well, it was Tuesday, the day of my lecture. I wanted to sleep late but didn't do so – I keep waking up at 7 like clockwork. I went and settled down in the hotel bar – which was deserted – and, contrary to what Bost and you say, I worked very well there for the whole morning. That was on the novel. I went for lunch to L'Auberge, came home to get ready, and at 3 they came to pick me up and cast me to the old women of the French Institute. There I saw a sinister individual called Bidard, whom Camus with his usual wit nicknamed 'Bidasse',[389] and who complained that you'd been outrageously rude to him. I spoke for an hour – much too fast and over-complicatedly, Lévi-Strauss told me afterwards. But that was of no importance, because those old bags don't understand French anyway. After that, Lévi-Strauss took me to cocktails at Dolores's place. I was very moved to be entering that apartment where you'd lived for so long; to see Calder's bird,[390] and the view, and so many people you'd told me about – the Condit woman, the Grazon woman, and above all J. Breton,[391] resplendent in her Indian blanket and a feathered redskin headdress. I spoke in English to Hare, whom I found charming, and in French to Jacqueline, who looked stern and expectant. Dolores was as

[389]In French slang, a *bidard* is a lucky fellow, while a *bidasse* is a squaddie or grunt.
[390]The sculptor Alexander Calder, whom Sartre had met on his first trip to New York and on whose work he was to write an essay in 1946.
[391]André Breton's former wife Jacqueline, now remarried to an American sculptor, David Hare.

dainty as a little Annamite idol and truly charming to me – I'd quite like to know what she was actually thinking. I had a good time, and was very upset when we had to leave – already an hour late – and go on to D. Nordman's place,[392] since she was giving a dinner party in my honour. I arrived somewhat tipsy and horribly embarrassed, especially since the door was opened for me by a young woman in black whose dress left bare all her shoulders and half her bosom. Everybody was at table (Dolores had rung ahead to say they should sit down without me) and – horrors! – there were oysters on my plate.[393] I greeted the Nordman woman, blushingly pushed away the oysters, and attacked a magnificent dish of chicken cooked with cherries. Luckily R. Wright[394] was there, and so nice that I could have hugged him. He at once put the situation to rights, and for as long as he was there I found the evening very enjoyable – especially as I was speaking only English and managing very well, which delighted me. People understand me when I speak, but the only trouble is I don't understand them. I strain to catch the first half of a story, but then it's the second half, of course, that's funny and I don't catch that. Once he'd left there was an abominable hour, because they'd invited French people of the De Roulet sort[395] – officials, real swine – who were talking a load of bullshit about France. I left at the first opportunity and collapsed into bed. I had angst-filled dreams the first few nights, and would wake up thinking: 'Something's happening to me, but what?' – not knowing if it was good or bad.

Oh! I was forgetting – I saw the Ball.[396] He really is as fat as an elephant, completely round, with huge horn-rimmed spectacles. It's quite monstrous to see him beside the diminutive Dolores – but he looks amiable enough.

On Wednesday morning, in magnificent weather, I first went to collect a cheque from Marion Saunders on 35th St. and had a prowl round that area. Then I took a taxi to Columbus Circle, and from there walked north, via Broadway and the banks of the Hudson, as far as [1]25th St. I came back to have lunch with Dolores, who took me to a seedy little Greek restaurant near her place and talked to me about herself – a bit too volubly, since she found the silences distressing. After leaving her I made heaps of phone calls, dropped in at the French

---

[392]Dorothy Nordman, 'A.M.' in *America Day by Day*.
[393]See note 253 above.
[394]Richard Wright, the novelist, and his wife Ellen (a literary agent) had met De Beauvoir and Sartre on a visit to Paris in the summer of 1946: she was to dedicate her book *America Day by Day* to them.
[395]Her brother-in-law was a state cultural functionary.
[396]Dolores's husband.

Institute, then went to call on the Gerassis. They welcomed me with a warmth that touched my heart. Stépha became quite faint from emotion over dinner. The kid's terribly nice,[397] with an American straightness and French intelligence. We drank martinis and went to dine at the Veau d'Or, where I had a marvellous duck à l'orange. I enjoyed seeing Stépha again, she's really very sweet. On Thursday there was still that same weather, in which it's impossible to sleep late. I wrote to you from the Bristol, then went to say goodbye to Dolores, whom I found surrounded by suitcases, harassed by phone calls, and consumed by fear of the plane – which I can understand. She really put herself out to organize articles for me, so I think everything will go all right on the cash front. We laboured away a bit, because we were saying goodbye without ever basically having got to know each other – so had no regrets and no prospects. I really do find her extremely pleasant and likeable. Just a bit too much of a 'good lady', as Bost puts it, for my own taste. But if you're male, and what's more inspired by an imperialistic passion of generosity, no more appropriate person could be met with. Let me know if she arrived safely and talk to me a bit about her. After leaving her, I went to snatch a bite at random. I've already told you, I think, that I like the way people eat here: without giving it much thought, lightly, cleanly, and quickly. I went for an enormous walk: the banks of the East River from Queens[boro] Bridge northwards; the German neighbourhood; and the fantastic 125th St. and Harlem which – when you're fresh from American crowds – is staggering, with all those people strolling about and chatting and enjoying themselves. I returned in a taxi all the way down Park Avenue – it's quite extraordinary seeing the transformation from seediness to opulence. I picked up Gerassi at his place and he took me to the Museum of Modern Art, which was spellbinding. Then dinner at their place, and an evening with Billie Holiday – but there I was pretty disappointed – there was just a little black band, nothing out of the ordinary. Café Society – the show's at midnight – I'm too tired to go there these evenings. Finally, yesterday [Friday], a big walk in the morning to Brooklyn returning by Brooklyn Bridge, which is fantastic – even terrifying. In the afternoon I had lots of appointments. At the Cultural Section. I phoned Sorokine – I was really moved to hear her voice and she sounded so happy. The 'general idea', as Dolores would say, is that I give lectures at Washington, Lynchburg, New London, Rochester and Oberlin, from 13 to 20 February roughly. Then 3 free days in Chicago. Then plane to Los

---

[397]John (Tito) Gerassi, born in 1935.

Angeles and stay at Sorokine's – with lectures in Los Angeles and San Francisco – until 10 March. Then departure by car or bus for the South, with side-trips on the way. Then return to New York where Sorokine will stay with me for a fortnight, and for another fortnight I'll be on my own and give a few more lectures. Isn't that wonderful? Only I'll have to find some money for the trip, because she won't have a sou – but I can live comfortably on $13 a day, room included, and with lots of little purchases: stockings, beauty products, etc. After that, I went upstairs to *Vogue* – on the 19th floor – which decided me to go up the Empire State Building this very day: it's fantastic. Then I saw Jean Condit about an article. After that the Knopf woman,[398] who wants me to cut *She Came to Stay* line by line, adjective by adjective. I won't do it – unless she pays me $200. After that I began writing to you in the Oak Room at the Plaza, while waiting for Odette Lieutier[399] and a friend of Piscator's.[400] We just started discussing, so I'm having dinner with Piscator on Sunday. Then I went home to sleep for an hour, since I was dropping – I have a cold – and I found your letter. My love, my dear love, I feel you so close to me! I read it, then slept for an hour clasping it to my heart. After that, a party at the Nordman woman's, where R. Wright spoke very appealingly about France. I saw Abel there,[401] and found him very nice. He invited me to have lunch later on with him and Chiaromonte.

It's now Saturday morning, the weather's fine, and I'm going for a walk. I adore New York – at all hours – and am as happy as a queen. Your letter brightened my spirits. Do keep writing to me. My little one, my dear little one, it's you I meet everywhere about New York, and it's you again whom I love when loving the skyscrapers. I kiss you so passionately.

Your Beaver

---

[398]Blanche Knopf, wife of De Beauvoir's U.S. publisher Alfred Knopf.
[399]Owner of a bookshop in Rue Bonaparte designed by Toulouse, where Dullin had signed his books.
[400]Erwin Piscator, German anti-fascist director with two theatres in New York, who was thinking of staging *The Flies*.
[401]Lionel Abel was an editor with Nicola Chiaromonte of the left-liberal, Trotskisant journal *Politics*, founded by Dwight Macdonald after he split from *Partisan Review*.

Alumnae House
at Vassar College
Poughkeepsie, N.Y.

7 February 1947

Dearest little yourself, my love

I'm writing to you from the most marvellous, cosy little room in the guest house at Vassar. There's snow all round the house and a fine misty moonlight. I've just finished my lecture, before a theatre-full of young girls fit to drive Camus to distraction, and had tea with the old ladies – I feel happy as a queen. It's my first college. I came from New York on a train that followed the Hudson for 2 h. – it was superb, that enormous river all clogged with snow and ice. The sky was unsullied, over white hills. It was strange being out of New York in the countryside. At the station there was an old, white-haired American Quaker lady and a former girl student of Souvarine's. I saw my first American small town, so classic it might have been a film set – but at the same time it resembled Megève, because of the snow. Then I saw the college, with all the girls in ski-wear conscientiously making their way down pathetic little slopes. I found the charm of the place quite breathtaking, with its library, its ski-runs, and its little bedrooms in the English style. I dined with some old ladies and gave a good lecture, I think. Now I'm delighted to have plenty of time and a pleasant spot for writing to you. There's only one shadow on my happiness – the fact that I've had no letter from you. I know for sure that you've written and it's due to the planes: no mail's getting through from France, and Teddy[402] tells me Dolores spent two days grounded at Shannon. Nevertheless, it's a tiny bit sad. Your dear face was there, laughing, on one of the college walls (do you have that article? – the Macht woman swears she'll send it you, but she gets everything screwed up) and my heart was suddenly quite smitten with love. Did you know that the pupils here are putting on *The Flies*? The old lady who's in charge of it told me they've never shown such enthusiasm for any play. I was shown the sets and costumes, which are being made up with the help of specialists brought in from New York. There'll be two performances, one on 5 April that I'll try and go to.

I'm going to start again from the beginning. I was in a bar and writing to you. Then I went off to 13 Charles Street to see R. Wright, who received me like an angel. He's the only person I'm really fond of here, and whom I see with warm pleasure. He says I've made extraordinary progress in English, and it's true that I could almost give lectures – I

---

[402]Dolores's husband.

talk for hours – and I understand almost everything too, though understanding's still the hardest part. He introduced me to his little daughter, who's as cute as can be, and along with his wife – whom I like a great deal too – they took me first of all to an excellent Chinese restaurant in Chinatown, after which we went to Harlem to pick up two black friends of his (a couple) and then on to the Savoy. Did you go there? It's phenomenal. The Kos. sisters would go crazy about it. At any rate Bost has been there, I think. We were the only two white women, and not a single white man. We drank whisky and watched the marvellous Negro women dance. Then we went to a little club – Jack's or Jackson's, perhaps Bost knows – with very good jazz. At around 1 we went home. The young woman was tired, because she has to work hard in the morning. These outings are rather awkward in a sense – like the other day at the *Politics* party – because lots of the girls there also work, and what's a pleasure and curiosity for me is a strain for them. Wright's wife told me too how stressful an American woman's life is. I was so delighted: on Sunday morning, that angel Richard Wright's going to take me to a Gospel Church in Harlem – apparently it's astounding. I'm also going with his recommendation to see the authors of *Black Antiquities*,[403] in Chicago. He has taken charge of my interests in a fantastically kind way.

On Tuesday, which was the next day, I had to work a bit in the morning, then I went to the Metropolitan Museum – there's a fine English exhibition on: Hogarth, Turner and especially Constable, whom I don't know but who's a good painter. I visited the picture galleries and there are some fine paintings; but it's all too muddled up to be very agreeable and by the end of two hours I was bored stiff with it. I went back to my neighbourhood and ate in a cafeteria. There was snow in New York, which was suddenly a totally new dimension and wonderfully agreeable – children were tobogganing and skiing in Central Park. I went to the cinema and saw Montgomery's *Lady in the Lake*,[404] which interested me because it has that technique you want to use with Clouzot,[405] of seeing everything through the eye of the camera. But he hasn't done much with it. It comes over as contrived, and strikes me as being unsuitable for a thriller. Then I went to doll myself up a bit before

---

[403]Possibly a garbled reference to Arnaud d'Usscurt and James Gow, authors of the play *Deep are the Roots* (1946).

[404]Robert Montgomery's *Lady in the Lake* (1946), based on the book by Raymond Chandler, is entirely shot as though from the viewpoint of the detective Philip Marlowe (Dick Powell).

[405]Sartre had been a scriptwriter for Pathé since 1943, beginning with *Les Jeux Sont Faits* – though it was only shot in 1947, not by Clouzot but by Delannoy.

meeting up with the Macht woman at the Plaza. She wanted to introduce me to some guy from *Town and Country* – but the guy was drunk, and anyway I was to meet some far more important people an hour later at Jean Condit's. I hate that [Macht] woman: it's her fault I shan't get your money in time, which I need (I'll borrow it from L[évi]-S[trauss] for a month, but it's the principle of the thing). You're amazingly indulgent towards women like Macht or Knopf – in fact, towards American women in general, it seems to me. I'll speak of this again. At all events, Macht is a real bitch and I bawled the living daylights out of her. She persecutes me by telephone because I haven't asked her for anything. I have another persecutor, that Collins friend of Piscator's, who wants *The Flies* and is just like Génina-Rassini.[406] Eventually, after I'd bawled out the Macht woman, we went to Jean Condit's. Arrival at 6, cocktail, then they took me to dinner and kept me till midnight. For 6 hours I argued in English, alone against them all, passionately. I was battling with Greenberg, Phillips, Rahv,[407] and a tall, pretentious young man who says we have no right to dabble in philosophy because we don't know Russell. We discussed politics and they simply turned my stomach. Abel and Chiaromonte had already disappointed me, with the total emptiness of their thinking: but they're nice and I like them. Whereas this lot, with their so-called cultural internationalism and freedom of spirit, are pure American imperialists. They attacked me about Merleau-Ponty,[408] and came out with two real gems: 'It wasn't Stalin who fed you, but UNRA', and: 'Stalingrad? Of no importance! We're the ones who won the war for you.' For them, dollars count far more than all the blood shed by others. We went at it hammer and tongs. I felt like quitting the table – and at any rate left all the steak on my plate. They were very upset, because personally they were congratulating me on my success and feting me. They served me up the argument of the firing-squad victim, of course. They don't give a shit about anything, except *Partisan Review*: they'd send the whole world up in flames to ensure the survival of their worthless rag. I'll never give another article to that filthy outfit. And all with such arrogance! You feel UNRA and dollars behind them, just as you feel 160 million people behind Ehrenburg. But it's less candid. I've been pretty disgusted these past two days. With the people from *Politics* and *Partisan Review*;

---

[406]Paris Theatre manager.
[407]Clement Greenberg, William Phillips and Philip Rahv, editors of *Partisan Review*, now entering upon a slide to the right under the impact of the Cold War.
[408]Doubtless a reference to Merleau-Ponty's article in *Les Temps Modernes*, No. 3 (December 1945) 'The Yogi and the Proletarian' – a critique of Koestler's *The Yogi and the Commissar*.

with publishers and magazine editors; and with that purely commercial way of inspecting your brain, as if it were a dancer's legs. They talk about existentialism as they would about a worm powder, and they award marks: Camus so many, Sartre so many – My God! by the end I was quite scared. I thought: Bost began with fear when he was alone; I'm scared now that I know people. What is everything we write for them? A product that's consumed in six months. As I don't think there's any more to be hoped for from the 'other side', it's discouraging – for I don't have any impression of hope here. And yet, though it's perhaps the worse world at present, it's the only one concerned with intellectual matters. I'll see what conclusion I've reached a month from now.

Anger had so exhausted me that for the first time I slept, really slept, from 1 to 11.30 in the morning. I felt 'relaxed', despite everything, and really at home in N.Y. It was a fine, icy morning. I went to the N.Y. Times, which requested just a short article for $75 – that's how it always is. I took the opportunity of visiting the building. An American newspaper is something quite phenomenal. After that I went to meet Chiaramonte, who'd been kind enough to telephone, and who organized lunch for me with Abel and Schapiro in a little Italian restaurant in the Village. Afterwards I went to see D. Nordman, who gave me a $100 advance against *Prostitute*[409] and my article. Aaahh!

Very important

1. send me immediately, in small packages, the last section (4th and final) of *Ethics of Ambiguity*;[410]

2. do *not* publish the Pilorge, which R. Wright says is full of crude mistakes and would risk having the most disastrous effect.

Reply on this point, and act.

After that, I went to see a very nice German woman whom you met, and who gave me heaps of tips for the German issue. Then: evening with the Gerassis, who are quite angelically kind to me. We had dinner at Café Society Down Town – but there was only a half-hour show, because it was empty – then on to Nick's, very agreeable but equally empty. Apparently, for the past two months there has been a 'recession', as they now call it rather than 'depression', and the nightclubs are emptying.

Yesterday, Thursday, telephone calls and work in the morning – I'm doing the article for *Vogue*. Lunch with the abominable Knopf woman, who no longer wants to publish me – she's a pain in the neck. Excellent

---

[409]*The Respectful Prostitute* had been staged in France in November 1946, together with *Men Without Shadows*.

[410]De Beauvoir's *Ethics of Ambiguity* was published later in 1947, and this refers no doubt to the proofs.

afternoon with the Boubou. We went to 155th street on the top of a bus, all along the Hudson – there was snow everywhere and kids playing. We saw a Spanish library with very good paintings, and next door the Indian museum. Then by taxi over Washington Heights to the tip of New York, where there's a cloister full of mediaeval objects imported from Europe by Rockefeller. Did you go there? You can see Washington Bridge and the Hudson, and big cliffs, and with the snow and the setting sun and the children playing on sledges it was fantastic. I returned by subway to La Fayette, where I drank whisky with Chiaramonte's wife and Abel's girl friend, who are very nice. I made an appointment to talk about American women. Then 5 hours at the cinema, until 1.30 in the morning. I saw Lawrence Olivier's *Henry V* in technicolour, with L. Olivier. I'm not yet quite sure what to think of it, but I wasn't bored, which strikes me as a success. Then *Conflict*,[411] with Humphrey Bogart. This morning, a bit of work. Then day at Vassar.

My dear love, goodbye. I still have so many things to tell you. I'm going to sleep now. Write to me. I'd be so totally happy if I could keep some contact with you. You're so present to me everywhere here. Goodbye. I still love you just as dearly, I feel myself at one with you. How we'll talk, when I get back! A big, big kiss.

Your charming Beaver

For Bost

Best beloved Little Bost. Write to me too, if you're not a brute. I've already told Sartre to explain to you how much I think about you over here. However, just to make more certain, I'm writing it down for you. Has he told you everything properly? I'm enjoying myself madly – I haven't been scared so far, but perhaps I'm about to start.

A big kiss.

Your Beaver

[New York]

Tuesday [11 February 1947]

My dearest love

As soon as I arrived back from Vassar on Saturday morning I found your Thursday letter, and then yesterday the Sunday one arrived. My

---

[411]*Conflict*: 1943 film directed by Curtis Bernhardt.

beloved, I do so hope you've received mine and seen how I experienced the whole of this N.Y. with you. That's over now, though. I mean, I think just as much about you, but it's no longer your N.Y., it's mine. I'm writing to you from the Sherry-Netherland: there's a little band and people eating, since it's 2.30 in the afternoon. There's a beautiful blue sky over the park, and I feel completely at home. It even makes my heart ache – this beautiful day, when N.Y. has recovered all its mildness – to think how tomorrow's my last day. It's yet another departure for me, and one that causes me some pain – even though I'm terribly happy to be going to California, to be seeing Sarbakhane,[412] and to be taking a big trip. But I enjoy this life so much. On Saturday I came back by train. Being a weekend, it was full of little, twittering college girls, who'd exchanged their 'pants' for fur coats and little hats and looked like real ladies. I went back to the hotel, collected my telephone messages, and made some telephone calls: it's crazy the time you spend on the telephone here. It starts at 8.30 and lasts until I go out, and after that there are ten messages every evening – it's quite entertaining. I went to have lunch with Prolers from *France-Amerique*, who's a filthy creep but he'll bring me in $150-200. I promptly got him to stand me a meal at the Chambord. There was some other woman too. It was entirely devoid of interest, but we ate well. After that, I spent an hour at the Frick Gallery. Did you see it? It's on 5th Av. – there are some fine Vermeers and Holbeins, and I thought about the museums in Holland where I went with you.[413] Then I had one of my best moments in N.Y. A very nice white friend of Wright's took me to the Carnegie Hall, to a Louis Armstrong concert. Apparently it was the most fantastic stroke of luck, because these days he himself does commercial jazz and there's never any real jazz in New York; but this time he played first-class jazz and the whole hall was carried away, me included. Armstrong casts quite a spell too, and the best record's no match for that kind of live jazz. I went for a drink at the home of a guy who's very famous here in his milieu, because he's the only white man who can play with a black band, having lived for twenty years in Harlem exactly like a black man, after marrying a Negro woman.[414] They gave me a book they've written together: it's called *Really the Blues* and is being translated by Duhamel.[415] I think it would be a good idea to get an extract for *Les*

---

[412]Sorokine.
[413]In December 1946, see *Force of Circumstance*, pp.117-8.
[414]Mezz Mezzrow.
[415]Marcel Duhamel, editor of the *Série Noire*.

Temps Modernes. There was also a very young American writer, a friend of Farrell[416] – to whom he's going to introduce me – and Wright, terribly American with his red hair and all of 24.[417] He gave me his book – about a military academy in the South – and it looks quite good. I was in seventh heaven with those people, it's the only milieu I really like. But I had to leave them, loaded down with books and records, in order to go and meet the people from *Partisan Review*. We had dinner in a charming Spanish restaurant in the Village, then drank a lot of reconciliation whiskies at Phillips's place. They were profuse in their apologies and assented to everything I said – they even made a mistake once or twice and assented when I meant the opposite. They were so nice, in fact, that they disarmed me somewhat and I no longer detest them so much. There's one called Barrett who's quite charming.[418] Do you know him? But why do they have such a high opinion of Georges Blin,[419] that's a real mystery. I spoke English all the time yesterday and drank at least 6 whiskies. I had quite a head on Sunday, but was really pleased because Wright – whom I've come to love with all my heart – came to fetch me and took me to the big Abyssinian church in Harlem, the biggest Gospel Church in the world. We heard the singing and the sermon, and saw how the people reacted – they were middle-class Negroes and pretty restrained, but very impassioned all the same. In April he'll take me to another one, smaller and more popular. He took me back to lunch at his house. He has a little daughter who's a real little marvel, and even I who don't like children am friends with her. His wife is very nice too, and they're like a proper family for me in New York, something really warm and agreeable. The friends I'd seen the evening before came, just two of them, and we chatted peacefully till 4. I'm having lunch with them again on Wednesday and I'll take the little girl a nice present.

After that I went to visit Mme Perrier, the woman from the Institute who wanted to give me a Rorschach Test. It's really very amusing, more than those ones of Van Lennep's.[420] After my own test, she showed me

---

[416]James Farrell, the Trotskyist author of *Studs Lonigan* who, with Nelson Algren and Richard Wright, made up what was often known as the Chicago School.

[417]Reference to *End As A Man* (1947), by Calder Willingham.

[418]William Barrett, later to be the author of *The Truants: Adventures among the Intellectuals* (1982).

[419]Georges Blin, the literary critic, had published his *Baudelaire* in 1939.

[420]At Utrecht, on the trip mentioned in note 413 above, De Beauvoir and Sartre had enjoyed undergoing 'personality tests' at the Psychological Institute headed by Van Lennep.

some very odd responses from the American war veterans she has been studying for the past two years. She has a whole file of them, really interesting.

After that I went to have dinner with little Mary Guggenheim,[421] who'd invited me with a girl from *Harper's Bazaar* who was much nicer than she was. She's very unlikeable, an old maid riddled with neuroses. I barely saw her, because she spent the two hours of the meal laboriously concocting a *zabaglione*, which she ended up by ruining and had to throw away – that too seemed pretty neurotic. When I left she said, very indiscreetly: 'I'm sure you're off to see Dolores, aren't you?' In fact I was going to the Gerassis, who are as nice as can be. I explained to them how spiteful they'd been to you with all those reproaches, and now they're keeping mum. We talked about Tito, who's a very interesting example of the confusion in the younger generation today – exiled and rootless, without a country and strongly affected by it. They're having problems with him, but I don't have time to tell you about those. Then the Boubou took me to the Bowery – to Sammy's Follies[422] – and I must admit that you and Bost weren't kidding me, it's a fantastic place. The clientele in particular is amazing. There was one woman of about 35, the Scottish type, very tough, all alone, who was drinking whisky after whisky and watching everything avidly. I was in seventh heaven. In a sense it's disgusting, and I think Dolores must feel quite ill when she goes there. But it's the culminating point of the whole sordid side of N.Y. and America, and as such takes on a certain poetry and is ultimately less revolting than the real reasons that allow it to exist. Well, once again it would take too long to discuss it now. (Make certain you keep these letters, which will be my only memento from here and which I really want to get back.)

On Monday, which was yesterday, I worked in the morning on my article for *Vogue*, made telephone calls, and went to the hairdresser's. After that, a lunch I couldn't avoid with Thineray and a lecturer from Columbia, very glum. We ate at the Beaujolais, and the occasion lacked gaiety. But I dropped them very quickly. I went to work on the article at the Sherry-Netherland, where I felt like a princess. After that, an interview with Brun from *France-Forum*: a wretched nobody who's

---

[421]Mary Guggenheim (called D.V. in *America Day by Day* and Nelly Benson in *Force of Circumstance*) met De Beauvoir through a friend at *Harper's Bazaar* responsible for entertaining distinguished visiting foreign contributors, and introduced her to her former lover Nelson Algren.

[422]A bar where elderly actresses and female singers and dancers – aged between sixty and eighty – used to perform.

organizing this evening's lecture, along with M. Morton and an American – Sweeney – who's supposed to introduce me. After that, an interview with an exiled German poet whom O. Lieutier absolutely insisted on presenting to me. After that, I spent a very enjoyable evening. Do you remember that charming American from Berne, a friend of Moffat's, who was my neighbour? He came to a party the other day just to see me and invite me out, so yesterday we met up. He took me to visit a young American novelist called Mary McCarthy, who's the rising star of *Partisan Review*. She's very beautiful and seems intelligent, but without the least charm or interest other than documentary (and as such she fascinated me), being so typically the American intellectual woman – I could write pages about her. She has a very insignificant husband (No. 3, not counting two official lovers). The four of us went to a restaurant called Lindy's – I'd wanted one that was typically American, and it really was. Do you know it? One couldn't imagine anything more like Hell. Then the new 'in' nightclub, The Blue Angel, with an agreeable funereal decor and good numbers. After that, a place which seems to me the best I've seen in N.Y., Torcy's, just opposite Billie Holiday. It's the place you'd go to every evening if you were a New Yorker, intimate and a bit shady, with a dash of music, whisky and hookers.

We talked about Koestler. Apparently, before him, Mamaine[423] was with a sadist who once left her for dead: she remained alone for three days in an abandoned house, more dead than alive. Torcy (the American, he has the same name as the bar we were in) is obviously homosexual, knowing Larronde and all his gang.[424] But he's very amusing when he talks about people, and very nice. I spent an excellent evening, drinking 4 different cocktails and at least 6 whiskies without the least trouble.

Sleep, telephone. I finally finished the article for *Vogue* – which is a relief – and am just off to dictate it to a typist. Then I'll prepare my lecture a bit. Then deliver it. Apparently there'll be a huge crowd, and cocktails afterwards at Lévi Strauss's. Farewell, my love, I must leave you. Do you admire all I've done in these past two weeks? Almost all the districts of New York, and all the museums and galleries, the cinemas, all the nightclubs you'd told me about and others too, and so many people. In April I'll know exactly whom not to see, which will be better still. Old Macdonald[425] from *Politics* made me a nice phone call

---

[423] Alfred Koestler's wife.
[424] A poet who had been published in *Les Temps Modernes*.
[425] Dwight Macdonald (1906-82) had been an editor of *Partisan Review* from 1937 until 1943, when he left it to found *Politics*. He was De Beauvoir's senior by just two years!

this morning. There were ten times as many people to see as I wanted. But I've almost always had long, empty hours just to myself – that's what has been so agreeable. Today the weather's very mild and clear, people are skating in Central Park, and New York has never been more engaging. Goodbye, my love. You're more lovely and more beloved than all the New Yorks in the world. Write to me, dearest little one.

Your Beaver

[New York]

Monday Morning 17 February [1947]

Most dear little being, my dear love

I had two letters from you at the beginning of the week. Finally you'd received mine and were answering me – I was very happy, my love. This morning I'm back from my trip and there's nothing. Perhaps something will arrive in the course of the day. I've so many things to tell you. And yet I haven't written all week – so you can see how busy I am, and therefore how much I'm enjoying myself, my sweet little one.

Listen then. I wrote to you on Tuesday from the Sherry-Netherland, I recall – that was before my lecture. All that day was spent writing letters and articles and preparing the lecture. I gave it at 8.30 at the Modern Museum, and even according to the Gerassis – who, as you know, are objective friends – it was a success. Stépha told me I looked radiantly beautiful in my 'concession' dress[426] (which is, in fact, a necessity here) and the lovely necklace. I spoke about the writer's responsibility, and had the impression it went down well. After that Lévi-Strauss had organized a cocktail party – deadly boring, of course. I saw Hessel, whom I didn't much care for. Thineray introduced me to some people from *Reader's Digest*. Perhaps it'll work out – it would bring in $1,000, which would be fantastic. Whole procession of people: Mme Parodi[427] (who'd apparently invited me round ten times; I'd never had her message and apologized), and other ladies who thanked me 'in the name of France' – I'm not sure for what. After that the Gerassis took me to the most charming bar, very plebeian, with a Negro singing

---

[426]Shortly before this, De Beauvoir had for the first time bought a dress that she considered expensive (25,000 F.). She felt very guilty about it, calling it her 'first concession'. See *Force of Circumstance*, p.120.

[427]Wife of the inspector-general of schools, who had always been very kind to De Beauvoir and Sartre, appointing them to schools close to one another even though they were not married.

– the Tally-Ho, on one of the big avenues – I don't know why you didn't tell me about it. We drank whisky till one in the morning, while Stépha told me very entertaining stories about the Bowery.

Wednesday was my last day in New York and I was quite overcome to be leaving. I had piles of things to do. I had to go to *Vogue*, in order to dictate my article to the typist and collect some cheques; an interview on the radio, with the Day woman's husband; another at the hotel, with a guy from the *New Yorker*. I had lunch at midday with R. Wright and Abel in a little tavern in the Village, then we had coffee at their place. I'd brought a big jar of candies for the little girl, who flung her arms round my neck. She's ravishing, and though I don't usually like children I adore her. Actually all three of them are adorable with me: they've given me addresses in Chicago, and it's like having a real family in New York – I feel at home with them.

[. . .]

This evening I'm leaving New York for good. But now I'm thirsty for travel, so I've no regrets.

My love, my dear love – there's a letter from you and nothing more is lacking for me to be completely happy. It contained the cheque, which has come at just the right moment. All the same I'm going to borrow $300 from Lévi-Strauss, in order to be rich in California. Actually I'm going to find fortunes here when I get back: from *Vogue*, *France-Amérique*, *Town and Country*, some lectures, and perhaps *Reader's Digest* as well. I spent the morning busy with those articles, now I'm off for lunch at the Gerassis'. I have a few things to tie up, then a walk or a film and I leave this evening for Rochester.

It's quite true that twice in Washington I felt an electric shock while touching the elevator button, and at the same hotel my key gave off sparks while being inserted in the lock. But what's not true is that it's hard to find 'Ladies' in New York – there are sumptuous ones in every cafetria. It seems strange to be leaving. It's as though I were leaving you to some extent. Till *10 March* I'll be c/o Mrs Moffat, 411 South Barrington Avenue, Westwood 24, Los Angeles. Afterwards Moffat will forward mail. So write there. I'm still writing to Rue Bonaparte. Tell your mother to forward my letters, or else cable an address to Sorokine's.

Goodbye, my love. I'm the happiest of queens because I'm at once travelling and not separated from you. Do tell Bost about everything. Oh, yes! Tell everybody that there never was any book called *I'll Spit on your Graves* in America, or any author called Sullivan. It was Vian who did the whole thing himself.[428] Did that bitch Macht send the splendid article from the *New Yorker*?

My love, I kiss you with all the joy in my heart. Do write. Your letters give me such happiness. I'm with you all the time.

Your charming Beaver

[train – Kansas City]

Sunday 23 February 1947

Here I am in the great train going to California. There's a long halt at Kansas City and I can start writing. I'm really delighted, and even rather moved, to think that I'm going to see this country, and that I'll have a real home out there – after all this time being just a tourist. It's agreeable to think there's something waiting for you: that it's not up to you to try and make a place for yourself in the unknown, but a comfortable one's all ready for you.

[...]

Next day, that's Wednesday, I spent all morning in the train. I saw the great lakes, just as I'd wished. We travelled all along Lake Erie, for 4 hours – it was frozen and unending. However, I read an excellent book, from which we absolutely must publish huge extracts in *T.M.* It's called *Class and Caste in the South*,[429] by an American sociologist – and the method's as interesting as the content. It's a kind of counterpart to your *Portrait of the Anti-Semite* but on the Blacks – and also scholarly in character. It contains everything on the problem of the South. It was old Dwight Macdonald who lent it to me – all those people were so kind. I read till Cleveland. There, for 25 cents, I put my luggage in a little locker and took the key – I'm always delighted by such 'gadgets' – and asked a driver to take me round Cleveland. A million inhabitants, and a bit less dreadful than Rochester or Buffalo because of the lake, which is very beautiful. But I was beginning to feel crushed by all these 'hopeless' cities. The driver took me round for almost an hour for $2, and we had a long conversation as I always do – and what enchants me is that almost all of them were in Paris as soldiers. They're terribly nice, and so proud of being Americans. This one put me down at the Cleveland Museum where there's a very fine collection of paintings, with a big blue Picasso and, on that very day, a big Degas exhibition. It was a

---

[428]Boris Vian, novelist and jazz musician friend of De Beauvoir and Sartre, had pretended to have translated the book which he had in fact written himself, hoping to cash in on the vogue for all things American.

[429]*Caste and Class in a Southern Town* (1937), by John Dollard.

relief to see how that world still contained things that could be looked at with pleasure. After that, I went and took the Greyhound to Oberlin. For 1½ hours – the city, other cities, always houses. At Oberlin it was 5 o'clock. It's just a village surrounding a college, there was plenty of snow and peace, and I was very happy – especially since they'd booked a superb room for me in a very pretty country hotel. I took a bath and spent a long time dressing. Then I met up with a professor and his wife – she's André Masson's sister[430] and they're as like as two peas in a pod. So conversation was easy. I had dinner at the Maison de France, gave my lecture, and three very nice students took me for a drink at a bistro. We drank coffee, since no alcohol is drunk in Oberlin, and talked a lot about American intellectual youth: I'm beginning to understand them properly and it seems to be a 'hopeless' case, alas! I'm afraid I'm going to come back from here an out-an-out communist – there can't be less freedom in Russia than here. Well, it would take a long while to explain it all. I think you had exactly the same feeling anyway. Then I went to sleep. And this morning: departure for Chicago.

Monday

My dear love. I stopped the letter yesterday evening, I'm going to finish it this morning. I'm in seventh heaven. I woke up as the sun was rising over a great desert and for the past two hours we've been travelling through spectacular landscapes of red earth, scrub and mountains under a fantastic sun. What a contrast with the ice of Buffalo and Chicago! I was up by 7, because I'd gone to bed early. I had my breakfast and am now in the 'Lounge', where there's a bar, a radio, all the magazines you could want, and tables for writing. A long train journey like this is very enjoyable. So I set off.

Tuesday

The train is jolting too much and I haven't been able to write. I'll tell you about Chicago tomorrow. It's now 7.30, I've just woken up and I'm crossing huge fields of orange-trees covered with oranges. In half an hour I'll be in Los Angeles. I'm hoping for a letter from you there. I dreamed about you and you were very nasty – that tells you how satisfied with you I still am. Goodbye, my dear love. I kiss you with all my love. Write to me.

Your charming Beaver

(Address as letter 26 January 1947)

---

[430]André Masson (1896-1987), the surrealist painter.

[Los Angeles]

Friday 28 February [1947]

My dear love

How happy I was to find your letter here. You're writing faithfully, o yourself, and that counts for a lot in my happiness. I'm beginning to feel a bit distressed to think that you'll be heaven knows where when this letter arrives, and that you'll have to reply to me back in New York. Write c/o Mme Gerassi, 215 E. 57th. I'm writing to you from a room at Sorokine's. It's marvellous: you can see the whole of Los Angeles in the distance, and the sea, and there are big eucalyptus trees and horses and hens – it's countryside and town at the same time. On the table there's an immense basket of oranges and orange-blossom that some unknown admirer sent me. Also, I'm writing to you with an everlasting fountain-pen given me yesterday by Annabella[431] – though actually, I don't find it very comfortable and will probably abandon it along the way. I'm enjoying myself more than ever, though a piece of my heart remains firmly in New York.

First, you should know that Chicago wasn't terrible. On the contrary, I liked Chicago a lot, perhaps because I liked the guy with whom I saw it. I took the train at a little station near Oberlin College, and we travelled for six hours along a frozen lake while I read. At Chicago, they (the consul) had reserved a room for me at a splendid hotel. I at once went off to spend an hour at the Museum, then had a walk round and a taxi-drive down Michigan Avenue and all along the lake. Then I phoned a certain Nelson Algren,[432] a friend of Wright's and beloved of that wretched Mary Guggenheim. He replied that I had a wrong number, because I wasn't pronouncing his name properly. I tried three times to explain to him, but as soon as he recognized my voice he'd shout: 'It's a wrong number!' with growing exasperation. I gave up and hastily did some work on an article for *France-Amérique*, which I was supposed to send off in a great hurry. But I wanted to go out for the evening with this guy, so I got an American woman to ring up and she pronounced his name right. We made our explanations, and at 9 I met up with him at the hotel. He's a typical American, poker-faced and physically inexpressive, who started off travelling across America on freight trains and working a a 'pin-boy' – the person who picks up the skittles in bowling-alleys. Then he started writing, had a bit of success, and now for two years he has been living on a publisher's advance, after which he'll start again earning his living as best he can. He writes books about Chicago – where he has always lived – that remind you of both Saroyan and Damon

---

[431]The actress.
[432]Nelson Algren (born Abraham, 1909-81) had published his first novel in 1935 but was not to achieve success until the publication of *The Man with the Golden Arm* in 1949 (see notes 416 and 421 above).

Runyan. And he's more or less a communist, of course. I found him very nice, and intelligent, and human – as they can be when they're successful. He immediately grasped where he should take me first: to the Chicago Bowery – to a dance-hall rather like Sammy's, but even more sordid and less commercial; to a little club where magnificent women stripped naked and danced obscenely under totally indifferent eyes; to a Negro club; and to a little Polish bar. The streets outside were cold, full of snow, entirely deserted – it was very different from New York and in a sense more potent. He put me in a taxi – kissing me clumsily, but very seriously and intently – and I had a long conversation with the driver on the way home.

The next day, I was intending to spend the whole day with the guy and was beside myself with fury when a telephone call came from the consul, who'd 'arranged' my day. I had to accept a lunch at the Alliance Française and dinner with the consul – I was livid. I returned to that fantastic museum, got a taxi to drive me to the Bowery, and also took a long taxi-drive along the lakeside and round the downtown area – which I find almost as beautiful as New York. Then a horrible lunch at the Alliance, with horrible old ladies and a fake French woman of letters. The consul wasn't too disagreeable, in a loutish way – it's possible to put up temporarily with that type of man. A friend of his, a well-informed but revolting American businessman, took me for a big tour round in his car before dropping me off at Algren's, where I had an appointment. He lives in a scruffy little house in the Polish neighbourhood, and you should have seen those gentleman's shocked faces when they had to stop the car in that squalid street. I found my guy in his little, indigent intellectual's room and he took me to the streets and bars of the Polish neighbourhood. The bars were very agreeable: outside the wind was bitter and we'd hurry inside to down a vodka in the warm. He showed me old gangster bars and told me lots of stories. I had the impression of leading a little neighbourhood life – it was all very informal – and we got on very well despite my English. I was terribly upset, because he'd arranged a dinner for me with one of the two authors of *Black Antiquities*, and I couldn't go. He also rushed to the phone to order the books I wanted for me – he was so nice – and in the end he asked me so insistently to return to Chicago, and kissed me with such feeling outside the taxi when I left, that I was moved myself. It gave Chicago a very genuine and very intense savour. After that I went and had dinner in a magnificent restaurant beside the lake with the consul and the businessman, and it was boring and irritating. They took me ceremoniously to the train, the businessman bought me quantities of books and magnificent reviews, and I went to bed in my berth full of excitement at the idea of that big journey – three nights and two days. The 2nd day did in fact drag a bit, but all in all it was very agreeable. I read the latest Steinbeck and lots of other things – and how beautiful that scenery is on the second day, when you're crossing deserts. A guy approached me on the first day, (a guy of 50 or 60) in the dining-car, with that nice, direct manner of theirs, and asked me over lunch my opinion on Russia. And he gave me a book of his. He's a journalist – a war correspondent, who also used to teach at Harvard, but was thrown out because he'd written too favourably about Russia. He's going to carry out a big survey throughout Europe, with a whole team, to try and understand where Europe's future lies. He's not a communist, but an idealistic sympathizer. Once again, I was staggered to see how the political problem is posed in different terms for those people and for us. He got out at Emporia, where he was going to give a pro-Russian lecture. I put his book, adorned by a huge portrait of Stalin, down beside me. The face of the Negro who does the sleeping-berths lit up, and he pointed at it with a broad grin: 'Oh! this is a good guy!' And he did me lots of little extra services throughout the journey. It's all these tiny things which make relations with people here so warm and pleasant, and which enliven a journey so much.

On Tuesday at 8, I arrived. Sarbakhane was at the station, her hair and face magnificent, but more enormous than ever. She had a little car that Moffat has bought her especially for us, which is truly kind. I was terribly glad to see her. She brought me here, which is a charming spot where Moffat was waiting with a lovely little breakfast on the table. O yourself! – I'm madly excited, since it's possible Capra might film 'Immortal Man'[433] with Claude Rains and Greta Garbo. It seems very serious. Moffat is a 'writer' under the orders of Stevens, the director of *Gunga Din*[434] and a friend of Capra's. Stevens is very interested by the subject as presented to him by Moffat, and he has asked Moffat to do a treatment of 'Immortal Man' before taking on any other work. Moffat's going to do that this week, and he says it's almost certain that either Capra or Stevens will accept it – and that otherwise he'll find someone else. Stevens, with whom I had lunch yesterday, seemed also to like me very much, so much so that he's going to accompany us on part of the trip we're going to take round California. We talked about the project a bit and he was very interested. I promised Moffat – who'll do the cutting and the dialogue and everything – half the net profits. It would mean at least $30,000 for me – doesn't that make your head spin? We'd live for a whole year in America, you and I. My head's already buzzing with plans. I know quite well that lots of things like this fall through, I've got no illusions, but I find just the idea so enjoyable.

I've had three fantastic days here. Sorokine has taken me gallivanting

---

[433]De Beauvoir's novel *All Men Are Mortal*, published in 1946.
[434]George Stevens (1904-   ) had made *Gunga Din* in 1939, and De Beauvoir had seen it before the war.

about everywhere: to the seaside; to the cemetery, which is extraordinary; into the hills; to Pasadena, etc. I gave lectures at Los Angeles on Tuesday and at Pasadena on Wednesday. We'd leave at about 10 and drive round till the lecture at about 3. Then, in the evening at 6, we'd meet Moffat over a scotch-and-soda in the prettiest bars. The first evening they took me to the Mexican quarter, which is very, very agreeable, and we ate in a restaurant so pretty it would have reduced the Kosakiewitch sisters to tears. The band, the cabaret, the cuisine and the drinks were all Mexican. Afterwards we went to a very pretty nightclub, with good jazz. On the second day we went to a kind of Los Angeles Montparnasse, at the bottom of a canyon beside the sea. There was a French café of the artistic kind with French cuisine, also very agreeable. We made a trip to Venice, to the Luna Park which Sorokine talked about in *T.M.*, and went on to the most terrifying 'scenic railway' of my life. Moffat was marvellous – with his abstract despair and his puritanical disapproval – as we plunged into abysses. Some day I'll try and find the time to tell you about Sorokine and him. They really couldn't love each other more intensely, and they're aggreeable together. I have a lot, really a lot, of affection for Moffat.

Yesterday was cinema day. In the morning I went to the hairdresser's and visited the village of Westwood, near where we're living – it's close to Beverly Hills. The village itself is very pretty. We went and picked up Moffat at the studio. Stevens invited us to lunch at Lucy's, in between the three by Hollywood studios – it's the big restaurant of the stars – and the clientele was indeed very diverting and the food magnificent. After that, we visited the studios and watched bits of scenes being filmed. I had my photo taken between two magnificent, half-naked 'glamour girls', each holding one of my hands – I'll send you the photo – you'd have *had* to laugh, and Bost too. After that, the consul had arranged a tea party at Annabella's – she'd had to sit through my lecture on Tuesday, poor thing. What was very convenient was the fact that the consul's a friend of Moffat's – he's the one who has arranged lectures for Sarbakhane, whom he introduces everywhere as my adoptive daughter – so people always ask us all together. Annabella was charming, she gave me this fountain-pen and we exchanged kisses. J. P. Aumont was there,[435] looking like a butcher's boy. It wasn't very enjoyable, but we stayed only for an hour. Afterwards, a sumptuous Chinese dinner in the smartest restaurant in Los Angeles – truly the most beautiful setting I've ever been in – a kind of aquarium or Haitian conservatory with the most marvellously pretty and astonishing lights and decor. The consul was host. I drank a monstrous zombie[436] and ate delicious things. But the

[435] Jean-Pierre Aumont: see note 103 above.
[436] A cocktail containing seven different rums of contrasting colours.

discussion about Genet's *Thief's Journal* turned sour. We parted with effusive cordiality, but I detest the fellow and he returns my sentiments. After we left him, Moffat took us to the very top of a hill from which you can see all Los Angeles at your feet. An immensity of twinkling lights and silence. It was very mild, and we stayed for quite a while smoking cigarettes and gazing. We were very happy. We went to bed at 2 in the morning. But I rose at 8 and spent two hours writing to you while they still slept. Sorokine is bustling about, since we're leaving for Ojaj where she has her daughter staying, in the mountains between Los Angeles and San Francisco. After that to San Francisco, returning via Reno and Death Valley. Sor. drives very decently. On Wednesday 12th, Chaplin is presenting his film on Landru[437] and there'll be a party and everything – I'm terribly pleased because we'll just have got back. Stevens is also going to show me *The Oxbow Incident*[438] and other films, and perhaps there'll be a jazz jam-session. And I have to work with Moffat too on 'Immortal Man'. As you see, I'm full of fine plans.

I received Bost's letter. It gave me a grat deal of pleasure, but he should write to me more often. I'd like him to have news of me, if you're far away. You might perhaps send him this letter? At all events, don't lose my letters, I beg of you – they'll be my only memory of here.

Goodbye, my love. I'm hoping for one or two letters more here. I'm happy when I have your letters and feel myself not forgotten. I'd like to live in America with you for a good long while. I live with you all the time, and kiss you with all my might.

Your charming Beaver

(Address as letter 26 January 1947)

[San Francisco]

Tuesday 4 March [1947]

Most dear little being

Where are you? I'm beginning to feel really far away from you, and to feel great yearnings of desire to see you again. Write to me now c/o the Gerassis, 215 E. 57th – I'll be there in a month. If it weren't for this separation that I'm beginning to experience with some distress (especially at night), I'd be the most shamefully blissful of Beavers. Here I am now in San Francisco. It doesn't have the mystery and depths of N.Y. or Chicago, but

---

[437] *Monsieur Verdoux* (1947).
[438] 1943 film by William Wellman, which indicted bigotry through the story of a lynching in the last century.

I don't know any city more charming. I know you roamed about – and even got a bit lost – among these hills, and that's a little concrete link with you. My love, after writing to you on Friday morning Sarbakhane and I went and made lots of little purchases in the village of Westwood, then valiantly took to the road in her little grey car. It was a mountain road, with views over the sea – very, very pretty. We stopped on the way at one of those charming roadside inns (one of them had a flesh-and-blood *elephant* in lieu of a sign), had lunch, and arrived at about 4.30 at Ojaj, a dreadful little village in a fantastic valley of orange trees in the middle of the mountains. Did you know there are little stoves set up between the rows of orange trees, and they're lit on really frosty nights to stop the buds from freezing? They're amazing to see. We first went for a long car drive all round the area, with views over the valley and everything. Then we went and picked up Soroki-ne's daughter, who's being wet-nursed by a bloated monster of obesity, and took her with us to the house of Moffat's mother Iris. It's 4 miles from the village, a house to make the two Kosakiewitch sisters cry their hearts out, with the landscape, colours and flowers of an earthly paradise, and inside the most marvellous Mexican and Indian objects. We were alone there, and we wandered about and chatted and played with the child, who appeals to me neither more nor less than any other child of that age – six months – i.e. not at all. Then Moffat turned up, with Iris and a man friend. She resembles a thin, old, American version of Wanda. In the valley she has a little theatre, where she stages plays by Shakespeare and by herself, with amateur actors living in the vicinity who fill the house like parasites from dawn till 2 in the morning. She's a fantastic bohemian. We dined in haphazard fashion off a few salmon steaks that Sor. had bought and grilled, then drank whisky and listened to some very fine records, about which Sorokine wants to write a little article for *T.M.*: they're old mediaeval English songs taken over by the Americans a long while back – it was a nice evening. They put the little girl to sleep in my room, which didn't bother me except that in the morning she was dreadfully smelly. In the morning, Iris's room was full of men arguing and the garden full of actors gesticulating as they learned their parts. Everyone ate what they could – luckily Sor. had brought some eggs – and I wrote some letters and we went for a bit of a walk. And at about 1.30 we set off amid general encouragements for San Francisco, in the big red car that Moffat was lending us. Sor. doesn't drive badly, just over-cautiously – nothing crazy about her anyway. We followed mountain and coast roads, ate hamburgers in a dreadful village, and as evening was falling – at about 6 – arrived at a very pleasant little out-of-the-way place on the edge of a creek. We dined in a sea-food restaurant beside the sea, with tables lit by multicoloured candles – as is the way here – then went to bed in one of the little cabins of a motel. It couldn't have been more poetic. I read for an hour beside Sorokine, who was already sleeping, and by 9 I was asleep too.

On Sunday we were on the road by 7.30. A fantastic corniche road, totally wild. We did about 300 miles, or 450 km., during the day. We had breakfast in an isolated seaside inn, and lunch in a very pretty town, Monterey, do you know it? It dates from Mexican times, before the Gold Rush, and there are old, studiedly elegant houses that once sheltered famous (in the locality) brigands or governors. There's above all a fishing-port, very bustling and agreeable, where we had lunch on a boat in the open air. I felt as happy as a queen. I was very keen too to arrive at San Francisco by about 5.30 in the afternoon. But it was strange, because we didn't know exactly where the city was, and Sor. was afraid of driving in town with all those terrifying ups and downs. We arrived at the Golden Gate Bridge, and then all of a sudden we did catch sight of the city and the bay – how beautiful it is! – but we were by then on our way and could no longer retrace our steps. Eventually, though, we were helped to return and easily found a hotel, just near Market Street – i.e. right in the centre. That very evening we went up to the Top Mark on Hopkins. They didn't want to let Sorokine in, because they took her for a minor, but they did let her in all the same and we had drinks and looked. After that we had dinner at a good restaurant with quite agreeable music. Then a stupid film in which Bette Davis plays two twins.

Yesterday I saw San Francisco from one end to the other. In the morning on foot: to Chinatown; Telegraph Hill, with its charming little houses and magnificent view; and Fisherman's Wharf, where we had lunch in a pretty harbour restaurant looking out over all the little boats. Then we went for a big tour round by car, crossing the Golden Gate Bridge and following the coast – it's fantastically beautiful. Then we wandered on foot round Down Town, and went to the cinema to see *The Killers*,[439] based on the story of Hemingway – it's enjoyable. But after it there was a silly film which worried me a bit in connection with *The Chips Are Down*:[440] once again dead people coming back to earth, and there's exactly your gimmick – they sit in the laps of people who don't realize it. Sor. says she has seen that gimmick *10* times. After this we had a drink in a bar, ate a snack at a lunch-counter, and went home.

I've just got up. I have a lecture at Mills this afternoon and another on Thursday at Berkeley, so I'm staying here for another three days, which I'm very glad of. I'll be going back to L.A. by way of Reno, a big national park, and Death Valley. I'll tell you all about it later. Sorokine's terribly nice. She says something has died in her, and that gives her an angelic character. It's funny seeing her drive, but she manages; except that here she engages first

---

[439]Version by Robert Siodmak (1946).
[440]Sartre's *Les Jeux Sont Faits* was due to appear later in the year: see note 405 above.

gear whenever she goes down a hill, so that the engine acts as a brake and we go down like a funeral amid cars plunging headlong into the void.

Goodbye, my love. I think you too have seen and loved these things, so I feel less separated from you. Write to me, think about me, don't forget me. I kiss you with all my might.

Your Beaver

Tell Bost I'm still thinking about him too and wish he'd write.

[Lone Pine, California]

Sunday 9 March [1947]

My dear love

I'm quite astounded when I think that I've been here for six weeks already, yet not for one minute have I so far felt that slight nausea which, even together, we experience at the end of a journey. On the contrary, the more time goes by, the more I feel myself taking root – to the point where I can hardly imagine really leaving America. It seems to be part of my life, my culture and my world. I'm attached to it as though to a kind of motherland, in spite of all the horror and above all disappointment it causes me on the political side. I know you felt exactly this mixture of affection and anger.

My journey through California is as wonderful as my stay in New York was. The agreeable thing is that I have a home in Los Angeles. Though I stayed there for only three days and shan't be staying any longer, it's a base. And then I have all of New York as a home, with friends and plans awaiting me, so that I feel myself drifting across America not as a Frenchwoman but as an inhabitant of New York.

[. . .]

At 5 we arrived at Lone Pine, which is an out-of-the-way little place at the entrance to Death Valley, which you've seen in *Greed*.[441] We have an appointment here at midday with Moffat and Stevens – his boss, whom I told you about, who's the director of *Gunga Din* and interested in my 'Immortal Man'. He's going to take us to Death Valley. It was delightful having a long peaceful evening yesterday. We stayed reading on or in our beds from 6 till 11, with just a quick visit to the cafeteria opposite. I read a big Thomas Wolfe, which I found interesting, and an

---

[441] By Erich von Stroheim (1924).

odd book that Miller regards as a work of genius, by a certain Patchen[442] – I'm not yet sure quite what to think of it. But I want to read at least twenty books in these last two months (I have a list of about 50) and bring back a good harvest for the *T.M.*. It makes a very important additional bond to know the literature properly of the country you're in. This morning's a big free morning. It's 9 o'clock, I've had breakfast, and they're not arriving till noon. I'm going to do my correspondence and read. Moffat said on the phone that there was a lot of mail for me in Los Angeles and I'm waiting for him impatiently, since perhaps there'll be a letter from you.

[. . .]

My love, I've had three letters from you and a telegram. I'm wiring at once. I'm terribly unhappy that you're no longer getting my letters. I've read your letters and feel really upset not to be with you. Everything suddenly strikes me as a bit tragic, and you so far away with that trip to Italy. My love, I've written long letters twice weekly, thought about you all the time, and been so happy getting your letters. You've written so nicely. I love you, my little one. This separation is suddenly painful to me – two months to go. I know I'll find you just the same, all tender and warm – and so very close to me. I haven't left you either. Cable me your address if necessary. Meanwhile, I'll write c/o your mother and she should forward everything. My love, I don't want to leave you – here I am, all upset. I'll write again from Los Angeles. I love you. You're my life.

Your charming Beaver

[Los Angeles]

Thursday 13 March [1947]

My love

Here I am, on my own for the afternoon, in the Moffats' pretty house. I have cigarettes and martinis, books and a magnificent sky. I've lain down on the terrace, I can see the sea and I can see the eucalyptus trees – here I am like a real queen. Just one thing saddens me, which is that I no longer quite know where you are – perhaps already on the train to Italy – and you no longer quite know where I am. Have you finally

---

[442]Kenneth Patchen (1911-72), poet and novelist (*Memoirs of a Shy Pornographer*, 1945). The 'Miller' in question is Henry Miller, whose influence on Californian writers De Beauvoir had already noted.

received my letters and telegram? Those signs from you – so close – overwhelmed me. Your last letter was only 4 days old. It's so strange for me to be as happy and carefree as this for weeks on end, and to know nevertheless that my life is not in my own hands but back there in Paris, and that I depend entirely upon you. It would be almost painful if I didn't have such a strong feeling, my dear love, that we are as one, and that at the beginning of May you'll be just as I left you. And I'm so accustomed here to a life entirely on the surface – a life of pure pleasure and indifference – that it shook me to rediscover my love for you in all its intensity; rather as though I'd started thinking, really thinking, about death in the middle of a pleasure outing. And what I felt last Sunday has still not dissipated.

[. . .]

This journey by car has really been marvellous. I adore all the 'service stations' and 'drug stores', the records, the brief halts, the villages. And the landscapes of cactus and boulders and snowy mountains and desert are magnificently lavish. It breaks your heart not to be able to like as you'd wish the people inhabiting this beautiful stretch of the planet. But only the day before yesterday Truman was proposing his anti-communist crusade, sending planes to Greece, etc.[443] You feel more and more that you're living under fascism in this country – it's scary. I less and less feel any hope for this country. Well, since yesterday, I'm part of a family again. It's really agreeable. Sorokine and I did the shopping – in those wonderful grocery-shops they have here[444] – then prepared blinis and pineapple. When Moffat came back from the studio, we spent a long while with him drinking cocktails and eating while we discussed 'Immortal Man', on which he's working away relentlessly – and very well. I must tell you all about him, and about them both together. He's very interesting, as an American from England: anti-American yet so very American in certain ways. We get on amazingly well – I enjoy his company a lot and he enjoys mine. We went to a nightclub full of queers dressed up as women, and to a very nice Hungarian nightclub. But everything closes at midnight in Hollywood, and it's really dead. After Las Vegas and its dissolute pleasures, we were a bit disappointed. This morning I gave a *lecture in English* at the University – big success! I'm overjoyed. I can give lectures in English, and that will bring me in some money. It will also allow me to come back here very easily. I want to come back to America, and I want to come back with you, my love. I've

[443]The so-called Truman Doctrine, intensifying the Cold War.
[444]There were no supermarkets in France at this time.

just been to the village with Sorokine to have my hair done, then I came home while she went off to town till this evening. Moffat's working at his studio. I'm alone and comfortable. I like the way people leave their houses open here, and the way delivery vans drive right into the garden, and how everything's easy and relaxed. The evenings are marvellously mild. I'm staying another two days, then on Sunday I'm leaving with Sor. by bus for the Grand Canyon, Sante Fe, Houston and New Orleans, where I have lectures. Write now for 27 March – if there's still time – c/o Marcel Morand, head of the Romance Languages Dept., Rice Institute, Houston, Texas. Otherwise c/o the Gerassis, 215 E. 57th, for 5 April. My love, I'd like so many letters! I'll still write to your flat. Keep these letters for me, please. I'd like Bost to have them too, and know that all this time I'm thinking tenderly about him. My love, do whatever you think best, but above all feel me right there with you. I kiss you with all my love.

Your charming Beaver

My Chicago friend has sent me a big parcel of books, and such a nice letter that I was moved by it. I can't get over the kindness of people on all sides.

[Williams, Arizona]

Monday 16 March [1947]

My dear little one, my love

Where are you now? I'm afraid it may be a really long while before you receive these letters and I yours. You can wire me an address at the Gerassis' on about 5 April, if we find ourselves too far separated. For my part, I left Los Angeles yesterday and am writing from my bed in a room at Williams, where I arrived yesterday evening with Sorokine and from where we'll be leaving shortly for the Grand Canyon. My feelings are somewhat confused, because I miss that house where I so enjoyed myself, the red car, and – especially – Moffat. Of course, our departure more or less upset what had been a peaceful, tender friendship. Sorokine, Moffat and I spent all Saturday night together, at the house of some very nice friends who'd assembled for me some interesting directors, some very pretty girls, and a splendid collection of records. I met Man Ray there,[445] among others, which brought back to me all my

---

[445]Man Ray (1890-1976), American artist and experimental film-maker influenced by Dadaism and Surrealism.

old memories of the Ursulines and avant-garde cinema. We played records and talked and drank whisky till 3 in the morning. At 5 we got up and Moffat took us to the bus, through a Los Angeles bathed in dawn like a European city and absolutely unfamiliar in its solitude and its silence. Meanwhile, and again at the bus depot, we kissed one another overcome by the emotion of our departure, we said the right words (more or less), he quarrelled with Sorokine, and everything became heavy and separation painful. You see what I mean. It's above all such a definitive separation: not the least future, for all those pleasant days of friendship or those last hours of emotion. But it'll pass, especially since Sorokine's such a nice companion, and the bus journey should be magnificent. But what a funny thing it is to travel like that, leaving little fragments of one's heart more or less everywhere. Through this departure I'm scared of my departure from America too, despite all the happiness of being back with you again. Here I am, at exactly the halfway stage, and I feel such strong bonds with this whole country.

[. . .]

Yesterday we caught the bus,[446] then, and drove from 7 in the morning till 10 in the evening through magnificent scenery. It's not at all tiring and I'm grateful to Bost for giving me the idea. Do tell him how I'm thinking of him as I repeat this journey in his tracks, but in the opposite direction. Tell him I don't forget him for one moment.

My love, goodbye. I'm in a state because of you too, and this break in our letters, and all that worry you had in Paris with the cinema and so on and so forth. Now I'm writing at the cafeteria while waiting for the bus. Basically, I'm extremely happy, because everything's potent and so full and so rich – I'd never expected so much from this journey. And with you basically it's security, joy, and calm love. Even this superficial melancholy doesn't taste bad. Goodbye, my love. I kiss you with all my love.

Your charming Beaver

[New Orleans]

Monday 30 March [1947]

My dear little one, my love

Once again you weren't lying, and once again here I am full of

---

[446]A Greyhound.

emotion at finding myself on your trail. How agreeable New Orleans is, perhaps the most agreeable of all. I wrote to you from Houston, I think, which is on the contrary really ugly, but where I wasn't bored. I had a gloomy lunch with old university people, but in the afternoon they took me for a car jaunt – and it was very striking to see all those estates and opulent colonial residences belonging to the oil barons, with tall, calm Negroes mowing their lawns in the sunlight. Do you recall those trees bearing great veils of grey foam on their branches? I love that Southern vegetation, that rotten, melancholy side of the landscapes and houses which goes so well with the tragedy of the races. There was a dinner – in a nice spot that was typically Southern – and however dumb people are, they always have stories to tell the first time. After that my lecture, in a marvellous University full of azaleas and camellias. Then some guy took me to a wrestling match. It was very funny, totally faked in the style of a bad film, but with a delirious crowd shouting: 'Kill him!' or throwing the referee over the ropes, etc. Then the guy took me to drink beer (since whisky's forbidden in Texas, except in the form of bottles purchased in advance and which people pull out of their pockets), in a typically Texan place decorated with steers' horns and photographs of cows.

The next day was a long bus drive. Sorokine groans and suffers as though I were making her do the journey on foot, but (as I've already told you) I quite like it. I read a lot and let myself be caught by the scenery – and this scenery in the South is incidentally pretty fascinating. We had a room reserved at the luxurious Roosevelt Hotel – is that where you stayed too? I'd so like to know, in order to follow you more closely. I just had time to eat dinner before we were fast asleep. Yesterday morning, the enchantment began. All morning we traipsed on foot round that neighbourhood you described so well to me, with its balconies of wrought iron; then by taxi through the parks and along blossoming avenues. It's just the season for blossom and fresh leaves, and the spring here has marvellous autumn colours under a sultry, tropical sky. Lunch at the Louisiana Restaurant, with French cuisine. Afternoon in a boat on the Mississippi. Meanwhile, I'm reading a gripping book on Russia: it's by Kravchenko,[447] who used to be at the Soviet Embassy in Washington but left the party during the past few

[447]Victor Kravchenko defected from the Soviet embassy in 1944 and published *I Chose Freedom* in 1946. Its French translation was to provoke a big controversy in 1949, when *Les Lettres Françaises* denouncd it as an American intelligence fabrication and Kravchenko successfully sued for libel (see *Force of Circumstance*, pp. 173-4). The surrounding disputes were to resurface, lightly transposed, in De Beauvoir's *The Mandarins*.

years. He tells the story of his own experience, which exactly matches Koestler's accounts, and I think we honestly should publish extracts in the *T.M.*

[...]

On Wednesday I leave for N.Y. by the coast: Jacksonville, Savannah, Charleston and Virginia. It will take 4 days by bus, and a night in the train at the end since I know the last part of the route. And Sunday – N.Y. and your letters. I feel myself drawing closer to your letters and drawing closer to you. I'm quite overcome with joy at this, at the same time that it breaks my heart to be leaving America. How I'd love to find myself here with you! Where are you? In Italy? Have you got my letters? Wire me an address, perhaps, c/o the Gerassis. Where's Bost? I know nothing of him or of Kos, or of anybody. I feel quite lost. But always close to you and with you, my love. I kiss you with all my might.

Your Beaver

Williamsburg Lodge
Williamsburg
Virginia

Saturday [6 April 1947]

Most dear little being

I'm writing to you from a place that strikes me as really strange: it's an entire town that the Americans have reconstructed just as it was 200 years ago. I haven't yet seen it, because it's dark; I've merely had dinner in a fine hotel full of tourists here for the Easter holiday. Tomorrow evening I'm taking the train for N.Y., I have a Pullman ticket in my pocket and am really excited. Write to the Lincoln – I've booked a room there. My heart's racing at the thought of seeing N.Y. again, but at the same time this scares me a bit. I'm going to find letters from you there, my love, and will write to you at once.

My dear little one, how I did love New Orleans! More than anything – along with New York. I wrote to you from there, but before I'd been for an evening out. Apparently it wasn't as good as it should have been, because due to Holy Week the places they really should have taken us were closed – but it was fantastic all the same. I had dinner with Sor. at the Patio Royal, which is charming. Then at the Absinthe House we found our jazz band with its 3 Negroes again, and also our white friend:

a little Italian of 22, crazy about jazz and James Joyce and Stravinsky, but not out of snobbery – since he's from the most modest middle-class background – but through a true vocation. He was remarkably intelligent and nice and lonely. And this, too, was a strange experience: to find in reality someone who seemed to come straight from the pages of Dorothy Baker's *Young Man with a Trumpet*, or of *Really the Blues* – a book on jazz that I like very much.[448] We listened to those three black men and chatted with them and we had the charming impression of being at home. And then we went to another place with an excellent little black band, and our guide (who had with him a very nice Spanish friend) knew them too, which made for a powerful complicity in the midst of that white audience – as ugly, upright, and ill-flavoured as a Berlin crowd. We went to the Negro neighbourhood too – to clubs closed to whites – and felt a great deal of friendship for one another and a great joy in that jazz, which is the only really good jazz I've heard in America. What's more, the weather was quite extraordinary – a pearly grey fog shedding an extremely bright light – so that at 2 in the morning you'd have thought it was dawn, while the lights of the city itself seemed to come from another planet. The air was as humid as in a greenhouse. It was one of the most poetic evenings of my life, perhaps the most poetic of all, and was so rich in meaning that a great deal of care would be needed to describe it properly. New Orleans was still extraordinary next day. In the morning there was still a pearly grey sky with great squalls of rain. In the afternoon, the people from the University took me by car to visit patios and old houses. There was such a downpour that we often couldn't get out of the car or see through the windows – but it had a cataclysmic grandeur. At about 6 the storm abated and I saw the strangest sky I've ever seen, yellow and grey over the flooded city. How I did love that putrefaction, and that splendour of the vegetation and the houses and the whole civilization of the South. In the morning I'd walked a lot through the parks and streets, and my spirits were quite overwhelmed. I gave one lecture in English and one in French – with the aid of whisky and orthedrine, since I was exhausted by two almost sleepless nights. I saw some people who knew you – some of them idiots, others nice. We drank and talked. Again I went to bed late, and rose early to catch the bus. I drove all day on Wednesday – across Louisiana, Mississippi, Alabama and Florida, all along the Gulf of Mexico, across muddy rivers and towns in blossom and tropical forests – it was intoxicating. This South says more to me than all of

---

[448]Mezz Mezzrow's autobiography.

California and the Far West, yet at the same time I abhor it. On Thursday we went from Jacksonville to Savannah, a marvellous old city full of flowers and statues of the heroes of Independence: those men look as old as Caesar. Time is as contracted here as space is expanded – a century's an enormous past. We went for a walk through the black part of town, and the women spat as we passed and the children shouted out: 'The enemy! The enemy!' There was a weight of hatred everywhere that made your heart bleed. And so deserved! A pregnant Negro woman fainted in a bus, and *all* the whites including the driver laughed themselves silly without taking care of her – only Sorokine came to her aid. And the country areas, with all those squalid, unkempt 'cabins', are somehow pathetic. Yesterday we saw Charleston, a very pretty old English town, and some marvellous romantic gardens full of flowers, lakes, little bridges and great trees veiled in grey – gardens dating from 1700 in the middle of big plantations, the ultimate luxury in that delicious, horrible civilization. You can still see the slave market at Charleston on your way back from the gardens. Here, towards Richmond in the northern part of Virginia, the atmosphere is less stifling. But I shall never forget the black towns of Jacksonville, Savannah, Charleston, etc. – and the hatred and fear of the whites, which you can feel at every moment.

My love, how I'd like to talk to you about all that. Today we reached northern Virginia, just 8 hours from N.Y.: it's really the North and seems insipid to me. But finally it will be N.Y. the day after tomorrow – and other days. I've read a lot during these three weeks on the bus, and am starting to feel intensely something of America – with despair, on the whole.

Write to me, my dear little one. How I'm longing for your letters! I'll rush over to the Gerasssis' place at 8 in the morning on Monday, to pick them up. In a month I'll be close to you. I'm going to start waiting for that return. I still love you as strongly, my love.

Your Beaver

Hotel Lincoln
New York 19, N.Y.

Monday 14 [April 1947]

My dear love

What a joy to have some letters at last! The Lincoln one was 'returned to sender', while the Houston one I did receive was very old. But finally

I've received the one from Paris, dated 25 March, and the one from Rome. Agreed for 10 May. I was just in the process of booking my seat for the 6th, but that makes hardly any difference. I'll let you know for sure next time whether I'm arriving on the 10th or the 11th. I think it'll be the 11th. All I ask is to have you for a fortnight to myself. Fix up a nice return for me (I mean seeing you and seeing Bost, but nobody else), for I'm a bit scared – in spite of all my joy at seeing you again – at the idea of leaving the life here, which is one perpetual party. It's abnormal, and monstrous, and you know it can't last, but at the same time it's enchanting, and it seems terrible to have to return to a real life and return also to one's own self. Above all, I do so love New York.

[...]

On Saturday morning, after 5 hours' sleep, S. and I went to see the Charlie Chaplin film which has just opened on Broadway, *Monsieur Verdoux* – it's not fantastic. Then an idiotic lunch at the Bruxelles, with Prolers from *France-Amerique* and a stupid American princess (?). Afternoon at the Sherry-Netherland with S., to talk to her about her book (the Sarbakhane family), and then whisky at the home of Dwight Macdonald from *Politics*, whom I like a lot. Everyone admires the way in which I've seen America and know it, and how fast I speak in English – I'm very proud. After that, a whole group of us went to the Chinese theatre – the Gerassis, S. and I, Odette Lieutier and some friends of hers. She took us backstage, which was fun, but it was much less good than in San Francisco. The Gerassis and S. gave up, but I went to eat and drink in a charming old café in Greenwich Village, which finally decided me to spend my last weeks in a Greenwich Village hotel.

Tuesday

Goodbye, my love. I had to go and give my lecture at Columbia and this morning I'm leaving for Smith College. I'll write the continuation tomorrow. My love, I'm beginning to feel I'm going to see you again. I kiss you with all my might.

Your Beaver

Tell Bost I'll be glad to see him again, though he's a little bastard for not having written to me.

Wellesley College
Wellesley, Massachussetts

Wednesday 16 [April 1947]

My dear love

Thank heavens, here I am far away from New York for a few days – I think I'd have died of alcohol and lack of sleep. In these wholesomely boring colleges, I suddenly feel how exhausted I was. It's perfect, since otherwise these retreats would seem unbearable to me – I was terribly depressed taking the train yesterday. I had to stop my letter abruptly, so I'm going to pick it up again from Saturday. It's a whole journal I'm sending you, but I know that every word is pregnant with memories and meanings for you and, through these listings, you'll assuredly recognise the excitement and wonder of life here.

[. . .]

Then I went to write to you in a bar next door to Columbia. Dinner and lecture at Columbia: deadly. Drink with O'Brien and Thineray: deadly. At 11 I met Saenz at the bar of the Pink Elephant, and we drank whisky till 2 in the morning – partly because he's nice and partly because, with my heart broken over leaving New York, I couldn't make up my mind to go home to bed. Yesterday I left for Smith College, while S. took a plane in terror to go and see her father-in-law, on an island 1 hour away from N.Y. The people were nice at Smith. Today it was Wellesley and dreadfully boring. Tomorrow Wellesley again, then Harvard, then back to New York for three days, another three days of colleges, and two weeks of N.Y. which will certainly be fantastic, because everybody's preparing parties, jam sessions, outings, etc. for me. I'm dead with exhaustion, my love. But I feel really happy. Happy, with a touch of dread and almost of tragedy, because I've attached myself very strongly to things and people here, but at the same time it's such a fragile bond. I think I'll be in agony till I see you again. Goodbye, my very dear love.

Your Beaver

University of Pennsylvania
Philadelphia
The College
Romance Languages and Literatures

Thursday 24 April [1947]

Yourself, my love

Well then, in a fortnight's time (18 days to be precise) I'm going to see you. I'm as moved as I was 3 months ago at the idea of seeing New York. I have my aeroplane seat booked on *Saturday 10th*. So I'll get to Paris at about 3 on Sunday. Ask Air France for the exact time. Come to the Invalides, or perhaps just wait for me at the Louisiane – you'll be better off there if there's any delay, and for me it's only a quarter of an hour's difference. Tell me what you decide. At any rate, of course, we'll remain alone till the next day. I'd like to see Bost with you on Monday, and then for you and I to go away for the promised fortnight – anywhere. I have so many things to tell you, my love. The week before this was sweet and reposeful. Smith; Wellesley, from where I was shown the pretty villages of New England; Boston, where I lunched on the harbour in a charming restaurant, and from where I was taken for a drive up the coast. On the Friday evening I was speaking at Harvard, and I discussed with the students then returned to New York by plane, which delighted me. I spent three days in New York with Sarbakhane, in a real whirl because the articles are piling up and the invitations too. On Saturday I *spoke in English* on *The Flies* at the New School: it was a contradictory lecture, and I think people admired my courage more than my accent. After the lecture, dinner at Sweeney's with Duchamp,[449] which was very agreeable. After leaving them at midnight, big party in my honour at Piscator's place: Kurt Weill was there, Le Corbusier, lots of important people, and above all Charlie Chaplin with his wife. The dreaded Collins made a speech that invited me in some way to acknowledge Chaplin as an existentialist – it was grotesque and embarrassing. Chaplin held forth for almost 3 hours, and I found him more or less as Sorokine had described him, but it was fun actually speaking to him. I went to bed at 4 in the morning.

[. . .]

This morning I arrived at Philadelphia at 10 – and was once again driven through lovely countryside on the way to the University. Memories of you abound here. I saw Bryn Mawr, that girls' college

---

[449]Marcel Duchamp (1887-1968), Dadaist painter and inventor of readymades, was living in New York at this time.

where you went, and Coindreau[450] and Seizener spoke to me about you – it's odd finding oneself on your trail like this. I feel I'm on the home slope now, but I'll have two marvellous weeks at N.Y., I think. I'll have no regrets at leaving, in a sense, since this journey has more or less worn itself out. The main thing is to come back here, and now I know that's going to happen, I'm thinking about seeing you again, my love, which overwhelms me. Write to me quickly that you're expecting me. And do keep me my fortnight just for me. I kiss you with all my love.

Your Beaver

Hotel Brevoort
Fifth Av. at Eighth Street
New York 3

Wednesday [30th April 1947]

My love, my sweet little one

How happy I've been feeling since Monday. There was a long letter from you, all tender, and with a glow of warmth I felt how I'd soon be back with you. There's a place in your heart waiting for me in Paris, and that makes leaving easy – even delightful. So it's true, my love, in ten days you'll be there, I'll touch you, I'll speak to you – I'm in raptures. You see, more than the Liberation, more than my journey to New York, it's you every time who are the most astonishing experience in my life, and the strongest and the deepest and the truest. My love, I'm so happy to feel you close at hand that it radiates across New York. This imminent departure doesn't destroy N.Y. – quite the contrary. Never has N.Y. seemed so marvellous to me, and the fact of leaving it is a sufficient occupation, giving full meaning to every walk and every look. Add that the spring is warm and tender, and that to cap it all I'm really raking in the dollars and am beginning to buy some lovely things. The new circumstance is that since Monday, instead of the tormented nights I always used to have, I've been sleeping like an angel, with that sense of justification that your presence gives me.

When did I last write? From Philadelphia, I think. I gave my lecture there on Thursday evening, then caught a train at about 11. I fell asleep at once and by 8 in the morning was in Boston. The same charming spinster lady who'd taken me round a week earlier was waiting for me

---

[450]Maurice Coindreau, translator of Faulkner and other American novelists.

with a car, and she took me for a big trip northwards to Cape Ann, Marblehead, Rockport and lots of old New England villages. She was as joyful as a child and I too was very happy. Then I went back to the hotel, to work on an article called 'An Existentialist Looks at America' for the *N.Y. Times*. It's terribly hard on them – but so what? I think the country has grown worse over the past year and the atmosphere's becoming unbreathable – if I stayed I'd become a Communist. The students from Harvard and Yale speak of war with Russia in resigned, positive tones that send a chill down your spine. I saw them on the Saturday. First, I finished off the article in the morning. Then lunch at the Alliance Française, with the old ladies you know and that imbecile Benouville, the dreadful Moringe, and Chambon the Boston consul, who by some miracle is a decent man, utterly disappointed – as a Catholic – by American Catholicism. Lecture: I spoke about you, which I enjoyed. Cocktail party with some students. Dinner at Gurvitch's – I like him.[451] He was in seventh heaven at being able to give vent to a hatred of 7 years' standing, and told me shattering stories about American anti-Semitism. At 10 a group of students came to collect me and we went out drinking in the evil haunts of Boston (!! as my mother would say) till 3 in the morning. That's when I got the creeps. There's a real 'red scare', and people no longer dare to be liberal because they get labelled as Communists. 'We *have* to get business jobs', they explained to me, 'and if we're suspected of being reds, that's bad for us. What can we do?' Posed in this way, the question obviously has no solution. The most depressing part of it is that they were well-intentioned kids. The next day in the morning I caught the plane, which bounced me about dreadfully all the way to N.Y. What a joy to see N.Y. again! I'm also savouring my solitude, since it was really agreeable having S., but what freedom to find myself alone after these past two months of almost constant presence!

[. . .]

I'm going to spend another ten good days. First, between now and Sunday I'm finishing off my articles. After that it will be glorious freedom. And then you, my love. Cable to the Brevoort, to let me know where you'll be meeting me. I advise the Louisiane. Fix up a good return for me. I love you so much, o yourself, my love.

Your happy Beaver

---

[451] Gyorgy Gurvitch, the sociologist.

[New York]

Thursday 8 May [1947]

My love

I was really shattered when I found your cable. It seems so close – you, and Paris – and I could have seen you on Sunday. Now I'll have to wait another week. But it's you who've requested it. I found the idea of returning earlier than you wanted so unbearable, that on Saturday it made me quite ill when I couldn't exchange my seat. But on Monday I grovelled to everybody so successfully that by Tuesday it had all been fixed. So I'll be at the Gare des Invalides at about 10.30 on *Sunday 18th*. Send another cable to confirm. It made me ill because, of course, it's a wrench for me too to be returning, and I really do want to feel completely calm and free of problems in Paris, at least during the first days. I beg of you, my love, fix everything nicely so that we can be on our own for a long time, and nothing spoils the happiness of being back with you. I can't write to you properly, because I've been too overwrought for the past week. I've been sleeping 4 hours a night, not eating, and drinking like a fish. All the same, I'm going to try and provide you with the dry bones of a diary, since I know that it will come to life for you. I last wrote on Wednesday, I think.

That evening, an inept evening out with Millie and the Days, who give me the creeps, in an avant-garde night club with hot jazz designed for whites, which I can no longer stand because of all it implies in terms of blacks and whites. On Thursday I made a recording and worked on some articles. In the evening, Bernie Wolfe[452] took me to smoke marijuana in the apartment of a marvellous black dancer, with a party of homosexuals and lesbians. They were all 'high', as they say, and I was told that with *one* cigarette I would be too; but I smoked *six*, inhaling all the smoke, without anything happening. In a fury I drank more than half a bottle of whisky, which didn't make me drunk but certainly made me merry. I must say their eyes were popping out of their heads. Certainly, too, I found myself at 4 in the morning in front of the hotel engaged in kissing B. W. with all the pathos of my imminent departure. And the pathos was still there when I woke up, because I care for him a lot. I whiled away Friday working on urgent articles. I saw Bernie again at 5, and spent the evening with the people from *Partisan Review*, who didn't leave me until 2. It was Saturday morning and a dark rainy day when I had your letter and a dreadful 'breakdown', which kept me in tears all day – an anguish I just couldn't manage to

---

[452]Bernard Wolfe, a former secretary of Trotsky's now working as an editor and subsequently a novelist, appears in *America Day by Day* as L.W. and as Z.

cast off. I went to see *Open City*[453] – which is a beautiful film – but that didn't help me. I arrived all puffy-eyed at Charley Harrison's place,[454] where he'd cooked me a marvellous dinner. There was Bernie and Richard Wright and their wives. They were all angelic to me and R. Wright was marvellous – as he can be when he really relaxes, which hardly ever happens. I like him more and more: he's as surprising as Genet, in his own way. In short, we went to see dawn break over the East River and I went to bed at 8 in the morning. I dawdled around in bed – and after that in Greenwich Village, which won my heart on that damp Sunday afternoon with children playing ball in the streets. I feel as much at home here as at St-Germain-des-Prés: you meet people in the street, pay neighbourly calls, stroll about, sit in Washington Square to read or watch – it's incredibly pleasing. I drank an insipid cup of tea with students and teachers from Columbia, then an evening with Miró and the Certes couple at Gerassi's place, where he put me in a frightful rage by reproaching me in the name of N.Y. 'liberals' with keeping company only with Trotskyists – which is absurd seeing that neither Wright nor Wolfe nor anybody else is a Trotskyist, they're simply not Stalinists. Even so, again went to bed at past 2 o'clock against a background of whisky. On Monday I had a nice lunch with the Wrights, then worked; after that, lecture in English to 600 people, followed by a discussion. Then at 11 Bernie W., and a long night lasting till 5 in a charming Greenwich bar with 'No Music' – but with whisky. He told me about his life in Mexico, during the three years when he was Trotsky's secretary, and about his whole youth as a Jewish kid – it fascinated me, I felt I was really reaching America.

On Tuesday I left by train and bus to visit the Hares. I spent a charming, restful evening with Jacqueline, who was terribly nice and whom I really like. At last I slept. At 11 in the morning the Sweeneys and Duchamp turned up in a car stinking of gasolene. We had lunch at Tanguy's place,[455] then took tea with an old lady who owns 'The Bride Stripped Bare . . .'[456] At 7 I met up with Bernie W., who was taking me to dinner at the house of some homosexuals from Kiev, with Harold Rosenberg[457] who's a very intelligent guy, an art critic and former Marxist, with whom I argued about politics and philosophy till I was

---

[453]*Roma, città aperta*, by Roberto Rossellini (1945).
[454]See note 125 above.
[455]Yves Tanguy, the surrealist painter, had lived in the United States since 1939.
[456]Duchamp's famous glass 'The Bride Stripped Bare by her Bachelors Even' is now in the Philadelphia Museum of Art.
[457]Harold Rosenberg, close to *Partisan Review*, was the author notably of studies on Thomas Mann.

half-dead from exhaustion and exasperation (it's hateful in English) – the situation here really does get you down. After that, in an attempt to raise my spirits again, I stayed on in a Greenwich bar with B.W. till 4 in the morning. We continued the discussion amiably, but it was going round in circles all the same. This morning, an avalanche of telephone calls. At 1 I went with B.W. and his girl to see some very interesting ballet rehearsals, then I did some shopping and finished off my last article. In half an hour I'm having dinner with Wright and the local equivalent of our *Société des Gens de Lettres*,[458] then I'm speaking at their meeting. Tomorrow: evening out in Harlem with Wright, Wolfe and their wives. On Saturday I'm leaving by plane for Chicago for three days, to provide me with a change of mood. The guy I liked there[459] has been entreating me for two months to go back, and I think it'll be nice. Then I'll return for three days and leave on the Saturday. There. What's new is that for the first time I feel myself in America, I belong – because of the neighbourhood where I'm living, and the people to whom I've become close. Oh, I hate this country, and like the people who suffer from it, and would be appalled if I had to stay here – yet leaving it is having a strange impression on me. I've told you all this in a higgledy-piggledy way. Overall, of course, as you realize, I'm very happy. But so wrought up that once, when I was sleeping dreamlessly and relaxed and with a sense of peace, it woke me up in astonishment and almost in fear. My love, I know I'll be happy this Sunday when I see you again. I love you.

Your Beaver

I'm rolling in money and have already bought a magnificent white coat.
    Tell that swine Bost I'm ridiculously glad to be seeing him again, and think about him far more than he deserves.

<hr />

[458]A writers' association founded in 1839 by Louis Desnoyers and still flourishing.
[459]Nelson Algren.

﷼ 1948

Hôtel Colon
Merida – Yucatan – Mexico

Thursday 27 May [1948]

Write from now on to
Guatemala, Poste Restante[460]

My dear little soul, my heart. It was fantastic, you know, leaving New Orleans yesterday at 8 and disembarking at noon in the heart of Merida: you really do leap straight from one world into another.

[...]

Now It's 1 and I'm off to lunch. At 4 we're leaving in a tourist car for Chichen-Itza, which is an old, dead Maya town which looks astounding from photos: pyramids, tombs, temples. We'll stay a day or two. Then more ruins, a bull fight here on Sunday, and by next Wednesday I think we'll have seen Yucatan (what can be seen, since it's very hard to visit) and we'll go on to Guatemala, 2 hours by air.

I'm in a real muddle here with all these languages. I try Spanish, which I remember a bit, but then when I talk to A. I lapse into French. Or, on the contrary, feeling I ought to be talking to him in an exotic tongue, I talk Spanish to him. I mix everything up.

About the last two days at N.O. there's little to tell, but it was very agreeable: tramway rides, taxi rides, walks, boxing matches, burlesque shows, whiskies, little bars. And a sumptuous meal at Antoine's. A.'s eyes opened wide – he'd had no idea cooking like that even existed. And the place is incredibly pleasant, I wonder how I could have missed it the first time. No wire from you, but perhaps you never went to London. I'm hoping for a letter here in three or four days. Go on working well, my little one. Fix up a nice summer for us – I'll be glad to be working again, like in Abisko.[461] Think a bit about your Beaver, tell yourself your Beaver's as happy as can be – and will be still happier when back with you again. I haven't abandoned you, my little ally, my heart. I kiss you with all my soul.

Your charming Beaver

---

[460]For this trip, see *Force of Circumstance*, pp.157-9; it is also used in *The Mandarins*.
[461]Town in the far north of Sweden where De Beauvoir and Sartre stayed in August 1947 (see *Force of Circumstance*, p.134).

Hotel de Cortes
Av. Hidalgo numero 85
Mexico

Wednesday 16 June [1948]

My most dear little one. I've done and seen so many things since Saturday that I haven't had time to write and am quite dazed.

[...]

We'll come back on Sunday for the bull fight. I'm hoping for a letter then, but that poste restante where they stick the names up tells me nothing useful. I wrote to Gerassi, telling him to book me a seat for *13 July*, or failing that the 14th or 15th. I'm beginning to have an immense desire to see you again, o yourself, my life, but at the same time it distresses me to be beginning to lean towards separation, because when I leave you I don't leave you, but with A[lgren] presence is all. The thing is, the idea of leaving – my *desire* to leave – calls the days I'm living through into question. I'm explaining this badly, but it's just to tell you I'm beginning to feel strange inside.[462]

Goodbye, o yourself, my life, my soul. In less than a month we'll be together again. Write to me *here*, then: Hotel de Cortes, *Mme* de B.[463] I was asked whether it was the U.N. that had sent me here, and at Maheu's name[464] the manager's face lit up. I'll write as soon as I get back, on Sunday.

Goodbye, my love.

Your charming Beaver

---

[462]A year later, when Algren came to Paris for three months and he and De Beauvoir travelled to Italy and North Africa, she was to write (*Force of Circumstance*, p.184): 'We had never got on better together. Next year I would go to Chicago; I was certain when I said goodbye to him that I would see Algren again. And yet there was something terribly tight around my heart as I accompanied him to Orly.'

[463]After having problems cashing her traveller's cheques at hotels where she was registered under Algren's name, De Beauvoir had on this occasion registered them as M. and Mme de Beauvoir.

[464]René Maheu was already working for UNESCO, whose director-general he was to become in the sixties, and had recently returned from a Latin American conference when De Beauvoir saw him just before leaving Paris for this trip.

❧ 1950

[Chicago]

Wednesday [early July 1950]

O yourself, my dear life. I was really moved when I saw you vanish in your little grey suit, and for a long while wanted nothing in the world except to see you again some day – which will happen, so everything's all right. The journey was perfect. I was sitting beside a Jew from Mexico who was reading *The Second Sex*,[465] and made conversation with him as far as Shannon. After that I slept, without the least fear. Gander was fogbound, so we came down at Sydney, Nova Scotia – the scenery's like Newfoundland and it's extremely pretty. At New York I found the Gerassis – Stépha had just come out of hospital. Gerassi asserted – and Algren and the newspapers confirmed it – that there was absolutely no question of a war,[466] so in that respect everything was going well. On Monday it was frightfully rainy in New York. I walked through the rain to Aubry's office, but he'd received no instructions from Gallimard (the secretaries hadn't, I mean). Aubry himself was travelling and will get back late. Could Cau perhaps see what the situation is? – I've written to Claude.[467] Then at the Guild they told me you hadn't got a penny left – which is all the same to me personally, since I didn't need the coat. I did the errand for Michelle.[468] Fernand has shown me some good canvases, but bored me with his idiotic philosophical arguments. I left on Monday afternoon for Chicago. Arrived at 8.30. It didn't take me 24 hours to see things had changed – exactly as I'd predicted to you, that night when I kept you up so late. I asked Algren yesterday evening what the matter was, and he explained. It's just what I felt from his letters, and from the rhythm of our affair: he's very glad to see me, but with the resigned idea that I'm coming only to leave – that we'll never have anything more than these arrivals and departures – which has given him a detachment bordering on indifference. I think these are the last months we'll ever spend together. He says, moreover, that he's incapable of ever loving a woman again. I'll tell you all about it later. I'm still pretty upset. But then I knew this

---

[465]*Le Deuxième Sexe* had been published in 1949.

[466]A reference to fears that the Korean War, which had just broken out, might lead to a third world war.

[467]Jean Cau was working as Sartre's secretary at this time; 'Claude' is Claude Gallimard, publisher of De Beauvoir and Sartre.

[468]Michelle Vian, wife of Boris (see note 428 above), who began an affair with Sartre probably soon after their first meeting in 1946; she was to remain a lifelong friend of both him and De Beauvoir.

affair had to end, and soon. It has died from within, because Algren realized that it was already dead, ossified. We're not leaving for Lake Michigan until the beginning of August.[469] I'm not too sorry, because I love Chicago. It's possible, once the shock and the explanations have been cleared away, that I'll spend three very good months here – I even believe so. At any rate don't worry about me, since I know that in three months we'll be together again; and that you're my life; and that I can't regret this affair being dead, since its death was implied in the life I've chosen – which you give me.

Goodbye, my dear little one. Do write. Extract yourself as best you can from your own troubles.[470]

Your charming Beaver

(Address as letter 26 January 1947)

[Chicago]

Monday [July 1950]

My most dear little one. How nice you are to have written so quickly. I had your first letter by Thursday, and it was a great help. This morning I've received the second, and I think it's really stupid that we should have gone rushing off independently into a whole heap of problems, when we were so happy together. The compensation is that in three months we shall both find ourselves free – for depending on one another doesn't mean depending on anyone. Three months strikes me as being very long and unbearable, but at the same time necessary for that 'work' we were talking about – which I was rejecting but must indeed do.

I first have to tell you that nobody here's interested in the war. That's what Algren – whom I've interviewed at length – asserts and I believe him, going by the general look of the streets and the people. The papers try to enthuse the public by alternately announcing victories and huge defeats; but even the 'atrocities' – seven GIs shot with their arms tied behind their backs – leave people unmoved. MacArthur has been trying to kick out two war correspondents who announced that the soldiers considered this war idiotic and pointless, but public opinion is protesting. The atmosphere couldn't be calmer. In spite of this, I feel

---

[469] Algren had won the Pulitzer Prize and used it to buy a little house at Miller, on Lake Michigan, near Gary, Indiana.

[470] Sartre was attempting to end his five-year relationship with Dolores.

Chicago has something poignant about it: that's the only appropriate word to describe the days I'm spending. This city is so close to me, I love it so much, I remember it so well – it's at once so exotic and so familiar. And it's already in a world that's no longer mine; already radically separated from me, by coming world events as much as by my own history. That history – it's strange how I'm reliving it street by street, hour by hour, with the mission of neutralizing it, and transforming it into an inoffensive past that I can keep in my heart without either disowning it or suffering from it. That's not easy. It's at once painful and poetic. I suppose it's better to be in my shoes than in yours, but at moments I feel seriously distressed. The weather's as muggy as in Bobo-Dioulasso,[471] as stormy as in Paris; it rains a lot and is terribly close – weather entirely appropriate to the state of my heart.

I'll try and give you a coherent overview of events. Well, I arrived here on Monday evening, all ready despite my forebodings to carry on from the last days of last year, when Algren had told me: 'I've never been so happy; I've never loved so much.' That night and all next day I felt a reserve, let's say – or an absence – that was absolutely striking in someone who used to be warmth itself. On the Tuesday night when we were going to bed I asked for an explanation. He told me fairly tersely that he didn't love anyone else but that something was dead. I spent a bad night, as you may imagine – it was the following morning when I wrote to you. In the afternoon he explained it all to me at length. In Hollywood[472] he half took up again with his ex-wife: she wanted to go back to living together, but he refused and got out of it by offering her a car. After that, there was a little Japanese girl about whom he'd been telling me for a long time, who threw herself at his head and wanted to get married. He ended up sleeping with her – after warning her clearly not to expect anything – then dropped her. He says all these struggles and disputes have left him weary of women; that he awaited me with indifference, and didn't feel much when he saw me again. I come, I'll go away again – it's agreeable but nothing more. I understand. It greatly relieved me (I say this for your instruction) to know that he hadn't fallen in love with another woman, and that the change has occurred within our affair rather than from outside. I more or less got some sleep that night, and the next day we talked about lots of things and in the afternoon spent two hours with some friends of his. The evening was very nice, we even slept together very tenderly. The next

---

[471]In Burkina Faso (then Upper Volta): for the trip made by De Beauvoir and Sartre to Black Africa in the spring of 1950, see *Force of Circumstance*, pp.204-23.
[472]Where the Pulitzer Prize had taken him.

day – a classic reaction with which you're familiar – I was ill. I'd caught a dreadful cold on the first night, it had simmered gently away, and then I'd taken too many Corydranes and drunk too much whisky. Now, I had a firm temperature that kept me in bed all day. It was rather pleasant – we played records and told each other lots of stories. On Saturday I slept twelve hours on the trot and my temperature fell more or less to normal; so we went for a walk through lots of pleasant places, had dinner in a charming French restaurant, saw a spectacular operetta, etc. Yesterday (Sunday) too, the day was perfect. We get on very well and – except for this tension inside me and that stormy weather outside – it's like it used to be. I revisited lots of Chicago places, and in the evening we talked till late and very agreeably. But then there was a little disaster, because we slept together again and it was so pitiful that it horrified me. I brooded over my horror for a good part of the night, then as soon as Algren woke up tried to talk to him; but he hates explanations – he just runs away. I do try and keep them to a minimum, but this one was really necessary. For him it lasted five minutes, but I dragged it out, this way and that, from midnight till noon – I barely slept at all. Luckily at 4 he had to spend almost an hour in front of a contraption at the television studio, so we made our way together to the Loop, then I went and sat down in a cool, dark 'cocktail lounge' with some whiskies – and now I'm writing to you and feeling better. It's a pity we can't go up to the Lake before 1 August. Impossible to work in his room – it's too small, and the rhythm of our outings doesn't allow it. Besides, I'd need another week to be capable of it. But a big house, separate beds, a bit of swimming – that would help. On the other hand, I love Chicago and this room. Last night I was thinking about returning to France pretty soon, after seeing Sorokine and New York for a bit. On the other hand, I like being here and don't want such an abrupt break-up. Apart from last night's incident, I've nothing at all to reproach Algren with and continue to feel good with him. I think it's better to allow these three months to do their work.

Tell Michelle the following: two days ago, a young woman who runs a jazz club in Chicago telephones Algren: 'Do you know Sidney Bechet's address in Paris? His nephew has just been arrested for shooting at someone – he wounded him in the shoulder.' And the woman adds: 'I know he plays in one of those two cafés the existentialists own in Montmartre, but I don't know which.' I give her the address. And then, yesterday, I go with Algren to see a 'line-up', and among the guys on display there's Bechet's nephew – a rather good-looking boy who passes himself off as Spanish, and who looks overcome with shame at finding himself there. I've in fact been to that jazz club of hers: the young woman's half Japanese, half Irish – a strange mixture – and very nice. She has a charming bracelet that Bechet gave her, with a ruby-eyed devil – because she sometimes used to chuck him forcibly out of the club, calling him a demon. The jazz in that little nightclub is actually as cold as its decor and its clientele. A white American can rarely play jazz – that's perfectly true. I've had a strange little letter from Sorokine, who's furious because I talked about her to Oreste.[473] She says: 'Those two faggots are a pain in the neck', complaining that for me she has remained eternally the girl who sticks pins into people's bottoms. 'And yet', she says, 'I feel as though I've flushed away the last people I knew' – and adds: 'Well, you never know!' I'll see her in August.

That's all, my little one. It was cosy writing to you and now I feel at a bit of a loss. Especially as it's raining outside and there's no film to see in this town. Perhaps I'll go to the Museum. As you can see, I'm doing what I said I didn't want to do: taking responsibility for an affair that was lived jointly, and making it into my own affair in such a way as to be able to dominate and liquidate it. But it's not I who began, and there's no other solution. Above all, don't worry at all about me. I'm not overwhelmed, except at moments and for a moment. By and large, moreover, I'm happy through all this. I'm happy that this affair should have been, such as it has been. With a bit of luck it will end gently.

Do write to me. What helps me most is the fact that I've remained anchored in Paris, with you. So nothing else is really important. And you, little one, remember that those sad days you're going through aren't absurd or gratuitous, but necessary to our life. You'll see what a beautiful life we'll have from now on, as soon as we're back together.

I kiss you with all my might.

Your charming Beaver

Algren
1523 W. Wabansia
Chicago

Wednesday [July 1950]

My dear little soul. I had to finish my letter in a hurry on Saturday, because a friend of Algren's was coming to pick us up by car to go up to the Lake. The weather was fine and we first crossed Chicago for ever, then a vast zone of refineries, factories and blast furnaces – which was

---

[473]Oreste F. Pucciani, a Californian friend of Sorokine's.

extraordinary to see in the evening on the way back, spitting fire everywhere. Algren has bought a ravishing little house hidden in the trees, with a garden running down to a little lake. You cross the lake by boat and on the other side there are dunes and the immense Lake Michigan with a lovely sand beach. I think it'll be really agreeable living there. But the present owners won't be leaving till the first of August. They cooked hamburgers for us in a kind of big oven in the middle of the garden. We swam in the lake, then ate and drank scotch till dark. It was a bit long, but not boring. I'd terribly like to be settled in there. On Sunday and Monday we stayed at home and I worked almost all day. We go out to dinner at about 8 in the evening and after that for a drink. We walk a bit. It's a good arrangement for work. On Monday evening, as we were coming back at midnight from a little Italian restaurant, at the moment of climbing the stairs Algren sensed a presence on the wooden balcony in front of the door – and, in fact, there was a woman in a grey smock waiting. 'It's Florence, an old friend,' said Algren, affably ushering her in. She was a bit overawed: 'If you're busy, I don't want to disturb . . .' But she accepted a coffee and then asked for some whisky. After that, propped against the stove, she began telling the story of her life in a pathetic voice, complaining of numerous unhappy marriages and a great, interrupted literary work. When she'd finished talking, she began collecting all the scraps of paper that were lying on the table, screwing them up and throwing them into the rubbish bin. Then she forced us to put away the ashtrays and shoes, on the pretext of tidying up, and demanded more whisky. She swallowed a nice big glass in a single gulp, then gave the tap a powerful buffet, filled the glass with water and swallowed that. Algren asked her where she was thinking of sleeping that night, and she said: 'Here, of course, when you've thrown this other woman out.' He said that was difficult. 'Leave him to me for this night, and I'll leave him to you for your whole life,' she entreated me. 'After all, that's only fair. It must be ten years I've loved him, and I need to talk to him.' And then she threatened him: 'If you don't keep me here, I'll never see you again – I'll marry someone else tomorrow morning.' Algren eventually told her we were married, which cast her down for a moment. She demanded more whisky, but he'd hidden it. Then she hunted for razor-blades to shave her legs, and – apologizing, laughing, applying herself – did in fact set about conscientiously shaving first her legs, then her armpits. Then she looked at herself satisfiedly in the mirror: 'That makes all the difference in the world.' She did her hair, but haughtily rejected my make-up. 'I don't use any powder and I have my own lipstick.' Then she violently assailed Algren, saying he was responsible for all her misfortunes and trying to hit him. Meanwhile, she'd continually go off to the lavatory, where she'd remain each time for a quarter of an hour. Eventually we rang for a taxi, but she refused to leave before doing the washing up. She heated some water and furiously washed every plate in the house. Then she did agree to go down, however, and Algren put her into a taxi. I'd realized from the outset that this was yet another of the crazy women who prowl round Algren, but what I didn't know was that she'd just escaped from the asylum, as her grey smock testified. The next day at 10 she was back again, shouting angrily through the glazed door. Algren decided to ring the asylum: what else was there to do? They told him they'd been searching for her since the evening before, that her mother was distraught, and that they'd send two orderlies to pick her up – which they did. The woman was sleeping in front of the door when they arrived. She has been confined for three years. Algren knew her ten years before that, not very well, but when his last book was published she wrote to him to ask for a copy, which he sent her with a nice note. So as soon as she escaped, she rushed off to his place. The neighbours have told us she'd been waiting for three hours.

Yesterday we went back to the races, in the car of the same friend and with some rather nice people. I had a pretty enjoyable time, because the trip was agreeable and I placed some bets (and lost). We had dinner in a kind of country hostelry – American style, of course. All in all, the days are going by agreeably. The weather's now cool and sunny, which is extremely pleasant. I'm working pretty well, at least in terms of quantity, and we don't talk about anything: I mean neither about our feelings, nor about the future. Sorokine, to whom I explained at length that I could spend only a week with her, is inviting herself for a fortnight in September. Actually, it's all the same to me now.

I've read that *Psychologie de la Colonisation*.[474] There are lots of interesting things there, and Leiris's viewpoint is indefensible. However, it's woolly and very suspect in its conclusions. You should read it yourself, in connection with the 'gift', because there's a curious inversion of 'potlatch' in that idea of dependency.

I'm expecting a new letter soon. I've had a note from Kos., who tells me she has signed for *The Flies*[475] – I'm very glad. She seems on excellent terms with me. What do *you* think about the war?

Goodbye, my sweet little one. Don't forget my address: 6228 Forest Avenue, Gary, Indiana. The time seems very long without you, you

---

[474]*Psychologie de la colonisation* by Octave Mannoni (1950).
[475]The play had an unsuccessful revival in 1951 at the Vieux Colombiers (see *Force of Circumstance*, p.238).

know. And how anxious I am to know you're safe and sound at That Lady's.[476] I suppose those days of parting were the worst. I'm with you, with all my heart.

Your charming Beaver

(Address as letter 26 January 1947)

S. de Beauvoir
6228 Forest Avenue
Gary
Indiana

Monday 31 [July 1950]

My dear, dear little one. I was impatiently waiting for your letter. Ten days without a thing – I was beginning to worry. Send just brief notes if necessary but do write, my sweet little one. I become distraught as soon as I feel you're not there. I'm longing desperately for details about Claude Day and Dolores. If only you don't forget to send your next letter to Gary! We're moving in tomorrow, and from now on nothing will be forwarded since the house will be empty. Your letters arrive in two or three days, which is wonderful. I'm glad to be leaving tomorrow. It's beginning to become close and humid here, and it's really not comfortable for working and life's a bit dreary. I feel it's terribly absurd to be spending another two months far away from you, when we want so much to be together. And this prospect of war makes our separation even more painful for me. If it weren't for that, I'd just tell myself: 'It's the last time we'll leave each other for such a long time.' But with this uncertain future, it wrings my heart to be losing two months of our life. On the other hand, though Algren didn't buy this house for me, of course, he did so based on the idea of my coming here, and he's terribly sweet – I can hardly say to him: 'Since you're no longer in love with me, I'm leaving.' And now there's Sorokine, who's coming at the beginning of September. I don't know. If I could press a button, I'd go back to France. Especially as half the time I'm full of dread. The American papers are so downcast that I think the USSR's return to the

---

[476] At her villa in Juan-les-Pins.

UN is a good thing for peace.[477] But they talk all the time about a Communist attack on Formosa, and some even say it's all set for 10 August. I know that's part of their domestic propaganda – they have to terrorize the country, in order to get the new taxes and their anti-democratic policy accepted – but I'm afraid and Algren's blind optimism doesn't reassure me. There's a series of astonishing articles in the *Chicago Sun* at the moment, explaining to people how to defend themselves against the atomic bomb: stay calm; wear clothes of light colour and as loose as possible, and gloves; obey orders – and so on. People seem as much influenced by propaganda as the ones on the other side of the curtain. A hairdresser asked me the other day: 'Is it still as *terrible* in Paris? How about the Communists? Are they still laying down the law in your country?' All Algren's friends are 'progressives', of course (though very disappointed in Wallace,[478] who eventually came out in support of the Korean War). They believe we'll have war in a year or two's time. I warned Algren that I'd go back to Paris if things grew worse.

I've had a very nice letter from Sorokine. She says you intimidated Oreste dreadfully, making him feel like 'a third-class gigolo disguised as an intellectual'. She's definitely coming to Gary in September. Long letter from a Lebanese who spends two pages expressing his enthusiastic admiration for *The Second Sex*, but then entreats me to change the title, because it seems to point to some inferiority of women – and he spends two more pages explaining to me that women, though doubtless not identical to men, are not beneath them! I'm in contact with the zoology professor who's translating me, but he's still only halfway through the first volume.

Life is calm. I rise late, work between noon and eight – putting in about five hours – and we go and have dinner in a good restaurant, then on to listen to some jazz or something. There have been some very agreeable evenings in black South Chicago; and others on the lakeside, where people bathe at night, light campfires, rig up lines and complicated nets – a whole nocturnal life. A very nice black musician, with whom we were chatting the evening before last, told us as though it were the simplest thing in the world how one day, when he was

---

[477]The USSR had temporarily withdrawn from the United Nations, which allowed the Security Council to endorse the US-led intervention in Korea on the Southern side, following the outbreak of war in June 1950.

[478]Henry Wallace, Roosevelt's vice-president 1941-4, had opposed the cold war policies of the Truman administration and run on a Progressive Party ticket in the presidential elections of 1948.

twelve, the Mississippi burst its banks, his house was swept away, and the whole family – 12 children, father, mother, grandmother – swam 5 kilometres to a hill where they stayed for two days. You get the impression in this country that half the people have endless stories behind them.

Not a film to be seen. The papers claim 'Films are better than ever' – it's a slogan in big letters – but the truth is that the cinema seems completely dead after those big political trials, among other things.[479]

There you are. It's the opposite from you. My life's calm outside, hectic and somewhat distressed inside. Do write – and tell me at once if there's just *one* reason to come back. I'd go back much more easily than I anticipated when I left, you understand. So don't hesitate about bringing me back for nothing. I'd so like you to have untroubled holidays, my little one. When are you leaving Dolores? I hope you're not waiting till she leaves for Spain, that might be never-ending. It's as well that she has work in October.

Goodbye, my little one, my dear little one who's everything to me. I've never felt all my love for you more strongly.

Your charming Beaver

[Gary, Indiana]

Friday 4 August [1950]

My most dear little one. How happy it makes me to be sending this letter to Juan-les-Pins, and to know you're at last going to have a peaceful holiday.[480] Your letter yesterday (the one you wrote on Tuesday) really cheered me up and I'm starting to feel a bit more balanced. I can tell you at once that I've booked my return air seat for 1 October. I'll be in Paris on the 2nd, between 4 in the afternoon and 10, I don't know exactly. Just as you were writing to me on Tuesday, I was overwhelmed by dread. First, it was my bad day and I could clearly sense a kind of madness seizing hold of me. We moved that day: we left Chicago at noon, stopped for three hours at a race-course, arrived here, had dinner with some friends, and began to move in. I was dead tired, I drank a lot, and I read in the newspaper that Russia was recalling all its European ambassadors and consuls, which probably meant an

---

[479]This was the high point of the MacCarthyite witch hunt in Hollywood.
[480]In other words, that he had completed the break with Dolores.

imminent attack. I lapsed into despair and wanted to go back to France immediately. It seemed all the more absurd to remain because A.'s feelings – and mine simultaneously – have changed. But he once again pointed out to me how the American papers deliberately scare everyone by announcing every day how the Soviets are going to attack tomorrow. Furthermore, he told me he was personally keen to keep me here for these two months. I had a great deal of trouble getting to sleep, seeing myself separated from you for ever and thinking how if that happened I'd throw myself into the lake. On Wednesday I was a bit better, but the weather was grey here and your letter didn't come. It's yesterday that I came back to life, since you assure me I'll have time to fly to France if the worst happens. Gerassi has written to me saying he absolutely disbelieves in war this year, and I'm feeling slightly reassured. But these newspapers are dreadful. The attack on Formosa is presented as imminent. The truth is, they have to present it as such in order to justify MacArthur and American policy; even so, it has set me all of a flutter day after day. All last night I dreamt I was combing Paris for a café where we were supposed to meet, but which I could no longer find.

If it weren't for this constant dread, and my regret at losing two months of life with you, I'd feel good here. Removal men have just brought some bits of furniture and Algren is busy fixing up the house. As for me, I'm in the garden in the sun, with a little lake at my feet. The weather's fine and it's pleasant and solitary. There are at least a hundred books I'm dying to read (not to speak of all the others), and I've started working again. We haven't been swimming yet, because I was tired and Algren was busy getting settled in, but the beach is just a step away. Now the cupboards and refrigerator are full of food, and we can live for a month without going to the village, which is 2 km. from the house. I'm not yet accustomed to these luxurious cars which come every so often to call on us, and from which a grocer's boy, a cleaner or the gas man emerges. But it's terribly convenient having everything brought to the house like that. Yesterday evening we took the boat out on the little lake, and made a big fire in the garden: there's a kind of oven where you can cook sausages and steaks in the open air. Then we went down to the cellars to look out lots of old papers, albums, books and photographs that Algren has been collecting there for weeks. Among other things, there were a few stupid articles about you – as usual. All in all it was a really pleasant evening, and if the outside world leaves us in peace – and if I know you're peaceful and contented – I think I'm going to be spending two almost agreeable months here.

I've had a long letter from V. Leduc, in the same vein as always: she's at Montjean close to La Pouèze, but not overjoyed with it; she's very glad she's not jealous of all those women currently admiring and flattering me on the American beaches; a worker tried to rape her on the banks of the Loire, but she escaped.

Goodbye, my little one. It would be great if Dolores made that trip to Africa. If people would only leave us in peace, we could still have such a good few years. My only wish is to see you again. Do write. I love you with all my might.

Your charming Beaver

Envelope:
M. Sartre
c/o Mme Morel
Villa Sull'Onda
Juan-les-Pins (Alpes Maritimes)
France*

[Gary, Indiana]

Tuesday [8 August 1950]

My most dear little one. It's going to be another whole week without a letter. I suppose your departure from Paris wasn't so easy, and then letters doubtless take longer from Juan-les-Pins. But I'm more patient than last week, because I've finally more or less found a balance in my own life. The papers aren't too worrying (but what am I to do if China attacks Indochina? – that's something you haven't told me) and existence here is very agreeable, though a bit austere. I get up late. By about 11 I've settled down to work in the garden. Often at about 1 or 2 we take the boat, cross our little lake and then – on foot – some burning sands and arrive at the big lake, where we bathe. It's really like the sea, and on windy days there are huge waves and the water's a bit salty. The beach is endless and there are lots of deserted spots, which is where we go. As soon as we get home we take something from the icebox, have a snack, and I work till evening. Then we generally cook a steak or something in the garden. We often go for a little walk, and I read till late at night. What makes this landscape strange is the blast furnaces rising at the far end of the beach, only a few kilometres from here. Without them the area's already hard to categorize – it's certainly not the suburbs any more, but it's barely the countryside – but when

_____

*Letters 4 to 24 August 1950 addressed as above

you do see them, you're back in the city. And what's very beautiful is that in the evening the sky has urban colours: in one direction it's all mauve and murky, like in Paris or Chicago. It's 10 at night and we've just been out in the boat: the chimneys were spitting huge red fumes in the distance, while our little lake was all darkness and silence amid big clumps of trees. I see almost no one. Algren has friends round here, but has told everyone I hate company and have some urgent work, so I keep out of sight when people come to see him and don't accompany him when he goes out – which is not very often anyway. There's a certain Christine, however, whom I really can't avoid, seeing as she furnished the whole house for us, takes care of all our grocery and laundry deliveries, etc. She's a tough-looking woman of 40 – Greek, with a mild, colourless husband who has $200 pension each month and is frantically learning French to become a teacher, two children, a housewife's existence, and all manner of aspirations. She has slept with Algren in the past and there's still something left over from that. This house fascinates her – and so do I. She comes over and talks frenetically, like someone who never gets any chance to talk. One evening – Saturday – she turned up at midnight, and left at 2 only because I got up deliberately to go and make the beds. The next day she arrived at 7. I worked without taking any notice of her. She cooked hamburgers in the garden with Algren till 9.30. By the end he wasn't uttering a word, and eventually trod on her hand in the dark while she was picking something up. 'All right, I've got the message', she said good-humouredly, 'and thank you for a really boring evening!' But she's tough, she'll be back. There's also a certain Joyce in the vicinity – who weeps and talks about herself all day because she so wanted to be a great writer and has only produced a fifteen-page illustrated book about a cat. She spent 15 years writing a novel with a hundred characters, which nobody was ever able to do anything with. She literally refused to sell her house to Algren (there had been negotiations) because she couldn't bear the idea of his writing his next novel under her roof. And she kicked out a girl friend who'd done some moderately successful scribbling, and who was down for a weekend, because she touched her typewriter. She wanted to give a big 'party' in my honour, but I declined.

I'm in difficulties with my novel, as usual.[481] But I think it will all work out. I feel like writing. I just need to get the whole thing hanging together properly, then I'll be able to enjoy myself polishing up each chapter.

---

[481] *The Mandarins*, on which she had been working since 1949.

I've read Faulkner's *Intruder in the Dust*, which I don't like at all – boring, prophetic, complicated for the sake of it. 'If you persist long enough in evil, it becomes good. Everything's good if you do it for long enough', and so on and so forth. I've read Fitzgerald's *Crack-up* – notes and essays, very moving. A whole epoch that was almost our own. A genius at 22, who knows he's finished at 30 and survives till he's 40. There are a few short stories and essays I'd really like to bring back for the *Temps Modernes*, by various people. It seems to me that if we could collect pamphlets and writing by left-wing people fighting against the America of today, that would be interesting. I'm going to have a look around. I'm also reading lots of things on the old America, which fascinates me.

I'm sending you a stupid article from the *N.Y. Times* on your *Baudelaire*, published last Sunday.

That's all. Things would be more or less all right, if it didn't seem so absurd not to be with you when you're free and we could be so happy. Because what bothers me is the fact that I don't exactly understand *why* I'm here, shut up in this little garden with aeroplanes and helicopters passing over my head. I'm infinitely happier with you – and I don't know to what extent my presence has any meaning for Algren. From time to time this absurdity becomes an overwhelming sadness. I have the impression of being attached here by old desires, whereas the novelty and romance and happiness of my life are with you, my little companion of 20 years. I'm counting the weeks, if not the hours.

Goodbye till 2 October, my love. Write to me. I kiss you with all my soul.

Your charming Beaver

S. de Beauvoir
6228 Forest Avenue
Gary, Indiana, U.S.A.

Sunday 20 [August 1950]

My dear little one. Yesterday I had your letter of the 13th. I'm so glad you're having clear blue weather at That Lady's, and that you're working well. Don't let anybody bother you, my little one, and don't worry about money. You know quite well our finances always come right at the last moment. It gave me a real pang of regret when I pictured you on that terrace, enjoying those mornings I recall so clearly – and that I'd so like to be sharing with you. But we'll share others, won't we? Lots of others.

As for me, my life here is working out better and better. In appearance, things are almost like they used to be between Algren and me – one could easily be deceived. Was it my own sadness that made him gloomy that first month? Or did he in a sense hold it against me that he hadn't rediscovered his love for me? Or was he afraid I'd interpret any affection wrongly? At all events he was stiff and distant – but he isn't any longer in the least. Now the days – with their tranquil routine of work, bathing and reading – pass swiftly. The most obvious change in our relations is that we no longer sleep together, by a common, tacit agreement. The most surprising thing is that we no longer can: there were one or two stabs, discreet attempts of no consequence, when he was impotent and I was frigid. In a sense that helps to liquidate an affair in which sexuality held a big place. But it remains mysterious to me that an emotion of that kind can die so radically during an absence. For we'd left one another at fever pitch – yet, from the moment of my arrival in Chicago, everything was dead from that point of view. Perhaps you can understand, you who are on the masculine side. I understand how it can wear out. But what I don't understand is how it can disappear from afar, never to be reborn. For my part I followed suit, which is only natural – indifference creates indifference, luckily. That said, in the background of these days there's always a troubling uncertainty. I remember too much of the past for the present not to be melancholy. But the present is still far too precious for me to accept burying it, along with all the regrets it enfolds. Obviously, it'll all be settled by oblivion once I'm in Paris – but I don't like to think that.

I don't think much at all, actually. I live from day to day and these days taken singly are pleasant. I haven't taken much advantage of the lake since my drowning accident.[482] Yesterday it was so rough that absolutely no one was bathing in it – I just took a dip, nothing more. On Sunday it's too crowded, so we never go. On the days before that, even in the safety zone I was feeling uneasy. Never have my fears – in planes, on bicycles, up mountains – survived for as long as this one. At nights, I think about it anew with fresh dread. Perhaps it's because it's such an obvious image of death, when you feel yourself losing your footing and the ground gives way. I wonder if I'm going to get used to swimming again this year. This lake makes a loud and beautiful noise

---

[482]On 14 or 15 August, De Beauvoir – always a poor swimmer – was almost drowned (see *Force of Circumstance*, pp.226-7). Unfortunately, the letter relating the episode has disappeared, though it is recorded in a drawing by Algren on an envelope.

all night. It's funny, on the beach I hadn't noticed it made that noise and all through one night when Algren was in Chicago I was wondering what that great factory racket was, coming from the woods. I can hear it at this moment as I write to you.

Algren has bought himself a heavy red bicycle which you brake with your feet. I'm in a period of decline, since I haven't yet dared ride it. It's a man's bicycle, I find it off-putting not to have any brakes to grip, and I'm no longer used to the machines. All the same, I'll have to pluck up courage.

I've had another letter from V. Leduc, who's still enjoying herself a lot at Montjean. Mops has done wonders. Sorokine's turning up in ten days' time, which I'm only half looking forward to. That's all, my dear love. Here I am today, just half-way away from you – it's starting not to seem so far away any more. You're always with me, and I'm waiting for you with all my being. Say hello to everybody from me. I kiss you, my dear little absolute.

Your charming Beaver

[Gary, Indiana]

Thursday [24 August 1950]

Dear little yourself

I'm definitely receiving only one letter a week – couldn't you write a bit more, if only briefly? It's sad when I go hopefully to open the letter box in the morning and there's nothing. I suppose you're more shaken than you thought, but I keep imagining something terrible has happened, in connection with Dolores or whatever.

Well, Sarbakhane turned up, without a by your leave, radiantly beautiful (she has grown thinner, cut her hair and taken on just a touch of American style; she's tanned and magnificent – Algren was quite impressed) and full of impossible stories.

[...]

I'll add a note this evening to tell you how we spent the day. I'm 'ambiguous' towards her. It seemed warming, familiar and agreeable to see her again, and as always I'm sensitive to her presence. But the stories she tells and her attitude to them give me gooseflesh. Her daughter looks virtually like a battered child, thanks to a total lack of care and affection from every side. Goodbye for now, little one. Yesterday I began swimming well again. I've gradually retaught myself, but I no longer trust the water and when it reaches my chin I become filled with dread. At all events, I shan't leave the safety zone for a long while. This lake is superb by night – we've been out on it twice with Algren. There are all the blast furnaces spitting fire on the horizon, the headlights, that kind of ocean with big waves, and hidden in the trees cosy little cottages – it all adds up to a fairly striking miniature of America.

Here are a few English idiocies published in the *N.Y.T.* The same imbecile did a more general and even more idiotic article in an English paper, which I've read but can't cut out for you. It should be noted that in this particular rubbish, he bears you out virtually all along the line.

Farewell, dear little one – I don't have time to add anything, except that S. has been delightful all day, with some really pretty amazing stories about Hollywood. I'll tell you next time. I kiss you with all my might.

Your charming Beaver

[Gary, Indiana]

Sunday [28 August 1950]

My most dear little one. Your letter, at last! It makes such a change in my days when there is one. My heart really rejoiced – how shameful, you dirty rascal! – tell me the sequel truthfully. I'm still longing to be with you just as much, and it wrings my heart whenever I think: 'Another month!'

[. . .]

When Sor. had left, Algren told me that his friends had been struck by her Lesbian side. It has to be said, she does caress and kiss me in front of people in a way that must appear odd. But Christine had thought her a Lesbian simply from hearing her voice on the telephone, and Algren says she made the same impression on him as soon as she got out of the taxi. She isn't one, though – she had one ludicrous, failed experience with a professional Lesbian, that's all – she's above all sexually infantile. Algren doesn't like her much. He finds Olga far more interesting (infinitely more attractive, of course). With S., he feels the same kind of revulsion that you and Bost feel. And as for her, it's strange how awkward and embarrassed she is in a man's presence. When she doesn't frankly adopt a stance of sexual challenge, she's like an adolescent girl terrorized by the male. I remember Olga and Michelle with Algren, and the contrast with Sorokine is striking. I have the impression that on this point Algren feels the same revulsion you do – he dislikes her as a woman and likes her in moderation as a person.

I'll tell you the rest later. I'm in a hurry – I got up early to finish off the letter before the postman came. Do write, little one. My heart is always with you.

Your charming Beaver

[Gary, Indiana]

Friday [2 September 1950]

My most dear little one. I'd like lots of addresses if you go travelling. Will this letter be forwarded? I do hope so. The one I received from you this morning wasn't too cheerful. I think the Dolores business is still weighing on you, and that you're a bit worried concerning Michelle. How impatient I am for us to be together again, at Cagnes or elsewhere, working peacefully and seeing only one another. I don't think this last month's going to be much fun. The weather has turned grey and I have too. Sorokine's visit was pretty disastrous, without it being her fault – unless you say it's her fault to be what she is. The fact is that Algren deeply and radically disliked her. Yet, on the Sunday and Monday afternoons they talked nicely, telling each other stories. And she tried hard to be discreet, did the washing up and cooking with me, etc. In spite of that, on the Tuesday A. didn't open his mouth all day and on Wednesday morning he informed me darkly that he was going off to Chicago for a few days. I said it was I who'd go off there with Sorokine. Luckily, Oreste had been imploring her for several days by letter and telephone to join him in Boston, so when I filled her in on the situation she said she'd rush off to Boston at once, then come back by car with Oreste and meet me next week in Chicago, where we'd spend a few days on our own. She was quite aware that the situation wasn't pleasant for anybody. Besides, she says her affair with Ivan has so knocked her out that she has become indifferent to everything. I think she really did go off with no regrets, especially since she could see I was pretty upset about things turning out that way – and that it wasn't my fault. I was upset, because for the first time in my life I had a real grudge against Algren. He has two excuses: first, he knew (I'd told him so too often myself, perhaps) that I too found Sorokine a burden; secondly, nice as she is, I suppose she is hard to put up with. For example, on the Sunday evening when A.'s friends came, she spoke only to me and left abruptly in the middle of the evening, making it clear she was bored. He says he felt she was so frozen, so distant, so shut up in herself, that he was always embarrassed to be there. All right. But he should have discussed the problem with me, instead of ill-temperedly announcing a decision which forced me into a decision of my own. Actually, he's aware that he behaved strangely, since he has never been so attentive and talkative and considerate as since Sorokine's departure. As for me, I'm in two minds. Just as you used to be delighted to find Dolores at fault, if something destroys my feelings for Algren in a sense I'm delighted too. But introducing resentment into this affair really does mean signing its death warrant. In connection with this, I was thinking how we can accept a person's faults lovingly so long as they seem like a given, through which – against which – freedom is sought and found. But as soon as we feel people are complicit with their faults, we may still excuse them but we no longer love them. I've always known A. was selfish and – like Dolores's avarice – thought of this as a defence against a difficult life: a wish to save oneself first. But this business has revealed his selfishness to me as a choice – which was being renewed for no valid reason – and something in me suddenly collapsed.

I'll tell you how things develop, but I'd be surprised if the old affection could revive. In a sense, I'm glad the situation has been resolved. Being caught between Sorokine and Algren was wearing, and for these days to have any meaning I need to work. But I'd like to be sure she's having a good time now, poor creature, and I'd like to be really nice to her in Chicago. She so *wants* to be interested in other people, to be nice and not quarrel with anybody any more. And she is nice in her own way – but so stunted, so congealed inside. Ivan seems unbearable, judging by the letters from him she showed me – utterly corrupted by Hollywood.

Yes, my little one, do write – I *need* your letters. I'd asked you for two tubes of Corydrane and a box of ear plugs. So will you please send them by air, as quickly as possible? I hope you'll have a pleasant trip with Michelle, with some work and no intruders. I can't wait for us both to be happy again. I kiss you with all my soul.

Your charming Beaver

Envelope:
M. Sartre
Grand Hôtel
Sainte-Maxime (Var)

Alexandria Hotel
Rush and Ohio Streets
Chicago 11

Saturday [10 September 1950]

My most dear little one

I haven't had a letter this week – but through my own fault, because I left on Tuesday for Chicago with Sarbakhane. She turned up by car from Boston – with Oreste and Jacques – and entreated me to come and spend the evening with them that very day. So I rolled up by train at 8 p.m. and we had quite a good evening out, first at a good French restaurant, then at that black nightclub where I once saw a one-legged dancer.[483] I was delighted to see Chicago again, after my long retreat of over a month. We saw the dawn and sunrise over the lake and it was really very beautiful. But that Oreste, though he does actually have some good points and is quite nice, is horribly stingy. He thought I was going to pay for the whole evening and was awfully disappointed when I reimbursed him only half. I thought it was crazy: for him to come and look me up, with the idea that I should make conversation with them, show them the city – and also maintain all three of them. Especially since S. asked me to pay her trips to Boston and Los Angeles, her upkeep here, etc. and I don't have a penny left of the money I was keeping privately to buy a few things for myself. So I let them go off in their magnificent Buick hanging their heads. Oreste's relations with Sorokine are not, I think, wonderful. Left alone with me, he complained about her a great deal – and always for the same reason: she wants to sleep with him and he doesn't. I tried discreetly after that to tell S. to give up sexual relations with him, but she's as stubborn as a mule. She was very nice actually during those few days, as she can be when you're utterly at her disposal and do everything she wants. She's distressed and annoyed because Algren didn't like her. She realizes there's something not quite right in her relations with people, but she's obviously incurable. We had lovely clear weather and went for all kinds of outings – on foot, by boat, in taxis, on buses. It was pleasant for me, because for the first time I was in Chicago on my own and I was finally finding my bearings, the city was taking shape, and I felt rather as though it belonged to me. I know it well. It was pleasant but a bit disappointing, because lots of unsituated places – places from my past, whose earthly existence had remained very vague and mysterious to me – now found a banal location in the streets of the city. Chicago became real and lost its enchanted character.

---

[483]In July 1950.

We went to the cinema – nothing very good. I finally read *Sheltering Sky*, by Paul Bowles. It's less bad than Algren had told me (he hates that book and is the only person to have given it a foul review, which has actually earned him some abuse), but it's far from being very good – and from our standpoint is quite without interest. It's not Africa at all, but a journey through Africa as seen by some American snobs, with a rubbishy story of adultery and an extravagant ending. There are descriptions of buses, hotels, food, and the tourist aspect of the towns – nothing else. I also bought Mary McCarthy's *Oasis*, which is a dreadfully boring book.

This morning I'm meeting up with Algren and going off again to Gary. He has been so nice that my resentment has more or less dissipated. But I'm still in a strange state. I long passionately to be in Paris. This conjugal life I lead here is especially absurd because it implies eternity: the days are agreeable in the perspective of an indefinite repetition – which is, however, simultaneously rejected by circumstances and by my own heart. A journey somewhere wouldn't have had this absurd side.

My little one, I hope Algren will have brought me your letter. Otherwise I'm sending this to That Lady's. My only unalloyed happiness is to think of the moment when I'll be with you again – it's coming closer. I kiss you with all my soul.

Your charming Beaver

Here's your Sunday letter – one has been missed out in the meantime – and I have your address. You've done *very, very* well with respect to Dolores. I've had my fill of people screwing us about. See you soon, my dear love.

(Address as letter 2 September 1950)

[Gary, Indiana]

Monday [late September 1950]

My most dear little one. Just a note, since my letter will precede me only by a few hours. I *ought to* be in Paris at 3 in the afternoon – i.e. at the Invalides at about 4, I suppose – on Monday 2 October: ring and find out the exact time. It's pointless having a Slota,[484] I'd really rather walk

---

[484]Name of a taxi firm.

round Paris and above all be with you. How good it will be, to be together again! I'm quite radiant with joy and consumed by impatience. This last period has been very pleasant, to a great extent because I'm so happy to be seeing you again. Last night there was a fantastic eclipse of the moon and now, in a dazzling sky, the moon's veiled by an orange dawn. It was incredibly lovely on the lake.

I think – I hope – that I'll leave here entirely serene, with the idea that after all things are probably best this way. At any rate, I'll arrive in Paris in raptures at finally beginning our happy old age. Goodbye, my dear little one – in a week you'll be returned to me just as you were when I left you. I kiss you with all my soul.

Your charming Beaver

Can you warn my concierge[485] – by phone, perhaps – that she should tidy things up for my return? If you forget, it's of no importance.

🦫 1951

Hotel Lincoln
'The House of Hospitality'
44th to 45th Streets at Eighth Avenue
New York, 19 N.Y.

[September 1951][486]

Yes, of course, now that I'm in New York sitting in front of a whisky and writing to you I feel very good. And I like the idea of a long, peaceful month in the country – it's moving around so much that was making me sick.[487]

I was prepared not to find the journey agreeable – and it really wasn't. Everything was fine as far as Shannon, where I bumped into Sidney Bechet who was travelling at the same time as me by T.W.A. – he looked quite lonely. The air hostess was that former pupil of mine whom I'd encountered on the way to Nice (or coming back?) with you, and who was so scared of planes – do you remember? And the captain was the same one who flew us from Dakar to Casa: he knows you and your

---

[485]Since October 1948, De Beauvoir had had an apartment in Rue de la Bûcherie.
[486]After a year of languishing correspondence, Algren had invited De Beauvoir to spend the month of October with him at Miller: it was to be her last visit.
[487]In the immediately preceding months, Sartre and she had been on a cruise to Norway, revisited Iceland, toured Scotland and stayed in London.

mother and gave me endless greetings for both of you. I was on familiar territory. But after Shannon – in spite of three Belladenal tablets – I couldn't get to sleep for more than quarter of an hour at a time, and was pretty much overcome by dread as long as we were over the ocean. We were going directly to Montreal (a scheduled stop-off where passengers were getting out), because Gander was impracticable. That made 13 hrs, including 9 over the ocean, and we were at only 2,000 m. because of the storms, which were still worse higher up. They were quite vigorous enough as it was. We were shaken about somewhat the whole time – and a great deal at moments – and had to make such detours that skipping the landing at Gander didn't gain us anything in timetable terms. The night lasted till noon (Paris time), it was long, and we felt terribly lost between sky and water in the grey-black dawn. I started to live again once we were over Labrador, and in broad daylight. Then the last four hours to Montreal were charming. The stewardess admitted to me that she'd been scared too, and to distract me she told me about lots of accidents. The story of the two Paris-Saigon ones is odd. The first accident's simply explained, because the airfield merges quite naturally into the sandbanks alongside it and at night – with sandstorms into the bargain – nothing's easier than to make a mistake. The second, however, was apparently psychological: the pilot was an intellectual – someone who thought too much. He thought all the time – something which won't happen to me! He'd begun a good landing when, just to be on the safe side, he decided to fly over the field one more time and shouted to the flight engineer to raise the undercarriage. But the engineer, who was expecting to be told to open the landing-flaps, did so and the plane dived into the sand. At least that's what people presume. In both cases the passengers could almost touch bottom, but in the darkness and panic they [turned] their backs to the coast. So – greatly cheered by this conversation – I landed at Montreal, which struck me as a dreadful place though the weather was fine and cool there, quite worthy of Iceland. What I saw of Canada – from the coast to Montreal – is monotonous and beautiful in the same style as Newfoundland: lakes and endless pine forests. After that, there was only an hour and a half left – a mere outing. I was astonished on arriving because they asked me hardly any questions, either on my political ideas or on my financial resources – you might have thought you were entering a free country. It was close and damp, but that kind of weather suits New York. The driver took a magnificent route along the coast, entering New York by a big tunnel leading to the Battery, and from there all along the Hudson embankment: it's the whole of New York in a few minutes and is never disappointing. There was a helicopter touching down on a roof and it was all so teeming, teeming – one always forgets how vibrant it is.

No Sorokine at the hotel,[488] and no boat due next day (i.e. today) – she must have been delayed by the storms. Her cheque is worthless without her, but luckily my 50 dollars were more than enough. I ate in a drugstore, then went for a walk and located the cinemas I'd go to in the evening. Deciding to get some rest by taking a nap, I went up to my room at 4 and slept until this morning at 8. I just broke off to phone Algren – who'll expect me in Chicago at 8 p.m. – with the same indifference as if he'd been a travel-agency clerk. And while drawing the blind I saw the splendour of New York in lights – I was on the 23rd floor and the view was fantastic. But all that really went by in a dream. This morning I did errands, went to the hairdresser's, had a sumptuous lunch at the Café Arnold (chosen in your honour), and am beginning to feel very well, though still a bit sleepy. It's very hot and stormy, which is tiring, but New York is more magnificent than ever. What a city! And how pleasant relations with people are! How easy everything is – even crossing the street! I've bought an enormous volume of science-fiction stories, which I'll bring back with me. Now I'm off to catch my plane. Two and a half hours' flying, it's just like taking a suburban train. I'll write again soon from Chicago or Gary. You write too, little soul of mine. I thought about you all the time in that horrible plane – and again today, in this New York you loved so much – not in bad terms either. Have a good time, write nice things, and don't get too fat. I've slimmed so much I needed new notches in my belt before I could fasten it. Give Michelle lots of greetings. I kiss you with all my Beaver's heart.

                                                    Your charming Beaver

[Gary, Indiana]

                                    Wednesday [late September 1951]
My dear little yourself. It's already a week since I last wrote, the time has flown. I wanted to finish the little chore on Sade,[489] and finally the

---

[488]Sorokine had arrived in Paris at the end of June with Oreste and Jacques, and was now returning to the United States by sea.

[489]In June De Beauvoir, after finishing a first version of *The Mandarins*, had undertaken a twofold writing assignment on the Marquis de Sade, in whom she had been very interested since reading *Justine* a couple of years previously. She was working simultaneously on a short essay requested by Raymond Queneau for a forthcoming volume on 'Famous Writers', and on a longer essay intended for *Les Temps Modernes* and which was to become her *Must We Burn Sade?*.

last word has been written and I'm sending it off by the same post as this letter. I've still heard nothing from you, but I imagine a letter will arrive at any moment. Let me tell you at once I'm leading an excellent life here. First, Algren's in an angelic mood – just as in his best periods. And then I'm nicely installed in a room of my own, with all the leisure needed to work. So, given that you aren't with me, I can't see where I could be better off than here. I left New York just after writing to you: 3 hours flying time, without a bump, with a magnificent twilight and sunset over the great lakes Erie and Michigan, and that really sensational arrival at Chicago. The only irritation was the fact that my neighbour began making conversation. He was a physics teacher from the University of Notre-Dame, where that dreadful Guineau teaches, and he wanted me to explain existentialism to him – and to give him my address. I had to be rude in order to get rid of him. I arrived at Algren's at about 8, we had dinner in a pleasant Italian restaurant, then we went to hear Billie Holiday – who's fat and ill and hasn't any voice left at all, and who's singing in a crummy dive. We stayed in Chicago for only one day. Algren's little apartment is completely empty, and as uncomfortable and gloomy as could be. We went walking near the lake, the weather was marvellous, and in the evening we saw *The Member of the Wedding* based on the Carson McCullers novel – it's a very bad play. We went straight from the theatre to the train and came here. When we arrived, at about 2 in the morning, I found a cable: Sarbakhane, announcing her arrival for a half-day visit. So she showed up early on Friday morning, with *all the money* she owed me, and I had to insist on leaving her with 50 dollars, which she'll send me later. Algren couldn't get over it and, though he doesn't quite like to admit it, found her very nice and agreeable this time. She'd been caught in that same huge storm that buffeted my plane, which delayed her by three days. As soon as she arrived she jumped into the train, and got out at Gary just to see me for a few hours. I took her to the lake shore – the beach was all sunny and absolutely deserted – then accompanied her by bus to Gary, where I put her on her train. There were a few friends of Algren's Saturday evening – and again on Sunday evening – but not for long, and the rest of the time is utterly peaceful. The time passes terribly quickly, though I get up early. I work for a good 6 hours a day – and there are lots of books I'm trying to read – but the weather's so fine we always go out somewhere in the afternoon or evening, Algren has hundreds of stories to tell, and above all there's that accursed television. I think I'll learn to stop paying any attention to it, but for the first few days it's fascinating having all those films and concerts and puppet-shows in one's home. It's almost always bad – yesterday there was an appalling old Charles Boyer/Jean Arthur film – but I allow myself to be trapped. Well, I shan't read a quarter of what I'd like to, but for working it's perfect and won't be a wasted month. I'm hoping to finish the 'big' Sade between now and the end of the month, then I'll get back to the novel.

Tell Michelle that Algren never stops talking admiringly about her. He says she's the most interesting of all the individuals I've introduced him to, and entertains a host of tender little dreams regarding her. He's helping me collect matchboxes for her, and last Sunday we pillaged all his friends. He'd like her to translate the Chicago book (which I'll bring back with me) herself.

Goodbye, my dear soul. I'm sure you're having a good time, but I'd really like to know what you're writing. As for me, I've had a lot of trouble compressing more than 100 pages into 5 pages. Do write to me. I kiss you most tenderly.

Your charming Beaver

Last night there was a sensational storm lasting for hours, and this morning for the first time the weather's all grey. Yesterday at about 11 the night was truly splendid at the lakeside, with the blast furnaces spitting fire to the heavens and the lights of Chicago in the distance.

[Gary, Indiana]

Wednesday 3 [October 1951]

My dear little soul – I've had two letters from you, so you're in Naples at this moment, or Capri or somewhere. I'm glad the weather's fine and you're enjoying writing about the baroque. Thank you for attending to the car,[490] I hope that dreadful fellow will look after it for us. I'm the one basically who's not writing much, but I've very few things to tell. The days go by very quickly and repeat one another. There have been big storms here too, but the weather has become magnificent – it's what they call an 'Indian summer'. The countryside has all the colours of autumn, yet the weather's as hot as in August. I sunbathe as I work in the garden, and today we bathed in a lake as blue as the Mediterranean – immense, and absolutely solitary – we feel as if we're the owners of an ocean. The nights are as warm as the days. I'm working five or six

---

[490] De Beauvoir had just bought her first car, an Aronde.

hours every day, without having yet quite finished Sade; but it's a matter
of a day or two now and, after all, it is a very long article. We listen to
a bit of good music on the radio; we watch a bit of boxing and a few
entertaining programmes on television; I read a bit; we go for a walk
by the lakeside in the evening, or a boatride on the lagoon during the
day – and our day's over. I'm in the middle of reading S . . . . Boy,[491]
an account of that business of the kidnapped prostitute by one of the
guys who was convicted for it, who spent 17 years in prison and
eventually escaped – it's a pity Bost hasn't read it. There was also a
sensational book on the sea. You're always saying one ought to know
some geography in order to understand landscapes, so I hope it'll be
translated so that you can read it. It's pure, exact science and
fantastically poetic at the same time. I wonder if we might do something
with it for the Temps Modernes. I've also found a big book on Oliver
Goldsmith, all about his relations with Dr Johnson – whom I come
across everywhere: as soon as you touch the English 18th century, there
he is.

Algren has bawled out all his friends in the course of the year, so
nobody disturbs us. He's more cheerful than I've ever seen him. His little
book on Chicago has come out, and I find it excellent. On the other
hand, he has vaguely started a novel which goes over exactly the same
ground as the others but less well. I didn't hide the fact from him that
I didn't find it at all good. He's not pleased with it himself, actually –
but he really must renew himself. He busies himself with trifles –
lectures, short stories – but without conviction.

I enjoyed your story about the Silone's and Carlo Levi – yes, they
must have odd ideas about us. I don't have any news from Paris, except
from my mother – I hope Queneau will have received the little article
on Sade.

Yes, I'm having a very good time here, although upon reflection it
strikes me as pretty strange. If I don't reflect, however, but live in the
present, it's just a good time, agreeable and put to good use. For anyone
not wanting to budge, it would be impossible to live better. There are
some shocking and astounding American stories I must tell you about:
the affair of the so-called spies, the Rosenbergs, condemned to death
without a scrap of evidence; and the repercussions of the Cicero affair,
when people wrecked the apartment of a black man who'd moved into
a white neighbourhood. It's the owner whom they're suing, for having
rented him the apartment – thus provoking a riot, and lowering the

---

[491]Illegible.

value of the neighbouring buildings – pretty unexpected, isn't it? Apart from that, I see nothing of this country – I'm in total retreat.

I'm sending the next letter to Venice. Do write again, my sweet little one. It still seems so close – our journey and your own self. But I'll be seeing you again soon. I kiss you with all my might.

Your charming Beaver

Envelope:
M. Sartre
Hotel Hassler
Piazza di Spagna
Roma, Italy

[Gary, Indiana]

Tuesday 9 [October 1951]

My dear little yourself. I've just seen a strange photo of you in a Chicago magazine on the theatre, all done by double exposure: it was to illustrate a big article on 'Devil . . .',[492] which simultaneously showers praises on you and reproaches you for not doing justice to your adversaries. I'll try and send it to you. I've had another really peaceful week, which has allowed me to finish off the Sade. It has given me so much trouble, I'd almost like to offer it to Gallimard as a short book. But you'll see whether it's worth it. The weather continued with blazing sun and blue skies for two days, then: storms, rain, high wind. But it's poetic here, when it's warm in the house and outside everything's in motion. On Saturday evening some people came round – as they do every Saturday – to watch a television programme that's really very funny. There's a woman who's a first-class comedian, which is rare. They suggested we go off to a 'frontier town' on the state border between Illinois and Indiana, i.e. between Gary and Chicago. That means a big sector's given over to gambling and prostitution, and that's where you find far the best burlesque shows. It's not so much the burlesque shows which interest me as seeing the place: it's so artificial – in the middle of a landscape of blast furnaces, at the end of a little provincial town – that kind of Reno which suddenly appears. There were a few really good sketches. But the astonishing thing in that area at night is the spectacular sky,

---

[492] *Le Diable et le Bon Dieu* had been staged in the spring of 1951.

with its chimneys spitting fire and the clouds which look as if they'd been painted by hand.

Algren has shown me a truly extraordinary letter, sent him by one of his friends who's a drug addict. The guy makes a general confession covering his whole life, accusing himself among other things of having ruined his wife by making her into an addict, regretting not having written a big book in collaboration with Algren, etc. And to get out of his tragic situation (he's deep in debt – he's a jazz musician who has ruined himself with morphine), he proposes to sell – to a friend who specializes in pornographic films and rubber Johnnies – a film representing in full colour a decapitation: his own. He describes the mechanism of the guillotine minutely, and the way in which the camera would be set up to catch the facial expressions properly, once the head was separated from the body. Algren's role is supposed to be that of 'silent partner': he'd go and pick up the camera, negotiate the film rights, and give the money to the guy's wife. He didn't answer. A few days later, he read in the newspaper that the guy had jumped under a subway train; he didn't kill himself, though, and was treated in hospital along with his wife. It's not known what has become of them since. I'd like the letter as a document for the *Temps Modernes*.

Wednesday

There's a blazing sun again, but I'm disgusted: I'm rereading the novel in order to work on it again, and it's terrible how stale it smells. I have my return seat booked on the 31st. I'm leaving at midday, which puts me in Paris about 14 hours later – or at 8 in the evening, Paris time. I imagine I'll be at the Gare des Invalides by about 9. If you've got back the day before, come and pick me up. Otherwise send a note – or a wire – to Rue de la Bûcherie, where I'll go if I don't see you. And I'll do what you tell me to. How glad I'll be to see you, my sweet little one. How nice you were, reading that rotten novel and giving me such good advice.[493] Here's the photo of you and the article. I'm also enclosing a letter from Algren for Michelle. Give her lots of greetings. I kiss you with all my heart, my dear little soul.

Your charming Beaver

Envelope:
M. Sartre
Poste Restante
Venice, Italy

---

[493]During their cruise to Norway.

LETTERS

JUNE 1953 – JULY 1963
Later Interludes

✿ 1953

[Trieste]

Friday [June 1953]

Dear little yourself. It was nice seeing each other in Venice and made me really happy. Lanzmann was loud in his praises of you when we left – and I agreed, of course. Did you see your article came out in *l'Unità*?[494] It must have caused quite a stir – and it sounded good in Italian too.

Anyway, we left Venice at about noon and circled the lagoon in the other direction – it's really the most astonishing kind of landscape. Bidding farewell to Venice in the distance, we lunched beside the sea in a little resort looking a bit like the Lido – we even bathed. From there to Aquileia which is a staggering place, with three superimposed layers of mosaics (Roman, 3rd C. Christian and 4th C. Christian) – it's amazing and very beautiful, you must see it one day. We went on to Grado, which looks rather like Venice in the middle of another lagoon, and arrived at Trieste after dark. An astonishing city. You have the impression the people are prisoners in this free territory so arrogantly occupied by the English,[495] who've taken up residence in the castles, ban access to the beaches, etc. The location is fantastic – there are hills and stairways like in Genoa – yet the city manages to have no character. The people are very friendly, but dull – nothing Italian about them. It's reminiscent of Geneva, but an oppressed Geneva. They look punished, but you don't know what for. The porter told us nothing was simpler than getting a Yugoslav visa, so yesterday we took the necessary steps and will have our visas in ten minutes – it's midday now. We've bought six litres of oil for the car and a reserve supply of petrol, and we're going to buy some salami, because everyone tells us that sustenance for people

---

[494]The Rosenbergs had just been executed, and Sartre wrote an article in Venice for *Libération*. Since July 1952, De Beauvoir had begun a seven-year love affair with Claude Lanzmann, a young journalist who had recently joined the editorial committee of *Les Temps Modernes* (see *Force of Circumstance*, Chapter 6).

[495]Trieste, nominally at this time a 'free city' under UN protection, in effect remained under a continuation of wartime British occupation until 1954, when a settlement was concluded between Italy and Yugoslavia dividing the city from its hinterland.

and motors is equally dreadful in Yugoslavia – and the roads appalling. This would be of no importance if the car were new, but just yesterday it had a breakdown which was easy enough to get fixed in Trieste, but in Yugoslavia would probably have been impossible to repair. Apparently they don't have garage mechanics or, above all, spare parts. Well, we'll soon see. Living seems to be dirt cheap and the scenery very beautiful, so we're fantastically excited at the idea of going there. Write c/o Putnik, Sarajevo. Putnik is the in-tourist agency that takes care of everything and is reckoned to save the tourist from every ill. Our itinerary is still uncertain, but we'll certainly go to Sarajevo. Write as soon as possible, because letters are sure to take ages to arrive.

Goodbye, little yourself. May you flourish. All my best wishes to Michelle. And tender kisses for you.

Your Beaver.

[Cahors]

[Summer 1953] Friday morning
Dear little yourself. I felt quite touched as I left on Wednesday morning. It was very sweet and helpful of you to keep me company to Lausanne.[496] I hope they woke you up in good time, that you arrived punctually, and so on. As for me, that dawn departure couldn't have been more poetic. It was still dark – huge deserted road as far as Geneva. When I reached the border, the frontier guard pulled a face at your name and looked at me suspiciously: 'Jean-Paul Sartre. So he lends you his car, does he?' 'Oh, yes!', I said. I drove at top speed to Lyons, which I bypassed: 220 km. in 3¼ hrs. But afterwards on the way to St Étienne, with the traffic now terribly heavy, I felt ravenous and realized I was all in, because I shot a red light and a policeman bawled me out. I stopped for an hour to drink cups of white coffee, read the papers, and ring Lanzmann. I got his father: the son was being bandaged and doing fine. Cheered by the rest and this news, I set off again. Busy road as far as Le Puy, where – in order to save 30 km. – I made the mistake of trying to reach Espalion by minor roads. Still, it was fantastically beautiful – one of the most beautiful roads in France, across the heather and limestone plateau of the Aubrac – but impossible to go fast, and at

---

[496]De Beauvoir and Sartre had just spent a month in Amsterdam, then driven down the Rhine and the Moselle to Basel. Lanzmann was supposed to join them there, but instead had a car accident near Cahors.

Nasbinals there was a cattle fair harder to get through than that one in Sicily last year. I almost did myself in too on a bend, pitching from one precipice to another before emerging safe and sound with thudding heart and weak knees. I realized I was all in again, so I stopped at Aubrac to have lunch (it was 3.30) and telephone again. This time I got Lanzmann and suggested his father should take him to Cahors, which would save me the 80 km. I'd have had to do at night. His father didn't have a car, but said they'd hire a taxi. I had only 180 km. left, on main roads. I set off again at 4.30 and was able to take my time. The sun in my eyes did rather . . . .[497]

. . . . which is very reprehensible with a little Renault. He remained at the roadside for an hour and a half, since the doctor had forbidden his being moved without an ambulance, fearing a fracture of the spine. He was in dreadful pain, and dictating his (sentimental) last will and testament to his photographer pal who'd landed painlessly on the grass. Finally they took him to the clinic. He didn't want to send a telegram, clinging to the idea of being in Bâle at the appointed hour without having warned me at all. But, of course, first *France-Dimanche*[498] and then his father intervened. His father showed up and was rewarded by a frightful scene, in which he was accused of being the one responsible for wrecking our plans and obliging me to put myself out. L. was aghast when I told him that his second telegram had thrown us into panic. In fact, he was living in the clouds for 48 hours without being at all aware of it. Anyway, we had dinner with his father, who went off again into the darkness. He amazed me by his youth – he seems younger than you and I – and you'd say he was a total mediocrity if you didn't know him to be capable, in his own way, of wild flights of passion. After that I slept, though badly, because L. was in pain; and yesterday I spent the whole day sleeping, rising only to send off the cables and have lunch. Since his watch had been broken in the accident, we never even suspected how late it was; when I woke up after lunch, I thought it was 4 – whereas it was already 8. We went for a tiny walk, had dinner, then went back to bed again. Which means that I couldn't write to you yesterday, but this morning am feeling as fit as twenty fiddles. It's bright sunshine and I'm in a dentist's waiting-room with no paper, which explains why I'm writing on these scraps. In an hour's time it will be midday, my tooth will be fixed and the car too, and we'll leave Cahors. We'll drive gently round the region until Wednesday.

---

[497]A fragment of this letter, written on various scraps of paper including the back of an 18 June letter from Violette Leduc, is missing.
[498]Newspaper for which Lanzmann was then working.

Here I am again. I have my tooth and am just leaving. Listen, I'd like to show you the Lascaux caves. So, instead of coming to Cahors, get out at Brive. The train leaves at 8.50 and arrives at 14.39.* I'll be at the station to meet the first and second trains – or at the Poste Restante, if so instructed. We could also arrange to meet at the Truffe Noire hotel, 21 Bd Anatole-France, and you can also wire me there on Wednesday.

Instructions

1. Ring Morazzani to transfer your total royalties for last month to your bank account, as he did before. Morazzani knows about it.

2. Ring Hirsch to sign the final proofs of *Henri Martin*.[499]

3. Ring Germaine about the T.M.[500] Does she have the [article] by Dzélépy which Grenier was supposed to deliver to her? Mediocre, but there's nothing else. Germaine should be in contact with Péju about the issue.[501]

4. Call at my place. Ask the concierge for shirts, socks, underpants and handkerchiefs.

My mail is scattered over the centre table (letters from Algren, my sister and another American) and on the mantelpiece, in a bundle of letters where there are two or three for you as well. They could be on the gramophone too.

The *Kean*[502] is on the centre table, in a yellowy-beige folder.

On the little table, there's some work of Lanzmann's in a notepad-wrapper: take the *whole packet*.

Till Wednesday, o little yourself. A big hug and lots of kisses.

Your charming Beaver

*There's one at 13 hrs too, which arrives at 18.37. You choose.

---

[499]Sartre's *L'Affaire Henri Martin* (1953).
[500]Germaine Sorbets was then secretary to *Les Temps Modernes*.
[501]Marcel Péju was to be the effective managing editor of *Les Temps Modernes* from 1954 until 1962.
[502]Sartre's play *Kean* was to be published in 1954.

❧ 1954

[Bou Sââda, Algeria]

Sunday [late January 1954]

Dear little yourself. I'm writing from Bou Sââda – not the hotel where we stayed,[503] but another even prettier one right at the foot of the dunes. Do you remember those dunes, with the little children and their teacher, and the pretty colours of the children against the sand? It really is a lovely place here, and the weather's very fine, with very cold evenings. But I'll tell you everything from the beginning. Well, as the meeting of the Left proceeded I slipped out again, and an hour later we were leaving Paris. We couldn't go very fast at first, because the car wasn't properly run in yet, but we still made good time overall. An hour for lunch at Auxerre, an hour for dinner at Vienne (not in the great restaurant,[504] but in a little one attempting to ape it), and by 2 in the morning we were at Marseilles. We slept at the Hôtel Bellevue – which has become quite squalid, believe it or not (as the Little Subject[505] did not fail to observe irritably). In the morning, I phoned to ask if it was yet time to load the car: Yes! The boat was leaving at noon, so the Aronde was taken along a bit beforehand and they hoisted it by crane to an upper deck. We then found our own way on board. At first the ship was rolling dreadfully, and some families left the table during lunch. I'd taken a travel pill and held up well, but I'd slept only four hours the night before so I spent the rest of the day recuperating. I dozed, vaguely read thrillers, vaguely had dinner, then slept again – this time for real. Our arrival at Algiers at 7 in the morning was very beautiful – we passed an enormous American aircraft carrier, on which people apparently move about only by jeep, and disembarked in a fine drizzle. We then drove up to the St Georges. A fairly contingent day. We had hundreds of little things to do – in connection with the car, our itinerary, etc. – and when it came to looking round Algiers, it rained. The Casbah was too dismal anyway, with all those beggars and cripples: it struck me as even worse than the other times.[506] We repeated that very pretty excursion you and I made through the forest to Bouzareah – which was very beautiful. But in general there was nothing enchanting about being in Algiers. So we decided to leave in the morning – which was yesterday – and that's what we did.

---

[503]In 1948 (see *Force of Circumstance*, pp.162-4).
[504]Chez Point.
[505]Lanzmann.
[506]In 1948 and 1950.

First stopping-place: Bou Sââda. We didn't take the same road as the bus you and I went in, but we too followed a very pretty route, along the coast and through the mountains. We even climbed to a winter-sports resort – third-rate as such, but with a fantastic view over the mountains and desert. It was strange coming into contact with snow above those reddish landscapes already redolent of the Sahara. We arrived at Bou Sââda after dark. At the St Georges (of which this hotel is a kind of branch), we'd been approached by a fellow I've told you about – because I heard Olga talk a lot about him – a certain Alain (who'd screwed A., and caused a scene with N., and run off with Brunbach's wife – does that ring a bell?). He'd approached me very nicely, in fact, not saying 'you're S. de B.' or anything of that sort, but simply 'I'm a friend of Pardo's'; and then he'd mentioned Bost, and eventually I'd asked him his name. He'd been on his way to Bou Sââda, so we met him there yesterday evening. Actually, he'd caused quite a scandal at the St Georges, by leaving a message in my name fixing where and when to meet – but I'd registered in the name of Lanzmann, while there was a Mme de Beauvoir there who was handed the billet doux under her husband's vengeful eye. Well, it was all explained eventually.

Anyway, we met up with this Alain here yesterday evening. Something sensational was going on: forty American sailors – the guys from the aircraft carrier – on leave here. The Ouled Naïls had been brought along to the hotel for them. You just should have seen it – the Ouled dancing and the sailors watching! The girls danced fully dressed – festooned with the gold coins that apparently constitute their dowries – not looking at anyone and their bellies writhing prodigiously. The Americans were clapping their hands and staring at them wide-eyed. Yet one more example, where the presence of so-called civilized man in nature (or folklore, which is the same thing in this case), far from impairing its truth, emphasizes and recreates it. Those dancing girls were far more real as a result of that paying American presence, since they dance precisely in order to be paid. However, not content with this incomplete spectacle, we went off to the street of the Ouled Naïls and saw them dance again, first dressed and then naked, but always with that utterly non-commercial, distracted air which (according to Alain) they retain even when they're screwing. He knows two of them very well (he's doing his military service in the area, and lives most of the time at Bou Sââda – out of love for Bou Sââda). They're sisters, living there with their mother. They invited us to drink mint tea after their dance – an invitation with a price-tag, of course, but they were very charming and quite chatty. The eldest – she's 17 – had a big love affair with the hotel boss, a Russian married to a rather beautiful half-Jewish woman.

They're the most amazing creatures seen close up, and not the least bit trashy. But the most interesting thing was seeing them with someone who knew them well.

Today we walked round Bou Sââda and the dunes. You know, even after having seen the real Sahara it's very appealing. It made a powerful impression on me to see sand and palm trees again, with that African sky and African aroma – there's honestly no other kind of landscape that I prefer. We took the car and went to see a holy town nearby that you'd really have liked, and also some mirages and another little oasis. It's very, very beautiful everywhere.

Tomorrow we're leaving for Laghouat. And the next day on to Gardhaïa, where we'll stay for a while. After that, our plans diverge. But I'll write and tell you, or even wire an address as soon as we've decided. It will depend on the condition of the tracks. Perhaps it will be El Golea, or else Ouargla. At any rate, I'm in seventh heaven finding myself back in the Sahara. I've lots of memories, which makes our own trip seem very close – and I really long to go on a long journey with you again one day. My sweet little one, I'm gripped by the most violent longing for news of you. Tell me honestly how your blood pressure and all that is.[507] It gave my heart quite a wrench to leave you in that semi-run-down condition – it's so essential for me to think of you as completely well all along the line, both health and the rest. I'm hoping for a letter from you the day after tomorrow. I'll write again at once. How I wish I could send you a bit of salt, if that's what you lack! I kiss you with all my soul.

Your Beaver

Hôtel du Hoggar, Touggourt
Algeria

30 January 1954[508]

Dearest little yourself

I just received your wire at Ouargla. I did think it was all the fault of the mails, but even so I was a bit distressed when yesterday, yet again, I found no letter at Ghardaïa. The stupid thing is, I won't get hold of yours before Algiers. It's impossible to have it forwarded, because we're

---

[507]For the past year Sartre had been overworking and suffered from high blood pressure.
[508]These letters correspond to *Force of Circumstance*, pp.298-301.

following tracks linking places that aren't officially linked. Well, I'm hoping for news at Tozeur.

I'm really enjoying myself. It's rather cold – very cold at night – and the days are rather short: at 5.30 they're over. But anyway, this Sahara's an utter delight. I wrote to you on Sunday evening from Bou Sâada. The next morning we took the road you know, to Djelfa – it's really very lovely. We carried on to Laghouat, which you also know, but we didn't go to that hotel where we ate flambéed dates; there's another nicer one now, so we had lunch there. From there to Ghardaïa. Surprising arrival at 6 in the evening: an exhibition of modern painting in the hotel (reproductions) and thirty-odd people vigorously discussing: 'Painting has to be understood' – 'Yes, but you can understand with your gut, too', and so on. The manager commented: 'It's a secular sect.' They were mainly people who were acquiring culture in order to go and impart culture to others, and who were travelling around to that end in a big coach. There was also a four-person 'expedition', consisting of three men (one with a beard) and a woman and two lorries covered with (printed) inscriptions: 'Demeyer Electric Cookers, Lille, Nord', '30,000 km. through Black Africa', and a map of Africa with names and arrows. A news item from *L'Écho d'Alger* announced that the aim of the expedition was to study 'the possibilities for installing electric cookers in Black Africa', and also 'African parasitology' – or the parasites of Africa. Meanwhile, the bearded man was interviewing the branch manager. We saw the two lorries again next day on the market-place at Ghardaïa: they never went a hundred metres without the two lorries. The hotel has expanded since our day, but you still eat just as badly there – and there's still camel on the menu. Ghardaïa's really miraculous, and Lanzmann was as captivated by it as we were. Thanks to the car we were able to visit some of the towns and oases round about – Mozabite towns, like the ones in the valley, and very lovely too: Berriane, Metlili, and especially Guerrara, which is 100 km. away and quite astonishing, all on its own in a red amphitheatre with strange, wild inhabitants. We stayed only two and a half days – which was a bit short – to see all that M'zab region, but after all I already knew it and found it quite familiar. Its beauty is really extraordinary, which strikes one as oddly outrageous in view of the fact that the Mozabites are so unappealing.

Those two days at Ghardaïa were enlivened by a dispute that had been brewing ever since Algiers: should we go to El Golea in the Aronde or not? The Algiers Touring Club had given the reply: 'It's humanly possible.' But after Bou Sâada people told us: 'It's possible, provided you buy another car afterwards.' The hotel-keeper said: 'It's impossible.'

But you know how mendacious, mythomaniac and generally unreliable everybody is in this country! All the same, for my part – as I knew the road a bit – I refused to make the experiment. L., who didn't yet realize the extent to which a road can be 'impossible', was hopping mad at the abstract obstacle. We argued pretty fiercely for two days (intermittently, of course). And then, luckily, there was a crushing consensus of evidence against the route. The only cars that took it were jeeps, etc., made expressly for the purpose. Above all, the Guerrara road began to convince Lanzmann. And the next day – that was yesterday – after we'd decided to drop El Golea and go to Ouargla, he was utterly convinced. The way things worked was as follows. The road surface is corrugated, so you have to maintain a speed of 80 km. per hour. But it's also crossed by gutters, which jolt the car to pieces if you don't take them slowly. So what's to be done? ᴡᴡᴧᴊᴧᴧᴜᴧᴊᴧᴧᴜᴧᴊᴧᴜᴜ (that's the road). Even if you're not transporting nitroglycerine, it's a problem. In addition, every so often you cross a thick sandbank, in which you get stuck. Yesterday we got quite seriously stuck, 100 km. from anywhere. Luckily, after an hour of fruitless effort, a lorry went by and helped us out.

So yesterday evening it was Ouargla, where I've been before.[509] A crazy homosexual colonel built a European town there in pseudo-Sudanese style which really makes one's eyes pop out. The native town isn't particularly beautiful, but its inhabitants are black and the Negro women stroll about with their faces uncovered, which is a pleasure to see after all those white ladies. The landscape's sensational, nothing but sand dunes, and this morning there was a terrifying sandstorm: we climbed on to high, faraway dunes and it felt rather like being in a big storm on the open sea. We got stuck once on the way to the dunes, but we're gaining experience – we've bought a spade and some boards – so we managed to extract ourselves all on our own. This afternoon on our way to Touggourt – on a quite good and very beautiful road through dunes – we got stuck twice: once we freed ourselves on our own, the other time a gang of roadworkers lifted the car out. We came across a lorry stuck fast, which often happens when there are big sandstorms. The car's holding up well. After each run we have it checked and all the nuts tightened, because it takes a dreadful shaking, poor little thing. Apart from that, you know the kind of landscapes – there are honestly none in the world more beautiful. You know the climate, too. And the hotels, where all people talk about is the roads. And the roads

---

[509]In 1946, when she gave lectures in Algeria and Tunisia.

themselves, with all those countless people working on them. And the Saharans, and the myths – it's all just like what we saw on our big journey.

Now we're going to go to El Oued, Tozeur, the Tunisian south, and back via Tunis. I think I'll be home on Monday week. But nothing's certain yet, I'll wire you another address from Tozeur. I'm hoping to find a letter – yes, I'm sure it'll have had time to get there. I do so miss it when I have no news of you. My head's stuffed with memories, and I'm consumed by yearning for another long period when I can be with you from morning to evening. Goodbye, my sweet little one. I'd so like to be sure everything's going really, really well for you. I kiss you with all my soul.

Your Beaver

Envelope:
M. Sartre
42 Rue Bonaparte
Paris 6

[Gabes, Tunisia]

Wednesday morning – Gabes
[early February 1954]

Dearest little yourself. I've no luck with your letters and it makes me so unhappy. Either there's a strike in France, or the mail's being sabotaged here. The Tozeur letter wasn't there either, though I'd had to make heroic efforts to go and collect it. I've had everything forwarded to Tunis, where I'll be the day after tomorrow; but in the meantime, for the past fortnight I've had nothing from you but a cable – and that rather distresses me. I'm going to wire you to write once more to Tunis. I'm coming back on Monday evening. Send me a note to Rue de la Bûcherie, to tell me when I'll see you on Tuesday. Make it as early as possible, as I'll be longing to be with you again.

If I hadn't this nagging fear in my heart, I'd be utterly content. We're having a truly fantastic trip – albeit not easy. The most difficult and most beautiful parts began at Touggourt. I wrote to you from there, one evening. The next morning we decided to leave for El Oued, that city in the dunes where the gardens are at the bottom of big sand funnels – I've already told you about it and was absolutely determined to see it again. There was a bit of a wind, and the people at Touggourt wrinkled up their noses when we said we were leaving – but without giving any explanation. The women from the hotel simply said they'd telephone to El Oued to find out whether we'd arrived – and if not have a breakdown truck sent out to us. After 3 km. we began to understand: sandstorms are worse than fog, a real white shroud, the full horror of whiteness that Melville and Poe talk about. And since the road was corrugated, you had to speed along at 70 per hour in that pitch darkness. Luckily, we're assured we won't meet anyone on the road in places like that – though that's not quite true, since one car with front-wheel drive did overtake us, saying: 'Follow me!' It was an Arab chauffeur driving a chieftain, and he really knew his stuff. We followed him – unable to see anything but the tail of his car – at top speed, with sand beneath our wheels and all around us. After 50 km. he left us on our own. Eventually the wind dropped a bit and we managed to cover half the distance without too much trouble. We ate our sandwiches, then set off again. But there the road was covered with thick sandbars: three times we got stuck. Luckily, once there was a crew of workers on the tiny railway running from El Oued to Biskra; the second time a train was passing and I stopped it (you can just imagine the kind of train: four Arabs on tip-trucks); and the third time we got out on our own, with spade and boards. We drove a bit further on a 'hard' surface, then got stuck definitively in a dune. We were getting ready to spend the night there – darkness was just falling – when, by some miracle, a Dodge came by: the station-master, his wife and two drivers. They took an hour to get us going again. We drove on ahead of them – but 20 km. further on we were stuck again. Impossible to extract us this time. So we locked up the car and stowed the luggage and ourselves into the Dodge. Arrival after dark, for dinner in a fine, deserted and rather sinister hotel – but we were really glad to be there. Next day we spent the morning in the dunes, walking around full of admiration (you know how beautiful sand is, and this was the most beautiful sandy desert in the whole Sahara). But we were in some perplexity, having tumbled into the middle of an obscure intrigue pitting the station-master (two trains a week, just freight – 120 km. in 10 hours – and threat of imminent abolition of the service) against the Hôtel Transat, with a coach service. The station-master wanted us to have our car got going again by a certain Salem, then put on a wagon as far as Biskra. The hotel-keeper wanted us to take the coach as far as our car, and for the coach to get us going again then escort us to Biskra, giving us assistance if the need arose. As for us, we wanted to go to Tozeur – but that was certainly out of the question, since the track was blocked by sand dunes as big as houses.

The station-master warned us against the coach ('He won't do any

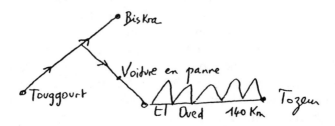

repairs for you') and the hotel-keeper against the station-master. Thereupon, the driver Salem declared: 'I'll take you to Tozeur in the Aronde.' The station-master's clan said: 'If he says so, he'll do it.' The other clan: 'You'll take a week to get to Tozeur.' Perplexity. We lean towards the more prudent option: returning to Biskra. Then we meet Salem in a jeep in the dunes, and he suggests: 'Come for a drive.' And he begins a series of demented manoeuvres, climbing vertically up dunes and so on. He swears: 'With an Aronde, it'll be better still.' The fact that I wanted your letter at Tozeur decided the matter. We went that afternoon to fetch the car with a breakdown truck, and Salem took it to El Oued – crossing the sandbars without the least hesitation. And next morning we left for Tozeur. The whole of El Oued swore we wouldn't get through. A truck was holding itself in readiness to come and look for us if we hadn't telephoned by 5. And we stuck in the sand for the first time only 4 km. from El Oued – which we didn't like the look of. But it was merely a minor accident, and that driver was a true genius. He crossed immense sand dunes for kilometres without once getting stuck, without putting a strain on the car, finding a way every time. Every so often I thought we were going to overturn, but he always righted himself. Lanzmann, who'd tackled the sand a bit the previous evening – from necessity, and without success – was round-eyed with admiration. We eventually arrived at Tozeur for lunch, where people looked at us admiringly since it never happens – a tourist car getting through on that road – just Dodges and things of that kind. It was into the bargain the most amazing jaunt 'from the scenic point of view': we were lost in an infinity of sand.

At all events, we were very pleased and the driver filled with pride. We walked round the Tozeur oasis. Yesterday morning we went to see the one at Nefta, which is the prettiest of all. But the days of *Les Nourritures Terrestres*[510] are, in fact, long gone. In these oases, the men

---

[510]By André Gide (1897).

work bare-footed and in rags and misery; the people have all the illnesses in the world; and on top of that you feel yourself hated. It's perfectly plain that there's an enormous difference between Tunisia and Algeria. In Algeria, there's a patriarchal atmosphere. Here, there's a sub-proletariat sunk in black poverty and hatred. We drove off to Gabes. We'll see this whole Tunisian south in two days anyway, then go back up to Tunis, from where we'll leave on Monday evening by air. The car will travel to Marseilles by boat, and we'll pick it up later. Yesterday afternoon there were more sandstorms, and cold: such a violent storm that we turned back, after trying to go beyond Gabes – it was as bad as that. But it's lovely seeing this southern region in a fury of sand and wind. The landlord here recognized me – after 8 years – and asked me to give a lecture![511]

Good. I'm off to post this letter and wire you. In two days, I'll surely have news of you. Till Tuesday, my dear little yourself. I kiss you with all my Beaver's heart.

Your Beaver

[Lac des Settons, Morvan]

Friday morning [late May 1954]
Dearest little yourself. Well, on Wednesday we read long extracts of your speech against the bomb in *L'Huma* and *Libération*[512] – extracts approved by the pilots. You spoke last – did you prepare your speech during the first part of the meeting? And yesterday morning the papers were announcing your arrival in Moscow,[513] which provoked the comment from Lanzmann that: 'Russian air transport's truly admirable.' Eventually your mother gave me your address yesterday on the telephone. It's strange to think I'm going to send this letter to Moscow, I can't really believe it'll get there. But I'm hoping for one myself when I get back to Paris on Sunday evening, or on Monday. I'm longing for details. Hour by hour since Tuesday morning we've been keeping track of you: 'He's in Berlin – He's leaving Berlin – He's in Russian airspace – He's in Moscow.' Last night I thought about your teeth, and as I had

[511]In 1946, 'the man who owned the hotel slipped a poem under my door in which he deplored, between courtly compliments, the fact that I was an Existentialist' (*Force of Circumstance*, p.58).
[512]Delivered in Berlin at a meeting of the Peace Movement: see *Force of Circumstance*, p.304.
[513]Sartre had been invited there by the Writers' Association.

insomnia I imagined your whole trip ruined by horrible sufferings. I do hope it's not true.

I'm writing to you from a ravishing spot, the Lac des Settons in the Morvan. L. is still sleeping behind me, I have my desk in front of the open window, you can see the water through the pines and the weather is sensationally beautiful. But I'll start from Monday, after I left you. At 8 I met up with L., who'd just learnt from the *F[rance]-D[imanche]* printers that *Preuves*[514] was publishing a vicious article attacking him, but hadn't been able to get hold of a copy. Apparently *Rivarol* and *Aspect de la France* have crudely insulted him too, not to speak of the *Dauphiné Libéré*. We decided to go to the cinema. What could we see? We tried *Animal Crackers*,[515] but left after ten minutes; it wasn't just bad, it was unbearable. We decided to have dinner, and found seats on the first floor at the St Moritz. At once we realized that the occupants of the next table – whom we couldn't see very well, as we were sitting sideways on to them, but who could easily feast their eyes on us – were Françoise Giroud, Servan-Schreiber and a third party.[516] It made us rather ill at ease. After that we went to see *M. Ripois*, which is an excellent film – a strange film, because of the gap between the novel and the screenplay and between M. Ripois and Gérard Philipe – but an excellent film precisely for that reason. Queneau's dialogue is marvellous, so is Philipe. We promptly felt like going to London next week or the one after – it depends on Évelyne,[517] but I think we'll go for four days in any case.

Tuesday: Bibliothèque Nationale in the morning, where I noted down some sensational admissions by Jules Romains.[518] A gloomy session with my sister and De Roulet at the May Salon. Her idea was to prove to me that the other painters of her age are as bad as she is –which is almost true. To cap it all I met Laure Garcin, who has managed to make herself unrecognizable – but to no avail. Then I saw Olga, who was nice but we had nothing to say to one another. And I took Bost out to dinner at Montfort-l'Amaury. We met L. at midnight at the Falstaff. Bost didn't

---

[514]*Preuves* was a violently anti-communist journal, the counterpart of *Encounter* in Britain, funded by the Congress for Cultural Freedom.

[515]One of the Marx Brothers' earliest films, (1930).

[516]Françoise Giroud and Jean-Jacques Servan-Schreiber were the chief reporter and editor respectively of *L'Express*, then a left-of-centre weekly which was to oppose the Algerian War increasingly firmly.

[517]Évelyne Rey, actress sister of Claude Lanzmann, with whom Sartre had an affair starting in 1955 and who played the main roles in several of his plays. She committed suicide in 1966.

[518]De Beauvoir was doing preliminary reading for her article on right-wing thought, 'La pensée de droite, aujourd'hui', written for *Les Temps Modernes*.

want to go to bed and he had us walking round Paris till 3 in the morning.

Wednesday: hard day with Violette Leduc. She'd just got out of bed, where she'd retired with a 39-degree temperature after her conversation with Lemarchand. The doctor told her that was what had brought it on. I took her to lunch at the Bois, then for a walk at Bagatalle, and comforted her as best I could. The taxi scene literally outrages people: Queneau, Lemarchand, Y. Lévy – I have the impression it wounds them directly as males. She'd really like to try and publish the book without cuts.[519]

In the evening, we went to Évelyne's. Jacques[520] was there with Dianna, getting on well together and very nice. Évelyne was in bed, ravishing – and so happy because of her film plans in Germany: it would be a fantastically good thing. I don't know yet if she'll have the operation tomorrow or on Monday, I'm going to phone her. At all events, you can rely on us to look after her. L. told us a lovely story about a sexual orgy involving the B.s and the T.s (veterans of earlier partner-swapping sessions with Paul Éluard, and with Denise D. too). The B. woman told Mama and Mony[521] the whole story, with a wealth of details even Violette Leduc wouldn't dare describe. All cloaked in the most frenzied spiritualism. B. didn't join in the orgy, but he encouraged his wife – and ended up being unfaithful too. He promptly realized he wasn't impotent, and abandoned his quest for God.

So yesterday we set off for the Morvan, after settling the money matters with Cau and Évelyne. It was Ascension Day, so it was difficult getting out of Paris. But we eventually found ourselves on fresh, green little roads and it was very agreeable. At 6 in the evening there was still quite a throng on the bar, but gradually everybody left and we remained alone in this hotel, where we're going to spend two or three days. We've brought what we need to work – tons of books – and I think we'll get some work done.

That's it basically, dear little yourself. Have a good time and do get some sleep, won't you? And try to remember everything faithfully, so that you can tell us it all properly when you get back. I suppose the weather's fine in Moscow, which is lucky.

I kiss you with all my soul, sweet little one, and implore you to take good care of yourself.

Your charming Beaver

---

[519]The book in question is *Ravages*, which appeared in a savagely cut form in the spring of 1955 (see *Force of Circumstance*, pp.522-3).
[520]Lanzmann's brother.
[521]Lanzmann's mother and stepfather.

The last issue of *T.M.* is out. It's excellent. The next one will be very good too.

[Paris]

Tuesday [1 June 1954]

Dear little yourself

No letter from you – nobody has one. Everybody's a bit downcast, but hoping you're having a good time. Yesterday in *Combat* there was a short item: 'Malenkov and Jean-Paul Sartre on Red Square'. It looked good. Two days before in *Le Monde*, Jouve was letting it be known that you hadn't warned the Embassy about your visit, but that if you thought it a good idea to drop in you'd still be received with the consideration due to any French citizen. He seemed to be hopping mad. I'm reading the Schapiro book[522] to get myself into the atmosphere – there are some very entertaining things in it. But I'd prefer a letter. L.'s waiting avidly for one, because of the stamp – I promised to make him a present of it.

Did you get my first letter? And the wire? I saw Évelyne yesterday when I got back to Paris. She'd had a lot of pain in the kidneys from her colon bacilli, and she had bronchitis and a temperature of 39 degrees – which is not serious, I don't think, but tiresome. She'd received your flowers, and was surrounded by her whole family and Fifi, but looked very tired. L. and I will be staying in Paris this week, and he'll try and see the doctor tomorrow to get some accurate information about her condition. I'll go back there this afternoon.

As for me I'm doing fine, despite having caught a cold on the Lac des Settons. We spent three good days – Friday, Saturday and Sunday – walking in the Morvan and Burgundy. We worked in the mornings (I'd brought along an entire library), then went walking until nightfall. I saw Vezelay, Autun and Dijon again, and heaps of little towns, lakes and minor roads. On the Sunday afternoon, as we were passing another car, a big pebble was flung up against our windscreen and it was unbelievable – in a fraction of a second the whole windscreen was covered with a close network which spread by chain reaction, with a tiny and utterly ravishing sound, till we couldn't see a thing except through a disc that remained intact just at the level of the driver's eyes.

---

[522]Leonard Schapiro's *Origins of the Communist Autocracy* was written in 1954, so perhaps De Beauvoir had got hold of an early copy of it.

That's how 'Securit' glass breaks and it's quite amazing. Everything stays in place, even though reduced to powder. The disc is expressly designed so that the driver won't be blinded in the event of breakage. We drove like that as far as Dijon, not really quite sure what to do – especially as it was Sunday. Eventually a garage-mechanic advised us simply to break the windscreen out. We picked it out piece by piece, as if we were crumbling a cake. But it was a bit chilly driving after that. We went for our jaunt all the same, in good schizoid fashion. The only painful moment was twilight, when thousands of midges swarmed down on to me in lieu of the windscreen. And the next day – yesterday, Monday – as we drove back to Paris very fast, insects were hitting me on the forehead like stones. (L., as driver, was somewhat protected by a piece of mica.) To cap it all there was a bit of rain. But even so we made it back by around 2 o'clock.

I had lunch with mother and sister, then took sister out for a drink. More dreadful than ever. Not a word about my trip or about you. She spent an hour describing the schemes people get up to in Paris to launch a painter. She's distraught because she has had wretched reviews ('The critics seem to think it's just a show like any other! Oh! people don't have any courage . . .'), and also because she hasn't sold anything, except one picture compulsorily to the State. But she won't admit that. Even to Mama she says she has sold 4 pictures. Greuze is displaying four 'Sold' tickets. The fact that there are no sales mustn't be admitted to anyone. She says: 'I thought Milan would have been harder to conquer than Paris!' And the real disaster is that they're definitely holding themselves ready to go to Greece if we should go! Lionel has left, but she's staying till Friday and I'm seeing her this evening.

Well, yesterday afternoon I went to see Évelyne, then in the evening we took Michelle out. We didn't do much, because L. had to spend an hour – from 9 to 10 – at the Cirque d'Hiver, as one of the Bouglione brothers had died. I had a couple of drinks in a bar with Michelle, then we had dinner at the Coupole. It was very nice, she seemed in good form.

Hard day today. I've just spent four hours with Olga; I'm off in a minute to the clinic; and this evening I'm going out with my sister. Well, tomorrow I'll be getting back to work, which I always really enjoy. The weather's turning a bit finer again this afternoon.

I'll add a few words when I leave the clinic, to give you news of Évelyne. I've given Wanda her dough, told Michelle to ask Cau again for some, and told Cau to give her some – everything's working out nicely. I had your mother on the phone this morning (after I'd been to see Cau), she seemed in good form. Your whole little world is doing fine in fact. Bye for now.

Well, I've seen Évelyne and she was transformed since yesterday. No more temperature, colour in her cheeks – or almost – and in excellent spirits. It must be said that she'd received your letter and was radiant about it. An envelope from Moscow looks splendid. But it breaks my heart to think how they've been tiring you out again. I'm really hoping for a letter myself soon, with more detailed news. Don't get overtired, dear little yourself.

A big hug and kisses

Your charming Beaver

[Paris]

Tuesday 8 [June 1954]

Dearest little yourself. I haven't the heart to write a real, long letter, because I have the impression the letters don't arrive. All the same, it was a great joy to have the one from you this morning: a long one dated Sunday 30 – the other little one dated Thursday 27 had arrived after *12 days*. It really came at the right time this morning, that letter, because I'd had dreadful nightmares during the night, in which I met you somewhere in a chalet with a face made out of big studs and resembling Prévert; I was tearing off a stud and asking: 'What does that mean?', and you were saying: 'That I'm on the other side – I'm paying for the life I've led' – and I realized that you'd a cancer on your face, or God knows what nightmarish thing of the kind. Actually, despite the lack of letters, there was some news of you in the papers: 'Sartre spoke on Radio Moscow. He is captivated by Soviet kindergartens.' Above all, there were the two photos of you in *France-Soir*, on the banks of the Moskowa and coming out of the cathedral. Your guardian angels were visible, and they didn't look any too enticing. But you seemed young and happy. L. is going to try and get me the originals.

In a nutshell: week spent working on the pseudo-thinkers of the Right (who this week *produced*: an article by Aron in the *Revue de Paris* against *The Communists and Peace*[523] – worthless; and the article of a complete nonentity in *Preuves*, in which he amalgamates the business of the editorial, *The Communists and Peace*, and L.'s paper – worse

---

[523]*Les Communistes et la Paix* had been published in *Les Temps Modernes*, the first two parts appearing in 1952, the final part in April 1954.

than worthless). I've also comforted Évelyne, who though suffering acutely from the lack of letters was angelically sweet. I like her a lot. They've given her a blood transfusion, and she was really brave and made no fuss. On Sunday they brought her home from the clinic, and she was so happy to find herself back in her beautiful flat that she seems to be getting better twice as fast. Her spirits are high now. Jacques and Dianna are taking care of her very nicely indeed.

I haven't seen Michelle again, because when I rang on Saturday she wasn't in Paris.

I rang your mother in Vichy just now, and gave her some news of you. We had one very nice outing with Bost and Olga, and I saw Bost alone one evening too. I'm seeing him again this evening. He's going to sell his thriller script and make some dough out of it. They seem to be in good shape. Olga still adores Évelyne.

To my very great pleasure, I've learned – through an indiscretion of Monique Lange's – that Queneau has written a 4-page notice on the novel, [524] enthusiastic, in which he says that it's a 'masterpiece', *War and Peace* and *The Princess of Cleves* rolled into one, etc. etc. I'm like Poupette writing this – but the fact is, it was the first opinion from outside the family and I was pleased. Cau has been rotten about money, but we managed to pull through anyway thanks to Bost. I'll tell you the story. He really goes too far. I'd warned him days in advance and again before the deadline, but he left É. without a penny to pay the clinic. I borrowed from Bost, who by a miracle had some. But it was shabby, not to speak of other little tricks.

The Little Subject is an absolute angel. He was as moved as I was when your letter arrived this morning. He dragged me off yesterday to see his parents, but it was really funny, what with those stories about the B.s' orgy with the T.s in the name of 'the communion of saints'. He now says coolly: 'As Paule (or Grenier) knows that *I am a commun- ist . . .*' They were heaping shit on you again yesterday at *France-Dimanche*: 'Sartre hasn't noticed there's no lavatory paper in the USSR', says Vidal-Lablache. – 'Obviously he never uses it', answers Guyot. – 'Or else he uses thousand-franc notes', Vidal Lablache adds.

OK. I could go on for a long time about it, but it's too insubstantial. Tomorrow we're leaving for London, the Little Subject and I. I'll have your letters forwarded on, if there are any. I'll be back on Monday: in other words, certainly before you. Your letter has really cheered me up – you seem so happy. Here, the weather's dreadful. At present, for example, there's a storm on. But life isn't going badly. Everyone's

---

[524] *The Mandarins*, which was to be published in October and win the Prix Goncourt.

waiting impatiently for you, me included. I was very moved to see your photos. I kiss you with all my soul, my dear, sweet little beloved.

Your charming Beaver

Envelope:
M. Jean-Paul Sartre
National Hotel
Moscow, USSR

🦫 1955

[Marseilles]

Sunday evening [early February 1955]

Dearest little yourself. I haven't written till now and this will be only a short letter, because the Slave of Hunger and I are really working like slaves – I hope the result will be worth such pains.[525] But look, I'd better tell you straight away: I made a mistake about the dates and we're not coming back for *a fortnight*. So it'll be 15 February when you get the article – is that soon enough? Otherwise, it just might be possible to have almost all of it typed here and send it off on the 10th. What do you think?

It was very agreeable hearing your voice on the telephone, especially since you seemed sprightly and in good spirits. Ring from your end as soon as you can, morning or late afternoon. It's nice here. We're at the Hôtel Mediterranée, which you know, on the left-hand side of the port: a very large room with two windows, very bright. There are two good desks and they've put in neon lamps especially for us. We briefly thought of installing ourselves at the Réserve, on the Corniche. Upon reflection, however, Lanzmann like me is sensitive to the melancholy of having the sea 'just a stone's throw away', and we preferred being surrounded by houses, boats and people. As we spend long hours in our room, we'd feel in exile there – whereas here we're having the benefit of Marseilles even while we work.

They've reconstructed the Old Port in a really shameful way – it's hideous. But it doesn't matter, the charm's still there. And the weather's pretty fine all the time. Yesterday it was even superb – we could see Martigues in bright sunlight.

---

[525]De Beauvoir was working on her article 'Merleau-Ponty ou le Pseudo-Sartrisme', a reply to the latter's *Adventures of the Dialectic* which had been published in June; Lanzmann – the 'slave of hunger' – was writing an article on 'The Leftwinger' (see *Force of Circumstance*, p.317-19).

We left at 10 in the morning on Wednesday. We passed through Nevers, Moulins, St Étienne and Roanne: do you remember how you and I did that stretch of road by bicycle, and it was such terribly hard work getting over the Col de la République. We stopped at Montélimar at about 9 in the evening. In that way we followed the Rhône valley by daylight and saw the floods: they were starting to go down, but they were impressive all the same – with lots of farms surrounded by water. We couldn't get through by Avignon. Arrived in Marseilles at 1 o'clock. For Lanzmann, who barely knew it, it was love at first sight and the spell still hasn't been broken.

We had lunch in a restaurant on the Old Port, selected our hotel, then immediately got down to work. We work every morning till about 1. After that, excursion – with lunch on the way – and work again from 5 to 9. On Friday, we saw Cassis and the *calanques*; on Saturday, Martigues: today, the Corniche as far as the end of the coast road (which goes a long way now), and N.D. de la Garde, and some odd corners of Marseilles. On Monday, I took time off to go to the cinema to see an appalling English thriller. On the newsreel they had an item about skiing, which said that it's raining non-stop in the mountains and the snow's dreadful – so, no regrets. Anyway, it's a positive delight to be here.

I'm waiting for your letter and telephone call. Be funny and be happy, if the two can be combined. A big hug and kisses, my dear Little yourself.

Your Beaver

[Salamanca, Spain]

Friday 22 July [1955]

My dear little yourself. I got your telegram, and this morning your letter. Moreover, the French papers aren't announcing your death, so I suppose Michelle's still driving with skill and prudence – and without any bad luck. I've never had any doubts about Michelle, but luck's treacherous, so sometimes while dropping asleep I've felt the odd tremor of fear. As for the Slave of Hunger, he cried in his sleep all through one night, so affected was he by the story of Hugo coming across the announcement of Leopoldine's death in a newspaper in a café – I'm reading Maurois' *Olympio*.[526] Anyway, today I'm reassured – and glad to know that

---

[526] A life of Victor Hugo (who personified himself in his poetry under the name Olympio).

Michelle has been converted to mountains, and that you enjoyed Bellagio. Did you like Aosta? – you don't say. I couldn't find our little hotel again either, in Bellagio. I forgot to ask you the other day whether you remembered the 'Papa-Moscas' at Burgos, who swallows flies as he strikes the hours: in those days when you and I were so nice, we found him really entertaining.

We left Burgos and sped off to the North-West, across the plateaux of Old Castille and some 'terrifying' mountains – very beautiful, actually. We followed the north coast – boring and desolate – till we reached La Coruña, a charming town. First, it's a port with a good smell of fish and tar. Secondly, all the apartments have verandahs for every room – they call them miradors here – which means that the facades are perfectly flat, white, and made of glass. The town's known as the crystal town, and it's quite true that it glitters amazingly in the sunlight and all the buildings look as though they were made of crystal. There was a fiesta, and crowds of people, and it was charming – even though since Pamplona we'd had a horror of the technique consisting in using firecrackers to keep the populace amused. The delight at being in Spain remains, but against that background – since it's familiar to us after last year – we're far more sensitive to the horrible aspects of the system: the priests and the poverty. Santiago de Compostella – all churches (amazing ones) and beautiful old arcaded streets, but ringed by filthy hovels – sickened us. And Salamanca where we are this evening – which has the same colours as Rome, a big 18th-century square, and lots of little squares: marvellous, but so poor, so harsh and so desperate under the sun – has made us intensely sad.

Between La Coruña and Salamanca, after visiting Santiago, we stopped for three days in a Galician island.* We bathed and sunbathed and toured the coast by car. It's rather like Brittany, at the same time as being southern. It's very beautiful, but the Galicians are sad and glum like Portuguese, and the fishing ports have the same gloomy air. They hate tourists – but out of Galician separatism, not at all out of class consciousness: they were Franco supporters from day one. It's a strange, lost region, very interesting to see, and from which Andalucia seems a very long way away.

Yesterday, we drove all day through wonderful landscapes before re-entering Castille and arriving in the evening at Salamanca – where we've just spent the day. It was hot, and I have an idea we're going to be hot every day from now on. Up to now, it has been ideal: sun and wind, a heavenly climate. I've already told you that we're leaving tomorrow for Valencia, where we'll spend three days seeing big bullfights with the best matadors of the day. Then we'll go back down into Andalucia, and up again into Estremadura – ending up in Madrid. On about 31 July I'll be in Seville, and on about 6 August in Madrid. Write if possible, or at least send a telegram to each address, so that I don't have bad dreams.

So, I've read *Olympio*. The beginning's entertaining, and the private life quite well told – though not always. But the way in which it passes over Hugo the public figure and man of the Left is shameful, and in general you get a very poor idea of the fellow. As you warned me, that Maurois's too petty-minded. Did you know too that Hemingway's sickeningly anti-Semitic? *The Sun Also Rises* – quite entertaining to read in Pamplona – is, from that point of view among others, a disgusting piece of work.

I've had a note from Violette Leduc, in transports about an article on her by Dominique Aury in the *N.R.F.* Monique Lange has told me some stories about her. Among other things, when I got the Goncourt[527] – speaking of the lunches which we take turns in paying, according to a custom imposed on me by her – she said to Monique Lange: 'I hope that now *we won't be going Dutch any longer*'. M.L. also has the impression that in a sense she hates me.

Do you have any news about *Nekrassov*?[528] Is it confirmed that they'll revive it in September, as Lanzmann has told me? Do you have any news about Merleau-Ponty, or about Paris in general? We get the occasional newspaper, but at least 3 days old (though today we have Wednesday's) and all full of pictures of Madame Edgar Faure[529] – we feel a long way away from everything.

I'm really longing for a letter at Valencia. I'll write to you again from there, to tell you whether the corridas were fine ones. I'll post this letter tomorrow in Madrid, which we'll be driving through. I think you must have had the first one, even though I left out part of the address. Do congratulate Michelle warmly on my behalf and on Lanzmann's. Make the best of Rome, and have a good rest. Are you working on *Jean Sans Terre*?[530] And car accidents apart, how's the blood pressure? Do reply. I'm so happy when I get a letter. I kiss you with all my soul, dear little yourself.

Your Beaver

---

[527] See note 524 above.
[528] Sartre's play *Nekrassov* had opened on 8 June 1955, but had lasted for only sixty performances.
[529] Edgar Faure was French prime minister (not for the first time) from February 1955 until January 1956.
[530] *Jean Sans-Terre* (John Lackland) was a first version of *Words* (1963), on which Sartre began to work in 1953.

Dear Michelle and dear Sartre, a big kiss to both of you.

Lanzmann

*An island connected to the mainland by a big bridge, which made car trips possible.

Envelope:
M. Sartre
Albergo Nazionale
Piazza Montecitorio
Roma

🦋 1958

[Paris]

Sunday [late August 1958]

Dear little yourself. Forgive me for 'breaking in on your mood', but I really must communicate to you what's being said to me insistently from every quarter: people are calling for *some* article by you that could, as a 'test case', also be published as a lampoon. What people are saying – in the Committees, etc.[531] – is that publication after 15 September would be too late. Whereas if you send an article at once, it will be a basis for the anti-referendum campaign[532] during the whole month of September. I don't like having to say so, but I think you really must do it: your silence is beginning to make a bad impression, now that the 'anti' campaign is seriously getting under way. They're making a real effort, you know. Lanzmann alone is going to speak at Nantes, at Montargis, and in the Doubs – all within the space of a fortnight. Bulletins are being published, they're holding meetings in the provinces, and the Communists are determined to pull out all the stops. Things will happen on 4 September if De Gaulle persists in his intention to speak. So an article signed by you seems absolutely indispensable to people here. No need for it to be all that long or complicated. But if you go on remaining silent, it will look dubious: bear in mind that dubiousness is rampant. (Did you see the sickening Merleau-Ponty interview in *l'Express*?)

[531]Local committees set up by the Comité de Résistance Contre le Fascisme, to combat the authoritarian tendencies in the new Gaullist administration that had been in place since May.
[532]De Gaulle had called a referendum for 28 September, to approve a new presidential constitution for the Fifth Republic.

Basically, what people are asking of you is to *declare yourself*; and obviously that can be done only in the shape of an article. I swear to you, little yourself, I know that you've got the play to do,[533] and that Huston must have been after you,[534] and so on. But it contradicts everything you've done previously if you don't speak *now*. Perhaps Servan-Schreiber came and spoke to you? But perhaps he didn't convince you either.[535]

I've seen lots of people again. Of course, I quarrelled more violently than ever with De Roulet. He says with a snigger: 'I'm Soustelle's left hand',[536] and claims that by participating in Soustelle's campaign against abstentionism he's helping the Left. I was really naive to think he'd withdraw! He thinks that with 'good elections' in November, De Gaulle will be forced to carry out left policies! In the end he left the table in fury, and we made up only very lamely. Bienenfeld, on the other hand, has become a thoroughgoing activist, and despite her self-importance she's very estimable. Bost is still lost in his amours, Olga sweet but very dejected.

Poor Lanzmann went to *L'Express* on Saturday morning, to do his article on Joliot-Curie (which they signed Thomas Lenoir). He came back twenty-four hours later, haggard and in despair, not having stopped working for those 24 hours – and moaning.[537]

✿ 1963

[Villeneuve-les-Avignon, Gard]

Saturday [July 1963]

Dear little yourself

I'd really like a few words, just to reassure me that you're alive, and that Arlette's a bit less pale than when we said goodbye.[538] If it's raining

---

[533]*Les Séquestrés d'Altona*, staged in 1959.

[534]John Huston was pursuing Sartre for the screenplay on Freud eventually published as *The Freud Scenario*.

[535]Sartre did in fact write three articles in *L'Express*, on 11, 18 and 25 September. He was still in Italy, at Rome, when De Beauvoir wrote this letter.

[536]Jacques Soustelle (1912-) was, like Malraux, a Gaullist with a left-wing, anti-fascist past. Appointed governor-general of Algeria in 1955, he had been instrumental in De Gaulle's return to power in France in 1958.

[537]This letter is unfinished.

[538]Arlette el-Kaïm had been with Sartre since 1956, and was to be adopted as his daughter and legal heir in 1965.

back there, have no regrets. As I write to you the rain's coming down in bucketfuls, after a storm that lasted all night (it's now 9 in the morning) – and it rained the whole of Wednesday morning too.

So, on Monday I met up with Lanzmann, went for a spin on the motorway to get myself used to the car again, listened to his exasperated account of how the Fanon woman and her man had reduced him to slavery, and of the disastrous situation in Algeria (though in Blida he'd seen some interesting people, who'd actually spoken to him about Fanon[539]). Dinner with him and Judith,[540] who was in a great state because she'd just been offered a play that's very bad but has a big role. I left them at midnight. At 5.30, woken up by impatience, I took to the road. What with motorways and widened roads, one can drive amazingly fast now and I went like the wind. By 4.30 – having lunched on the way, after Vienne – I was at Villeneuve-les-Avignon. I have a lovely big room opening onto a mediocre garden, with no view and invaded by tennis courts, but where it's not unpleasant to sit and read or have dinner. In the mornings I work half-heartedly (at that article on women, and subbing V. Leduc[541]). Then I go for a walk and lunch, come home at about 5, and read. Dinner at the Châteauneuf-du-Pape, *one* scotch in bed while reading, and to sleep at 10. I've revisited the Pont-du-Gard, the Fontaine-de-Vaucluse, the Tour-du-Ventoux, some lovely villages, and the countryside – unfortunately overcast by stormy skies. On Thursday evening Lanzmann and Judith dined with me, and we had a few drinks at Avignon. He has gone off again, she's rehearsing. I'm going to be obliged to see a bit of her – which doesn't wildly appeal to me. Overall, I'm fine here.

Here's a letter that was sent directly from Paris to the Prieuré for you[542] – it's a pity we can't accept.

Have as good a time as possible, get some rest, and write me the odd word or two. I miss you. I'll be very happy on the 31st. Kisses from me, o little yourself.

Your Beaver

---

[539]Frantz Fanon (1925-61), author of *The Damned of the Earth* to which Sartre wrote a long preface.
[540]Judith Magre, an actress who had performed in several of Sartre's plays.
[541]The book in question was *La Bâtarde* (1964).
[542]Hôtel du Prieuré at Villeneuve-les-Avignon, where Sartre was to join her. The letter presumably contained some invitation.

INDEX